Explorer's Mind

A Map to Freedom

Carolyn Eberle

Explorer's Mind: A Map to Freedom is a step by step guide and workbook to achieve Self-Mastery so "pain transforms to power!". It is the curriculum for our full certification program and is quite intensive. We recommend you join any of our online or in person trainings to deepen the value of this curriculum!

The Art and Science of Mind Energy Body (Me-B Transformation) is detailed in this book. **It teaches us how to turn pain into wisdom and difficulty into triumph in our mind, energy and body (Me-B) systems.** This creates Choice Points for peace. We do this by learning to reconnect to our wholeness, true self, source, good self whatever word you want to call it. We call it Core Being.

Core Being holds high vibrational consciousness and can be used to transform illness, negative beliefs and insecurities that create our life challenges. To do this we use advanced mindfulness, body-centered trauma-release techniques combined with subtle energy skills. By connecting us back to Core Being we learn how to be the light in the dark and the clear, balanced "I" in the hurricane of life's challenges.

Life has suffering and pain in it; this cannot change and will not change, but we can learn to not be the suffering.

We can use the energy of suffering as an energetic resource to transform and connect us to life, love and joy. We can move through the challenges before us, without merging with the pain and negative identification. **We learn to use the energy of pain, illness, stress, anxiety, depression and difficulty as a raw material to reconnect us to our wholeness and light.**

Just as a diamond needs polishing before it shines, we need to remember our shine. Polish with compassion and acceptance...

Author, Carolyn Eberle, LPC, educator and lecturer, has traveled the world studying meditation, psychotherapy, Reiki, Healing Touch and the Fundamentals of Brennan Healing.

"This is the next evolution of psychotherapy, energy work and personal transformation." - Hakomi Therapist

Table of Contents

TRANSFORMATION and INTERVENTION SKILLS INDEX

Void Transformation (death of old self, re-birth of new)

Which System Holds The Truth?

Whole Feminine/Masculine and the Good Enough Mother/Father

BLUE BOX EXERCISE INDEX and ORANGE BOX EXAMPLES INDX

Mind Energy Body Transformation^{TM} Definitions

3 Rings of Healing: the transformational process of moving through the outer-most ring of your defenses, through the middle ring where trauma/wounding is held, and back to the center ring of Core Being. **Pages** 19-22, 57, 67, Chapter 10: 132-144 (*Exercise: 144*), 152, 162, 168, 173, 175, 178, 282, 324, 332, 385, 385, 403

5 Seeds of Distortion: Before conception, consciousness exists in/as a sea of bliss, love and joy. After conception, we enter this denser dimension of earth. Still somewhat protected, we enter the liquid warmth of the womb.

This love and bliss fades further as we move through the birth canal out into the air. As a result, we all start life with the need to be loved. Unfortunately, because this need for love is not always met by ourselves or others in a perfect manner, a separation from our Core Being evolves at deeper and deeper levels. This separation, caused by our attachment to joy, love and bliss, is where we forget our Core Being. As we develop a false understanding of who we are in the world, our distortions around love increase and **we carry these distortions into our intimate adult relationships.** These distortions are the 5 Seeds and they characterize our Adult Attachment challenges. At the most fundamental level they signify your disconnect from Core Being. As you find which of the 5-Seeds negatively influences your life, and as you heal them, you empower yourself to manifest healthy relationships. **SEED 1:** We attract what is familiar, even if it is unhealthy; **SEED 2:** We accept unhealthy behaviors as loving; **SEED 3:** What happens inside us when we are not loved? **SEED 4:** Unhealthy programming of how we "act out" self-love; **SEED 5:** We can make unhealthy "choices" around showing love for others...see all the unhealthy ways I love you. **Pages** Chapter 16: 306-437 (*exercise 319*) also review Chapter 10: 136-144 on Boundaries, 5 Seeds Chart p.289, Betrayal Bond Test p. 290-291.

5-Steps the process you engage in so you can lead yourself and others to self-mastery and to consciously create your best life. This is the most important skill Me-B Guides teach to clients and themselves. You must work the 5-Steps many (100) times a day. Step 1 is Self-Awareness. In Steps 2 and 3 we use Aligned Intention to examine and label what negative beliefs and emotions are triggered within us and we gain wisdom as to why they are triggered. In Step 4 we sense where in the Mind, Energy, Body (Me-B) System the Low Vibrational Consciousness (LVC) is held and we listen to any wisdom or lessons held there. In Step 5 we allow the energy of our LVC to transform to High Vibrational Consciousness (HVC) of Core Being in our Me-B System. **Pages** *16, 143-147* (exercise on 150), 178, 283, 324, 418, 421.

10 Stages of Consciousness: the various stages that you pass through on your journey towards anchoring deeper and deeper into Core Being and transforming Low Vibrational Consciousness (LVC) such as negative emotions, depression, anxiety and insecurity back into High Vibrational Consciousness (HVC) of Source. **Pages** 21-23, 47, 67, 70, 81, Chapter 12: 167-194.

Aligned Intention: the ability to choose the highest good for ourselves; occurs when we allow the flow of source to move through us. It comes from the Manifest Energy Intention Line (Hara Line in Barbara Brennan's System of healing). **Pages** 13, 21, 25,27, 27, 31, 34, 36, 39, 39, 47, 49, 62, 68, 72-74, 86, 90, 113, 133, 143, 144, 227, 239, 288, 298, 399, 411, 413.

Ancestral Energies: patterns that we are born with and that are held in our bodies and in the blueprint of our DNA as it is passed down through centuries. **Pages** 192, 241, 418, Chapter 21: 383-388.

Anxiety: A feeling of worry, nervousness, or unease, typically about an imminent event or something with an uncertain outcome and/or you feel you have made a mistake. Energetically, anxiety is when our Ego has been triggered and we are launched into a hyper-arousal state as if there was a tiger attacking us. Yet, with no tiger in the room, our system becomes dis-regulated and confused. Usually the "tiger" in the room is our over-activated negative ego because it feels attacked or less than. Anxiety also happens when we feel we have too much to do but we feel there either is not enough time to do it or we are not capable of doing it well enough. Because each person has a unique chemical makeup, the type, number, intensity, and frequency of anxiety symptoms will vary from person to person. For example, one person may have just one mild anxiety symptom, whereas another may have all anxiety symptoms and to great severity. All combinations are common. **Pages** 15, 23, 27, 42, 47, 81, 109, 126, 173, 183, 191, 203, 230, Chapter 15: 281-306, 316, 331, 343, 355, 389, 402, 412, 430, 435.

Archetype: patterns that are derived from the universal collective unconscious. By accessing the energy of higher vibrational archetypal structures that we would like to embody, we can shift ourselves or a client deeper into aspects of their divine spirit. Conversely, we can also help ourselves or our clients tap into negative archetypical patterns held in the Me-B system. **Pages** 105, 145, 252, 258, 362, 391, Chapter 21: 385.

Attachment Disorder "Attachment" is an emotional bond to another person. An attachment disorder is an overly needy bond, an unhealthy bond, or an inability to bond. Psychologist John Bowlby was the first attachment theorist, describing attachment as a "lasting psychological connectedness between human beings" (Bowlby, 1969, p. 194). Bowlby believed that the earliest bonds formed by children with their caregivers have a tremendous impact that continues throughout life. The central theme of attachment theory is that mothers who are available and responsive to their infant's needs establish a sense of security. The infant knows that the caregiver is dependable, which creates a secure base from which the child can then explore the world. Unfortunately, rarely were our environments and parents perfect. And even if they were, I still believe we would have attachment challenges *no matter how perfect our childhoods*. This is because the vibration here on earth is very dense, and this dense energy feeds our ego-based personality and our false sense of self and a disconnect from Core Being. **Our disconnect from Core Being is the source of attachment challenges. Pages** Chapter 16: 277-290, also review Chapter 9: 126-131 on Boundaries, 5 Seeds Chart p.321, Betrayal Bond Test p. 278-279.

Awakening Process: a process that unfolds as we choose to live our life more consciously from Core Being. As a result, joy, happiness, and safety grow within, regardless of external challenges. **Pages** 55, 329, 389.

Awareness: the ability to know when you have been triggered out of your center and your ability to utilize Choice Points to realign with your Core Being. **Pages** all!

Cancer: Is a Chronic Illness that on the emotional level often deals with not having enough space and not saying no often enough. Energetically, cancer is a very sticky energy so be careful you don't let it enter your field when you are working with it. Also, don't send loving energy into it. Instead align with the cancer telling it that it does not support you and align your intention for it to leave. Strong boundaries are needed with the cancer. Core Being frequency often destroys cancer cells. **Pages** 41, 197, *400.*

Chakras: a set of energy vortexes that exist within the Auric Dimension. There are seven major chakras that we work with in Me-B Transformation™. Chakras hold the energy of consciousness and promote health and well-being when aligned. When distorted the offer us lessons for personal transformation as we collect the wisdom from them and bring in the energy of Core Being into them. **Pages 195-279, Chapters 13-14 primarily.**

Character Structure: There are 5 major body-centered Character Structures developed and used by Alexander Lowen and William Reich. In Mind Energy Body (Me-B) Transformation™ we have renamed the character structures by their gifts and not their expressions of ones' defenses. We all have parts of us represented in each character structure. As we adopt the gifts of each we realize our balanced potential. Names: Excel (Ridged), Spiritual (Schizoid), Heart-Centered (Masochist), Leader (Psychopath), Compassionate (Oral). **Pages** 73, 76, 77, 81, 83-157; 186, 225, 241-245, 251, 255-257, 282, 312, 326, 358, 375, 377, 380, Intervention 386, 390, 399, 415, 418, 422, 427

Choice Points: Are the moments when we correct our life course. They are the opportunities we experience moment-to-moment as a result of developing our centered awareness and connection to Core Being. As we open to create Choice Points, we are more able to eliminate negative patterns and realign with our Core Being. Just as a ship only one degree off course, over time, will soon become 500 degrees off course if not corrected, we can use Choice Points to correct our life course and undo our negative patterns of the past. **Pages** 13, 15, 21, 22, 24, *35,* 55, *57, 62,* 64, *68,* 70, 73, 74, 83, 102, *(102 exercise),* 110, (142 *exercise-boundary choice points*), 150, 151, 158, 163, 170, 176, 178, 230, 244, 246, 268, 282, 346, 347-348, 411 *(trauma choice points exercise 418).*

Chronic Illness: any re-occurring symptom or pathology that is persistent, long-term and/or terminal. Both physical and emotional challenges can be considered chronic. In chronic illness, there is sometimes low-vagal tone and high dorsal-vagal tone. Chronic illness in itself is trauma. Working to mitigate any additional trauma or stress to our emotional system is important. **Pages** 25, 26, 41, 76, 90, 225, 241, 270, 285, 315, 325, 331, 332, 408, 409, Chapter 22: 398.

Consciousness: Energy is consciousness and is the blueprint for everything. Energy is the medium that connects the mind with the body. As we change our consciousness, we change our energy system, our physical body and our reality. **Pages** all!

Consciousness Container (energy and biology): Teaching ourselves and our clients how to strengthen our consciousness container is vital if we want to more consciously create our life and transform Low Vibrational Consciousness (LVC) into High Vibrational Consciousness (HVC). We have an energetic and biological consciousness container. Our **biological consciousness container** is made up of our brain and its components such as its neuro-plasticity, neuro-network, limbic system, frontal lobe. Our DNA, cells, and nervous system are also part of our biological consciousness container. Our biology can limit our ability to raise our consciousness and thus our ability to think/act differently. As we bring the energy of source/Core Being into our biological consciousness container we support our awakening and healing process. Self-mastery advances as our consciousness container strengthens and expands. **Pages** 79,

152, 178, 205, 225, 286-287, 325, (Intervention *329-334*), 337, 346, 391, 397.

Contact: Contact is one of the most important skills. It means that we are aware of our level of connection to Core Being, Programmed Personality, ego and defenses. Contact with another means we are seeing them in their Core Being yet can also be aware of their programmed personality, ego and defenses. True contact is non-judgmental. **Pages** All, it is the essence of the book.

Core Being: (Core Star it is called in Barbara Brennan, *Hands of Light*) the dimensional expression of our deeper truth, the deeper reality of our unique divinity; who we really are before we have been programmed or altered by life experiences. It is our unique note in the symphony of all the notes that make up the wholeness in the universe. **Pages** all! (*Meditation/Intervention are on pages 48, 49, 360*)

Core Distortion: Is anything that causes us to lose our connection with Core Being and dramatically impinges upon our ability to be present. Typically, they are located in the lower levels of the Auric Field. The external situations of trauma, genetics, developmental wounding, stress, relational attachment issues – and even everyday life – create our Core Distortions. Core Distortions also include our reactive feelings of anger, fear, pain, hurt, depression, anxiety, and confusion. These distortions perpetuate our negative beliefs and cause us to maintain a false identity. **Pages** 16, 17, 21, 22, 24, 27, 42, 45-48, 56, *(62 exercise)*, 80-83, 132, 136, 139, 144, *152-157 touch and non-touch interventions; Trauma Intervention* – throughout the book.

Defenses: Unhealthy ways of protecting the false self (ego) that were programmed into our nervous system, brain, body chemistry, energy system and consciousness. Defenses replay the energy of the past and are the "tipping point" that recycles the negative past if we don't develop more balanced and coherent methods and reactions for self-protection. As we unwind and re-pattern our negative reactive patterns, we empower ourselves to consciously create our reality and achieve our life-task. **Pages** 14, 16, 20, 21, 72, Chapters 4-8; 72-136, most of the book.

Detachment (Also see Intention): the experience that occurs when we access the Manifest Energy Intention Line (Brennan's Hara Line) and feel difficult emotions without being overwhelmed by them. We are present, but not collapsed, disassociated or merged with the challenge. We feel strong and have more clear perception. **Pages** 16, 22, 28, 34, chart 41, *(exercise p. 79)* 54, 123, 144.

Depression: Anxiety and Depression usually go together. It is a serious biological disease that affects millions of people each year. The encouraging news is that it may be successfully treated. What causes depression? Although no single cause of depression has been identified, it appears that interaction among genetic, biochemical, environmental, and psychosocial factors may play a role. The fact is, depression is not a personal weakness or a condition that can be willed or wished away, but it can be successfully treated. *Dorsal vagal complex often heightens depression symptoms and the energy of anger, when transformed back into personal power can help heal it.* An estimated 33 to 35 million U.S. adults are likely to experience depression at some point during their lifetime. The disease affects men and women of all ages, races, and economic levels. However, women are at a significantly greater risk than men to develop major depression. Studies show that episodes of depression occur twice as frequently in women as in men. Although anyone can develop depression, some types of depression, including major depression, seem to run in families. Whether or not depression is genetic, the disorder is believed to be associated with changes to levels of chemicals in the brain such as serotonin and norepinephrine. Our ego re-activity and a negative sense of self I believe can cause depression and create biochemical changes that enable depression. **Pages** 15, 25, 27, 36, 41, 42, 45, 128, 173, 179, 231, 389 (Chapter 22-Chronic Illness - 390.

Digging in the Dirt: stage One of Me-B Transformation where we begin to explore who we are; the first stage where we are just beginning to discover our unhealthy defenses, false beliefs, and Public Personality. **Pages** 21, 169.

Discharge of the Freeze: Lack of discharge of our bodies freeze response could create vulnerability to our body and health. As we learn to discharge any leftover freeze energy, we could support a more balanced system. In addition, we could reduce unhealthy hypo or hyper-arousal states that can cause stress on our body. (Robert C. Scare, MD; *The Body Bears the Burden*). As Core Being or HVC comes into our body, we often shake and quake away the freeze energy. As we can move our body in a healthy defensive manner in all Me-B Systems, we invite health and happiness. **Pages** 26, 435.

Dissociative Capsules created by procedural memories: According to Scare, the number of one's Dissociative capsules is determined by the sum total of one's cumulative life traumas. He said that capsules consist of procedural memories from the past trauma, but are perceived as being present, and are therefore dissociative. This "living in the past" could stress our body-mind system. (Robert C. Scare, MD; *The Body Bears the Burden*). **Page** 436.

Dimensions: in Me-B Transformation we work with 5 dimensions: 1) the Physical Dimension (our body) 2) the Auric Dimension 3) the Manifest Energy Intention Line (Hara Line in Brennan work) 4) the Core Being (Core Star in Brennan work) Dimension, and 5) the Multi-dimensional Fabric of Interconnectedness. **Page** Chapter 13- p. 195.

Dorsal Vagal: "Among body centered practitioners when we say someone has gone into "dorsal" we mean the nervous system has gone beyond overwhelm. For instance, you may have at times in your life felt overwhelmed, that you could not take on another thing. Imagine feeling this way *all the time*. When this state becomes chronic we believe the nervous system has *decelerated* into a state called dorsal. The problem is that this state – as with all states – become *normalized*. That is, the individual becomes so accustomed to the state that it becomes the norm for them. They acclimatize to the flatness of their demeanor. Sometimes the change in behaviour is noticed but is *falsely attributed* to getting older! One friend of mine described it as a ship in calm waters, in the doldrums...nothing to look forward to, nothing to pick up her sails. As the nervous system moves into dorsal it selectively shuts down to conserve energy. In doing so, it becomes restrictive in how much stimulation will be taken in. In response, the individual, quite unconsciously, gradually moves into a lifestyle that serves to preserve energy. He or she moves into what is referred to as 'living in the minimus'. This restrictive state is not conscious but it will unknowingly influence the choices we make. I might choose for instance to get a video rather than go to the theatre. Not a big deal once and a while but maybe it now reflects the pattern of how I approach every activity. "The way you do anything is the way you do everything". By Dr. Suzanne LaCombe, April 7, 2007. **Page** 408, 414, 416, 436.

Ego: the part of us that works extremely hard to prevent personal growth, because change means death to this part of us. Our Ego is lower in frequency than our Core Being. **Page** 17, 18, 22, 23. 59-60, 119-124, 408, 418.

Ego Death Process: an ongoing death-rebirth process of our Ego, that never ends for the spiritual warrior. The warrior engages this process as an opportunity and a gift. **Page 22, 23, 179.**

Energetic Tool: The mind is a powerful energetic tool for transformation when filled with the HVC of the Enlightened Observer. Sound, acts of kindness, our words, actions, hands and body can also be energetic tools. **Page 53, Chapter 1.**

Enlightenment: the ability to move from the programmed personality level back to Core Being. This can only be done when we create a stronger state of presence. **Page 42, 45, 47** and all of the 5 steps and skills.

Enlightened Observer (EO): the part of our mind that is connected to our Core Being and holds enough HVC to enable us to move through the 5-Step Mindfulness Process with compassion, kindness, and ease. The EO is the single most important skill to master because you can't move through the 5 Steps without it. Without the EO, you can merge with the pain of challenge and lower your vibration so there is no detachment (this means your sense of self is negatively defined by the pain) and thus you lower your level of consciousness and can re- traumatize yourself. Without the EO victim consciousness can take over and you can feel life is hard instead of life being a playground of opportunities and lessons to learn. **Page 29, 30, 134, 303.**

Explorer's Mind: the internal detective that examines the deeper issues of what is really going on within and around us, so we can move out of blame or judgment and into self-empowerment. **Page 14-24 all!**

False Self: what we adopt as a result of life experiences, trauma, prenatal, birth and childhood experiences that create false images and beliefs within us. This False Self can limit us from achieving our life's passions and joys, and it also creates LVC. **Page 28, 30, 39, 45, 178** and throughout.

Heart Rate Variability: Heart rate normally increases with inspiration and decreases with expiration. In his book, Scare calls it the Respiratory Sinus Arrythmia (RSA). The greater the difference between these rates, the healthier and more stable the autonomic nervous system, a measure of homeostasis or optimal autonomic balance (Robert C. Scare, MD; *The Body Bears the Burden*). **Page 417** and Chapter 21.

High Vibrational Consciousness (HVC): the energy of our Core Being when it is felt as a sensation in the body and a thought and concept in the mind. **Page 1, 3, 6, 19** and throughout.

Holding Two Places At Once: stage 4 of Me-B Transformation, where one learns how to hold the dark in the light and the light in the dark. One is able to be in connection with the emotional challenge as well as the Enlightened Observer/Core Being without over-identifying with Core Distortions and traumas. **Page 161.**

Intention Line. See Manifest Energy Intention Line.

Kindling and Autonomic Dysregulation: Kindling is the development of self-perpetuating neural circuits through repetitive stimulation, said Scare. In other words, continued and repetitive stress and/or trauma causes an imbalance in our neural circuits. Kindled posttraumatic procedural memories provide repetitive, unconscious cue-related input to the sympathetic limb of the autonomic nervous system, leading to increased dysfunctional cycling and dysregulation, according to Scare. (Robert C. Scare, MD; *The Body Bears the Burden*) **Chapter 21.**

Levels of the Field: vibrational frequencies that are accessed through the chakras and are part of the Auric Dimension. Chapter 13, 201.

Low Vibrational Consciousness (LVC): The unbalanced energy of our Negative Programmed Personality that holds negative beliefs, trauma, ego, false sense of self, illness, and difficult emotions. **Page** 1, 3, 6, 19 and throughout.

Manifest Energy Intention Line: (Brennan Healing Science's Hara Line) runs through the middle of our Central Channel but is on a different dimensional frequency. It allows us to feel difficult emotions but not be overwhelmed by them, because this dimension helps us detach (not disassociate). Energetically, it feels like a safe and solid base. From it, we sense strength, clarity, and solidity. **Page** 71, 72, 208, **Chapter 13.**

Manifest: creating the outcomes that we want through tuning into the Manifest Energy Intention Line and realigning with positive intention. **Page** 85, 93, 99 and throughout.

Mindfulness: is an *energetic tool you can learn to use to cultivate presence and transformation of pain into joy.* In Mind Energy Body TransformationTM we look at the energetics of Mindfulness. What frequency is your mind resonating at when you think a thought and when you put your mind in the body? You can learn to track how low in the body your mind can resonate a high enough frequency for transformation to happen. We use the frequency of an **Enlightened Observer** and **a 5-Step Mindfulness process** for deep energetic transformation in our mind and body. **Page** 1-6, 48, 240 and throughout the book.

Merging: What results when people who are processing trauma become energetically, cognitively, and somatically over-identify with the trauma in a way that creates further discomfort and fear. **Page** 3, 46, 50, 324.

Multi-Dimensional Fabric: the energy that we experience when we remove "us" from the equation and connect to the frequency of universal oneness. This fabric weaves through all of us and connects dimensions, worlds, universes, consciousness, and concepts of time and space. It resonates brightly and is reminiscent of the beauty seen in the Aurora Borealis (Northern Lights). **Chapter 13,** *(exercise 213, 348).*

Negative Cycles: Cycles that occur when one merges and over-identifies with pain, illness, trauma, and difficult emotions. Our biological consciousness container programs into us habituated responses so we often repeat our negative past. Bringing Core Being into our body and noticing our unhealthy orienting responses helps prevent negative cycles. **Page** 24 and throughout book.

The Polyvagal Theory of Emotion: This is a very complex theory. It deals with Vagal Tone/Dorsal Tone, the vagal break and Dorsal Vagal Complex. A whole book can be devoted to this topic. Basically, high vagal tone is healthy and promotes balance because you can be socially engaged. Yet you don't want high doral tone because it brings you to a more shut down mode to run your life. A short review of Polyvagal theory begins with noting that the dorsal and the vagal tone are two parasympathetic nerve centers in the brainstem medulla: dorsal and ventral vagal nuclei. Dorsal vagal complex governs digestive, taste and hypoxic responses. In part, it provides primary neural control of abdominal organs. It also promotes change from mobilization to immobilization (the freeze response). High dorsal vagal complex tone may promote immobilization and freeze. In our normal day to day life, this in not healthy because it could deal with fear, helpless, dissociation, collapse and lack of body awareness (Robert C. Scare, MD; *The Body Bears the Burden*). **Chapter 20**.

Procedural Memory: Memory programmed into us by the past. It is held in our cellular script. Specifically, it involves learned patterns of behavior, movement, gestures, autonomic arousal patterns, and emotional and cognitive tendencies. Procedural Memory is often unconscious and reactive in nature. **Procedural Memory can prevent us from being in charge of our actions. It can put us on autopilot. Because most often we don't know we have lost choice, we later judge and ridicule ourselves for our negative reactivity.** Trauma from the past prevents us from functioning at a higher level of choice instead of taking action out of a programmed defense. So we can get stuck in the outer ring of healing and never make it back to center. **Chapter 20**.

Programmed Personality: a false sense of self that occurs when our identification is linked to our negative past. Our programmed personality is greatly orchestrated by the state of **our biological consciousness container**. **Page** 69, throughout book.

Presence: is Core Being and is the result of energy, intention and mindfulness. When presence is experienced not only in the mind, but also in the body and energy systems its quality increases as we learn to anchor into Core Being in all Me-B Systems. See Core Being. **Page** 31, 136; throughout the book.

Public Personality: the inner actor within us that pretends it knows who we are but is afraid to sink in and really see the truth. It is a mask covering who we really are. **Page** 92,93.

Saboteur: the internal part of us that thwarts our forward movement. **Page** 24

Golden Shadow: Page 303.

Self-Mastery: the ability to experience Core Being in all mind, energy, and body systems. Occurs when you recognize you have been triggered out of Core Being and you can consequently follow the 5 Step Mindfulness Process to return back to Core Being. It is a life-long exploration. Although we are never done, self-mastery is when you feel free and happy, even when there is LVC to transform and your negative ego is activated. **Page** 1, 4, 5, 13, 14, 19, 53, 56, 91, 241, 406.

Spiritual Junk Food: also known as "Spiritual Bypass." Consists of self-delusions designed to allow us to artificially boost the ego and avoid owning our Core Distortions and imperfections. Spiritual Junk Food is present when we think we are connected to our Core Being, but we are really escaping to higher frequencies to avoid pain, instead of transforming that pain into HVC and Core Being. **Page** 53.

Star Child Energies: represents the lessons our soul has learned over its many lifetimes. Specifically it represents the insights, gifts and talents we have developed from living on many different planets and many different dimensions across the cosmos. We can learn to access the memory of these lessons so they can be helpful to us in this lifetime. **Chapter 13.**

Structured Levels of The Barbara Brennan Auric Field: levels 1, 3, 5, and 7 of the Auric Field. They are part of the meridian structure and look like fiber-optic grids of light. Level 1 is blue grid and represents the health of the physical level. Level 3 is a yellow grid and represents the health of our mental/thinking level. Level 5 is a cobalt blue template, reverse negative for what will happen on the 1st level of the field. Level 7 is a golden grid of divine wisdom. **Chapter 13**

Transformation: the result of shifting the energy and the consciousness so you can returning to Core Being by bringing the HVC of our Enlightened Observer into the dense LVC of the Programmed Personality (thoughts, beliefs, feelings, emotions, trauma, past lives, ancestral wiring…) and then return to Core Being. It is spiritual alchemy where emotional pain, illness becomes fuel to help us reconnect to Core Being. (**See 5 Steps, Enlightened Observer, Core Being**.)

Transition (death): We believe death is a transition from this earthly form to the spiritual dimension that is formless. So when someone is "transitioning" we call this the death process. Me-B students learn to help people transition through death. (**Page** 403-406)

Unstructured Levels of the Brennan Auric Field: levels 2, 4, and 6 of the Auric Field. Level 2 is our relationship to self, level 4 is our relationship to others and level six is our relationship to divine ecstasy, unconditional love. They are infused with beautiful colors. (See Levels of the field**) Chapter 13.**

Trauma: Harsh programming in the mind/energy/body systems that makes it difficult or impossible to reconnect to Core Being. It holds the energy of ego, negative emotions/beliefs, negative defenses, fear, anger and our false sense of self. **Chapters 20, 21 (whole book).**

Vagal Tone: High Vagal Tone means a person's nervous system is aligned for "Social Engagement" and no trauma is creating a **Core Distortion.** Low vagal tone signifies a dysregulation in the nervous system and probably the need for a Core Distortion intervention to address issues of safety, trust and/or attachment issues. Following the 5 Step process, can restore Vagal Tone. The Ventral Vagal Complex fosters social engagement and maternal infant bonding and complex social behaviors. High vagal tone promotes health and communication and social engagement (Robert C. Scare, MD; *The Body Bears the Burden). Chapter 20.*

Void: the place of the unknown; the time in between the death of the old sense of self and before the birth of the new sense of self; the metaphorical womb. Self-mastery means entering the void with passion and trust. **Page** 46, 112, 164, 174, 324.

ACKNOWLEDGEMENT

All my teachers, friends and petty tyrants who have helped me along the way! Barbara Brennan School of Healing and all their teachers

Franny Harcey

All my students and clients

My family, husband, Maya and Ethan

My inner wounded and awake child that has taught me so much!

My horses Billy, Leo, and Zeus and my dogs Shanti, Tara, Bear, Caribou and our cat Sydney

FORWARD

The adventure of writing, living and implementing the practices in this book and brought me to a place of peace and conscious creation I didn't think was possible. I too move in and out of Core Being. But more and more, I live in bliss and gratitude. More and more I have choice about who I am and therefore I create my reality more and more from my higher self. And, when I do find I am creating my reality from my wounded parts, I see the lessons and wisdom needed to move through the challenge and reclaim my light.

This book outlines the code for success and conscious creation. It is the code to change your neuro-network, alter your negative reactivity and negative programming of your personality, negative beliefs and misaligned energy system. As a result, you anchor deeper into a whole spiritual truth of who you really are.

As you journey through this book, you also journey within. You observe the areas where you create your relationships, love, career and finances from your wounded parts you manifest a distorted and difficult reality. Yet this books helps you live from the ancient secret code, so that more and more you create from your wholeness and as a result you achieve the goal of manifesting your life task. In addition, you begin to experience how the magical moments throughout your day become magical minutes, then magical days, weeks and years.

This is enough for me. I live my life imperfect, humbly human yet with enough moments of the divine to feel whole, joyful and complete. I am empty, yet full. I know I will always have more low vibrational consciousness (wounded parts) to uncover, heal and transform and this is O.K. It is even grand because there is always more god consciousness to incarnate into the physical body and reclaim. This is living life from my aliveness and light.

This book is a map to help you navigate the challenges of this world. In it, we learn to bring in the high vibrational consciousness of the divine into our human form in our mind, in our energy system and in our body. If it is useful, thanks can be given to yourself. Take with you only what truly helps you.

INTRODUCTION

Consider that you are much more than what you appear to be, and that you choose who you are and who you become. Every moment is a CHOICE POINT of creation!

When emotional pitfalls prevail, overwhelming our clarity, we too often lose the connection to who we really are and become reactive. Just like an amoeba contracts from external stimuli, we react to a challenging environment. Learning to be the calm, clear "I" in the emotional hurricane of this reality is paramount to owning your own creative nature and to creating joy. Since few people are born with the skills to navigate this complex and contradictory environment we live in, the *Explorer's Mind* provides a systematic map to help us gain the clarity to consciously manifest your highest good.

This book is written for people who want deep personal health, self-knowledge, and the ability to feel joy even in times of darkness. It is also written for healing and mental health professionals who want to expand their current way of working with clients and embrace a new multi-dimensional system that accelerates healing as it unravels faulty perception of self, illness, negative beliefs, trauma and emotional pain. As you detach (not dissociate) from difficulty, pain and challenge, you can regain enough presence to learn how to use the energy of challenge as fuel to create peace, wholeness and understanding.

Faulty perception keeps us from wisdom. Wisdom can turn difficulty into wholeness.

In this book, you will learn about the *3-Rings of Healing* to Shape Shift your Emotions by following the *5-Step Energetic Mindfulness Process* for self-mastery. It uses aligned intention, advanced mindfulness techniques, cultivated presence and subtle energy awareness to work your mind, energy and body (Me-B) systems together. Energy, chi or whatever you wish to call it, is consciousness and is the medium that connects your mind with your body. As you learn how to sense, feel and convert energy's low vibrational consciousness (LVC) into high vibrational consciousness (HVC) you give yourself the power and skills to return to the deeper truth.

You can't always stay connected to the HVC of wholeness, true self, Jesus, god or source (use the name that works best for you). **In Mind Energy Body (Me-B) Transformation, we call this HVC (high vibrational consciousness) your Core Being.**

Negative feelings and thoughts in your mind and body eventually invade any peace or calm you have temporarily mastered. As a result, the LVC grows and can spiral us into despair and overwhelm. But as your mindfulness and subtle energy skills advance, you can engage your Explorer's State of Mind to master these 5-Steps which provide us with the ability to shift, transform and return to Core Being.

The Explorer's State of Mind Leads to Mastery

What is the Explorer's State of Mind and why is it an essential ingredient for personal transformation? The Explorer's State of Mind allows us to examine situations and yourself with honesty and openness. If you engage life from the view of an explorer, you can view challenges as adventures to be overcome and as riddles to solve. From the Explorer's State of Mind, you more easily move out of your negative ego and programmed personality and back to your bigger more whole spiritual truth. Next is an example of a client using their Explorer's State of mind to release pain and trauma and reconnect to their wholeness.

Explorer's State of Mind Case Example

Roselyn called me in distress. Apparently her partner had just come home from a trip to confess that he was in love with another woman. He was moving out of their apartment as soon as possible.

Her world crashed down. He was everything to her. Not only did he pay most of the rent, she also felt that his love for her proved to the world that she mattered. He was successful, good-looking and he validated her net worth.

As we worked together, Roselyn gained a broader perspective on her situation. She opened to the energetic frequency and expanded consciousness of the interconnectedness of all. As her consciousness expanded, she moved out of her small, wounded self and into a more accurate and whole perspective. It was as if she was part of an Apollo flight and she looked down on the tiny dot called earth. From this vantage point, she gained a clear view of her inner and outer world.

She experienced herself as a light body that traveled to earth so she could experience loss but not become lost. She remembered that her soul was meant to journey and visit the emotion of rejection and abandonment just so she could learn not to abandon herself.

When she left my office, she was grateful she no longer needed Rick to love her in order for her to feel worthy. Roselyn had gone into the pain of her negative ego and negative programmed personality and returned back home.

This is the journey of the true explorer – one who investigates difficulty in a manner that helps them anchor into their light! *As you travel through this book, you will practice the following 5-Mindfulness Steps over and over again until they become an automatic positive reaction to a negative circumstance.* When you do this, you lead yourself back to your Core Being.

Later you will learn how the 5-Step Mindfulness process will help you move through the 3-Rings of Healing. In the 3-Rings of Healing the center ring is your Core Being. The outer ring represents your negative defenses, and the middle ring represents your trauma and false sense of self.

Examples of HVC and LVC

Energy is Consciousness and holds both high and low vibrations

High Vibrational Consciousness (HVC) = Core Being, Presence, Positive Intention, Balance

Low Vibrational Consciousness (LVC) = negative beliefs & images, depression, anxiety, false self, illness

5-Step Mindfulness Process Helps Us Move Through the 3-Rings of Healing toward Mastery

There are 5 Mindfulness Steps we use in Me-B Transformation to lead ourselves and help guide others to self-mastery. Step 1 is self-awareness. This is beginning (Level 1) Me-B Process. Specifically it is the ability to experience Core Being in all mind, energy and body (Me-B) systems and then to know when you have been triggered out of our center. As you develop centered awareness, you are more able to have choice. In Me-B Transformation, we call this creating **Choice Points for Change**. The more you create Choice Points, the more you help foster peace and harmony.

In Intermediate (Level II) Me-B, you master Mindfulness Steps 2 and 3. In these steps you examine and label what negative beliefs and emotions triggered us and why. You do this in all Mind, Energy, Body (Me-B) systems. Advanced Me-B Guides (Level III) master Steps 4 and 5. In Step 4 you sense where in the Me-B Systems the LVC is being held and listen to any wisdom or lessons held there.

During these mindfulness steps, you endeavor to use your **Enlightened Observer**. Your Enlightened Observer is the part of your mind that is connected to your Core Being. It holds enough HVC to enable us to move through the 5-Step Mindfulness Process with compassion, kindness and ease.

Step 5 is when you allow the energy of your LVC to transform to HVC and Core Being in your Me-B Systems. This last step of transformation is essential for the deepest healing to happen. Some mental health professionals negate this last step and tell clients it is important to just feel and understand an emotion. However, I have found that simply feeling an emotion rarely creates the deepest healing. In fact, the latest findings in neuropsychology seem to demonstrate that catharsis is not healing.

As you develop your ability to sense subtle energies and consciousness you can also learn how to feel an emotion or difficult life pattern in a way that reconnects us to Core Being and cultivates HVC. Eventually you can all learn how to follow this 5-Step process, and reclaim your center and deeper truth. It takes time to cultivate these skills. Remember that being kind and gentle to your self is essential to developing a higher level of consciousness.

Mindfulness Example

I felt the front of my third chakra begin to spin backwards. I stopped, connected to the energy and consciousness in my body that created that backwards spin and asked why this distortion arose. Fear was held there and it reminded me of the fear that arose when I told my father I was going to study energy work. I knew he wouldn't be pleased and I was afraid to reveal myself in such a vulnerable manner. Letting my mind connect to my Enlightened Observer, I send myself compassion. As a result, I feel able to move through the Mindfulness process of letting this LVC transform to HVC. By moving through all 5 Steps, I self-regulate back to Core Being.

Explorer's 5-Step Mindfulness Practice to Self-Mastery

Step 1: Awareness of when you are in Core Being and when you are not in Core Being. Step one is the ability to experience Core Being in all mind, energy and body (Me-B) systems and then to know when you have been triggered out of your Core Being. As you have awareness you are more able to have choice. Awareness is the first step.

Step 2: Detachment (versus dissociation) comes from an aligned Manifest Energy field. Manifest Energy lets us feel the difficult emotion (LVC) yet not merge your identity with the negative feelings. This helps you know you are more than the energy and challenging emotions that run through us. As you become detached from your pain, it helps us reconnect to Core Being. This is because detachment helps us assess what is happening without collapsing or defending against it. It also prevents us from over-identifying with the pain and the challenge you are experiencing. As your subtle energy skills advance, this process becomes easier.

Step 3: Naming, owning and locating the LVC in the mind, energy body systems. The process of placing a label on your particular trauma, pain, and Core Distortion helps us own it. For instance, is the LVC anger, collapse, hopelessness, sadness, fear or insecurity? Where is it held in the body and energy system? Owning it is essential and is very different from being over-identified with the trigger. You are not your unhealthy defenses or distortions; they are just energy moving through us. You use them as ineffective methods to protect yourselves. If you name them, versus identifying with them, you are self-compassionate and centered. If you identify with a defense or trigger, it activates your ego and you collapse back into the negative programmed personality.

Also, in this step, you learn to connect to the energy and consciousness in the body to identify the difficulty. This is because you can't always trust what your mind tells us. For instance, when I notice my belly fat with my mind, at the cognitive level, I am ready to let it go. However, subconsciously, when I actually feel the energy in my belly, I get a different response. The energy there does not want to leave. It says it holds loving protection. This is an example of how your mind might give us one answer, but the actual consciousness in the body may hold a different vibration and perspective. This is why you move toward unifying all three systems: mind, energy and body.

Step 4: Insight - Linking the trigger to your past negative programming in all three Me-B Systems. For most people, insight into what is happening is helpful in supporting change and transformation. If what you named in Step 3 is anger or hopelessness, how might this reflect back into your past negative programming?

For example, Roselyn learned that Rick was leaving her for another woman. As Roselyn worked through these 5-steps, she noticed that the feelings she experienced reminded her of when her own father left his marriage for another woman. It felt to her as if the trauma of the past was replaying again in the present and as a result, it felt even more painful.

You can gain insight into your present day triggers to see if they have any roots in your past. You can learn to assess what past trauma or negative belief is supporting the core distortion and misaligned energy in your mind and body. As Roselyn felt the grief in her chest and heart chakra and in her stomach and 3rd chakra, she noticed the negative belief that she would never be good enough to be loved.

_____

It can take time to master the skill of feeling the energy of the trigger in the mind and body and then to uncover what LVC is held there. The exercises in each chapter build upon the skills of previous chapters. As you focus on what you can do, your skills grow and soon you succeed.

_____

Step 5: Transformation - shift the energy in the mind, energy and body systems and return to Core Being. You do this by bringing in HVC into the dense LVC of the negative programmed personality. An advanced energetic technique called the Enlightened Observer is used throughout this 5-step process. It is especially important during the transformation phase. This is because in Step 5, you allow and invite the HVC of your Enlightened Observer to fill your Me-B Systems. As a result, you reconnect to your Core Being. As you learn to return to Core Being, transformation is complete. In any one day, you may need to follow this process numerous times.

In life, you all disconnect from your wholeness, yet as you gain the ability to (1) notice this disconnect and (2) understand why it happened, you then are closer to transformation and reconnection.

Further details of this 5-Step Mindfulness process are outlined in later Chapters.

Using this 5-Step Mindfulness process, along with the other techniques taught in this book, you develop the ability to use the energy in your negative programmed personality that holds LVC and transform it into the energy of your Core Being that holds HVC. Self-mastery happens as you learn to self-regulate your Me-B Systems and cultivate this high vibrational shift back to Core Being. Just as silt rises to the surface when the bottom of a lake is disturbed, your Explorer's Mind helps you uncover your next personal growth work so your Enlightened Observer can use the silt to create HVC, happiness, and peace.

No Self, No Ego — Emptiness

Different spiritual philosophies discuss the concept of evolving your consciousness so you become egoless and transcend all concepts of self. To describe this experience, some use the words wholeness, emptiness, unity and oneness. Nirvana, or spiritual enlightenment, is another term to describe this state of being. *In Me-B Transformation, we use the term Core Being.*

Words fail to adequately describe these expanded states of consciousness. When I am there, I notice no sense of self and no separation. To me, it feels like pure presence and clear acceptance of what is here now. The practices in this book can help you develop skills to raise your vibrational consciousness. *Ultimately, you can be just as present, content and balanced whether the energy of anger or sadness runs through you or the energy of Core Being runs through you. This is the ideal. This is freedom.*

Any time you have an ego, you also have a self. Your ego can hold negative or positive feelings. The battle of not letting your ego tell you that you are bad can feel intimidating and overwhelming. This is why in Me-B transformation you let Core Being become a healthy and tangible resource. I have found that to get even near the ideal of no ego and no self, some of us need a transitional object. Just as a child will use their blanket for comfort when their mother leaves, we need to connect to a concept of Core Being. To date, I don't know anyone that maintains an egoless state 24/7, yet it is an ideal I still hold possible for all of us. Until this happens, we can, hopefully, at least experience Core Being more and more throughout the day.

The 5-Step Mindfulness process and various positive resourcing meditations and exercises are included throughout the book to facilitate the experience of some *level of Core Being*.

So what do I mean by "some level" of Core Being? You can examine to what extent you are connected to Core Being. For instance, the level of Core Being I experience today holds a much higher vibration than the level of Core Being I was able to experience five years ago. In fact, when I look back upon who I was just five years ago, I am slightly embarrassed by my lack of awareness. And five years from now, as I look back upon who I am today, I hope to have advanced so much that I am "embarrassed" again. Each deepening of our connection to Core Being allows for even deeper connections. The process continues and is never-ending because there will always be higher vibrations of light we can allow within us.

What Is the Negative Programmed Personality and LVC/HVC?

Your negative programmed personality is a false sense of self and occurs when your identification is linked to your negative past. Life experiences, trauma, prenatal experiences, birth and childhood experiences can create false images and beliefs. As a result, you adopt unhealthy defenses and a false sense of self. This false sense of self can prevent you from achieving your life's passions and joys. It also creates LVC.

Low Vibrational Consciousness is the unbalanced energy of your negative programmed personality that holds negative beliefs, trauma, ego, false sense of self, illness, and difficult emotions. High Vibrational Consciousness is defined as the energy of your Core Being when it is felt as a sensation in the body and a thought and concept in the mind. *Of course there is a continuum of frequencies between high and low vibrational consciousnesses.* It is not as if you always perfectly switch off LVC and then switch on HVC.

It can take a day, week or more to fully return to our average baseline of energy and consciousness.

For instance, there are *10 Stages of Consciousness* in Me-B Transformation. Although most days, my baseline is Stage 6, during times of intense stress, I may fall to Stage 4. During more expansive times, I tap into Stage 8. (Benchmarks for each stage and a self-assessment test are provided.) As we advance our consciousness and our skills, we more quickly regulate our Me-B Systems back to Core Being.

The baseline Core Being vibration I can currently achieve is much higher than the baseline Core Being vibration I could achieve five years ago. For most of us, as we grow and progress, so does our ability to reach and maintain a higher vibration of Core Being. I believe this opportunity to continually grow and reach higher states of consciousness never ends.

However, any <u>need</u> to be in a particular vibration in order to feel whole and content can prevent you from mastering higher states of consciousness. I find that when people reach at least Stage 4 of Me-B Transformation, they become more able to feel whole and content, even when the energy of pain and hardship runs through them. This is when you are somewhat able to be your own life preserver on an ocean of challenge.

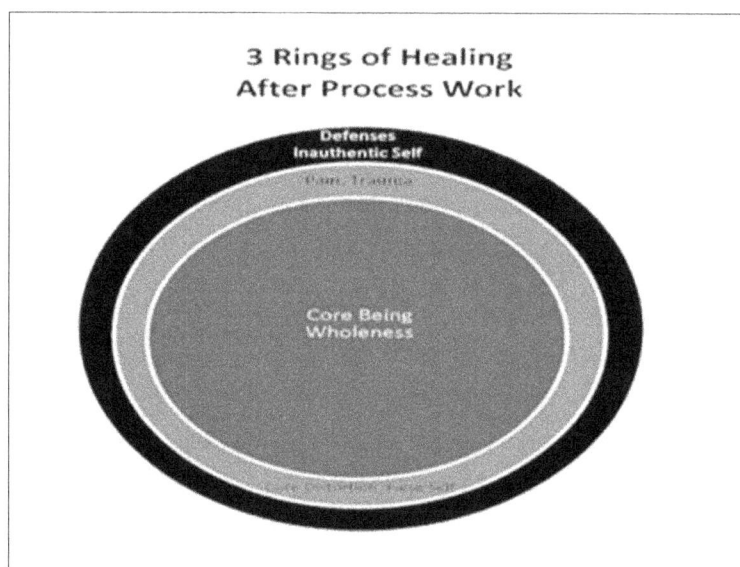

**3 Rings of Healing
After Process Work**

Defenses
Inauthentic Self

Pain, Trauma

Core Being
Wholeness

Notice center ring – Core Being—grows stronger

The more personal growth work we do in Me-B transformation

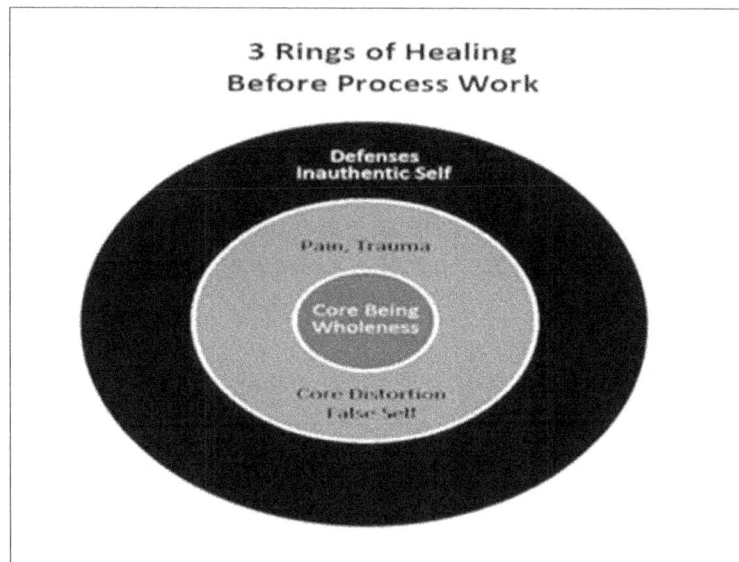

3 Rings of Healing
Before Process Work

Defenses
Inauthentic Self

Pain, Trauma

Core Being
Wholeness

Core Distortion
False Self

With practice, cultivated wisdom, self-love, and compassion, we move from the outer rings to the center ring and master higher stages of consciousness

What are the 3 Rings of Healing and the 10 Stages of Consciousness?

As you advance your level of consciousness, negative life experiences become gifts, whereas when you are locked into the energy of LVC you can feel trapped and stuck in the negative aspects of your ego and personality.

As you engage your Explorer's State of Mind, you discover more about yourself.

The outer (black) ring represents your unhealthy defenses. In future chapters you will examine your idealized self-image, your tendency to minimize the reality before you, or your tendency to dissociate, or judge others or yourself. We do all these things. In Me-B Transformation you simply notice when they arise and discover how to move out of these unhealthy defenses.

> This means you must feel and move through the emotional pain and challenge that the unhealthy defense is trying to protect. Emotional pain, illness and trauma is what is held in the second, blue ring. As you learn to feel the challenge as energy, you can then transform its LVC and return to Core Being — the purple center ring.

The middle (blue) ring represents your Core Distortions and traumas in life. Trauma can be a physical illness, the result of a car accident or the pain you feel when another is hurtful or judgmental. Often it is when your ego feels attacked or damaged. It also includes developmental trauma, and unresolved challenges that happen in your childhood.

The center-middle (purple) ring is Core Being. As you use aligned intention to be mindful of the wisdom needed to transform the LVC, you can move through the outer two rings back to the center ring, Core Being.

Throughout the day you travel back and forth between these three rings. The more skillful you are at following the 5-Step Mindfulness Process, the easier it is to move through the outer 2 rings and into the center ring of Core Being.

Learning to track your energy field to notice when it becomes unbalanced and then be able to self-regulate your Me-B Systems throughout your day is a vital life skill. This is because if you are aware of your negative defenses and distortions, you then have choice. **Choice Points** *are found when you are aware you are out of balance. You then can choose to develop and use your skills to return to balance.* This is essential in creating your map to freedom and self-mastery.

The 10 Stages of Me-B Transformation map our journey from being imprisoned and ruled by our negative programmed personality to being free of its influence over us. *As you have aligned intention to follow the wisdom you gain from your Mindfulness skills, you become more present to follow that wisdom. The more present you are, the more connected you are to Core Being, and you then progress to higher stages of Me-B Transformation.* A brief summary of each stage follows.

Me-B Transformation Skill Levels for the 10 Me-B Stages

- Skill Level I – Me-B Stages 1-3 (Step 1)
- Skill Level II – Me-B Stage 4 (Steps 2 and 3)
- Skill Level III – Me-B Stages 5-7 (Steps 4 and 5)
- Skill Level IV – Me-B Stages 8-10 which represent various degrees of Enlightenment. (Rarely does anyone get above Stage 7 of Me-B Transformation.)

Stage 1: Digging in the Dirt. Stage One is when you begin "digging in the dirt" to understand – at the mental level – your unhealthy defenses, Core Being, and negative programming. You know Core Being exists, but you cannot yet experience it. In Me-B Stage 1, Core Being is simply an ideal or concept of the mind. This is when a part of us feels, "How can it possibly exist, and how can defenses/emotions be in the body and energy system? I want to believe, but is it all true/real?"

Stage 2: Where are we digging? At this stage, you are beginning to label the outer and middle rings of the 3 - rings of healing. You are not yet sure where they are held energetically in your body. Also, at this stage of Me-B Transformation, you are not yet convinced this "stuff" works, so you are "faking it to make it." You are focused on knowing the answer to the Zen Koan, "Who Am I?" in all 3 Rings: the outer ring (unhealthy defenses); middle ring (trauma, false self); and center ring (Core Being). (In Stage 2, we develop the gifts of the 4th chakra — compassion for self and others.)

Stage 3: Transformation. Finally, at this Me-B Stage, you have enough HVC to begin to transform LVC. This is because you can finally experience, feel, and sense all 3 Rings. You can feel Core Being, notice our Trauma and Core Distortions in the blue middle ring, and identify our negative defenses in the black outer ring. At Stage 3, you are just beginning to be able to toggle back and forth between experiencing your HVC and then experiencing your emotional pain. We go back and forth because we can't yet keep our HVC of Core Being strong when we feel emotional pain.

Transformation Choice Points happen more often at this stage, because we have a stronger awareness of our Core Being and we have stronger Mindfulness skills so we also are more present to follow the wisdom the mindfulness brings. Our ego still over-identifies with the pain, but we are starting to believe/experience and move beyond faking it to make it. We are much closer to knowing the answer to "Who am I?" (At this stage we are developing gifts of the 3rd chakra — a positive ego/sense of self.)

Stage 4: Holding Two Places At Once. Holding two places at once means we can somewhat maintain the Level II Mindfulness Skills of detachment and naming the LVC. This means we are learning **not to** identify with the energy of the negative emotions/thoughts/beliefs flowing through us. For instance, if we are feeling grief, we are not merging our identity with the grief. Instead, we feel the energy of grief moving though us. If we are feeling insecure, we know it is the energy of insecurity that is running though us and we don't completely merge our identity with the insecurity.

Stage 5: Ego Death Process. In this stage of Me-B Transformation, who we thought we were is now changing. At Stage 5, there is a conscious death of our old self-identity. Yes, once we finally answer the question, "Who am I?" that ego-based understanding of self must die and eventually be reborn. I find this process is a continuum. Just as a snake must shed its skin, as we grow we must shed our concept of self. This is why snakes are such a potent symbol of transformation.

For me, this process happens every few years. I shed my old concept of self and a new one is reborn. And, as long as we still have an ego, this process will continue to take place until one day, we notice no concept of self or ego is found.

In Me-B Transformation, then, we constantly discover who we are—and then let it go, so we can discover the next deeper truth. Then again we ask, "Who am I?" and then again we let it go. Enter the void. Come through the other side and once again discover who we are. Let it go. Enter the void. Come through the other side and once again. . . over and over again. This is how we grow, change and transform.

The experience of the void occurs when the ego's old self-identification is gone, and the new one has not yet been put in place. At Stage 5 — Ego Death Process — often we can notice and take responsibility when our ego is activated. Also at Stage 5, our Mindfulness Skills are advanced, to Level III. This means we can maintain HVC, and we don't over-identify with emotional triggers. (This happens about 60 percent of the time.) The void still feels difficult, like climbing Mt. Everest without oxygen. (At this stage, we are developing the gifts of the 2nd Chakra — Personal Power).

Stage 6: Through the Void. At Stage 6, we have come though the void and are deeply anchored into Core Being. We understand that the Ego Death Process will happen again and again throughout our lifetime. We know it will always feel painful and difficult – like climbing Mt. Everest without oxygen.

It can be okay because we have already walked that path and know we can succeed. At this stage, 70 percent of the time we can own our ego activation and be in Core Being. We can also confidently transform anger, anxiety, and sadness into personal strength. (We are starting to use the 2nd Chakra's gifts.)

Stage 7: Self-Mirroring, Loneliness Mastered—Joy and Bliss Multiply. Self-authority is strong at this stage. Even when we are alone, we are never lonely, because we are anchored so deeply into ourselves. When someone negatively projects upon us, we know the truth of what is ours and what is not ours – because *we* define who we are in the world. The statement "no one can abandon me but myself" now feels true. Existential fear is still difficult to transform, but we are not over-identified with it. Our ego gets activated and we still live from our programmed personality, but 80 percent of the time we are in Core Being. (At this stage we are mastering skills of the 5th Chakra — self authority. We feel whole even when someone of authority issues harsh judgments about us.)

Even if you are able to master all the skills of Stage 7 of Me-B Transformation, it doesn't necessarily mean you have enough HVC to stay at Stage 7. At this stage you know your unhealthy defenses, and have worked though much of your childhood wounding. You are proficient at transforming LVC and HVC and you are proficient at the 5-Step Mindfulness Process. You easily sense subtle energies and can effortlessly connect to your body and assess where there are Core Distortions. Most of your personal process work is devoted to uncovering your subconscious (*shadow*) aspects that were previously hidden from your conscious awareness.

As you master all of the skills in the book, if you find yourself at Stage 7 but later discover you have dropped back down to Stage 4, just know you are exploring your shadow aspects. You are still human. You are human, and, as humans, there will always be LVC to transform into HVC. It is very important to continue looking for those difficult Choice Points where you own your past negative programming, chose a different reaction, and create a different reality. This process may not be easy — so you can at least be kind and patient with yourself as you develop the skills outlined in this book.

Stage 8-10: Degrees of Enlightenment. Very few people can consistently maintain Stages 8-10. These states represent varying degrees of Enlightenment. When we are at Stages 8-10, we use the gifts of all the Chakras and all the Dimensions. (Even though few people evolve past Me-B Stage 4, think of how much more joy and peace would spread if we all mastered at least Stage 4.)

How I Developed This System

I developed this system after I graduated from college and began to investigate how to overcome my own pain and insecurities. In 1984 I began my professional career as a Community Organizer in Washington, D.C. helping out in low-income neighborhoods. Then I worked in national organizations as a policy advocate on Capitol Hill for the disenfranchised. Later my work expanded to Bangladesh, Nepal and Cambodia where I developed woman empowerment programs, and began to study healing. I became a Licensed Professional Counselor (LPC), learned body-centered psychotherapeutic approaches, studied advanced trauma strategies, meditation, and energetic practices such as Reiki, healing touch, Barbara Brennan Healing Science, Chi Kung and others.

Each system I learned had valuable components and life skills but none felt complete and comprehensive so I began to look for the missing pieces.

The missing pieces I found include the need to master subtle energy awareness, Core Being and the Enlightened Observer skills. It is also important to incorporate all 3 mind, energy and bodily systems together in a coordinated manner.

Next is a summary of why people get stuck in negative cycles and how subtle energy awareness, advanced mindfulness and presence of Core Being help us overcome personal challenges such as: chronic illness, depression, loneliness, and repetitive negative cycles.

Each task has a tool to help us: **Aligned Intention, Mindfulness** – from the Enlightened Observer to gain wisdom – and **Presence** of Core Being to follow the message mindfulness delivers. (Additional discussion of these three tools will be presented in the next chapter.)

3 TASKS TO SELF-MASTERY: OVERCOMING NEGATIVE CYCLES

As a healer and psychotherapist, I began to notice three reasons why people get stuck in the same negative life challenges and three tasks you can master so you move forward. As you master these tasks, you are also more able to follow the *5-Step Mindfulness Practice,* move through the 3-rings of healing, and anchor back into Core Being.

TASK ONE: Don't Merge and identify with the pain.

You get stuck any time you merge and over-identify with pain, illness, trauma and difficult emotions.

> What do you mean I am not the fear, anger, anguish and insecurity that runs through me? If I am not my pain, what am I?

Too often you identify your sense of self with what you are feeling about yourself in the moment. If you are happy and others act loving, you feel good about yourself. If you are sad, make mistakes and others are judging you then you feel bad about yourself.

Manifest Energy helps align your intention so you are able to be in relation to the pain and difficulty — yet detached enough so you can listen to its wisdom. Pain and difficulty always has a gift, but can you be wise enough to discover the gift? Manifest Energy also helps you be present enough to follow through with the wisdom Mindfulness provides you. Learn to let the energy of pain and challenge be energy, and not a self-identification of who you are. Then learn to let the energy of pain and challenge run through your Me-B system. Don't hold on to it!

I believe freedom comes when your wholeness is a consistent force you can tap into for support. This promotes long-term positive change and healing. So learning not to merge with the negative energy, emotions, trauma and false sense of self is pivotal if you are to create your map to freedom. I feel free when I am so deeply anchored into my Core Being that I feel complete, even when in pain. Freedom is also when I no longer feel alone because I am deeply connected to the oneness within me. This book is devoted to helping you achieve this goal of freedom.

TASK TWO: Discover the negative aspects of our personality that sabotage us.

The second reason people stay stuck is when a subconscious harmful intention toward healing and self-mastery takes charge of our actions. For instance, we all have positive aspects of our personality that help us. But you also have negative aspects of your personality that can sabotage you. If you are committed to healing and growth, you must learn to see how your internal saboteur thwarts your forward movement.

A saboteur might make you feel frozen — as if you are waiting for someone or something to come to our rescue. Sometimes we wait for years to be rescued. For instance, a talented writer I know attended a workshop to get support on her new book. At the workshop, she was ostracized and shamed by the other participants. She hasn't written a word since. She so wanted the external support but didn't receive it. Sometimes we must move forward even when there is no external support. (This does not mean we can't get external support to augment our internal light. In fact, asking for help is often an indicator of strength. The problem comes when we can't move forward without it.)

Trauma actually programs this freeze (saboteur) into your body's nervous system. Polyvagal Theory explains (in part) our immobilization and is discussed more in the trauma and chronic healing chapters.

Another way our saboteur can limit us is when it makes us stay in pain and darkness. The saying "the devil we know is better than the devil we don't know" is an example of this. It can feel safer to stay in the pain than to leave it and move into the unknown. In fact, the latest advances in neuropsychology suggest we all become programmed to stay in the same patterns by our brain and body systems. This is why it takes relentless, strong and focused intention to reprogram.

TASK THREE: Master subtle energy awareness and the ability to transformation Me-B Systems.

The final reason we stay stuck is lack of self-awareness at a subtle enough level to change. Too many of our problems cannot be solved through cognitive reasoning alone. Many of our negative patterns are held at such a subtle level in the body and energy system that it can be hard to find the distortions and heal.

For instance, trauma wires our brain to repeat its negative patterns. It is a physiological programming that happens in both the body and brain. Because it gets so deeply wired within us, it is rarely solved only through talk therapy. Therefore, it is vital we learn to tap into the body and energy systems and reveal the subconscious core distortions and negative programming held there. (A core distortion is anything that keeps us from Core Being. It can be an emotion, negative belief, trauma or pain.)

Carl Jung suggests that it is the unknown that has the most power over us. Arguably, our subconscious is 99.9 percent of total awareness. Or we are only 0.1 percent aware. Because the subconscious can conspire against us, it can be a reason we get stuck. As we learn to use subtle energy awareness to reveal what is hidden in our subconscious, we can discover the parts of us that need support and the parts of us that can support us.

Growing up, I suffered from a haze I now know was depression and Post Traumatic Stress Disorder. As an adoptee I worked to heal abandonment issues, prenatal trauma and overcome the challenges of growing up with an emotionally abusive alcoholic father and a distant mother. At the time, I never felt I belonged anywhere. The harsh treatment people inflicted upon one another made no sense to me. I wondered what was I doing on this crazy, harsh planet?

As I grew older, I had a sense that there was something important I was supposed to do. I believe the Science of Me-B Transformation is the important work I came to do and I couldn't have developed it without all the very difficult challenges I encountered in my life. Every time I am grateful that something bad happened to me, I know I received the gift the difficulty was meant to deliver to me. Wisdom and self-awareness can sometimes only be born from hardship.

One of the best known proverbs from Buddhism is: life is suffering. My interpretation is that life has suffering and pain in it. This cannot change and will not change. **But, we can learn to not be the suffering and we can look for the gifts difficulty can bring.**

Just as a diamond needs polishing before it shines, we need to remember our shine. As we move through the challenges before us without merging with the pain and negative identification, we learn to use the energy of pain, illness, depression and difficulty as a raw material that will reconnect us to our wholeness and light. Just as splitting an atom creates a burst of energy, I find if we have:

(1) aligned intention, then
(2) our mind has a high enough vibrational frequency as we connect to the center of the painful emotions in our body, and
(3) we don't merge with the difficulty but bring light into it, and a burst of energy moves through us too. As a result, healing and wholeness happens.

In this book we use a combination of positive intention, advanced mindfulness techniques and subtle energy awareness to convert LVC into HVC. Through our Explorer's State of Mind, we also learn to listen to any wisdom and lesson that difficulty and LVC brings. From wisdom, we facilitate connection to our wholeness. As a result, the HVC of Core Being is felt in the thoughts of our mind, in the sensations in our body and in our energy system. It is truly a map to wholeness and freedom.

3 Tasks to Overcome Negative Cycles

- **TASK ONE**
  Don't merge and over-identify with pain, illness, trauma and difficult emotions. Manifest Energy helps with this by fostering the energetic alignment to achieve a balanced level of detachment from the challenge. Learn to let the energy of pain and challenge run through you and then reconnect to Core Being.
- **TASK TWO**
  Discover the negative aspects of our personality that can sabotage us. If we are committed to healing and growth, we must see how our internal saboteur thwarts our forward movement.
- **TASK THREE**
  We must master subtle energy awareness and transformation in all three Me-B Systems. Too many of our problems cannot be solved through cognitive reasoning alone. Many of our negative patterns are held at such a subtle level in the brain, body and energy system that it can be hard to find the distortions and heal.

We can think of Me-B Transformation as a form of spiritual alchemy. This is because you connect to the metaphorical lead of your past negative programming (trauma, negative beliefs and emotional pain). You then surrender into the center of it with high enough consciousness and wisdom (advance mindfulness) to allow it to transform into the gold of your Core Being.

Since you are human, you move in and out of your negative personality aspects throughout the day. Wouldn't it be nice if you were to notice how you do this and then have the skill and aligned intention to return to the truth of your Core Being? As you learn to consciously cultivate the energy of your Core Being, you can use its HVC to heal the LVC of the negative aspects of your out-of-balance programmed personality.

Then, from the clear and whole perspective of Core Being, wisdom can be gained and your path more easily revealed. In addition, the energy of Core Being's HVC can be used to change your cells, your thoughts and your concepts of self so you can overcome illness, depression, anxiety and manifest our dreams.

When I am asked what my definition of empowerment and enlightenment is, the answer I give is: **simply the ability within us to know when we are out of our center and wholeness and then return quicker and quicker back to Core Being.** For most of us who do this diligently throughout the day, it is a difficult yet rewarding challenge.

Skills To Develop

When we connect to difficulty and challenge with the LVC of our negative programmed personality, we create more negativity. As we learn to align our intention, use mindfulness to receive wisdom and develop the presence to follow that wisdom, we are more able to self-regulate back to the wholeness of our Core Being in our Me-B System. As a result, we cultivate HVC and foster health, happiness and abundance. I call it learning to be the light in the darkness and the metaphorical "I" in the hurricane.

Happily, we can learn how to notice when we are creating and running LVC within us and we can learn the techniques taught in this book to reconnect to our wholeness and live more often from the HVC of our Core Being. So although we can't control if the energy of HVC or LVC is going to run through us anymore than we can control the weather, as our skills increase, we are more able to:

- self-regulate our mind-energy-body system so we can
- transform the energy of the LVC,
- see what lessons or wisdom it holds, and
- through the power of subtle energy awareness, positive intention and advanced mindfulness techniques, we become present enough so we can return back to the HVC of Core Being.

To be successful in this process, it is vital that you cultivate a connection to your wholeness or Core Being and not base your identity on the negative aspects of your personality that have been programmed into you throughout your life. In this book, you learn how to move out of your negative programmed personality and deepen your connection to Core Being in your Me-B System.

This book serves as year-long training in Me-B Transformation™. It is a guide and workbook in one. Take your time to master the skills and set goals to do a little bit every week. (If you need help, seek guidance from Me-B trained Guides, and/or organize classes in your area.)

INTRODUCTION REVIEW and PERSONAL MASTERY QUESTIONS

1. Explain HVC and LVC.
2. Explain your programmed personality – both the positive aspects and the saboteur aspects.
3. List 5-steps to use mindfulness and self-regulate our Me-B System back to Core Being.
4. What is easy for you in mastering these steps and where might you need additional support?

5. How might you organize your life to get that support (or have you already done this — explain)?
6. Just as splitting an atom creates a burst of energy, I find if we have (1) _(2) ____ and, (3) then as a result, healing and wholeness happens.
7. What keeps us from wisdom?
8. Explain Choice Points for Peace.
9. Draw the 3 rings of healing before and after process work. Explain the difference.
10. List three reasons why we get stuck. Now relate these reasons to you and your life challenges.
11. To be successful in self-mastery, it is vital we cultivate __ based on ____.
12. Explain why life is suffering and that is the good news.
13. Explain why Me-B Transformation is a form of spiritual alchemy.
14. Look at your life and explore what gifts you gained from past hardship.
15. For the next two weeks, look for Choice Points. You don't have to change any behaviors, just notice them.
16. What is your identity based on? How might that need to be deepened into a more universal support system of Core Being?

CHAPTER 1

THE MIND AS A POWERFUL ENERGETIC TOOL

How does healing happen? What is the magic bullet?

Energy is the primary substance that connects our mind with our body and is the foundation of everything. Physics tells us that the primary substance everything is made out of is energy and that we are nothing but energized particles. Physics also states that these particles can move from lower to higher vibrational states.

This is why in Me-B Transformation you learn to connect to subtle energy with holistic awareness, intention and presence. As you learn to sense subtle energy and transform the low vibrational consciousness (LVC) of suffering into high vibrational consciousness (HVC) of Core Being, you master the skills to create deep personal health, self-knowledge, and the ability to feel joy even in times of darkness. Subtle energy awareness, combined with mindfulness and aligned intention are pivotal tools to our success. All three together, when used artfully, are the magic bullets for self-mastery.

Awareness used with clear intention is the power behind energy transformation.

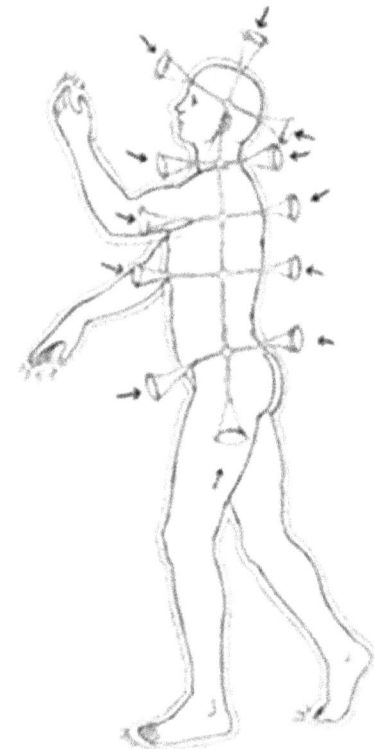

Through Me-B Transformation, you develop a deep understanding that the body is energy and that energy is consciousness. All three — the mind, energy, and body systems — are distinct aspects of one continuous state of being. This is illustrated most clearly within the Auric Field, which is one of the four types of energies you will learn to work with. I will introduce them now and you will delve deeper in future Chapters.

Only two types of energy hold negative personality distortions: energy in the Auric Field and Manifest Energy. Other energetic configurations you access in this book are conduits to receive spirit and HVC into our mind and body. (Chapter 14 teaches you how to feel, sense and track energy and Chapter 13 outlines the various energetic frequencies you work with in Me-B Transformation.) Specifically, you work with four types of energies:

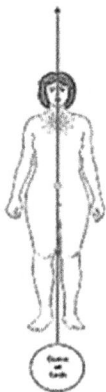

Auric Field includes 7 chakras (front and back), the Central Channel where the chakras connect into (see above picture), outer energy egg, and the 7 levels of the Auric Field that include your physical, emotional, mental, relational, and spiritual energy bodies. (See chapter 13 for details.) Trauma and negative beliefs are held in the chakras, and in the emotional and relational energetic bodies. When the Auric field is balanced, it connects you to your life force, aliveness, health and the positive aspects of your personality.

Manifest Energy and its Intention Line helps you align your Me-B System to create your dreams. To me it feels like magnetic particles that align through the center of your body and create a strong steel rod. What feels like a strong steel rod is the Manifest Energy Intention Line (see diagram below). You can use this energy to attract your dreams to us. However, it manifests to you both your hidden harmful intentions and your constructive intentions. Sometimes a subconscious part of us wants to stay in our pain and separate from our Core Being. When this happens, you can learn to realign your intention and move out of your LVC and reconnect to Core Being. I believe we would all be instantly enlightened if all parts of us were aligned toward that higher intention. Unfortunately, the LVC in our past programming can create a blend of negative and positive intentions. Learning to realign our Manifest Energy and thus our intentions is a very powerful tool to use for consciously creating our lives.

Manifest Energy responds to our intentions by organizing in a manner that attracts our intentions to you. For instance, if you are not able to attract to you what you think you want, you can assess your Manifest Energy Intention Line to discover why it has not showed up in your lives. (Manifest Energy is similar to the Hara Dimension as outlined In *Hands of Light*, by premier healer and scientist, Barbara Brennan.)

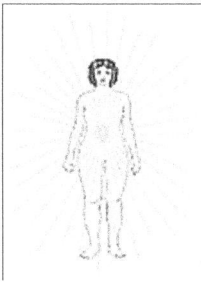

Core Being. At the energetic and spiritual levels you are all connected and one. Core being energy is your unique one note in the universal symphony that represents the oneness of all. You have a part of yourself that has never been damaged or hurt — this is Core Being. As you learn to cultivate this energy in every aspect of your Me-B System, you can undo the negative programming of the past. (In *Hands of Light*, Barbara Brennan names this the Core Star Dimension.)

The *Multi-dimensional Fabric of Interconnectedness.* Whereas Core Being is our one unique note, the Multi-dimensional fabric of Interconnectedness is the symphony of all — including all universes, planets, stars and galaxies. From this broader view of reality, you can better evaluate and solve your challenges.

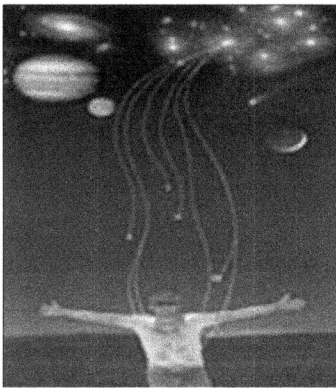

Star Child Energy. Star Child energy represents the lessons our soul has learned over the many lifetimes. Specifically it represents the insights, gifts and talents we have developed from living on many different planets and many different dimensions across the cosmos. Many of these gifts have been lost from our memory and thus from our ability to use them. We can learn to access the memory of these lessons so they can be helpful to us in this lifetime. Unlike Core Being and Multi-dimensional Fabric energy, soul energy is not always whole and complete. It represents the light and the dark aspects of our personality. However we can learn to retrieve the HVC from the lessons our soul has collected. As we are able to remember these gifts, it can be a boost to help raise our consciousness.

Since energy is consciousness, as you learn to make energy a tangible resource that you can sense, see, touch and evaluate, you can then use it as a raw material to increase your self-awareness and raise your consciousness. Then you can connect to the energy that holds LVC in your body and in your mind (Mindfulness Steps 1-3), gain wisdom and insight (Mindfulness Step 4) and transform misaligned energy into HVC and Core Being (Mindfulness Step 5).

THE POWER OF "RIGHT" MINDFULNESS, PRESENCE AND ALIGNED INTENTION

Why Are They So Important?

I have noticed a wonderful increase in psychotherapeutic practices incorporating mindfulness techniques to help clients. As a result, I think it is important to further define mindfulness. Are mindfulness and presence the same thing, or how do they differ? What role does intention play? Are there various qualities of presence and mindfulness that hold a range of energetic vibrations? How can exploring this further help you in your own healing processes?

Let's start with the first question: are mindfulness and presence the same? Mindfulness is a tool you can use to cultivate presence. For instance, by following the 5-Step Mindfulness Practice outlined in the previous section, you activate and energize presence within you. There are many different mindfulness practices that can invite deeper levels of presence.

Mindfulness Techniques to Invite Presence

Yoga, Chanting, Dance, Exercise, Chi Kung, Breath Work, Meditation, Energy Work, Emotional Freedom Techniques, Lovemaking, Sensory Integration, Psychotherapy, Nutrition, baths, Hypnotherapy, Massage, Rolfing, and more. Almost anything can be a mindfulness technique if done with the right intention.

Of course, if you don't have clear intention for deeper presence, then whatever mindfulness technique you use will fail. This is because *it is intention that moves energy.* Energy is a tangible representation of consciousness and is the blueprint for everything. Energy is also the medium that connects the mind with the body. As your intentions align so does your energy and consciousness. **Mindfulness is only the tool. Intention directs the tool of mindfulness to create presence.**

For example, if I place my hand on my leg and I don't have intention for energy to flow, it won't. But if I place my hand on my leg and I align my intention to have the energy flow, then it will. **Where intention goes, energy flows.** If while exercising, doing yoga or meditating your intention migrates out of your body so will your energy. As a result, you become less connected and less – not more — present with yourself.

...subtle energy is conscious. Subtle energy bodies are able to transmute one type of energy into the other, with each energy center performing its own unique function within the anatomical structure of the body's energy system. As such, these centers tie together different parts of the body, the body with the cosmos, and all aspects of being with one another physical, emotional, mental and spiritual. (*The Subtle Body*, Cyndi Dale; page 245)

When I am not present or balanced enough to solve a problem, I often go for a bike ride. On the bike ride, I set my intention to let my mind wander off to connect with HVC outside of my body. Usually it takes about 15 minutes before I notice my mind is focusing on the wisdom I needed to solve the problem. I then use intention to be present with that wisdom, and apply it in my life.

Intention is the force that directs energy to use the tool of mindfulness. Mindfulness is the tool to create presence. Therefore, you can't accurately discuss presence without also talking about energy, intention and mindfulness.

Presence then is the result of energy, intention and mindfulness. When presence is experienced not only in the mind, but also in the body and energy systems, it results in a higher quality of presence.

So what is the energy and consciousness of presence? In Me-B Transformation the highest quality of presence is experiencing Core Being in our Me-B System. As your connection to Core Being vibrates at a higher frequency, so does your presence.

As I align my (a) intention to use (b) mindfulness to be (c) more present, I notice my unhealthy defenses. Awareness leads me to my Choice Points. I then find my Choice Point; follow the 5-Step Mindfulness Process, which helps me realign my negative programmed personality, transform LVC and reconnect to center.

Making Energy A Tangible Resource For Change

The more present I am, the more empowered I am. It becomes easier for me to see and sense energy and use it as a practical tool for transformation.

For instance, while meditating, I look at my body and intend to be even more present with the reality before me. As I do this, I notice the energy in my legs begin to shimmer. I see my legs turn to silvery light. As the silver glows, I invite even deeper presence. As a result, the light dissolves into a haze of dancing energy particles. Bliss fills me. I regulate my field with the intention of returning to solidity and I see the world as a grid of solid lines. Slowly form returns.

This level of presence helps me sense the deeper reality before me. I notice the truth of my light while at the same time I am aware of my earthly personal work. In fact, I believe because we acknowledge our light, it can make it easier to also acknowledge our own personal growth work.

As we deepen our self-mastery, we also raise the vibration of our Core Being. So as my intention is aligned, my mindfulness skills advance and I become more present. The more present I am, the higher the vibration of my Core Being I can experience. As this happens, maybe shimmering legs of light will become commonplace.

As outlined previously, awareness is the first step to healing. As you clarify what the energetic vibration of intention, "right" mindfulness, and presence are, you can better self-assess and regulate back to a higher vibration.

The term "right mindfulness" comes from the Fourth Noble Truths of Buddhism.

The Four Noble Truths

1. **Life means suffering.** To live means to suffer, because human nature is not perfect, and neither is the world we live in. During our lifetimes, we inevitably have to endure physical suffering—such as pain, sickness, injury, tiredness, old age, and eventually death. We also have to endure psychological suffering — sadness, fear, frustration, disappointment, and depression. There are different degrees of suffering, and there are also positive experiences in life such as comfort, and happiness. Because our world is subject to impermanence, life will always fluctuate and change. Ups and downs will always happen. What can be permanent is a continuous flow of aligned intention and mindfulness that knows our happiness is linked to an internal constant of Core Being and not an external flux and change. Change can feel safe just as sadness can deliver the gift of wisdom and strength.

2. **The origin of suffering is attachment.** Suffering is caused by clinging to something or revolting against something. Non-attachment happens when we have deep connection and knowledge of Core Being.

3. **The cessation of suffering is attainable.** The cessation of suffering can be attained through nirodha. Nirodha means the unmaking of sensual craving and conceptual attachment. Nirodha extinguishes all forms of clinging and attachment.

4. **The path to the cessation of suffering is the Eightfold Path**. This path leads to self-mastery.
   Eightfold Path
   - Right View
   - Right Intention
   - Right Speech
   - Right Action
   - Right Livelihood
   - Right Effort
   - Right Mindfulness
   - Right Concentration

Our Enlightened Observer helps us get closer to wholeness.

Valerie Hunt has done some research into this general topic of measuring energy that holds HVC.

When people in her studies were thinking of daily situations, their energy fields measured frequencies in the range of 250Hz. This is the same frequency as the heart. When psychic individuals had their energy fields tested on the electromyography, their frequency ranged in a band from 400-800Hz. Trance specialists and channelers fell into the 800 to 900 Hz range, and mystics, connected continually to their higher self had an energy or etheric body above 900 Hz. Hunt's findings correlate with traditional chakra lore: the chakras can be stepping-stones to enlightenment, each inviting a different spiritual awareness and increasing the frequency of the subtle body. In fact, the manufacturer of the equipment adapted the machine to measure higher frequencies, and it was found that a mystic had an average subtle energy field frequency of 200.000Hz. Hunt also found changes in coloration emanating from the chakra points when subjects were being Rolfed. (*The Subtle Body*, Cyndi Dale; p. 247)

To date, I don't know of any device to measure our exact vibrational range of "right" intention, "right" mindfulness or presence. But in the following charts, performance indicators for intention, mindfulness and presence are outlined. They are organized according to skill levels I, II and III.

IT BEGINS WITH RIGHT INTENTION— RIGHT INTENTION CREATES MINDFULNESS, PRESENCE, and CORE BEING

Where intention goes, energy flows.

Some meditation techniques use chanting, yoga positions and ceremony to raise the vibration of the mind. I support these approaches and I also want to emphasize the importance of constructive intention. Intention is the force that moves energy and consciousness. You can't be mindful or present without right intention. If the intention is to separate, you separate. If the hidden intention is to be a victim, you become a victim. However, as you cultivate enough intention to be mindful and invite presence you heal. Is it this simple?

It is simple, but not necessarily easy. Because your subconscious is so large, hidden saboteurs have mixed intentions. There are many reasons you may have misaligned intentions that don't serve your highest good. For instance, to align your intentions, you often must first experience your negative beliefs and negative ego. This means you may need to feel the LVC of something very harsh. It might feel painful to your idealized self-image. This makes it very difficult to notice a misaligned intention.

Our self-identity wants to feel whole, but if you have a positive intention to heal, you often must go through the pain and into the light. *The danger is that you could get lost in the pain and link it to your self-identity.* When this happens, your ego tends to chime in and confirm your negative image. If this happens you become stuck in the pain and your negative ego takes charge. As a result, you can't move through the 3-rings of healing and back into Core Being. Pain becomes your barrier. So...it is the power pain has over you that creates your negative intentions.

Emotional pain that slashes your sense of self, also destabilizes your energy system. *In this book, you develop the skills so you can split your awareness into two parts — one part connected to the emotion, and the other part with enough presence to know who you really are. When you can do this, you don't merge with your negative self-identity, but instead maintain mindfulness and presence.*

With enough aligned Intention:

- you don't merge with your negative self-identity,
- you can then learn how to feel the pain as an energy and sensation and not as a litmus test for your self-worth.

Remember the earlier story of Roselyn. She had enough constructive intention so her consciousness could expand. As a result, she moved out of her small, wounded self and into a more accurate and whole perspective. She experienced herself as a light body that traveled to earth so she could experience loss but not become lost. I believe this is the real truth we can embrace. Yes, it is hard to muster that level of aligned intention, but it is this positive intention that creates the deepest healing.

Intention does not mean you have an agenda, and does not come from a place of judgment or tension. **Intention is simply an alignment within yourself of what you want to create or manifest.** You don't hold onto it, or think you are bad if it doesn't show up, but you can investigate why it doesn't show up. This is because there may be a contrary intention that has LVC. As you investigate why it doesn't show up, you can see if some part of you is preventing it from happening. (See future chapters for exercises on developing aligned Intention.)

Levels I, II, III — Indicators of Intention to Transform LVC Energy and Consciousness into Core Being

MIND: At Level I you understand the harmful aspects of misaligned intention and the benefits. Cognitively you can begin to assess negative and positive intentions. At Level II you are getting better at aligning your Manifest Energy Intention Line to promote positive change. At Level III you are much more skillful at manifesting your intentions.

BODY: At Level I you can only begin to feel the sensation of aligned/misaligned Manifest Energy in your body. At Level II you can often feel the sensation of it and know where in the body it is aligned and misaligned. At Level III, you can easily feel the sensation of it in the body and know where in the body it is aligned or misaligned. You also know what deeper personal work must be done so you are more likely to manifest your intentions.

ENERGY: Level I is more "faking it to make it." You don't yet know how to align your Manifest Energy into right intention. At Level II you can begin to self assess/track/realign your Manifest Energy. At level III you can easily assess and realign our Manifest Energy in yourself and others. When you can't realign, you usually know why and what deeper personal work is needed to be successful.

Energy and Consciousness Transformation	LEVEL I (Stages 1-3)	LEVEL II (Stage 4)	LEVEL III (Stage 5-7)
MIND	We are more faking it to make it. We don't yet know how to align our Manifest Energy into right intention.	We can begin to self assess/ track/ realign our Manifest Energy. For instance, we know when we are in contrary intention - even if we can't always realign it.	We can often assess and realign our Manifest Energy in ourselves and others. When we can't realign we usually know why and what deeper personal work is needed to be successful.
BODY	At Level I we can only begin to feel the sensation of aligned/misaligned	We can sometimes feel the sensation of its alignment and misalignment and know the location in the	We can easily feel the sensation of its alignment and

	Manifest Energy in our body.	body where it is misaligned or aligned.	misalignment and know where in the body it is misaligned or aligned.
ENERGETICALLY	Level I is more faking it to make it. We don't yet know how to align our Manifest Energy into right intention.	At Level II we can begin to self assess/ track/ realign our Manifest Energy.	At level III we can often see, sense, assess and realign Manifest Energy in ourselves and others. When we can't realign we usually know why and what deeper personal work is needed to be successful.

ADVANCED MINDFULNESS — Uses the Vibration of the Enlightened Observer

The mind is a powerful energetic tool. In fact, I argue that it is the most powerful energetic tool available to any of us — as powerful as hands-on healing, or an acupuncture needle. Used skillfully, your mind can heal anything. Used skillfully *in the body*, it can make the impossible, possible. I have seen clients heal breast cancer, torn ligaments, deep trauma and chronic depression simply by putting their mind in the body. Yet, as an energetic tool, it is important you notice what vibration the mind is holding when you use it in your body and energy system.

If your mind fixates and loops through negative images and thoughts, the energy loses its healing qualities. As a result, the energy of LVC spreads like a virus throughout your mind and your body. Yet if your mind focuses on connecting with the Enlightened Observer, HVC flows.

Over time, as you remember to invite connection to your Enlightened Observer, it becomes a positive habituation throughout the day. On days that I find this difficult, I often exercise, ride my horse, dance, sing or chant and before I know it, my mind is reconnected to its HVC. If the mind is running judgments and LVC you risk creating more judgments and LVC. But if the Enlightened Observer raises your mind's vibration, it can more effectively transform energetic distortions, trauma, and painful emotions into wisdom and light.

Many mindfulness techniques teach about the objective observer. Meditators can use an objective mind so they don't judge feelings, images, pain — or anything else that arises during the meditation practice.

The objective observer is a technique used to achieve a balanced and nonjudgmental meditative practice. Unfortunately, too often meditation students get lost in the illusions and pain that arise during deep practice. They think their mind is objective, but in subtle ways the observer's objectivity dissolves and people can feel victimized by meditation practices. So in Me-B Transformation, you develop the Enlightened Observer to raise the vibration of your mind to promote your highest good when it is used in the body and in your energy system.

For instance, imagine a bucket of beautiful white paint (representing the Enlightened Observer and HVC), to which you only add a dropper full of black paint (LVC) representing a painful emotion. If you mix the two paints together, your white paint will still have its beautiful white color (or HVC). But if you dump too much black paint (LVC) into your white paint, it turns grey or even completely black. So if you don't engage your Enlightened Observer in times of stress, you risk creating more pain for yourself.

Think of our Enlightened Observer as a scale of HVC and LVC (white and black energetic paint). If we connect to pain and challenge in our lives with too much LVC, it tips the scales so we keep creating LVC. As we commit to cultivating energy that holds higher vibrational consciousness in our Me-B Systems, we gain enough high vibrational energy to transmute our LVC.

This is why you learn to develop an authentic connection to your "white paint" or Enlightened Observer before you jump too deeply into feeling and resonating at the level of your negative ego and Core Distortions. Over time, as you develop your skills, you can more easily return to HVC when life becomes challenging. This helps you re-anchor into Core Being. If too much "black paint" is created, you cannot re-balance. This can re-traumatize you and activate your nervous system so that the energies of fight/flight, freeze, ego, anxiety and depression are magnified.

There are many ways to cultivate "Right" Mindfulness and thus HVC. They range from Level I (beginner) to intermediate (Level II) to advanced (Level III). **Developing a strong Enlightened Observer is the most important ingredient in this process**. As you invite your mindfulness to resonate at the vibration of the Enlightened Observer, it will have enough HVC to be clear, focused, wise, and knowing. It holds bucketful of "white paint." It doesn't judge or collapse or merge with the LVC. It simply resonates at a high enough vibration so when it connects to a thought, a sensation in the body, illness or distorted energy, it promotes health and healing.

People processing trauma can energetically, cognitively, and somatically merge with the trauma and create further discomfort and fear. We can't heal trauma if it overwhelms us, developmentally regresses us, or suppresses our ability to believe in ourselves.

When mindfulness connects to the body and feels emotions, energy and sensations, it is a powerful tool for health or harm. *If mindfulness is vibrating at the frequency of the Enlightened Observer, it protects us from lowering our energetic vibration and from losing our insight.* With its help, we heal and re-pattern the traumatic past—and create a productive future. The Enlightened Observer is like a life preserver in an ocean of pain: it keeps us afloat so we don't drown. It is our metaphorical anchor in the hurricane—the calm, clear eye that sees that we are more than the trauma inside of us or around us.

A STRONG ENLIGHTENED OBSERVER

Shaking, heat building, with stomach cramps and nausea, I quickly excuse myself from my client. I close the door behind me as I crawl to the bathroom, almost blacking out. The trauma from my client's recent operation has triggered my own trauma from birth. Using my Enlightened Observer, I regain my balance, and within minutes I am able to finish the Me-B session. Mentally, I note to revisit my birth trauma at my next supervision session.

A strong Enlightened Observer can assist us even under harsh circumstances. At my next supervision session, I invited the trauma to reappear. Once again the shakes, confusion, and fragmentation ripple through me. Tears run down my cheeks as I sob. On my mind screen was the vision of me being pulled from my birth mother's arms and taken away for adoption.

Even though part of me was feeling the effects of the past, my Enlightened Observer was strong — even happy for the opportunity to release and move forward. *This is because the Enlightened Observer allowed me to self-acknowledge my own divinity while at the same time experiencing trauma, pain, and sorrow. Its frequency was high enough to transform pain into higher consciousness.* I had enough "white paint" to transmute the pain.

As you use your clear intention to move energy, you better support transformation. As you learn to work the different parts of your **Me-B System** in coordination with one another, you may be surprised at how natural it can be to live life with your Enlightened Observer.

ENLIGHTENED OBSERVER CONNECTION

(Practice this when difficulty sets in. It melts the intensity away to find the gifts beneath.)

- **Step 1**
  Imagine that your energy field is charged and balanced. To help it balance, dance, exercise, and imagine it charged and balanced — from front to back, top to bottom, and left to right. (More technical methods to balance and charge your energy field are taught later.)

- **Step 2**
  Imagine, feel, or sense the energy of your Enlightened Observer floating downward from above through the top of your head. As it melts into every cell, it fills every cell. Head, forehead, center of head, chin, jaw, tongue, lips, neck — receive it in —shoulders, chest front and back, mid-back, mid-chest, stomach, all of your internal organs, receive it in. Keep moving downward though the body. Sometimes its high frequency will bring up challenging emotions as it melts deep within, cleansing and cleaning along the way. Let the emotions come, and then let them go as you soak in the love, acceptance, and wholeness of your Enlightened Observer.

Levels I, II, III of Mindfulness/Enlightened Observer

MIND: Level I is when someone can conceptually understand the Enlightened Observer but can't yet use it to transform LVC into HVC of Core Being. Level II is when we can begin to use the HVC of the

Enlightened Observer to self-assess and self-regulate so LVC (negative thoughts/emotions and core distortions) transforms to HVC. Level III is when this process is more effortless and more effective.

BODY: Level I is when we are only beginning to feel sensations of our Enlightened Observer and LVC and describe them such as cold, soft, tingling and flowing. Level II is when we can sometimes feel the Enlightened Observer as a sensation in the body and are beginning to be mindful of how its HVC is transforming LVC. At this level we can reduce unproductive thoughts and emotional looping. At level III we can clearly identify the consciousness (feelings, trauma, negative beliefs...) of the sensations, we know where they are located in the body and can easily engage our Enlightened Observer to transform the LVC into HVC.

ENERGY: At Level I, we might be using the strategy of faking it to make it. Sometimes we need to pretend we know what we are doing in order to succeed. So at this level we are only imaging and inviting the energy of our Enlightened Observer into the mind and body. At this level we can cognitively describe the Auric field (such as chakra functions, outer energy egg and Core Being) but can barely feel or self-asses it in the body. Level II is when we can somewhat invite the energy of the Enlightened Observer into the body. We can also somewhat self-assess the Auric field and higher energetic vibrations.

At level III our mindfulness skills are advanced. We can easily invite the energy of our Enlightened Observer into the body and mind. We also use our Enlightened Observer to easily self-assess all energetic vibrations and identify the Core Distortions that create any misalignments.

Indicators of "Right" Mindfulness/Strong Enlightened Observer in our Me-B System

Energy and Consciousness Transformation	LEVEL I (Stages 1-3)	LEVEL II (Stage 4)	LEVEL III (Stage 5-7)
MIND	Noticing thoughts/ emotions. Conceptually understands LVC and the Enlightened Observer.	Using Mindfulness/ Enlightened Observer we can begin to reduce un- productive thoughts/ emotions and LVC.	Many times there are no thoughts; just direct input of knowledge. Experienced use of Enlightened Observer.
BODY	Beginning to feel sensations in the body of their Core Being/ Enlightened Observer and LVC and describe them such as cold, soft, flowing...	Can somewhat use the Enlightened Observer feel sensations in the body. Sometimes can identify basic neg / pos. emotion and know where they are held in the body. Can sometimes feel Core Being/ Enlightened Observer as a sensation in the body.	Can clearly identify the consciousness (feelings, trauma, negative beliefs...) and feel the sensations and know where they are located in the body.
ENERGETICALLY	It is more faking it to make it to invite the energy of the Enlightened Observer into the mind and body. Cognitively describes the Auric field such as charka functions, outer energy egg and Core Being but can't feel or self-asses it in their body.	Can somewhat invite the energy of the Enlightened Observer into the body. Can somewhat self-assess the Auric field and higher energetic vibrations in the body.	Can easily invite the energy of the Enlightened Observer into the body and mind. Can easily self-assess all energetic vibrations and identify the Core Distortions that create any misalignments.

PRESENCE —From a Strong Connection to CORE BEING Thanks to our Enlightened Observer *Presence is a State of Being. As we move higher in the 10 Stages of Me-B Transformation, we cultivate our connection to Core Being and increase our ability to be present.*

Understanding your life patterns can help you map out solutions. In Me-B Transformation™, you learn to identify and transform our **Core Distortions** and let the higher consciousness of our Core Being anchor deeply within us. As we do this, we become more present.

Everyone has a divine Core Being or spirit that is part of the oneness and wholeness around us. Being fully present is being fully in Core Being. However, there are many degrees of presence. Each higher stage of Me- B Transformation™ represents a stronger ability to be present.

When you are present, you can use your aligned intention to be mindful and engage your Enlightened Observer, cultivate HVC, transform (LVC) Core Distortions and return to Core Being.

As mentioned earlier, Core Being has many names. Some call it the God Consciousness, the light of Jesus, Spirit, True Self, Core Being, or Higher Self. Our Core Being is an actual energetic vibration that each of us can claim. It is your right to embody this Core Being—it is your path to freedom, god, and joy. *As you learn how to resonate at this vibration, you cultivate presence and return to it more quickly. Your life changes for the better.*

A **Core Distortion** is anything that causes you to lose your connection with Core Being and it dramatically impinges upon your ability to be present. It is located in the lower levels of the Auric field. The external situations of trauma, genetics, developmental wounding, relational attachment issues — and even everyday life — create our Core Distortions. Core Distortions also include your reactive feelings of anger, fear, pain, hurt, depression, anxiety, and confusion. These distortions perpetuate our negative beliefs and cause you to maintain a false identity.

Lost my Presence — Lost my Cell Phone

For instance, today when I was riding my horse, my business phone fell out of my pocket. I borrowed someone else's phone so I could walk the 40-acre field to find where my phone might have landed. It was like finding a needle in a haystack. I was flustered. My ego was in charge. It said, "My phone is my livelihood. How could I have been so 'stupid' to leave it in my pocket?"

I definitely was not present. In fact, the first time I called my business number, I accidentally called my home number instead. My husband answered. "Oops," I said to him. I dialed the wrong number.

Heck, I wasn't present enough to even remember what number to call so I centered, engaged my Enlightened Observer and reconnected to Core Being. I assessed the energy in the field. I sensed where it was. I walked toward the spot and dialed the correct number. I could hear the ring four steps away and I had it!

PRESENCE invites CORE BEING

Core Being is the expression of our own musical note, which, when combined with other notes, makes the music of Universal Oneness.

Your Enlightened Observer helps you reconnect to Core Being and you become more present. Ideally, you would all be in Core Being 24/7 and so always be completely present. Realistically, you are only human and you travel in and out of contact with yourself. Kindness linked with awareness can help you return.

The primary goal of Me-B Transformation is to help us become more present so we can move out of our programmed personality with its Core Distortions and back to Core Being. Me-B Transformation teaches roughly 100 techniques to invite more presence so that we can bring the balanced high frequency of our Core Being into the Low Vibrational Consciousness (LVC) of our pain, illness, anger, overwhelm, insecurity, and ego.

By using these techniques, our Core Distortions transmute into the innate wisdom, joy, and bliss of Higher Vibrational Consciousness (HVC). Such transformation allows us to create health, peace, and empowerment.

An essential ingredient in the Me-B Transformation formula is our Enlightened Observer. As we are more present, we can better learn to maintain the high frequency of our Enlightened Observer. Transformation is possible!

The Enlightened Observer helps us learn how to track energy at its most subtle levels. Energy is the medium in which the transformation takes place. By tuning in to the various aspects of our Energy System, we can learn what personal process work has been successful and what work is still ahead of us.

Your Core Being is the dimensional—mind, energy, and body — expression of the deeper truth, the deeper reality of our unique divinity. Your Core Being is who you are *before* you have been programmed or altered with life experiences. As you use the state of being of presence to connect to Core Being, Core Being helps us become more present.

You know you are in our Core Being when you experience the following:

- We have no judgment or denial of our imperfections.
- We have clarity that the pain and difficulty in the moment is perfect.
- We completely accept our mistakes as learning opportunities.
- We acknowledge that we are the metaphorical "I" in the hurricane which we can anchor into in times of stress.
- We are glad that we are who we are, and not someone different.
- An island of safety exists within us that we trust for support and security.
- We feel like a beautiful sunny beach, and our imperfections are only grains of sand that help us learn, grow, and transform.
- Negative AND positive emotions are energies that run through us, versus concepts that define who we are.
- We can feel the sensations of tingling and flow throughout our body and outer energy system.
- Our ego and defenses don't define our actions and words.
- It is easy to acknowledge the deeper truth of a situation even when we are attacked and told we are "bad."
- We can easily mirror our positive sense of self back to ourselves.
- We love and comfort ourselves even when we wish someone else would save us.
- Positive intention flows effortlessly.
- Our positive and negative ego is silent. There are no judgments, just understandings.

When a Me-B Guide sees a client's, friend's, or partner's Core Being, you are seeing clearly. Unless you are willing to put aside your judgments and see a person's Core Being, it is much harder to assist the person. How can you invite them to see their own Core Being if you can't see it too? In addition, if you don't acknowledge your own Core Being, it is much harder to acknowledge others' and assist them in the process.

Enlightenment is the ability to move from the programmed personality level back to Core Being. This can only be done as we are able to create a stronger state of presence.

> *When we make a mistake or someone tells us they don't like us, we may feel pain, but we are not defined by the pain—This can happen because we have enough presence to connect to Core Being.*

When a difficult emotion or trauma moves within you, if you are present with Core Being, your ego remains calm and knows the challenge is a life lesson and not a judgment of your worth.

For example, the love of our life can reject us and leave us. We feel despondent, yelling with rage, tears streaming down our faces—but at Stage 7 of Me-B Transformation, we also remain so empowered that we are grateful, safe, and whole. At this higher stage of Me-B Transformation, if a part of our consciousness regresses to a younger age, we experience two qualities. We are present enough to know: (1) that we are regressed; and (2) how to transform the energy of the regressed consciousness within us, and return back to our Core Being.

Core Being is the answer — the only answer for any problem or challenge. From the place of Core Being, you become present enough to solve any challenge and overcome any hardship. It is that simple. The ease of finding, remaining in, or returning to your Core Being is linked to your aligned intention. When you focus on what you can do, it fosters the ability to be mindful of the wisdom needed to be present.

CORE BEING CONNECTION MEDITATION FOSTERS PRESENCE

(Practice every moment of every day)

- **Part I**
  Ground deeply and do movements—such as dancing to music—to balance and charge your energy field. Imagine it balanced front to back, top to bottom, and left to right. Once you feel more connected and   balanced, place your awareness on the Core Being energy vortex located 1½ inches above your belly button, in the center of your body.

- **Part II**
  Imagine a ball of energy the size of a dime glowing with your unique essence. To the extent possible, notice its color, light, sensation, image, smell, taste, and sound. Breathe deeply into that space, and imagine the glowing ball of your unique essence expanding to the size of a tennis ball. Just as a balloon expands, imagine the energy of your Core Being increasing in size. Once again, spend time breathing into its center, feeling its sensation. It is the conduit for the divine source of you. Sense it, know it, and intuit it.

- **Part III**
  If you want, place your hands on the Core Being area to help it charge and expand. The sensation of it often feels like tingles of wholeness. Begin to feel your wholeness. Melt into the center of your Core Being again, and this time let it expand further—to the size of a volley ball. Imagine it front and back, top and bottom, left and right. With every in-breath, go back to the center of the energy ball. With every out-breath, expand outward until this sphere of light fills your physical body and your outer energy field, an egg-shaped zone of energy extending about 2.5 feet from the body (see Chapter on Energy Fields).

- **Part IV**
  As you anchor into your center during the in-breaths, you may notice negative emotions. You can expand through these outwardly to connect to your Core Being. With every in-breath, go back to the center of your light. With every out-breath, expand further until your light fills all

Some days, your presence with Core Being may not expand very easily or very far. This is because a Core Distortion — perhaps more than one — needs love, attention, and transmuting. But if you are present enough with Core Being, this means you can be ok, even when you are lost and in pain.

In the beginning of Me-B Transformation™, you only focus on cultivating the positive higher frequencies. Once you have enough skill to resonate at the higher frequencies, you then can bring the high frequencies into the difficult emotions created by our Core Distortions.

Until we reach Stage 4 of Me-B Transformation, we are simply cultivating HVC and strengthening our ability to anchor into Core Being. Once we reach Stage 4, we can stay somewhat connected to Core Being as we are also noticing stress and overwhelm. So, at Stage 4, when we feel negative emotions, we are so present with the truth of who we are at the Core Being level, we are much more able to learn from these emotions.

The more present we are with ourselves, the more we are able to know how to feel emotions in a manner that doesn't overwhelm our ego, energy system, and negative defenses.

One solution to reducing the amount of overwhelms and distress in ourselves, is to practice invoking HVC. As we learn to bring the HVC of Core Being into the negative emotions, they dissolve and melt away. Just as butter melts on the grill, LVC melts away when the HVC of Core Being is brought into it. (This technique is called a Core Distortion Intervention and is discussed later in the book.)

Levels I, II, III Indicators of Presence (Core Being)

MIND: Level I is when we are available enough for ourselves that we can notice thoughts/emotions and Level II is when our presence/Core Being is strong enough so that we actually reduce LVC. Level III is when we are so present that thinking/awareness flows from our connection to Core Being most of the time.

BODY: At level I we can just begin to be present enough to feel or imagine sensations in the body and describe them as hot, cold, dense, soft, flowing, solid, etc. At this level, we are not sure what the sensations represent. We are just happy to be present enough to feel them. Whereas at Level II we not only can feel sensations in the body, but also are present enough to describe them and identify what Core Distortion, negative believe of LVC is held there. We can also begin to be present enough to feel the HVC of Core Being and our Enlightened Observer in the body. At Level III, we are anchored so deeply into Core Being that we are present enough to do this easily.

ENERGY: At Level I we are only present enough to describe Core Being energy and other energetic configurations. We cannot yet see/sense/track/assess much of the Auric Field; Chakras; Colors; Manifest Energy; Outer Energy Egg and more. At level II we are present enough with ourselves to begin to sense energy in others and ourselves. At level III we are deeply connected to Core Begin and thus can easily sense energy in others and ourselves. We can sense where in the body someone is present and where they are not.

Indicators of "right" Presence (Core Being) in our Me-B System			
Presence	LEVEL I (Stages 1-3)	LEVEL II (Stage 4)	LEVEL III (Stage 5-7)
MIND	Noticing thoughts/emotions at least in the Mind. Beginning to be able to label the positive aspects of Core Being.	Reduction of LVC and unproductive thoughts/emotions and Experience of Core Being.	More often, no thoughts. Experiences of Core Being easily transforms LVC.
BODY	Can just begin to be present enough to feel or imagine sensations in the body and describe them such as hot, cold, dense, soft, flowing, solid, etc.	Can identify basic negative/ positive emotions from the sensations and might know where they are in the body. Beginning to Experience Core Being as a sensation in the body.	Can clearly identify LVC/HVC consciousness (feelings, trauma, negative beliefs, etc.) and feel the sensations of the consciousness in the body and know where they are located in the body. Can easily experience the sensations of Core Being in the body and transform LVC into HVC.
ENERGETICALLY	Can describe Core Being energy and other energetic configurations. Cannot yet see/ sense much of the Auric Field; Chakras; Colors; Manifest Energy; Outer Energy Egg and more.	Beginning experiences of Core Being in mind and body and energy system. Can begin to sense/ assess/ track the Auric Field; Chakras; Colors; Manifest Energy; Outer Energy Egg and more.	Can sense where in the body someone is present, and where they are not. Experiences of Core Being in Mind and body and energy system. We are present enough to see/ sense/ assess/ track energy in ourselves and others such as the Auric.

Learning Me-B Transformation is learning a new system, yet ancient art form. It is important we focus on what we can do and not on what we wish we could do better. Be kind, compassionate and patient with ourselves. In addition to this book, you can get individual support from me so you continue to be successful. You can also attend our 12-class Certification program to become a Mind Energy Body Transformation™ Guide and attend on-line trainings and tele-classes.

CHAPTER REVIEW QUESTIONS

1. Define mindfulness. What are your personal challenges in this area and how can you support yourself to overcome them?
2. Are mindfulness and presence the same thing? Explain.
3. Explain the various qualities of presence and their range of energetic vibrations.
4. Outline where you are in your ability to be present/ mindful-level I, II or III.
5. Outline your challenges related to Intention and Manifest Energy. How can you better support

yourself in overcoming these challenges?

6. What is your saboteur to mastering the next level and what can you do to overcome the saboteur? Remember to keep our negative ego in check when answering this question! It is not our friend. Kindness is!

7. Explain the following terms: Core Being, Core Distortion, Enlightened Observer, Low Vibrational Consciousness (LVC), and High Vibrational Consciousness (HVC).

8. Why is the Enlightened Observer important in transmuting lower energy frequencies?

9. Why is gentleness and compassion to yourself so important? What part of your personality needs more gentleness and compassion?

10. Why is Mind Energy Body Transformation™ new yet ancient?

CHAPTER 2

INTENTION + MINDFULNESS = PRESENCE

Let go of our programming – Embrace our CORE BEING Follow the Map!

As we travel through this book, we can open ourselves to question our current perspectives and see the illusion in every moment. Since the reality we see only holds a shade of truth, as we detach (not dissociate) we gain the necessary perspective to move forward and achieve our greatest potential. An aligned Manifest Energy field helps us achieve enough detachment so we don't merge with the LVC.

Through Me-B Transformation™, gradually, over time, we can discover more and more about the nature of illusion-based reality, the roots of our pain, and the ability to influence our destiny. The skills we learn in order to accomplish this goal range from Level I, Level II and Level III.

Most often, it is our *inaccurate perception* of ourselves, our environment, and those around us that helps *create* our choices and manifests our discomfort. Since energy is the blueprint for the physical level, as we learn to sense, see and track its configuration, the illusions before us change, and we see life from a clearer and more objective perspective. To achieve such clarity, we can use our Explorer's State of Mind to:

1. **embrace uncertainty**, and release ourselves from being invested in a particular outcome;
2. **see light in the darkness of a difficult situation**, even if a part of our psyche feels threatened and afraid - in fact, fear is often a warning sign that we are getting closer to an answer; and
3. **use emotions**, instead of being abused by emotions.

These skills are cornerstones of Me-B Transformation™ and are essential components for consciously creating our lives.

Throughout the day, there are so many "wrongs" and "rights" that it can be difficult to know how we should react. What career, partner, or place to live in is the right one? Who has the answers? What is the reality of the situation? Am I right or wrong to feel this way? What is the deeper truth?

Simply asking the question can help to generate the answer to the question. At the very least, it creates the energetic opening to explore. Socrates once said that the only thing he knew was that he didn't know. This perspective represents the Explorer's State of Mind. As we read this book and study this modality, we can maintain the Explorer's State of Mind, find our CHOICE POINTS, and be a detective solving life's vast mystery.

There are multiple layers of reality to travel through; each layer we transcend leads us to the next, and we wake up further and further along our path. As we wake up to our own wisdom of life, we empower ourselves with the perspectives to see, feel, and know what we are creating and how we create it.

THE AWAKENING PROCESS

With this knowledge, we can choose our life more consciously. We can see life in a very different light.

We awaken. As we awaken, joy, happiness and safety grow regardless of the external challenges. The Explorer says:

"I am not finished with the need to examine myself, grow, learn, and transform. I don't think we are ever done—yet, now I journey through life more consciously than ever before and more joyfully than I ever thought possible."

Does pain still happen? Will we still feel discomfort, mistrust, and insecurities? Yes. Anything else is Spiritual Junk Food. Emotions are part of this Earth-bound frequency. They are inevitable and necessary. They create biochemical reactions and provide information that serves as clues to help The Explorer's State of Mind uncover the next deeper reality available for us to see. We can learn how to question our pain and insecurities so we can use them to wake up to our reality even more. Our personal lessons repeat but at deeper levels. *As we watch our repeated mistakes, they point out to us our core life lessons.*

Core Lessons—Blowing in the Wind

Too often, we let others' opinions dictate to us who we are. Just as a leaf must follow where the wind blows, we let our confidence blow in the direction of someone else's opinion. We lose our center and inner knowing. I was no different. My life's pattern was to be happy when someone loved me and to collapse when someone disliked me or accused me of being wrong. It was exhausting to never be secure anywhere unless someone else made me secure.

But this is how I grew up—this was my programming as a young child. No one ever stood up to my father or set boundaries. If they did, they were verbally smashed and left eviscerated, all love from them withdrawn.

So I took on others' truths as being real, instead of anchoring into my own divine core truth. I couldn't maintain happiness because I was so reliant upon others' positive opinions of me. If their moods or opinions faded, my confidence faded, too.

I was easily projected upon and manipulated to meet other people's needs. Their egos became my guides. If I protected their egos, they would like me and then I could like myself.

Over many years, I worked hard to change this. I identified my negative beliefs, such as *"if I say 'no' to you, I am bad."* I uncovered my unhealthy defenses—pleasing everyone else's egos so I felt loved—and I reconnected to my inner knowing and light. Gradually, I began to stand in the light of my Core Being when con- fronted or dismissed.

I found the "I" in the hurricane of life's challenges and others' judgments. I was no longer a leaf being blown in the direction of someone else's wind.

This is part of my personal story, but the wisdom gained can apply to all. As we learn to anchor into our Core Being, we raise our consciousness and heal our negative Core Distortions. We all have them, and we can all change them.

SPIRITUAL JUNK FOOD

Our Enlightened Observer and Core Being, when applied skillfully, allow us to avoid Spiritual Junk Food. Spiritual Junk Food, also known as spiritual bypassing, consists of self-delusions designed to allow us to artificially boost the ego and avoid owning our Core Distortions and imperfections. *Spiritual Junk Food is present when we think we are connected to our Core Being, but we are really escaping to higher frequencies to avoid pain instead of transforming that pain into HVC.* This is a common way we avoid the truth of "Now" because the ego feels threatened and overwhelmed. This happens to all of us! **However, staying in this state of denial is Spiritual Junk Food.**

There is no easy magic bullet to healing. Pain and discomfort will always show up from time to time. Spiritual Junk Food is when we ignore our "black paint" and pretend it isn't there. As we move higher in the Me-B Stages of Transformation™, we are more able to stay present with the "black paint" of our trauma, pain, and Core Distortions—while at the same time bringing in the energy of higher vibrations of consciousness (Stages 4-10 of Me-B Transformation™). We eventually become able to deal with buckets full of "black paint," and we don't get overwhelmed or retreat to Spiritual Junk Food.

> **NOTE:** Not all of us will choose to reach Stage 4 of Me-B Transformation™. Some of us will always just want to melt away the pain by calling in higher vibrations of energy, Manifest Energy, and the HVC of our Core Being. This is NOT Spiritual Junk Food—*as long as we are still acknowledging our negative programmed personality, ego, negative defenses, and Core Distortions and are clearly working toward healing them.*

> One key reason to move beyond Stage 4 is to obtain a higher level of self-mastery. Plus, life doesn't always present itself in easy, comfortable chunks of challenge. We can't always CONTROL how much "black paint" is thrown in our direction. As we move above Stage 4, we become more skillful at feeling deep emotional pain and negative ego — and yet not letting it lower our HVC!

We all escape; we all go into defense. However, some of us cling to spiritual and self-help practices to find a "magic bullet" that lets us escape from looking at the negative aspects of our programmed personality. This is NOT Me-B Transformation™, nor is it Core Being—but it is a great example of Spiritual Junk Food.

Me-B Transformation™ works to help us become aware of our Spiritual Junk Food and find an authentic Core Being connection. We do this by using the Explorer's Mind to catch ourselves when our ego has triggered us into Spiritual Junk Food. The Explorer's Mind then helps us to transmute our Core Distortions and LVC and return to balance.

UNDERSTAND CHALLENGING LIFE PATTERNS AND AVOID SPIRITUAL JUNK FOOD

Using the Explorer's Mind, look back upon your life patterns. Remember, the Explorer's Mind is a detective, helping us solve life's puzzles. Now write down the answers to the following. What unwanted experiences repeat?

What are the teachings, common lessons, insights, and understandings of our negative patterns? Write these down.

What is the negative belief that underlies these patterns? (For instance, if I take care of them, they will like me. Or, if I am small, I am safe.) Write this down.

Where do you feel/imagine the distortions are held in your body? Write this down.

- Then -

Using the Explorer's Mind throughout the day—with the understanding that unwanted experiences repeat, and using your Enlightened Observer—begin to watch yourself. Using intention, call in the HVC into your body. Imagine it, feel it, and visualize the HVC taking the place of the negative patterns. (Practice the Core Being exercise in the previous chapter to help you do this. It holds the HVC.)

Notice when these patterns repeat and how the old patterns feel or present in your body. Then imagine your Enlightened Observer calling in the HVC of your Core Being.

Eventually you will be able to use the Explorer's Mind to find your CHOICE POINTS and choose to vibrate at a higher level of consciousness more often. By the end of this book, you will know how to feel, visualize, and imagine the new healthy patterns taking hold in your mind, body, and energy system. You will be able to actually feel the energy of the old, dissipating unhealthy consciousness as the new, higher vibrational configuration takes its place.

William couldn't seem to get himself below $24,000 in debt. He worked hard to pay it off, only to find himself back in debt weeks later.

During a Me-B Session, William used the Explorer's Mind and examined this cycle. As he connected deeply inside himself, he was able to sense where he held this cycle in his body.

He stayed connected, breathing into the area for a few minutes, and then his eyes opened. He smiled as his inner light bulb glowed and he said, "I always want a little more than what I have. I am never satisfied with what I, alone, can provide for myself."

He committed to working his Me-B System so he could experience himself fully and live within the boundaries of his income. Every difficulty we face has at its root a negative belief about ourselves and others. For example: "He should take care of me," or "I am not strong enough." As we acknowledge the root of our financial challenges, we create a vortex of energy. Just as splitting an atom discharges energy, splitting open a false belief releases the energy needed to change it. We need only to follow through by bringing in the HVC of our Enlightened Observer to heal the past.

EGO CHALLENGES TO SELF-WORTH

Our self-worth cannot be a commodity based on perfection, money, or external love and support. The true test is when we can shift into balance even when we feel hurt, unloved, and imperfect. *Me-B Transformation*™ *doesn't stop the pain from coming. It empowers us to shift the pain into learning, growth, and transformation*. As we raise our consciousness, we also increase our empowerment—so even when difficulty visits, we are free, whole, and in gratitude.

Acceptance of our light and dark is part of the process. Pain, pleasure—it is all the same "clay." One is not better or worse than the other. As we move out of our ego, we can use whatever clay is before us to make a masterpiece.

Energetically, the ego presents in the third chakra. (See Chapter on Energy Field for details.) The ego can split our intention and fragment our energy field. It also distorts the sixth chakra's ability to perceive accurately. We project our fears into the world, where they are more likely to manifest and grow. Taking pain and "misfortune" and turning them into gifts can become a way of life—and it is a great way to stop the negative effects of the ego.

The "clay" laid before us nags agonizingly until we focus its shape. As we begin to see life challenges as clay that **can** be molded and transformed into art, we let go of judgment and create! Create and journey through this book and learn to raise our consciousness and shape-shift our lives!

TURN MISFORTUNE INTO THE CLAY OF TRANSFORMATION

1. Write down one recent misfortune, such as an illness, a mistake, a death, breakup, or job loss.
2. Now write down how this "misfortune" supports an old negative belief. We can use difficulty to change negative beliefs that shape our lives.
3. List your negative beliefs, and then design a positive alternative to adopt in its place.
4. Every time you feel the negative belief, imagine it leaving your body and energy system, and reprogram the positive belief in its place. Later chapters will teach other skills to help us turn misfortune into clay. Each skill set builds upon the next.

(See the chart below to help identify the negative/positive beliefs.)

Check the ones most meaningful to you and discover others that hold you back.

Negative Belief	Positive Alternative
If I set boundaries, I will be abandoned.	As I respect myself, others do too.
I need to be in control.	It is safe to trust.
I must be perfect.	I am enough even when I make mistakes.
The universe is against me	I am supported
I can't succeed.	I choose success.
I am a victim.	I connect to my power.
I will always be alone.	I choose relationship.
To be alone is bad.	I am whole, even when alone.
The unknown is scary.	I am safe in the unknown.
I must be full. I must be empty.	I am peaceful.
What happened to me is bad.	I choose to learn and grow.
What I feel now will never change.	Change is inevitable.
Emotional pain is bad.	Emotional pain happens.
I sabotage myself before others sabotage me.	I support myself
How I feel about myself is true.	I accept all parts of me.
How others feel about me is true.	I know who I am.
Negative emotions feed my self-hate.	I use negative emotions to transform /grow.
If I succeed, something will go wrong and ruin it.	I overcome my challenges to success.
If I succeed, someone will attack me.	I am empowered to achieve self-mastery.
If I succeed, I will sabotage my success.	I heal my saboteur.
I can't be abundant.	I am abundant.
Being an adult is boring and can't be fun.	Being an adult is fun.
I can't grow up.	I am strong and achieve my goals.
I will always be addicted to____.	I succeed.
____ will never change.	I am empowered.
My marriage/family will never change.	I change the unhealthy patterns within me.
If he/she/they would change, I would be happy.	I am happy.
Being vulnerable is a fault.	It is safe to be authentic and real.
Emotions are bad, especially anger.	Emotions are energy that runs through us all.
Either choice is wrong.	It is safe to choose.
I am unsafe.	I experience inner safety.
I can't trust.	I experience internal trust.

I am not enough.	I am whole and accept all parts of me.
If I stand up for myself, I will be attacked.	I receive support and love.
I expect kindness.	I am whole, even when I feel hurt.

The negative beliefs we have created are scripted into our cells, brain, and energy systems. As we re-experience tragedy, it validates these negative beliefs. Nothing likes to die, especially negative habituations. Often it seems as if there is no way out, and we say, "I knew this was going to happen . . . it *always* happens." These thoughts perpetuate victim consciousness. If we can only see that it is our negative programming from the past that created these negative beliefs in the first place, and that the repeated patterns are not destiny or reality, then we can become more empowered.

Consciousness creates an energetic blue print that ensures the perpetuation of negative beliefs in the mind, the cells of our body and energetically on the 5th Level of our Auric Energy Field. Since energy is consciousness, changing our consciousness changes our energy system. The Explorer's Mind and other techniques taught in this book help us raise our consciousness so we can reprogram our negative beliefs into supportive, positive beliefs.

MINDFULNESS STRATEGIES TO ELIMINATE NEGATIVE LIFE PATTERNS
TRANSFORM CORE DISTORTIONS/RE-CONNECT TO CORE BEING

To summarize, as we practice the following strategies, we begin to master advanced mindfulness skills — Level II and Level III of the 5-Step Mindfulness Process.

Begin to examine our current way of being in the world, find our Choice Point, and discover a positive alternative. As we are skillful, we learn how to locate Low Vibrational Consciousness (**LVC**) within our **Me-B System** and replace it with Higher Vibrational Consciousness (**HVC**). This helps us find our **CHOICE POINTS** and avoid Spiritual Junk Food. **Core Distortions** create **LVC**. A **Core Distortion** is anything that causes us to lose our connection with our **Core Being. Core Distortions** form the basis for our false identity and negative beliefs. **Core Distortions** are created by trauma, developmental wounding, and relational attachment issues. In addition, Core Distortions are born from our ego-based personalities. Strategies to transform Core Distortions back into higher consciousness are outlined below. As we master these strategies we are also more able to master Mindfulness Steps 3, 4 and 5.

Use the Explorer's Mind (previous exercise) to examine negative cycles/beliefs and determine where we imagine they are held in our body. (Often, Core Distortions are held in the stomach, front and/or back of heart, throat, and/or pelvis.) Pick one of these body-centered locations if you are not sure where your Core Distortion is located. Slowly start developing your skills by focusing on what you can do, not on what you can't do! (Step 3)

Breathe into that area of the body. Connect deeply and ask, "Why do I stay trapped in this cycle/belief?" Open to receive the answer. It may come as a symbol, picture, feeling, taste, smell, knowing, and/or intuition. Much support on developing this skill is provided throughout the book. (See the Pin Wheel Technique for collecting psychic information.) If we work too hard to receive an answer, it interferes with the receiving. Trust that the answer will come! If it doesn't, then dance, draw, or write— use your imagination and see what comes. Practice, practice, practice. It took me years to develop this skill. Give yourself time, patience, and practice. (Step 4)

Take any new insights, and experience the negative cycle being replaced by a positive alternative. Use all of your senses (intuit it gone; smell, taste, visualize, know, and feel it leave the body and energy system). Release the LVC of the old and receive the new HVC. Receive it in our Me-B System. Since it is intention that moves energy, simply having clear aligned intention means HVC is coming in. Just trust it. (Step 5)

Understand that often we need to feel the emotional pain and low vibrational energy of the old leaving before the positive belief, emotion, and high vibrational energy takes hold. If we don't feel it, we may be in Spiritual Junk Food. As you feel the pain of the old leaving, don't let the ego identify with the pain as being the truth of who you are, or else you will be creating more "black paint." Your Enlightened Observer prevents this from happening. It is the ego frequency and hidden negative intentions that keep us from changing. Many chapters are devoted to helping us learn this complex skill. (Step 5)

Every time we notice the negative return and take hold, we must repeat this process. Even if it takes 100 times—for we are never done. The old tends to return in times of stress and discomfort. Therefore, it is vital that we stay aware and commit to change again, and again, and again. Use the **Explorer's Mind** to help you experience the joy that accompanies change and growth. Remember it takes: Aligned Intention, Advanced Mindfulness to listen to the wisdom and enough Presence to follow through with positive and balanced action.

Me-B TRANSFORMATION SEQUENCE OF SKILLS

EXPLORER'S MIND

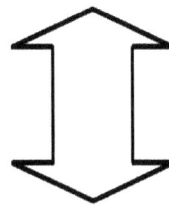

IDENTIFY WHEN WE ARE IN CORE BEING AND WHEN WE HAVE BEEN TRIGGERED INTO THE LVC OF OUR NEGATIVE PROGRAMMED PERSONALITY

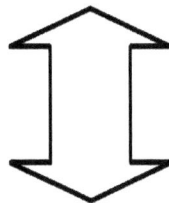

ENGAGE OUR ENLIGHTENED OBSERVER
Follow the 5-Step Mindfulness Process

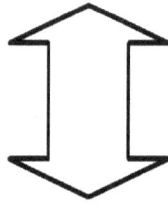

MOVE THROUGH THE 3-RINGS OF HEALING TRANSFORM

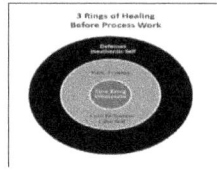

Low Vibrational Consciousness (LVC) into HVC AND MASTER HIGHER STAGES OF Me-B TRANSFORMATION™

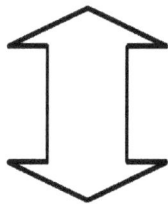

CHOICE POINTS BECOME OPPORTUNITIES TO ALIGN INTENTION

TO BE MINDFUL OF THE WISDOM

BECOME PRESENT ENOUGH TO FOLLOW THROUGH WITH POSITIVE ACTION and RECONNECTION TO CORE BEING

As a result you CONSCIOUSLY CREATE YOUR LIFE AND ACHIEVE SELF-MASTERY

CHAPTER REVIEW QUESTIONS

What does the Explorer's State of Mind say?

1. The Explorer's Mind is an important tool that helps us examine unsupportive life patterns. Explain why Me- B Guides and clients need to understand and review these life patterns.

2. Does pain still happen? As we move through the stages of Me-B Transformationc™, will we still feel discomfort, mistrust, and insecurities? Why is faulty perception the cause of emotional pain?

3. How is energy the blueprint to negative beliefs? How can I use this understanding to better support myself?

4. Who/what defines our truth?

5. How can we end debt cycles?

6. Explain the concept of "ego challenges to self worth." Also explain the ego in energetic terms. Where is it held in the body? How do we confront the ego by using the Me-B System and open the way toward self- mastery? Why must we accept our dark and our light in order to return to

balance?

7. Explain how pain is the pathway to magic and how to turn misfortune into the clay for transformation.

8. Me-B Transformation^{TM} teaches over 100 interventions to _____.

9. What is Spiritual Junk Food?

10. Explain how we avoid Spiritual Junk food and how the ego will want to perpetuate it.

11. List three cornerstones of Me-B Transformation^{TM} that are essential components for consciously creating our lives.

CHAPTER 3

THE SCIENCE BEHIND Me-B TRANSFORMATION™ AND WHY IT WORKS

Sensations are a physical representation of energy and consciousness felt in the body. Feeling sensations with an Enlightened Observer alters our body chemistry, raises our frequency, and creates a vortex for higher consciousness.

In this chapter, the science behind Me-B Transformation™ is explained. We begin to understand: (1) why our bio-chemistry and its somatic memory are vital parts of the healing process; (2) the physical science supporting transformation; and (3) how energy work alters consciousness and supports deep and powerful change.

Increasing our ability to believe in the power of Me-B Transformation™ allows us to transmit this belief to ourselves and our clients. Even if we are not scientifically minded, we can explore the basics of how this system of transformation is grounded in body chemistry and physics.

An organized system of transformation that integrates cognitive, energetic, and body systems together is unique and powerful. It attends to the abundant resources in our subconscious. Numerous studies document that it is the unknown that has the most power over us. In this book, we learn to work with all three parts of our Me-B System together, and to find out what is hidden in our subconscious so that we can become more aware of ourselves.

Awareness creates Choice Points that we can use to tap into our subconscious. For instance, in relation to the room where we now sit, studies suggest that the conscious mind represents only the space of a small dime; the rest is lost in our unconscious and subconscious. This book helps us awaken to see deeper into our sub- conscious, and promote choice, health, and happiness.

Through utilizing the information in this book, we gain an internal reference and source of strength that can launch us upon our path toward individuation and a deep realization of our Core Being—the spirit within all of us. This spirit transcends our personality and dissolves our idea of self so we can evolve into much more.

The first step to transformation is acknowledging that we create much of our reality. This understanding empowers us to claim responsibility for what we have created and to make better choices. The second step is to learn how to connect to our internal Core Being. This vibration is identifiable within each of us. We can alter ourselves back to wholeness again and again and again throughout the day. Most of us may not be able to stay at the frequency of Core Being, especially in times of stress or attack—but all of us can learn how to return to it more often and more quickly.

THE BODY FACTOR: BIO-CHEMISTRY AND SOMATICS

We finally have scientific documentation of what many of us already knew—our emotions are not just in our head. Humans are programmed by our body chemistry into emotional responses. These emotional responses shape our reality and our ability to live in joy and abundance.

Researcher, author, and biologist Bruce Lipton outlines that our consciousness creates the blueprint for our DNA. Lipton noticed that to promote health, it is imperative we begin with the source of consciousness. Lipton explains that the SIGNAL (perception, emotions, thoughts, and body chemistry) interacts with our beliefs systems, and from these raw materials, the universe creates.

This means that when we want to prevent a "bad" signal and work with the laws of attraction and manifestation, we must consider all three systems of mind, energy, and body. If one system is not aligned, we cannot succeed. The great news is that each person has a natural ally in at least one of these systems. This book helps us identify which system is our ally, and it will help us learn how to make the other systems allies as well.

Candice Pert, author of *Molecules of Emotions,* provides us with the scientific basis to understand the relationship between our emotions and our physiology. The emotions, Pert explains, are located within a part of the brain structure called the *limbic system* or *neopallium brain*. The emotions reside in the brain in the form of neuropeptides—chemical signals that control mood, energy levels, pain and pleasure reception, body weight, and the ability to solve problems. Neuropeptides also form memories and regulate the immune system. They are the biochemical messengers running throughout the nervous system, providing emotional communications somatically felt as sensations in our bodies.

These somatic sensations represent biochemical reactions, and they are physical representations of healthy or unhealthy energy configurations. For example, good sensations in the body are indicators of positive energy configurations, and painful sensations are indicators of low vibrational energy configurations. Somatics are energy, and energy is felt as somatics—which in turn influences us at the biochemical level. ***This means that sensations are a physical representation of consciousness running through the physical body.*** Only deep awareness and self-mastery prevent us from being controlled by the chemical explosions taking place within us.

In Me-B Transformation™, we learn specific techniques to reprogram our body chemistry into HVC. We learn how to establish a relationship with our body sensations and energy system that promotes the cultivation of higher consciousness. We do not judge or try to eliminate negative sensations. We meet them with kindness, compassion, and the Explorer's Mind, to discover more about our own map to living in this earthly dimension. To ignore this primary component in our healing and self-mastery process would be to ignore a magical pathway for achieving empowerment and manifesting our dreams.

PHYSICS SUPPORTING Me-B TRANSFORMATION™

In my own life, through years of meditation, I experienced how my internal observer influences reality. For instance, I saw solid objects, including my body, dissolve into particles of energy, and I experienced the interconnectedness of oneness. Later, when the popular book and movie *What the Bleep Do We Know!?* were released, I was excited to begin the search to understand the physics behind my experiences and behind Me- B Transformation™.

Heisenberg's Uncertainty Principle

A key component of Me-B Transformation™ is Heisenberg's Uncertainty Principle. According to author Stephen H. Wolinsky, this principle states that our reality is created by the observer. During countless hours of meditation and self-observation, I found that if our internal observer is operating in distortion, then we create pain and illness. If our observer is operating coherently and with HVC, then we create positive change.

Such change allows us to feel and examine incoherency and distortions and then re-pattern old ways of reacting in the world that no longer serve us. As we change our unhealthy patterns, we also change our reality. Years ago after my first two-week silent meditation retreat, I wrote in my journal, "change your mind, change your reality."

I wrote this after observing how my mind wanted to label experiences during my meditation retreat as being "bad" or "painful." As I permitted myself to question what my mind told me was true, my experiences changed from negative into positive. Hour after hour I *noticed how my mind was like a computer program creating my reality.* I was amazed by the power of my mind to create my life experiences. At the end of the meditation retreat, I effortlessly let my thoughts and mind flow. It was as if I was finally able to unhook the computer from the electrical socket and, as a result, bliss flowed though me as well. Knowing replaced thoughts and mind chatter. And when the mind chatter returned, it was easy to dismiss its view of reality and investigate the deeper truth.

In Me-B Transformation™, we learn to develop our own *Enlightened Observer.* Our Enlightened Observer holds HVC. High Vibrational Consciousness creates positive change because it uses the deep pain in our mind and body systems as raw material with which to build awareness, wisdom, and personal power. So, from the raw material of challenging life circumstances—negative beliefs, painful emotions, ego, stress, trauma, and illness—we manufacture our creations. Shouldn't we learn to make them positive creations that support our own life force as well as the world's?

If our observer is **not** empowered with HVC, then it isn't strong enough to change negative beliefs, emotions, and life experiences. When this happens, there is no transformation of energy. Instead, we risk continuing unhealthy life patterns.

In a future Chapter, the 10 Stages of Me-B Transformation™ are introduced. Stage 4 of Me-B Transformation™ is the point when our Enlightened Observer is strong enough to transform LVC into HVC. This means it is empowered enough so that when we have an overwhelming life experience, we can transform it into a life lesson. We reap from it wisdom and a deep connection to Core Being.

If all of us can aspire to obtaining at least Stage 4 of Me-B Transformation™, non-violence, compassion, and love will abound. Changing the world is not so much about changing governments and political systems. It is about each of us taking the oath to work diligently to raise our consciousness in all areas of our lives.

Self-Mastery Story

In times of deep stress, my ego leads me to lose my connection to my Enlightened Observer. Its frequency decreases, and my connection to my Core Being fragments. I react in the world and perpetuate negative life patterns.

So I listen, learn, and set my intention to improve. Although sometimes my progress is slow, I at least have my sense of humor and enjoy the journey of staying committed to self-mastery, change, and growth. I choose many situations in my life where my ego can be stressed to the extent that my dark shadow is revealed. Horses, work, and relationships are my teachers.

Attractors: Why Negative Patterns Repeat and How to Stop Them

"Attractors" is the name given to specific patterns that emerge from a seemingly chaotic mass of data, according to David Hawkins, author of *Power vs. Force*. Ostensibly, Attractors show that coherency can be found by examining the incoherent. For instance, in the previous chapter, we explored the incoherent — our negative life patterns. We then looked at how our negative beliefs were attracting those patterns. We then did an exercise where we developed strategies to eliminate these negative trends (in coherency) thus cultivating coherency.

Hawkins uses the example of a ship in the ocean that is only a few degrees off course. If not corrected, the ship will quickly find itself miles adrift. As we correct our few degrees "off course" in our lives, this correction has a profound impact as well.

With aligned intention, mindfulness, and presence of Core Being, we can all find these critical points so we return to the path of our highest good.

Critical point analysis, states Hawkins, is derived from the fact that in any highly complex system, "there is a specific, critical point at which the smallest input will result in the greatest change." In Me-B Transformation™, we use our **Explorer's Mind** to uncover our Choice Points by unraveling the complexity of thoughts, energies, and somatics in our Me-B System. Then, when we use our **Enlightened Observer**, find our Choice Points and transform LVC into HVC.

Hawkins goes on to explain that the causal A ⟹ B ⟹ C

started with an unobservable ABC (mind-energy-body). Our Me-B System makes the unobservable, observable. For instance, it takes abc (mind-energy-body) and breaks it down so we can observe our mind, then observe our body and then our energy system so we can see clear enough to end our complicity with the unhealthy patterns of our past.

In the movie *The Butterfly Effect,* the lead character's super power is the ability to go back in time to find the exact action that he can alter in order to save the woman he loves. In Me-B Transformation™ we call this our Choice Point. (As was true of the movie, Choice Points tend to feel very emotionally painful.) This is when we find our own "butterfly effect" and alter our programmed low vibrational responses.

61

Quantum Effects:

Our Mind Attributes Meaning to Energy and Creates Physical Reality

On the quantum, subatomic level, Wolinsky explains, "there is no difference between space (emptiness) and physical matter." He reports that Einstein said that *everything is emptiness and emptiness is everything*. This view helps us understand that our mind attributes meaning to energy, to create physical matter.

When we were guided by Newtonian physics, western society only saw ourselves living in a world of solid objects made up of "building blocks" called atoms. Then quantum physics outlined a more accurate view of the world that described a less solid and more malleable universe. Evidence suggests that the human mind attributes meaning to particles. The particles then interact in relationship to each other and to the meanings we attribute to them. Some suggest this is what creates reality. In meditation, I notice how as I change my mind, my reality changed. For instance, as I sat, I noticed how my body began to ache. Hour after hour I was sure I had hurt my back by sitting so many hours in meditation. However, as I allowed my mind to relax and return to the HVC of the Enlightened Observer, the pain disappeared and bliss filled every cell.

Our Programmed Mind Can Limit Us

Our mind's programming can be so strong that simply naming the programming isn't always powerful enough to reprogram it. This is why our life can drive us crazy and overwhelm us. It is also why traditional cognitive therapy and some meditation and healing strategies can be limited in their effectiveness if they don't also include the body's energy system.

Most of us find it very difficult to undo our negative belief systems, our ideas of self, and many other false concepts of reality. This is because these are not only held in our mind system, they are also held in our body chemistry and its energy system.

My daughter used to complain that she saw everything in her room turn to energy at night. The multitudes of particles and color distracted her from falling asleep. She begged me to teach her to make it stop. Ten years later, she can't see energy. She successfully trained her eyes to see the world from the Newtonian perspective of solidity. When she goes to sleep, she sees only a table, chairs, and bed in her room.

We tend to conform to the acceptable because we think it is easier. In Me-B Transformation™, we use the Explorer's Mind to examine the acceptable and open to a deeper reality. By this I mean, we bring the HVC of the formless into our solid body. As we learn to do this more skillfully, we become the architects of our lives.

As mentioned earlier, during meditation retreats, I have disappeared into particles and so has everything around me. There was no I, there was no-thing. As we experience energy and consciousness, we can more accurately see what is really programming our lives. Shifting the energy and thus the consciousness helps us create and choose our lives. It is the ultimate power that fuels transformation.

Thoughts Create!

According to Lynne McTaggart, author of *The Intention Experiment,* quantum theory suggests that matter, at its most fundamental levels, gains its meaning through a web of dynamic interrelationships. She adds that particles retain a remote hold over each other. There is an orientation for one subatomic particle to instantaneously influence the other, no matter how far they are separated.

If we carry this analysis into our lives, it means we are all connected. For instance, our nations' leaders' thoughts influence us, and our thoughts influence them. As one of us finds peace, it influences us all. Thoughts and intentions are tangible energies interacting and inter-relating. Let us do so as consciously throughout our day as possible. The collective power we have is amazing, especially if we use it for a common purpose—be it to end global warming or to better love our children.

Oneness is Wholeness is God

Physics supports the theory that all is oneness and everything is inter-related. Those of us who have experienced the bliss that has come when all three Me-B System are cohesive and unified can attest to the validity of various Eastern philosophies. We can attest to the existence of an internal experience of spirit; we know that oneness and higher consciousness are real.

As we move through the 10 Stages of Me-B Transformation™, we gain the ability to experience our Core Being and oneness more and more throughout the day and at deeper levels. We avoid Spiritual Junk food and find our painful Choice Points and create coherency and positive change.

Although we may not be able to remain in our Core Being, we learn to at least return to this vibration more quickly and more often. This is the power of this work. This is the power we all have! It is not an easy magic bullet. In fact, it just might be the hardest thing we ever do. Yet it is real. It is obtainable and it can feel quite magical.

Self-Mastery Alert

My young, very thin, loving but insecure horse was left out, again. For months, I watched the other horses bullying him, kicking him, and pushing him away. The harsh treatment was too stressful for his young soul, and he nearly died. So I moved him to what I thought was a gentle environment to give him time to grow and find his strength.

Once, on a visit to the new ranch, I realized something was wrong. As I saw my horse's head hung low, searching for the absent food, my heart broke, and anger filled every cell. The ranch manager had forgotten to feed him that day. I yelled out, trying to move the anger and dissipate the fury. My Explorer's Mind, quiet amidst the fury, became curious about this outburst. Who was this really about? What old pain did this event bring to the surface, again? The quantum exchange of relational particles brought the consciousness of my young self into the time of now in a very deep, painful way. It was me being hurt now. It felt real and raw, and my Enlightened Observer was almost lost.

We all can be triggered in our daily lives. And we can all take personal responsibility to examine that trigger and seek the gift it brings.

ENERGY—If we can't see it, is it there?

When working energetically, we can wonder if the energy is real or imagined. Our society is accustomed to quantitative and qualitative data. As we journey through our understanding of energetic healing, we can notice that there is no separation between energy and consciousness. In fact, consciousness *creates* energy— and energy is a form of consciousness.

Energy is a tangible manifestation of consciousness. Energy is the precursor of matter. Without consciousness, and the resulting energetic blueprint created by it, matter cannot be formed. More and more research is now available to substantiate the power and existence of bio-energy. In Me-B Transformation™ we learn to take the energy of consciousness and bring it into matter to raise the vibration of the matter so it can become formless (egoless) again.

In his book *Energy Medicine: The Scientific Basis,* author James Oschman presents the research conducted in the early 1980's by Dr. John Zimmerman. Zimmerman studied the energy of a therapeutic touch practitioner with a SQUID magnetometer at the University of Denver. This device is used to detect incredibly small energy fields, such as those found in living organisms. The healer held his hands close to the client without the intention of shifting energy, and a baseline recording was made. Then, the healer entered a healing trance, and additional readings were made. Oschman reported that the energy field was so strong that the amplifiers and recorder had to be readjusted so that a more accurate recording could be made. Oschman added that the therapeutic touch signal pulsed at a variable frequency ranging from .3 to 30 Hz, with most of the activity in the range of 7-8 Hz.

In another popularized study, participants were hooked up to body sensors and were shown a series of unrelated pictures. Before a violent picture appeared on the screen, the participant's body sensors reacted. How was this possible? How could the body react to a picture it hasn't yet seen?

Apparently, the body read the energy of the upcoming picture before the mind saw the picture. Actually, we do this all day long. When I go to the supermarket, I notice how people are reading and reacting to each other's energy fields but are not consciously aware of it. As we pay closer attention to our energy system, we become more aware of how our energies interact with one another.

For instance, I can feel the energy when someone is going to win the Lottery. I can tell when someone sent me a very happy or very sad email. In this book, we will learn how to cultivate this skill of energy reading, so we can better assist clients and ourselves.

THERAPEUTIC ENTRAINMENT

Oschman discusses the importance of a phenomenon called *therapeutic entrainment*. This process occurs when the energy of the therapist is directed in a manner to positively influence the energy of a client. Oschman states that there is evidence to show the coupling of both cardiac and brain rhythms between two individuals in the same room, who are sitting meditatively facing each other and not touching. He adds that, "such synchronization is present, and it is enhanced if the subjects are connected electrically, such as by a wire held in the left hand of one person and the right hand of the other." He suggests that hands-on, touch therapies could be even more effective at facilitating healing energies.

Barbara Brennan discusses a similar concept that she calls *harmonic induction*. As one person raises his or her vibration, that frequency harmonically spreads to the other. As an example, Brennan states, "the phenomenon of harmonic induction is that which occurs when you strike one tuning fork and another in the room will sound."

Based on the impact of therapeutic entrainment and harmonic induction, the touch and non-touch therapies outlined in this book can have profound healing effects on both clients and therapists. The more skillful a client is at receiving these high vibrations, the more enhanced the benefits.

If your thirst for more research on energy and consciousness has deeper longing, I recommend contacting The International Society for the Study of Subtle Energies and Energy Medicine (ISSSEEM). Also, some Healing Touch sources include:

www.healingtouchresearch.com/articles.html and www.healingtouchresearch.com.

CHAPTER 4

THE COMPONENTS OF CHANGE CHOICE POINTS

It is the expectation of kindness that creates our unhealthy defenses. As we release this expectation and learn to find peace, even in discomfort, we are more able to accept that emotional pain will happen. Acceptance of what is happening in the moment reduces pain, balances our energy field, and allows happiness, wholeness, and joy to spread.

Me-B Transformation™ works three systems together to access wholeness. We are all whole; we just don't always interact from that deep connection within us. We sometimes get lost. The **Explorer's Mind** and its **Components of Change** can lead us home and are vital to our success.

The Explorer's Mind is an essential part of Me-B Transformation™ because it allows us to move toward self mastery by helping us become our own spiritual detectives. It teaches us **not** to be invested in any outcome; it allows us to see both the dark and light of a situation, even if the psyche feels threatened and afraid. It knows fear is a sign that we are getting closer to an answer, and it uses difficult emotions as resources to raise our consciousness. With it, we can understand that what we see in every moment is an illusion. This then helps us muster the detachment necessary to manifest change, and become much more than what we think we can become.

The Explorer's Mind must be the internal detective to examine the deeper issues of what is really going on within and around us, so we move out of blame or judgment and into self-empowerment.

The **Explorer's Mind** uses the following **Components of Change so we use Choice Points** to move us out of the frequency of our programmed personality so we connect back to our **Core Being**. One of the most important **Components of Change** is **aligned intention**. It is the first ingredient needed to bring our awareness into the present moment so we can assess if we are vibrating at **Core Being** or **Programmed Personality**.

As we are mindful of the Components of Change, we can be present enough to find our Choice Points and move from the Programmed Personality back to Core Being.

Components of Change

Mindfulness, Presence, Intention, Unhealthy Character Structure Defenses, Public Personality, Misaligned Intention, Core Distortion, Separated Self, Ego, False Beliefs, Transference/Counter Transference, Projection, Unhealthy Boundaries, Relationship Coherency—Core to Core, Rhythm of Flow Shapes Reality, Shadow.

As we read and understand the nuances of the concepts described below, we can be more mindful throughout the day of which Components of Change need support so we can return to the higher consciousness of our **Core Being**.

The 3 Rings of Healing, Shape-Shifting Emotional Realities approach is introduced later. It provides a very structured process for how to travel back to Core Being. As we get better at locating Choice

Points—where our old, unhealthy programmed responses can be replaced with new and healthier responses to stressful circum- stances—we move closer to self-mastery.

PROGRAMMED PERSONALITY LEVEL

When we act from the programmed personality level versus our **Core Being,** we find our self in any of the following states: Misaligned Intention, Defense, Core Distortion, Negative Beliefs, Unhealthy Boundaries, Public Personality, Separated Self, Transference, Ego, and/or Shadow.

Most of us operate from the **Programmed Personality** level throughout the day because we don't know the truth of who we are. Unfortunately, we don't know our **Core Being**. In part, this is because our society doesn't support the positive mirroring most of us needs in order to believe in ourselves. This is reflected on a national level in terms of crime, abuse, illiteracy, poverty, terrorism, pollution, inequitable health care system, and even global warming. If we all lived from our **Core Being**, we would take better care of ourselves, our Earth, and those around us.

Even though our ego-based **Programmed Personality** holds distortions of reality, it is not always in distortion and defense. It can become a cohesive field that aligns with our **Core Being**. This can be an aligned intention in all of us and thus a possible reality we can create. Given how difficult this earthly dimension can be, we do need to support each other in these ideals. As one candle is lit, it can shine the light for the others to follow.

Incoherency on the personality level can trigger our Misaligned Intention, Public Personality, Defenses, Separated Self, Negative Ego, and Dark Shadow.

Energetically, the programmed personality is held in the lower Auric field—usually levels 1 through 4. Although all of us have levels 1-7, each person's frequency can be slightly different: some resonate more softly or at a higher vibration, and some are fuller and more expansive. As humanity evolves to embrace more HVC, we bring this energy into the Auric field. As this happens, it is easier to live from a multi-dimensional reality that connects us to the oneness within all.

INTENTION

Aligned Intention is the ability to choose the highest good. **Intention** moves energy and is the force that helps us transform lower vibrations to higher vibrations. Aligned Intention, helps us be mindful and present. Misaligned intentionality exists whenever there is a feeling of "stuckness," or when we repeatedly don't achieve our goal(s).

Aligned intentionality supports flow—misaligned intentionality inhibits flow and freezes our creations.

On some level, we would all be enlightened if some aspect of us wasn't saying "no." Sometimes we and our clients get attached to disappointment or failure. In addition, over our lifetime, we become programmed in our brain and body's neurobiology to respond in our old patterns. *Misaligned intention* keeps us from receiving and manifesting the gifts of life:

- It makes us dissociate from the present.

- It keeps us merged with the pain.
- It prevents our ability to transform LVC into HVC and Core Being.

Using our **Explorer's State of Mind** can help us examine our unhealthy intentions and discover the underlying causes. This information and wisdom then helps us create a shift so we realign our intentions to our highest good.

FEELING STUCK

Joshua, a 38-year old software engineer, is very successful at what he does. He makes a six-figure salary, yet feels stuck and unhappy at work and in his relationships. He has been diagnosed with chronic fatigue and often feels depressed. A Me-B Guide worked with him for over a year on the "stuckness" issue.

She noticed that when she worked with him, she felt inclined to "do all the work." She noticed how she would get an overwhelming sense that she *had* to come up with a solution. *When a therapist or family member feels this, it is a good indicator that negative intention is being held by the client.* As the Me-B Guide reflected these feelings back to Joshua, he acknowledged that he didn't want to do the work and hoped the solution was somewhere else.

He then was able to feel the deep-seated anger anchoring the negative intention in place. Anger is usually the emotion that prevents us from moving toward positive intention. We may feel angry that we have to do it ourselves, or angry over questions such as, "Why can't I be saved?" or "Why is it just so darn hard?"

Our two-year old "tantrum" energy can subconsciously control us. It says, "I won't move forward until I get my way." Unfortunately, life doesn't work that way. No "good enough mother" will come to our rescue. When things are not working out, we need more forward motion, not less. This forward motion also helps us release the trauma "freeze" response in our body and parasympathetic nervous system. (See Chapter on Trauma.)

Within a year of this session, Joshua had internalized his own "good enough mother. " He got married and was enjoying a new job. Positive intention was once more a part of his life.

As we study this material and learn more about our own energetic patterns, we become adept at assessing where we hold our misaligned and aligned intentions, and become even more successful at seeing the deeper reality within. The body-centered Character Structures developed by Alexander Lowen also have intention challenges. Review the chart below and see which ones might be similar to yours.

CHARACTER STRUCTURE CHALLENGES

INTENTIONS ENERGETIC ALIGNMENTS	SPIRITUAL (SCHIZOID)	COMPASSIONATE (ORAL)	HEART-CENTERED (MASOCHIST)	EXCEL (RIGID)	LEADER (PSYCHOPATH)
Unhelpful Intention	I will not be here.	I want someone to take care of me.	I will be a victim.	I will be perfect and judge you if you are not perfect.	I will dominate and control.
Necessary Aligned Intention	I commit to being here.	I take responsibility for myself.	I am empowered and can save myself.	I am whole even when I make errors.	I trust and am safe in relationship, even if I don't do everything my way.
Energetic Misalignment	Manifest Energy disconnected from Earth. Auric field weak in lower chakras and outer energy egg.	I am strong enough to support myself. Manifest Energy weak, fragmented. Auric field can't hold strong charge of power.	Manifest Energy split at 3rd chakra, and weak in upper chakras. Auric field armored.	Manifest Energy aligned toward needing perfection. Auric field disconnected at 4th chakra, diaphragm, and 2nd chakra. Undercharged 4th level	Manifest Energy aligned toward domination and control. Back of 4th chakra blocked; overcharge on neck, shoulders, upper back. Weaker in lower body

Aligned Intention is an ideal we can create. It occurs when we allow the flow of source to move through us. It also happens when we maintain zero mind, and a centered and balanced energy system that is anchored into our **Core Being** and accentuated by a strong **Manifest Energy Intention Line**. We know this is happening when our body is relaxed, accepting the truth of what is happening in the moment without judgment, collapse, or push.

This is the most effective state of being for a Me-B Guide
when he/she is guiding a client.

We may not always stay in **Core Being** during life or during a session with a client. However, we can learn how to track ourselves and return (more quickly and frequently) to this frequency by using our **Aligned Intention**. (Remember to practice the techniques in this book that help you move through the 3 Rings of Healing and Shape-Shift your Realities so you can return to Core Being.)

Energetically, Manifest Energy determines our aligned intention. Anytime we are not moving forward toward our goals, we can reconnect our Manifest Energy Intention Line (see the intention exercise in the energy chapter.) In the body system, contrary intention is often held in the lower body and is felt as a compression of energy or holding down of the life force.

When working with **Intention**, keep in mind the following:

1. By working on your Me-B System together, we shift out of contrary intention. By strengthening and realigning your own **Manifest Energy**, you can harmonically shift another's Manifest Energy

and Auric field.

2. The **Explorer's State of Mind** will help you watch your thoughts and can help you catch misaligned intentions as well. Connecting to and learning from what is being held emotionally in our bodily sensations usually reveals important information on **Intention**.

3. Working at the level of **Intention** is one of the most powerful ways to promote healing. Energetically, Manifest Energy is a primary force that creates what is happening on the physical level. Any distortion in Manifest Energy eventually creates a distortion in the physical world.

MANIFEST ENERGY INTENTION LINE

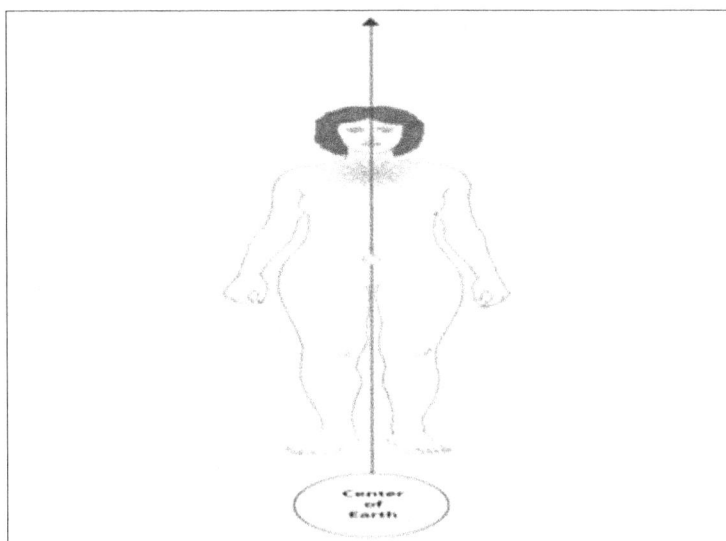

CREATING POSITIVE INTENTION

From your **Explorer's Mind**, beginning at the top of your head, scan-down your body. Pause for 10 seconds or longer in any area of the body that you can imagine feeling sensations of comfort. Feel all parts of your body— dismiss nothing.

MANIFEST ENERGY LINE

- Eyes, nose, ears, teeth, tongue, lips, jaw Neck—front and back Shoulders—front and back
- Chest, upper back Arms, elbows, hands, fingers Mid-back and Core Center
- Lower back and lower abdomen
- Pelvis—Sacrum
- Legs, thighs, back of thighs, front/back of lower legs, ankles, feet, toes

Scan through the body five times, each time stopping at sensations of comfort. Melt into the sensations of comfort and notice if they grow, intensify, or expand. Simply by focusing on the comforting sensations, you are charging them energetically, helping them multiply. Let them move to areas of low or no sensations. Be careful not to judge sensations as being good or bad or harmful or helpful. We are just focusing on the comfort because what we focus on grows. We are building an energetic and biological consciousness container of HVC to help our nervous system relax before we going into LVC. Remember the scales of white and black paint. We are building white paint so we are strong enough to realign our contrary intentions.

Now, name what your misaligned intention is and what you want your aligned Intention to be. Write this down. Then, once you have a strong charge of comfortable sensations growing, imagine bringing those sensations into the center of your **Manifest Energy Intention Line.** Remember, it extends through the center of your body from the top of your head— straight down—and out your perineum like a steel rod, anchoring deep into the core of the Earth.

Imagine filling the center of that line with sensations of comfort as you let any negative intention melt away. Then feel and imagine aligned intention/sensations taking the place of the contrary intention. (Also review the Manifest Energy Intention Line Alignment Exercises outlined in this book.)
**When doing this exercise, if you only feel/imagine negative sensations,
then review the exercises for positive resourcing, safety, and containment.**

NOTE: If you can't feel any sensations, go to the end of the energy assessment chapter and review the Body Connecting Sequence (BCS) meditation that will teach you how to cultivate positive sensations. Those of us with Excel and/or Spiritual Character Types will find it more difficult to feel any sensations in our bodies. This is because Excel types often have energy fields that are too tightly structured, and Spiritual types tend to be very disconnected from their bodies. Get support from a Me-B trained guide and be kind and gentle to yourself.

CORE DISTORTION

As very young children, most of us are connected to our **Core Being**. We don't have to work at it; we just know who we are. Unfortunately, given that humans, not gods, surround us, this Earth-bound lower vibrational dimension can result in our essence getting smashed and dishonored.

When someone else is not consistently mirroring back to us our Core Being, we can forget who we really are. This is why it is important to develop the skills so we don't need someone else in this manner. As we follow the 5-Step Mindfulness Process, and use our Enlightened Observer, we can bring that HVC into our Core Distortions and heal them.

*We can see Core Distortions as an energetic resource to gain strength, wisdom, and compassion. This is when our **Core Distortions** become **core wisdom.** We develop our deepest gifts when we learn to use the energy of pain and difficulty to heal our distortions.*

Core Distortions are found in all three systems: mind, energy, and body. Energetically they are held in the Auric

Field and in Manifest Energy. Core Distortions are the birthplace of false belief systems, unhealthy defenses, and distorted energies.

Most often, the deepest Core Distortion is felt like a hole in the abdomen, usually in the third chakra. This is because our ego, held in the 3rd chakra, can easily be torn when difficulties are present.

When we first begin to work on our **Core Distortions**, usually the first energetic block is in the heart. This is because as we remove our **Core Distortions**, the energy of our Core Being moves more deeply into the body. Each block we remove makes space for more of our **Core Being** to incarnate into the physical. As a result, our consciousness is raised and our mental and physical health improves.

Often much grieving and emotional release happens when the heart dissolves its **Core Distortions**. As we learn to receive more love into our heart we may temporarily feel the pain of the times when we were not loved. As we clear this energy, we heal the energy in our heart. As a result, over time the energy begins to move lower, and the next station that usually holds blocks is the diaphragm.

Unblocking the energy in our diaphragm heals some of the Excel personality type's challenges. It gives us the opportunity to make peace with our humanness and our imperfections.

From there, the energy can stop at the 3rd chakra or solar plexus. Fear and/or anxiety are often found here. It is also where our sense of self and ego energetically resides. If we are feeling unworthy, the 3rd chakra will wobble in distortion. The Compassionate Character Structure's negative reactivity receives healing at this stage.

After we work some of the Core Distortions in the Solar Plexus, we move even lower in the body and release Core Distortions in the pelvis/sacrum or 2nd chakra. This is when we often feel suppressed anger from the past. As we learn how to access it and transform its LVC it turns into the HVC of personal power. Usually, when we get to this level, we can master Stage 4 of Me-B Transformation^{TM} fairly easily.

Once we have incarnated our Core Being energy this deeply into our body, the next levels of healing is often the throat—surrender and trust in the divine. The Heart-Centered and Leader Personality types receive healing at this stage (Stages 5-7 of Me-B Transformation^{TM}).

Because many of us can feel betrayed and abandoned by god, it might feel hard to trust others and the divine within us and around us. When this happens, our throat chakra (inner authority/communication) and second chakra (personal power) can shut down. When they shut down, LVC runs throughout our body and we lose connection with our Core Being. This often results in life getting much more difficult and we can feel even more alone and disconnected from god.

However, as we transform the Core Distortions in our throat chakra, both the throat chakra and the 2nd Chakra open. This allows a huge energy boost to move through the full length of the Central Channel. Often at this time, our life changes dramatically because as we successfully heal our Core Distortions and bring Core Being energy deep into our body, we metaphorically re-birth ourselves. As a result we heal additional Core Distortions in our 1st chakra (achieving our life task).

Healing our Core Distortions in the body is a deep spiritual journey that results in the death of our old ego identification and a re-birth of the new sense of self. As this happens, we become more aligned with our Core Being. Joseph Campbell, a mythologist, describes this process as the Hero and Heroine journey.

Mastering the 5-Step Mindfulness process and moving through the 3-Rings of Healing helps us transform our Core Distortions. In our lifetime, depending upon how deep we want to work, we may consciously take this journey 15 or more times. I find that every five or so years I complete this cycle. I am 49 now, so I expect I could do it another 10 times. Each time I move through this cycle, more of my ego and false sense of self dies and I move higher in the 10 Stages of Me-B Transformation^{TM}. Because this earthly dimension is so dense, the healing process is rarely a spontaneous event. Just as an inchworm moves slowly forward, step by step, so do most of us. This is why strong intention is needed, and so we use our advanced mindfulness skills to collect the wisdom and understanding needed to become more present with Core Being.

The higher we are in the 10 Me-B Stages of Transformation, the more aware we are as we journey through each of our Core Distortions. Even though the process feels painful, we can learn to let the energy of the pain become the fuel for transformation.

Typically, Core Distortions release in the sequence outlined below. This is a "rule of thumb." Our Explorer's State of Mind helps us determine what is true for us.

The heart (4th Chakra) is often the first station to release. The pain around love and relationships can be easiest to access and have the most impact on our lives. We learn self-compassion and to receive and give healthier forms of love.

The diaphragm then releases, as we learn to make peace with our imperfections.

The solar plexus (3rd Chakra) is next. This release helps us to honor our positive sense of self and ego, which is often negatively influenced by love and relationships.

The pelvis (2nd Chakra) usually releases next. This is where we reclaim our personal power and healthy sexuality. This area's energy often gets depressed from distortions in our ego or false sense of self.

The pattern of release then moves toward claiming our own authority and ability to communicate that authority in the world. The release occurs in our throat area **(5th Chakra)**, both front and back. There is a relationship between the **throat chakra** and our **2nd Chakra.** When one releases, it influences the other—just as if you sit on one side of a teeter-totter, the other side is affected. Once the **5th Chakra** opens, it then initiates an additional release in the **2nd Chakra,** opening up the energetic channel between them.

The following sequence is called the Integration Phase. At this point, most of the main chakras have released deep distortions. Integration of our energy field then happens as a result of **Core Distortions** being released between our heart and our perineum. The whole central channel has longer periods of openness and flow.

The perineum (1st Chakra) is usually the next station to release its Core Distortions. With our personal power intact, we then move to manifesting our life task, the goal of the **1st chakra.**

The top of the head is the **7th chakra**. It then can open even more, which connects through the center of the head to prompt the forehead/back of the head **(6th chakra)** to open. (Completion of the Hero/ Heroine journey.)

Over our lifetime, this process repeats again and again, releasing **Core Distortions** at deeper and deeper levels so we move higher in the Me-B Stages of Transformation.

PROGRAMMED CHARACTER STRUCTURE DEFENSES

A defense is a protective reaction to cover a **Core Distortion and to dissociate from the present moment**. At one time, these defenses felt vital to our survival. As we grow up and heal, they become unhealthy responses to stressful situations that are programmed by our past.

Previously, we discussed the concept of finding Choice Points to foster peace and community. *In order to find a CHOICE POINT, we must be willing to reprogram our self so we are able to choose more healthy ways of interacting with others and ourselves.*

This section will give you more self-awareness tools that your Explorer's Mind can use to track your own negative defenses. Hopefully, this will help us better locate our Choice Points, where old negative actions can be replaced with healthier options.

Negative belief systems and false images keep unhealthy defenses in place. As we use our **Explorer's State of Mind**, with kindness and compassion, we become more skillful at aligned intention and advanced mindfulness. As a result, we move out of defense and become present with **Core Being**.

As we look at the negative belief systems beneath our defenses and heal our Core Distortions, we more easily choose supportive ways to protect ourselves. The 5-Step Mindfulness process and the 3-Rings of Healing return us back to Core Being.

Healthier defense systems empower us to more consciously create our dreams. **Unhealthy defenses send out the energy of the past and are the "tipping point" that recycles the negative past**. Healthy defenses come from a healthy connection to our **Core Being** and are a positive "tipping point" to rewrite the script so we better manifest our dreams. Wishes can become reality.

Me-B Transformation^{TM} explores the gifts and defenses of the five main body-centered Character Structures developed by William Reich and Alexander Lowen. Each Character Structure has typical defenses used as unhealthy ways of protecting the self. *We are all "**multi-defensed**," meaning we all use multiple unhealthy methods of protecting ourselves at times, and we all operate from aspects of each of the five Character Structures.* We can learn to use these defenses less often. This is the ultimate realistic Me-B Transformation ^{TM} goal.

In this book, the five Character Structures are renamed to reflect their gifts and not their challenges. Review the self-assessment test at the end of this chapter to help identify your primary Character Structure. Feel free to take the test now to have a sense of which Character Structure defenses are prominent at this point in time. *Ideally, we can find a part of ourselves in all five Character Structures. At certain times of our life, we heal different aspects of each Character Structure.*

For instance, I spent three years healing many aspects of my Spiritual and Leader types and then moved onto healing aspects of my Compassionate and Heart-Centered Structures. Each Character Structure has gifts, negative defenses, negative programmed personality traits, and Core Distortions. Below is a chart describing each of the Character Structures.

CHARACTER STRUCTURE NAME	SPIRITUAL (SCHIZOID)	COMPASSIONATE (ORAL)	HEART-CENTERED (MASOCHIST)	EXCEL (RIGID)	LEADER (PSYCHOPATH)
Age of Trauma	Pre-birth to six months	Six months to 2.5 years	1.5 to 3 years	Early Childhood	
Energetic Holding Pattern	Hold together	Hold on to others, Collapse	Hold inside	Hold back	
Core Distortion	Terror; disconnected from the body; too much in the mind Maintain a sense of the right to exist and be in the body.	Abandonment; rejection; feelings of "not enough"; collapse into hopelessness	Shame; takes the victim role; anger stuck inside	Not confident in feeling emotions and imperfections; disconnected heart and sexuality	
Goals Toward Owning Core Being	Connect to others, not only through the mind but also through the body and emotions. Overcome feelings of abandonment; feel good enough and able to support the self, even if abandoned. Learn not to collapse into hopelessness. Become own authority on value and give up the need for external confirmation.	Overcome feelings of abandonment; feel good enough and able to support the self, even if abandoned. Learn not to collapse into hopelessness. Become own authority on value and give up the need for external confirmation.	Learn to save the self from victim consciousness. Set stronger boundaries. Just say no! Learn to receive support from others. Release anger.	Feel Core Being even when imperfect. Reconnect to emotions.	
Main Negative Belief	"I am not safe."	"I am not enough	"I am a victim.		
Parental Shock	Angry, hostile, or vacant mother	Deprivation, abandonment	Controlling parents; invasion, enmeshment	Sexual rejection	Sexual betrayal; authoritarian parents
Programmed Personality—Mind	"It is only safe in my mind—to exist means to die."	"If I ask, it's not love; if I don't ask, I won't get it. I can't give to myself. I'm not enough."	"I can't say 'no' or be angry. I am a victim. You can't save me, and I can't save me."	"Either choice is wrong. I must be perfect."	"I'm right, you're wrong. I must control and manipu-late. I can't trust. I won't give in to

					you."
Programmed Personality—Body	Elongated body, vacant eyes	Pleading eyes, sunken chest, too fat or too thin, pale and lacking energy	Stocky, compressed, thick and confused eyes, fluffy and soft body.	Bright and focused eyes; structured, tight, closed heart; active pelvis. Athletic body type	Strong upper body; wide shoulders and back
Programmed Personality—Energy	Upper chakras strongest. Connected to spirit. Disconnected from Earth. Manifest Energy is also disconnected from Earth. Outer Egg split or fragmented; Mani-fest Energy needs to be set toward safety on Earth.	Very undercharged. Sucks energy from others to supplement depletion. Can't fill 3rd Chakra. Very weak Manifest Energy. Manifest Energy needs to align toward saving/sup-porting self instead of getting support from another.	Levels 1, 3, and 5 very unstructured, loose/wide grid. Split at 3rd Chakra separating heaven and Earth. Stronger energy in lower body and on 4th level. Strong Heart Chakra. Manifest Energy needs more clarity towards self-empowerment and setting good boundaries.	Levels 1, 3, 5, and 7 are overly structured grids, too tightly woven together. They are disconnected from 2nd and 4th levels of the field. Strong Manifest Energy, but it needs to be set toward feeling emotions and being connected to Core Being—so emotions can be felt and imperfection can feel freeing.	Very structured in upper body. Back chakras strongest, Strong Manifest Energy, but needs to be set to trust and not to control others.

The defenses we use get programmed within our brain's neurobiology through interaction with people, care givers, DNA, and our environment. Some research indicates that this programming process begins before we are born. The brain is malleable enough to be molded and healed, but current research indicates that the old defense patterns remain indelibly written into the script. This is why connecting to a vibrational dimension – the **Core Being**—that has never had a defense pattern written into it becomes so important. The **Core Being** is the key to overriding our physiological programming. *Learning to transition out of the programmed defense and into* **Core Being** *can be a vital goal – and the only way to overcome neurological/physiological programming.* We don't always use the same energetic defense. Different defenses come up with different people and different situations. Energetic defenses of fight or flight are operated by our sympathetic nervous system and energetic defenses of freeze are often part of our parasympathetic nervous system. The **Explorer's State of Mind** helps us become aware of our defenses and develop healthy new patterns of interaction that are not based on our past **Core Distortions**. Each energetic defense has a body (physical) and mind (mental) component and is related to a particular stage of developmental wounding.

THE SPIRITUAL CHARACTER TYPE – ENERGETIC DEFENSES

Escape

This defense occurs when the Spiritual Type energetically leaves and withdraws toward higher frequencies to escape real or projected danger. The Spiritual Character Structure enjoys this pattern. The defense initiates from the primal brain, which reacts in a "flight" response. Our higher brain shuts down, and the primal brain and limbic system take over. We then "leave" energetically, often before we even know we have left. The first step to coming out of this defense is to re-engage our higher brain so we become aware that we have left. (Mindfulness Step 1 combined with aligned intention.) Then, we can learn how to: (1) feel safe enough to be grounded in the physical dimension and the emotional levels of the field (2 and 4); and (2) make our outer energy egg more solid.

Review exercises outlined in later chapters on programming safety and trust into our cells and energy system. If we, or our clients, present with this defense, those exercises are a great place to start. Usually, the withdrawal defense presents when we have had prenatal, birth, or in-utero trauma.

We all "space out" at times. Having the expectation of ending this defense forever might be unrealistic. We can, however, set a goal to quickly catch ourselves when we dissociate.

As a Me-B Guide, if we are with someone who withdraws, we can energetically raise our vibration to match their vibration. Then, we slowly reground and bring ourselves and the other person back.

Diffuse Outer Energy Egg Fragmented by Fear

Another typical defense of the Spiritual character is an outer energy egg that is diffuse, fragmented, and not solid. It provides no clear sense of when the boundaries of the "self" end and the boundaries of the other begin. A diffuse egg makes it easier to energetically escape to the higher frequencies, but it also makes it easier for other people's energy to invade us.

Doing the Energy Egg exercise outlined in a later Chapter is a healthy way of healing this defense. If this exercise doesn't work, bringing in anger to eliminate the fear works as well. This "anger" approach is considered an advanced skill in Me-B Transformation™, because for it to succeed, our Enlightened Observer must be strong enough to transform the anger into power so that the fear dissolves.

THE HEART-CENTERED TYPE - ENERGETIC DEFENSES

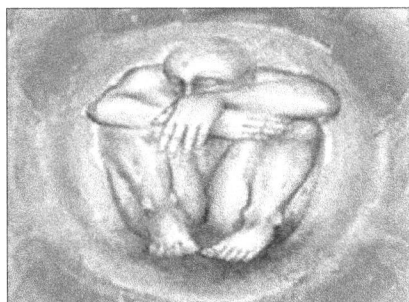

Boundary Thickening and Shielding

Energetically, this defense looks like a very strong and reinforced outer energy egg or shield. Physically, such reinforcements can look like extra fat and/or muscle.

This energetic defense provides protection, but it can prevent both positive and negative energy from entering our fields. If we or our clients are in this defense, energetically cracking open the shell of protection can feel overwhelming and create a sense of vulnerability. A person in this defense can feel stuck, like they are in a box. If a Me-B Guide is conducting a session with a client who has this defense, the Guide might need to help the client feel safe enough to receive the higher frequencies.

If we are patient and have a strong intention to vanquish our unhealthy protection, we will succeed. How- ever, keep in mind that this defense is also a productive coping mechanism to keep external low vibrations from harming us. As we find healthier ways to energetically reinforce our positive identifications, these approaches can help us feel safe.

As always, a more supportive protection is the high frequency of our **Core Being**. If our ego doesn't engage with the negative energy coming toward us, and our frequency is very high, then any energy (even if it is angry and attacking) will transform to HVC.

Porous as a Sponge

The Heart-Centered Character Structure's field is often too porous and, as a result, this individual uses other unhealthy defenses as protection. Often the negative defenses of Boundary Containment and Armoring with muscles or fat are used. A healthier way of protection is to invite more structure and a tighter energy grid in Auric levels 1, 3, 5, and 7. (See Energy Chapter for details.)

The overly porous energy fields developed because when these individuals were young, they were constantly invaded by others. Their energetic boundaries were broken so often that they now remain too open—just as elastic can be overly stretched, so were their young energy fields. Some people were abused physically and/or emotionally; all were somehow shamed and their boundaries disrespected.

In a too porous field, the outer energy egg's structured grid is too loose, and the unstructured levels (2—relationships to self and 4—relationship to others) soak up the negative energy like a sponge. Unfortunately, these mirrors back to them the negative invasions from childhood. To heal this programming, we can practice the Energy Egg exercise and practice having strong boundaries in our daily lives.

Also refer to the chapter that discusses how to transform anger into personal power. Anger is often a signal that our boundaries have been invaded. As we learn to use the energy of anger to reconnect ourselves to our personal power, our ability to set healthy boundaries increase.

The most startling example of my field being too porous happened about 10 years ago at a party. I went to welcome the guest of honor's husband. He was from Ireland and loved his gin. As I entered his field, the effects of his intoxication penetrated my overly porous field. A friend watched on, in amazement, as he saw me slur my words and stumble through the greeting. He knew I didn't drink and was disappointed at my apparent over-indulgence. As soon as I left the intoxicated guest's side, I returned to normal.

Most of us are influenced by the energy fields of others. We can learn to regulate our field so when it is in our highest good to receive HVC, we can let our field be porous—and when we need a less porous field, we can adjust.

Porcupine Defense

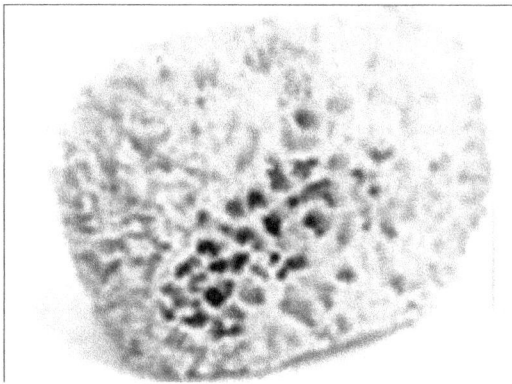

Prickly-attacking energy that spikes into us as if we were a pincushion is used by the Heart-Centered type. This defense is often used when someone feels their space has been invaded. If we notice this happening to us or if we notice we are doing this to another we can literally take a step back. As we reclaim our space and help another reclaim their physical and emotional space the porcupine defense dissolves.

When we are in these Heart-Centered defenses, and someone comes in to help us, it might ignite our anger or it might make us freeze, and become confused. The anger or freezing might increase as others try harder to help us.

This is because their help doesn't feels supportive. In fact, no matter how kind and gentle someone may be in their offer of help, when we are deeply in this defense, nothing feels supportive. Yet, the double bind is that we also feel we can't move forward without their help. This creates a metaphorical box that traps us from moving forward.

We feel like a victim — we can't save ourselves and we can't be saved by another. As a result, this activates a trauma freeze (immobilization) response in our nervous system. Just as a deer freezes in the headlights of an attacking car, we too can freeze when we feel trapped and unable to receive help from others or give help to ourselves.

Connecting to anger and the power to fight back can bring us out of this defense. In fact, simply moving the body or even the hands can create an unfreezing in our brain neurology and reconnect us to Core Being.

THE LEADER TYPE—ENERGETIC DEFENSES

No One Has My Back

Sometimes we only shrink the back part of our energy egg, so the field is full in front but collapsed behind. It might feel like someone is going to, or is already, stabbing us in the back. Our field shrinks in anticipation and reaction to the energetic strike.

Often, we also shrink our back when we feel guilty about set- ting (or wanting to set) a boundary with someone—such as telling someone "no" or speaking our truth. *Ironically, on some level, the others sense our hesitance, and they can be more reactive than if we energetically "have our own back" and keep our Manifest Energy clearly aligned to our highest good.* Having our own back in life helps us stay centered in our Core Being and be less reactive to others' actions.

THE COMPASSIONATE TYPE—ENERGETIC DEFENSES

Collapse

Energetic Collapse occurs when our ego is activated to the extent that we feel there is no hope. We forget that our Core Being exists. We feel that the universe is against us, and we hook into the negative belief that someone else must come save us. Energetically, this defense looks like a deflated tire or a balloon that has lost all of its air. To come out of this defense, we must call in our Leader/Excel energies and give up hope that anyone else will rescue us.

If we often find ourselves in these defenses, feeling how it presents energetically in the body is a key—as well as looking at the **Core Distortion** that created the energetic misalignment. Drawing a picture of how this presents in our field can help us own what we are doing to ourselves. We can also connect to the positive aspects of the Leader personality type so we are more able to bring in HVC and move out of this defense. (You can refer to the previous chart.)

It is important to use aligned intention and have a relentless commitment to succeed. It is also important to release any need to have someone else save us. People with chronic illness and those who have had severe trauma often present with this defense.

Because the energy in this defense is so undercharged and depressed, there is often an inadequate amount of "aliveness" running through us. This makes it almost impossible to engage our Enlightened Observer, and use the aligned intention needed to move through the 3-rings of healing and the 5-Step Mindfulness process.

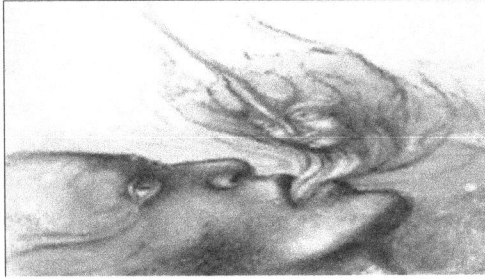

Sucking Others' Energy

Compassionate Character types try to suck energy from others because it is easier to digest, just as a mother's milk is easier for a baby to digest. A Me-B Guide may choose to energetically "feed" the client presenting with this defense and over a period of time slowly wean them and teach them how to access their own internal source of power and support.

If we use this defense, we can explore the circum- stances under which it tends to arise. Does it come up mostly during intimate relationships, and how can we learn to provide energy/support to ourselves? Later we discuss three aspects of **Adult Consciousness**. The aspect of **Adult Consciousness** that the Compassionate Type needs to master is *to learn how to give to self when we would rather receive from another.*

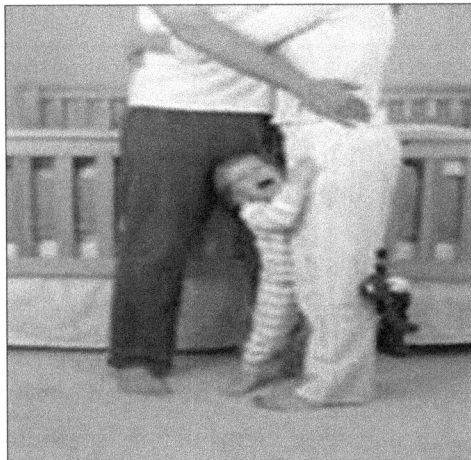

Tentacles and Energy Hooks

If someone walks away, the **Compassionate Type** using this defense will energetically want to hook onto the other person. They do this so they can energetically feed off of another. A two-year old child uses this defense when he or she clings to their mother's leg as she tries to leave the room. It is like the tentacles of a jellyfish holding on to its catch.

The core issue behind the tentacles defense is primal—fear and survival. Helping our client move out of a primal response pattern and back into their higher brain can help them move out of this defense. Sometimes simply asking, "What are you feeling now?" or, "What are you afraid of?" will reinitiate the higher brain functions. Mirroring the "good enough mom/dad" energy until they can do it for themselves can be important as well.

Sometimes we hook into another simply because we are programmed to follow. It can be an energetic habituation that we are not even aware we are doing. For instance, I often attend spinning classes where stationary bicycles are lined up next to each other in rows. They are stacked very close so that one person's energy is next to another person's energy. Spinning instructors encourage us to work individually and at our own rate.

During class, I notice that when I move into the standing run position, the person next to me often follows. Or sometimes I follow someone else's lead and sit when they sit and stand when they stand. This happens mostly when my mind is wandering and I am not present enough with myself. As a result, I subconsciously let someone else be in charge of my choices while thinking I was the one in charge. I hook my energy into them and/or they hook their energy into mine, and we simply respond from past programming.

In life, we do this all day long. Let us use aligned intention, and advanced mindfulness to notice when we are doing this so we can regain our choices in life and our power.

If we find ourselves in these defenses, we can explore what Core Distortion, childhood trauma or negative beliefs are the fuel behind these actions. Then we can investigate healthy methods of self-comfort and safety so we return to **Core Being**.

Shrinking is one of the most common energetic defenses. We energetically shrink our outer energy egg when we are attacked, scared or triggered. This makes our consciousness smaller and as a result, it makes us *less able* to protect ourselves. Shrinking is an automatic fight/flight response. We can (1) recognize, then (2) move out of our fight/flight sympathetic nervous system response to (3) regain our higher brain, parasym-pathetic nervous system response and (4) reconnect to Core Being. This then allows us to find a healthier way of defending ourselves. These four steps bring us out of the **Shrinking Defense**. Also see the grounding exercises.

THE EXCEL TYPE—ENERGETIC DEFENSES

Pushing away the truth through denial is often an indicator that the ego has been activated. If our clients are in this defense, what would our healing response be to help them recover? Also, when we enter this defense, how can we support ourselves?

When we are with someone using this defense, we can check our **Central Channel** to see if we are pushing our will upon them and if we need them to agree with us. If they are in **Denial**, then a part of them feels threatened, and they don't want to look at themselves. We can slow down, back up, and give them and us space to reconnect to **Core Being**. Then reconnect to them from Core Being and ground deeply into the Earth for love and support.

If we find ourselves using this defense, it is important to wonder why we feel the need to deny. Is there something we are afraid to accept or see about ourselves? None of us are perfect, and of course, there will always be something uncomfortable to look at within. As we valiantly do so, we grow, learn, and raise our frequency. This defense is primary for the Excel Type, but it can be used by all Character Structures.

To the sensitive, **verbal daggers** feel like knifes being thrown in our direction. The **Leader Character Structure** can use this defense, for instance, when their issues of trust/betrayal get activated. Who in your life does this to you, and how might it feel if a client sent this defense in your direction?

If someone is directing negative energy our way, use **Core Being** to fill our field. It is also important to survey our **Central Channel** so it runs solidly in the center of our body.

If we find ourselves doing this to someone, own it. We may not be able to do so in the heat of the moment, but once we are alone, we can explore what **Core Distortion** and/or **Child Consciousness** within us was brought to the surface. Then we can begin the process of transforming it to HVC. Usually, we need to feel the pain and then let the higher frequency of our **Enlightened Observer** melt it away. We may need to re- peat this process 1,000 or more times over our lifetime.

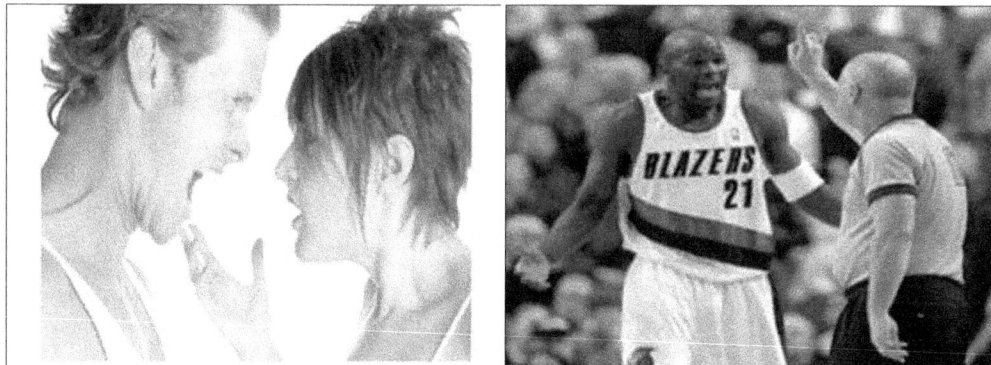

"You must accept my reality" is how it feels when we are experiencing this defense. The energy feels as if we are being controlled by another person. The **Leader/Excel** types are good at this defense because they always have the answers and know what is "right." Or at least, they feel they do.

If our client/associate is in this defense, we can energetically release their grasp by disconnecting our outer energy egg from theirs, then ground and fill our field with Core Being. If we are in this defense, we can explore why we need the other to accept our views and what part of us is in distortion. Then, we can come into our heart and feel the pain we are avoiding.

Confusion is a defense usually caused because the energy of a past trauma has been brought to the surface. The nervous system becomes activated, clouding higher brain functions. Confusion can be ego-related, because a part of us doesn't want to feel pain or go deeper into our personal process work.

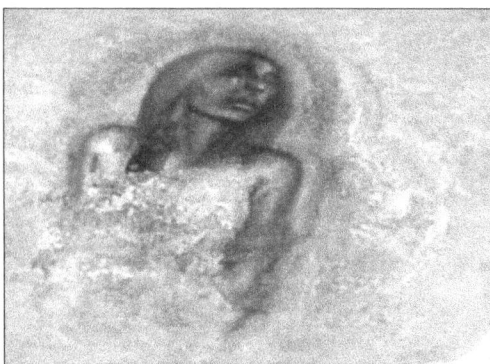

All **Character Structures** become confused. It takes strong intention to move out of this defense. Simply knowing it is a defense has helped many clients move through it. If we or our clients are in this defense, we can ground, align our Manifest Energy, and balance our Auric Field with any of the exercises already discussed. Give kindness and compassion for the parts of us that need support in order to move out of **Confusion** and reconnect to our aliveness.

PUBLIC PERSONALITY

The **Public Personality** or In-Authentic Self has become a popularized term. It is the inner actor within us. It pretends it knows who we are but is afraid to sink in and really see the truth. It is a cover, plastic and pretend. This mask can also be considered a defense because it protects the ego.

Yet it does have its uses. For instance, when someone asks us how we are, and we say fine or good—even when our pain may be very close to the surface—this can be an appropriate response under some circumstances. Learning to choose when Public Personality serves (or doesn't serve) us is a useful skill.

MY PUBLIC PERSONALITY IS IN CHARGE

Jessup was 29 years old. She dressed impeccably and "put on her face" every morning before she left her house. She had the perfect job, house, car and boy friend. However, as perfect as she looked from the out- side, underneath she felt deeply insecure and feared someone would find out the truth beneath her public projection.

As we incarnate, we start uncovering our **Public Personality** and discover our **Core Being** beneath. Then there is choice. In self-help circles, people discuss the value of finding our **Authentic Self**. The **Authentic Self** can resonate at a very high frequency but it is still part of the ego-based **Auric Dimension**. We support moving as close as possible to our non-ego-based dimension, Core Being.

In Me-B Transformation™, we can learn how to raise our consciousness to the frequency of **Core Being**, where eventually, there is no ego and no self. As explained in the previous quote by Deepak Chopra, "reality increases the closer one gets to the source." As we are close to source, confusion goes away and we see things as they really are. The illusion of life fades and we come out of negative projection and a need to use our Public Personality.

In Me-B Transformation™, we are hoping to return closer and closer to the "source." There is no self; we be- come a vessel of wholeness that transcends ego and is the home of pure consciousness. Although most of us won't reach this ideal, the higher we set the bar, the closer we may come!

CREATE THE MASK OF YOUR PUBLIC PERSONALITY

Supplies: glue, markers, colored paper, scissors, tape and imagination.

Close your eyes as you touch the supplies. Using your imagination, watch your mind screen (what you see when you look with your eyes closed).

With the materials before you, make one or more masks that represent your Public Personality. Put them on. Sense the Public Personality in your body and energy system. How does it serve you? What images or beliefs support your Public Personality?

Now imagine how your Core Being could take the place of the mask. Then, in your daily life, practice living from your Core.

Our Separated Self holds Painful Child Consciousness. It keeps us in Negative Intention and Spiritual Junk Food because we don't want to feel pain. Feeling the pain from our Core Being heals the Separated Self and raises our consciousness.

Anger, judgment, and even humor can be used to keep us separate

SEPARATED SELF

The **Separated Self** is the part of us that chooses to use emotional triggers and Core Distortions to judge, blame and separate from others and from our Core Being. Sometimes we yell, sometimes we leave, and sometimes we use humor. All of us have a **Separated Self**. Biochemically and physiologically, all of us have a killer and an aggressor inside of us. If we don't look for and own our **Separate Self**, it controls us. Despite our wish to suppress it, it will come out in a sloppy, hurtful manner. Its typical sources of energy are our primal brain and hormones. Our **Separated Self** is part of the human experience and it has much to teach us, if only we will listen.

As we look deep within, we own the parts of ourselves that are not deeply connected to our **Core Being**. If we are willing to listen to the wisdom behind the need to want to separate, we can heal.

By listening to the underlying need to separate, judge, react, blame . . . we learn. We learn more about our **Core Distortions**, our lack of boundaries and our needs. By listening to and learning about our **Separated Self**, we find the path to freedom and enlightenment. By ignoring this aspect of ourselves, we create **Spiritual Junk Food** that sickens our soul when we feed on it. We miss the boat to self-awareness and growth.

Every time our vibration rises, we can be sure that life will show us our next piece of personal process work through the reactions of our Separated Self.

The higher we go in vibration, the more deeply we have to look at our Separated Self.

The good news is that as we listen and work to transform, we maintain that higher vibration and adopt a bigger piece of our Core Being. Without the wisdom from the **Separated Self**, we would never find out who we really are. Ironically, this part of us is our link to the "source." Energetically the **Separated Self** holds a split between the upper and the lower chakras. The **Central Channel** is usually twisted at the second and/or third chakra, and we disconnect from our **Core Being**. (See energy chapter for a summary of the Central Channel/Auric Field and other important energy anatomy details.)

There is no light without darkness – there is no darkness without light. As we own our light, it shines upon our darkness so it can heal!

SEPARATED SELF

- **Step 1:** Which of the Separated Self Statements best describes you?
- **Step 2:** Where do you imagine it is held in your Manifest Energy/Auric Field and your body?
- **Step 3:** What part of your negative ego encourages your Separated Self (arrogance, hurt, feeling you are not enough)?
- **Step 4:** Bring Core Being Energy into those aspects of your body/energy systems to reconnect to others and yourself.

SELF ASSESSMENT TOOL FOR THE 5 CHARACTER STRUCTURES

Take a piece of paper out and write down the answers to the following questions. Don't think of what the answer should be, just give your first initial response.

When I feel challenged in a relationship, the person challenging me is more likely to respond in which of the following manners?

1. Intellectualize what is happening
2. Be mothering
3. Be submissive
4. Tease
5. Be in competition

When I find myself in a situation where my abilities are publicly shown and tested, I can:

1. Withdraw
2. Become needy or dependent
3. Control or exert energy
4. Feel guilty and shameful
5. Hold back and be reserved

Which negative belief statement do you most identify with?

1. To exist means to die.
2. If I ask, it's not love; if I don't ask, I won't get it.
3. I have to be right or I'll die.
4. If I get angry, I'll be humiliated; if I don't, I'll be humiliated.
5. Either choice is wrong.

My public personality most closely resembles the following statement.

1. I'll reject you before you reject me.
2. I don't need you.
3. I'm right and you're wrong.
4. I'll hurt myself before you hurt me.
5. Yes, but...

I tend to offer the following statement when I am in my Separated Self:

1. You don't exist either.
2. Take care of me.
3. I will control you.
4. I will spite and provoke you.
5. I won't love you.

Which of the following is my Core Being Statement?

1. I am real.
2. I'm satisfied, full and whole.
3. I can give in and trust.
4. I am free.
5. I commit to someone and I love.

My most common challenging feeling is:

1. Fear
2. Passivity
3. Feelings of Defeat
4. Tension
5. No feelings, just thoughts

My pattern in life is to:

1. Hold Together
2. Hold On
3. Hold Up
4. Hold In
5. Hold Back

My negative Intention in relationship is best expressed by which of the following?

1. I tend to separate from others, to split.
2. I'll make you give it to me and when you give it, it won't be enough.
3. It has to be done the way I think it should be done. If you don't do it the way I think it should be done then I cannot trust you.
4. I love negativity.
5. I won't surrender, let go and be messy.

I feel I most need to:

1. Strengthen Boundaries
2. Own Needs and Stand on My own Two Feet
3. Trust
4. Be Assertive, Free, and Open to Spiritual Connections
5. Connect Heart to Genitals

The following describes my physical body best:

1. Elongation, Scoliosis, Cold Hands and Feet, Cold Core
2. Thin, Collapsed Chest, Cold Chest, Depleted
3. Inflated Chest, Top Heavy; Cold Legs and Pelvis, Upper Body Holds More of a Charge
4. Head Forward, Heavy and Cold Buttocks; Boiling Inside
5. Ridged Back, Pelvis Tipped and Cold, Withheld from Core

My negative energetic defense is best described in the following manner:

1. Withdrawal, Beside Myself, Porcupine
2. Oral Sucking, Verbal Denial, Hysteria
3. Hook, Mental Grasp
4. Silent Brooding, Tentacles
5. Power/Will Display and Boundary Containment

The chakras I use the most include:

1. 7, front of 6th, 3rd front, 2nd rear
2. 7, 6th front, 2nd front
3. 7, 6, 4th rear
4. Front of 6th, front of 3rd
5. Back Chakras, 6th front

Total the number of 1s, 2s, 3s, 4s, and 5s. Bring your totals to the first day of class.

1._____   2. _____   3. _____   4. _____   5. _____

1 = Spiritual 2 = Compassionate 3 = Leader 4 = Heart-Centered 5 = Excel

List your primary type and your next highest type _____

Exercise: List the lessons you can learn, in the following categories, based on the answers you gave in this inventory – not necessarily just those related to the personality type you rated highest.

1. Energetically

2. Relational Challenges

3. Body Types

4. Core Being

5. Separated Self

CHAPTER REVIEW

1. Explain how our expectation of kindness can cause us pain.
2. Why in Me-B Transformation™ do we develop the ability to move out of our Programmed Personality and into Core Being?
3. List the components of change.
4. The Explorer's Mind must be __.

Intention

1. There are two types of Intention. List them.
2. Positive Intention supports ____; Negative Intention ___.
3. We would all be enlightened if _.
4. What moves energy — negative or positive intention or both?
5. What do negative and positive intentions do, and how do they present energetically?
6. What is the dimension of Intention?
7. What are your gifts/challenges in this area?

8. What can you personally do to solve our world's problems?
9. The programmed personality level is held where in the Auric Field?

Core Distortion

1. Explain Core Distortions.
2. What are your Core Distortions, and is there one that keeps repeating more strongly than the others? Explain.
3. List the typical order in which distortions release.

Defenses

1. Is there a relationship between our brain chemistry and our programmed defenses? Explain.
2. List the energetic defenses you use most often, and describe the circumstances under which you typically use them.
3. What Character Structures tend to use which defenses?

Public Personality

1. When is this useful and when isn't it useful? What is yours? Explain.

Separated Self

1. Explain the Separated Self and your challenges in this area.
2. Identifying when we have regressed to our Separated Self can help us __.

CHAPTER 5

HEALING OUR DEFENSES IN RELATIONSHIP

It is never about the other person. As we learn to take responsibility for our own actions and investigate why we are triggered, we can then use our Choice Points for peace and reconnect to the other person with adult consciousness and not regressed anger and hurt. We can't control them or make them act aligned. But we can be mindful of our reactions in response to them.

The partners we choose create different challenges for us depending upon how our energies and Core Distortions interact. Since none of us are perfect, our defenses will eventually collide. For instance, if we are a Spiritual type who feels terror about existing, and we select a business or relationship partner who runs strong, some- times attacking Leader energies, the marriage between these two very different energies can cause suffering for both people. The Explorer's State of Mind can help us take advantage of these relational collisions and turn them into learning opportunities. The Explorer's Mind does this by being the inner spiritual detective that helps us see when we are reactive, in child consciousness and out of our center. When we are in these states, it helps us understand why we are acting that way and it can help us align our intention, be mindful of the wisdom so we can return back to Core Being.

The richest ground for us to achieve self-mastery is through interaction with one another. Relationships by far present the most profound challenges because, if the relationship lasts long enough, we can't avoid triggering each other's Core Distortions. The programmed personality interacts with another's human parts and before we know it, we can feel hurt, boundaries are crossed, and the seeds of anger and resentment are laid.

Saying this will not happen is naive and an example of Spiritual Junk Food. Instead, we can: (1) acknowledge that intimacy will eventually lead to us being triggered out of our Core Being and into defense; and then (2) develop a plan to deal with this certainty. (The 3-rings of healing outlines an action plan to bring ourselves out of defense.) This can be everyone's loving commitment to others and our selves—and it can be everyone's personal responsibility.

Take the character structure self-assessment test if you haven't already and have your partner/family take it as well. Then investigate which relationship dynamics you might need to negotiate in order to find your choice point opportunities and return to Core Being.

Relationship Defenses CHOICE POINT Opportunities

Either way, whenever our defense strategy prevails, love and relationship fail; it is our responsibility to find a new way by noticing the Choice Points in our lives. Under the anger and defense is love. Isn't love worth the effort? After all, it is only the ego that wins—we don't.

Spiritual and Compassionate: The Spiritual might give the Compassionate intellectual love. For the Compassionate personality type, it probably won't be enough. In turn, the Compassionate might trigger the Spiritual to withdrawal because of their neediness and their demands for too much support. Both tend to run undercharged fields, so that could have a negative influence on their sexual life and on finding personal power in the relationship.

Spiritual and Heart-Centered: Anger might escape from the Heart-Centered partner toward their Spiritual love. This will be sure to initiate a quick withdraw by the Spiritual, which in turn could trigger the Heart-Centered victim consciousness. The overcharged field of the Heart-Centered could provide comfort to the Spiritual's undercharged, more fragmented field. However, Spirituals tend to be very intuitive, and if the Spiritual senses the overcharge in the other's field as suppressed anger, the Spiritual might feel the urge to escape.

Spiritual and Excel: Inherently, both of these Character Structures tend to be disconnected from their emotions. The Spirituals are disconnected because they are not present with themselves or others, and the Excels are disconnected from their emotions because the rigid structures of their energy field suppress emotions. In these defenses, the partnership might work well, in the beginning. As one or the other comes out of their distortion, they might demand a deeper emotional connection with the other. If it is the Spiritual demanding the deeper connection, but their Excel partner doesn't follow through, the Spiritual might reject the Excel and leave. They will reject another before they are rejected. If it is the Excel that is demanding the Spiritual to change, the Excel will look for ways to do it so perfectly that she will try to "ensure" success. If the Excel doesn't immediately get a positive response from their Spiritual partner, they may shut down their heart and harbor resentment toward the defended Spiritual that can't or won't follow through.

Spiritual and Leader: The control and manipulation can make the Spiritual withdraw. With no one to lead, because of the Spiritual's withdrawal, anger can spill from the Leader onto the Spiritual – making the Spiritual withdraw all the more. For success, Spirituals can ground and stay strong, yet loving. The Leader can heal his or her trust and fear issues around betrayal.

Compassionate and Heart-Centered: The Heart-Centered has a tendency to give, even when they want to say no. The Compassionate, in their neediness, could take advantage of this. This could illicit feelings of victim consciousness for the Heart-Centered. As a result, it might trigger the Heart-Centered to release his/her suppressed anger upon the Compassionate, which in turn can make the Compassionate collapse into hopelessness, fear of abandonment and feelings of not being good enough.

Compassionate and Leader: Co-dependency could dominate this relationship. The Leader might be controlling and taking charge, with the Compassionate being submissive to the Leader, very willing to be dominated and controlled. The Compassionate might be needy, and the Leader might feel that safe he or she won't be betrayed by the weaker, needy Compassionate. As one or the other comes out of their defense, those puzzle pieces won't fit anymore, and the chain of co-dependency will break. As this happens, turmoil can initially set in. Healing the turmoil is important, so the Compassionate can learn to support him/herself and the Leader can learn to surrender and trust.

Compassionate and Excel: The Excel could "excel" at supporting and mothering the Compassionate until...the Excel becomes resentful toward the Compassionate. The Excel's disconnect between heart and sexuality could accentuate spilling anger toward the Compassionate, triggering the Compassionate into the old pattern of neediness, collapse and lack of self-worth.

Heart-Centered and Excel: The perfectionist in the Excel might seek solutions while the stuck, angry energy in the Heart-Centered withholds any forward progress. If this happens, be careful the Excel doesn't push or work harder than their Heart-Centered partner to heal the problems in the relationship. As each person balances their defenses, ideally the Excel will meet the giving/loving nature of their Heart-Centered love. This in turn will help the Excel heal his or her heart so it can re-connect to their sexuality and Core Being.

Heart-Centered and Leader: The Leader must be careful not to shame and humiliate his or her Heart-Centered partner. The Leader also needs to be careful not to try to control/manipulate the giving nature of the Heart-

Centered so the Heart-Centered feeds the Leaders' needs. And, the Heart-Centered can work his/her anger and victim issues to eliminate feelings of being trapped, stuck and victimized by the distortions of his/her Leader partner.

An Excel and Leader: A match between a Leader and an Excel can go very well. Both are focused toward success, yet both can be disconnected from their hearts and sexuality. They have different parental shocks, yet they are similar in terms of seduction and betrayal. Giving up needing to control or manipulate—and learning to connect heart energy with sexual energy—are both important in this paring. Each will have to learn how to deal with the anger that is sure to eventually come to the surface.

Excel/Excel: This pair could work well. They might both try to out-perform the other and be competitive in the relationship. This could be helpful and passionate, or it could become a problem to overcome. As they learn to be in both heart energies and sexuality and as they learn to adequately deal with anger, the long-term success of this pair could be strong. A lot depends upon what other minor Character Structures may be interacting within them. For instance, we are rarely just one Character Structure. We are often working minor Character Structures at the same time, such as Excel-Compassionate and Excel-Leader energies. (More will be presented on this topic below.)

Leader/Leader: Two leaders needing to be in control and manipulating might lead to war. The pairing could be perfect or disastrous. Whether the two interact from Core or interact through control, fear of betrayal and manipulation will determine how well this pair is able to love and appreciate one another. Depending upon what other minor Character Structure energies may be influencing the defenses, this pairing could be more or less challenging. For instance, one person in the relationship may have Leader energies combined with Compassionate or Heart- centered energies, and the other person might be a Leader type combined with Excel traits. The former may feel dominated by his or her partner and will need to learn how to stand up for him/herself or collapse and/or feel victimized.

Heart-Centered/Heart-Centered: At some point, both people may feel stuck as this personality type often does. And, because they both don't have good boundaries, this too could cause tensions between them. Both often give too much and then feel angry because they gave too much. This couple must deal with their victim energies, anger and lack of boundaries if they are to create a successful partnership.

Compassionate/Compassionate: If both present as needy, undercharged, and wanting the other to save them, it could create deep challenges for this relationship. The relationship could feel very co-dependent—both confirming the other's value and commiserating but not empowering themselves. On the other hand, they could both find anger; transform it to personal power and save themselves by finding their own internal "good enough" mother. A lot will depend upon what minor Character Structure energies are colluding with the Compassionate energies. For instance, if one or the other or both call in the positive aspects of the Leader or Excel energies to help them, balance, joy and mutual support can be maintained.

Spiritual/Spiritual: Both of these character types are not present/stuck in head. Both also need to connect to the body for healthy sexual and emotional connections, and deeper spiritual connections. If they call in the positive qualities of the Compassionate, Leader or Excel types, great balance could be created.

COMPASSIONATE

EXCEL

HEART-
CENTERED

SPIRITUAL

LEADER

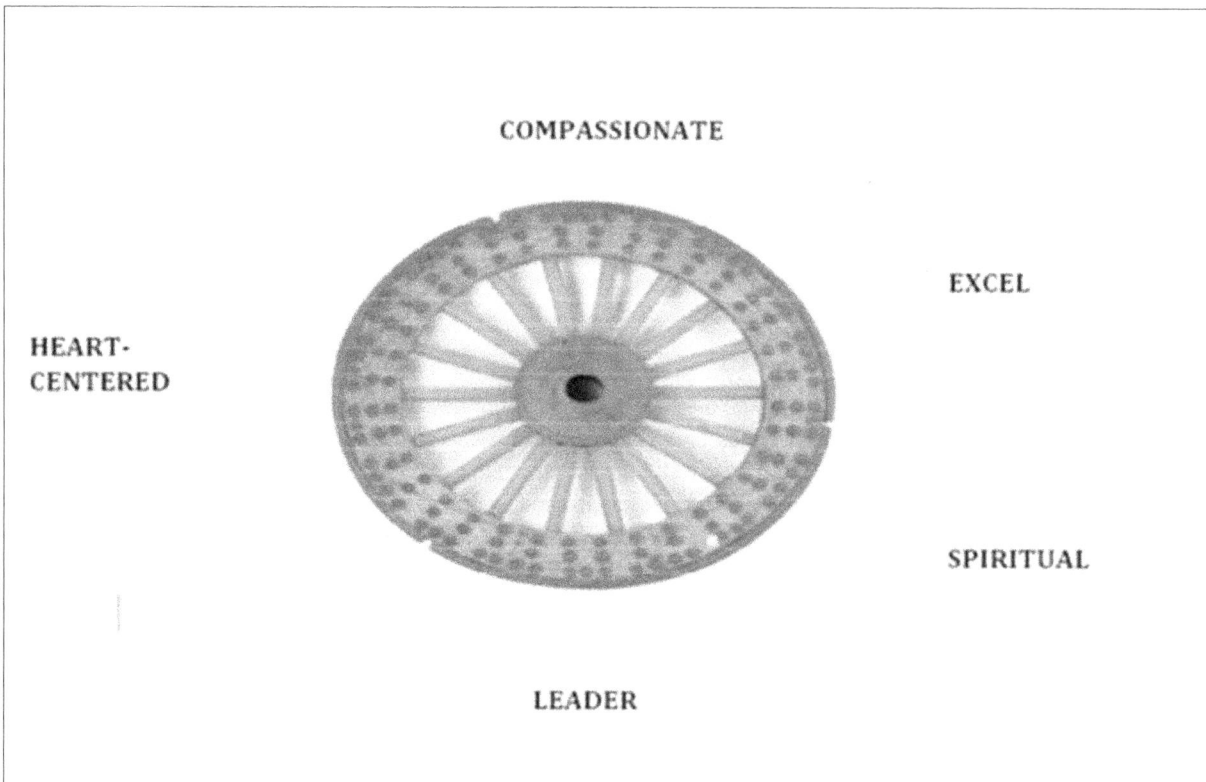

We Cycle through the Wheel of Defenses

Most of us cycle through different defenses. As one defense fails, we move to the next. For instance, think of the challenge of learning to see/sense energy. We might begin this task with our **Leader** and **Excel** gifts of trying to follow the procedures perfectly, taking charge of our learning and seeking success. Gaining some success in the process, but not doing it as well as we want can then trigger our **Spiritual** defense and we can withdraw, quit, runaway. If we come out of this defense, it can then trigger our **Compassionate** defense: feeling hopeless and not good enough, and collapsing our energy into "I will never be able to do this."

If we stay in this defense, it can spiral further, and we may find ourselves in the **Heart-Centered** energies of feeling trapped and stuck. We demand help, and even get angry at the teacher or anyone who comes into our energy field to help us, but their help never feels adequate. As much as we need their help, we can't take in their help. Anger bursts and feelings

HE SAYS/SHE SAYS?

SHE SAYS:

"Doesn't he know I love him? I am the one scheduling the counseling sessions. I am the one noticing what needs to be done to heal our marriage. We go to counseling, he agrees to change, and then nothing. I can't afford to leave. I am too old and haven't worked out of the house in years. The kids are gone. It is just the two of us now, and he is absent and withdrawn. I feel alone—trapped. He has victimized me because he won't show up; he won't change."

HE SAYS:

"Nothing I do is ever enough. I try but fail. Why should I try again? Why isn't she happy? I pro- vide a house, pay all the bills, but still she wants more. She is so angry I can't stand to spend too much time with her or else she finds something to fight about. I don't know what to do."

Both began the marriage in love, with excitement and with the positive aspects of their programmed personalities in place. Twenty-five years later, they have spun through all of the Character Structure defenses and are now in victim consciousness, angry and lost. Too often when it gets to this stage, one or the other has an affair, leaves, or decides to settle and remain in pain.

Instead, we can use the energy from our anger, transform it into personal power so we find our way out of defense, and begin the long, hard road back to ourselves. As one person stays out of defense and connects to Core Being, miracles happen—and often, love returns. That is, if we don't project any expectations of change upon the other. This is very important. We can't expect change yet we can become secure in our own future happiness *without it being contingent* upon another's ability to change. You see, the only way to succeed is to lead ourselves out of pain. There is no external source or savior except for the one we can provide for ourselves.

Solutions for Coming out of Defense

Given that none of us are only just one Character Structure, we might need to use more than one of these solutions to we move out of defense and return back to Core Being. These solutions may sound simple, but the energetic structures might feel impossible in the beginning. Just like it took time to learn to ride a bike, practice, practice, practice.

Even if we fall off—or rather, *especially* if we fall off—we serve our highest good when we commit to coming out of defense with our loved ones, associates and friends. Let there be NO other option. Coming out of defense is the deepest expression of love we can give one another. Come out of defense and back into love—even if the other person doesn't! After all, the hardest things to do are often the most worthwhile. It is the ego that keeps us in defense, and our connection with source that brings us back out.

Solution for an Excel to Come out of Relationship Defense

Parental Shock: sexual rejection in early childhood. We so love our dad. He is perfect and can do nothing wrong. My arms go around his neck as I hug him tight to give him a kiss, but he is angry now and is pushing me away, yelling at me, rejecting me. My heart shuts down.

For an Excel to come out of defense, she must accept that she can't fix the other person, and she needs to keep her heart open to release the resentment. Excels tend to separate heart and sexuality (4th and 2nd chakras). As they keep their heart open, the anger in their 2nd chakras can release. They can reconnect to the relationship based on their wholeness, instead of their defenses. As always, this helps them move out of the personality level and into their Core Being. From here, clarity about the relationship is possible. In addition, they can invoke the positive loving qualities of the Compassionate type, who is able to feel so much love.

Solution for a Spiritual to come out of Defense in Relationship:

Parental Shock: hostile/angry parent, pre/post natal trauma from 0-6 months of age. Light fills the young unborn soul, the bliss of Core Being strong inside her. The amniotic fluid is warm and protective, as month after month she grows. She barely notices how crowded it has become when the contractions start. The pounding pressure against her body becomes tight and uncomfortable—she notices her heart race, her head pound, and something pulling at her neck. She loses consciousness as the cord gets tighter and her skin becomes blue from lack of oxygen. Cognitive thinking is not yet available to her, just pain, feelings, and tears as she reawakens to a cold, sterile environment. No more amniotic warmth—she is in a clear box now, alone. No touch, just tubes. She is poked and pricked.

Spirituals can seek to align their Manifest Energy Intention Line deep into the Earth. They can open their undercharged root chakras and ground more deeply into their bodies. As they process and eliminate the deep terror, they will be able to be present enough to connect to Core Being and then to their Excel partner (or any other type of partner). Bringing in the positive aspects of the Compassionate can help them feel instead of just think. Bringing in the strength of the Leader energies can also help them overcome the terror of existing.

Spirituals also need to be careful not to use connection to Core Being as a type of **Spiritual Junk Food** and as a way to bypass what they are really feeling. One of the Spirituals' gifts is that they can be very creative. Using their creativity to reconnect to the earthly world can be very helpful. Sometimes it helps for them to even create a physical place (e.g. a meditation room) where they can practice feeling safe and connected in their body in silence and solitude. Doing physical exercise on their core and lower body can be a necessary ritual, as is practicing the Centered Oneness Intervention.

Solution for a Compassionate to Come out of Defense in Relationship:

Parental Shock: Parent was negligent or depriving, and caused feeling of abandonment between 6 months and 2.5 years. Imagine a baby in his crib crying for his mother to comfort him. For some reason, she doesn't or can't come to his side. He cries harder, hoping she will come, making as much noise as a young baby can muster, and desperately pleading for help—until . . . he eventually gives up, numb and frozen by hopelessness.

It is vital that the Compassionate give up needing someone else to save them. They must learn to overcome their tendencies to collapse into feelings of "not enough." Ignoring their negative, ego-based self-talk might be very difficult, but it is absolutely necessary if they are going to triumph over their internal saboteur.

Compassionates *must become their own authority on their value* and stop looking to others to provide that for them. They can learn to look at mistakes as learning opportunities instead of as confirmation that they are failures. Since we each have all of the Character Structure energies hidden within us, the Compassionate can find and nurture the structured, strong energy and Manifest Energy of the positive aspects of the Leader and Excel types.

Compassionates must remember that they are perfect right now, as they are! Finding, feeling, and anchoring into their perfection can be the Compassionates moment-to-moment choice. The "No Excuses" intervention is great practice for this personality type. It can also help the Heart-Centered type.

Solution for a Heart-Centered to Come out of Defense in Relationship:

Parental Shock: controlling, invasive, enmeshed parents between the ages of 1.5 and 3 years. I am only two years old, yet I know what it means to be invaded and humiliated by my parents. They control my hand as I scribble the horse picture; they control what to eat and when to eat. They make me sit on the potty for hours until I . . . The character of Raymond's mother on the T.V. show *Raymond* is a type of mother who creates the Heart-Centered Child. With the best of intentions, our boundaries are invaded, and our "no" is taken away. We feel controlled by our caregivers and enmeshed with them. We have no space and feel trapped.

Heart-Centered types feel stuck in a box – they can't get out without someone else's help, yet they can't let in that help. They are the quintessential victims. By releasing their suppressed anger, they can find the strength to set strong boundaries, say no, and strengthen their Manifest Energy Intention Line so they can find their own way out of the box. Their life's Rhythm of Flow of energy is slower than the Leader and Excel types. They can give themselves the space they need to heal the trauma of the past and move forward.

Solution for a Leader to Come out of Defense in Relationship:

Parental Shock: seductive/authoritarian parents during puberty. I don't understand why my father acts that way toward me. He drinks and I can smell him come too close . . . way too close to me. His breath is on my neck. He is too close! God, please. Why did he betray me?

The Leader, underneath their defenses, is simply afraid of being betrayed and attacked. They act like a puffer fish when they feel threatened. They can have an inflated ego and are arrogant at times.

Discovering what they need in order to release this fear of attack and begin to trust others is the first step. One aspect of this process is to find safety and trust within themselves so that when someone does attack them, they can still feel whole and safe. At some point of our life, we will be emotionally and/or verbally at- tacked. Accepting this and knowing that attacking back perpetuates this cycle can help us find other, more positive ways to defend ourselves.

Collapsing as the Compassionate is not the answer either. Learning how to better stay in Core Being (or resonating as close to the Core Being frequency as we can) is the ideal to work toward. From Core Being we can assess the "attack," own our part, and in a balanced way set boundaries, speak our truth and stay centered.

Character Structure	SPIRITUAL	COMPASSIONATE	HEART-CENTERED	EXCEL	LEADER
Spiritual	Both not present/stuck in head. Both need to connect to body for healthy sexual, emotional, and Spiritual connection.	Spiritual might give Compassionate Intellectual love, but it won't be enough. A Compassionate might trigger the Spiritual to with-draw, because of their neediness and demands for too much support.	Anger from Heart-Centered might trigger Spiritual to withdraw, which could in turn trigger the victim energy in the Heart-Centered because the Spiritual is absent.	It might work well until one or the other heals their defenses, and then the Excel will work very hard to fix it. If the Spiritual doesn't show up, the Excel's anger will make the Spiritual withdraw even more.	The control and manipulation can make the Spiritual withdraw. With no one to lead, because of the Spiritual's withdrawal, anger and difficulty can occur. For success, the Spiritual can ground and stay strong, yet loving. The Leader can heal his/her trust and fear issues.

Character Structure	COMPASSIONATE	HEART-CENTERED	EXCEL	LEADER
LEADER	Co-dependency could dominate this relation- ship. The Leader might be controlling and taking charge, with the Compassionate being submissive to the Leader, very willing to be dominated and controlled. The Compassion- ate might be needy, and the Leader might feel that safe he or she won't be betrayed by the weaker, needy Compassionate.	The Leader must be careful not to shame and humiliate his or her Heart-Centered partner. The Leader also needs to be careful not to try to control/manipulate the giving nature of the Heart- Centered so the Heart-Centered feeds the Leaders' needs. And, the Heart-Centered can work his/her anger and victim issues to eliminate feelings of being trapped, stuck and victimized by the distortions of his/her Leader partner.	A match between a Leader and an Excel can go very well. Both are focused toward success, yet both can be disconnected from their hearts and sexuality. They have different parental shocks, yet they are similar in terms of seduction and betrayal. Giving up needing to control or manipulate—and learning to connect heart energy with sexual energy—are both important in this paring. Each will have to learn how to deal with the anger that is sure to eventually come to the surface, so they too don't get triggered and regress.	The pairing could be perfect or disastrous. Whether the two interact from Core or interact through control, fear of betrayal and manipulation will determine how well this pair is able to love and appreciate one another. Depending upon what other minor Character Structure energies may be influencing the defenses, this pairing could be more or less challenging. For instance, one person in the relationship may have Leader energies combined with Compassionate or Heart-centered energies, and the other person might be a Leader type combined with Excel traits. The former may feel dominated by his or her partner and will need to learn how to stand up for him/herself or collapse and/or feel victimized.

98

Character Structure Defense in Relationship	COMPASSIONATE	HEART-CENTERED	EXCEL
COMPASSIONATE	This could be a disaster if both stay in their defenses. Both might be needy, needing the other to confirm them, or both might be codependent—confirming the others value and commiserating but not empowering.	The Heart-Centered has a tendency to give, even when they want to say no. The Compassion- ate, in their neediness, could take advantage of this. This could illicit feelings of victim consciousness for the Heart-Centered. As a result, it might trigger the Heart- Centered to release his/her suppressed anger upon the Com- passionate, which in turn can make the Compassionate collapse into hopelessness, fear of abandonment and feelings of not being good enough.	The Excel could "excel" at supporting and mothering the Compassionate until...the Excel becomes resentful toward the Compassionate. The Excel's disconnect between heart and sexuality could accentuate spilling anger toward the Compassionate, triggering the Compassionate into the old pattern of neediness, collapse and lack of self-worth.

Character Structure Defense in Relationship	HEART-CENTERED	EXCEL
HEART-CENTERED	The relationship can stagnate if each gets stuck in their metaphorical box. Improvement won't hap- pen unless the other person makes it happen— but each partner won't let the other person help. They must learn how to listen to the wisdom of the anger held inside to better set boundaries and move out of victim energy. This will enable both to release the stuck/trapped feelings and find personal power.	The perfectionist in the Excel might seek solutions, while the stuck, angry energy in the Heart-Centered could withhold progress. This pair must be careful that the Excel doesn't work harder than the Heart-Centered to heal problems in the relationship. As each person balances their defenses, ideally the Excel will meet the giving/loving nature of the Heart-Centered with his or her healed heart.

Character Structure Defense in Relationship	EXCEL
EXCEL	This could be a very effective relationship, as the partners learn to be in both heart energies and sexuality and to adequately deal with anger. Much will depend upon the minor Character Structures they also hold. For instance, if one partner is an Excel type combined with Leader energy and the other is an Excel type combined with Heart-Centered energy, one partner may dominate another. The Heart-Centered/Excel might give too much and resent it, becoming the victim in the relationship. The Leader/Excel might feel betrayed when the Heart-Centered sets boundaries and attacks back, reconfirming the Heart-Centered/Excel's hidden victim energy.

ANGER, THE SECRET TO A HAPPY MARRIAGE

The common aspect of all these Character Structure combinations and interactions is anger. Each Character Structure deals with anger in different unhealthy ways. The most common reason relationships end prematurely is because of our failure to acknowledge and work through our anger with one another.

Leader attacks, controls and manipulates with anger and feels betrayed if anger comes at them.

Excel attacks and seduces with anger and tries to do everything perfect to prevent anger from coming at them.

Spiritual withdrawals from anger. Anger reinforces their feelings of terror on earth.

Heart-Centered holds anger within them until it burst out uncontrollably. Anger reinforces their feelings of being a victim.

Compassionate collapses when anger comes at them, and they feel insecure and inadequate when it does. To prevent anger from coming at them, they try to please others.

Another whole book will be devoted to this topic. In the meantime, we can look at our anger as wisdom that holds a red flag saying, "PAY ATTENTION TO ME; I have a message to deliver." (Also review the Chapter on Anger and Anxiety.)

Most of the time, the message deals with a boundary being invaded. If we are mad at ourselves, then the boundary needs to be internal. For instance, we may need to say no to addiction or an unhealthy choice. If the anger is at someone else, then usually someone is invading us or they have triggered a Core Distortion within us. Listen to the wisdom behind the messenger and don't judge the anger. This helps us heal our Separated Self energies and come out of defense.

If we are in a co-dependent relationship, it will be very hard for us to follow through with action, based on the wisdom we receive. We get fearful if we change the dynamics of the relationship on our end because often the other person reacts with rage and discomfort.

For instance, look upon our interactions with another person as a puzzle. If one person changes then the puzzle pieces will no fit with ours. This can make them feel abandoned, fearful and confused. These are positive indicators that the puzzle pieces were not aligned to everyone's highest good. As we more skillfully re-arrange the pieces to our highest good and are more aligned with our Core Being, there is a good chance that the other person, too, will find their highest good and their Core Being.

CHOICE POINT Exercises For Identifying Defenses and Developing Healthy Solutions

Part I

Engage your **Explorer's Mind**, charge and balance your field, and remember to keep kind humor and love toward all aspects of you. Judgment of ourselves **hardens not heals** our unhealthy defenses. We are trying to eliminate or at least reduce them.

Part II

Then list your healthy and unhealthy defenses. Write out the typical defenses you imagine you used with your parents and in relationships as a teenager growing up. Watch yourself over a period of a few days.

Imagine which defenses you use now and in which situations. Write this down.

Part III

Imagine which healthy defenses might replace the old programmed responses. Write them down and practice integrating them into your life. Remember, we are never done with these exercises; they become a daily practice. Thinking we are done is a defense in itself.

Part IV

What defenses coming from a client/partner would be most difficult for you to handle? Who uses these defenses with you when you were growing up? Design a plan that will help you better deal with them today.

CHAPTER REVIEW

1. Explore your relationship challenges based on character structure types.
   Specifically list strategies that will help you find and use Choice Points and move out of defense in relationship and back to Core Being.

CHAPTER 6

RELATIONSHIP COHERENCY – CORE BEING TO CORE BEING

Can a healthy relationship happen if we are not connected to our self?
Is it the chicken or the egg?

We cannot have true connection with another until we are connected to ourselves. Yet, loving connection from another helps us connect to ourselves. As we take time to connect (or reconnect) to ourselves before we connect to another, we can clear the slate of transference and counter transference. We can raise our vibration so it is coherent with the energies in the moment.

Relational incoherency is created when our Enlightened Observer loses its HVC and we project unhealthy attachment issues upon the present moment. This is when our Defenses, Separated Self and Core Distortions take the lead. We all do this at times.

Relationships come and go sometimes as a natural rhythm of life. But some leave prematurely because we lose ourselves and paste our past upon the present. If both people in the relationship are doing this, the energetic discharge can be strong and raw. (See the energetic examples of Defenses presented earlier.)

Whenever we interact with another, our Explorer's Mind can help us discover if we are relating from our Core Being, Core Distortion, Separated Self or Defense. If we discover our own incoherency, we can adjust. However, if we take too long to adjust, we might trigger another into relational incoherency resulting in a domino effect. Or was it their incoherent energy in the first place that threw us off? Either way, we surely notice how easily we react to each other.

The longer the relationship, the more domino moments have happened. So, if after many years of marriage, there have been too many incoherencies ignored, all the dominos can fall. The past becomes stacked up against us and the relationship ends. As we look back at the relationship we find that it either ended prematurely or we stayed too long. Either way, collecting these lessons and using them in our next relationship provides depth for empowerment.

It is ignoring incoherency within us and within the relationship that creates the problems—not the actual issues that cause triggers. Sociologists say that money, sex and religion are the most common reasons marriages end. I say it is the *continued failure to adequately address these issues* that are the actual cause of the relationship's untimely demise (or why we stayed too long).

This is because we lack the skills:

- to notice we are incoherent, to discover why, and
- to resolve our own incoherency within the relationship. Miracles happen when we master these three steps.

Quantum physics suggests that merely by being coherent within ourselves, it cultivates coherency around us.

Relationship problems resolve. By "resolve," that may mean we become clear that it is time to let go and move on—or, we rectify the triggers by being coherent within ourselves.

Coherency fosters connection to our Core Being. From this place, clarity about our relationships happens more quickly and cleanly. Students of Me-B Transformation™ comment often about how their husbands and families seem very different by the end of the year's training; it is as if their family members, too, had completed the classes. We are all so very powerful. Finding the courage to implement that power in conscious relationships is probably the most difficult action we take in our lives. But when we do, the results are profound.

When working with clients or others in our lives, we can use this knowledge in many ways:

Track our field and our client's field and assess incoherency. If our field is incoherent, rebalance. Reassess, to see if the client's field follows. If not, make a mental note to eventually address the incoherency. It might be negative transference, trauma or a Core Distortion that got activated. It also may mean that it is time for the therapeutic relationship to either deepen or end. Usually, the sooner the incoherency is addressed, the greater the benefit.

If a trusting relationship has been established, we can **purposely trigger the client into incoherency and invite them to engage their Explorer's Mind** to discover what was triggered and how they can readjust back to their center. If possible, have them link the trigger back to their childhood, past lives, archetypes or ancestral issues to see if deeper work is needed. An advanced client can do profound work using this technique.

Notice when a client's field becomes incoherent during a session and **invite him or her to discover what is happening energetically in the room** that could have caused it. This too can be very profound – especially if both client and therapist are skilled at tracking the subtleties of energy. For instance, what level of the field was activated and how did that influence Defenses, Core Distortions, Manifest Energy and Core Being? If we can name these reactions in the moment, as they are happening, the impact becomes more obvious.

> If the client is in aligned intention, the Rhythm of the Energy flows and deeper transformation takes place. If the client is in negative or contrary intention, everything stops and they have the opportunity to see how the strength of their contrary intention impedes them. Of course, if their contrary intention is too strong, even the most skillful therapist can't help. We don't have power over others choices. It is up to each and every one of us to take responsibility for our incoherencies and work to address them. There is no magic bullet other than willingness to engage our Explorer's Mind and take responsibility for our own creations – be they happy or sad.

What is Relational Coherency/Incoherency?

A cohesive field is one where we are self-aware, and in deep contact with what is going on within, even if it is difficult and messy. Coherence enables us to own any internal challenges that arise without ego, arrogance or denial. Incoherency is created by our Separated Self.

When we are in relational coherence, we are in aligned Intention to be in relationship, our Enlightened Observer is vibrating at a high frequency, and we are aware of our Core Being as well as the other's Core Being. Clearly, maintaining this state during a relationship challenge is one of life's most difficult tasks.

In Equine Psychotherapy, horses act as therapists. This is not because of their cognitive acumen, but rather because of their innate ability to track and respond to coherent relational-energy fields.

> For instance, Paul, a recently separated businessman, came to work with my horses for an Equine Session. Paul began the session by softly stroking Billy and speaking to him in a loving voice. Billy, a veteran therapy horse, bumped him gently with his nose, then turned his back and walked away.
>
> As Paul paused to consider what happened, I asked, "What might Billy know that we don't?" Paul was normally someone very in charge and confident that he knew exactly what should be done. He took a moment, and then asked, "Why doesn't Billy want my love and affection?"
>
> This made me curious about how his wife responded to Paul's affection and what was underneath his kind gestures. As Paul explored what was going on in his energy field that made Billy leave, tears formed in his eyes and his face darkened. "I guess I was angry that I had to give Billy affection when I thought this session was about him giving me support."
>
> Paul connected more deeply to his feelings, letting the energy of his anger, and sadness move through him. When he looked up again, not only had Billy returned to his side, but he was surrounded by four other kind and concerned equine faces.

So, as we engage our Explorer's Mind to see what emotion, Core Distortion, Separated Self or Defenses present, we reconnect to ourselves and create a cohesive field.

Connection with self, even if it is with a part of us that is messy, emotional and regressed, leads toward cohesion. Denial keeps our ego in charge. When we connect deeply to whatever it is that has kept us separate from ourselves, we win—as do those around us. This process can be monitored continuously throughout our day and during a Me-B Session.

CHARACTER STRUCTURE NAME	SPIRITUAL (SCHIZOID)	COMPASSIONATE (ORAL)	HEART-CENTERED (MASOCHIST)	EXCEL (RIGID)	LEADER (PSYCHOPATH)
Relationship Incoherency	I must reject you before you reject me.	If I ask, it's not love; if I don't ask, I won't get it.	I will hurt me before you hurt me.	Yes, but	I am correct; you are wrong. I must be controlling and manipulate.

"Right" listening involves learning to listen with our divine mind (7th Level of the Field), to feel the communication kinesthetically in our body, and to sense it with our ears, taste, smell and energy system. This type of listening is an indicator of deep connection with our self and with others. The "right" listening mode allows us to be deeply aware of ourselves and the client's Core Being. No judgments are made, just pure awareness of what is here now.

If we are in defense or out of our Core Being,
do we know how to come back as quickly as possible?

We all go into defense at times. The skillful Me-B advocate can recognize it, own what is happening, re-center and then reconnect to the other person. This is at least the ideal to work toward. On some days, and with certain individuals, we may need to do this 20 times an hour.

This is definitely true when someone is in negative transference with us in a manner that perfectly reflects our childhood wounding. For instance, if our father or mother used to abuse us, and someone enters our life who holds a similar energy pattern in his or her personality, we can easily become overwhelmed and lose ourselves.

Trauma is the cause of relational incoherency.
It makes our system disorganized and either over or under-reactive.
This makes healthy boundaries difficult and takes us out of our center.

Obviously, the deeper the emotional trigger, the more focus it takes to reconnect to the Core Being present in each of us. (The next chapter reviews the 5-Step Process for How to Reconnect to Our Core Being.) Our Separated Self can and will sabotage us. Constant vigilance and compassion for our own imperfections is needed. Remember, it is about us gradually raising our HVC and being humbled by how human we really are. *Perfection* is for the gods. Being humble disengages the ego and allows us to be more realistic in our goals and self-appreciation. We are often way too hard on ourselves.

The **Explorer's Mind** can help us have the courage to reexamine ourselves throughout the day. *We must re- examine and then shift, reexamine and shift back to center again, and again, and again.* The process never ends because there is an infinite supply of light that we can allow in. After all, connection with self and connection with another is ideally the process of unraveling the deeper truth of our divinity.

Be divine. Work our process back to center, all day, all week and all the time. Accept that some days, we will be more skillful in this process than others. *Let's just not give up—especially on the days that feel very painful and difficult, when our child consciousness recreates the pain of our past with the person we happen to be with, in the moment.* We can help each other by working together to remember why we are here. Relationships can either wound us again or lead us to our Core Being. We decide which outcome occurs—not the other person!

DOMINO EFFECT EXERCISE

With the following categories of relationship, list your typical incoherent responses. Review the answers you wrote for the Defenses and Core Distortion Exercises to help you better investigate this exercise.

Mother _____

Father _____

Siblings _____

Children _____

Partner _____

Authority Figures (teachers, bosses...) _____

Friends _____

Clients _____

People you don't like and/or prefer not to be near _____

List similarities/patterns. For instance, do you tend to want to please others to receive love then resent giving too much? Do you expect them to love you and are surprised when you are judged? Do you only feel safe when you are the boss or are controlling and manipulating? Do you wait to be helped or saved by others? Does your mistrust in others ripple and cause the mistrust to come back to burn you? Do you think life is safe, and then become surprised when others try to dominate you—or do you think life is unsafe and re- peat that in your relationship incoherencies? Do you see your partner's light so well that when he/she interacts from the darkness, you think you can help him/her change? Do you want to fix them because you love them so much?

Earlier in this chapter, we discussed energetic Character Structures and Personality Types. You might gain more insights into these exercises from a deeper understanding of the Character Structures and choose to review that material again.

Note: you can repeat this exercise every few years, because our dark shadow will always need to be revealed into the light. Some of my more challenging relationship issues I am only now beginning to understand.

CONFLICT AND SAFETY GUIDELINES FOR COUPLES

1. **Maintain awareness of what is happening.**
2. **Take a moment to slow down the interaction and reconnect to yourself.**
   De-escalate. For instance, breathe deeply for a moment, close your eyes, and feel positive sensations in your body. Step away so there is more distance between you and the other. This may mean postponing discussion until later. Remember, conflict cannot be resolved if either of

you is in defense. (Postponement should not be longer than 24 hours unless violence is possible.)

3. **Explore what childhood issue or trauma might have been triggered, and own your part.**

   For instance, "when you did that, it reminded me of my father, and I did not feel loved or safe. As a result of feeling this way, I spoke with deep anger."

4. **Remind yourself that you are in defense, and connect to your Core Being by sending love, strength and compassion to the pain.**

   Our Core Being is the part of us that can feel whole even when someone else is judging us. It is adult consciousness and is connected to our inner divine self.

5. **Remind yourself that the other is in defense, and imagine them connected to their Core Being.**

   Energetically and/or verbally send understanding to the other person's defenses and pain.

6. **Notice what you need from yourself—and give it to yourself.**

   Notice what you would like from them and tell them what, if anything, you need from them.

7. **Return to adult consciousness and out of defense.**

   When in adult consciousness, you will be able to give love to yourself when others can't give it to you. You will also be able to give love to others and receive love from others.

These skills may be new to you. Discover which ones are most difficult to master. If needed, get support in mastering them by working with a therapist, friends, and/or family.

Chapter Review

1. We cannot have true connection with another until _____.
2. What gets in the way of intimacy and connection with others?
3. Outline what transference (positive/negative) could interfere with true connection with another.
4. What tool(s) have you learned thus far that can bring you back into relational coherency?
5. It is _____ within us and within the relationship that creates problems in a relationship.
6. Why does connection with self, especially if it is messy, promote coherency (think of Paul)?
7. What is the deepest reason most marriages/partnerships end or last too long?
8. How can you use the concept of relational coherency to improve your life?
9. Explain listening with divine mind.
10. Why might we need to repeat many, if not all, of the exercises in this book (especially the Domino exercise)?

CHAPTER 7

DEFENSES IN THE SUBCONSCIOUS AND THE POWER OF THE EGO

As we look at what is hidden beneath, we reveal the answers to our unanswered questions.

We have both a **Golden Shadow** and a **Dark Shadow**. The **Golden Shadow** represents the light we are but have not yet completely realized. It reflects where we are headed in our self-growth, our **Core Being**. We may get glimpses of our **Golden Shadow**, but the challenges of this world and our humanness can make it difficult for us to know that part of ourselves — and even more difficult to anchor into that knowing.

Our **Dark Shadow** represents the parts of us that we are not aware of that hold lower vibrational frequencies. It is this unconscious material that tends to create the difficulties in life. As we work to uncover our **Dark Shadow** aspects, more flow and rhythm are possible.

As a client or Me-B Guide, we can remember to stay at this place of unknowing so the **shadow** can reveal itself. It is important to keep opening to what we don't know so we can invite a deeper perspective. This place of not knowing is where true miracles come through. It is definitely the road less traveled.

Energetically, the **shadow** is held in the sensations of the body. When doing or receiving an energetic hands-on healing and we or our client falls asleep, it is a signal we are working on a part of the subconscious. For instance, being able to handle higher (or harsh) vibrations without dissociating or falling asleep is an indicator that we are making progress on healing our shadow.

What is a way to assess our subconscious?

We can connect to a part of our energy system within our physical body. Then, using the PIN Wheel Technique (taught in the sensing energy chapter), we can collect information about the consciousness that is held somatically in the body and in the energy itself. We can practice feeling, sensing and accessing the energy and sensations in different parts of our body. This will help us learn to reveal the subconscious. Ask yourself, what message is held there—what **Core Distortion**, **Core Being** aspect or false belief?

When I began to learn this process, I spent 30 minutes to an hour every day connecting to my body and feeling emotions and opening to letting the body reveal to me what is hidden there. At the time I ran the structured levels of my Auric energy field very tightly (like an excel personality type). I was also very dissociated and disconnected from my body (like a Spiritual type). I found this process very difficult and in the beginning I couldn't feel much. I got support from my teachers and therapists to work through the parts of me that didn't want to be connected to my body, and to feel them. Over time, I became masterful at this process because I didn't give up and I focused on my successes and not my failures.

When we learn to ride a bike, it takes time and practice. We fall, get up, fall, and get up, but eventually we learn and never forget. This next exercise may be a similar experience. Just remember, practice, practice, and practice. As we focus on what we can do, we learn, grow and succeed.

EXERCISE TO UNCOVER OUR SHADOW

Sensations in the body are the window to our subconscious. Over time, our **Explorer's Mind** can teach us how to connect to areas of the body, assess the energy held there, and feel sensations in the body that send messages to our mind about our subconscious or shadow. Do not give up. Eventually we all can learn how to master this skill.

Step 1: Begin by scanning your body. Start at the top of the head and work downward, assessing the body, the chakras, **Manifest Energy** and the **Levels of the Field.** Notice where you feel flows and where there might be uncomfortable sensations or no sensations at all.

Step 2: Now, go back to an area where there are either no sensations or where there are uncomfortable sensations. Pick one area — other than the head. (When we are skilled at this practice we can explore the head to uncover the subconscious, but not until then.)

This is where you can call upon your creativity and your imagination to help. Breathe into the area, melting deeper into the skin, energy and emotions/images held there.

Using the **Explorers' Mind**, ask the question, "What wisdom is here and what can I learn from this part of my body?" Discount nothing. Allow visions, intuition, emotions, false beliefs and energy held in that area to flow toward consciousness. If nothing comes to your mind, you can try to allow your hand to write the answer or draw a picture of the answer. Remember, discount nothing.

Over time, our practice pays off and we learn how to read the wisdom in our body.

CHARACTER STRUCTURE NAME	SPIRITUAL (SCHIZOID)	COMPASSIONATE (ORAL)	HEART-CENTERED (MASOCHIST)	EXCEL (RIGID)	LEADER (PSYCHOPATH)
SHADOW ASPECT Golden / Dark	Spiritual / Terror	Self-Love / Neediness	Giving / Hate	Capable / Can't Accept Self	Leader / Manipulator

EGO/SUPEREGO

The concept of the **Ego** can be difficult to understand because it can be illusive and a trickster to find in our Me-B System. For instance, most of us can say, "I feel angry or sad." However, how often do you hear, "oh, I can feel my ego!"?

Even though it may be a difficult concept to understand, the **Ego** is an essential supporter to or detractor from our and our client's transformation. The **negative ego** and the **Superego** work extremely hard to prevent personal growth because change means death to these parts of us. In the archetypical "Hero's Journey" and its dark night of the soul, the ego undergoes a death and rebirth process. The pain and the struggle of this journey are profound because the ego doesn't want to die.

We can use the **Explorer's Mind** to help us and our clients identify which part of the **Ego** is acting upon us. The **Explorer's Mind** can teach us how to identify the ego's presence in the mind, energy and body so we make choices to either accept or reject its effects upon us.

What are the effects the negative ego or superego may have upon us? Some people equate the superego to the judging voice of a parent. For instance, a parent's voice may say "you can't succeed at that," instead of "I believe in you."

This energy of the parental judge can be felt physically, mentally and energetically. For example, your negative ego may show itself as an upset stomach every time you work toward a goal, a congested block in your **2ⁿᵈ or 3ʳᵈ Chakra**, or a voice in your head saying you will never make it. As we identify the effects of the negative ego, our **Explorer's Mind** can help us transform these obstacles in all three parts of our Me-B System.

LET GO MY EGO

Andrea acted like she wanted to do deeper work. She wanted to learn to connect to her Me-B Systems and transform her pain, but every time I guided her, she became agitated. It became clear that her negative ego was in charge, and she was lost. As we started to uncover the negative talk in her head, she was able to put names and faces to the words. Her mom, her dad, her Great Aunt, and her sister were all yelling in her ear. If all those voices were someone else's, where was there space for Andrea?

She cried as she realized the strength and control her superego had over her. And then she said, "OK. How do I let it go and regain my life?" Her strong positive intention, combined with using her Explorer's Mind, made the letting go easier. She still hears the voices. Now, she knows whose they are, and she doesn't listen!

Therapeutic Ego Strength Can Be a Trap

Psychologists, psychotherapists, and counselors discuss the level of *Ego Strength* a client has in order to assess how deeply they can go into their emotions and trauma. If a client doesn't have "enough" *Ego Strength*, it is said that their Negative Ego is too strong and their Positive Ego is not strong enough. In Me-B Transformation™, we believe this type of analysis to be a trap. Because the ego vibrates at the Programmed Personality Level, it is based on duality (one aspect is good another is bad).

Instead of prioritizing the positive ego over the negative ego, we can acknowledge that in our human forms, we will always have our ego. Sometimes our ego will speak kindly to us and sometimes it will speak to us with negative self-talk. We need to learn how to be OK, regardless of what our ego does. It is very important that we learn to detach from any negative or positive effects of the ego and live from our Core Being.

Anytime the ego defines us, it lowers our frequency, even if it is the positive ego. This is because our Core Being has the highest vibrational consciousness, higher than the dualistic energy of our positive ego. Core Being lets us anchor into our divine truth so we are better equipped to transcend the effects of ego. Positive ego vibrates at the level of our Programmed Personality, a lower frequency than Core Being. As we learn how to feel/sense the difference between the negative ego, positive ego and Core Being, we support our own empowerment.

The Explorer's Mind must learn to train our Me-B System so it knows not to react to **any** ego vibration. Because the **Negative Ego/Superego** does not want to die, it will fight to stay alive. If we learn to unhook our energy from the ego, then it has nothing to fight against.

The negative ego/superego may have lived lifetimes repeating the same patterns, and it feels threatened when we begin to see ourselves in a more expanded and whole state. It attempts to trick us into remaining the same.

The stronger we are, the more talented is our ego trickster. **Excel** and **Leader** character types can have very elusive egos, and their positive ego can be very strong. Heart-centered and compassionate character types can have very loud negative egos. The **Spiritual** character type tends to have an ego that is hyper-vigilant, looking to withdraw toward safety.

From the **Manifest Energy Intention Line**, we are more detached and less emotional. While in our Manifest Energy, we can let our **Explorer's Mind** teach us to watch the effects of the ego upon us. This is especially true when we are able to watch the ego's effects from the place within us that is deeply connected to **Core Being.** Then transcendence and healing is promoted. If the negative ego or superego acts upon us from the place of our **Core Distortion**, it feels very painful. Learning how to watch the ego from a healthy place within us **(Core Being)** allows us to re-pattern the negative and accept the positive.

DEATH-REBIRTH PROCESS OF OUR EGO

Practice connecting to the **Manifest Energy** and then watch the ego and its effects on our state of happiness. Get to know the games the ego plays in order to prevent us from changing, and write these down. Then, energetically unhook from the ego and connect back to Core Being!

1. Notice in our Me-B System the effects of the negative ego or superego, then
2. Let the Explorer's Mind teach us again and again how to allow the old identifications of ego-based self to die. We can let ourselves become metaphorically reborn by unhooking our 2nd and 4th levels of the Auric Field from the Ego vibration and reconnecting to Core Being.

Using intention, feel and imagine the frequency of Core Being filling the 2nd and 4th levels of the field and filling the 3rd Chakra. Then realign your intention in the Manifest Energy, so it knows that when ego is present, you will disconnect from the ego and realign to support Core Being.

The death-rebirth process of our Ego is an ongoing life-long process. For the spiritual warrior, it never ends. The universe will always invite a situation into our life where we find our self bumping up against the edges of our negative ego. It is the warrior who sees this as an opportunity and a gift.

Maybe life does this so we have the opportunity to see ourselves at a deeper level and see our next piece of personal work. I sometimes call this another *"blankety-blank"* growth opportunity— the expletive being that it is usually quite difficult and painful!

However, as we begin to view what is happening from the detachment of the **Manifest Energy** and **Explorer's Mind**, we can use our Enlightened Observer to help us reconnect to our **Core Being**. When this happens, our relationship to the pain can change. We can become aware of what is happening instead of feeling victim to what is happening. We learn how to transform versus collapse, dissociate or reject.

Some believe the human ego supports our individuation and supports our ability to co-create. It is a trickster because it also prevents our individuation when the negative ego takes hold. In expanded states of consciousness—such as when we connect to our **Core Being**—the negative ego dissolves, the positive ego emerges and our **Core Being** can be accessed.

In psychological trainings, much is said about supporting Ego Strength. *In Me-B Transformation™, we strive to move out of the dimension of Ego and into Core Being. We don't teach Ego Strength; instead, we teach using our Explorer's Mind so we have the positive intention to use our Enlightened Observer and connect to our Core Being!*

This process is much simpler to explain than to actualize. Yet, as we focus on what we can do, we get more of what we can do. The **Explorer's Mind** can send kindness and compassion for the parts of us that get lost along the way.

CHARACTER STRUCTURE NAME	SPIRITUAL (SCHIZOID)	COMPASSIONATE (ORAL)	HEART-CENTERED (MASOCHIST)	EXCEL (RIGID)	LEADER (PSYCHOPATH)
Ego Distortion	Fear	Inadequacy	Humiliation	Arrogance/ Imperfection	Arrogance/Fear Manipulation/ Control

EXERCISE – WHERE IS WALDO?

Remember the <u>Where Is Waldo</u> Book for children? In it, we look at a busy page of images and find Waldo somewhere hidden on the page. Our ego is very similar. Our minds and lives are packed full with so much throughout our days that it takes effort and strength to find our activated ego in the midst of the chaos.

Step 1: Using the **Explorer's Mind**, set your intention to watch your ego for one day. Simply notice it.

Step 2: The next day, watch your ego and assess how it affects your body and energy system.

Step 3: The third day, watch, assess and imagine how you can shift out of an activated ego and come back to center. To let go of the activated ego, you must let go of the negative self-images and emotions it evokes. Let the images and emotions become simply energy that runs through you, instead something that defines you. The negative ego lowers your vibration. To shift out of it, you must find ways to raise your vibration and connect to **Core Being**.

Step 4: Do the positive resourcing techniques described later. Practice feeling the pain without <u>being</u> the pain. Accept the dark and light within, without energetically merging and over-identifying with the dark or light.

Remember, it is our programming at the personality level that creates the pain we experience. It is the Core Being that can rebalance us to the deeper ribbon of truth.

We enter arrogance, denial or collapse when the Ego takes charge!

Shadow

1. Explain your Dark/Golden Shadow and how it might make it difficult for you to view reality clearly.
2. By connecting to _____ in the body/energy system, we can reveal our shadow/subconscious.

Ego

1. Explain superego, negative, and positive ego.
2. Explain why "ego strength" is not the highest vibration. What might work better for you?
3. Where is the ego held energetically?
4. What is the death-rebirth process of our ego (the Hero's Journey)?
5. What are your ego challenges and some solutions to help you so you more clearly see yourself, others and the reality before you?

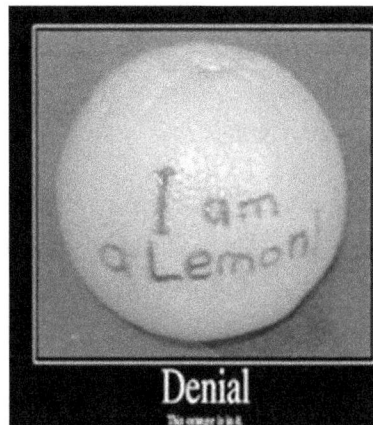

Denial

CHAPTER 8

WHAT SHAPES OUR REALITY?

Imagine you are a newborn baby. You are innocent, open, connected to the divine within you — an energetic and body sponge. Over the years, this "sponge" is imprinted upon. Many factors are involved in the imprinting that creates the personality of you.

BELIEF SYSTEMS

When we are first born, our **Core Being** is already formed, whole and complete. It is our personality that gets molded at this stage. Some people believe we incarnate into this world with karma, wisdom, and challenges from past lives. Our genetics, environment, and family lineage also play a role in shaping our mind, body, and energy systems at the personality level.

The analogy of computer programming works well. We are programmed, and we program ourselves, in all three systems: mind, energy, and body. *As we become more aware at the most subtle level – energy – we can consciously reprogram ourselves and invite the expression of our Core Being. Unfortunately, when we lose our connection to Core Being, we operate at the ego-based personality level. At this level, we can get confused, and false images and beliefs take hold.*

When we live our life from these false beliefs, inaccurate images and unhealthy life systems distort our view of reality. With a distorted view of reality, we also distort relationships and what we manifest in life. We self-limit because we hold a belief (subconsciously or consciously) that what we wish to manifest is not attainable or we don't deserve it.

Beliefs such as "I cannot be loved"; "life is unsafe"; "if I am big and beautiful I will be attacked"; "life is hard"; and "I can't be happy" are just a few common belief systems. Each personality type develops unhealthy beliefs related to their past trauma and challenges.

CHARACTER STRUCTURE NAME	SPIRITUAL	COMPASSIONATE	HEART-CENTERED	EXCEL	LEADER
Main Negative Belief	"I am not safe."	"I am not enough if you leave, so I please you or get you to mother me so you stay."	"I am a victim. I am trapped in a box. Save me, but I won't let	"I must be perfect."	"I must be in control or I will be attacked."

Throughout my life I notice how friends take advantage of me. I am the giver and am always supporting them, but they never help me. I notice how I hold this problem in my solar plexus.

As I connect to and melted into the area with my mind and breath, I remember feeling this way when I was 4 years old. My father was busy working on his car and wouldn't pay attention to me until I agreed to hand him the tools he needed. Whenever I helped him, or anyone, I finally felt important and loved.

Of course, I attract clients who hold the belief, "I will only be loved and supported if I give and don't receive." The image behind this belief is — if I stop giving, they will hurt and betray me.

June came into the office complaining that all her boyfriends expected too much from her. She would give and give and give and still they would leave her. She examined this and her life choices. Over time, she understood how this false image and belief created stress and unhappiness in her life. June placed her hand on her solar plexus and imagined that she was lovable and important *even if she didn't take care of everyone around her*.

The sensations in her stomach began to change. Warmth filled the space. I didn't see June again for six months. When she returned this time, she was radiant. Her red hair shined and her eyes sparked blue. She thanked me for helping her see she could make different choices and attract friendships that were mutually supportive.

Exercise on Belief Systems

Step 1: Charge and balance your field, and connect to **Core Being**.

Step 2: List a problem. Using the **Explorer's Mind**, examine what negative images or beliefs relate to that problem.

Step 3: Imagine where in your body that problem is held. Feel the sensation of it and notice the youngest moment in your life you remember having that feeling or the sensation of the problem.

Step 4: Now list the negative image or belief associated with that problem. (If there is more than one, then work on each one at a time. Muscle test or a use a pendulum to help you chose which one to start with.)

Step 5: Imagine the positive image or belief system that could replace the unhelpful one. Using your breath and positive intention, feel/visualize it as energy in the body and sensations in the body. Feel/visualize the sensation/energy of the old belief system leaving and the new positive belief system taking its place. Take your time. Make it as tangible as possible. Does it have a color, taste, smell, sensation, and/or symbol? The more tangible your experience, the more deeply you will be able to transform LVC into HVC.

RHYTHM OF FLOW SHAPES REALITY

Every life experience, every moment has a Rhythm and Flow of energy. This rhythm is best described as a force of energy that expands outward and inward. It speeds up and slows down, it increases and decreases. The rhythm dictates the flow of energy in our bodies and in our lives. *It can distort or clarify reality depending upon how we hold onto it or let it go. The objective of regulating our rhythm is to cultivate HVC and the pleasure it creates.*

When Defenses, Separated Self, Negative Intentions and Core Distortions go unattended, our intelligent rhythm will slow so we can attend to the underlying issues. As we are able to use our Enlightened Observer and meet the internal challenges with HVC, the flow of rhythm continues and we foster synchronicity. Our life operates in unison to effortlessly achieve a confluence of diverse yet supportive positive intentions. Me-B Transformation™ teaches us how to consciously influence our life's rhythm to realize our highest good. These lessons can be used to support our community, country and world.

A balance is needed in the rhythm. If it is always expanding outward, there is no time to go inward. If it is always running fast, we may get sick or have an accident to slow the rhythm down. Just as a wave expands and contracts, so must our rhythm. The latest financial recession is a slowing down of our economy's rhythm because it has been running out of balance. As each one of us addresses our out-of-balance finances, we can regulate our country's financial rhythm back to balance. This is the power of tracking our own rhythm and supporting its flow; it helps us and the greater good.

Diagnostically, if the rhythm slows, it is a signal to slow down, to self-assess, and to literally and metaphorically clean our closets. As our rhythm slows and invites us inward, we can cultivate energy by transforming LVC— such as guilt, sadness, anger, judgment, and insecurity—into HVC. By doing this, we support the next Rhythm and Flow to expand outward and speed up. In the context of the Rhythm of Energy, an apparent tragedy such as a job loss can be seen as a natural ebb in the flow **and** an opportunity. That is, if our negative ego doesn't get in the way of us learning from the slower, inward flow.

Mental and physical Illness results when the Rhythm of Reality is interrupted.
Restoration of the rhythm supports health and joy.

Depression is a symptom of us failing to support our internal rhythm. The energy literally gets depressed, and the wave is stymied from its natural progression. Anxiety occurs when the energy is revving its engines and wanting to move forward, but it can't because we haven't supported its flow (this is usually related to a threatened ego). An extreme case of us not supporting the rhythm is mania. This is when the rhythm accelerates and expands too quickly; we lose our grounding and our center just as if we have been shot out of a cannon. It can feel exhilarating but can't be sustained; the wave of energy will eventually recoil in the other direction, as painful now as it once was stimulating.

As we become more skillful at regulating our rhythm by anchoring into our Core Being, the too intense highs in our life and the too intense lows begin to even out, and a higher bar of consciousness is set. We still have the expansions and contractions, but we are more skillful in supporting ourselves during each aspect of the rhythm.

The Rhythm of Flow of energy during a Me-B Transformation™ session can also become artificially slowed or stopped. Me-B Guides can stymie the flow of energy or support it, depending upon how we interact with a client and how we run our own energy.

Why Do the Successes in My Marriage Never Maintain?

George and Alice have been married close to 30 years. Alice explains that as soon as she attends to the marriage and it is working well, eventually the marriage tanks and all the advances they have made fall away.

She sighs, "I am exhausted. I am always the one to initiate the next level of work in the marriage, and I don't want to do it anymore! Why does it fall apart? Why do we fail to maintain the great successes we gained?"

The answer: The Rhythm of the Flow Is not being supported by both participants.

If we don't support the rhythm in our life, our family, our relationships, and our jobs during a slight downward slump, eventually the slight slump becomes a massive crash. Constant care to our rhythm takes less energy than letting it break down and stall.

Even if just one person in a relationship works to maintain the flow, they will at least bring more clarity. Our internal distortions make the rhythm shift into extremes. As we heal our internal distortions, the ups and downs of the rhythm gently flow, instead of jumping too high and getting manic—and then dropping too low and being depressed.

If we speed up the rhythm and jump ahead of a client or go too slowly or inadvertently (or purposely) trigger a person into transference, the flow will change. This is not necessarily "bad" or "good." Our Explorer's Mind can help us access and use the HVC of our Enlightened Observer, our Manifest Energy, and our Auric Field to adjust the rhythm as needed.

All of these techniques support a client, friend or family member as long as we are able to track what is happening and are aware. Awareness supports choice, and choice supports healing.

Sometimes it is the other person that either consciously or unconsciously stymies the flow of energy. This usually is an indicator that the negative ego has been activated. We can then support the person, so the flow can be reinstated. The Explorer's Mind can support examining why the flow was interrupted and rein- state the flow by connecting to the next deeper level of reality ready to be revealed.

Too often when we are in an expansion, we also want to cling to that expansion in the hope that it will never go away. During an expansion we can forget that the slower, dense wave of the rhythm cycle ever took place. It is the classic issue of duality – life is either good or bad. In Me-B Transformation™, we look at the "bad" with the Explorer's Mind to reconnect to our Core Being.

Helping ourselves or a client learn to hold the light in the dark or the dark in the light supports balance and unity. Unity supports our connection to our Core Being and reinstates any disruption in the rhythm.

RHYTHM PACE

Our Rhythm Pace can be looked at throughout a day, a week, a year or five years. We can examine it in terms of our family unit's rhythm, or our business, community or nation's rhythm. Energy from the planets plays a role in influencing our rhythms as well. You can have your astrological chart done to assist you in taking advantage of each expansion and contraction of your Rhythm's energy.

STEP 1: Notice your day/week. When is your energy strong and when do you have less?

STEP 2: Write out an action plan to rearrange your day/week/month to support slowing down when your rhythm slows and taking advantage of doing more when your energy is strong. If you don't have enough energy (or have too much) for the tasks at hand, deeper investigation for self-empowerment might be needed. Have a medical physical to determine a possible cause. You may need to get additional support from a naturopath, acupuncturist, herbalist, Me-B Guide, and/or doctor.

STEP 3: Feel free to examine your job, business and family's rhythms too. What can be done to better support the natural ebbs and flows?

Surrender to the Rhythm to Cultivate HVC

There is a saying, "surrender to the god within you." Other sayings are: "just relax" or "let go, don't hold on to it." Sayings are much easier to name than to do. We so often hold on to the past pain and Core Distortions so tightly that it is hard to know how to let go. This is partially because letting go can mean letting go of old belief systems, old ego identifications and defenses. So just let go of all of these and move on. No problem—all you have to do is relax!

If only it were so easy. Surrendering to the deeper truth of the moment is a very vital skill, and it takes deeper work to support the rhythm's flow. Space, time, compassion and positive intention are instrumental to the process of surrender. In fact, without these four elements, letting go rarely happens.

SURRENDER AND RETURN TO OUR BEGINNER'S MIND

I was in Nepal when I met someone who did this weird new thing called Reiki energy healing. As a new student, I was very much in my beginner's mind. I was extremely skeptical and had no idea what to expect. As he laid his hands on me, and the first time the energy came in through the top of my head, it flowed effortlessly downward, filling my central channel down to my pelvis.

I had never felt anything like it before, and I never have since. No defenses prevented my energy system from completely aligning. And then, I felt it: the pain of 32 years of life filled me, overwhelming me. I could barely move or speak. What was happening to me?

The surge of undefended energy expansion that first aligned me also brought to the surface deep wounding for my conscious mind to finally meet. Emotionally, it was the most intense pain I had ever encountered.

Over the next year, I tried to find a healer who could repeat the experience for me, but my beginner's mind was gone and my defenses were alerted. It was hard to feel anything now, either the good or the bad. A subconscious armor surrounded me.

When we let go and surrender, usually LVC (such as fear of the unknown) will try to block us. Often it is the ego fearing that if we let go of our pain (or if we surrender to accepting more of our light), part of the ego will die. And if it dies, it enters the place of – who am I now? This can be very frightening until we are able to adopt a new self-identification and integrate our expansion into HVC.

As we learn to anchor into our Core Being, the death and re-birth of the ego can feel less traumatizing because we at least have a sense of our connection to the god within. This is true even if at the personality level, a part of us may still feel lost.

> The ego and its programmed personality ask: "What will it be like to surrender and let the Rhythm of Energy flow? If I let go, what will replace it? Will the next wave of life be better or worse? I know the devil I have, and I have developed coping skills around it – so who will I be without it?"

If we could all surrender completely to the rhythm, we would all be enlightened. Surrender does not mean giving up or being less responsible! On the contrary, it means being willing to use our Enlightened Observer and melt into and move through our past distortions, false images and beliefs systems, defenses, separated self, and negative ego to clean the slate and increase our vibration.

Energetically, the process of letting go is really about receiving and trust. We submit to allowing something bigger and more aligned to assist and move through us, because we created the space to allow the help to enter.

When working with ourselves or a client, practice melting into and receiving the energy and support from:

- the universe,
- spirit guides, and
- Core Being.

Then, inviting our beginner's mind, let the energy of the surrender move through and guide us throughout life, and during a Me-B Transformation™ session.

RHYTHM OF FLOW SUPPORTS REALITY

Why do we get stuck in our life? Why on one day we are happy and think life is perfect, and another day we feel hopeless? As we learn to support the rhythm of energy, we also learn to *choose our life's passage*. Spend a few days using the Enlightened Observer and doubt the reality before you.

Watch how there are times during the day when life flows easily and times when you feel overwhelmed by the reality you observe before you. Each time, doubt the reality and hold the question, "What is the deeper truth?" Notice what happens when you don't attach to the reality before you.

When we don't attach to anything at the programmed personality level, we support the rhythm to create a more aligned reality. Contractions become expansions; expansions, contractions – neither better than the other – both opportunities to evolve. Use aligned intention and advanced mindfulness to discover the wisdom of the expansion or contraction of the rhythm and flow, and then, following that wisdom, invite the presence of Core Being.

TRANSFERENCE/COUNTER TRANSFERENCE

Transference is the state of being where we project upon the outside world something from our past and it distorts reality. According to psychodynamic theory, "important people in our lives, such as our partners, are represented unconsciously in our memories and exert an influence on our thoughts and behaviors. "

Transference often occurs when we interact with someone who *reminds* us of someone from our past. For instance, a male teacher may remind us of a father or grandfather. Or, a work associate might remind us of an important friend from our childhood. Often, we are not aware of the connection that we are making psychologically between the individual in the present and the person from our past. The connection happens subconsciously, beneath our conscious awareness. Yet we behave with the current person as if they were the person from our past. We assume they will treat us similarly to the way that the previous person did in the past. And, because of our expectations, this may be exactly what occurs.

Another way of explaining Transference is to place our hands in front of our face, with our fingers close together. Now look outward. We certainly wouldn't want to drive a car this way, yet we drive through relationships in this manner. As we open our fingers, we can see through the blinds. As we move out of transference, we see clearly again. Some researchers believe we are in transference 98 percent of the time! Issues arise when we don't know that the energy of transference is interacting upon us.

Transference often occurs within therapy relationships, when a client projects certain expectations of behavior onto the therapist. However, it is also possible for the therapist to have transference with a client. This dynamic, known as "counter transference," creates a situation in which the therapist is not seeing the client clearly. The therapist projects upon the client his or her past experiences and isn't in clean and clear relationship with the client.

When we break through transference or counter transference and re-orient ourselves to our inner world, we can look at the Core Distortions that cloud our perspectives. These are often related to mother/father and/or authority issues. Gaining internal clarity then allows us to release the energy in our mind, energy and body systems, and once again, we allow god to work through us.

Transference distorts reality; yet emerging from it can create a
profound healing and a deeper appreciation for those around us.

Often, projecting upon the other is the only way we can allow difficult subconscious material to emerge. Unfortunately, if we stay in the state of transference, we lose the opportunity to grow and understand ourselves. Instead of understanding who the person we are dealing with really is, and accepting them for their humanness and uniqueness, we continue to project onto them a false image based upon expectations from our past. If unresolved, transference can inhibit the progress of what might be a truly loving and supportive relationship.

I TRANSFER MY PAIN TO YOU

Lilly attended a training to learn more about her profession. She felt she was the expert and wondered if anyone could teach her anything. In the first class, another student made a supportive comment to Lilly. Instead of responding to the support, she lashed out and said, "Don't call me that!" Obviously, she was in such deep transference she couldn't hear the support. In subsequent trainings, she saw enemies everywhere.

Growing up, Lilly felt constantly attacked by her mother. Because of her unconscious transference, she re- peats that experience with every group she attends. She expects to be attacked, and so she looks for it within interactions. Because she expects it, she manages to see it—even if it's not there.

To move out of our transferences, we must take responsibility for them so we can grow and learn. When we don't, the pain of our past keeps repeating. If we blame others for our pain as Lilly did, we lose our power. But if we feel our own pain, find the trigger from the past, and come back into alignment, we empower ourselves.

Up until now we have been talking about negative transference, when we project negative expectations upon another because of our past difficult experiences. Transference can be positive as well as negative. "Positive transference" occurs when we idolize a favorite teacher or lover and think they are perfect. We don't really see them for who they are – human, with positive and negative qualities. Instead, we focus only on their positive qualities, and create a false image of them in our minds. Positive transference is involved, for instance, when we "put someone on a pedestal."

Although positive transference feels good while it's happening—certainly better than negative transference!—it, too, has its drawbacks. Eventually, the person who is idolized will come "down off the pedestal," and the fall can be hard. Often when the person starts to reveal their imperfections, we go into negative transference and see only their faults. It is hard not to live in a black and white world when we think people are either "all good" or "all bad."

All of us are human and imperfect and make mistakes. Imperfection does not make us "bad," it makes us human. As humans, we often act from the Programmed Personality level instead of from our Core Being.

Learning to honor and respect differences and to move out of transference is what peace is all about.

USING TRANSFERENCE CONSTRUCTIVELY

Working with negative or positive transference in the therapeutic setting can be very helpful. For instance, positive "mother transference" can secure the therapeutic relationship and create a safe space for deeper work. However, this dynamic can be abused if we don't eventually help the client through the transference. The client can become too reliant upon us, the good mom. We might even go into counter transference and want to "please" our client. Whenever we are afraid to have our client displeased with us, we might be in counter transference. Develop the ability to use transference therapeutically and be able to move out of counter transference.

Any exaggerated emotion— such as rage, love, or lust, especially if it is out of proportion to the situation— could be Transference (or Counter Transference). Use it as a flag to look within and rebalance. This can be noticed in all three systems as a thought, as a sensation and as an energetic defense.

Energetically, transference presents on the second level of the field as heightened emotions and clouds. It also presents on the third level as too thick and over-charged yellow lines of light, and on the forth level of the field as mucus. It is supported by our negative belief systems such as, "I will be attacked," as represented in the case of Lilly above.

We all tend to like some energy fields better than others. For instance, models and athletes have very structured energy fields. The typical "grandmother" field can feel soft and fluffy. Even though we may not yet be knowledgeable of the particulars of someone's energy field, we all are reactive to fields we like and don't like.

CHARACTER STRUCTURE NAME	SPIRITUAL (SCHIZOID)	COMPASSIONATE (ORAL)	HEART-CENTERED (MASOCHIST)	EXCEL (RIGID)	LEADER (PSYCHOPATH)
Negative Transference We Subconsciously Attract to Our-selves	People will move away or get angry because we are so disconnected and in our heads.	Others may mother us or leave us because we are so needy.	Others may take advantage of our giving nature or shame us.	Others may depend upon us to do everything correctly.	Others may expect us to lead or they may betray or attack us.

EXERCISE TO ELIMINATE TRANSFERENCE AND COUNTER-TRANSFERENCE

Step 1:

List the people in your life that you either like very much or dislike very much. List at least four people. Now write the qualities that you most appreciate or least appreciate about them.

People I Like Most   Best Qualities/Characteristics

People I Like Least   Worse Qualities/Characteristics

Step 2:

Using your **Explorer's Mind**, investigate any common qualities of those you don't like. What do you imagine you dislike about their Auric fields and how they run their energy? What negative belief system might support those qualities? Write down the name of the person(s) they most resemble (such as family members/past authority figures).

Repeat this with the people you like the most as well. What about their Auric fields feels good? What positive belief systems might support those qualities, and what are the names of those who they most resemble?

Step 3:

Now, with each set of people, do the opposite. For the people you like least, discover positive qualities they have. With the people you like most, see the qualities that aren't so positive.

Step 4:

Now, sit in meditation. Charge and balance your field using any of the techniques already taught: balance it front/back; left/right; top/bottom. Do the Core Being exercise taught earlier. Be in your core and explore seeing them from their core. See both their light and any darkness of their programmed personality.

Step 5:

Practice interacting with them from your Core and not from any idealized image or negative defense. How might your Enlightened Observer help you meet them with love and an understanding of who they are in their entirety, instead of seeing them through the eyes of transference?

Hopefully, we all are humbled by the level of difficulty this exercise reveals. Negative transference keeps our vibration low and dishonors others. Self-compassion and positive intention can offer comfort to us when it is difficult to let go of negative or positive transference and love the other anyway.

REVIEW QUESTIONS

1. How might your ego cloud your view of reality? List some specific life examples.
2. Explain the analogy of computer programming in relationship to our negative beliefs.
3. What are the negative beliefs that cause you the most pain and how do they negatively shape your reality?
4. What is the purpose of being aware of the Rhythm of Flow of Energy? How can it help us manifest our dreams and create deeper intimacy?
5. What disrupts the Rhythm of Energy and clouds reality?
6. What supports our rhythm to flow again?
7. What does death of the ego have to do with supporting, slowing or disrupting the Rhythm of Energy?
8. The Rhythm _____ when we are depressed, anxious or manic.
9. In life, is your Rhythm of Energy too fast, too slow or balanced? If it is out of balance, write up a "5 year Me-B Action Plan" to balance it in the areas of Family, Career, and Relationship. Explore what core emotional issues interrupt its balance and list aspects of your Core Being that can bring it back into balance.
10. Letting go and surrender are methods to achieve _____. Why is beginner's mind so important?
11. What does surrender bring to the surface?
12. Why is it so hard to surrender? What four elements are needed to surrender?
13. If we completely_____, we would be enlightened.
14. What are some common misunderstandings of surrender? How can you correct them?
15. What are your personal challenges in this area? Solutions?
16. What is Transference? Explain and provide an example from your own life.
17. Throughout the day, how often are we in Transference?
18. What is the difference between positive transference and negative transference? What are the problems associated with both?
19. What is Counter-transference?
20. Any exaggerated emotion out of proportion to the situation we are in signifies what?
21. Why should we be humbled by the level of difficulty involved in moving out of negative transference? What is most difficult for you?

CHAPTER 9

ENERGETICS OF BOUNDARIES

"Good fences build good neighbors," is a wise saying that illustrates the value of adopting healthy relationship boundaries.

Where do we begin and end? What does that look like energetically, in our thought process and in our bodies? Many of our Core Distortions and trauma came from invasion of boundaries, over/understatement of boundaries, and/or confusion around boundaries. Boundaries differ depending upon cultural norms, political views, religious beliefs and spiritual states of being.

When Might Loose Boundaries Be Fitting/Un-Fitting?

During meditation, when alone, when making love with someone we trust, or when we are in nature, we can practice expanding our energy field and consciousness to a higher frequency and feel one with everything. Boundaries are rarely needed in these circumstances.

However, when we go to the supermarket, are in class, or are being social with other people, we may want tighter boundaries. The term "healthy boundaries" may differ in meaning depending upon our situation, our safety with the people we are with, and our level of consciousness. For instance, if we or our clients are developmentally regressed, we have different boundary needs than when we are in our Adult Consciousness.

In addition, different Character Structures and personality types have varied boundary tendencies. The Heart- Centered (masochist) Character Structure's boundaries can be too loose and they can invade others and easily be invaded. Subconsciously they do this to repeat their "victim" status in the hope of healing it. It is very important that they learn to have tighter boundaries; this is a life-long challenge for them. Tighter does not mean too tight. In reaction to being invaded, sometimes they use the defenses of armor and/or boundary containment to protect themselves after an invasion. The Manifest Energy of a Heart-Centered person can be separated in their third chakra and more strongly connected through the lower body than the upper body.

Spiritual (schizoid) types have diffuse energetic boundaries and/or an energetic hole in their outer energy egg so they can escape quickly if they feel threatened. Their Manifest Energy Intention Line is often disconnected from the earth. More rigid boundaries are held by the Excel (rigid) and Leader (psychopath) types. The Structured levels 1, 3, 5, and 7 of the Auric Field are weaved extremely tight. Just as a basket is woven so water can't run through, emotions are compressed and are more difficult to feel. Tight boundaries help them to exert self-control and to control others.

The Manifest Energy of the Excel is often broken around the diaphragm, and the Manifest Energy of the Leader can bend off to the right side, especially as it connects upward toward heaven.

The Compassionate (oral) Character structure tends to have a very small outer energy egg that is undercharged. Because they aren't adept at fueling themselves, they can suck energy from others and will invade someone's boundaries to achieve this goal. Being subtle so as not to get caught is a trait they hold. Compassionates *have upon who we are with, how much stress we are under, and the level at which we are connected to our Core Being.*

If you haven't already, take the Character Structure Self-Assessment Test at the end of this chapter to get an idea of your prominent Character Structures. Also, do the exercise in the energy chapter where you learn to assess the levels of the field. If we feel we are with someone and are displaying too rigid or too loose boundaries, explore what it would be like to adjust them into balance. Go slow and begin in situations where we feel safest and with people who love us.

Often, if we have too loose boundaries and then we start setting stronger boundaries, people become mad and reactive. They may even end the relationship because we are no longer giving them what they expect and want from us. Staying strong in our resolve and being willing to change the unspoken co-dependencies of the past is necessary for boundary redefinition. Every one of us has a need to redefine and improve our boundaries. Below is an exercise to guide us in this process.

BOUNDARY ISSUES TO EXPLORE IN LIFE

- What are healthy Boundaries and in which situations?
- What are unhealthy Defensive Boundaries?
- How can we energetically tell if we are invading someone's boundary?
- How can we energetically tell if someone is invading our boundary?
- How do we learn to adjust our boundaries in all three parts of our Me-B System?

There is a direct link between our ability to connect to our Core Being and our ability to discern healthy, balanced boundaries. This is related to the ability to know where we end and where another begins (differentiation/individuation). On one level, differentiation may appear simple. On another level, when someone is sending us judging energy, projections and demands, we can get confused and not know what is us being in distortion and what is being projected upon us.

Also, if someone is leaving us—for instance, when we are breaking up or when we feel abandoned by another—boundaries can be confusing too. It is so easy to "lose ourselves" to the point that we often don't even know when we are invading and when we have been invaded. We can lose our grounding, get defensive and react emotionally in a manner that doesn't reflect our Core Being. Anger, sadness and emotional reactivity are the messengers that our boundaries may be out of alignment. Usually when we are angry, it might mean our boundaries have been invaded and we need to say "no" and firm them up.

TIGHT BOUNDARIES BUILD GOOD NEIGHBORS

When I first brought my horse to Sudden Stables, there were only 30 other horses. Within two years, more than 100 horses and their owners occupied the same space. Every morning when I arrived, I inevitably ran into Penny and her 19 year old daughter, Rose. They were stereotypical Excel types with very rigid boundaries, and I, at the time, ran my energy in a very Heart-Centered manner. In the beginning, we developed a strong and supportive relationship. Over time, however, as more boarders arrived, the space available for Penny and Rose to work their horses seemed to shrink, and so did their tolerance. My more open, flexible and different ways soon wore them thin, whereas their controlling ways wore the owner and other boarders thin.

Before we knew it, throughout the stables, a boundary war had begun. Rules that hadn't been there before were now being posted prominently on every door. And I was a partial cause of it. Negative energy was flying about to the point that I had to laugh. If we couldn't even negotiate these basic challenges at a stable, how the heck were countries going to negotiate world peace?

Yet, I had to take responsibility for my part. I was a good Heart-Centered type and made some supreme boundary mistakes. So I started the deeper journey of looking within and owning the related Core Distortions, transferences, and Separated Self aspects of my programmed personality. I vowed to live from Core Being and with good tight boundaries.

I am not yet perfect with it, but am closer to the ideal. I just heard that Penny and Rose left to find a more solitary environment. I so wish them well and am grateful for the boundary lessons they, and others like them have taught me. Although just yesterday my young lab stole a carrot out of a boarder's box, I am getting closer to the goal!

Differentiation and individualization reflect the ability to define ourselves and not let others' opinions, cultures and ideals be accepted by us, unless they are complementary with our own. When our boundaries are enmeshed, this can be more difficult to assess.

A young child naturally becomes enmeshed with her mother and father. Ideally, the parents help her discover who she is, and over time they help her individuate and differentiate from them. This will help her discover where they end and she begins. They can do this in part by honoring how she is different from them.

If they don't allow her to be different, or don't honor her differences, then she may need to separate physically and emotionally in order to find herself.

Some families never resolve these issues. Parents don't always want to honor their child's uniqueness and children don't always want to energetically break away and grow up. Plus, there are different cultural norms to consider—such those in Asian, Indian and Latino cultures compared with some European and American cultural norms. It can be a complex web to discover what is right for us versus what we have been raised to believe.

Ideally, healthy adult boundaries are present when our outer energy egg snuggles next to another.

There is no separation or overlap. Yet, separate boundaries are often needed if a Core Distortion is triggered. We can use positive intention to separate and re-center so that we may eventually reconnect to the other per- son. If someone is violent toward us, or if we are violent toward them (or if there is a risk of violence), separation is healthy.

An unhealthy example of separate boundaries occurs when our ego has been hurt and we want to run away and hide. We succumb to our Separated Self, project, blame, become angry, and then want to leave instead of resolving the situation. Below are pictures of energetic boundaries that are:

healthy,
enmeshed and
separate.

Discover when each set is best for you and under which circumstances.

Healthy Boundaries

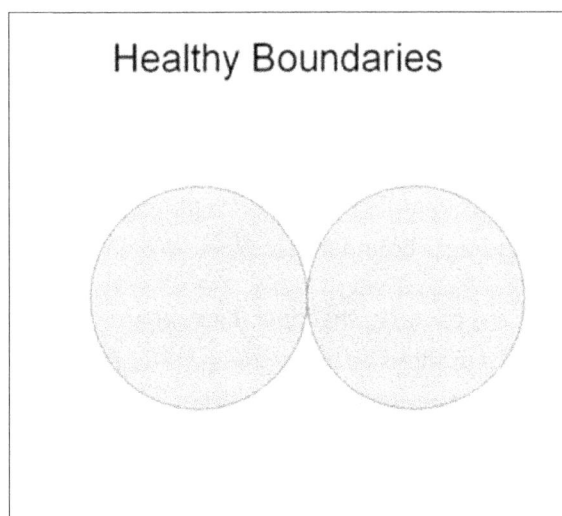

Enmeshed Boundaries

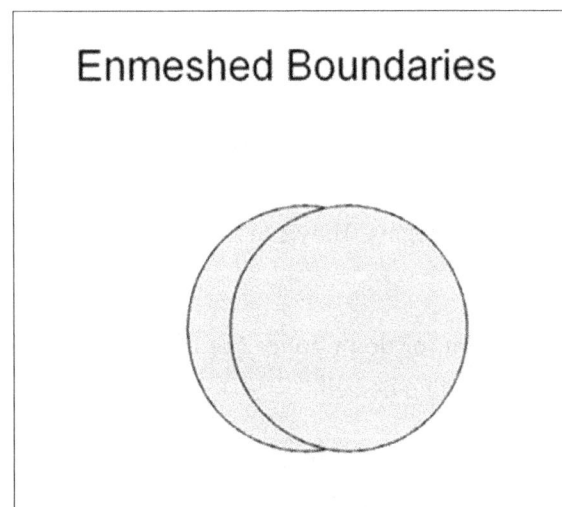

Separated Boundaries

Any time we need to take space and re-center, separation can help us reconnect to ourselves so we can eventually connect to another. For instance, enmeshed boundaries with our parents are healthy when we are young, and then when we individualize we might need to separate for a while before we can return to healthy boundaries. In another example, often during the initial stages of a love relationship, we become enmeshed with our partner and lost in positive transference. Over time, we may need to separate until we reorganize our interpersonal dynamic with healthy boundaries.

Sometimes, as in the case of Penny and her daughter Rose, we might leave something (or someone) to find a better situation that matches our personality more closely. In the following exercise, we examine our healthy boundary choices and determine which boundaries might need readjustment.

BOUNDARY CHOICE POINTS

As we watch ourselves throughout the day, we can notice our boundary expressions and work to influence them in a manner that promotes unity and wholeness.

List Boundary Successes: Who, Why and Positive Belief that Helped You

List Boundary Failures: Who, Why and Negative Belief

In the body, Manifest Energy and Auric Field, How/Where Do You Imagine the Failures Present and What Core Distortion Fuels Them? (For instance, the spiritual will have a hole in the outer Auric levels so they can escape easily if afraid, and their Manifest Energy might be disconnected from the earth but strong toward heaven. Depending upon who we are with, the boundary failures may present differently.)

Now, imagine, feel, and sense the negative aspects of boundary Choice Points leaving your Me-B System. Then allow your positive alignments to fill the space where the negative ones left. Practice this often. Depending upon who we are with and how safe we feel with them, we may have different boundary Choice Points to reorganize. All of us can review our boundaries and find aspects that can be improved.

REVIEW QUESTIONS

1. Explain typical boundary configurations in the Aura and Manifest Energies of the five Character Types: Spiritual, Excel, Heart-Centered, Compassionate, and Leader. Also explain their boundary challenges.

2. How can you tell if your boundaries have been invaded or if you have invaded someone's boundaries?

3. Do you know where you end and someone else begins? Explain why this can be confusing and what can be done to reduce confusion.

4. Discuss when separate, healthy, and enmeshed boundaries may all be appropriate and when they become an unhealthy defense. Use your life examples when possible.

5. List some negative beliefs that could support unhealthy boundaries.

6. Is a more structured Auric Field (levels 1, 3, 5, 7) supportive of tight boundaries? Why?

7. What boundaries are appropriate between an American mother and her young child? How might the boundaries change when the child becomes a teenager and then an adult?

CHAPTER 10

3 RINGS OF HEALING: SHAPE SHIFTING OUR EMOTIONAL REALITIES

It takes High Vibrational Consciousness to love ourselves when we are imperfect, messy, awkward and wrong. But this is when we need it the most! Anything else perpetuates pain and ego-based low vibrational consciousness. Enlightenment is overrated.

Using the Explorer's Mind, Me-B Transformation™ teaches important skills for tracking and shifting back to Core Being. At this point in the book, we are familiar with the concept of our Enlightened Observer, our Programmed Personality, the components of change, and Core Being. Next we will outline a detailed set of principles, a map of consciousness and cornerstones of Me-B Transformation™ so we know how to raise our level of consciousness successfully and invite effortless joy and balance into our lives.

IT ONLY TAKES 5-STEPS FOR TRANSFORMATION

Follow these 5 Steps to move through the **3 Rings of Healing**, and shape-shift your emotions back to Core Being. This process moves you upward through the **Me-B Stages of Transformation**. It takes (1) aligned intention to be (2) mindful of the wisdom needed (3) to be present with Core Being.

Self-Awareness (through deep connection within). Step one is **using the Explorer's Mind to master** the ability to notice when we are in our Core Being and when we are living from the programmed personality level. If we have awareness, then we are more able to have choice. Awareness is the first step. Using aligned intention, we can understand the components of change and better bring awareness to our present moment. **What are our unhealthy defenses/ programmed personality traits and where are they held in our body and energy systems?** (Outer-Most Ring.)

Detachment (versus dissociation) comes from Manifest Energy. It helps us know we are more than the energy and challenging emotions that run through us, and it helps us connect to our **Enlightened Observer**. With detachment we can begin to assess what is happening without collapsing or defending against it. (Outer-Most Ring and Middle Ring.)

Naming, owning and locating the Core Distortion/Defense/Trigger in the mind, energy and body systems.

The process of placing a label on our particular trauma, pain, and defense helps us own it. Owning it is essential and is very different from being over-identified with the trigger. We are not our unhealthy defenses or distortions; they are just energy moving through us. We use them as ineffective methods to protect ourselves. If we name them, versus identifying with them, we are self-compassionate and centered. If we identify with a defense or trigger, it activates our ego and we can collapse back to the programmed personality. (Outer-Most Ring and Middle Ring.)

Insight - Linking the trigger to the past so the mind can understand why we have been triggered. Divine mind is the 7th Level of the field and can help us. For most people, insight into what is happening is necessary before change and transformation can occur. What childhood developmental issue (past trauma, physiology, archetype, etc.) was triggered? *It is often important to actually feel the emotion* *behind the trigger with our **Enlightened Observer** in order for us to cultivate enough energetic boost to move into the center- most ring.* Our defenses prevent ("protect") us from feeling the pain in the middle ring. But if we do not meet the pain with our Enlightened Observer's HVC, then it remains—forever sabotaging and controlling us. Let the pain be energy moving through us, rather than a blockage to avoid feeling. (Middle Ring.)

Transformation in all three mind, energy and body systems. Shift the energy and return to Core Being by bringing the energy of our Enlightened Observer (HVC) into the dense LVC of the Programmed Personality. **Allow/Invite the HVC to fill the cells of our body: front/back; top/bottom; left/right. Also let it fill the** 2nd Chakra (and 2nd level of the Auric Energy Field-relationship to self) and 4th Chakra (and 4th level of the Auric Field-relationship to others). Allow it to fill the 3rd Chakra as well. Also invite HVC to fill the center of the Intention Line and realign it. Reconnection to Core Being in every cell completes this process. (Center Ring.)

Sometimes we can't reconnect completely to Core Being because our ego or negative intention is too strong. Sometimes our mind loops with negative thoughts. If this happens, we must be patient and compassionate with ourselves. We can engage our Explorer's Mind and be curious about why. We can also use a Containment Procedure as support until we can reconnect to Core Being. (See positive resources chapter for a summary of the Containment Procedure.) (Center Ring.)

We can use these **5 Steps** as a SELF-ASSESSMENT SCALE (not a self-judgment scale) so we have a system to track ourselves throughout the day and during Me-B Transformation™ sessions. We can teach our clients, friends, and associates to do the same. *Before Me-B Transformation™ work, our center ring (Core Being) is small in our consciousness, but after process work it grows, as our ability to anchor into it grows.*

We use aligned intention, advanced mindfulness to access the wisdom of how to use the 5-Step mindfulness practice and move through the 3-Rings and become present with Core Being.

As we Practice Moving Through the 3 Rings, Our Skills Advance

Level I: Uses the mental levels only to imagine and visualize moving through the 3 Rings. We guess at what is probably the trigger and emotion and are still trying to develop our Enlightened Observer. Core Being is not yet felt as an energy and sensation in our body; we are still using imagery and positive intention to imagine Core Being. (Me-B Stages 1-3.)

Level II: Uses imagination and visualization but is beginning to imagine and maybe even feel the sensation and emotion of the trigger, negative belief and **Core Distortion**. At this level, we are beginning to imagine and sometimes feel the energy of **Core Being** and **Enlightened Observer** and can often guess where in the body/energy system the trigger is located. At this level, only sometimes do we over-identify with the negative energy, belief and/or **Core Distortion**. (Me-B Stages 3-4.)

Level III: Can *easily* feel the sensation of the energy, know exactly how it affects the Auric and Manifest Energy, and know where it is held in the body. Can identify the negative belief, can feel the actual emotion and can bring in Core Being at least 80 percent of the time. At this advanced level, we never lose connection with the Enlightened Observer and never over-identify with the negative energy/feelings. However, even at this Advanced Level, we can't always act and react from this deeper wisdom. (Me-B Stages 5-7.)

3 Rings of Healing
Before Process Work

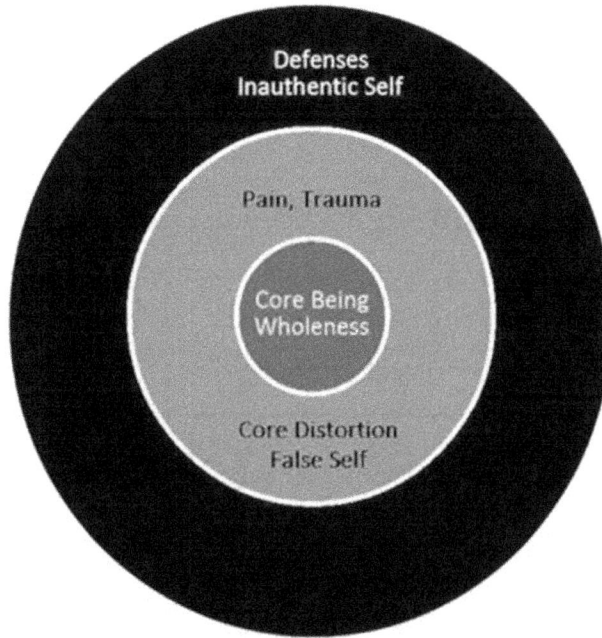

Defenses
Inauthentic Self

Pain, Trauma

Core Being
Wholeness

Core Distortion
False Self

3 Rings of Healing
After Process Work

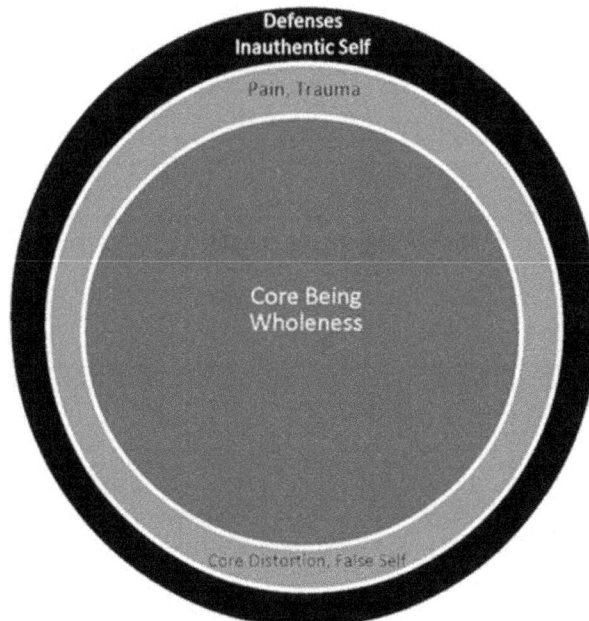

Defenses
Inauthentic Self

Pain, Trauma

Core Being
Wholeness

Core Distortion, False Self

FILL IN THE DETAILS OF YOUR RINGS ON THE FOLLOWING FORM

Outer most ring—List your unhealthy defenses/beliefs (such as withdrawal, porcupine, denial, boundary containment, collapse)

Middle Ring—List your traumas, pain, developmental trauma, negative Core Beliefs (such as abuse, bullying, not feeling loved, "if I stand up for myself, I will be smashed")

Center Ring—List your Core Being Qualities (such as compassion, creativity, hardworking, giving). If you are not sure what to list, ask your best friends/family members to help you.

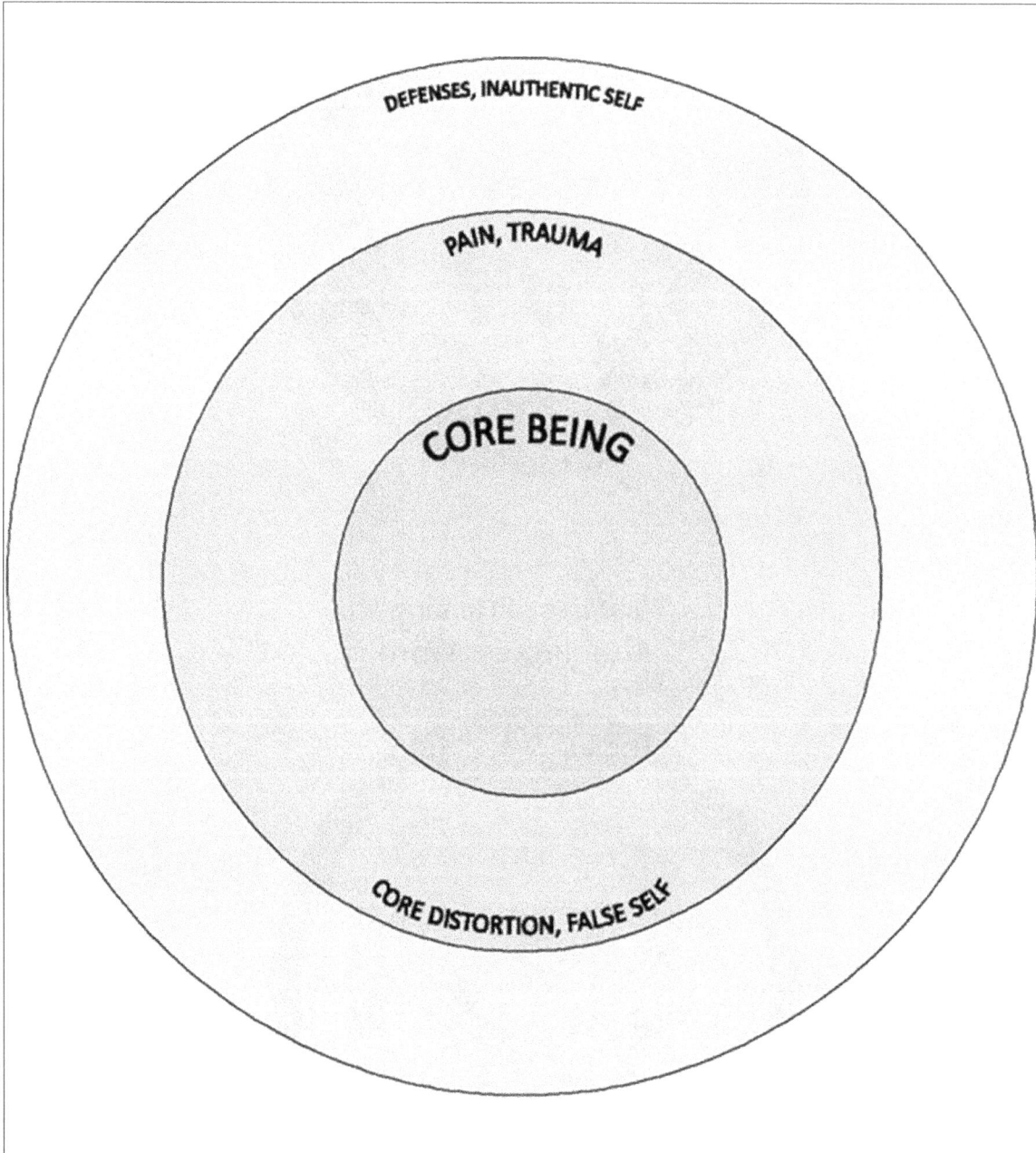

DEFENSES, INAUTHENTIC SELF

PAIN, TRAUMA

CORE BEING

CORE DISTORTION, FALSE SELF

5-STEP Mindfulness Process to transform pain into light and move through the

3-RINGS of HEALING AND SHAPE-SHIFT OUR EMOTIONAL REALITIES

All day long, we move through these rings, so let's do it consciously. Use the **Five Step Mindfulness process and practice moving through the 3-rings and return to wholeness.** Practice noticing what ring you are currently living from and why. Then you can practice moving through the outer rings and returning to your Core Being throughout the day (center ring). Core Being is described more below. Basically it is our true self or god self - the part of us that feels whole.

1. Self-Awareness (through deep connection within). Step one is the ability to notice when we are in our Core Being and when we are living from the unhealthy programmed personality level. What is the unhealthy programmed personality level? It includes all our negative beliefs, images and ego. It is the part of our brain neurology that reacts to the world based on habituated responses that are programmed into us from birth.

(Outer Most Ring)

2. Detachment (versus dissociation) comes from aligned positive intention. It helps us know we are more than the energy that runs through us and helps us connect to our Enlightened Observer. This is when we don't merge with the negative feelings, images, beliefs and emotions. We notice them but they don't define our sense of self. Instead, we view them from our Enlightened Observer. The Enlightened Observer is the part of us that is connected to our wholeness and sees us from "god's eyes" and not from the ego. It is different from the "objective" observer in that it clearly has our back and is very positively in our court, like a mother bear or the archetype of the good enough mother.

(Outer Most Ring) (Middle Ring)

3. Naming, owning and locating the defense and trigger in the mind, energy and body systems. In this step, we identify our defense and the trigger that prompted us to move into an unhealthy programmed defensive reaction. (Such as: I am feeling hopelessness, anger, insecurity. It is held in my throat and 5th chakra.) In this step, we take responsibility for the fact that we have been triggered out of our center. We name and own our reaction. "I am mad, in defense and out of my Core Being; I feel it in my 3rd chakra and my solar plexus."

(Outer Most Ring) (Middle Ring)

4. Insight - Linking the trigger to the past in all 3 mind, energy and body systems. This step helps the mind to understand why we have been triggered and to collect wisdom. For instance, in step 3 we have named and owned that we are in defense and in this step, we look at the reasons and the wisdom. We know it is our brain's programmed and habituated reaction to a perceived threat and/or stress. On another level, we might remember how the current situation is similar to how we were treated by (fill in the blank_____ mother/ father/ classmate/ teacher/ authority figure) in the past.

5. Transformation in Me-B System. Now, we shift the energy and return to Core Being by using our Enlightened Observer and bringing High Vibrational Consciousness (HVC) into the dense Low Vibrational Consciousness (LVC) of the Programmed Personality. This must happen in all 3 systems: mind, energy and body. Further discussion on what is LVC and HVC follows. Basically, an example of LVC is our negative beliefs, trauma, ego and challenging emotions. HVC examples are faith, Core Being, joy and positive intention.

(Center of the 3 Rings)

Sometimes we can't reconnect completely to Core Being because our mind, ego or negative intention is too strong. If this happens, we must be patient and compassionate with ourselves.

PRINCIPLES OF ME-B TRANSFORMATION™

The following Me-B Transformational Principles, when applied to our daily lives (or to our clients' lives), help us move through the 3 Rings of Healing and Shape-Shift our Emotional Realities. They act as fuel motivating us to move forward toward our center.

Principles Become Cornerstones for Change!

ME-B PRINCIPLES

It is Resistance that Causes Pain

Relationship Supports High Vibrational Consciousness (HVC)

As We Explore Our Self, We Become the Truth That Passes Through Us—
So We Evolve Toward Truth

Because We Don't Believe the Inner Turmoil

We Implode (Go Within) so We Can Explode (our Core Being),
Which Supports the Rhythm of Flow

We Release It to the Highest Good

Find the CHOICE POINT,
Which Tells Us "Less is More"

No One Heals Anyone and No One Needs to be Fixed

And Connecting to the Effortless Flow of Inner Joy Helps Us Get Out of Our Own Way!

It is Resistance That Causes Pain because *energy always distorts when we try to hold onto it, or revolt against it.* When a horse or dog gives birth, they don't judge the pain as bad or good. They simply relax into the pain to support the next Rhythm of Flow of energy. If they stiffen, resist and pull against the pain, it only intensifies their agony. This illustrates how we too can accept the pain in the moment and investigate its meaning, so we don't collapse into the pain or bury it. As we use our Explorer's Mind, we can discover the gifts hidden beneath the challenges we face and trust that the beautiful moments will someday return.

Relationship can Support High Vibrational Consciousness. As we know how deep to go, when to push, when to pull back, and when to stay neutral in our relationships (and with clients), we support everyone's highest good. Learning how to better leave our programmed personality behind and become a whole vessel in relationship, we can support the raising of everyone's consciousness.

However, it is inevitable that the longer we are in relationship with one another, the more our dark shadow will be revealed. This is where it gets much harder. At this depth, the *work becomes more of an art-form than a science* and life is our teacher — if we open to learn the lessons. To do this, we must **Explore Our Self at the same time** as we interact with others. **This helps us Become The Vessel Truth Can Pass Through (Stages 8-10).** In this way, without thinking, we adjust our field and track our defenses back to alignment with Core Being,

As our skills grow, we support our self, our family and our clients. We move forward with the hope that at the end of each encounter, we can learn something new and/or deepen what we already know. Every relationship is an opportunity to reclaim our Core Being and revitalize our own process.

Carlos Castaneda, a famous shaman, called this process "stalking." We stalk (explore) ourselves in relationship with others to discover how to stay connected to our whole self. This **Helps Us Evolve toward Truth Because We Don't Believe our Inner Turmoil (Stage 4 and above)** (Core Distortions), which relaxes our ego and connects us to our Enlightened Observer and Explorer's Mind. From this place, we learn how important it is to go within and explore what personal work is needed **(Implode).** As we do the internal personal work, we cultivate the energy so we can **Explode** our Core Being out into the world.

Going within and learning about our inner gifts—and the obstructions to those gifts—is the **Implode.** This helps us to be better equipped to **Explode** the gifts out into the world. A Me-B Guide must implode on a regular basis in order to create the momentum for the next expansion. Just as energy works in waves of expansion and contractions, so do our abilities to support our loved ones (and clients). If we work our contractions and uncover the shadow (golden and dark), it will help us to then bring that learning into the world.

This Supports the Rhythm of Flow of Reality and Releases it to the Highest Good. It is our job to allow healing energy to come through by tracking the **Rhythm of Flow.** It is the process of unraveling congested energy and supporting its evolution. Know how to use words, guidance, intuition, and Me-B techniques to gently promote the next unwinding within us and/or our family members and clients.

As we **Find the Critical Point, it Tells Us that "Less is More"**—we get more "bang for the buck." *Critical point analysis* is derived from the fact that in any highly complex system, "there is a specific, critical point at which the smallest input will result in the greatest (hopefully positive) change." In Me-B Transformation™, we use our Explorer's Mind to uncover our critical point by unraveling the complexity of thoughts, energies and somatics in our Me-B System.

Then, when we use our Enlightened Observer at the critical point, we raise our vibration, end our distortion, and with the smallest effort, exert change. Some know this process as the "Butterfly Effect."

So, **No one Heals Anyone and No one Needs to be Fixed.** We are strictly the facilitator or guide. Know from an egoless state of mind that we are not the one doing the work (Stage 7 and above of Me-B Transformation™). It is not our job to fix anything. We can surrender to the concept that the only work to do is to promote a healthy relationship and offer support. The real work can only be done by our clients/friends/family/employer. We *can't do it for them.*

(The website www.thework.com by Byron Katie outlines how to discover the perfection in every situation.)

DAMAGED TO THE CORE?

Some of us feel that even at the Core Being level, we are inadequate. Jillian felt she damaged herself so deeply over so many lifetimes that she even damaged her divine spirit.

What she couldn't yet hold for herself, I held for her. I met her where she was and acknowledged her feelings, and we did work around the "issue of repair." Now she knows, at least at the Core Being level, that she is whole. She works to return to that frequency throughout the day.

Every river's water smashes against rocks on its way down the steam. In life, we too hit many metaphorical rocks. So when we as the water (Core Being) hit a rock (Core Distortion), why do we get confused and believe that we are the rock?

Throughout our life, our programmed personality (lower levels of the Auric Field) can be built and altered by the rocks we hit, but our Core Being remains the same. Its frequency is too high to be smashed by a mere rock, as long as at least a part of us remembers who we are....

As we do our work from the place of wholeness, we access more wholeness. If all of us did our work from the place of being broken, we would manifest more brokenness. This is the *CHOICE POINT* we each must make to return to wholeness.

A meditation teacher explained that if we are bored or frustrated, we are not paying close enough attention. This is great advice! Another way of saying this is that if we are living our life (or in a session with a client) and the experience doesn't foster inner joy, effortlessness and flow, then somehow we are getting in our own way. **Connecting to the Effortless Flow of Inner Joy Helps Us Get out of our Own Way!** So, moving through the 3 Rings and not getting stuck at any one point is the key. None of us will be perfect at this. Thinking we will be or should be is Spiritual Junk Food. We can strive for growth and improvement, and to be kind to ourselves when we are imperfect.

The following can all help us in this process: supervision, healings, massage, therapy, dancing, Explorer's Mind, Enlightened Observer, Compassion, and Love. It is essential we (1) know and (2) follow through with what supports us in returning to Core Being. (See the No Excuses technique for help as well.)

Regardless of how much personal growth work we have done, there is never an end...yet there are as many new beginnings as we choose to create! Every moment is a CHOICE POINT!

Once we find our **Choice Points**, we will need to shift any **Core Distortions** preventing us from creating HVC with them. It takes time to completely transform all the LVC in our **Core Distortions** so we can fully

138

integrate the new more positive habituation. Giving ourselves time to fully integrate the new more positive habituation is realistic and compassionate.

CHOICE POINTS—NOT SO EASY

I have inadvertently programmed people to expect me to "give away the house" to them. As I mature and locate my Choice Points so I can transform my Core Distortions and work my 3 Rings of Healing, I am learning to say "no." Unfortunately, others are not happy about this at times. My cumbersome manner of saying "no" is definitely a work in progress. Too soft, too hard—trying to let my bruised ego go and say "no" from Core Being is humbling and challenging.

Fortunately, the Universe is giving me many opportunities to practice my Choice Points. I am finally get- ting closer to setting these boundaries from Stage 6 of Me-B Transformation™. Four months ago, I was barely hanging on to Stage 4 when I set them. "Progress, not perfection" is what we can tell ourselves! As we stay focused, we succeed. Then, using our CHOICE POINTS and transforming Core Distortions becomes a positive habituation.

TRANSFORMING CORE DISTORTIONS

When a Me-B Guide helps a client transform their **Core Distortions**, they can consider the following questions:

1. How much talk is too much talk, which could disconnect clients from their body/energy system and emotions?
2. What is the best timing of the Intervention so we support the client's Rhythm of Flow of energy?
3. How can practitioners more accurately track the client's field and make sure the Enlightened Observer is strong and engaged?
4. How much (if any) information is helpful to share with the client based on what we collect from a client's energy field regarding their Core Distortion, past lives, beliefs, trauma and emotions?

As a rule of thumb, we don't need to know what Core Distortions are held in the energy field for them to be successfully transformed. However, in some cases, it is wise to know what consciousness the Core Distortion holds. This is especially true if it is an issue that tends to repeat over and over again. The more awareness we bring to an issue, the more empowered we are to transform it. For instance, I have a father-related Core Distortion that visits once every year. Each year this uninvited guest knocks on my door, and each year I transform it at a deeper level. I now trust and am comforted by the fact that because I succeeded in transforming it be- fore, that when it visits again, I will be equally successful.

Ideally, as a result of following this Intervention, we all will feel the power and strength that comes as a by- product of this technique. In the beginning, guidance and support from a trained Me-B Guide are necessary. Eventually we (and our clients) become so skilled at this Intervention that only occasionally will assistance from a Me-B guide be needed to identify and then transform Core Distortions into the HVC of Core Being.

If you are doing a Core Distortion Touch session, do a simple energy clearing and/or positive resourcing intervention before clearing the Core Distortion. If a client is only Stage 1, 2 or 3 of Me-B Transformation™, we might not want to do deeper work with Core Distortions until their positive ego, Enlightened Observer and energetic and biological Consciousness Container is stronger.

TRANSFORMATION OF CORE DISTORTION - TOUCH SESSION

STEP 1:

Locate where the Core Distortion is held in the body and energy system. Always ask clients where they think, imagine or feel it is held. Sometimes they know and sometimes they think they know. If we are able to read it in the field, compare the information we receive with what the clients tell us. For the purposes of practicing this exercise on our self, select a part of the body (such as our ankle) and work only there. Later, after we have had more practice scanning the body and locating where the LVC is held, we can go where our client (and/or we) assess the Core Distortion to be.

STEP 2:

Assess what information is held in the Core Distortion and then energetically call in the positive opposite.

So if the Core Distortion is, "I am powerless." The HVC is, "I am powerful." If the Core Distortion is fear, we bring in the consciousness of courage and strength. If the negative belief is "I am bad," we bring in the HVC of "I am good enough." (See samples of negative/positive beliefs.)

When we connect to the body and sense into the Core Distortion, the energy looks dark, thick and sticky like tar. It is held primarily on the 2nd and 4th levels of the Auric Field. It may feel prickly, hot and sticky to the touch.

As we collect more information on the Core Distortion, also ask clients to self-assess themselves. If we feel clients are way off-base in their self-assessment, let this information be diagnostic for how to proceed with them. Usually, if a client's self-assessment is extremely off-base and incorrect, use this as an indicator that the client may not be ready to do deep work on this issue and we need to go very slowly.

If we have a deep trusting relationship with them, we might be able to suggest they might be misguided in their assessment. If not, it is best to always go slow. Begin in the area they identify and let the energy lead to where it needs to go next. **Always follow the energy because it has the intelligence.** No matter where in the body we start, if we just remain open and follow what the energy tells us, we will be on track.

Often when we think we know best, we can get in our own way. If we and the client are not sure where the Core Distortion is located in the body and energy system, then we can choose an area based on our best guess and once again follow what the energy tells us. The solar plexus is a good place to start. It is where our ego is held energetically and always has some Core Distortion trapped in the cells.

When we sense into the emotion, simply feeling mad, glad, sad, or fear is enough. We don't have to be too specific in order to bring in the positive opposite HVC. Often clients won't know what emotion/image/belief is held there. It takes practice. If they don't know and we don't know, then we can use intention to bring in the energy of Core Being. Core Being transforms anything willing to be transformed.

As we sense into an area, if the information we receive on the Core Distortion is different from what the client states, always go with what the client says. Often as we bring in the HVC alternative, a client will notice what the real issue is and then they can adjust the type of HVC they receive into the area. Also, there are layers to Core Distortions. We may begin thinking it is one issue—but as we deepen into the experience, the energy may change to clarify what is asking to be transformed. **This is why it is so important to follow the energy. Let it lead us toward transformation.**

Review for Step 2:

- If we only identify an emotion instead of more specific information, that is often enough.
- It is OK if we don't know details of the Core Distortion and just bring in the energy of HVC of Core Being.
- Remember to follow the energy.

STEP 3:

When doing touch table-work with clients, help them prepare their energy field for transformation by first charging below the location of the Core Distortion. Observe/sense how the LVC is linked to other body parts and to other energy systems. Observe/sense if charging the energy below shifted the LVC. If not, **then place one hand above and one hand below the LVC and charge the field by bringing in higher vibrations.**

Once again observe how the LVC is linked to other parts of the body and to the client's overall energy system.

Assess if we think another part of the body needs to be energetically cleared before the Core Distortion can clear. This takes experience and training. We encourage everyone to attend the Me-B Transformational Training for support in developing this skill. For instance, previously we discussed the order in which Core Distortions tend to clear. Usually, clients begin clearing in their heart area, then the diaphragm, then the solar plexus, and so on. If we are trying to clear something in their diaphragm, but the energy in their heart is shut down— stopping the flow from coming into the diaphragm—we might have to clear the heart and its Core Distortion first.

STEP 4:

At this point, the Core Distortion might have already transformed. If not, **we bring in the high vibrational consciousness of a positive image, belief or emotion. From Core Being, we place our hand over the particular Core Distortion and using intention, we bring in the energy of the positive alternative. Let that frequency flow out of our hand and into the client's body. At the same time, the client too allows the positive alternative to come into their body.** The client works with the Me-B Guide. We don't "do it to" the client. Usually we and the client feel the emotion/sensation of the negative and melt it away and then we can feel the emotion/ sensation of the positive. Because our subconscious is so strong, ideally it is best to be able to feel both the emotion and sensation of the LVC being transformed into HVC.

REVIEW:

Using intention, we allow our hand and body to resonate with the HVC in the form of a positive image/ belief/ emotion and feel, sense, see the energy of higher consciousness move into the client's field through their 7th, 6th, 5th, 4th, 3rd, 2nd, and 1st levels of the field. Allow it to fill and resonate, transforming and then replacing the negative belief/image/emotion. Have the HVC fill the client's levels of the field, especially the 1st level.

As we vibrate at the Core Being dimension and use our intention to bring in the energy of the positive alternative, we must continue to keep our own vibration high so we don't merge and accidentally charge the LVC. Modulate our hand to the high vibration and slowly let it melt away the LVC. As our hand dissolves the LVC, breathe – and pull multi-dimensional energy in from Top/Bottom, Left/Right, and Front/Back so our frequency stays high enough for transformation to take place.

Explore again what is happening elsewhere in the field. As outlined earlier, sometimes if the heart chakra shuts down (or any area above the Core Distortion), this prevents energy from flowing into the Core Distortion, so it can't transform. This means the energy field is in defense and needs extra support. It could also mean that another Core Distortion is preventing the transformation. In this case, do Containment and explore what negative intention, separated self, ego or other Core Distortion is prohibiting transformation.

NO TOUCH TRANSFORMATION OF CORE DISTORTION

- **STEP 1:** Identify where the Core Distortion is held in the body.
- **STEP 2:** Identify the image, emotion or negative belief.
- **STEP 3:** Identify the positive alternative.
- **STEP 4:** Ask our clients to place their hands (if possible), awareness and breath in contact with the area. Using intention, allow your mind and body to resonate with the positive image/belief/emotion and feel, sense, see the energy of higher consciousness move into the client's field through their 7th, 6th, 5th, 4th, 3rd, 2nd, and 1st levels of the field. Allow it to fill and resonate, taking the place of the negative belief/image/emotion. Using intension, ask your client do the same.
- **STEP 5:** Me-B Guide works with the client to invite the client's Core Being energy to fill and expand into each cell in the client. Then, connect to the area and assess if it has been transformed. Ask the client to also connect and assess. If it has not been completely transformed, do containment or, if time permits, return to STEP 1 and identify the LVC left in the body. Ask what it needs to feel safe enough to transform. Bring in the energy and consciousness it needs to feel safe. Often all it needs is to be heard. Remove the need for it to transform and instead send it understanding, love and compassion.

REVIEW QUESTIONS

1. What are the 3 Rings of Healing?
2. How do they help us Shape-Shift Our Emotional Realities?
3. What 5 Steps can we follow to travel through the Rings?
4. Which steps might be hardest for you, based on your Character Structure's negative defenses?
5. What solutions do you think you can follow (review solutions) to help you move through the 3 Rings?
6. Which Me-B principals might be the most challenging, and which solutions can you follow to support yourself? (Remember to leave the ego behind by sending love and compassion to your programmed personality as you answer this question.)
7. Why are relationships our best teachers?
8. What is most challenging about relationships?
9. Who heals us and why?
10. Write out a plan to support yourself so that moving through the 3 Rings of Healing becomes a healthy habit in your daily life.
11. Review the process of Transforming Core Distortions and outline what was easy. Focus on this and let it grow. Also, practice placing your hand on your own Core Distortions and melting away the LVC energy as you bring in HVC energy.

CHAPTER 11

UNIVERSAL ONENESS SKILLS FOR MASTERING Me-B STAGES

Our wish for Enlightenment is too often fueled by our wish to avoid the challenges of being human.

Exactly what do we mean by wholeness, and can we be whole without being enlightened? As we master the skills in the Me-B Stages, we increase our HVC and our ability to reconnect to Core Being during difficult and stressful moments. Without deep emotional work, rarely do people access their wholeness in all three parts of our Me-B System simultaneously. It takes even deeper work to maintain that connection to wholeness because *the energy on earth is very dense and we are surrounded by LVC. To advance to higher stages of Me-B transformation™, we must master the ability to create safety and security within us and give up our need for external approval or confirmation.*

Me-B Transformation's definition of enlightenment is the ability to return to Core Being. For most of us, this is a big challenge because we will always have an ego-based programmed personality triggering us out of our center.

So, if we are not enlightened, are we still whole? If the answer is "no," how might that affect our reality and our day-to-day view of ourselves and our view of our clients? How too might it affect our ability to heal and manifest our hearts' passions?

Consider that just because we don't always interact with others or ourselves from the place of wholeness, at our Core Being level, we are still whole. This means that even when we are (1) imperfect and (2) in defense, (3) in Core Distortion or (4) in our Programmed Personality, we can *also* be connected to our wholeness. Accessing our larger spirit — our oneness — when in defense, helps us to reconnect to our wholeness quicker.

Being imperfect is part of being human. How we deal with our ego when we face our imperfections can be a choice that reunites us to our Core Being or keeps us trapped in our Programmed Personality. This is the CHOICE POINT we all make many times a day.

It is possible to be in two places at one time (Stage 4). In fact, it is obligatory for all Me-B enthusiasts to someday become proficient at this high-level transformational skill. If we ignore our separated self and lower vibrational consciousness (anger, jealousy, inadequacy, arrogance) then we lose the ability to choose the deeper AND more expansive realities. We become lost in Spiritual Junk Food. We must own our LVC in order to transform it, otherwise it becomes stronger and will explode outward against our will; it can take control of us instead of us transforming it. Sometimes the higher brain doesn't know what is hidden below the surface. As we learn to "turn off" what we think we know and discover what is hidden, deeper healing can happen.

Our ego can be another reason we don't listen to what is hidden below the surface. If our ego over-identifies with a challenging emotion, we might miss hearing the message and thus miss an opportunity to transform.

EMOTIONS + OVER-IDENTIFICATION = MISSING THEIR MESSAGE AND THE WISDOM THEY BRING — resulting in a MISSED OPPORTUNITY TO TRANSFORM AND CLAIM CORE BEING

In addition, if we over-identify with our separated self and difficult emotions then we also miss an opportunity to learn what message it brings and we fail to allow these difficult emotions and separated self to transform us. When our Enlightened Observer is present, real healing happens. It is the most essential ingredient to remember throughout the day. It holds the detachment vital to seeing clearly, like a deep breath or pause in the rhythm of the flow of reality so we can re-center and awaken.

ENLIGHTENED OBSERVER + CORE DISTORTION, SEPARATED SELF, TRAUMA, OR PAIN = TRANSFORMATION AND WISDOM

ELIMINATE JUDGMENTS

Judgments are about separation and division both within ourselves and in our relationships with others. When we judge another, we usually feel we are better than they. This means we are interacting from the place of superego, not Core Being. It is our separated self that births our judgments. It is our Core Being that heals judgments.

We all have a separated self and thus we all judge. It is just part of our life's experience and it is Spiritual Junk Food to deny this aspect that exists within all of us. What we do with our judgments can be terrifying or healing. To the extreme our judgments can develop into prejudices, racial violence, hate crimes or even war. In schools we have seen the effect of judgment as breakdown, suicide and violence toward others.

JUDGMENT + SEPARATED SELF = FOSTERING PAIN, BLAME and NO SELF-RESPONSIBILITY

During group and family dynamics, it is easy to see others' judgments emerge. One person thinks the other should say, be or do something other than what they are saying, doing or being. Left alone, the person judging avoids looking at the source of the judgment within his or her self because their energy is directed externally toward the perceived source of their pain (the other) instead of the more accurate source – his or her own internal fears, pain and distortions.

Instead of judging others, we can acknowledge that our judgments are a symptom that *we* are out of balance. Judgments are devoid of understanding, compassion and care for the other. These negative attitudes toward others tend to be a mirror of that same lack of understanding and compassion for ourselves.

Judgments hurt and multiply. Criticizing others is easy. Understanding others, and setting boundaries, speaking our truth to create our own internal safety and comfort is more difficult, yet the benefits to the world are far greater. So let's campaign to end our own judgments and the Spiritual Junk Food that accompanies them. It is crucial that Me-B Guides explore their own judgments and assist others in doing the same. Peace cannot exist in the light of judgment.

JUDGMENT + ENLIGHTENED OBSERVER = UNDERSTANDING, COMPASSION, PEACE

Judgments will happen because we all are human; yet we can work to reduce their influence over us. As we remember that we are all connected and one, when we want to judge another, we can also understand that *they are acting out an aspect of us too.* It is an aspect that is in profound forgetting of the truth, which is the wholeness that is available to us all. Our separated self dislikes the person we judge, disharmony results and spreads. We can eliminate our judgments of others by remembering that judgments come from an imbalance within our own separated self and by opening to the possibility that we are probably in transference or counter-transference.

ASSESS JUDGMENTS AND HEAL SEPARATED SELF

Balance and charge your field front/back; top/bottom; left/right. To do this, use any of the techniques already taught. Now, image someone you hold judgments against. Pause the Rhythm of Flow of Reality enough to identify what aspect in them you judge deeply. Breathe in and feel/sense/see the energetics of that piece(s) of them you judge.

Using intention and your Enlightened Observer, allow your field to resonate with the energetics of that distortion and notice where you feel it in your body, mind and energy system. Keeping the vibration of your Enlightened Observer high, melt into the sensations of it and connect deeply. Allow yourself to receive understanding and information about that distortion and why you judge it.

Using the following 4 Step process, record on paper what the judgment reveals about their Core Distortions and what it reveals about your Core Distortions, and what could be the positive mindset to support you in moving out of judgment.

- **STEP 1:**
  I imagine they are (name what you imagine is their Core Distortion) so they are acting (list the characteristics about the action they took that you judged).
  EXAMPLE: I imagine (they are in fear) so they are (acting controlling and attacking).
- **STEP 2:**
  As a result I feel (list the emotion you are feeling) because (link it to your own history and list the reason you are responding that way).
  EXAMPLE: I notice that makes me feel (I can't trust them) because (they are acting like my father used to react and I hate that).
- **STEP 3:**
  Instead I could think (*list mind solution*) so I can see them more clearly.
  EXAMPLE: Instead I could think that they are in their own Core Distortion, I could feel compassion for both of us and understand that they are not my father, move out of transference and know I can learn how to keep myself safe even when someone is trying to control me.
  It is vital to pause the Rhythm of Flow of Reality long enough so we can invite detachment from our reaction and create understanding. Connecting to the Intention Line will help as well.
- **STEP 4:**
  Let go of the distortion in your energy system, mind and physical body. Using Intention, visualize and feel it leaving you. Give it to your spirit guides, and/or your god figure. Feel the sensations

of it leaving the body. Visualize it leaving using colors, pictures, symbols and energy. Now, connect to the positive mindset you listed in STEP 3 and feel, visualize, intend the positive alternative to fill all three-systems-mind, energy and body. Finally, experience them and yourself reconnected to Core Being.

Note: Some judgments are extremely difficult to shift in just one exercise because they are linked to deeper cultural, past-life, ancestral or archetypical issues. Using our Explorer's Mind, we can work with a Me-B Guide and succeed in overcoming our negative transference and judgments of others. *As our skills in feeling our Core Being — and thus our wholeness — expand, we more easily move out of judgment.* Strong motivation is needed to heal our separated self and succeed.

An aspect of higher energy consciousness is universal oneness. It is the deepest intelligence where ego and judgment dissolve. Any judgments, ego or resentments in our day-to-day actions prevent us from living the divine fabric of our life. If our CHOICE POINT is ignored, we miss an important opportunity. Owning our separated self and strengthening our ability to transform it, and bring in higher consciousness, can be a moment-to-moment intention. (Review the Core Being, Centered Oneness and Multi-Dimensional Fabric of Interconnectedness meditations.)

The Multi-Dimensional Fabric connects us to the greater frequencies available. As a result, our current fears, problems and pain shrink in importance. We no longer feel lonely or alone. Our place in the universe is gently aligned and our perspective altered. By bringing in our greater parts, we also bring in our humbleness. At the personality level, we are nothing, insignificant. Our internal ache that once echoed so loudly quickly is seen as lacking importance.

When we access our Core Being, we access a place where everything is peaceful. This is where conflict can't exist. When we are not in this place, we are in our separated self — separated not only from us, but from those around us.

Use the Explorer's Mind to help you stretch to see deeper. Watch how you create reasons, excuses and realities where your longings can't possibly be met or where you think you can't be happy if they are not met. It is often helpful to do this with fun and with intense passion. Risk throwing away any rules, barriers and restrictions your mind conjures. Question those excuses and false realities we all create— yet don't question yourself and your own divine right to your light and to your longings.

At the same time, don't cling to them. For if they are ours, they will return in the form that is in our highest good. So if we don't win the lottery, maybe there is something more important that we are winning but can't see.

As we find our inner home we also find our deepest joy and can understand what fulfillment really means.

We let ourselves guide our clients to access the same level of joy, peace and grace within us. This is the gift Me-B Transformation™ offers; it only takes patience, courage and relentless commitment.

It is often long-term work. This level of energy psychotherapy can continue and deepen over time. The analogy holds true that this work is like peeling away the "layers of an onion." It is not uncommon for clients to participate in Me-B Transformation™ sessions for three or more years, take a break to integrate, and then return. From time to time everyone needs support, and one is never "done." There are always deeper levels of transformation available to us. The length of time it takes to: access our Core Being, develop our Enlightened Observer, and use our Explorer's Mind and its Components of Change so we can travel through the 3 Rings of Healing — differs greatly from person to person.

The diathesis stress model used in psychology offers insight into the differing lengths of time. It considers the following factors:

- environmental conditions such as culture, family system, and physical and emotional trauma, genetic and bio-chemical makeup, and
- resiliency.

In addition, I include:

- level of intention,
- passion toward spiritual and personal growth, and
- evolution of the incarnated soul and the lessons he/she has chosen to learn in this life.

Regardless of the challenges faced in the transformational process, let us all find our inner guide and then let that knowing expand to help us guide our clients and ourselves!

IS THERE HOPE?

Alice felt her mother was doomed and hoped she could save her mother from the torturous life she lived. I told her a story about an enlightened mystic. This mystic walked the streets of India with his students every morning. Some days he would bless and heal the crippled and blind so they could see and walk again—and some days, he walked by, ignoring their plight. A student became very angry at this mystic and asked him why he was so heartless, healing some and ignoring others.

The mystic explained that some people have chosen to have certain challenging experiences and if he were to heal them, they would miss out on their life tasks. I suggested that Alice's mother might be more enlightened than she appeared, and that maybe she chose to incarnate only the challenging aspects of herself. Maybe she really wasn't as lost as Alice thought.

When we admit we don't know what is good for another person, we take a humbling step that facilitates our own personal transformation. Unless we are an enlightened mystic, we really don't always know what is best. One of our most difficult lessons in life might be accepting our powerlessness to heal anyone but ourselves.

Review Questions

1. Explain the meaning of the charts/pictures below.

   - Arrows Below/Chart

   - Picture 2

   - Picture 3

   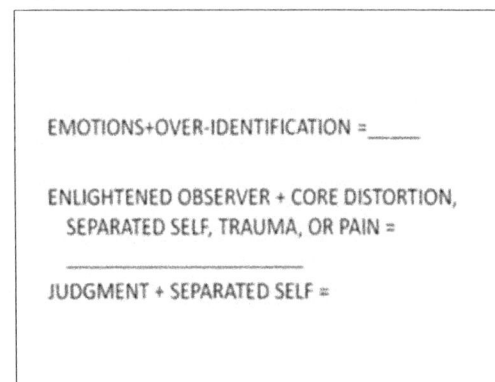

   - Picture 4

   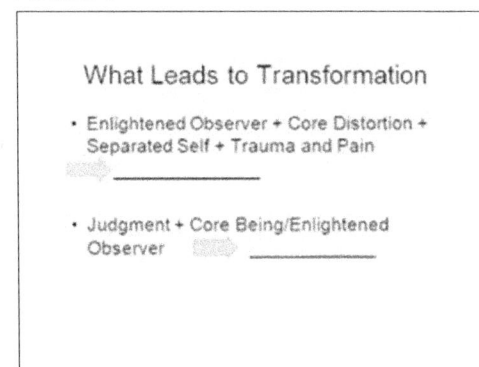

CHAPTER 12

CONTINUUM OF HEALING

It IS about not being controlled by the energy that runs through us, around us, and within us.

It IS about having the freedom to choose the deeper reality.

Learning how to anchor into our Core Being during the downs of life — so we can more easily return to a higher state of consciousness — is empowering! Me-B Transformation™ teaches us how to return to wholeness even in times of pain and stress, creating opportunities to find deep joy and freedom. At this point, we have learned how to move through the 3 Rings of Healing and Shape-Shift Our Emotional Realities. Below is a summary of the 10 Me-B Stages and a self-assessment test. Feel free to take the test now to discover which stages you have mastered and which you are still working toward. The 5-Step Mindfulness process helps us move through the 3 Rings and it also helps us master higher levels of Me-B Stages of consciousness.

WE CAN BE FREE AND LIVE FROM DEEP JOY WITHIN

I have gotten to the point where I am often living from Stage 7 of Me-B Transformation™. However, in times of stress I can quickly drop to Stage 4. I feel it is a great achievement that I never drop below Stage 4, the place where I can hold two places at once: (1) the pain, and (2) the knowing that I am *much more than* the pain. In times of stress, movement downward to lower Stages of Consciousness is not bad. In fact, *the normal Rhythm of Flow of Reality creates ups and downs. There is no way to stop it.*

As we use our Explorer's Mind to investigate why our consciousness level lowered, we cultivate the energy needed to raise it again. Staying connected to our Enlightened Observer, we can use the positive energy of our Intention, and more effortlessly return to Core Being, gaining valuable lessons and wisdom along the way!

Our programmed personality is an elusive animal. Just when we think it is gone, it returns stronger than before. This is a diagnostic indication that HVC is waiting to enter; only a little house-cleaning is needed first.

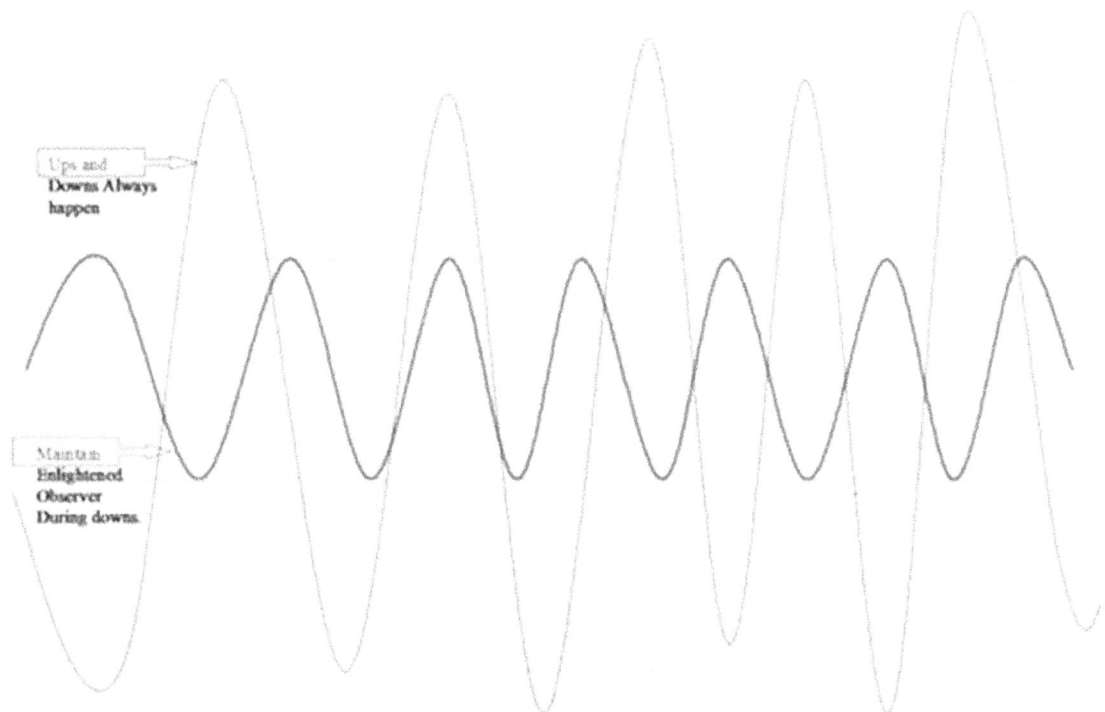

The Rhythm and flow will always create ups and downs in life. As we move through the Me-B Stages of Transformation we have more balanced ups and downs (blue line); Stage 6 and above. But there will ALWAYS be ups and downs in the Rhythm and Flow of Reality. Our Enlightened Observer and Explorer's Mind help us return more quickly. Being able to (1) recognize when we lose connection to our Core Being and then (2) return more quickly to Core Being, is the Me-B definition of Enlightenment.

WHY SELF-ASSESS OUR Me-B STAGES?

Since we move upward and downward to higher and lower Me-B Stages, why bother to self-assess which Me-B Stage we are holding?

It is helpful to self-assess because this is an important tool the Explorer's Mind can use to reconnect to HVC. For instance, if our Explorer's Mind senses we have dropped to Stage 4, we can discover what we need to do to raise to a higher stage. We do this by moving through the 3 Rings of Healing. We discover what defense (outer black ring) is triggering our trauma and pain (middle blue ring) and then transform that LVC so were- turn to Core Being (purple center ring). Also, if we sense we are at Stage 2 but hope to be at Stage 4 of Me-B Transformation™, we know what skills to master so we can support ourselves and advance to Stage 4.

151

STAGE ONE - DIGGING IN THE DIRT

Just beginning—intellectually only and outer Ring mostly.

Mentally, we are beginning to identify elements in the outer ring: the ego-based personality level of negative defenses and public personality. We are not yet able to feel, sense these aspects in the energy system and body as a tangible experience. (Energetically, we are using the ego and only the upper/mental energy constructs of the Auric Dimension).

Digging in the Dirt is the process where we begin to explore who we are. We uncover the source of our Core Distortions and Public Personality. All this work is done at the programmed personality level and mostly the outer black ring. In this stage, we are **just beginning** to discover our unhealthy defenses, false beliefs, and public personality. It is an initial self-discovery stage. Usually at this stage we only look at the dark shadow and are not yet aware of a golden shadow (Core Being). Our ego tells us we are either "good" or "bad" and we live in a very dualistic manner.

This is because, at this stage, we are so focused on digging up the past and understanding the personality level that we have a single point of focus. During this stage we might think that what we are digging up is who we are. In reality, what we are digging up is the "lead" we will use to transform and reveal the gold of our Core Being. When we over-identify with these negative aspects as being "who we are," and we cannot distinguish yet between the personality level and the Core Being level, it is very easy to get lost and feel overwhelmed. In fact, unless we come from a more spiritual tradition, the concept of a Core Being can be very confusing.

I find some Buddhists who don't believe in the concept of "self" can get lost in the intellectual discussion of the self. The language is confusing. If this is the case, as a Me-B Guide, we can alter our language so it better matches the energy of what we are discussing so that we don't get lost in mental concepts. In fact, it is purely an intellectual discussion to separate the Core Being from the false self or personality level, but usually it is a necessary one because our human ego/mind needs a concept of self in order to eventually let it go.

Quantum physics says that all that is real are wave/particles of energy. Just as we observe the solid table in front of us as real, our mind seems to need a solid concept of self until we are strong enough to let it go and connect to a broader view of Core Being. Eventually we let that go and become an empty vessel or nothingness (Stages 8-10 of Me-B Transformation™). After all, we are just labeling different vibrational frequencies of consciousness as being different aspects of a self until we find there is no self and there is "no thing" in the oneness.

Energetically, the movement of self begins at the programmed personality or lower Auric Dimension. We can then move our identification to the more expansive concept of the Core Being Dimension (Stages 4 and above), and eventually (Stage 8-10) we can become the vessel consciousness moves through - the Multi-Dimensional Fabric of Interconnectedness.

Clients who cling to the language debate around the concept of "self" can have a part of themselves refusing to advance, and they only use the "wording" as an unhealthy defense to remain stuck and separated from the deeper truth of who they are. (Often Heart-Centered and/or Compassionate

Character Structures do this.)

As we become more skilled within our self and understand that "digging in the dirt" is not deep personal process work, clients can understand this and move more quickly toward Stage 4. Stage One is uncovering awareness of mostly the outer most ring by using our upper chakras, i.e. the mental level only.

REVEAL OUR OUTER RING

Using the Explorer's Mind, watch yourself and those around you throughout the day. Write down the Public Personality and defenses you use and the ones you see others use. Then look at what you hide beneath the mask and defense. Often times the negative defenses and Public Personalities we most dislike in others are those we subconsciously use ourselves.

Watch closely and uncover the shadow in the outer ring! Reviewing the exercises in that Chapter will remind you of your prominent defenses, boundary challenges, character structures, and relationship coherency negative programming.

Energetic and cognitive defenses can be numerous. Usually defenses in the outer ring are unhealthy defenses programmed into us as part of a primal reaction to life's challenges. We sometimes copy our parents' unhealthy defenses and/or create our own based on how our parents treated us.

WE MUST QUIET OUR EGO, IN ORDER TO HEAR

Gene clearly was a beautiful, powerful, smart and wise woman. Yet there was a part of her ego that kept her from seeing too much of her false sense of self. She felt she had done her work and had transformed. She was excellent at convincing you that she didn't need to do any more personal work. From her forehead she used a strong mental focus that energetically grasped onto another person. She backed it up by clear words. Even though you knew something was off, you couldn't overwhelm the strength of her focus. You had a sense that if for some reason you looked to the deeper truth, she would either run or attack.

In order to look deep enough to see clearly what we need to see, but don't want to see, our ego must quiet so it can reveal the vulnerable and most tender obstacles in our personality.

A Clue: Any time we think we don't have any more personal work left to do, we know we are in Spiritual Junk Food.

Our ego must quiet so we can dig deep enough to discover healthy methods of creating a loving and safe environment for ourselves.

DIG DEEPER TO UNCOVER MORE

Watch yourself and others for one week and look at the sometimes unhelpful methods that you or they protect themselves with. Notice and then describe in writing how you use different defenses with different people and why. Begin to uncover your Core Distortion that created these unhealthy defenses. Write down your unhealthy defenses and the negative beliefs that created them.

Now, imagine connecting to your Core Being and positive beliefs. How might you react differently from this perspective? Be as specific as possible. This will help you find the Choice Points for Peace.

Lastly, as you are talking with someone who you find to be difficult, and you are in defense, invite your Enlightened Observer's HVC to descend down upon you and fill you up. See if you can come out of defense.

The second inner ring of the diagram represents our Core Distortions and traumas of life. Our Core Distortions are also the source of our false images and beliefs. They are the traumas and painful moments that happened to us and keep us anchored in our false sense of self. Abuse, neglect, death of a parent, and unfair treatment all are severe sources of Core Distortions. Regardless of how "perfect" our childhood might have been, everyone has Core Distortions that create a false impression of ourselves and those around us. *As we learn to uncover and reveal the Core Distortions that influence who we are in the world we then open to the possibility of change.*

LIFE IS PERFECT

Dean had the perfect family. Everyone wanted to be him. Money came easily to him—until one day, the stock market crashed and he lost most of his wealth. Along with his wealth, he lost the foundation his positive sense of self was built upon. He collapsed into a deep depression. As Dean was growing up, his father and mother had been hyper-critical of him. They only saw value in him when he became successful financially.

Dean eventually discovered that his Core Distortion dealt with not feeling "good enough." Instead of looking inside and discovering his internal self-worth, he pursued an external source of value—money. When the money disappeared, he had to face the deeper Core Distortions in his life and discover a more permanent, internal source of value, his Core Being.

The innermost or center ring represents our Core Being, the divinity of who we are. This is not part of the personality level. It operates in a different energetic dimension and vibrational frequency than does the personality. *During the 10 Stages of Me-B Transformation*[TM] *process, the center ring is the most important one.* It represents the truth of who we are, and allows us to choose our reality versus letting the energy of our emotions chose it for us. As we "Dig" at the personality level, our objective can be to eventually unearth our Core Being. In Stage 1, we explore unhealthy family dynamics and reveal unhealthy dynamics that we repeated in the history of our daily lives. During this stage, we begin to see that misery is something we *do* to ourselves as a result of programming and our reactions to what was *done* to us in the past.

Misery is something we do to ourselves as a result of what was programmed within—be it through trauma, past lives, parents, partners or genetics.

During Stage One, we usually focus on the negative aspects of our personality. We dwell on our mistakes and personal challenges. As the digging continues, often we will over-identify with these negative aspects as being "who we are." At this point, we can get overwhelmed, and our negative ego becomes activated. If we are not careful, we will drown in our own misunderstanding of ourselves.

DON'T GET TRAPPED BY THE DENSE FREQUENCY OF STAGE ONE!

The dense frequency of Stage One Consciousness can feel as sticky and thick as molasses. Sometimes we must use Herculean effort to release ourselves from the hold of this denser consciousness so we can then move toward Stage 4.

To help yourself, take a moment to contemplate times when you have over-identified with the darkness of your programmed personality. Write, draw, and describe when you have observed yourself feeling drowned by the negative aspects you have uncovered within you. Specifically, look at when it was hard to see that the deeper you was not your negative actions AND when you felt uncomfortable about owning your dark aspects. Investigate how this looked in your Auric Field, levels 1-5 and the chakras.

Now connect to the Manifest Energy that allows us to be connected yet detached. Practice noticing these aspects of yourself — feel the emotion. Direct your attention to it as if it were a movie you are watching and not something you are attached to or something that defines all of you. Notice how it feels in your body/energy system to watch those challenging aspects of your programmed personality in a more detached and balanced manner. From Manifest Energy our ego calms and our anxiety lessens, which allows our nervous system to relax. This helps us release and move forward to the next goal.

Lastly, imagine the HVC of Core Being melting away the negative energetic and emotional challenges. Feel yourself whole again, and acknowledge the aspects of your programmed personality that need extra support to change.

It can be very challenging for the Me-B guide to help clients see and understand the past without also thinking they are the things they have done or continue to do. *Therefore it is vital that the Me-B guide help clients to at least consider the possibility that these negative aspects are who they are NOT—and NOT who they ARE.*

Many people refer to this first stage as "working their process." I often hear students, clients, therapists, and couples say, I am working my process but I don't seem to be changing. This is because we all have to do more than just dig, uncover and intellectually understand. *In Me-B Transformation*™, *the intellect is just the beginning. For there to be transformation, we must also bring the energy of HVC into the body and energy systems.*

STAGE 2 — WHERE ARE WE DIGGING?

Just beginning—intellectually only, but now, firmly in all 3 Rings

We can label our defenses in the outer ring, Core Distortions and trauma in the middle ring, and list the qualities of our Core Being, center ring. At this stage, we are investigating "Who Am I?" in all 3 Rings. We are documenting who we believe ourselves to be at the programmed personality level and Core Being Dimensions. We practice using imagery, visualization and imagination to sense into the energy and body systems. We are reactive to our attachment issues and often need someone else to mirror our positive sense of self to us. (Energetically, we are using the ego and only the upper/mental energy constructs and gifts).

Often digging is done with no real idea of where we are digging. We just know we want to dig out of where we are. People forget to look for the metaphorical buried treasure and rarely taste enough of the riches of our Core Being.

The concept of Core Being becomes more tangible and real in Stage 2 — at least at the mind level of Me-B Transformation™. Rarely at this stage can it be felt either in the body or energetically. The Enlightened Ob- server also becomes more present. We can't yet transform Core Distortions in all three systems, but we are moving closer to being able to.

ACCESS OUR CORE BEING

At this stage, it would help to write a journal of what our Core Being might:

- feel like,
- look like energetically, and
- how we would describe its characteristics.

Also, we can practice the Centered Oneness, Multi-Dimensional Fabric and Star Child interventions to help our Core Being become more tangible. At this stage, any of the positive resourcing interventions can be practiced as well.

In Stage 2, intellectually, we can name our defenses in the energy system and body more easily, and can begin to self-assess. This means we can connect to energy or sensations in the body and guess what might be held there. We can also imagine/guess where a negative feeling or emotion is held in the body/energy systems.

At this stage, we are still guessing and imagining—although often very accurately. We are not yet able to trust our ability to self-assess and we don't yet trust that energy is real and that the body holds the past. Energy/somatic awareness is an intellectual understanding, or accepted as a matter of faith, but is not yet grounded in our day-to-day experiences.

Often in the therapeutic process, the timing of when a specific type of healing can be done depends upon various factors. The Multi-Dimensional Fabric Alignment, Star Healing and the Centered-Oneness Healing are examples of positive resourcing and can be done at almost any time. Positive resourcing is a psychotherapeutic term that describes the technique of helping a client develop INTERNAL positive resources, skills, and attributes so they can overcome:

- EXTERNAL criticism, judgment, and trauma, and
- INTERNAL effects of their false self and negative ego.

STAGE 2 CLIENT JOURNEY

Depending upon the consciousness level of the client, he or she may or may not be able to clearly connect to their deeper positive reality. Yet that is the magic of energetic work. Positive resourcing can play a large role in helping a client transform and eventually open to receiving their truth—even if the client's current level of conscious awareness isn't ready. This is because energy works profoundly on the subconscious. As we increase our awareness and skills at seeing and assessing energy during a Me-B Transformation™ session, we will easily understand to what extent the subconscious has been affected. The deeper the energetic shifts, the deeper the effect upon both the subconscious and the conscious. Through interaction with the client we can assess at the conscious level, and through tracking the energetics we can assess the sub- conscious levels.

For instance, if our field (or a client's energy field) is not absorbing the energy of the centered oneness intervention, then their subconscious is in defense. This is especially true if they tell us they think it is easy to receive the energy but we notice the energy is blocked. Me-B Guides gain the ability to assess if the energetic intervention was effective, and if not, why and how best to proceed.

Stage 2 Aspects

We are still digging in the dirt and uncovering our defenses, Core Distortions and public personality.

We are also exploring the possibility of uncovering the "treasures" found within our Core Being and are exploring the possibility that negative beliefs can be changed.

The differences between Stage one and Stage two are that Stage two is slightly further along; we are more connected to Core Being, and as a result our consciousness is slightly higher.

STAGE 3 – TRANSFORMATION

Somewhat able in all Me-B Systems and beginning to develop the Enlightened Observer and beginning to experience, feel, sense all 3 Rings in the body and energy system.

At Stage 3, we are beginning to be able to toggle back and forth between (1) experiencing our Enlightened Observer (Core Being) and (2) experiencing our emotional pain in the body/energy system; yet cannot hold both at one time because our ego still over-identifies with the pain/emotional challenge. We are starting to believe/experience and move beyond "faking it to make it" and are closer to knowing the answer to the Zen Koan "Who am I?" We begin to ask, "Where is my true Tribe?" (We are starting to explore the 4th and 3rd Chakras' gifts and energy Levels and are starting to move beyond the intellect.)

Uncovering the true self or Core Being provides the energetic vibration so we can turn LEAD into GOLD or transform our negative identification of self into HVC. Done skillfully, the uncovered "dirt" feeds the energetic field to allow the higher vibrations of our Core Being to enter. Using elements such as our Explorer's Mind and its Components of Change, it completes the transformation of the lower vibrations.

Some of the following may be triggered within us during the course of reading this book:

- negative ego,
- separated self,
- Core Distortion,
- transferences,
- boundary issues,
- relationship coherency,
- public personality,
- Spiritual Junk Food,
- unhealthy defenses,
- pain, and
- difficult emotions such as sadness, anger, anxiety and insecurity.

As we presence ourselves with them, there is the opportunity to allow ourselves and others to assist us to transform these internal triggers. Doing this creates the opportunity to deepen our understanding and skills so we can assist others.

Transformation CHOICE POINTS appear more frequently at this stage because we have a stronger Enlightened Observer and are somewhat connected to our Core Being. At this stage, we have enough contact with our Core Being that low vibrational material can be transformed in at least one of the mind, energy, or body systems.

Diagnostically, in Stage 3 someone can actually begin the process of transforming. We have dug in the dirt and found many negative defenses, Core Distortions, public personality and are looking at moving beyond the personality level into experiencing higher vibrations such as Core Being and upper levels of the Auric Dimension. As a result we are beginning to explore these higher vibrations so we can bring them into the "dirt" and darkness and energetically begin the transformation process.

STAGE 3 CLIENT JOURNEY

During Stage 3, a client prepares their energy field to resonate at higher frequencies so it feels more comfortable and less overwhelming to the ego. It is the stage where Ego Strength stabilizes so when they get to Stage 4, they can begin trauma work. It is a testing ground for whether they can go back and forth between their Core Being and difficult emotions.

The most helpful therapeutic intervention at this point is to mirror to them where they are and name it—to assist them in moving from Core Being to emotional/ego discomfort and then back again to Core Being. This is putting a toe in the pool to test the temperature before jumping into trauma work too deeply.

At this stage, their ego strength is not high enough to be able to spend too much time in the pain. Asking them to move out of it consciously (versus dissociate out of it) and shift to Core Being develops important "muscles" in the Me-B System which will raise their consciousness so they can graduate to the level of Stage 4, Holding Two Places At Once.

STAGE 4 - HOLDING TWO PLACES AT ONCE

Better able to feel/sense emotions, Core Being, Core Distortions and Negative Defenses in the body and energy Systems; and able to hold two places at once—the emotional challenge and Enlightened Observer/Core Being. In addition, we are just able to feel safe based on an internal source, our Core Being.

This internal source of safety allows us to hold two places at one time – the pain and the light. This is a new skill. (We are more deeply using the gifts of the 4th and 3rd Chakras and can access Manifest Energy and Core Being Dimensions.)

Stage 4 of Me-B Energy Transformation is the stage where people must learn how to hold the dark in the light and the light in the dark. *This takes practice and deep positive resourcing. Without deep internal resourcing, clients tend to over-identify with their Core Distortions and traumas. Sometimes they become frozen in their* defenses, and unable to access their internal safety. In times of deep challenge or emotional pain, it is impossible to connect to our internal light without an internal safe place. One step that helps us secure Stage 4 is to learn how to feel safe within ourselves and not have safety linked only to an external condition. An important energetic technique to reprogram ourselves for internal safety and trust is learning to feel positive sensations of safety and trust within the body.

In addition to feeling safe, we also must allow our current self-identification (ego) to be reborn to a broader sense of self. This does not mean arrogance. In fact, deep humility is necessary. Since the ego doesn't want to die, this rebirth is the stage where one's inner saboteur often rears its head. Fear also often comes in: fear of change, fear of letting go, and fear of the unknown.

It may be important to see a client more often during this initial phase. Going slow is recommended. Also, using the Enlightened Observer is key. It is important that the Enlightened Observer comes from the vibrational frequency of the Core Being and not from the vibrational frequency of the (1) personality, (2) trauma, (3) ego or (4) separated self. In other words, it is not an Enlightened Observer if it is not connected to wisdom and truth. It also is not an Enlightened Observer if it doesn't raise a client's vibrational frequency.

Learning that apparent reality is not real is what this Stage of Me-B Transformation™ mandates.

Since we are so programmed to believe what we see and feel — this is one of the most difficult stages of transformation! Much compassion and patience is needed. Me-B Guides' emotional issues can more easily be triggered during this phase, so supervision is recommended. Self-awareness and patience is key when working with clients so they don't collapse into the pain.

In the beginning, before the more expanded Core Being deepens, a client will either be able to access their light or their Core Distortions. Stage 4 necessitates they learn to do both at the same time! A transition Stage is usually necessary. This is when the Me-B Therapist learns how to help a client move back and forth between the light and the dark (Stage 3). As a client's skill to move back and forth increases, clients become more able to be in both places at the same time.

STAGE 4 CLIENT JOURNEY

For some clients, it takes years to master Stage 4. However, I believe with clear guidance and strong enough intention on the part of the client, everyone can master this stage. Once a broader sense of self is developed, a deeper part of the Core Being has been incarnated into the body, so more of the client can be present with him/herself. **Moving up in the Stages means more of our Core Being has been incarnated into our physical body.** Because more of the client is present, there is more of their Core Being to anchor into when the energy of darkness, emotional pain, defense, trauma, public personality and Core Distortion runs through them.

Because more of the client is present, there is more of their Core Being to anchor into when challenging life circumstances arise.

A technique to practice to help clients learn how to feel energetic "darkness," emotional pain and trauma as energy is called "Taking Out the Trash." By using the Enlightened Observer, clients can learn how to see the emotional challenge as energy moving through them instead of identifying the energy as who they are! It is a turning point in Me-B Transformation™ when clients develop the ability to see their negative ego, emotional trauma/pain and/or unhealthy defenses as energetic consciousness instead of self-identification. The Enlightened Observer has the ability to watch from the place of the inner ring or Core Being. That ability is very important in this stage of Me-B Transformation™. If the Enlightened Observer is not empowered with their True Self, a Client may just watch themselves be swamped and wounded deeply by the emotional pain.

IS CATHARSIS HEALING?

Catharsis is not healing. It overly activates our nervous system and programs us to over-identify with the energy and consciousness of the painful emotion. **Just because we can feel and express an emotion such as sadness or anger doesn't make it healing. What matters is HOW WE FEEL IT.** Assessing the type of energy and consciousness we use to feel it will determine if it either creates transformation and HVC or simply creates more LVC, anger and sadness and traps us in the dirt.

For instance, expressing anger through hitting something, as they do in some body centered psychotherapy programs, can actually reactivate and multiply the anger or sadness if clients (1) over-identify with the emotion by not having a strong enough Enlightened Observer and (2) they don't bring the HVC into the body, mind and energy system that once held the LVC. A metaphor for this is a garden that has been plowed and cleaned of all its weeds; if flowers are not planted, the weeds quickly return.

As we develop this art of self-transformation, we sometimes don't do it perfectly. Teaching ourselves and our clients how to assess if we are simply being cathartic or transforming the energy is important. As we advance our skill level, kindness and patience to our self is important. It takes time to be a solid Stage 5 and we are bound to re-grow some "weeds." When this happens, we can use the 5 Steps to move through the 3 Rings and replant our inner light. Me-B Guides learn how to track energy at its most subtle level so we can better guide clients until they can guide themselves.

It is important to master the difference between simply accessing an emotional issue and actually transforming the emotional issue so we don't invite too many weeds. **We must know what the difference is**

energetically,
cognitively and
based on sensations in the body.

To summarize, the following techniques help us master Stage 4, holding two places at the same time.

- Go slowly and be patient with yourself.
- Use the Explorer's Mind more often during the day and follows the 5-Steps so you move though the 3 Rings of Healing.
- Develop the ability to give love to yourself and to your child consciousness, especially when you feel hurt and not good enough.
- Feel negative emotions as energy/sensations passing through you.
- Get support more often (or see the client more often).
- Keep the frequency of the Enlightened Observer very high.
- Practice feeling safety and trust within your cells so it is based on an Internal versus external source.
- Master your fear of the Death of the Ego and void.
- Anchor into Core Being.

STAGE 5 – DEATH OF THE EGO

Often (60 percent) we can notice and take responsibility when our ego is activated; our Enlightened Observer is much stronger so we don't over-identify with emotional triggers.

Stage 5 is when we are experiencing the void where the ego's old self-identification is gone and the new one has not yet taken its place. The void feels difficult, like climbing Mt. Everest without oxygen. This is our first time in the void. We don't yet feel we belong or have found our true internal home.

Steps for Mastering Stage 5, Letting Go of Our Old Ego Identification of Self

- **Overcoming fear of the unknown**. We don't know who we will be once we let go of our old identification of self.
- **Void.** The place of the unknown. It is the time in-between the death of the old sense of self and before the birth of the new sense of self. We are in the metaphorical womb.
- Can **use the 6th level** of the field (divine compassion/bliss) **and the 7th level** of the field (divine mind) as personal support.
- Connect to **the 2nd and 4th levels of the field and** feel the negative emotions, and bring in the HVC of Core Being to transform them.
- Once these milestones are mastered, we naturally progress to the next stage of Me-B Transformation™— through the void at last!

STAGE 6 - THROUGH THE VOID

Most of the time (at least 70 percent) in all Me-B System. Often we are able to feel safe because we can anchor into our Core Being. When we feel the void/death of the ego/the unknown, most of the time we feel safe, even though it is painful. This is because we understand the ego death process will happen again and again before we die. We know it will always feel like Mt. Everest, and that is ok because we have already walked that path and know we can succeed. We can also confidently transform anger into personal strength and depression into wholeness. Using 2nd Chakra's gifts, we can more easily anchor into Core Being Dimension.

Even in times of challenge, the joy is stronger because joy becomes the new orientation and thus reflects within us and through us. Stage 6 clients and therapists become more connected to the greater wholeness of the benevolent universe. We still work our process but from a unique perspective. We know the universe is presenting this challenge because we are loved and supported, not because there is something wrong with us.

At this stage, it is important that we self-assess to see if this more positive orientation to life and ourselves presents equally in all three systems: mind, energy and body.

If it is not present in all three systems, the subconscious still has too strong an orientation toward the old ego structure and Me-B personal work should be directed toward addressing this need for deeper and comprehensive alignment.

SUPPORTING CLIENTS AT STAGE 6

If we are working with a client at this stage of awareness, we can usually see them less often. As a Me-B Guide, the ultimate goal is to work ourselves out of a job. All of us need regular support and "tune-ups." Some clients may want to take a brief break before choosing to move to the next level. This break can be an important integration period to help the client solidify their current consciousness level before they choose to continue. Of course, other clients may choose to enthusiastically pursue advancement toward their next personal growth phase with only a brief integration period. This too should be honored. The client always sets the pace for every stage.

Since we usually drop down to lower stages in times of stress or when we are uncovering deep dark shadow material, we can help clients understand that this is natural. When this happens, the ego can sabotage us if we are not careful.

At this stage, regulation of our energy field is a daily and moment-to-moment practice. It is a healthy habit we enjoy. As a result, our psychic and intuitive abilities naturally emerge and increase.

STAGE 7 – SELF-MIRRORING, LONELINESS MASTERED, JOY, BLISS and GRATITUDE ABOUND

80 percent of the time in all Me-B Systems synchronicity is a common experience. **All attachment** issues are healed and we finally feel **we belong and are at home within ourselves**. Joy and Bliss abound through most days. We feel safe in groups and new environments. Self-authority is strong even when we are alone; we are never lonely because we are anchored so deeply into ourselves. When someone negatively projects upon us, we know the truth of what is ours and what is not ours because we define who we are in the world. The statement, "no one can abandon me but myself" feels true. Existential fear is still difficult to transform but we are not over-identified with it. Our ego gets activated and we still live from our programmed personality. At this stage, we can use the 5th and 2nd chakras' gifts related to personal power, standing alone but strong and speaking our truth. We can easily connect to the multi-dimensional fabric.

When our identification of self is no longer linked to an external source or an internal defense or distortion, then we have graduated to this Stage of Me-B Transformation™. At Stage 7, we can easily feel our Core Being as a sensation in the body and when triggered into defense we can access our mind, energy and body systems to support ourselves.

163

Some key milestones must be passed before this internal self-knowledge is firm—we must l*earn to work with _external and internal self-mirroring_*. Our society in particular programs us to please others. We too often become dependent upon approval so that we feel ok about ourselves. Alternatively, we react by rebelling against needing approval. These are all symptoms of having attachment challenges. Yet as we orient our self to an internal source of approval, we can more easily become our own authority and self-mirror our Core Being back to ourselves. Too often we feel challenged when someone we respect doesn't respect us. We must learn to **feel our own authority on our own value as a sensation in our body**. This is an important milestone for Stage 7. At this stage, (1) *we become our own internal barometer of self-worth; and (2) we refuse to abandon our self even at times of stress, emotional challenge and adversity.*

The energy of our programmed personality might say, "but he/she abandoned me; I feel helpless, useless and alone." We can transform that energy and rejoice in the fact that, "the only one who can abandon me is me." We become *our own knight in shining armor and rescue ourselves.*

So Stage 7 is about discovering how to champion ourselves - not from an egoic personality level - but because we are beginning to live from our Core Being and can be humble in our humanness.

People with addiction issues have the most trouble with this milestone and might need much work on their positive Intention line. They might need to explore their subconscious internal saboteur that will prevent them from success.

Mastering the feeling of being completely alone and/or unloved is also important for mastering Stage 7. Feeling unloved and alone is hard. Yet if we don't face these feelings, they control us and limit our ability to make clear choices. From our Enlightened Observer, we can feel the pain—energetically and as sensations in the body—and then transform that pain and return to Core Being. If this is done at a deep enough level, we will be working on energetic ancestral wiring in the back of the heart chakra.

People who live from Stage 7 find themselves in deep gratitude even when times are difficult. We still have to work our process but we do so from a unique perspective: the perspective of knowing the truth of who we are. We may not always be as deeply connected to that truth in all three systems as we wish to be, but at this stage of consciousness we always "know" our Core Being and the blissful magic of the Multi-Dimensional Fabric of Interconnectedness.

The higher up in vibration we go, the deeper we need to go into our dark shadow. The process continues yet feels easier because we know who we are. Life becomes synchronistic.

Even when we feel overwhelmed with negative emotions, we are secure in the benevolence of the universe and trust we will eventually feel whole again and that there is a gift beneath the misery. As a result, joy and bliss in all Me-B Systems abound. We are adept at regulating our field so we can transform physical and emotional challenges and return to Core Being. Usually it is done easily. Occasionally it takes time. As a Me-B Guide, if we have a client at this level but we are not yet here, we might want to refer them to some- one else.

It is also important to make sure this reality is equally present in all three Me-B Systems. Sometimes the accomplishment of this stage is present only in the mind but we can't feel it and melt into it as an actual sensation in the body.

Our ability to feel the sensations of bliss and joy is directly proportional to our level of Consciousness. As we grow in our capacity to feel — throughout the day — positive sensations of trust, safety, joy and bliss, we are accessing higher and higher levels of consciousness.

At Stage 7, aspects of our shadow still emerge and much of our personal process work is to look deeper into bringing the shadow to the conscious level. Dream work, somatic experiencing and energetic work can be vital supports to us in this process.

Synchronicity becomes more noticeable. Our mind is less of a negative challenge and there are longer periods of time where there is "no mind." Awareness moves through us versus us thinking. No longer do we fear the future. We embrace the belief that the future will bring opportunity!

(A cautionary note: Many students of Me-B Transformation™ assess themselves at this stage when they aren't really living from Stage 7. It is very easy to be in Spiritual Junk Food and escape to higher frequencies and place our self at a higher stage than is authentic. If we are truly Stage 7, then even if extreme stress makes us drop down to Stage 4, we are still happy and able to love ourselves because we know that everything that happens is perfect and needed to happen and our only job is to find the lessons and gifts and not wish otherwise.)

STAGE 8 - NEGATIVE THOUGHTS ARE REPLACED BY POSITIVE ACTIONS, NO MIND

Most of us won't ever reach this stage. But if we do, once we are here, we notice that it is no longer "I" who creates and interacts. Instead, we become the vehicle that god moves through. Ironically, the beginning stages of Me-B Transformation™ are about connecting to Core Being, learning to be the "I" in the hurricane and discovering who we are. If we are to advance to Stage 8, we need to let go of our understanding of self and simply become a vessel for high vibrational consciousness to flow through. The ego and personality level die and life is synchronistic. What once was difficult is no longer a challenge. We manifest through intention very quickly.

Jill began to notice that she didn't have many thoughts to monitor during the day. When people gave her a compliment or complaint, she didn't feel attached to the person they were describing – although she knew they were talking about her.

When she walked into the store, down the street or to exercise in the local gym, people seemed to notice her as someone they wanted to be near. Jill too noticed this but once again, it did not have an impact on her because her ego didn't respond. In fact, she began to notice that her energy field used to react to all types of situations — both good and bad — but now there was almost a constant flow of Core Being and she was usually connected to the Multi-Dimensional Fabric.

Her old energetic defense strategies don't ignite anymore. Her mind became like a still lake and her body filled with tingles and flows.

STAGE 9 and STAGE 10: STAGES OF ENLIGHTENMENT

Wholeness is felt constantly and life becomes effortless. No ego, no mind. Any dense vibrations, thoughts, emotions, defenses run through and transform instantly because the HVC is so strong. Thought begets matter and synchronizes with everything within and around. We become all-knowing within the universal flow.

Boundaries don't exist because we are one with all.

Few people achieve this level of transformation. In fact, I don't know of any personally. This is because it is very hard to regulate at this level of awareness in all three systems, continuously and simultaneously. In fact, Jesus and Buddha and all the great masters that vibrated at this level have played extensive roles in helping assist the evolution of humanity. Is this an obtainable goal for us? Is it realistic or even attractive? Check the internal guidance and belief systems and remember that we are enough regardless of our current vibration/frequency and consciousness level. Let's follow our passion and live in the joy and grace that is always available to us — and then who knows what may happen!

Control of our external environment is not possible, yet as we get better at letting go, surrender is easier. There is a direct correlation between high consciousness and being highly skilled at being able to accept and surrender. As we follow our passion and live in the joy and grace that is always available to us, life becomes easier and more meaningful.

Sai Baba is said to vibrate near this frequency and consciousness. His Ashram is near Bangalore, India. Some call him a living avatar and believe that setting our intention to connect to his vibration (and others like him) will provide us with healings, wisdom and insight.

A personal note in relation to achieving this level of Me-B Transformation[TM]: I find that the happier I become, the more content I am and the less I crave for something different. The here and now feels complete and I am not sure if that means I will get to a higher stage more quickly or not at all. Yet, things are so OK now, Enlightenment seems less important. Yet, I am always up for fun and growth so, who knows what the future may bring?

CLARIFICATIONS

Being higher in the Me-B Stages doesn't mean we are better than another. We are all whole and one. It means we are directly working the gifts of the full rainbow of chakras. When we begin at Stage 1, we are working mostly the upper chakras and our intellectual capability. As we move higher in the stages we incarnate deeper into the physical body and bring HVC into the denser chakras that are lower in the body. So in the beginning, we are like the branches of a tree, beautiful and flowing but easily moved around by external forces. As we incarnate more deeply into the body, we become rooted within our Core Being and resilient to the external pressures and challenges. Our ability to create joy out of hardship grows, but again, this does not make us better than another.

Our skill level improves as we move though the Me-B Stages, which supports us in bringing in the HVC to create, manifest and facilitate health, abundance and happiness. This is not to say that those who operate predominantly at Stage One don't have happiness or wealth. But think of the potential as we grow and increase our awareness and our connection to Core Being!

Use this Self-Assessment as a guide to empower your Explorer's Mind so you know where you are and where you are going—and then decide where you want to be!

CONSCIOUSNESS SKILLS (Beginner through Advanced)

Check the skills that you have mastered

BEGINNER CHECKLIST OF SKILLS TO MASTER: Stages 1-2 of Me-B Transformation™

___cognitively, mental level only can identify negative defenses

___cognitively, mental level only can identify negative beliefs

___cognitively, mental level only can identify Core Distortions

___cognitively, mental level only can identify Emotions (Anger, Sadness, Fear, Anxiety...)

___cognitively, mental level only can identify energy systems/dimensions

___cognitively, mental level only can identify Core Being

___cognitively, mental level only can identify Enlightened Observer and adjust to support HVC

___cognitively, mental level only can identify Spiritual Junk Food and adjust to support HVC

___cognitively, mental level only can identify Intention and adjust to support HVC

___cognitively, mental level only can identify Transferences and adjust to support HVC

___cognitively, mental level only can identify when acting from Programmed Personality and adjust to support HVC

___cognitively, mental level only can identify Rhythm of Flow of Reality and adjust to support HVC ___cognitively, mental level only can identify Boundaries and are just beginning to adjust to support HVC

___cognitively, mental level only can identify Separated Self and are just beginning to support HVC

___cognitively, mental level only can identify Ego and are just beginning adjust to support HVC

___cognitively, mental level only can identify Relationship Coherency and are just beginning to support HVC

___cognitively, mental level only and are just beginning to identify "Who am I?"

___cognitively, mental level only and are just beginning to identify death of the old Ego

___cognitively, mental level only and are just beginning to be able to identify fear of the unknown

___cognitively, mental level only and are just beginning to identify safety and trust within

___cognitively, mental level only and just beginning to mirror our positive Core Being and sense of self back to us even when someone is judging us or when we have made a mistake

INTERMEDIATE CHECKLIST OF SKILLS TO MASTER: Stages 3-4 of Me-B Transformation™

___Visualizing, imagery, imagining energy systems/dimensions in the body and outer energy egg such as Auric Levels, Chakras, Manifest Energy Line, Core Being, Multi-Dimensional Fabric

___Visualizing, imagery, imagining where/what negative defenses are held in the body/energy systems

___Visualizing, imagery, imagining where negative beliefs are held in the body/energy systems

___Visualizing, imagery, imagining where Core Distortions are held in the body/energy systems

___Visualizing, imagery, imagining where/what emotions (Anger, Sadness, Fear, Anxiety…)are held in the body/energy systems

___Visualizing, imagery, imagining where Core Being is held in the body/energy systems

___Visualizing, imagery, imagining where Enlightened Observer is held in the body/energy systems

___Visualizing, imagery, imagining where Spiritual Junk Food is held in the body/energy systems and can adjust to HVC

___Visualizing, imagery, imagining where/what negative/positive intention is held in the body/energy systems and can adjust to HVC

___Visualizing, imagery, imagining where Transferences are held in the body/energy systems and can adjust to HVC

___Visualizing, imagery, imagining, assessing if we are acting from the programmed personality and where it is presenting in the body/energy systems

___Visualizing, imagery, imagining, assessing our Rhythm of Flow of Reality and what is happening and how to support it in the body/energy systems

__Visualizing, imagery, imagining where unhealthy/healthy boundaries are held in the body/energy systems and how to support it to foster HVC

__Visualizing, imagery, imagining where Separate Self is held in the body/energy systems and how to adjust it to create HVC

__Visualizing, imagery, imagining aspects of the Ego, where held in the body/energy systems and how to adjust to foster HVC

__Visualizing, imagery, imagining aspects of Relationship Coherency, where held in the body/energy systems and how to adjust to foster HVC

__Identification of the Death of the Ego Process is taking place by visualizing, imagery, imagining

__can identify "Who am I?" through visualizing, imagery, imagining

__can identify that we are in the void through visualizing, imagery, imagining

__can identify that death of the old Ego is taking place through visualizing, imagery, imagining

__can identify when fear of the unknown is taking place by visualizing, imagery, imagining and shifting to HVC

__can identify safety and trust within by visualizing, imagery, imagining

__can mirror our positive Core Being and sense of self back to self—even when someone is judging us or when we made a mistake—through visualizing, imagery, imagining

ADVANCED CHECKLIST OF SKILLS TO MASTER: Stages 5 and above of Me-B Transformation™ (Some Stage 4 people can feel energy too.)

These are more advanced skills because the physical level has the densest energy (and holds the subconscious) so it can be difficult to feel the sensation of HVC in the physical body. Also, most people are more accustomed to using the mental level of their field to think and it can initially feel intimidating to "think" and listen to the wisdom in the body. *(Note: Spiritual and Excel Character structures have difficulty feeling sensations/emotions in the body. Bringing in the energetic configuration of the positive aspects of Compassionate/Heart-Centered Character Structures can help. This means loosening the structure in the Auric field through imagery, intention, feeling and not letting our ego overwhelm us when we feel the challenging emotions. As we anchor into a sense of safety and Core Being within, everything is possible. Do the positive resourcing techniques to learn how to feel good sensations before you try to feel the challenging ones—create much white paint before touching the darkness...)*

__sensing, identifying and feeling the sensation of energy systems/dimensions in the body and outer energy egg such as Auric Levels, Chakras, Manifest Energy Line, Core Being, Multi-Dimensional Fabric

__sensing and feeling the sensation/energy of negative defenses in the body and energy systems and shifting to HVC

__sensing and feeling the sensation/energy of negative beliefs in the body and energy systems and shifting to HVC

__sensing and feeling the sensation/energy of Core Distortions in the body and energy systems and shifting to HVC

__sensing and feeling the sensation/energy of Emotions (Anger, Sadness, Fear, Anxiety...) in the body and energy systems and shifting to HVC

__sensing and feeling the sensation/energy of Core Being in the body and energy systems

__sensing and feeling the sensation/energy of Enlightened Observer in the body and energy systems

__sensing and feeling the sensation/energy of Spiritual Junk Food in the body and energy systems and can adjust to HVC

__sensing and feeling the sensation/energy of Intentions in the body and energy systems and can adjust to HVC

__sensing and feeling the sensation/energy of Transference in the body and energy systems and can adjust to HVC

__sensing and feeling the sensation/energy of Programmed Personality in the body and energy systems and can adjust to HVC

__sensing and feeling the sensation/energy of Rhythm of Flow of Reality in the body and energy systems and can adjust to HVC

__sensing and feeling the sensation/energy of Boundaries in the body and energy systems and can adjust to HVC.

__sensing and feeling the sensation/energy of Separate Self in the body and energy systems and can adjust to HVC

__sensing and feeling the sensation/energy of Ego in the body and energy systems and can adjust to HVC.

__sensing and feeling the sensation/energy of Relationship Coherency in the body and energy systems and can adjust to HVC

__Identification of the Death of the Ego Process is taking place by sensing and feeling the sensation/energy and bringing in HVC

__can identify "Who am I?" by sensing and feeling the sensation/energy and bringing in HVC

__can identify when we are in the void by sensing and feeling the sensation/energy and bringing in HVC

__can identify death of the old Ego is taking place by sensing and feeling the sensation/energy and bringing in HVC

__can identify fear of the unknown is taking place by sensing and feeling the sensation/energy and bringing in HVC

__can identify safety and trust within by sensing and feeling the sensation/energy and bringing in HVC

__can identify mirroring our positive Core Being and sense of self back to us even when someone is judging us or when we made a mistake by sensing and feeling the sensation/energy and bringing in HV

SELF-ASSESSMENT TEST: WHICH SET OF QUESTIONS BEST DESCRIBES YOU?

If you answer yes to **all** of the questions listed in a given stage, then you have mastered that stage of Me-B Transformation™. Since we move through the stages depending upon our level of stress, the highest stage we master can be considered our benchmark to return to more quickly. Although few achieve Stage 8 or above, as we set our sights high, and make our intention clear, who knows what may happen. Nevertheless, let's avoid Spiritual Junk Food by not pretending we are further along than we are. After all, our wholeness is ever-present regardless of the stage we are mastering—all we need to do is stay connected to it and remember!

Stage One: Answer Yes or No to the following questions. yes.

- Do you **over-identify** with the negative energy, images, beliefs and past as who you are? If so, write
- If you are *just* beginning the process of understanding at the mind level only your Core Distortions, negative images, beliefs, unhealthy defenses and past trauma (the outer two rings) write yes.
- If you feel your personality reflects **who you really are** write yes.
- If you are *just beginning* to understand, in your mind level only, that a Core Being exists—but you are not sure exactly what it is, write yes.
- Do you feel you are "**digging in the dirt**" and just beginning to uncover aspects of who you are? If so, write yes.
- If you are *just* beginning at the mind level only, understanding your ego, boundaries, separated self, relationship coherency, Spiritual Junk Food, and transferences, write yes.
- If you are *just* beginning at the mind level only, understanding the death of the ego, void, mirroring our positive sense of self back to us, and trust and safety within, write yes.

Stage Two: Answer Yes or No to the following questions.

- Can label aspects of our self in all three rings, mind level only. If so, write yes.
- At this point, is the concept that our body and energy system holds emotions, negative beliefs and Core Distortions **taken more on faith** and intellectual understanding versus direct day-to-day experiences. If so, write yes.
- Is the concept of Core Being only *slightly* more tangible to you now so that in the mind, you are **more able** to identify your own Core Being. If so, write yes.
- You try to use imagery, visualization and imagination to sense into the energy and body

systems, and you are not yet able to trust your ability to self assess what is happening energetically, write yes.

- You might not even trust that energy is real and that the body holds the past, because energetic and somatic awareness is still an intellectual understanding based on faith and not yet grounded in experience, write yes.

- You are developing your Enlightened Observer, only at the mind level now, write yes.

Stage 3: Answer Yes or No to the following Questions.

- You have a ***better understanding*** of who you are at the personality level and can experience the Explorer's Mind Components of Change in all Me-B System. If so, write yes.

- You now are ***somewhat able*** to feel or sense the energy of your Core Being in the Me-B System? You are moving past the stage of faking it to make it because energy and somatics are becoming a real first-hand experience. If so, write yes.

- You are now ***somewhat able*** to feel/sense the energy of your Core Distortions, defenses, negative images and beliefs (the personality level and components of change) in the Me-B System? If so, write yes.

- You now are ***somewhat able*** to sense the Core Being when experiencing some negative feelings/emotions/images/beliefs. This means your ego strength is more stable and linked to Core Being. This is still a new experience for you. If so, write yes.

- You feel you have already "dug in the metaphorical dirt" and can name your defenses, Core Distortions, transferences, boundaries, separated self, relationship coherency, public personality, Spiritual Junk Food…and you are **somewhat able** to look at moving beyond the personality level into experiencing higher vibrations such as Core Being and upper levels of the Auric Field, Manifest Energy Line, and Multi-Dimensional Fabric. As a result, you feel you are **somewhat able** to explore these higher vibrations so you can bring them into the "dirt" and darkness and energetically begin the transformation process. **It still feels diffi**cult and fairly new. If so, write yes.

- You are now ***often able*** to move back and forth between Core Distortion and Core Being. You can't yet hold two places at once – i.e., be in Core Distortion and Core Being at the same time. If so, write yes.

- Your Enlightened Observer is **getting stronger in all three Me-B System**, write yes.

- Your ego still over-identifies with the pain and you lose your Enlightened Observer if you stay in the pain too long but you can move back and forth between Core Being and Core Distortion. If so, write yes.

- You feel you are closer to knowing the answer to, "Who am I?" Transformation CHOICE POINT begins at this stage because we have a stronger Enlightened Observer and are somewhat connected to our Core Being. So diagnostically, Stage 3 is someone who can actually begin the process of transforming. They have dug in the dirt and found many of their defenses, Core Distortions, in authentic self and are looking at moving beyond the personality level into experiencing higher vibrations such as Core Being and the upper levels of the Auric Dimension. As a result they are beginning to explore these higher vibrations so they can bring them into the "dirt" and darkness and energetically begin the transformation process. If so, write yes.

Stage 4: Answer Yes or No to the following questions.

- You can cry and allow tears and sadness to be energy that runs through you—and know it is not the deeper truth of who you are. If so, write yes.
- You are *just beginning to learn how to feel safe* in all three Me-B Systems. This ability to have enough internal safety allows you to hold two places at once, Core Being and LVC. If so, write yes.
- Your Enlightened Observer has just gotten strong enough so you don't collapse into the pain and overwhelm of the material you want to transform. This helps you hold two places at once. If so, write yes.
- Holding two-places at once (Core Distortion/Core Being) in all three Me-B Systems is *a new experience for you* and you are still learning how to maintain it. If so, write yes.
- Being **somewhat** safe in the unknown is a new experience for you and you want to deepen this skill. If so, write yes.
- You are **just beginning** the process of mastering your fear of the death of the ego. If so, write yes.
- You have a **good knowledge** of your Core Being in all three Me-B Systems. If so, write yes.
- You can feel energetic darkness and painful ego and emotions as energy versus who you are. If so, write yes.
- You *know you are programmed to react to feelings and emotions* in all three Me-B Systems, and you *more often* question the reality that you experience, using the Explorer's Mind and your Enlightened Ob- server to help. If so, write yes.
- There is more of your Core Being to anchor into when the energy of darkness, emotional pain, defense, public personality and Core Distortion runs through you. If so, write yes.
- Because more of your Core Being is present, you feel somewhat confident in doing personal trauma work. You mostly believe you won't re-traumatize yourself. If so, write yes.

Stage Five: Death of the Ego Answer Yes or No to the following questions.

- *Often (60 percent)* we can notice and take responsibility when our ego is activated; if so, write yes.
- We are experiencing the void where the ego's old self-identification is gone and the new one has not yet been replaced. The void feels difficult, like climbing Mt. Everest without oxygen. This is our first time in the void, if so answer yes.
- You can use the Core Being dimension and the multi-level fabric dimension for support throughout the day. If so, write yes.
- You can use the Manifest Energy Line for support throughout the day. If so, write yes.
- We don't yet feel we belong or have found our true internal home, but feel very close to that goal, if so answer yes.
- We are making peace with our fear of the unknown, if so answer yes.
- Can use the 6th level of the field (divine compassion/bliss) and the 7th level of the field, divine mind as personal support. if so answer yes.
- Can connect to the 2nd and 4th levels of the field and feel the negative emotion(s) and bring in

the HVC of Core Being to transform them, if so answer yes.

Stage 6: Through the Void. Answer Yes or No to the following questions.

- Even in times of challenge, the joy is strong because the energetics and sensations of joy, bliss and gratitude have become the new orientation for who you are. If so, write yes.
- You are becoming more connected to the greater wholeness of the benevolent universe.
- **At least 70 percent in all Me-B Systems** we are able to feel safe because we can anchor into our Core Being. If so, write yes.
- We can transform anger into personal power and depression into wholeness. If so, yes.
- We can better mirror our Core Being to ourselves when attacked. If so, write yes.
- You remember well the many times you have felt the death of the old self and the void that it created before the new self was reborn. Being in the void and the unknown are places you have traveled. This experience is not yet effortless for you but it is much easier than before. If so, write yes.
- Using 2nd Chakra's gifts, you can more easily anchor into the Core Being Dimension. If so, write yes.
- Can transform anxiety and depression by using the energy of anger. If so, write yes.
- Can transform unhealthy fear to HVC. If so, write yes.
- When you feel lonely, you can become more anchored into your Core Being. If so, write yes.
- I still work my process but from a unique perspective. I know the universe is presenting this challenge to me because I am loved and supported, not because there is something wrong with me. If so, write yes.
- At this stage, regulation of our energy field is a daily and moment to moment practice. It is a healthy habit we enjoy. As a result, our psychic and intuitive abilities naturally emerge and increase. If so, write yes.

Stage Seven: Bliss and Joy Answer Yes or No to the following questions.

- I enjoy deep joy, bliss and gratitude on a regular basis, even when times are hard. The sensation of their energy and consciousness run through and around me 80 percent of the time. If so, write yes.
- Even when I am feeling overwhelmed with negative emotions, I am secure in the benevolence of the universe and trust that I will eventually feel whole again. If so, write yes.
- I am adept at regulating my field so I can transform physical and emotional challenges and return to the Core Being. Usually it is done easily. Occasionally it takes time. If so, write yes.
- Regulation of my field is a daily and moment-to-moment practice. It is a healthy habit I enjoy. As a result, my psychic and intuitive abilities naturally emerge and increase. If so, write yes.
- Aspects of my dark and golden shadow still emerge and much of my personal process work is looking deeper into bringing the shadow to the conscious level. If so, write yes.
- I am working with archetypical and ancestral energies and fewer developmental issues emerge. Never does a new developmental issue emerge that I hadn't already partially healed. If so, write yes.
- Synchronicity is more noticeable. My mind is less of a negative challenge and there are longer

periods of time where there is "no mind." Awareness moves through me versus thinking. If so, write yes.

- No longer do I fear the future. I embrace the belief that the future brings opportunity even in the form of hardship! If so, write yes.

- I enjoy deep gratitude on a regular basis, even when times are hard. If so, write yes.

- I still work my process but from a unique perspective. I know the universe is presenting this challenge to me because I am loved and supported, not because there is something wrong with me.

- I know the truth of who I am but am not always as deeply connected to that truth in all three Me-B Systems at the same time. But I do "know" my divinity. If so, write yes.

- Even when I am feeling overwhelmed with negative emotions, I am secure in the benevolence of the universe and trust that I will eventually feel whole again. If so, write yes.

- I am adept at regulating my field so I can transform physical and emotional challenges and return to the core divine being. Usually it is done easily. Occasionally it takes time. If so, write yes.

- Regulation of my field is a daily and moment-to-moment practice. It is a healthy habit I enjoy. As a result, my psychic and intuitive abilities naturally emerge and increase. If so, write yes.

- Aspects of my dark and golden shadow still emerge and much of my personal process work is looking deeper into bringing the shadow to the conscious level. If so, write yes.

- I am working with archetypical and ancestral energies and fewer developmental issues emerge. Never does a new developmental issue emerge that I hadn't already partially healed. If so, write yes.

- Synchronicity is more noticeable. My mind is less of a negative challenge and there are longer periods of time where there is "no mind." Awareness moves through me versus thinking. If so, write yes.

- No longer do I fear the future. I embrace the belief that the future brings opportunity even in the form of hardship! If so, write yes.

Stage Eight: Answer Yes or No to the following questions.

- 90 % of the time, life is synchronistic.
- It is no longer "I" that creates and interacts. Instead, I am becoming the vehicle that the divine moves through. My personality is gone. I live in effortless intention.
- I used to try to discover who I am. I learned how to be the "I" in the hurricane. Now I am letting go of my understanding of self and am only a simple vessel for high vibrational consciousness to flow through.

REVIEW QUESTIONS

1. Why does it empower us to know what Stage of Me-B Transformation™ we are currently in?
2. In terms of what has been taught so far, what can you do to move to a higher Stage of Me-B Transformation™? Write out your personal map of where you are today, where you want to be, and how you can support yourself to get there.
3. How can you better deal with the challenges around: death of ego, void, feeling lonely, being

abandoned by someone you love, attachment issues, and becoming the positive "good enough" parental authority on your self-esteem/value?

4. What can you do to help yourself feel subconscious challenging emotions on levels 2 and 4 and access the wisdom and HVC of levels 6 and 7 of the Auric Field?

5. The most important Me-B Skills for moving to higher stages of consciousness are: (1) positive intention, (2) Enlightened Observer, and (3) anchoring into Core Being (feeling the sensation/energy/consciousness of Core Being). What can you do for yourself to strengthen these skills? What do you find most easy/hard about these skills? Write out a short-term/long-term plan.

6. Does it make us better than another if we test higher in the Me-B Stages? Explain why or why not.

CHAPTER 13

ENERGETIC CONFIGURATIONS OF Me-B TRANSFORMATIONTM

Rule our lives! Clear the pain of the past by lovingly meeting the pain in the moment with wisdom and the energy of light.

Throughout the Me-B Transformation[TM] process, we learn how to track, feel, see, assess, and support energetic shifts in our self and our clients. Energy becomes a tangible reality that we interact with and regulate through- out our day. We learn how to accept the gifts of higher consciousness that the various dimensions bring.

Pain, Core Distortions, ego, and our programmed personality **only exist** in the Auric Dimension, the Physical Dimension, and Manifest Energy. Every other energetic dimension has only HVC. Through Me-B Transformation[TM] we can become more skillful at bringing these higher frequencies into the physical body and maintaining HVC longer. We wish there was a magic bullet, but it takes continuous focus throughout the day to remember to transform the lower frequencies into HVC.

In this chapter, we will review:

- The **Auric Dimension**, including chakras, the central channel, and the 7 levels of the field (Brennan, Barbara; Hands of Light, 1987)
- The **Chinese Energy Meridians**, including the 12 meridians and the eight extra meridians. These are part of the Auric Dimension.
- The **Core Being Dimension** (Brennan, Barbara Hands of Light, 1987)
- Manifest Energy and its Intention Line — also named Hara Dimension (Brennan, Barbara; Hands of Light, 1987)
- The Multi-Dimensional Fabric of Interconnectedness, which includes Centered Oneness. It also includes interstellar galaxies/universes and the **Star Child Frequencies**.

BASIC PRINCIPLES OF ENERGY HEALTH

On one level, energetic health can be easily explained in terms of overcharge, undercharge, or fragmentation. When beginning this work, simply noticing where in our bodies there is an overcharge or undercharge is a great start. We learn to move our awareness through the body and energy system and notice where we feel heavy (overcharged) or too light and weak (undercharged). In the next chapter, we practice doing this in our chakra system, but we can also do this throughout our body, in our Auric field, and even in our organs and meridians.

As we become more comfortable tracking and assessing our own energy field, we are also better able to notice what is happening with our loved one's/client's field. Because our energy system provides a blueprint for what happens in our bodies on the physical level, an undercharge or overcharge provides us with information about our health, personality, emotions and physiology.

Scan the body and trace the energy meridians (listed in the appendix) and/or scan the body from head to toe and assess if the energy is over- or undercharged or balanced. If we think an area is undercharged, we can in- crease the charge by placing our hand and awareness into the area to build the energy. If an area is over- charged, we place our awareness and hand on the area and invite the energy to move out of the area and spread to places that are undercharged. Remember, it is intention that moves energy. As we set our intention as to how we want the energy to move, and then connect to an area, the energy responds.

If we do this using the HVC of our Enlightened Observer, we raise our vibration and balance our Auric field. Energy has intelligence. As we learn to follow it better, we will notice how it will often balance on its own. If it doesn't balance, there may be a negative intention, defense, or Core Distortion in the way. Practice and patience is needed as you develop your energy skills.

Grounding Exercise

As we advance through the Me-B Stages, we also incarnate deeper into our physical body, bringing HVC into our cells. Grounding into our body— especially for the Spiritual personality type—can be a life challenge. The following Oak Tree exercise is a quick and easy method for grounding. (See also the Body Connecting Sequence for "release down" to help program grounding into your cells and energy system.)

OAK TREE

This Chi Kung energy grounding exercise can be used throughout the day to bring you back into your body and create the consciousness of strength. It can be done with and without the support of a tree.

Depending upon where you live, if possible, begin to learn this exercise by actually "hugging a tree." (If you don't have a tree, skip below to Step 1.) Wrap your arms around the tree as far as they will go and press the front of your body/legs against it. Oak trees are good, but any tree in your area can work. Then follow the steps below.

- **STEP 1:**
  Stand as tall as possible. Imagine your spine elongated, your neck in a neutral position so that your chin is tucked in, and your cervical vertebrae long and stacked squarely in the center of your shoulders (not tipped forward).
  Feel your head/neck in the middle of your body, squared over your hips, straight like the upper floors of a tall building. Arms are chest-high, making an open circle as if hugging a tree. Knees are soft and slightly bent.
- **STEP 2:**
  Use breath and awareness together as you imagine, visualize, feel, and sense the energy and grounded strength of a tree against the front of your body.
- **STEP 3:**
  Invite the energy of the visualized tree to penetrate and melt into your cells, filling you up as it expands toward your back. Let the energy fill your spinal cord and each of the cells in your vertebrae, the back of the coccyx, the sacrum and back of the legs, the hamstrings, and the calf muscles. Let the energy fill you up front/back, top/bottom, and left/right.
- **STEP 4:**

Now, feel your feet on the ground. Feel, sense, imagine, and visualize the grounded strong energy of the tree filling your legs. Allow that energy to extend through your legs, through the bottoms of your feet, and into the center of the Earth. Let your energy and the Earth energy meet and mix and become one. Feel, sense, and visualize the oneness of the energy throughout your whole body, your trunk, your neck, and your arms.

- **STEP 5:**
  Allow this energy to fill you and your Manifest Energy Line. Set your intention to allow it to stay with you and support you throughout the day!

Steps to Eliminate Energetic Over Charging

An overcharge or energy block in its most severe form can signify physical illness such as a tumor. Not all areas that are overcharged develop into tumors or cancer, but if they remain overcharged long enough, emotional or physical illness can develop.

This book is devoted to outlining numerous methods to eliminate energetic weakness and/or energy congestion. This greatly reduces the chance of ill health. (Remember, energy is consciousness, so energy under/over charge or fragmentation reduces HVC.)

To keep our understanding of the process simple and easy, remember the following:

- **CONSCIOUSNESS** <u>creates</u> **energy;**
- **INTENTION** <u>moves</u> **energy.**

All day long, whether we believe in energy or not, we are creating and moving energy through our conconsciousness and our intention. Me-B Transformation™ awakens us to the how's, why's and when's of our creations. It also provides us with tools to shift our mind, beliefs, emotions, and energy system so that unwanted creations can be eliminated or reduced.

The following are examples of negative emotions that become energetically overcharged when we hold on to them:

- arrogance
- violence
- mania
- anger
- rage
- hyperactivity
- attention deficit disorder
- lack of restraint
- controlling and manipulating
- abusive behavior
- narcissism
- borderline personality disorder
- engagement in risky behavior

Typical physical sensations of overcharge in the body are pain, texture, roughness, prickliness, bursting, heaviness, and too much heat. If we want **to decrease the charge** in a part of our body, we move our mind and/or hand over the area, and using the HVC of our Enlightened Observer, intend the energy to spread and dissipate.

Discharging Anger

Later in the book, we explore various methods to discharge anger and work with depression and turn it into personal power and strength. However, as a beginning step, we can invite our client or ourselves to touch an area of the body that is holding anger, such as the pelvis, heart, or diaphragm. (These are typical locations of anger. Some people think anger is in the head, and it is. But it is best to focus on a different location than the head when doing this exercise because it is too easy to overcharge the head, which can result in a headache or dissociation from the body.)

Then, use the mind and hand to discharge the anger by: (1) connecting to the area deeply, and (2) using our Enlightened Observer and intention, moving our hand over the area in a broom-like motion, and asking the energy to dissipate. This is a basic, but powerful technique.

If the overcharge doesn't dissipate, usually it is because: a part of us does not want to move forward there is wisdom we need to hear and the energetic congestion won't shift until we listen to it a deeper **Core Distortion** is holding the energy in place so we need to investigate further, and/or there is a trapped emotion we must feel in order for it to transform.

Note: We have already outlined various exercises to transform the energy of **Core Distortions**. For instance, we discussed the process of locating where the distortion is held in our body, finding the negative belief, and bringing in the frequency of the opposite positive belief. Remember to keep practicing this skill.

Undercharge or Fragmentation of Energy

In an undercharged area, we may feel:

- sadness self-hate grief
- worthlessness hopelessness
- lack of confidence dependency depression schizophrenia
- Dissociative Identity Disorder (DID)
- attachment disorder
- Sensations of undercharge or fragmentation include: no sensations, confusion, dissociation, and feeling ungrounded or spacey.

If we want **to increase the charge** in one part of our body or energy system, we can touch it (or just focus on it with our mind) and, using the HVC of our Enlightened Observer, intend the energy to build there. We can teach our clients to connect to their bodies and/or an aspect of their energy system so they can learn to increase or decrease the charge.

Meridians

Some of the most commonly known energetic structures are the 12 Energy Meridians and the Eight Extra Meridians used in Chi Kung and acupuncture. Chi Kung is an ancient Taoist practice. There are inner and outer Chi Kung practices that support both physical and emotional health.

Acupuncture uses specific energy points within meridians to activate and balance energy within the body. The 12 main meridians are interlinked and circulate energy throughout the body. The main meridians correspond to organ systems: Liver, Spleen, Stomach, Heart, Triple Heater, Kidneys, Gall Bladder, Bladder, Heart Constrictor, Lung, Large Intestine, and Small Intestine.

We can activate our own meridians by tracing the meridian with our finger (or mind) using our Enlightened Observer. Or, we can follow an inner or outer Chi Kung practice. Receiving acupuncture and learning Chi Kung can strengthen and balance us.

The Micro-Cosmic orbit, an Inner Chi Kung practice, is effective **for balancing our ability to move out of the dynamics of "pushing through life" or "collapsing into our emotions."** This is because the practice balances the back and front of our chakras. The back of our energy system holds the energy of will, and the front of our energy system charges the energy of emotion. We tend to overuse and push energy through the back of our chakras if we are in too much will. If we get easily overwhelmed and are too sensitive, we run too much energy through the front of our chakras. For instance, when we are collapsed into grief, fear, sadness, and stress, if we bring more energy toward our back, we can re-balance and find the "will" to proceed forward.

Specifically, the **Central Channel** runs from the heavens, through the crown chakra, then down the center of the body, and out the perineum into the Earth. The front and back chakras connect into it. If the Central Channel is too far forward, it will mean collapsing into our feelings—and if it is too far back, we push through life.

The following Chi Kung exercise helps us balance our will and our emotions so that we interact more from our internal center or Core Being. As indicated earlier, *will is energetically governed by our back chakras, and emotions are ruled by the front chakras.*

Because physical, energetic, and emotional distortions often present as an imbalance of will and emotion, personal power can come from balancing will and emotion in all aspects of our life. The essential underlying ingredient to achieve this goal is trust. Can we trust enough to let go and not push or collapse into life's difficulties? Practice the following exercise to support balancing will and emotion.

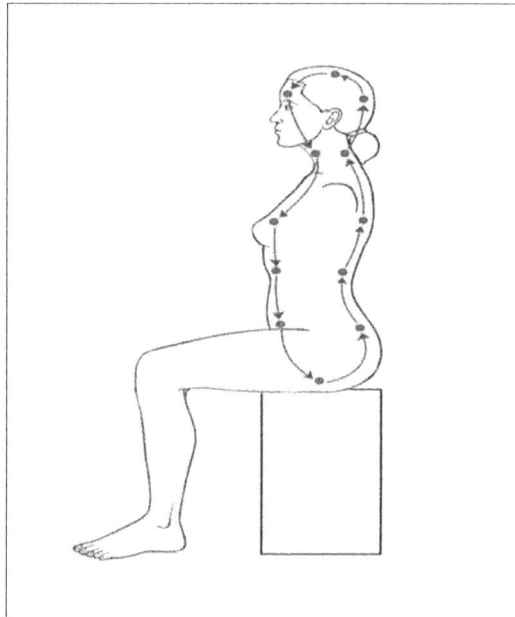

Micro-Cosmic Orbit Exercise

The Micro-Cosmic Orbit is an Inner Chi Kung exercise, and one of the more powerful foundational exercises taught in Chi Kung. This is my revised version of the exercise. It involves the Conception Meridian that runs down the front of the body and the Governor Meridian that runs up the spine. (See above diagram.) During this process, keep your **Explorer's Mind** available; use your **Enlightened Observer**; and be curious in a fun and playful manner.

1. Begin by bringing your conscious awareness to the center of your breastbone, a few inches below the Adam's Apple. To assist you in the beginning, trace the pathway down with your fingers.

2. Using the Enlightened Observer, sink in deep with awareness and energy from your fingers at the breastbone site. Breathe. Feel into the meridian. See it. Feel it. Sense it. Imagine it.

3. Now trace your awareness down a few inches, to the center of your solar plexus area. Once again, sink in deeply and breathe. Notice it. Where might this area be under or overcharged? Notice if there are any emotional issues you might want to collect information about for later work. Do you think there might be breaks in the line? See it. Feel it. Sense it. Imagine it using the Enlightened Observer and the Explorer's Mind.

4. Continue connecting deeply, with the intention for the energy to move downward through the meridian, to the perineum, and up the back. In the beginning, move only a few inches at a time and sink in deeply. Notice what you notice. Always energetically sink in deeply and open to feeling sensations such as flows, tingles, pain, roughness, smoothness, etc. Discount nothing. Notice everything and be curious about what is happening. A suggested sequence to follow is outlined next.

   Cautionary note: In the beginning, people tend to "will" the movement of energy. This sets up an unhealthy energetic agenda that movement is better than no movement. Instead, invite the energy to move using your Enlightened Observer, breath, and awareness as you trust and surrender into the moment.

Begin at the breastbone to solar plexus, travel down to the navel, then to the top of the pubic bone, perineum, and coccyx. Then follow each vertebra upward, including the back of the neck. Then follow the curve up the back of the head, over the head, and then back down the front. Keep your tongue at the roof of your mouth to facilitate connection as the energy travels through the meridians from the back of the body to the front.

Eventually you may notice the energy moving on its own, and you will just support the movement with focused presence. In areas of congestion, the energy will move more slowly, and you might want to investigate what emotional images or beliefs need support. In other areas, the energy may feel thin and undercharged.

5. Once you feel confident in the exercise, feel free to vary it. Begin by doing it on the body against the skin and then expand it to 2 inches off the body. Then try it 6 inches, 1 foot, 2 feet and 3 feet off the body.

   For some people, it will be much easier to imagine the process off the body than against the skin. Why do you think this might be true or false for you? How does you answer relate to your energetic gifts or challenges?

   Because some of us enjoy the upper vibrational frequencies and can get bogged down in the lower frequency of Earth, working off the body is easier. If this is true for you, it means that your energetic gifts are being able to connect to spirit more easily and that your mind will be a strong support to access high vibrations.

   If you find it easier to move the Micro-Cosmic Orbit on the body, most likely your energetic gifts will be to work with more grounded energy and to work with your physical body. Ideally, our intention is to have the micro- cosmic orbit flow smoothly whether we imagine it on or off the body.

   You can learn how to shift dense areas to fill in undercharged areas. It is also important to notice any negative Core Distortions within you as you do this exercise so they can be diluted and transformed. A Core Distortion is a false image or belief about our self or others that interferes with love, support, and compassion. Our energy system and bodies hold negative beliefs/images. The Micro-Cosmic Orbit can help us identify, clear, and transform them.

Activation of Meridian Systems

Simply tracing the energy meridians with our hand and/or mind using our **Enlightened Observer** can activate them into balance if positive intention is used. We can scan the body and connect to the various organs and meridians. If during the scan we notice a meridian or organ out of alignment, or we sense a particular emotion, we can trace the meridian with our mind and/or fingers to increase an undercharged area or decrease an area that is overcharged.

If we want to increase the charge on one part of the meridian, we can touch it with our finger (or just focus on it with our mind) and intend the energy to build there. If we want to decrease the charge, we move our mind and/or finger over it and intend the energy to spread and dissipate.

Learning how to sense under- or overcharge can take patience and practice. Working with a Me-B Guide or someone who can confirm our own assessment and help refine your skills is helpful. The book *Energy Medicine* by Donna Eden is a great resource for working meridians, and I highly recommend it.

EXERCISE FOR CLEARING ORGANS

Using Color, Emotions, Healing Sounds, Coupling Organ

Lung: white, grief/purity; sssssss; nose
Kidneys: blue/black; fear/courage; HOOOOOO; ears
Liver: green, anger/personal power; shhh; eyes
Heart: red, anxiety/joy; Haaaawwww; tongue
Spleen/pancreas: yellow; worry/anxiety
you are not enough/you are whole, Whhhhooooo; Mouth
Triple Heater: red, HEEEEEE, no specific organ,

In Chi Kung, there are depleting and beneficial emotions attached to the organs. I have listed them here as a guideline of what you may find in the organ. This is a slightly revised version of Chi Kung's Healing Sounds exercise.

LUNG—WHITE, GRIEF/PURITY; SSSSS: NOSE:

Using your **Enlightened Observer** and **Explorer's Mind**, bring your conscious awareness to your lungs and place your hand on your chest while you breathe deeply 3 times. Let the energy of your hands sink in and energetically connect to the organ. Notice what you notice. Do you sense dense sensations, blocks, or undercharge? What emotions/beliefs are there? Use the PIN wheel technique to collect wisdom. Vibrate the sound "SSSSSSSSS" and the color white with the intention of clearing. Let the imbalanced energy leave through the nose. Feel/ imagine/ intend that the sound and color vibrate in the organ and exit through the nose. Repeat 3-9 times.

When complete, reconnect to the organ and reassess. If it is not clear, make a note to return to that area later so you can collect any information about the LVC and what is needed for it to clear.

KIDNEYS—BLUE/BLACK; FEAR/COURAGE; HOOOOOO; EARS:

Bring your conscious awareness to your kidneys and place your hands on each kidney on your back, just below the ribs. Let the energy of your hands sink in and energetically connect to the organ. Breathe deeply 3 times.

Notice what you notice. Do you sense dense sensations, blocks, or undercharge? What emotions/beliefs are there? Use the PIN wheel technique to collect wisdom. Now, vibrate the sound "HOOOOOOOOOOO" and the color blue-black with the intention of clearing and the imbalanced energy leaving through the ears. Feel/ imagine/ intend that the sound and color vibrate in the organ and exit through the ears. Repeat 3-9 times.

When complete, reconnect to the organ and reassess. If it is not clear, make a note to return to that area later so you can collect any information about the LVC and what is needed for it to clear.

LIVER—GREEN, ANGER/PERSONAL POWER; SHHH; EYES:

Bring your conscious awareness to your liver on the right side of the front of your mid-chest area and place your hands on it while you breathe deeply 3 times. Let the energy of your hands sink in and energetically connect to the organ. Notice what you notice. Do you sense dense sensations, blocks, or undercharge? What emotions/beliefs are there? Use the PIN wheel technique to collect wisdom. Remaining in deep contact with the area, vibrate the sound "SShhhh" and the color green with the intention of clearing and the imbalanced energy leaving through your open eyes. Feel/imagine/intend that the sound and color vibrate in the organ and exit through the open eyes. Repeat 3-9 times. When complete, reconnect to the organ and reassess. If it is not clear, make a note to return to that area later so you can collect any information about the LVC and what is needed for it to clear.

HEART—RED, ANXIETY/JOY; HAAAAWW; TONGUE:

Bring your conscious awareness to your heart on the left side of the front of your upper chest area and place your hands on it while your breath deeply 3 times. Let the energy of your hands sink in and energetically connect to the organ. Notice what you notice. Do you sense dense sensations, blocks, or undercharge? What emotions/beliefs are there? Use the PIN wheel technique to collect wisdom. Remaining in deep contact with the area, vibrate the sound "Haaaaww" and the color red with the intention of clearing and the imbalanced energy leaving through your tongue. Feel/imagine/intend that the sound and color vibrate in the organ and exit through the tongue. Repeat 3-9 times. When complete, reconnect to the organ and reassess. If it is not clear, make a note to return to that area later so you can collect any information about the LVC and what is needed for it to clear.

SPLEEN/PANCREAS—YELLOW; WORRY/ANXIETY YOU ARE NOT ENOUGH/YOU ARE WHOLE, WHHHHOOOOO; MOUTH:

Bring your conscious awareness to your spleen/pancreas area on the left side of the front of your body, under the ribs. Place your hands on this area while you breathe deeply 3 times. Let the energy of your hands sink in and energetically connect to the organs. Notice what you notice. Do you sense dense sensations, blocks, or undercharge? What emotions/beliefs are there? Use the PIN wheel technique to collect wisdom. Remaining in deep contact with the area, vibrate the sound "whhhooo" and the color yellow with the intention of clearing and the imbalanced energy leaving through your mouth. Feel/imagine/intend that the sound and color vibrate in the organ and exit through the mouth. Repeat 3-9 times. When complete, reconnect to the organ and re- assess. If it is not clear, make a note to return to that area later so you can collect any information about the LVC and what is needed for it to clear.

TRIPLE HEATER: RED, HEEEEEE, NO SPECIFIC ORGAN:

Bring your conscious awareness to your whole body and breathe deeply 3 times. Notice what you notice. Do you sense dense sensations, blocks, or undercharge? What emotions/beliefs come into your awareness? Use the PIN wheel technique to collect wisdom. Remaining in deep contact with your body, vibrate the sound "Heeeeee" and the color red with the intention of clearing and the imbalanced energy leaving. Feel/imagine/intend that the sound and color vibrate in your body. Repeat 3-9 times. When complete, reconnect to your body and reassess. If it is not clear, make a note to return to it later so you can collect any information about the LVC and what is needed for it to clear.

As you trace a meridian or connect to an organ, you can feel what distortion is being held there. Always use the intention of bringing the highest positive vibration into the area. **Intention** moves energy. If you are new at this, you must trust that the energy is moving based on your intention in the moment. As you complete this book, you will gradually gain experience and increase your skills from Level I to Level III, advanced.

Knowledge creates power. Practice self-assessing your entire Auric energy system, even if you are just learning how to shift it. Always be the expert on your own system. Use doctors, therapist, healers, naturopaths, acupuncturists, and others as support and as a supplement to our own inner knowing. *No one can be the expert on us, except us. This is paramount to success in this challenging reality.*

If, at anytime, an area doesn't shift, explore what emotion or negative belief might be held there. There have been times when it took over a year (or more) for an area to release the LVC and completely reorganize to HVC. ***Needing an area to shift to feel whole is a negative belief in itself. Remember that we are never done. Finding wholeness even in discomfort is vital to success and joy in life.*** This is our challenge and our mission. Using the **Explorer's Mind** to assist us in examining an area can help—but sometimes, the answer just reveals itself at an unexpected moment.

The Unexpected Moment

I was sure I had done all the work I needed to do on my issues related to my parents and my developmental trauma. However, I kept noticing that the energy on my back (governor meridian) was very slow and static. It always was more difficult to shift the energy on my back versus the front.

As I lay in my room watching a sad movie, I spontaneously had a flashback to a scene when I was a child. I noticed how I couldn't remember my mom holding me, not ever. As I got older, the only hugs I got were when she needed something from me—my energy, my essence, my love.

Sobbing overwhelmed me, and a wave of energy on my back began to expand. The deeper my sobs, the more strongly it expanded. My **Enlightened Observer** remained present, even welcoming the next wave to move through me. I didn't need to hold onto this pain anymore.

Now, are these memories absolutely true? Who cares! What matters is that I successfully connected to the energy in the moment, released the negative perceptions of the past, and welcomed wholeness and happiness

---

AURIC DIMENSION

In Me-B TransformationTM we work with 5 Dimensions. They are as follows:

- the Physical Dimension (our body)
- the Auric Dimension
- the Manifest Energy (intention toward manifestation)
- the Core Being Dimension (our Core Being), and
- the Multi-dimensional Fabric of Interconnectedness (includes Interstellar Energies, Star Child, and Centered Oneness Frequencies)

The lower frequencies in the **Auric Dimension** hold the energy of our programmed personality and **Core Distortions**. *This is where most transformational work is done, because the other energetic dimensions hold predominantly HVC.* Within the **Auric Dimension,** there are three main energy structures:

1. The Central Channel
2. The Chakras
3. The Levels of the Field that make up our outer energy egg

Front Chakras Rule Emotion
Back Chakras Rule Will

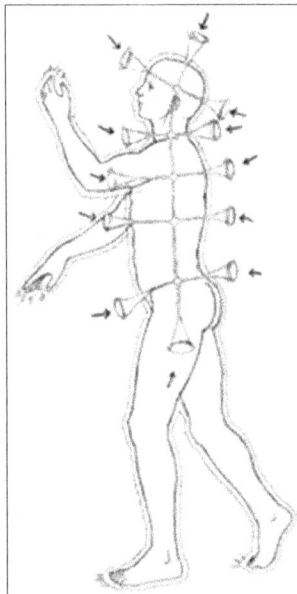

Central Channel runs through the center of the body

TIPS IN ENERGY WORK

1. Intention and surrendering to the highest good are what move energy. We connect deeply to ourselves and trust.
2. In the area of the body where we are working, we move our mind and hands and connect our breath and awareness deep inside the body.

   Connect as deeply with our awareness, hands, and breath as we can or need to in order to be in contact with any energy distortion. Do not force the connection. Melt gently in, like butter on a grill.
3. The deeper the connection, the more strongly the energy flows.

   Though we can use physical touch with our hands, we don't have to—because it is intention and energetic connection that are needed for a strong flow. We do need deep contact with ourselves.
4. Invite the cells, tissues, muscles, and bones to open and receive.

   Just ask them. They have intelligence; trust they can do the work. Then, assess and notice if a negative defense is preventing the higher frequencies from entering. If a defense enters, there are two choices. First, you can focus on where the defense is not presenting. Support the areas that want to receive, and let that good energy spread to areas of low or no

SOME COMMON MISTAKES TO AVOID

5. Don't will the energy, or use mostly just the back chakras or the front of the 6th to bring in or move energy. Intention and surrendering to the highest good is what en- gages energy.

6. Don't focus too hard or create an agenda of what "should" happen. If we NEED a shift, this very feeling of "need" itself distorts the energy. If we have positive intention and trust, and remain curious about what is happening instead of insisting on what we WANT to MAKE happen, the energy aligns to the highest good. We must be in the moment and track what IS happening.

7. Don't just PULL energy in from the top or just the bottom of our body—work multi-dimensionally and receive the energy in front/back, top/bottom, and left/right.

Central Channel

One main component of the Auric Dimension is the **Central Channel**. The Central Channel runs like a hollow pipe in the center of the body, from the top of the head and out the perineum where the root chakra is located. All chakras, front and back, hook into the Central Channel as shown in the diagram above. The chakras' primary job is to bring in HVC and energy to feed and fill the Central Channel, which pumps energy throughout the center of the body.

As we strengthen our energetic and biological consciousness container, the Central Channel widens. A strong Central Channel will be at least two inches in diameter. During Me-B Sessions, it might get as wide as six inches in diameter.

In the Auric Field, the emotional centers are in the front of the body, and the will centers are in the back. If the Central Channel is too far forward, we become overly emotional. If it is too far backward, we are pushing and overusing will. Ideally, the Central Channel should be equally balanced in front as well as in back. This balances our will centers (back chakras) and our emotional centers (front chakras). With will and emotion balanced, there is more energy to move out of our **Core Distortions**, and we can more easily connect to the wholeness of our **Core Being**.

BALANCE/CHARGE CENTRAL CHANNEL

During stress, illness, or emotional chaos, we can practice realigning **our Central Channel**. If it is too far forward, we become overcharged with emotions, if too far back, we become distant or pushy. Align it in the center, and live from balance.

STEP 1:

Engaging your **Explorer's Mind** and **Enlightened Observer**, bring your awareness to the top of the crown chakra. Allow energy to come in through the crown chakra and move down through the center of the head.

Imagine the crown chakra energetically feeding the Central Channel.

STEP 2:

Split your awareness between the front and back of the 6th chakra, and 3rd Eye. Allow energy to come in through both the front and back at the same time and energetically feed the Central Channel. If this is too hard, first allow the energy to come in the front, and then allow it to come in through the back. It can be more difficult to allow energy in through our back chakras, so be kind to yourself and patient. This is because in our fast-paced life, we can push ourselves to move forward to the next task instead of filling and expanding our field by balancing our central channel.

Imagine how wide the Central Channel is from the crown down to the sixth chakra. Let the energy fill and widen it slightly. Use all of your senses, and focus only on feeling good sensations and intending high vibrational consciousness to come in. If you sense a **Core Distortion** or **Negative Belief**, ignore it and focus on cultivating only good sensations and high vibrations. *Melt into the positive sensations* *and let them expand and fill areas of low or no sensation. Let the good sensations fill the Central Channel just as sand fills an empty glass. As the energy fills up the Central Channel, invite the channel to widen and fill up even more.*

STEP 3:

Continue working through all the chakras. Next is the throat chakra. Once again, receive energy in through the front and back, filling the Central Channel. Use all of your senses and focus only on feeling good sensations. If you sense a **Core Distortion** or **Negative Belief,** ignore it and focus on building only good sensations and high vibrations. Then move to the 4th chakra, front and back, and repeat the process. Focus on the 3rd chakra, solar plexus, front and back, and the 2nd chakra, pelvic center, front and back.

STEP 4:

Now receive energy from the Earth through the root chakra and let it fill and expand the connection between the root and the 2nd chakra.

STEP 5:

Lastly, allow your awareness/breath to sense into the Central Channel from the root chakra upward. As you sense, notice any areas where the Central Channel may narrow or seem to collapse. Also notice if it is equally balanced in the front and the back. Using breath, awareness, and intention, invite the Central Channel to balance in the middle and to widen where it narrows or collapses. Do not judge one way of being better than the other. We invite balance, but do not think we are less than if the energy and consciousness are not ready to expand.

STEP 6:

Draw a picture of your Central Channel and note which areas might need extra support. Usually the connection between the root and the 2nd, the 3rd chakra, diaphragm, and throat tend to narrow. Whatever is true for you, notice the areas that don't balance. Make a note of what negative beliefs, defenses, or Core Distortions might need more love and support so you can address them in a future Me-B transformation™ session.

Note: A commonly asked question is "what direction should the energy move, up or down?" For the purposes of this exercise, we are not running energy up and down, we are filling and expanding the Central Channel. We simply allow the energy in and allow it to fill. The energy has the intelligence and knows where to go.

Chakras

Another well-known set of energetic structures within the Auric Dimension is the set of energy vortexes known as the chakras. There are seven major Chakras that we work with in Me-B Transformation[TM], although the Chakra system extends beyond the seven.

Using the **Explorer's Mind**, we can balance and assess our Chakras daily to help us stabilize our emotions, increase the amount of energy available to us, and support our immune system. Eventually, we will be able to self-assess and balance our Chakras in just 5 minutes. The more we practice working our energy system, the more we are able to cultivate HVC and the skill of assessing a client's system.

> *No one has all perfect chakras or a perfect energy system.*
> *Knowing our baseline and improving it over time is a realistic goal.*

When working with a client on their energy system, a Me-B Guide can track how much a client's Auric Field improves over a month or a year. If our client's field (or our field) does not improve, it is important to explore why. What support do they (or do we) need? What **Core Distortion**, subconscious material, ego, or internal saboteur is getting in the way?

Barbara Brennan, author, founder of the Barbara Brennan School of Healing, and premier healer and scientist, outlines the psychological and physical expressions of the Auric Field in her book Hands of Light. As of this writing, she currently has three schools on three continents that teach her master form of healing—North America (U.S.), Europe, and Japan. Like many energetic teaching modalities, Me-B Transformation also follows Brennan's anatomy of the energy field with a few additions, variations in interpretation, and clarifications. We urge anyone interested in learning her life-changing hands-on healing modalities to attend any of her three schools. Her web site is www.barbarabrennan.com.

CHAKRA	COLOR	ENDOCRINE	AREA OF BODY
7th – Crown	Violet-White	Pineal	Upper Brain, Right Eye
6th – Head	Indigo	Pituitary	Lower Brain, Left Eye, Ears, Nose
5th – Throat	Blue	Thyroid	Bronchial, Vocal Apparatus, Lungs, Alimentary Canal
4th – Heart	Green	Thymus	Heart, Blood, Vagus Nerve, Circulatory System
3rd – Solar Plexus	Yellow	Pancreas	Stomach, Liver, Gall Bladder, Nervous System, Pancreas
2nd – Sacral	Orange	Gonads	Reproductive System
1st – Root	Red	Adrenals	Spinal Column, Kidneys

CHAKRA	LOCATION IN BODY	EMOTIONAL GENERAL	EMOTIONAL FRONT ASPECTS	EMOTIONAL BACK ASPECTS
1st	Perineum	Life Task	Connection to the Physical	
2nd	Pelvis/Sacrum	Personal Power	Quality of Sexual Energy, Giving and Receiving Physical, Mental, Spiritual Pleasure Passion for Carrying Out Life Task	Quantity of Sexual Energy
3rd	Solar Plexus	Sense of Self Ego	Who You Are in the Universe	Intention Toward Health/Healing
4th	Center of Upper Chest and Between Shoulder Blades	Compassion	Love of Self / Other	Will Ability to Love Self and Other
5th	Neck –Front and Back	Authority, Authority Issues	Taking in, Assimilation Ability to Communicate Feelings	Ability to Be in One's Profession Will to Stand Alone
6th	Forehead – Back of Head	Inner Seeing	Ability to Visualize and Understand Mental Concepts	Capacity to Carry Out Ideas in a Practical Manner
7th	Crown Center	Spiritual Connection	Integration of Total Personality with Life and with Spiritual Aspects of Mankind	

Some information came from Barbara Brennan's book, Hands of Light

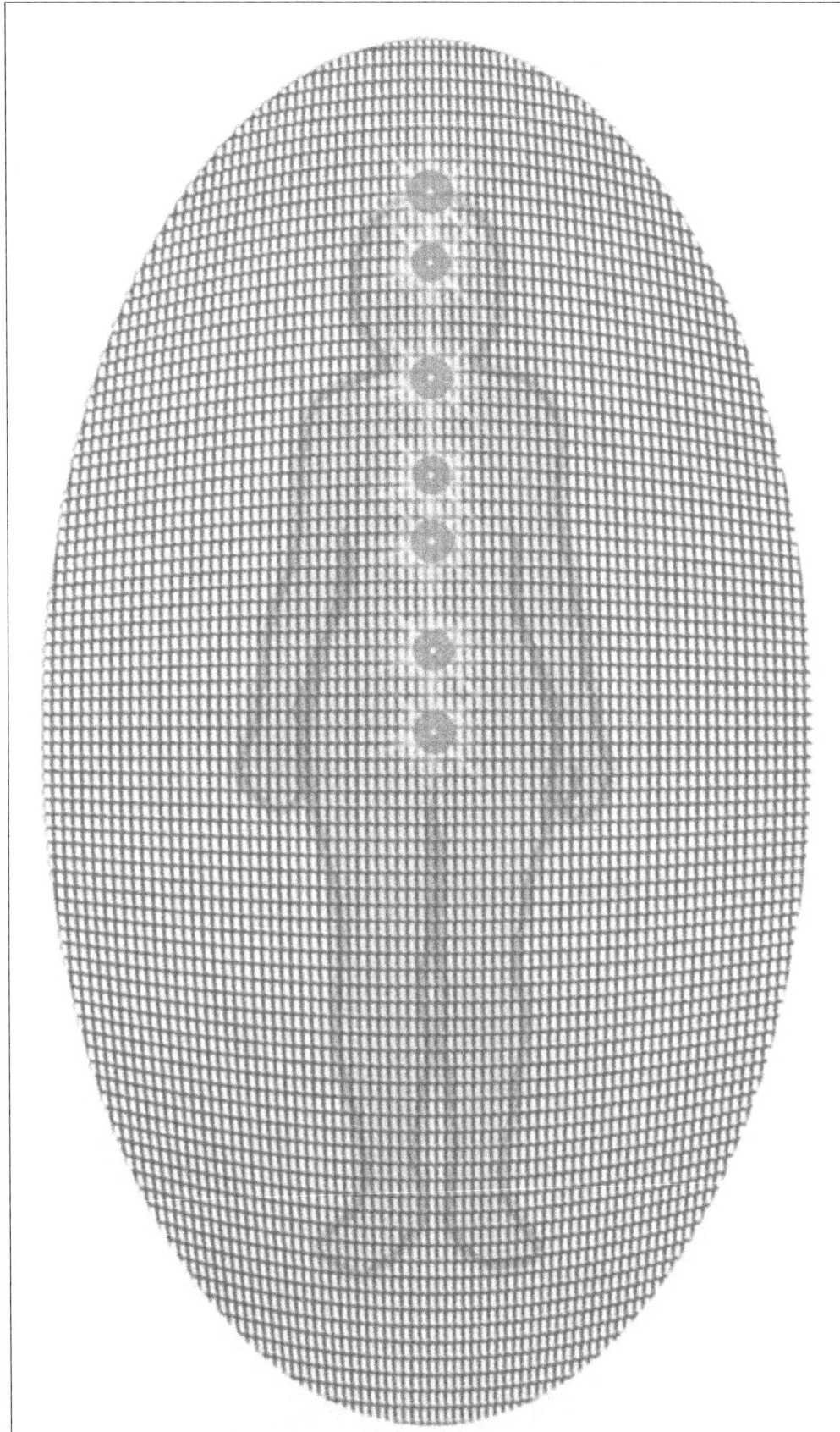

BASED ON BRENNAN'S LEVEL 2
EMOTIONS-RELATIONSHIP TO SELF

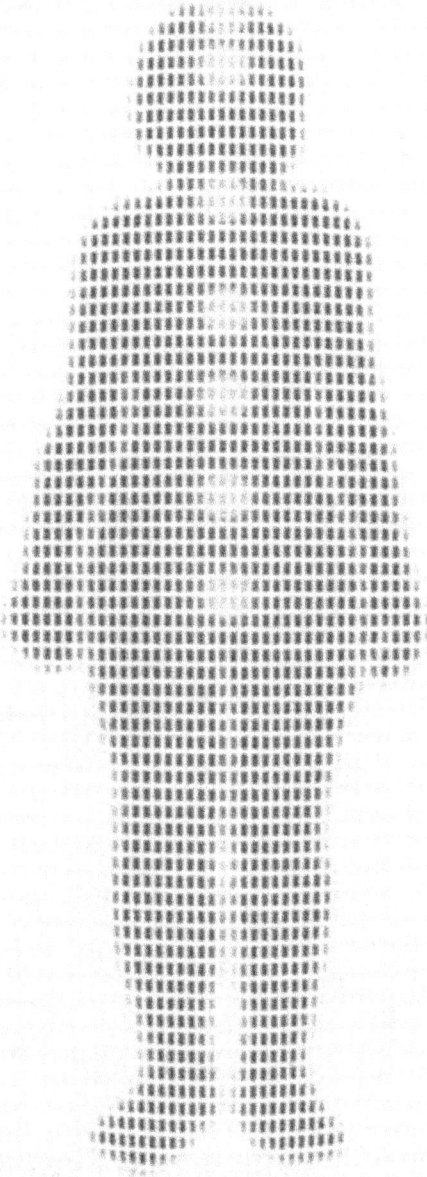

BASED ON BRENNAN'S LEVEL 3
MENTAL LEVEL

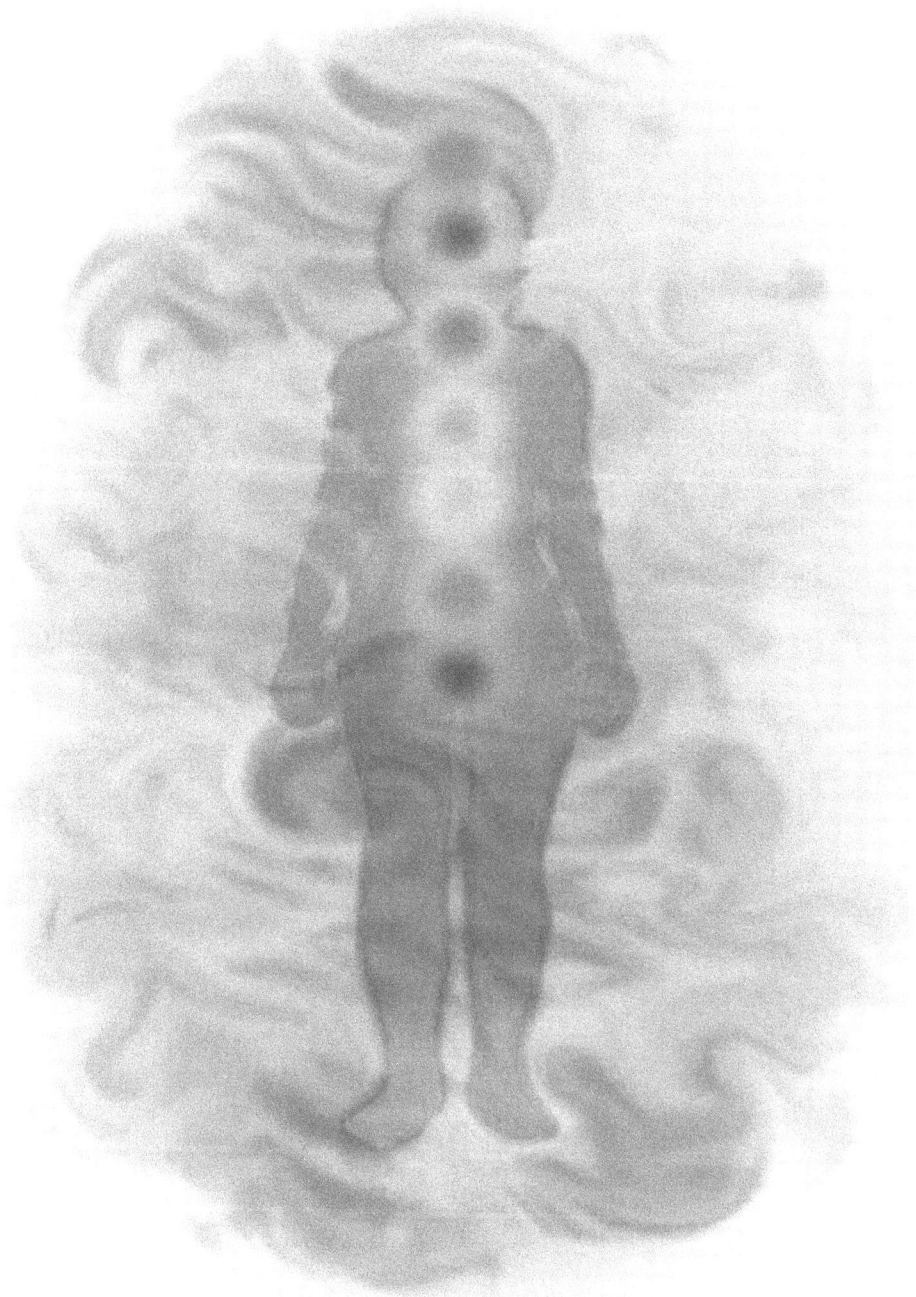

BASED ON BRENNAN'S LEVEL 4
TRAUMA, RELATIONSHIPS

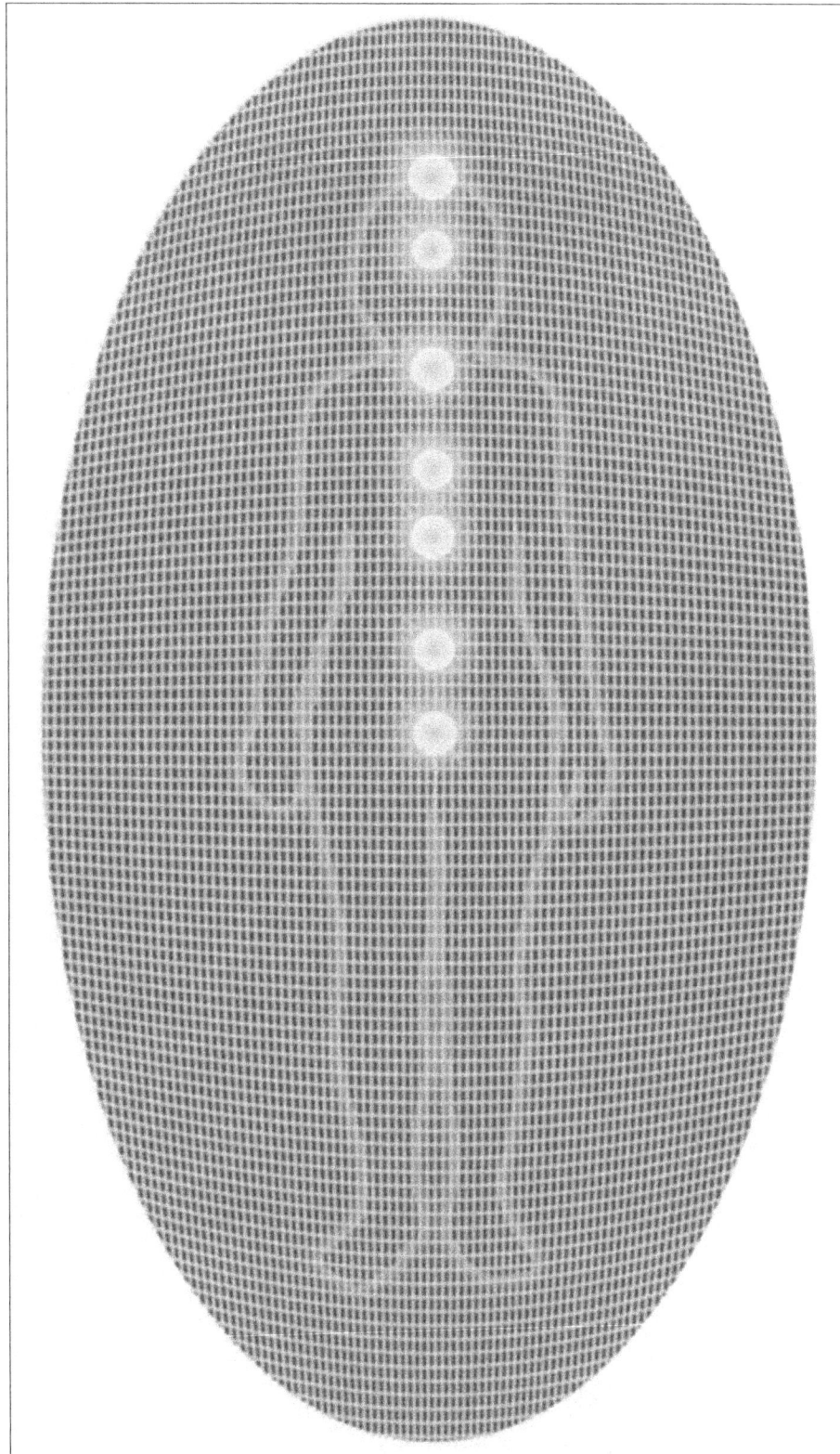

BASED ON BRENNAN'S LEVEL 5
BLUEPRINT FOR THE PHYSICAL LEVEL

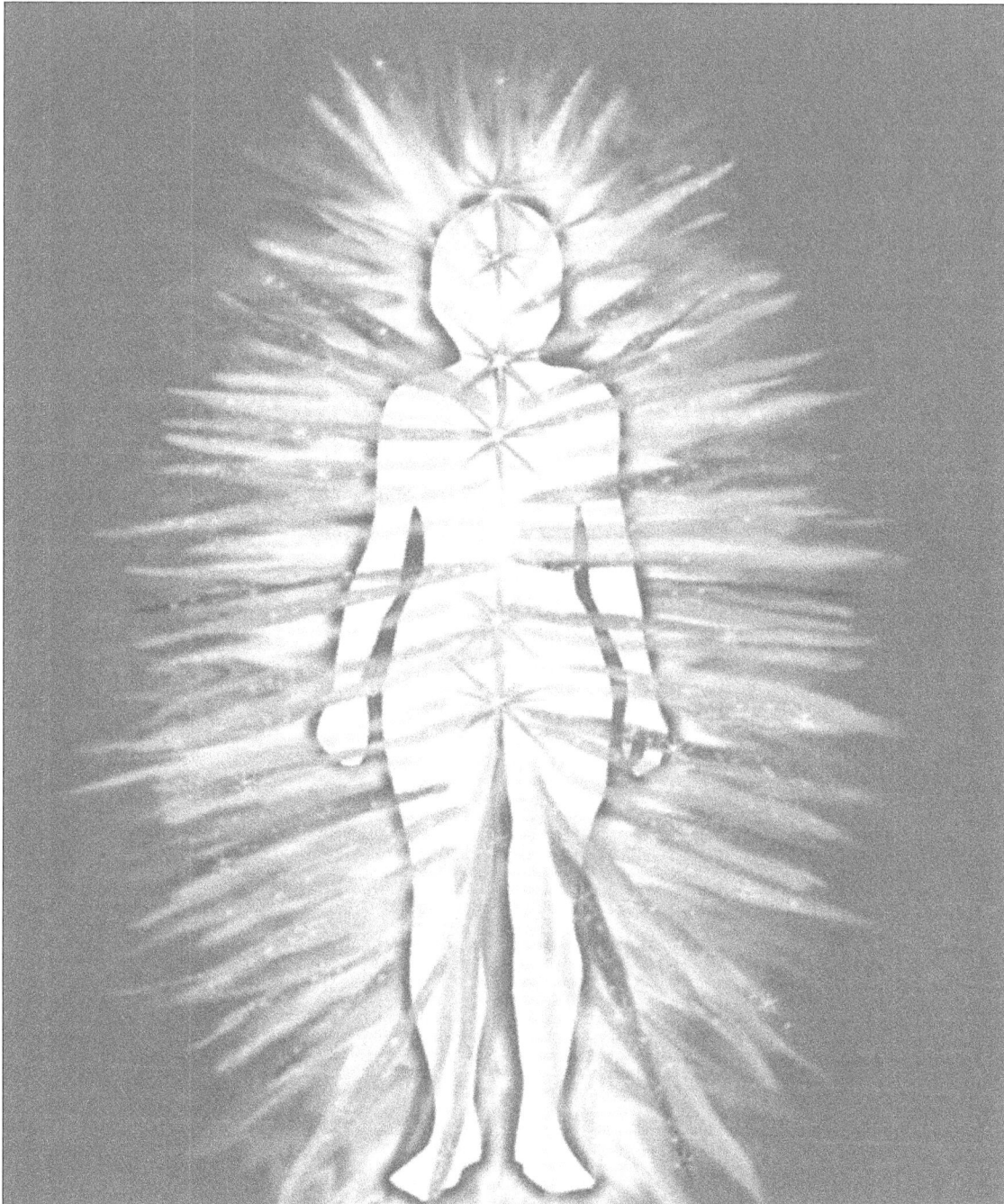

BASED ON BRENNAN'S LEVEL 6
DEVINE ECSTACY,
UNCONDITIONAL LOVE

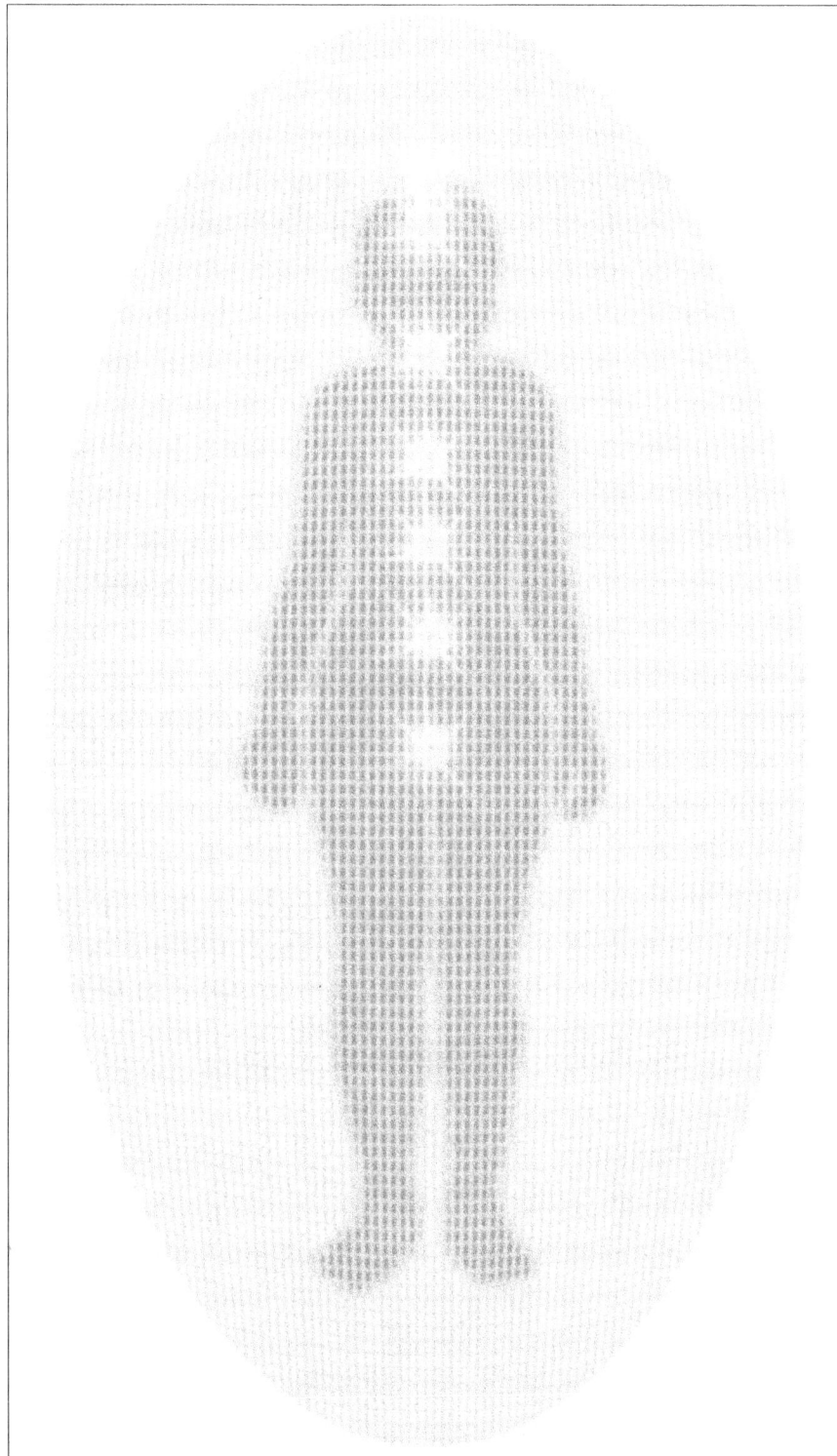

BASED ON BRENNAN'S LEVEL 7
DEVINE WISDOM,
A GOLDEN GRID OF ENERGY

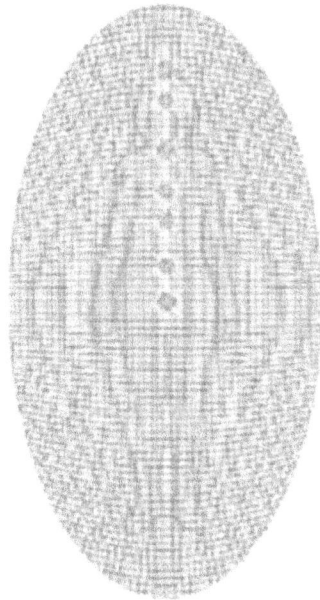
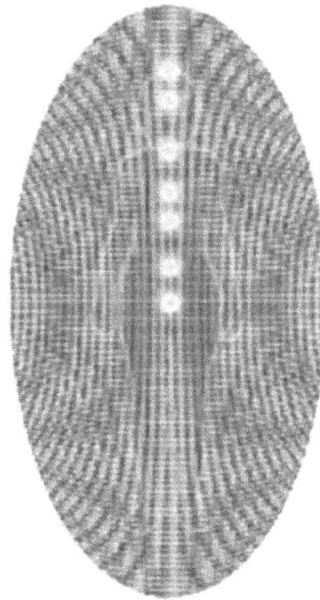

Level 1   Level 5

Levels of the Field

Chakras are the doorways to vibrational frequencies called levels of the field (Barbara Brennan, *Hands of Light*). The levels of the field and the chakras are parts of the Auric Dimension. The first chakra is the door way to the first level of the field; the second Chakra is the doorway to the second level of the field; and so on. The odd-numbered levels of the field (1, 3, 5, 7) are structured and look like a crisscross grid of light running horizontally and perpendicularly (Barbara Brennan, *Hands of Light*).

A web of light is the foundation of our physical, mental, emotional, relational and spiritual energy bodies as outlined below. *In Me-B Transformation*™ *we focus on bringing in the HVC of Core down through all the levels of the field and then into the physical body.* (See pictures shown above of the levels of the Auric Dimension. Brennan discovered these levels of the field.)

Structured Energy Grids Of the Auric Dimension—Levels 1, 3, 5, 7

The odd-numbered levels of the energy field are part of the meridian structure and look like fiber-optic grids of light (Barbara Brennan, *Hands of Light*).

- **1st level is a blue grid.**
  This level deals with the physical body, and the energetic doorway is the 1st chakra. A strong physical body that gets exercise will have a brilliant blue grid system, and a weak body will have a grid that is light in color or will have a broken grid (Barbara Brennan, *Hands of Light*).
- **3rd level is yellow.**
  The mental body is held in this yellow grid. A strong brilliant grid of yellow indicates mental clarity and intelligence. A broken or thin and pale grid suggests confusion and distorted thoughts (Barbara Brennan, *Hands* of Light).
- **5th is the etheric template.**

A cobalt blue, negative is what this level looks like. What is written into the etheric template will eventually manifest in the physical body. With intention, we can learn how to alter this level so we support conscious manifestation and promote health and happiness (Barbara Brennan, *Hands of Light*).

- **7th level of the field.**

The ketheric template or causal body describes this level of the field, and it looks like a beautiful golden grid.

It is the level of divine wisdom. Rarely are there any breaks or distortions found at this high frequency. Tuning into this level of the field can help us see the broader vision of our life. It is the level of the field we draw upon for divine guidance, wisdom, and inspiration.

A Me-B Guide will access this level of the field to help clients. From this level, wisdom is found when the Me- B Guide is in a place of not knowing. As they resonate at this level and open their 7th chakra, knowing can be effortlessly transported to them and the flow of the session expands. Anyone can use this technique to bring in their own divine wisdom! (Barbara Brennan, *Hands of Light*)

Level	Energetic Doorway	Structured	Gift	Challenge
1st	1st Chakra	Yes	Physical Health Blue Grid	Illness Broken, Under/Over Charged Blue Grid
2nd	2nd Chakra	No	Positive Relationship to Self Beautiful Pastel Colors—No clouds	Negative Relationship to Self, Energetic Clouds
3rd	3rd Chakra	Yes	Mental Clarity Yellow Grid	Too dark, Too Light or Broken Yellow Grid Confusion—Lack of Mental Clarity
4th	4th Chakra	No	Relationship Love Beautiful Pastel Colors Infused with Rose Light	Difficulty in Relationships Energetic Mucus Covering the Rose Light

Barbara Brennan, Hands of Light

LEVELS OF THE FIELD: DISTANCE FROM THE BODY

Level	Appearance	Description	Distance from the Body
1	Blue Lines of Light	Physical Level	1 – 3 inches
2	Chakra Colors	Relationship to Self-Love, Acceptance	3 – 8 inches
3	Yellow Lines of Light	Mental Level	6 inches – 1 foot
4	Rose Light	Relationship to Others	1½ – 2 feet
5	Cobalt Blue, Negative	Relationship to Authority/Divine Will Within	2 – 2 ¾ feet
6	Opalescent Light	Divine Love, Spiritual Ecstasy	2¼ - 3 feet
7	Golden Lines of Light	Divine Mind	2¼ - 3¾ feet

From Barbara Brennan, *Hands of Light*

Energy Emotions—Relationship Levels 2, 4, and 6 of the Auric Dimension

The even-numbered levels 2, 4, and 6 deal with relationship issues and are infused with beautiful colors (Barbara Brennan, *Hands of Light*).

- **2nd level is about self-love and our relationship to the self.**
  In *Hands of Light*, the 2nd level is called the Emotional Body. It has colored clouds of red, orange, yellow, green, blue, indigo, violet, and white (the same colors as are typically known for the chakras). Negative impressions of self look like too dark (overcharged) or too light (undercharged) clouds. Trauma can be seen on both this level of the field and the 4th level of the field. Me-B Guides are trained to work with this trauma in a manner that helps clients re-pattern the pain of the old to eliminate the past and create a positive future. Working with trauma in the field is described later.

- **4th level is about our relationship to love and others.**
  The 4th level is called the Astral Level in *Hands of Light*. The colors are the same as the second level but infused with the rose light of love. Negative energetic patterns on this level feel like mucus and present either as too dark or too light (Barbara Brennan, *Hands of Light*). A Me-B Guide will connect to trauma or LVC about relationships and help guide a client to transform them. As we practice transforming distortions about relationships in our Auric field, we are more able to connect to another from our Core Being.

- **6th level of the field can be seen as dealing with our relationship to the divine within ourselves and outside of ourselves.**
  Hands of Light calls this level Spiritual Ecstasy because when we are there, it feels as if we are whole and one with the divine. The colors of the 6th level look like the 2nd level colors but are infused with opalescence. If we can't access this level of the field, it is difficult to move out of the personality level and into our Core Being. Our divine Core Being energetically vibrates on a

different dimension from the Auric Field, but recognizes this level of the field as vibrating at the level of divine relationship.

Outer Energy Egg

We have energetic structures within our body as well as outside our physical body. The 7th level of the field is the outer covering of our Energy Egg. The sixth level is the next level in, the 5th level, further in . . . until we hit the 1st level of the field, about an inch from the body.

Those of us that experienced trauma at a very young age (Spiritual Character Structure) or who have a chronic illness, often don't have a solid external energy egg. There may be breaks or cracks in it, or the outer edges may be diffuse. If we want to have good boundaries and prevent other people's emotions and LVC from entering our field, a solid and strong outer energy egg is vital. In addition, a strong energy egg can hold higher frequencies. Just as a sieve cannot hold water, if our outer field has holes, it will leak higher vibrations.

The following exercise is designed to help us assess and strengthen our outer energy egg. The larger the egg, the higher/faster our consciousness can vibrate, until eventually we get to the point of not having an ego, a self, or an energy egg. In Me-B Stages of Transformation, this would occur at stages 8-10. The outer energy egg is about individuation and self-identification.

STRENGTHEN OUR OUTER ENERGY EGG

This practice strengthens our energy container and creates strong protection from any negativity entering our energy field. If our field is too sponge-like and soaks up external negative energy easily, we can practice this exercise over and over again to create more safety and security. For instance, if we enter a room where there is dirty energy or negative energy being projected toward us, this exercise will help prevent it from entering our Me-B system. However, it is important to note that our Enlightened Observer can take any energy, even LVC, and convert it into HVC. The purpose of this exercise is to supplement the power of our Enlightened Ob- server and make it easier to have a protective energetic structure around us.

- **STEP 1:**
  Balance and charge your field using any of the techniques already outlined, such as spinning your chakras, dancing, or exercise. Use what works best for you. Remember to stay in the playful, curious mode of the **Explorer's Mind**.
- **STEP 2:**
  Standing, bring your hands up next to you, palms down, up high, and on either side of your head. Breathe in deeply. Then, as you exhale, keeping palms facing downward, move your hands down and push any dense energy into the Earth. You can even bend your knees and squat as your hands move downward, eventually touching the floor. (Repeat 3 or more times until you can imagine all the dense vibrations swept away and your outer energy egg much cleaner.)
- **STEP 3:**
  Repeat the same procedure, except have one hand in front of you and the intention of having

the other hand behind you (place it as far toward the back of you as possible). As you exhale, push dense energy into the Earth. (Repeat 3 or more times until you can imagine all the dense vibrations swept away and your outer energy egg much cleaner.)

- **STEP 4:**
Now, bring your breath and awareness to the outside of your outer energy egg, a golden grid of HVC, Divine Wisdom. The outer energy egg is about 3 feet from your body. Imagine it firm, strong, and vibrant. Connecting breath with awareness, scan your outer energy egg for incoherencies. If you sense any cracks or holes, imagine them being repaired.

- **STEP 5:**
Now bring your breath and awareness slightly inside the egg to the 5th level of the field. Imagine that grid strong and bright. Then bring your breath and awareness slightly more inside the egg to the 3rd level, a yellow grid that is about 12 to 6 inches from the body. Imagine that grid strong and bright. Lastly, bring your breath and awareness to the 1st level, a blue grid about an inch from the body. Imagine that grid strong and bright.

Just as a radio tunes into other frequencies, the different levels of the field hold different vibrations. As we learn to tune into these frequencies, we can alter our consciousness and improve our way of life. *In Me-B transformation*[TM], *we learn how to move between the levels of the field to collect information about us and about our client's defenses and gifts.*

Just as playing scales on the piano helps increase a pianist's skills, moving through and assessing all the levels of the field improves our psychic and self-mastery skills. If we can assess what is happening in a chakra or level of the field, we can better understand ourselves and guide others. In addition, energetic awareness brings the subconscious to the conscious.

EXERCISE TO ASSESS YOUR LEVELS OF THE FIELD

Have pen and paper handy so you can record what you discover. Stay curious and open using the **Explorer's Mind**. Begin by placing your hand on the **chakra** that is the doorway to the level of the field you want to assess and follow the procedure outlined in the exercise below. The first chakra is the doorway to the first level of the field, the second chakra is the doorway to the second level of the field, and so on (Barbara Brennan, *Hands of Light*).

If you are assessing someone else's level of the field, it is easier to assess it in their outer energy egg. Refer to the chart that lists the distances from the body. For instance, the first level is an inch from the body, the second level is 3 to 8 inches, and so on.

Self-Assessment, Levels of the Field Exercise

Just as we practice scales of the piano to learn how to play more complex songs, practice assessing your (and others') levels of the field to help strengthen your ability to sense, feel, see, assess, track, and transform energy.

Practice, practice, practice all of the energy exercises in this chapter/book (assessing chakras, Central Channel, Core Being, Manifest Energy, Multi-Dimensional Fabric) and you will become strong, competent, and secure in your energy awareness abilities.

Draw a picture! Practice drawing your chakras, levels of the field, Central Channel, Manifest Energy, and Core Being. Don't think—just let your hand move. You'll be surprised how much you know.

- **Physical Body, Level 1:** Connect to your **1st Chakra** by placing your hand, intention, and mind there. Imagine the chakra is the doorway to the level of the field and intend this frequency to fill your body. Let your hand and whole body resonate to the 1st level of the field. Allow yourself to imagine entering that doorway and experiencing the blue grid that runs throughout your body. Feel, imagine, and intuit its frequency vibrating everywhere. Now place the other hand on an area of the body you want to investigate, such as the thigh. Notice the color and thickness of the lines of light on this level. Normally they are the thickness of sky-blue yarn in a grid pattern.
Slowly scan your body from head to toe, moving from one section to the next, and draw and describe your 1st level of the field. Where are the lines normal, too thin or too thick, too dark or too light? Where is there no grid, a break in the grid, or a dotted line? What does this level tell you about your physical health and your relationship to the physical body? What lessons are here and what support does this level need? Also practice assessing someone else's first level and determine to what extent it is balanced, over or undercharged. If it is over- or undercharged, where does it present that way in the body, and what might that mean psychologically in terms of gifts or challenges?
- **Relationship to Self, Level 2:** Put your hand on the **2nd Chakra**. Enter its doorway to the second level of the field and intend this frequency to fill your body. Feel, imagine, and intuit its frequency vibrating everywhere. Now place the other hand on an area of the

body you want to investigate, such as the thigh. Start in a small area and as your skill increases, you will eventually be able to assess other areas.

On this level, there are rainbow-colored clouds. Darker or too light colors provide information about your **Core Distortions** of self. Negative images and beliefs are held here as well as the positive. Darker clouds appear as lower vibrational energy. A Me-B Guide's field on this level can be triggered, sparking counter-transference issues. This is why it is so important that Me-B Guides do their own personal work and participate in supervision.

Describe your **2nd level** and/or draw it. What support does this level need and what lessons are held here? Also practice assessing others people's second levels to receive data on how to better support them. To assess someone else's level of the field, make sure you are resonating at the level you want to assess. Place your hands on their field, about 3-8 inches from the body. Experience their level deeply and see what you pick up. (Yes, we can resonate to a level by touching the body or by assessing it in their outer energy egg.)

- **Mental Level 3**: Put your hand on the **3rd Chakra**. Let your hand resonate with the energy of the third level of the field and intend this frequency to fill your body. Feel, imagine, and intuit the frequency vibrating everywhere. Now place the other hand on an area of the body you want to investigate, such as the thigh. Start in a small area and as your skill increases, you will eventually be able to assess other areas.

A grid of yellow lines of light creates the structure for our mental energy body, representing mental clarity and focus. The energy is a higher frequency on this grid than on the 1st level of the field. You may sense the energy running faster, and the grid may feel thinner relative to the 1st level of the field. (The 5th Level grid is a higher frequency, too, as is the 7th level grid.)

As you tune into the 3rd level of the field, what support does it need and what lessons are held here? Support can come in various forms such as nutrition, supplements, therapy, energy, and consciousness. If you were your own client, what would you recommend for yourself? Also, practice assessing other people's 3rd level. If the grid is too light or fragmented versus balanced or too heavy, what might that mean about their mental level of the field?

- **Relationship Level 4**: Put your hand on the **4th Chakra**. Let it resonate to the forth level of the field and intend this frequency to fill your body. Feel, imagine, and intuit its frequency vibrating everywhere. Now place the other hand on an area of the body you want to investigate, such as the thigh. Start in a small area and as your skill increases, you will eventually be able to assess other areas.

Pastel colors of rose light float in this level of the field. The movie *Where Dreams May Come* (with Robyn Williams) portrays this level of the field. It is known as the Astral level. There is the lower astral with "devil" like energy, and the upper Astral where angels appear. This level deals with relationships. Mucus is on this level and represents lower vibrational frequencies. If you attend the Brennan School of Healing, you can learn how to energetically remove mucus. As you tune into this level of the field, what support does it need and what lessons are held here? If you were your own client, what would you recommend and why?

- **Level 5**: Put your hand on the **5th Chakra**. Let it resonate to the fifth level of the field. This level is cobalt blue and looks like a photography negative. It is the blueprint for the physical level, so what appears on this level will eventually manifest on the physical level. As you tune into this level of the field, what support does it need and what lessons are held here? If you were your own client, what would you recommend?

- **Level 6**: Put your hand on the **6th Chakra**. Opalescence colors of unconditional love and divine ecstasy are found here. As you tune into this level of the field, what support does it need and what lessons are held here? Is the energy egg still formed on this level, or is it too diffuse? Do you allow this level of the field to be present in your life in times of trials? Can you help yourself or a client access this level of the field for support in difficult times?

- **Level 7**: Put your hand on the **7th Chakra**. Let it resonate to the 7th level of the field. A grid of golden lines of light creates the structure for divine mind. Can you assess your own or your client's outer energy egg? If the egg is too tight or too defuse, what might that indicate?

NOTE: To assess someone else's level of the field, make sure you are resonating at the level you want to assess. Place your hands on their field. Use the distance chart above to help guide you. Experience their level deeply and see what you pick up.

MANIFEST ENERGY and ITS INTENTION LINE

This is the dimension of intention. What moves energy? **Intention.** So if we "say" we want a relationship, but there is a break in our **Manifest Energy Line** toward achieving that goal, it simply won't happen.

As we tune into this frequency and realign our Intention Line, however, we support the outcomes we want. For instance, we can use this dimension to realign our energy field, creating abundance and love. What's the old saying? "Be careful what you ask for." If our **Manifest Energy** aligns toward something, it usually happens.

If our Central Channel is too far forward, and we move our **Manifest Energy Line** backward, the Central Channel follows. This is because our **Manifest Energy** aligns our life through intention. Where our Auric Field is weak, our Manifest Energy Line is weak, and vice versa. Strengthening the **Manifest Energy Line** strengthens the Auric Field. Diagnosing a break in the line will tell us where there is a break in our intention. For instance, we can explore the break further to discover what emotional issues, negative beliefs or self-sabotaging behavior is preventing us from manifesting our intention.

The **Manifest Energy's Intention Line** runs through the middle of our Central Channel but it is on a different dimensional frequency. Unlike the Auric Field, within the body, the **Manifest Energy's Intention Line** doesn't feel like tingles and flows. It can feel like a strong steel rod of strength or a metal bar running though the center of our body connecting heaven and earth. From **Manifest Energy**, we can feel difficult emotions but not be overwhelmed by them, because this dimension helps us detach (not dissociate). Energetically, it feels like a safe and solid base. From it, we sense strength, clarity, and solidity so trauma is more easily transformed.

Manifest Energy magnetizes our intentions, attracting them into this physical plane and into reality. Any misaligned intentions we hold are magnetized as well, *so it is important to notice what we think we want to manifest, but have not yet manifested. This helps us discover any hidden negative intentions.*

Use this dimension to manifest what you want, and to support you in not being overwhelmed by emotions.

First, we connect to our **Manifest Energy Line** and diagnose its strengths. If there is anxiety, trauma, or depression, spending time throughout the day focusing on our **Manifest Energy Line** eliminates much of the pain that these conditions inflict. Me-B Guides can conduct all of their sessions holding the **Manifest Energy Line** to promote more effortlessness in their exchanges of support. We can practice being in **Core Being**, Aura, and **Manifest Energy** all day, throughout the day. This is working multi-dimensionally and is a very sophisticated Me-B skill that we will practice later in this book.

To help us get a better understanding of this dimension, we can think of Martial Arts masters and tune into how they feel, how they move—their strength, grace, and focus. This is the potential we tap into when we are in **Manifest Energy.** There is a flow of effortlessness in actions. All mind chatter clears. Each cell, each thought, and each breath have **Manifest Energy Lines**. *We are constantly using this energy to magnetize and manifest. We might as well make it more conscious so we find our **Choice Points** in manifestation!*

MANIFEST ENERGY ASSESSMENT/ALIGNMENT BASIC ALIGNMENT MEDITATION

- **Step 1**: Ground, balance and charge your field. As you do this, remember you are in the Auric Dimension.
- **Step 2**: To move into **Manifest Energy**, bring your breath and awareness to the top of your head. With intention, begin to sense into your Manifest Energy just as you sensed into your **Central Channel** in the previous exercise. Unlike the **Central Channel**, Manifest Energy will feel like a strong metal bar that runs through the center of the **Central Channel** but on a different dimension. It magnetizes our intentions—attracting them into this physical plane and into reality. As you develop this skill, begin by trusting that your intention of being there brings you there.
- **Step 3:** Using awareness, breath, and visualization (using all senses), feel the Manifest Energy connect down from "heaven" as is shown in the diagram above, through the center of the head, to the center of the neck (Throat Chakra). A core quality of the Throat Chakra (5th Chakra) involves becoming our own authority in life; this means that we are able to mirror our positive sense of self back to ourselves even when someone is projecting negative attacks our way. Let the **Intention Line** support your own authority. As the line moves through the center of the Throat Chakra, feel the strength. Connect to how effortless it is to be in charge of your success.
- **Step 4:** Now align the **Intention Line** from the center of the 5th Chakra down to the center

of the 4th Chakra (Heart Chakra). As you do this, notice your intention to effortlessly receive and give love come into alignment also.

- **Step 5:** Next, align the **Intention Line** down through the center of the 3rd Chakra, the Solar Plexus. The energy of our ego and sense of self is held here. When our negative ego runs our life, it can create chaos. We can feel inadequate and unable to achieve our goals, and collapse into self-judgment. As the **Intention Line** runs through the center, let it magnetize balancing your positive sense of self.
- **Step 6:** Connect to the **Intention Line** as it moves through the center of the 2nd Chakra, our Pelvis. Let it resonate to support your effortless ability for personal power as it moves through the pelvis and then down to the Root Chakra, at the perineum.
- **Step 7**: From the Root Chakra, align to your life task being effortlessly implemented.
- **Step 8:** Then imagine, intend, and focus on the line moving down to the center of the Earth. Feel it anchor deep into the core of the Earth supporting your highest good in all areas of your life.

(Repeat this process three or more times) ASSESS AND ALIGN TO A SPECIFIC INTENTION YOU WANT TO MANIFEST

- Follow Step 1 and 2 from above.
- **Step 3**: Now, pick an area of your life that you want to change, but have been unsuccessful in accomplishing. (Such as money, career, relationship, health, etc.) As you connect to the **Manifest Energy**, set your intention to see how aligned it is toward your goal, and then to realign it.
- **Step 4**: With breath and awareness, follow the Manifest Energy **Line** and assess where it is strong and where it is weak. If you are not sure, you can tune into the **Central Channel**. It mirrors the Manifest Energy **Line**. Remember, Manifest Energy feels more like a steel beam, and the Auric Field feel like tingles/flows or electromagnetic energy. (Practice this 4 times, moving your awareness/breath up and down Manifest Energy to assess.)
- **Step 5**: Draw a picture of it.
- **Step 6**: Where you assess the Manifest Energy Line as strongest, place your awareness in those areas first. Connect your breath and awareness to sense into the strength, denseness, and clarity of your goal. Then, using **Intention**, invite the stronger areas to expand into the weaker areas.
- **Step 7**: In areas that don't align strongly, use the **Explorer's Mind** to investigate what **Core Distortion**, emotion, or negative belief is held there that is preventing it from aligning. With this wisdom, we begin deepening into the process of change. Work on healing any **Core Distortions** or Negative Beliefs that prevent your highest good from manifesting. Work with a Me-B Guide to assist you when needed.

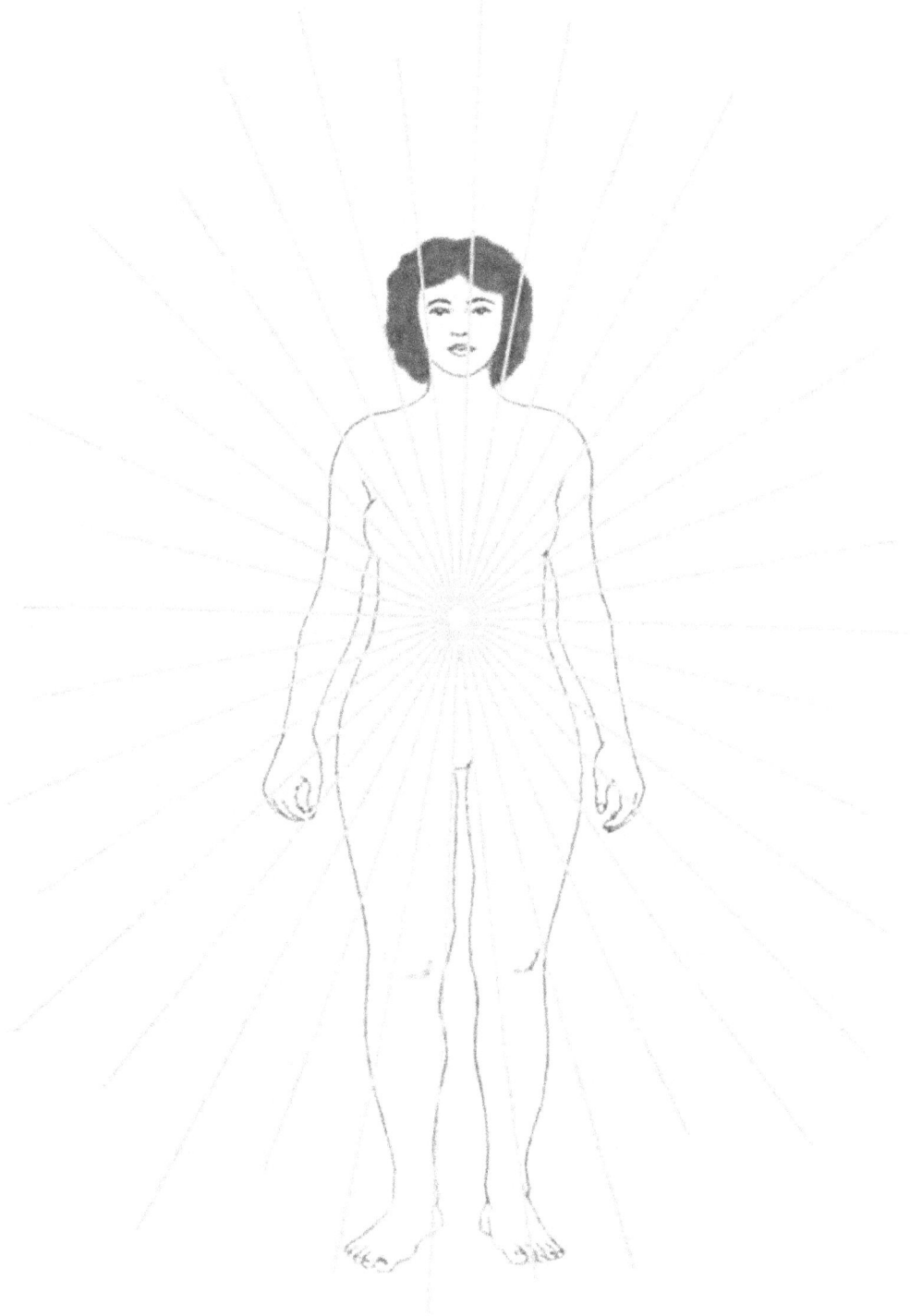

**Me-B CORE BEING
based on Brennan's Core Star Dimension**

CORE BEING DIMENSION

Just as we evolve physically, we also evolve energetically. Me-B Transformation™ understands that the Auric Dimension is evolving. We all can evolve to the level of bringing more of Core Being dimension into the physical world. As we become more skillful at this task, we significantly increase our level of consciousness.

The **Core Being Dimension** has no **Core Distortions**, no ego, and no illusions of self. It represents our whole self and its unique expression. The vortex to this dimension is located 1 ½ inches above the navel.

Living from this dimension by bringing it into the physical body is the goal of Me-B Transformation™. As we become skillful at returning to this dimension, effortlessness, joy, and abundance become commonplace. Magic and aliveness live everywhere.

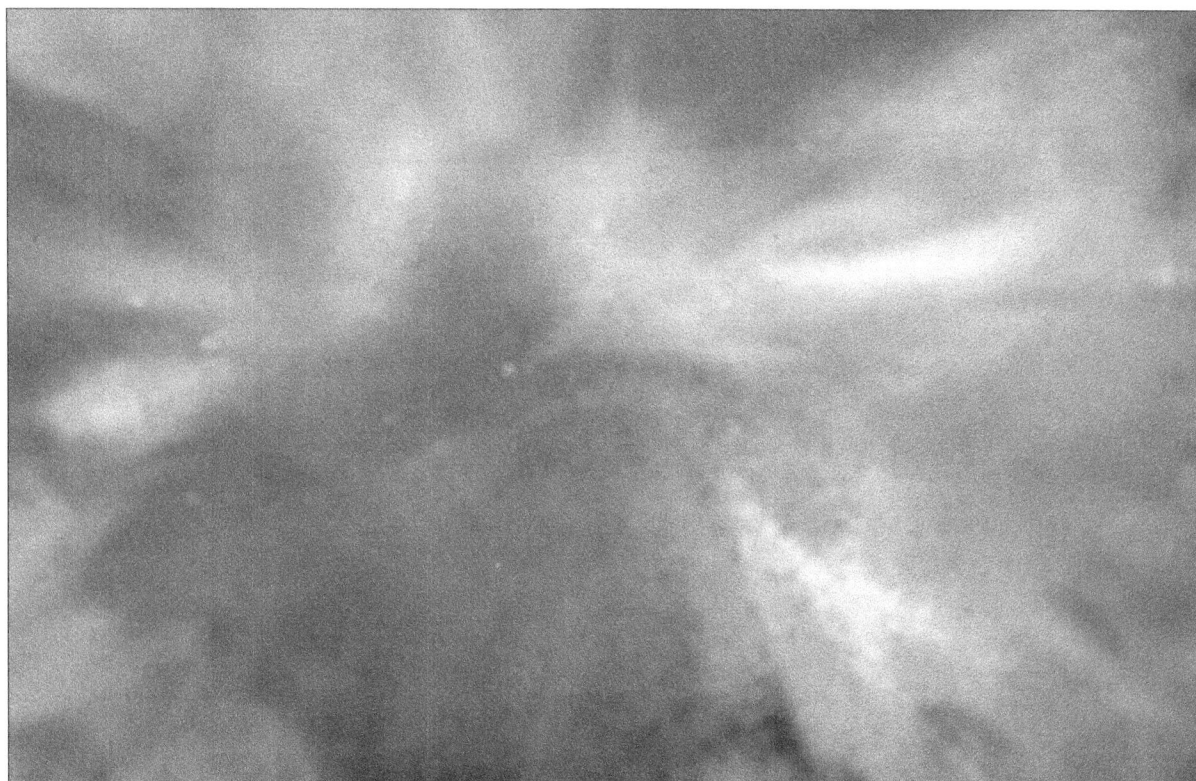

VISUAL OF STAR CHILD
FREQUENCY

GOLDEN "computer" CHIPS of
LESSONS LEARNED from lifetimes of living
STAR CHILD FREQUENCY

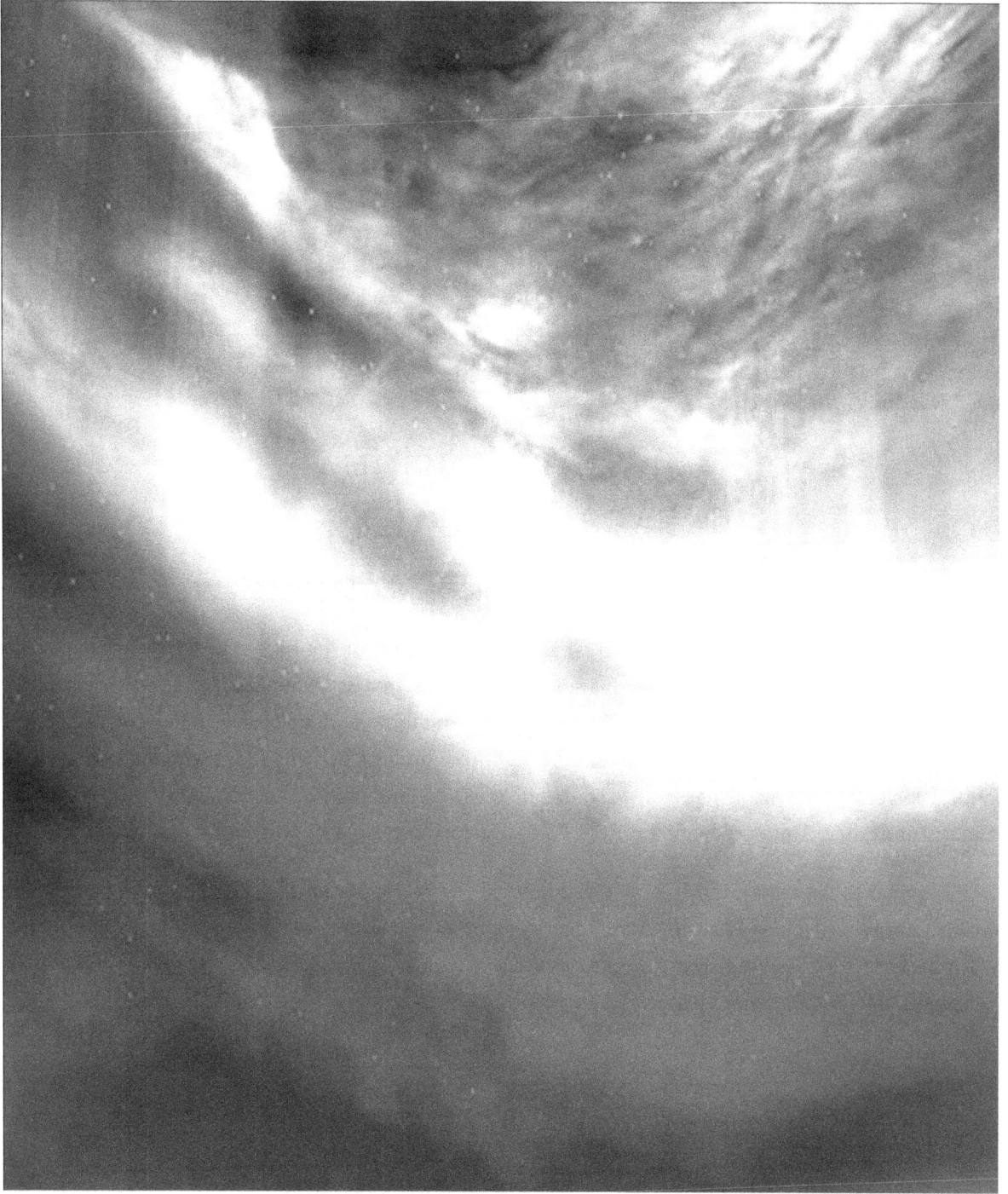

MULI-DIMENSIONAL
FABRIC OF INTERCONNECTEDNESS

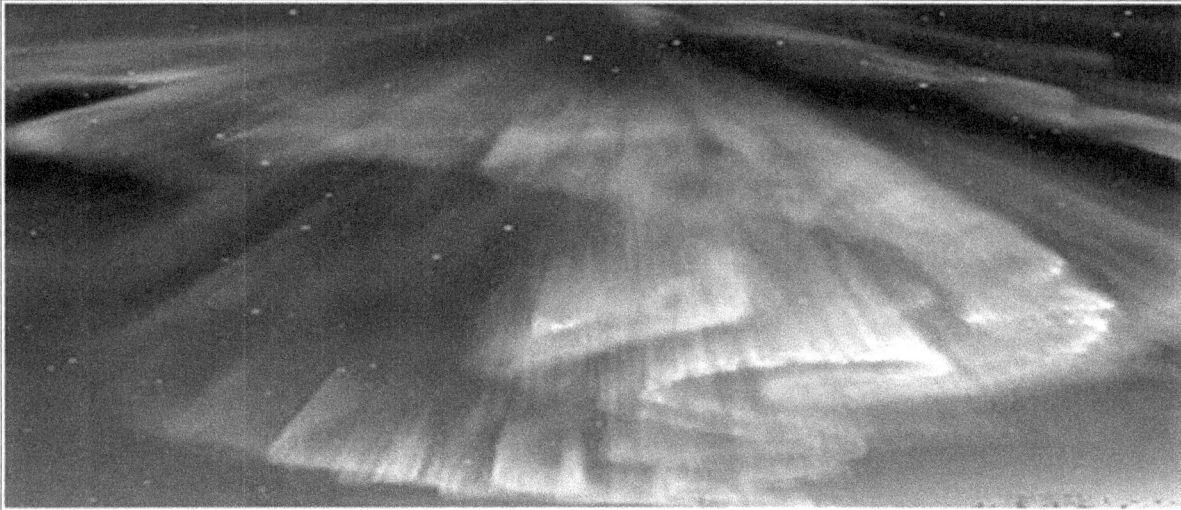

MULTI-DIMENSIONAL FABRIC VISUAL #2

MULTI-DIMENSIONAL FABRIC OF INTERCONNECTEDNESS—We are all one!

We can think of **Core Being** as our individual, unique expression of the higher energy consciousness of oneness. (It is our one distinct, individuated musical note that is connected to the divine spiritual symphony of the whole.) When we take "us" out of the equation, and we connect to universal oneness, it creates a **Multi-Dimensional Fabric** that weaves through all of us. This fabric connects dimensions, worlds, universes, consciousness, and concepts of time and space. It resonates brightly and is reminiscent of the beauty seen in the Aurora Borealis (Northern Lights)

There is an old saying about the "fabric of our being." The fabric of our divine or universal being can be seen as energy that links us all together regardless of race, culture, religion, planet, or even current consciousness. *It is the place where science and divinity meet in the miraculous truth.* In this deepest intelligence, ego and judgment dissolve.

Practice Accessing the MULTI-DIMENSIONAL FABRIC OF INTERCONNECTEDNESS Dimension

- **Step 1**: Begin by grounding and balancing your field. Connect deeply to yourself. Dance, sing. Return to that place of expanded oneness with the world. Feel it, image it!
- **Step 2**: Now imagine rainbow ribbons flowing through that oneness. (Pastels, primary colors, opalescence, gold, silver, brilliancy.) Let the colors come in and flow from head to foot down the middle of your body (head-torso-perineum). Invite the **Multi-Dimensional Fabric** in.
- **Step 3**: Imagine the colors flowing through your arm and leg on the left side of the body, then the arm and leg on the right side of the body. Let the ribbons flow. Watch which color comes next. If no color comes, imagine brilliancy coming in. Then wait to see if another color flows. If it doesn't, then move through the pastel colors one at a time, pausing between them in case the next color wants an opportunity to come without your directing it. Feel the universes and worlds flowing and connecting within you. Imagine the consciousness they bring. Let your consciousness resonate at that level. Breathe, bask, breathe, bask.
- **Step 4**: Record your experience on paper.
  Later in the book, we will adapt this exercise and teach a hands-on table work positive resource healing. Me-B Guides learn how to bring this dimension into a client's physical body to help them better access wholeness and to help them imagine, feel, and experience their connection to the worlds within and beyond the stars.

The **Multi-Dimensional Fabric** Exercise connects us to the greater frequencies available. As a result, our current fears, problems, and pain shrink in importance. Our place in the universe is gently aligned and our perspective altered. By bringing in our greater oneness, we also bring in our humble self. Our internal ache that once echoed so loudly is quickly seen as lacking importance compared to the vast consciousness of the **Multi-Dimensional Fabric of Interconnectedness**.

The difference between this dimension and **Core Being** is that the Core Being dimension is unique for each individual, whereas Multi-Dimensional Interconnectedness is universal.

STAR CHILD FREQUENCY

Star Child energy represents the lessons our soul has learned over the many lifetimes. Specifically it represents the insights, gifts and talents we have developed from living on many different planets and many different dimensions across the cosmos. Many of these gifts have been lost from our memory and thus from our ability to use them. We can learn to access the memory of these lessons so they can be helpful to us in this lifetime. Unlike Core Being and Multi-dimensional Fabric energy, soul energy is not always whole and complete. It rep- resents the light and the dark aspects of our personality. We can, however, learn to retrieve the HVC from the lessons that our soul has collected. As we are able to remember these gifts, it can be a boost to help raise our consciousness.

As a Me-B Guide expands his/her field to connect to the stars, the energy that comes in looks like **computer chips** made of gold energetic stardust. This energy contains the knowledge the client needs to fulfill their life task. If a client has never had or has had only a few incarnations on other planets/dimensions, only a few chips may enter. If they have had many, you may see the whole belly cavity fill. Practice expanding your field and Core Being out to the stars, and see what comes in.

CENTERED ONENESS FREQUENCY

This is an excellent positive resource for self-healing. It strengthens our connection to our higher self and to the higher consciousness of the oneness of everyone. Carl Jung might call it the energetic equivalent to the positive collective consciousness.

CENTERED ONENESS

- **STEP 1:**
  Using intention, imagine a hollow, thin, clear tube that might feel like plastic located at our belly button. Place our thumb and index fingers on either side of our navel.
- **STEP 2:**
  Using intention, presence, and deep contact with the oneness of all, invite energy down from the heavens through the "tube" or cord-like channel to enter through our navel and fill our belly. It is like a universal gas tank we are hooking ourselves up to—but the "gas" is our deeper connection to oneness. Allow the energy to first fill the whole belly. It will then expand to fill both up and down the body.

RELATIONSHIP BETWEEN DIMENSIONS

The Core Being Dimension, Centered Oneness, and Multidimensional Fabric are all related to each other. The Core Being is our unique expression of the divine spirit. (We are one perfect note, a part of the symphony of all.) The Centered Oneness state of being is all of our Core Being frequencies together as one. We, in our Core Being, are like a drop of rain, with the Centered Oneness being the source from which the individual raindrop was born. The Multi-Dimensional Fabric of Interconnectedness includes Core Being, Centered Oneness, and Star Child frequencies—plus it encompasses all universes, galaxies, dimensions, stars, and all beings of light.

HOW TO WORK MULTI-DIMENSIONALLY

In many of the leading types of energy work, students are taught to draw in energy through their heads or through their feet/root chakras. Me-B Transformation™ enthusiasts work Multi-Dimensionally. This entails inviting energy to connect through all vortices and all dimensions. We can resonate our field at all of these dimensions at the same time:

- Auric Levels
- Manifest Energy
- Core Being, and
- The Multi-Dimensional Fabric Dimension

Then we can allow the energy to flow through our feet, chakras, and head, bringing in energy from all dimensions in the room using mind/awareness and intention. It is still sometimes difficult for me to be in all of these frequencies at the same time, but each year it gets easier and becomes a positive habit and natural. Begin by practicing being in Core Being and Manifest Energy at the same time.

- **Step 1:** Allow Core Being to resonate throughout the Manifest Energy Line.
- **Step 2:** Once that feels comfortable, practice holding Core Being and the Auric Levels at the same time.
- **Step 3:** Then try Core Being, the Manifest Energy, and the Auric Dimension all together.
- **Step 4:** Add in the Multi-Dimensional Fabric Dimension once you have mastered the other three dimensions. Practice, practice, practice!

REVIEW QUESTIONS

1. Outline the basic principles of Energy Health.
2. Chakras are the doorways to what?
3. The relationship to self and ego strength are connected primarily to which level of the field?
4. What Chi Kung Meditation can balance will and emotion?
5. Describe how to energetically clear your organs.
6. If something is not manifesting in your life, what Dimension could you self- assess to discover a cause?
7. If you are overwhelmed with emotions or anxiety, what Dimension can help you?
8. Explain the psychological functions of the chakras.
9. Which chakras govern which organs?
10. When you assessed your levels of the field, what did you find?
11. What are the distances from the body of all the levels of the field?
12. What did you discover when you assessed your outer energy egg?
13. What is the purpose of the Manifest Energy, Multi-Dimensional Fabric, and Star Child Frequency? Why are these dimensions useful to you?
14. What levels of the field are structured and which ones are unstructured? How can accessing the levels of the field support you or your client? Explain.
15. List Tips of Energy work.
16. List Common Mistakes in Energy Work. What mistakes do you need to avoid?
17. What is the difference between the Core Being, Auric Field, Multi-Dimensional Fabric, Centered Oneness Dimension, and Star Child Frequency?
18. If you are overwhelmed with emotions, what can you do to adjust energetically?
19. If you are not manifesting something in your life, what do you adjust energetically to manifest it? Be specific to your life.
20. What is the best way to master energetic awareness? Why is this important to achieving self-mastery?
21. List three joys you receive when you work energetically.
22. Draw/describe your current energetic baseline and set goals for it to improve in the next year.

CHAPTER 14

YES WE CAN!

TOGETHER WE LEARN HOW TO MASTER SUBTLE ENERGY AWARENESS

*Energy is the pathway to the conscious mind—the mind is
the pathway to transformation. Each needs the other to succeed!*

Me-B Transformation™ challenges us to increase our conscious mind. Mindfulness happens when we follow these principles:

1. Look within.
2. Ask for and receive a deeper understanding of who we are.
3. Know who we aren't and who we can someday become.

To do this we use aligned intention (Manifest Energy Intention Line) to collect the wisdom from our mindfulness (Enlightened Observer and Explorers Mind) so we can be more present (connected to core being) and lay a steady path toward self-mastery and joy.

When doing this level of work, I don't use the term *psychic* because it connotes something out-of-the-ordinary. Instead, I believe these skills are very natural and normal. They get programmed out of us as we age and shut down our "naturalness," because what we sense is too often not matched with what people around us are saying. For instance, as a child, I knew my father was imperfect and angry—but when I confronted this, I was told I was wrong. So as I went to reawaken these most natural abilities, it was hugely important to me to have someone else confirm my perceptions and inner knowing. In the beginning, confirmation gives us the confidence to awaken.

Another definition of *psychic* is something that is "of human mind." This definition supports what is possible and confirms that its origin is very human. Being naturally "psychic" is one of the gifts we can all embrace if we get support, have confidence, and are willing to practice and focus on our successes.

WHAT INFORMATION CAN BE COLLECTED FROM OUR ME-B SYSTEM?

There may be no limit to what we are able to learn when we tune within for answers. After all, look what happened to Buddha! Life's mysteries can be unraveled. Yet often we must take it out of the head and into the body and transform it. If our **Enlightened Observer** is not attached to the material and the "story" behind the energy, it is more easily transformed into higher consciousness, wisdom, and compassion.

In Me-B Transformation, we find and collect information to promote Self-Mastery. See the following chart of opportunities available to us as our energy awareness skills increase.

- **Past lives are revealed that hold LVC and are transformed to HVC.**
  (We find energy of a **past life** that is negatively influencing us in this life. For instance, if we died of starvation and this energy of the past is negatively influencing us to eat too much in

this lifetime, we can locate where it is held within our body/energy system and heal it so our eating challenges can be finally resolved.)

- **Pre-Birth and Birth Trauma** are brought to consciousness so fear and pain evolve to confidence and internal safety;
- **End of Life, Death to Spirit Transitions**—we are able to help loved ones in the process of dying;
- **Archetypical Energies** are located within us so LVC (such as victim consciousness) is transformed into HVC archetype energy (such as the leader archetype);
- **Core Distortions** (false images, beliefs, traumas) are located and brought to HVC of Core Being;
- **Dream Work**—the subconscious message revealed by the dream is found in the body/energy system so higher alignment is achieved;
- **Adjusting Misalignments**—we can tune into our Energy System to adjust misalignments in our meridians, chakras, Manifest Energy, and levels of the field, realigning them so we vibrate at higher frequencies;
- **Ancestral Energies** can be rewired so we are able to find and receive the talents passed down through our DNA;
- **Chronic Illnesses** are located before they present physically, and/or gifts are found and lessons are learned from them, so healing and joy are promoted;
- **Subconscious/Shadow Material** is hidden in our body and energy system; we find it, learn and grow;
- **Trauma and Neurological System Adjustments** are found, so we re-pattern our programmed personality back to Core Being; and
- **More!**

We also collect information about our personality type. Below is a chart on body-centered Character Structures. More is discussed about this in subsequent chapters, but we will begin to investigate them here.

We all have parts of each Character Structure within us. As we learn to access the gifts and heal the challenges of our personality types, we become more balanced. The types given below are derived originally from the work of William Reich, Alexander Lowen, and John Pierrakos. In the chart below, the personality types are renamed to emphasize their gifts instead of their distortions: Spiritual (Schizoid); Compassionate (Oral); Leader (Psychopath); Heart-Centered (Masochist) and Excel (Rigid).

				HEART-	
				INTERPERSONAL RELATIONS	

GIFT NAME	**SPIRITUAL**	**COMPASSIONATE**	**LEADER**	**HEART-CENTERED**	**EXCEL**
CHALLENGE NAME	Schizoid	Oral	Psychopathic	Masochistic	Rigid
PSYCHOANALYTIC DEFINITION	Before or at Birth Hostile Mother	Babyhood Feeding Abandonment	Early Childhood Seduction Betrayal	Autonomy Stage Control Forced Feeding & Evacuation	Genital Sexual Denial Betrayal of Heart
EVOKES FROM OTHERS	Hold Together	Hold On	Hold Up	Hold In	Hold Back
COUNTER-TRANSFERENCE	Sex to Feel Life Force, Fantasy Fear Be / Exist	Sex for Closeness & Contact Greed Be Nurtured & Fulfilled	Hostel/ Fragile-Fantasy Untruthfulness	Impotence, Strong Interest in Pornography Hatred	Sex with Contempt Pride Have
REACTION	Fear / Anxiety	Passivity (Fatigue)	Be Supported & Encouraged Feeling of Defeat	Be Independent Tension	Feelings (Love / Sex) No feelings
COMMUNICATES IN **LANGUAGE**	"I will be split." Tend to separate from others.	"I'll make you give it." When you give it, it won't be enough. "I won't need."	"My will be done." If you don't do it my way, I cannot trust you.	"I love negativity."	"I won't surrender." I won't let go and be messy.
DOUBLE BIND	Unity vs. Splitting Strengthen Boundaries	Need vs. Abandonment Own Needs & Stand on Own Two Feet	Will vs. Surrender Trust	Freedom vs. Submission Be Assertive Be Free Open to Spiritual Connections	Sex vs. Love Connect Heart to Genitals
LOWER SELF STATEMENT	Elongation, Scoliosis, Cold Hands and Feet, Cold Core	Thin, Collapsed Chest, Depleted	Inflated Chest, Top Heavy, Cold Legs and Pelvis, Upper Body Holds More of a	Head Forward, Heavy and Cold Buttocks, Boiling Inside	Rigid Back, Pelvis Tipped and Cold, Withheld from Core

			Charge		
HIGHER SELF STATEMENT	Withdrawal, Beside Myself, Porcupine 7th, 6th front	Oral Sucking, Verbal Denial, Hysteria 7, 6th front	Hook, Mental Grasp 7, 6, 4th rear	Silent Brooding, Tentacles 6th front, 3rd front	Power/Will Display, Boundary Containment Back chakras, 6th front

INTERPERSONAL RELATIONS					
GIFT NAME	SPIRITUAL	COMPASSIONATE	LEADER	HEART-CENTERED	EXCEL
ARREST OF DEVELOPMENT	Before or at Birth	Babyhood Feeding	Early Childhood Seduction	Autonomy Stage Control	Genital Sexual Denial
TRAUMA	Hostile Mother	Abandonment	Betrayal	Forced Feeding & Evacuation	Betrayal of Heart
PATTERN	Hold Together	Hold On	Hold Up	Hold In	Hold Back
SEXUALITY	Sex to Feel Life Force, Fantasy	Sex for Closeness & Contact Greed	Hostel/ Fragile-Fantasy	Impotence, Strong Interest in Pornography	Sex with Contempt
FAULT	Fear Be / Exist	Be Nurtured & Fulfilled	Untruthfulness	Hatred	Pride Have
DEMANDS THE RIGHT TO	Fear / Anxiety	Passivity (Fatigue)	Be Supported & Encouraged	Be Independent	Feelings (Love / Sex)
PRESENTING COMPLAINT	"I will be split." Tend to separate from others.	"I'll make you give it." When you give it, it won't be enough. "I won't need."	Feeling of Defeat "My will be done." If you don't do it my way, I cannot trust you.	Tension "I love negativity."	No feelings "I won't surrender." I won't let go and be messy.
NEGATIVE INTENT	Unity vs. Splitting	Need vs. Abandonment	Will vs. Surrender	Freedom vs. Submission	Sex vs. Love
DEVICES BEHIND NEGATIVE INTENT	Strengthen Boundaries	Own Needs & Stand on Own Two Feet	Trust	Be Assertive Be Free	Connect Heart to Genitals
NEEDS TO	Elongation	Thin, Collapsed	Inflated Chest, Top Heavy, Cold Legs and Pelvis, Upper Body	Open to Spiritual Connections	Rigid Back,
BODY	Hands and	Chest, Depleted	Holds More of a	Head Forward	Pelvis Tipped

	Feet		Charge	Heavy and Cold Buttocks, Boiling Inside	and Cold, Withheld from Core
COMMON DEFENSE	Withdrawal, Beside Myself, Porcupine	Oral Sucking, Verbal Denial, Hysteria	Hook, Mental Grasp	Silent Brooding, Tentacles	Power/Will Display, Boundary Containment
DOMINANT CHAKRAS	7th, 6th front	7, 6th front	7, 6, 4th rear	6th front, 3rd front	Back chakras, 6th front

WHY COLLECT INFORMATION FROM OUR BODY/ENERGY SYSTEMS?

Empowerment. Information is power because it fosters self-knowledge and self-responsibility. *It strengthens the Explorer's Mind so we locate our **CHOICE POINTS** and can transform LVC into HVC.* We must know what is happening in our own system so we can adequately assist and assess another's system. Because energy is so subtle, we can easily become confused about what we are sensing—is it us or them? As we become clear about ourselves, then we are more able to energetically assess both ourselves and others.

Throughout our day, all of us use energy as the raw material for that which we create and manifest. Tracking and assessing energy brings this process into our conscience awareness so we are in charge of what we are creating. Energy awareness helps us uncover our subtle yet powerful internal saboteur and avoid painful mistakes.

For instance, in a couple's session, Albert and Sara were sitting next to each other expressing their goals for therapy. As I watched them talk, I noticed that Albert's field grew and invaded Sara's field every time she asked him to be a more equal partner. Without stating what I observed, I asked them to notice what was happening energetically in their bodies. I then separated them from each other. Albert stood on one side of the office, and Sara stood on the other side of the room and again, they noticed what happened to their energy fields. Sara's field expanded, returning to its full size, as Albert's field returned to balance around him and moved away from controlling hers.

A light bulb went off as each of them became aware of the subtle ways they interacted. Albert was amazed at his controlling and dominating energy field and Sara eventually learned to stand in her center when making a request. Each person owned their unhealthy defenses and practiced interacting with each other so neither energetically dominated nor collapsed into submission.

As our skills grow, we can learn to track ourselves and others. We can learn to track subtle family dynamics so we discover how we might be *subconsciously creating the reality we most want to avoid.* In the case of Albert and Sara, she didn't want to collapse into the victim role, and he didn't want to control or dominate his beloved wife, but that was exactly what was happening.

Neither Albert nor Sara was "energy aware" before this session. Sara had done some somatic work, but energy was a new horizon for them both. Yet in the moment, they found they could actually be aware of what was happening, as long as someone asked the question. I find that this is often the first step: asking the question. We all track and react to energy as Sara and Albert did. *Now, it is just a matter of noticing what we are already doing.*

Cautionary Notes

Issues can present energetically that never happened physically. For instance, in the case of remembering incest, it can be difficult to know if the action was an energetic invasion of abuse or a physical actuality. Wanting to know is understandable. However, any emotional attachment to needing to know distorts the energy.

Also, remembering past events that happened when we were preverbal can be difficult to clearly assess. This occurs whenever we or our client remember a past life or earlier event that is traumatizing but can't be confirmed as "true" or not, on some level. If the energy is presenting, then it is asking for attention and support. Instead of focusing on what is "true," and whether it "really happened," we can focus on meeting the energy and feelings in our Me-B System and transforming the LVC into HVC.

The exception to the rule is when there is psychosis or possible abuse of a child. In the case of child abuse, state laws need to be followed; in the case of a possible mental illness, further assessment is needed.

A Success Story of What We All Can Do
Question Asked, Wisdom Found, Negative Energy Transformed

Trudy came to my office. Her right rib kept going out of alignment, which then pulled at her neck and twisted her core. The pain was so great that she could barely walk, let alone work at her job as a Pilates instructor. She asked the question, "What negative belief, trauma, or energy is causing this extreme discomfort?"

We both connected to the area beginning at the right rib and followed where the energy misalignment originated. It took us to the left side of Trudy's third chakra. As we placed our hands there, we could feel the physical knot and the trapped, painful emotions. Trudy wanted to collect information from the area so she could heal whatever she found. She first connected to her Core Being, *remembering that the challenging feelings and emotions were just energy asking for love and support.* She then *engaged her Enlightened Ob- server* and placed her hands on her stomach, letting the warm energy melt into the knot. Knowing that if she "tried too hard" she wouldn't be able to pick up anything, *she let her mind wonder and move out of focus.*

It took a few minutes, and then Trudy noticed she had started thinking about a time when she was 12 years old. Ann, her older sister, had just pushed her into confessing her feelings for Joey, a boy in her class. Later that same day, she saw Ann holding Joey's hand. As she remembered this, the energy in her hands expanded and went deeper into the knot. Tears started to flow as she felt her young self's pain. Trudy remembered that when her young self confronted her sister's betrayal, Ann laughed at her and teased her. Shamed, Trudy was told she was overly sensitive.

Now, however, Trudy was determined to let the memory go. She melted the energy of her Enlightened Observer deep into the emotions and pain. As she did this, more energy entered her body, releasing the past and bringing in the energy of comfort, self-love, and acceptance. This process helped Trudy own the fact that too many of her past **Choice Points** had been missed because her low self-esteem had gotten in the way. At 42, Trudy had moved through a string of somewhat abusive, dead-end relationships. As a result of this session, she found her Choice Points for change: she broke up with her current unavailable boyfriend and found the love of her dreams!

To collect information from ourselves, clients, or a loved one, we begin by discovering how our energy system is uniquely designed to provide us with information. We simply need to pause long enough so we can (1) connect, (2) ask, (3) listen, and (4) receive the knowledge. To do this, we must first **find out our way in**. Practice the following Pin Wheel Technique. It can teach us how to find our way in.

PIN WHEEL TECHNIQUE: FINDING OUR WAY IN

How do we best collect information? Which sense is strongest? Is it direct knowing, sight, taste, smell, intuition, emotions, kinaesthetics (touch, sensations) and/or hearing? Chakras, literally translated as wheels or disks, are energy vortexes along the body's front and back (see diagram below). According to Barbara Brennan, author and premier healer, each chakra is designed to provide a different type of psychic knowing, as shown in the chart on the next page.

7th Chakra – Crown
Spiritual Connection
Integration of total personality with life and
with spiritual aspects of mankind
Pineal, Upper Brain, Right Eye.

6th Chakra – Forehead
Inner Seeing
Ability to visualize and
understand mental concepts

6th Chakra – Back of head
Capacity to carryout ideas in a
practical manner
Pituitary, Lower Brain, Left Eye,
Ears, Nose

5th Chakra – Back of Neck
Thyroid, Bronchial, Vocal Apparatus,
Lungs, Alimentary Canal
Authority, Authority issues
Ability to be in one's profession
Will to stand alone

5th Chakra– Throat
Taking in, assimilation
Ability to communicate
feelings

4th Chakra - between shoulder Blades
Ego, will - Ability to love self and other
Thymus, Heart, Blood, Vagus Nerve,
Circulatory System

4th Chakra – Heart
Center of Upper Chest
Compassion
Love of self/ other

3rd Chakra
Sense Of Self
Intention toward Health/Healing
Pancreas, Stomach, Liver, Gall
Bladder, Nervous System

3rd Chakra
Solar Plexus
Who you are in
the Universe

2nd Chakra - Sacrum
Personal Power
Quantity of Sexual Energy
Ability to carry out life task
Gonads, Reproductive System

1st Chakra – Root
Perineum
Life Task
Connection to the physical
Adrenals, Spinal Column,
Kidneys

2nd Chakra – Sacral
Pelvis/
Quality of Sexual Energy
Giving and receiving physical,
mental, spiritual pleasure
Passion for carrying out life
task

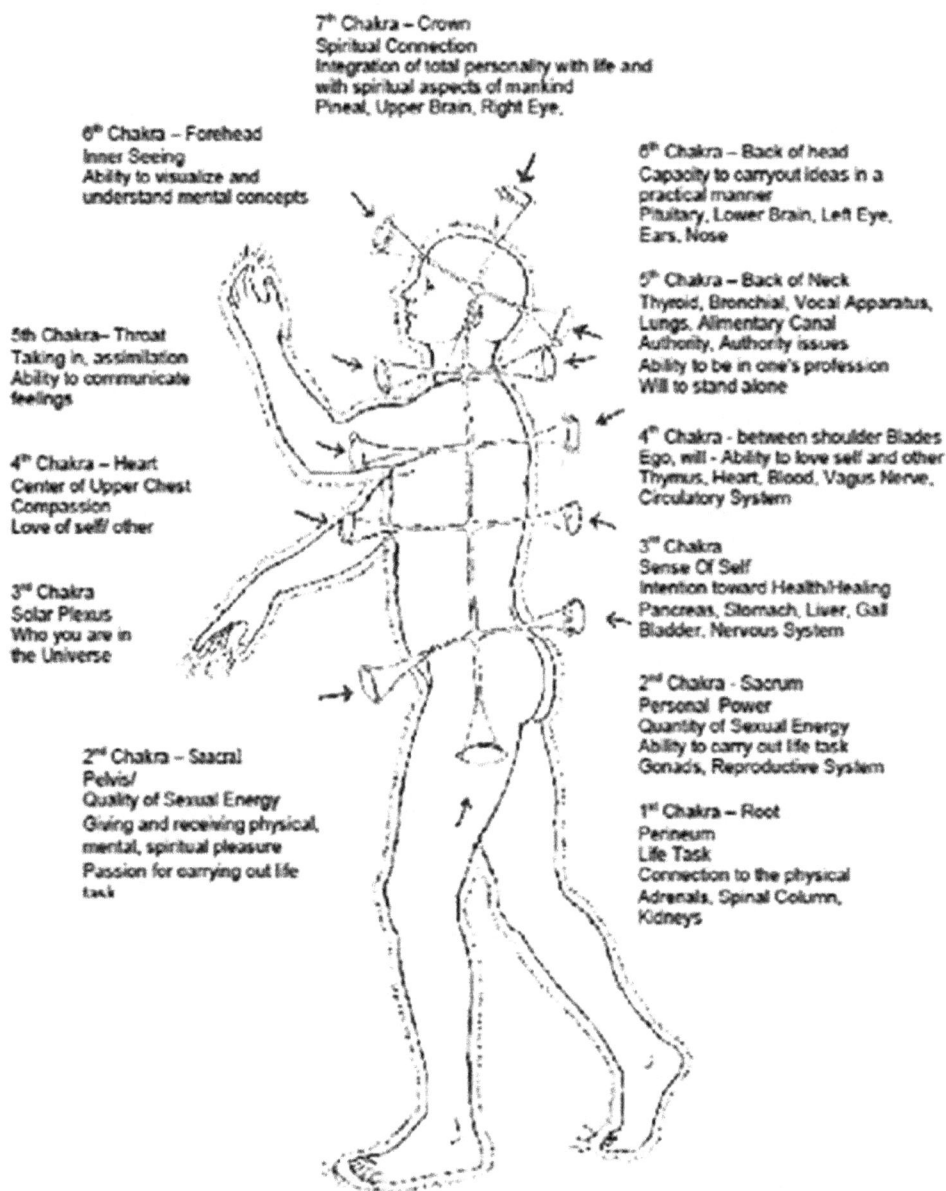

The Chakra System

CHAKRAS HELP US COLLECT PSYCHIC INFORMATION

- **7th Chakra; Crown**: Can give us information in the form of direct knowing, like when we just know someone is going to call us on the phone, and then they do. This book is written from the divine knowing coming through the 7th Chakra.
- **6th Chakra; 3rd Eye**: Governs sight in the form of direct seeing of energy, seeing on the mind screen internally, and in the form of symbols or visions. Have you ever seen a flash of light in a dark room, or colors coming out of someone's hands? If so, you are seeing from the 6th Chakra.
- **5th Chakra; Throat**: Provides the energy vortex to channel, hear, taste, and smell psychically.

Mediums use the 5th chakra to channel. I once smelled burnt pizza while driving in my car. I quickly called home to my son. He apparently forgot to take the pizza out of the oven when the buzzer rang.

- **4th Chakra; Heart**: Provides information about love, past life, archetypes, and relationship issues. The old saying, "what does your heart say?" rings true here.
- **3rd Chakra; Solar Plexus**: Is the chakra that gives us our intuition. When we are not quite sure, but have an intuition we shouldn't take a specific traffic route home from work, then later hear on the news that an accident had the traffic backed up for miles, is an example of our intuition working for us.
- **2nd Chakra; Sacrum/Pelvis**: This Chakra provides information on emotions. When I first learned energy work, I placed my hands on someone and began to notice I was feeling their emotions. Sometimes I felt sadness, anger, or joy. This information was picked up through my second chakra.
- **1st Chakra; Root**: Through the root chakra, we can collect information by feeling the sensation of the energy kinesthetically. For instance, sensations such as pain, pleasure, smooth, crisp, cohesive, pulsations, pressure, heavy, light, texture, temperature, flows, blocks, streams, steam, mist, and rough represent energetic configurations. Lightness is an undercharge, flow is balance and blocks are an overcharge of energy. Simply through touch, much information can be collected about energy and its consciousness.

Barbara Brennan, *Hands of Light*

Notice how a pinwheel spins—a continuous flow. As it spins quickly, we no longer see the individual segments of the wheel. Picking up information from the mind, energy, and body systems is similar to the process of ob- serving a pinwheel. At first, we may work slowly with each petal of the wheel—each chakra. The faster the pinwheel (energy) spins, the faster we receive information, until eventually we receive information from multiple chakras at the same time.

This is the ideal. But first, find out which ways of receiving energy are easiest for you, and then ground into that talent. Claim it as yours, so you can build upon it.

Remember to focus on what we can do, not on what we can't do. What we focus on gets charged with energy. As we focus on what we can do, we'll get more of what we can do!
How do we move a mountain? One stone at a time.

As part of our awareness tunes into a chakra, we train ourselves to collect information from our body. For instance, our awareness might tune into the 2nd chakra to pick up emotional information—as another part of our awareness tunes into the area of the body we want information from, such as our heart.

Doing this exercise strengthens our psychic muscles, just as playing scales on the piano strengthens our ability to play a song. Eventually we won't do this in such a methodical manner, but practicing this technique every day helps us notice which psychic pathways are strongest, and reprograms us to more easily receive information from our energy system.

When I first learned this approach, every day for a year, I spent an hour lying comfortably on my bed, tuning into a part of my body where I imagined the energy was blocked. I then practiced the following exercise. Collecting information from my body/energy system is now easy and effortless—as it can be for all of us.

FINDING OUR WAY IN

- **Step 1** *Charge and balance your energy field*. Many ways are explained in this book. For starters, here are some suggestions. Do 25 jumping jacks. Pat your body with your hands, starting at the feet and working up, front and back, and then working your way back down. Then, stop and breathe in the change—and feel, imagine, or sense the energy filling up our cells with HVC. Imagine the energy flowing and balancing front/back, top/bottom, and left/right

  Now, imagine your outer and inner energy field getting large and filling with acceptance and self-love. The more energy moving through us, the easier it is to pick up psychic information. Referring to the chakra diagram above, connect to the first chakra and imagine red energy coming in. Then connect to the second chakra (front and back) and imagine orange energy coming in; the third (front and back), with yellow energy coming in; the fourth chakra (front and back), with grass green energy coming in; the fifth chakra (front and back), with sky blue energy coming in; the sixth chakra (front and back), with indigo energy coming in; and the seventh chakra, with white or violet energy coming in. Then, imagine your energy field balanced front/back, left/right, and top/bottom. Later we will learn how to program these cues into our field so that just saying the word "balance" will raise our vibration.

- **Step 2** Connect to any area of the body or energy system and ask a question. **For the purposes of this exercise, we will connect to the heart area and ask, "What negative belief about me is held in my heart?"** Place your hands on the heart (when possible, always touch the part of the body from which we are collecting information).

  Using one chakra at a time, we will ask this question (or any question), as we split our awareness and tune in simultaneously to the heart and to the chakra we are trying to receive information from. Some- times the more specific the question, the easier it is to get an answer. Practice on your own and see what works best. An example of a broad question might be, "what wisdom is here?" An example of a specific question to ask is, "What negative belief is being held in the heart chakra?" Once again, for the purposes of this exercise we will ask **"What negative belief about me is held in my heart?"**

  With one hand on (or near) the area we want to receive information about—in this case, the heart—place the other hand on the specific chakra from which we wish to collect information. Start at the 1st chakra.

  For instance, the first chakra brings in information kinesthetically, through sensations such as pain, pleasure, smooth, crisp, cohesive, pulsations, pressure, heavy, light, texture, temperature, flows, blocks, streams, steam, mist, and rough. So, one hand is on the 1st chakra, and the other hand is touching our heart area. Make a mental note of what you feel through the hand touching your heart.

  Then move to the 2nd chakra, which picks up emotions. Now, one hand is touching our 2nd chakra, and the other hand is still touching your heart. Remember to let your mind wander and go out of focus as we gently invite our self to feel an emotion. Notice what you pick up emotionally: anger, betrayal, sadness, the child consciousness of not being enough . . . .

Connect to the 3rd chakra (intuition) with one hand and leave the other hand on the area you are sensing into (your heart). Notice what you receive intuitively about the energy in your heart. Remember to let your mind wander, and notice what wanders back in.

Continue to move one hand to each of the remaining chakras, while leaving the other hand on the heart. The 4th chakra is about relationships and love. Sense what you pick up when your hand is placed here. If you "need" a relationship or have just finished a challenging one, how might that get in the way of receiving information? Being clear and accepting of all parts of our self helps us more clearly receive in- formation and self assess.

Tune into the 5th chakra as you also connect to the area we are asking a question about, and ask, "What do you hear in your head about the belief held in your heart? What words want to come through? What, if anything do you smell and/or taste?" Again, don't focus too hard; invite the response to come through by letting our mind wander—or imagine the answer.

Tune into the 6th chakra as you also connect to the area you are asking a question about, and ask, "What do you see with your unfocused soft eyes, or what do you see on your 'mind screen' with closed eyes? (Seeing something on your *mind screen* occurs when you see it in your "mind's eye" – on your "mental screen" — and not tangibly in front of you.) Again, don't focus too hard; invite the response to come through by letting your eyes wander. Or, imagine what flies in front of your open or closed eyes. Is it a dragon, a symbol, or perhaps colors?

Tune into the 7th Chakra (direct knowing) as you also connect to the area you are asking a question about. Letting your mind wander, eventually notice what direct wisdom comes through. Always remember to pause and listen and receive the information. If it is hard for you to trust the information you receive, this could interrupt the flow. It is a way we self-sabotage. Be playful and make it a fun game. Over time, your information is confirmed and your self-trust grows—and then, so does your skill.

- **STEP 3:** Notice which chakras are easiest to collect information from, and write this down. **THIS IS YOUR WAY IN!** *Focus on what we **can do**,* and then other senses may come in. In the beginning, most people feel kinesthetically. Some others get an intuitive hit, see something on their mind screen, or get a knowing sense. It usually takes some practice before people see energy tangibly, if at all. Because seeing is often believing, this may be challenging to overcome. *No one way of picking up information is more accurate or better than another.* Don't judge the manner in which we receive! Patience and practice, patience and practice!

Different personality types have different talents in receiving psychic information. Generally, Leaders, Excel, and Spiritual types have more difficulty feeling emotions and feeling kinesthetically; they do better seeing or using direct knowing. Heart-centered types tend to feel kinetically and emotionally, as do Compassionate types.

As we are able to connect to the parts of ourselves that represent each Character Structure's gifts, we increase our skills in life, and in collecting psychic information. For instance, we can call in our Leader energies to help us problem solve and find solutions, so we succeed and move away from any negative feelings of not being good enough. Psychically reading energy can trigger our negative egos and create a CHOICE POINT. Remember, we are in charge of our developing skills for sensing and shifting energy, so let us be kind, patient, and receptive to help and support.

Also notice if you have difficulty relaxing. If there is tension anywhere, it stops the flow of energy and makes it harder to read what is happening. You can explore whether it is easier to listen or feel—and what the difference is between the two. How can you expand your gifts so you become skilful at both? Be curious and explore.

The next exercise expands upon this skill. Once we know our own way in, we can practice so it grows.

Meditation to Assess/Shift Emotional Aspects of Your Chakra System

Once we know "our way in," we can practice, practice, practice.

Have a piece of paper and pen nearby to record the information you collect. In the beginning, this assessment can take an hour or more. Eventually, you will be able to assess each chakra in a few moments. If you can assess your system, you will then be better able to assess another's system. *Working with a Me-B Guide (or anyone) that can confirm your skill is important as well. Confirmation builds self-confidence, which builds skill.*

<u>NOTE: How to Tell If A Chakra Is Turning Clockwise</u>

Place a clock or watch face over the chakra, facing outward. That is the direction that a clockwise-spinning chakra turns. Another way of understanding the direction is to take your right hand and place your thumb into the center of the chakra. The direction in which the fingers fold over is clockwise.

Beginning with the 1st chakra, follow the procedure below with all 7 chakras.

STEP 1:

Let your mind and breath focus on the area, and set your intention to collect information. Do this exercise from your **Explorer's Mind**. Stay in child-like joy and curiosity. Write the answers down. Is the chakra under or overcharged, or is it balanced? Is it turning clockwise—bringing in energy—or counterclockwise, taking out energy? Or is it wobbling in different directions?

Do you sense dark colors, congestion, and dense energy that doesn't flow? This suggests overcharge, whereas few sensations or light energy and colors suggest undercharged energy.

Learning how to access personal information by connecting to the body and/or energy system is an important skill in Me-B Transformation and in personal transformation, because it supports self-empowerment through self-assessment. Begin with imagining what you think is there. Trusting yourself to accurately collect information may take time and patience. Don't give up— remember, 98 percent of success is **showing up for ourselves**! Excel and Spiritual personality types will have the most difficulty with feeling energy/sensations in the body, because the Spiritual type energetically escapes from the body and the Excel type shuts down their feelings. So, continue to practice. Support by an Me-B Guide and patience are needed.

STEP 2:

Imagine what positive beliefs are held there, such as: "I love myself." Be curious—how do these beliefs feel, sensation wise, in the body? (Do you feel tingles, flows, heat, cold . . . ?) What images do you imagine support those beliefs? Images could be past experiences, symbols, archetypes—anything that helps you anchor into the positive beliefs. For instance, you can imagine a screen showing an image of when you did something well and were proud of yourself.

STEP 3:

What emotional blocks (negative beliefs) get in the way of the chakra's psychological functions? Read what you wrote down for Step 2, the positive beliefs/images. Now feel, imagine, and visualize the positive growing somatically, energetically, and cognitively—and the negative melting way.

STEP 4:

Now, go back to reassess the chakra. Do you imagine its frequency changed? Did the positive beliefs melt away the negative? What can you pick up?

If you have trouble picking up any information, it takes practice, practice, practice. Work with a Me-B Guide to learn how to self-assess and shift to a healthier vibration.

This journey is more about noticing that we already interact with one another and our world based on what is happening energetically around us. All we have to do is notice and bring it deeper into our conscious mind to claim that power.

DON'T GIVE UP

When I first began learning how to feel, track, and experience energy, I thought it was impossible. My friend Cindy always had the profound spiritual and energetic experiences. She saw energy, and even worked with a Shaman who froze time on a busy Washington, D.C. street. Then she would come home and ask me to explain everything that had happened to her. I was the explainer, <u>not</u> the person experiencing it.

And that is the first place I had to start. I had to redefine who I thought I was and open that definition to more! This was harder than I thought. My old identity kept coming in to talk negatively to me—"Are you kidding, you can't do this!" it chided.

When I first learned Reiki, I placed my hands on my teacher's head and felt strong sensations move across my palms. I jumped, my hands flew away, and I said, "What was that?"

Gradually, over time, my ability to feel energy grew. Eventually, I began to "know" (7th chakra) what was happening energetically. I couldn't really see it, but I knew what I was seeing (6th and 7th chakras working together). Teachers, clients, and friends confirmed my experiences, and I began to trust what I was sensing.

As my trust grew, so did my abilities. Now, I often see energy as clearly as I see the mountains framing my house. We can go slowly, be patient, and keep our focus toward success.

OPENING TO RADICAL INTUITION

Opening to Radical Intuition is really about the practice of radically opening to receive ourselves. If wholeness is the definition of healing, then connecting to our inner wholeness allows us to receive our inner guidance. All the information of enlightenment is there for us to reach out and receive as we better learn to get out of our own way. Practice the following exercise and investigate with an open heart our own radical intuition. In this way, we also learn to help others access theirs!

Deepak Chopra writes:

> To be completely free means waking up from all dreamlike states, and reclaiming who you are: the maker of reality. Therefore, nothing we can see, hear, and touch, whether in waking, dreaming, or beyond both, is ultimately real; they only represent shifting perspectives. The material world is projected from a nonmaterial source. The invisible world comes first. It contains the seeds of time and space. Reality increases the closer one gets to the source.

The source in Me-B Transformation™ is called Core Being but it is also sometimes known as the Akashic. By connecting to the Akashic, we can view our destiny and access a road map to help guide us on the way. The sole purpose of the exercise below is to discover more about us and our defenses, blocks, and gifts. This is our life challenge and a path to freedom.

MEDITATION TO OPEN TO RADICAL INTUITION

We are our own power source. External support such as that from doctors, therapists, healers, family, and friends can only supplement our own internal knowing. The following exercise helps us develop this skill and can be applied to any question we hold.

- **STEP 1:**
  From your **Explorer's Mind**, ask a question. Stay light and playful. In this example, we will ask, "What information is held in my Akashic Records?" The Akashic Records reflect the elements of our soul's journey, energetically outlined like an encyclopedia. For instance, we can ask about our lessons learned and those to be learned.

- **STEP 2:**
  Get comfortable.

- **STEP 3:**
  Balance and charge your energy field. Repeat Step 1 of the exercise presented earlier, Finding Our Way In.

- **STEP 4:**
  Find your center—between your navel and solar plexus. Place your hands here and let them sink in. Feel the spark—the spark that ignited your **Core Being**'s existence on Earth. As you breathe, imagine you can (1) recognize the truth of who you are; and (2) let that truth expand—as a sensation in the body, as a thought or image in the mind, and as energy flowing through you.
  As the truth of who you are expands, let it fill your body, and then the room. Continue to let it expand until it connects with the oneness of all. Imagine it even if you can't

feel, see, or sense it. Trust that some part of you is connected and remembers it is ONE.

- **STEP 5:**
  Send the question outward and pause to receive the answer. Sometimes it's helpful to see the image of a computer downloading information to us as the disk. If we try to get an answer, it rarely comes. Instead, let your mind wander and watch where it goes. Do words and/or images present? If so, keep letting them flow.

Follow them. Notice what you feel (emotions/sensations). Notice any images, symbols or pictures, smells or sounds. Do you hear voices or words, or do you just know the answer?

Maybe information will be disjointed at first or just felt as sensations. Record the sensations or disjointed images or thoughts. Let the information flow without needing to understand anything. Give yourself time to practice and evolve. After all, it is the process—not the result—that matters. In the process, you slowly begin to discover you, your defenses, your saboteur and your helper. As we find our internal helper, our skills grow.

Watch to learn what your next step is in developing your internal radical intuition. Eliminate the internal judge. Be in the place of "no excuses," and simply begin to understand what is easy and what is hard about this. The enemy is the false belief that you can't. You choose whether to remember, even if you are only remembering a part of yourself. Remember where you came from. Remember the truth of who you are. **Remember you can and practice, practice, practice!**

Even discovering what makes this difficult for you is a success. Get support from an Me-B trained guide or someone who already has this skill and knows how to help you.

CONNECTING TO SPIRIT GUIDES

Life can be so challenging; external spiritual support can relieve some of the pressure. Some people believe in angels, a higher power, god, or a higher self that can aid us in difficult times.

Clients often ask me about the name of their guide. "How do I get to know them? Why don't they answer my questions? Do I have a guide?"

I find great comfort in the wisdom and love I get from my spirit guides. We can collect all types of information from them. It is forever there, waiting for us to be open and willing enough to sense. However, I find that receiving the wisdom is only half the battle. *Our real tasks are: (1) believing and trusting what we hear, and (2) acting positively on the advice we receive.*

Many people who go to see "psychics" and those who channel spirits often want someone to tell them what they WANT to hear and not necessarily what they NEED to hear or what is true. If we open enough to receive wisdom from our guides or from a psychic, often we are not willing to follow through with the advice if following through means we have to change or necessitates deep personal work. Too often we want information from our guides because we hope there is another way out than the one that is right in front of us.

Deep change rarely comes without looking at our ego-based personality. When guidance does come through, how many of us are strong enough to follow the wisdom—especially if the wisdom takes us out of our comfort zone or demands a new way of thinking? Psychics, intuitives, and spiritual guidance can be used as Spiritual Junk Food to avoid something we need to investigate. If we are in a process of focusing on Spiritual Junk Food, we can't receive clear guidance, even if a gifted psychic is the channel.

When I was 24 years old, my two best friends and I went to a psychic. At the time, I was a community organizer and political activist in Washington, D.C. trying to help empower the poor. I had just graduated from Purdue University and was enthusiastically on my way to change the world. So when the psychic said I would become a healer and he saw me in a past life as a healer, I was sure he was crazy and that I had wasted my money. I wish I could tell him today how correct he was. I just wasn't ready to hear the truth. Not being ready to hear is one of the main reasons we have trouble connecting to guidance.

The next time I saw a psychic, I was 31, a young mom, and having difficulty in my marriage. I had just left my high-powered lobbyist job to follow my husband to Asia and support his career. I went from talking with congressional staff to being "the wife of." I felt lost and alone. This psychic too said I had a calling in the healing profession. But again, I couldn't hear it.

Receiving the information is easy for me, but following through with the wisdom and integrating it into my life is much harder. If we are having trouble receiving information from our guides, a first step to take is to use our Explorer's Mind and investigate what part of us might not want to know the deeper truth. What part (usually our ego) doesn't want to see clearly? This is the largest obstacle to overcome.

At the time, I didn't know what a healer was, and I didn't care to find out. I felt it was much more helpful to the world and also more prestigious to work on Capitol Hill than to be a healer or therapist. Funny, now I feel the opposite is true. As the saying goes, the only one in our way on the route to happiness and success is our self. That is why I believe the Explorer's Mind, my Core Being, and Enlightened Observer are so important. I so want to get better at getting out of my own way. The ten years that went by before I found my inner healer was not wasted, and I don't regret a day. I do, however, appreciate that I am much better at listening to my spirit guides, following through with the wisdom, and moving out of my own way!

Finding Our Way to Connect to Our Guides

1. Balance and charge your energy field.
2. To the extent possible, follow the exercise to connect to Core Being.
3. Ask a question and open to receive the answer. It may come as a picture, symbol, knowing, words/concepts, feeling, emotion, or some other way. If it doesn't come right away, then do something else for a while and notice what thoughts come into your head. Sometimes if we try too hard, we don't get an answer. However, if we let our mind wander, the answer can find its way back to us.
4. Practice writing the answer, using a Pendulum, and/or drawing an answer. If you have trouble receiving information — practice, practice, practice. Focus on what you can do and look for any part of you not willing to see the truth. Avoid Spiritual Junk food.

TIPS TO ASSESS ENERGY

Before Beginning, Facilitate Connection with Core Being

Before beginning to work with a client, or before we begin any connection with another in our life, we must first align our own field and resonate with our Core Being. We can't have deep connection with another if we are not in contact with ourselves. The more we can move out of the personality level and into our Core Being, the more able we are to assist another.

Some energetic shifting techniques we can use to balance, charge, and reconnect to our center are outlined below. (This entire book is devoted to offering interventions that allow us to more easily return to Core Being.) Patience and practice ensures success!

- Spin colors/chakras clockwise—front and back,
- Chi Kung practices such as the oak and the micro-cosmic orbit,
- Engage our Enlightened Observer and Explorer's Mind,
- Strengthen our positive intention,
- Solidify and balance our outer energy egg,
- Run second and forth level colors through the field,
- Align with Core Being and the Manifest Energy,
- Open the central channel and align all chakras with it,
- Practice centered oneness, and
- Connect with our multi-dimensional fabric and universal trust.

Next, Facilitate Deep Connection to self and other

1. Without deep contact, we can't asses our energy field or another's energy field. The ease of connecting to a client depends upon the following. (Using these techniques with our spouse, co-workers, boss, parents, and friends is also recommended.)

We may experience conflict simply because of the way our character structure relates to the other's character type. Sometimes, if we are too different or too much alike, it can be more difficult to connect. However, as we move out of the personality level and into our Core Being and honor their Core Being, connection happens more easily.

2. Transference and Counter-Transference can either facilitate connection or detract from it. Often there is positive transference from a client toward the Me-B Guide. We can use the positive transference to create a safe space. In the long run, the Me-B Guide must encourage a more real and authentic relationship.

3. Mirror back (repeat back) to the client what they say, and mirror their positive sense of self to them to help facilitate connection with them.

4. Track their negative energetic defenses and help them come out of defense.

5. Practice any of the positive resourcing techniques outlined in this book.

6. Be the "good enough mom." Eventually, we must wean the client from the motherly transference so the client learns to hold that energy for him- or herself. When we do wean them, they usually negatively project upon us their anger. Use this anger as a raw material for them to feel their own power.

7. Depending upon the client's character type, challenging them can deepen our relationship with them and thus deepen our contact. It can also detract from our connection with the client, so reading the field is important in order to know which approach is most supportive.

8. Sometimes we are imperfect in a session. Admitting we made a mistake can be a powerful tool to facilitate deeper connection with a client. This is especially true if the client's parents never admitted they were wrong.

9. Following and supporting the Rhythm of Flow of energy deepens connection—as does positive intention and good listening skills.

10. In addition to these methods for making contact, there may also be other approaches. List your gifts and challenges in the area of connecting to others. This is not about being perfect. It is about being genuine, even in our imperfection.

ASSESS ENERGETICALLY

Once we have deep connection with self and client, we can then begin to receive information on the energy and consciousness running through them. We can learn to assess: Core Distortions, beliefs, past lives, ancestral lineage distortions, archetypes, trauma, emotions, and more.

1. **Connection.** As mentioned, we must be in contact with ourselves and then expand to connect to our client. Otherwise, we will have trouble tracking the energetic blocks/flows. So, if we cannot receive information or cannot track the energy, then there is a good chance we are NOT in deep enough contact.

Sometimes a client will purposely or unconsciously break contact, so it is more difficult to read what is happening. This is not bad or good—it is just information. It tells us that the client has gone into defense. Being adept at working with the defense both energetically and cognitively will serve our client's transformation greatly. Yet ultimately it is up to them to do the healing. We can only do our best to help.

Usually, if a client shuts down, and they are lying on the table, I don't place my hands on them. I use this information to assess their character structure, developmental Core Distortions, images, and beliefs. This practical knowledge, combined with intuition and information from our client's guides, will support us in our next step.

Practicing, practicing, practicing is very important as well.

I often give the client space and ask them how safe or comfortable they feel. Sometimes they don't even know, but usually, they deeply appreciate my "seeing." This then deepens the relationship be- cause I see and honor what is happening with them. It creates trust.

With certain personality types, a client will shut down either during the first session or directly after a session where they felt deep emotional release. If this happens, help them notice what is happening. Explore this defense and how it might create hardship for them in life.

2. **Know our way in by practicing the pinwheel exercise.** Which of the following ways in are strongest: kinesthetic, seeing, hearing, direct knowing, intuition, emotions, taste, or smell? It helps to use our strongest channel as the doorway in to assessing a field. For me, kinesthetic is strongest. I use it to help me vibrate at the level that opens me up to seeing.

3. **Begin by assessing the basics—flow or no flow.** Sometimes it is enough information to simply determine where the energy wants to flow and where the energy either slows or appears dense. Again, tips to assist in this process include:

   - use our eyes to notice where in the body we are drawn toward;
   - use our mind—put our awareness in to the client's body to scan from head to toe, and as we scan, use our third eye to see and open to sense intuition, direct knowing, hearing, smell and taste;
   - feel in our body what is happening;
   - sink our energetic hand deep into the body to scan and sense flows or no flows, emotions, or any information that comes; and
   - find our unique way of assessing energetically.

4. **Assess the 5 dimensions** (Auric Field; Manifest Energy Intention Line; Core Being; Multi-Dimensional Fabric, and the Physical Body.) Remember to also assess the structured and unstructured levels of the Auric Field. Is the Manifest Energy aligned? Is our client connected to their Core Being? What do we notice in the physical body? Let your body/hand/senses vibrate through the Auric field and see what you discover. How connected is the client to the Multi-Dimensional fabric and Star Child energies?

   Here are some suggestions of what you might want to notice at each level:

   - Under- or overcharged (Auric levels 1,3,5,7)
   - Does the client have awareness of their energy/emotions/Manifest Energy/defenses?
   - Blocks and flows
   - Core Distortions (Auric, Manifest Energy, physical)

- Past lives, traumas (primarily Auric levels 2 and 4)
- Subconscious
- Ancestral issues, archetypes, cords
- Emotions (Auric levels 2, 4)
- Images/beliefs
- Developmental level
- Resourcing and positive sense of self

5. **What is too much information?** I tend to find that less information can often be more useful as a therapeutic tool. Getting flooded with too much detail can take us out of contact with the client. Sometimes the trick is to regulate the flow of information we pick up from a client's field and to learn how to discern what is most needed in the moment. To facilitate this, we can bring the thinking out of the mix and set our intention to receive only what is necessary.

6. **Practice.** Practice and notice what we can do, and then build upon what we can do. Use the Connection-Track-Intervention-Shift sequence below to help us.

CONNECTION-TRACK-INTERVENTION-SHIFT SEQUENCE

1. Connect to self and client.
2. Track what is happening energetically.
3. Offer a dialogue or energetic intervention.
4. Assess if and how the intervention shifted the client's field.
5. Gauge the next dialogue or energetic intervention based on how the client's field shifted or did not shift.

After each energy or dialogue intervention you make, assess if there was a shift in the client's field, and then gear the next energy or dialogue intervention based on what you observed.

In the beginning, you might not be able to assess subtle energy shifts. If you focus on what you can do, you will receive more of what you can do. Using the Explorer's Mind, remember to remain positive and give yourself credit for any successes. Some people like to use pendulums, their hands, and/or muscle testing to help track energy. You can also notice changes in our own body and energy system to track what is happening with a client's field.

USING A PENDULUM TO COLLECT INFORMATION

When using a pendulum, make sure your arm and elbow are relaxed against our side. If the body is tight and stiff, energy won't flow as easily. Make sure you are grounded so your energy field is large. The more energy that is flowing, the more accurate the reading will be, and the more the pendulum will move.

When asking a question, be clear that "yes" is clockwise and "no" is counterclockwise. If the pendulum does not go in either of those directions, then the answer is not clear, or you are not aligned to receive a clear answer. Wait a while before you try again and examine your own Manifest Energy to see if there is a break in the Intention line.

238

Also, since intention moves energy, be careful that you don't move the pendulum and control it with your intention. Don't look at it directly; keep your eyes soft and unfocused and glance at it.

To read energy with a pendulum, dip the pendulum into the chakra to read what direction the chakra is turning. The longer the pendulum stays in the chakra, the more our energy will influence a change in the chakra, so do the readings as quickly as possible. If using the pendulum to check the level of the field or Manifest Energy Line, make sure your energy field is strong and vibrating at the same frequency as the person's field you want to read. For instance, if you want to read what is happening with someone's Manifest Energy, you need to be in your own Manifest Energy Line. Or if you want to assess someone's second level of the field, you must be on the 2nd level of the field.

Also, be clear as to what you are asking the pendulum. For instance, are you checking where a negative belief is held in the body? Are you checking where the lines are broken or where they may be too dense? Are you checking for breaks in the Manifest Energy? The clearer you are in what you want to know, the easier it will be to collect the answer.

Some Me-B Guides rely heavily on the pendulum and use it throughout the session and throughout the day. It is important not to over-rely on anything but your own developing skills.

USING YOUR HAND TO READ ENERGY

Our hands pick up information kinesthetically (1st Chakra) but we can also assess emotions, child consciousness, and much more. What makes us able to read energy with our hand is connection. Any time we connect with our hand or our mind to ourselves or another person, we open the conduit to read energy.

Without deep connection to our self and the other person there is no energy flow and we will not be able to read/assess/track energy!

READING ENERGY WITH THE HAND

- **STEP 1:**
  Regulate a large amount of energy through our field and make contact with our Core Being. Also check to make sure we are grounded, that our shoulders and mid-back are relaxed, and that we can allow energy to flow through our whole body: front/back; top/bottom; left/right.
- **STEP 2:**
  When sensing energy with our hand, be very careful not to charge the area while we are sensing. This is because instead of collecting data, we will be changing the consciousness of the area. Doing both at one time can be confusing and is an advanced skill. (Learn one skill at a time.)
- **STEP 3:**
  Once we are connected, allow ourselves to receive information. What do we feel on our hand? Sometimes we can feel the client in defense. What do we feel emotionally from the client?
- **STEP 4:**
  Notice what we notice and then open to receive more information. Like riding a bike, at first we may fall—but if we practice, practice, practice it becomes easier.

USING OUR BODY TO READ/TRACK ENERGY

Ideally, it is not optimal to use your own body as a receptor for collecting information about others or your clients, because you must be able to distinguish between what is happening in your own energy field and body—and what is your body reading and reacting to another's field. Sometimes information or dynamics are occurring both in our field and in our client's field at the same time. It can get complicated.

To use our own body to read someone else's information, we must know at a very subtle level what is theirs, what is ours, and what might be in both our field and the client's field.

Before we use our body to read/track energy, therefore, we must first know what is happening in our field. Then, during the reading, if we feel a change in our body and energy system, and we know it is <u>not</u> something going on within our field, we can assume it is a change in the client's field.

What we assess as a shift in someone else (such as a client) can inform us as to what the next intervention with them could be. *Remember, the energy has the intelligence. It leads, and we follow.* If we are interacting with a client, our boss, a parent, or our partner, as we read what is happening in their energy system, we better know how to respond. If their field collapses or becomes reactive, we can investigate what is happening and why they went into defense.

Once again, I don't recommend using your body as receptor to assess another person's energetic patterns. It is not the healthiest choice. You don't want to take in LVC into your body from another's — especially if you are working with many clients a day.

Using your own body to assess another's energy system should only be used as a beginning step. This is because it may feel easier when you are first learning to assess and track energy. Eventually, however, it is ideal to graduate from this method and diversify your skills so you have more than one method at your disposal.

SEEING ENERGY AND SHIFTS IN CONSCIOUSNESS

There are many different ways to "see" shifts. Seeing is done primarily through the 6th chakra. Each of us will have our own favorite method of seeing energy based on what feels most comfortable for us.

Our method of seeing energy can be very different from someone else's method—yet equal. I find we tend to judge how we see instead of feeling grateful and appreciating our gifts. Gratitude for what we can do is necessary if our skills are to grow.

We can internally see shifts tangibly with our eyes, as if we are watching a movie.

We can see shifts internally on our mind screen, if we look at what we see with our eyes closed. Let's close our eyes now and ask a question, and then look to see what appears. Open to receive an answer. Notice whether we are trying to receive or "trusting to receive." It is a subtle distinction, but an important one. Sometimes, we will see an image or symbol that is a clue to the answer—whereas sometimes we see things directly.

We can see images flash before our eyes and mind screen. For instance, when with a client during one session, I saw a dragon flash before me. I first checked in with myself to see if the message was for me. I don't have a strong connection with dragons and haven't had them visit me before, so I asked the client about it. She said that the dragon was her power animal and that he comes to her when she needs support. We then used the dragon's energy to help her overcome a recent trauma.

We can intuitively see (third chakra) or see through direct knowing (seventh chakra). When we look at someone's field, we can be intuitively drawn to an area. When a client walks into the room, notice where your eyes are drawn to focus. Keep that information close, because you may want to investigate that area of the body later in the session. I find that 9 out of 10 times, the area I am most drawn to focus on is the area the client identifies as holding a challenging emotion or belief. As this happens more, you can relax into trusting yourself.

My favorite method of seeing is through direct knowing. As I scan a client's field, through direct knowing (7th chakra), I am able to notice where the energy flows and where the energy is blocked, and what consciousness is held there. With practice, we can find our favorite method of picking up information. On a regular basis, do the pin wheel technique to help develop your ability to sense and track energy.

Use "your way in" to open to seeing. As we deepen and trust our ability to sense energy, we can expand upon that method so are able to sense energy through other senses as well, including seeing. In the beginning, I thought I could only pick up information kinesthetically, through touch. It was the easiest for me, and it was "my way in." Later, I used touch as a way of opening to seeing energy.

When I was first learning, I didn't know I could see energy until I had to present a client's case to my supervisors. I described what happened in our sessions and the success the client made in her personal process work. I discussed how I "saw" the energy. Only then did I notice that I really did see energy. I just never gave myself credit for seeing it.

Over time, my skills grew, and I gained more confidence and accuracy. I first saw energy by "knowing" what I saw (6th and 7th chakras). Once I got comfortable seeing through direct knowing, I began to notice I could actually visually see energy as well.

However, I didn't just start out seeing energy. I first assessed what was happening by touching the energy with my hand and tracking it that way. Later, as I gained confidence in my ability to assess energy by feeling with my hand and tracking it that way. Later, as I gained confidence in my ability to assess energy by feeling it with my hand, I eventually opened to seeing it.

We can each find our own unique way into sensing energy—be it through smell, taste, touch, intuition, or direct knowing. Then, as we deepen that skill and trust it, the other methods of sensing energy can come through, too. **Remember to practice and take our classes to assist you.**

Sensing Energy Through the Chakras

Each chakra has a function to help you sense energy:

- **1st** — Feeling sensations and Touch, Kinesthetic
- **2nd**— Emotions
- **3rd**— Intuition
- **4th**— Love
- **5th**— Taste, Smell, and Hearing
- **6th**— Seeing
- **7th**— Direct Knowing

(Barbara Brennan, *Hands of Light)*

TRACKING BODY LANGUAGE

Another method of noticing energy shifts is to look at body language and facial expressions. Some believe that 85 percent of communication occurs through body language. Non-verbal communication is a powerful tool to use in Me-B Transformation™ because we work so deeply at the subconscious level. For instance, if you ask another, "What's here now?" and your child, friend, partner, or client claims they notice nothing—but their hand starts to clench and unclench—it is a wonderful indicator of a shift.

Ideally, all interventions during Me-B sessions are made based on the shifts that we notice. We connect, track what is happening, make an intervention, notice the shift, reconnect, track, and the process continues. Use the **Connection-Track-Intervention-Shift Sequence** outlined above.

Some non-verbal cues of a shift include: toe or finger Tapping, movement of the eyes, changes in facial expression, shifting in the seat, tightening or loosening of a body part, bent shoulders, leaning forward or backward, gestures, or looking in a different direction.

Two Case Examples of the Connection-Track-Intervention-Shift Sequence

EXAMPLE 1:

I noticed Joy would always look up and away from me when she talked about her alcoholic ex-boyfriend. I mentioned this, and she confessed that she felt guilty about leaving him and was considering getting back together with him. By tracking her body, I was able to gear my intervention based on what I saw happening in the moment and thus deepen the session to address the real presenting complaint and not the one she had originally stated.

EXAMPLE 2:

Prudence, an Excel personality type, came to see me after the death of her husband. It had been one year since his death, and she was explaining to me how well she was doing. As she talked, I noticed her field reacting strongly, as if it was screaming to be noticed. Her words, emotions, body language and facial expression were consistent with each other, but her energy field was up-in-arms in rebellion.

My next intervention was to follow where the energy was leading, so we began to explore why her energy field was so reactive. She explained that she felt stuck in her life and wasn't able to move forward, especially in the areas of relationship and career. She discovered that a part of her was afraid that if she moved forward, it would really mean she was leaving her husband behind. The energy showed her how and why she was holding back from moving on. Within six weeks of that session, Prudence quit her job, went back to school, and had a new love and new sense of self!

Eventually, the process of "Connection-Track-Intervention-Shift" becomes seamless. It supports the Rhythm of Flow of Reality so that work seems more natural and intuitive. It also helps us move out of the personality level and into our Core Being because we no longer "think" but instead are led by what we see happening. Contact with the self is *vital* to accurately tracking energy. The deeper we connect with ourselves, the more we are able to connect to another.

LOOK MOM, NO HANDS!

We can also practice moving energy with our mind alone, without using our hands. Begin practicing this technique on yourself. Practice the Chi Kung and energy techniques that have been presented. Also practice the Body Connecting Sequence outlined at the end of this chapter, and let the saying **"WHERE AWARENESS GOES, ENERGY FLOWS"** be your guide. The mind moves the energy within us and around us. That is why thoughts are so powerful. Once we can move HVC energy in our own system, we are more skillful at doing this in someone else's system.

Thinking during a Me-B Transformational Intervention can detract us from our goal. Negative thoughts, and distractions such as creating our mental "to do" list, all need to be done outside Me-B Transformation™ sessions. Even self-questioning or judging of the client moves energy in a manner that doesn't support the highest good.

Moving Energy With Mind

VARIATION 1:

1. Place the mind "in" the client's body.
2. Scan the body with your mind and notice where there are flows and where there are blocks.
3. Sink your mind/awareness/breath into the area that needs HVC.
4. Using positive intention, invite the client's Core Being energy into the area.
5. Allow the energy to shift.

VARIATION 2:

1. Place one hand above, and one hand below, an area of the body that needs to be transformed. For instance, if a client is holding dense energy in the knee, one of your hands might be placed on the lower part of the leg, with the other hand on the client's thigh. (Joints often have dense energy.)
2. Using your mind/awareness, melt the dense energy in the knee. Once it has melted away, invite Core Being energy to take its place.

MOVE AND TRACK ENERGY AT THE SAME TIME

It is important to be able to track where the energy is going as we move it. Practice, practice, practice using the techniques offered thus far. Clearly make it your intention to track as you allow and support the movement of the energy.

Whether we are doing touch or no-touch interventions, it is vital that we learn how to track what is happening in both our field and the field of our client, friend or associate.

SEEING ENERGY WHEN SOMEONE IS ABSENT

I often have clients who need support regarding a husband or boyfriend who is not physically in the room with us. Common questions asked include: Should I stay married? Is he cheating on me? Does he love me? Should I continue the relationship? Am I making the same mistake with this one that I made with the last ones?

Being able to tune into the field of someone who is not currently in the room can be very useful. Even energetically calling the person into the room can help the client gain enough information to know how to shift their internal triggers and answer their own questions. Usually just by mentioning the person's name, the room fills with their energy, and it become easier to assess that person. Two techniques to use for assessing someone who is absent are:

Use a chair or table and call in the energy of the person onto the table, pillow or chair. Using intention, tune in to the person.

Reading what is happening with the person not present can be very useful. **Also reading what is happening with a client's field while talking about an absent person** can provide us with vital information. For instance, a client discussed how much she loved and appreciated her friend. At one point of the story, the client's field went into distortion, and I noticed the energy of fear and insecurity. Because I picked up this information, I knew to go back and question the client about that specific part of the story to discover what was really happening.

I mentioned how her field had a reaction during that part of the story, and the client confessed to me that she was secretly envious of her friend's success, and had always felt inadequate next to her. We then took that information to a deeper level and discovered an event in the client's childhood that caused her deep trauma. We worked to shift the Core Distortion surrounding that trauma. By the end of the session, the client could hold authentic appreciation for her friend. She also rescued a vulnerable part of her child consciousness from blame, judgment, and insecurity.

This process of tracking emotions and shifting Core Distortions can be completed as a client sits in a chair or lies on a table. Assessing on the table can be easier in the beginning, because we usually are in deeper con- tact with clients when they are on the table—and we often have our hands on the actual energy of the distortion/emotion as well.

ASSESSING SUBCONSCIOUS SHIFTS

Assessing subconscious shifts can help us determine if there is a positive change in the energetic consciousness even though the client may not feel that there has been a shift. It is important to practice tracking the energy and improving our skills at assessing flows, blocks, defenses, dense energy, chakras, emotions, Core Distortions, and Core Being.

SELF-ASSESSMENT CHECKLIST
The following is a checklist to assess if we are using too much effort, holding back, or are out of balance when working with a client or anyone in our life!

— Your breathing is forced, shallow, or uneven You have an agenda of what must happen You are thinking too much
— You are not in contact with yourself
— You are not in contact with the client/other person
— You think you know what should happen, versus what might happen
— You are living In the past or future
— You are doing more work than your client
— You are making judgments (versus observations) of the other
— You are making judgments (versus observations) of your self
— You are in defense
— You have a sense of need (versus intention) that the other person heal or be different
— You are over-identified with the subject material being discussed (secondary trauma)

- You are hooked into Counter-Transference with the other
- Your ego is activated
- You are needing to do a "good job"
- You have a sense of knowing what is "best" for the client (or other person)
- You are not following the Rhythm of Flow of energy
- You are in negative intention
- You are in Core Distortion, or holding a negative image or belief
- Your Shadow self interferes in the session
- You are needing to please the client/other person
- You are over-identifying with an emotion such as sadness, anger, or fear
- You need the client or other person to like you
- The client/other person feels misunderstood or unsupported—and they are NOT in negative transference

Mental or physical challenges cannot be present if: (1) intention is aligned; (2) the energetics of our Core Being is complete in all three systems; and (3) no contrary alignments are held in the shadow or subconscious. To understand the subconscious, it is important that our clients learn to access the wisdom held within the physical body. Our cells, tissues, bones, organs, fat, and muscles hold vital information.

COMMON MISTAKES EASILY AVOIDED

Listed next are common mistakes to avoid when trying to read our own subtle energy and collect information from our body.

1. When bringing our awareness into the body, most of us use our 6th chakra to "see." When doing so, **all the energy often stays in the head, and we don't actually *connect* to the body**. In the beginning, this happened to 95 percent of my clients. I have found that when I put one hand on their forehead and ask them to bring the 6th chakra down into the body and feel, it usually rectifies the problem.

6th Chakra Seeing Vs. Feeling

Julie wanted to see what was behind the energy block held in her heart. Energetically, she immediately went into her head to "feel into her heart." This is a very common mistake. I placed my hand on her forehead and invited her to bring her 6th chakra down into her body and feel into her heart. With intention, she allowed the energy in her forehead to melt down into her body, finally feeling the grief over her friend's death hidden there.

2. **Working too hard to "find an answer."** This common mistake freezes the energy and prevents the flow of information. When we fixate on finding an answer, it freezes the energy. If you want an answer to come, allow your mind and vision to go out of focus, wander, and drift. Then, use your Enlightened Observer to track what information appears. The most accurate information effortlessly comes when we don't search too hard.

3. **Failure to trust the information we receive.** So often, we discount the value of what we receive and second-guess ourselves. Usually it is our first impressions that are the most accurate.

BODY CONNECTING SEQUENCE AND SENSORY INTEGRATION CHALLENGES

Sensory Integration is the vehicle that keeps the body-mind connection running smoothly. It is the interconnection of all our senses that allows us to move through space with a sense of safety and security. It coordinates what we see, hear, and feel in our environment. From an energetic perspective, sensory stimuli are consciousness tools that regulate our energy system. When our sensory stimuli are activated into a state of alert or hyper-arousal (or to a state of collapse or hypo-arousal), it deregulates our energy system. Since energy is better explained as consciousness, as we learn to regulate the sensations in our body (including taste, smell, visual, and hearing) we can modulate our consciousness, our nervous system and our energy system.

For instance, each chakra regulates a different part of our sensory input. As explained earlier, the 1st chakra regulates sensations, the second emotions, the 5th hearing, taste and smell. If we have sensory integration challenges, as we gain experience in regulating our chakra system, we can overcome these challenges.

We can practice the following Body Connecting Sequence (BCS) on a regular basis and discover the gifts, challenges, and wisdom within us. Our cells and energy system hold consciousness. By doing this BCS, we can reprogram negative aspects of LVC into HVC and create more **Choice Points** for change. When completing the BCS, it is paramount for a Me-B enthusiast to learn to feel the actual sensations in the body, because these sensations are the doorway to the subconscious. *Distortions in our subconscious create the misunderstandings, pain, and challenges in our lives.* Learning to feel actual sensations provides a clear path to identify and transform these distortions.

Excel and Spiritual personality types might have the most difficulty feeling sensations of energy in the body. Compassionate and Heart-Centered types tend to have the easiest time. The Excel's energy tends to be too tightly wound to feel sensations, and Spiritual types have energy that is not grounded into their bodies. As Excels and Spirituals learn to bring in the more expansive and porous energy of the Compassionate and Heart- Centered types, their fields will expand, ground and become more balanced. Find the exercises in this book that help, beginning with the BCS on programming positive sensations outlined next.

BODY CONNECTING SEQUENCE (BCS)

Pause for 10 seconds or longer in each area of the body/energy system, as listed below. Feel all parts of your body and chakra system—dismiss nothing. Connect deeply with your breath and awareness as you melt into each area, just as butter melts on the grill. Notice what you notice as you scan, in sequence, various locations in the body, holding the intention of health and healing. You may also wish to hold the intention to achieve one or more of the BCS objectives outlined below.

- Begin at 7th chakra, and the top of the head, 6th chakra, forehead, back of head, sides of head, eyes, ears, nose, teeth, tongue, lips, cheeks, jaw and cells/muscles bone.
- Then 5th chakra, neck—front and back, shoulders—front and back, 4th chakra, chest, upper back,

heart, lungs, arms, elbows, hands, and fingers, including muscles and bone.

- Move to the 3rd chakra, mid-back and core center, stomach, liver, pancreas, intestines, spleen, muscles, cells and bones.
- Now, melt into the 2nd chakra, lower back, lower abdomen, sex organs, large intestine, pelvis and sacrum down deep into the cells.
- Spend time assessing, feeling, and sensing the 1st chakra, perineum, thighs, back of thighs, front/back of lower legs, ankles, feet, and toes, including muscles and deep into the bones.
- Now tune into the Central Channel. Notice how thick it is, if it narrows, and to what extent the chakras (front and back) connect nicely into the central channel.
- Now assess the Manifest Energy Line as it runs through the central channel in the center of the body. Remember, it is on a different vibration than the Auric level.

*Repeat the BCS as many times as you want or need
in order to achieve any of the 8 BCS objectives.*

Eight objectives for reprogramming ourselves during the BCS process:

OBJECTIVE 1: To program positive sensations of HVC into the physical dimension, including our cells, organs, and bones. This is the most important exercise for all of us to master. If we have a chronic mental or physical illness, this exercise is even more important.

As you scan through the BCS outlined above, notice where you feel positive sensations, using intention, breath, and awareness. Then invite sensations to come into your body and to grow and spread simply by noticing them and melting into them. Imagine energy coming into and through each pore, as if it were an energetic conduit. DO NOT will them or "make them" spread. Simply invite and support.

Any time we judge positive flows and sensations as being better than or worse than others, we distort the energy. So if there are any areas of pain, don't judge them as being bad; just move more quickly through them and spend more time on the positive flows, tingles, and light. **Where awareness goes, energy flows**—*so simply focusing on the positive creates more positive, if done without an agenda, judgment, or the need for anything to be fixed.* **Invite the good sensations to grow and spread to areas of low or no sensations.**

What happens if we can't feel any sensations? If this occurs, three steps may be helpful:

1. Be patient and imagine your energy field as more porous; then practice receiving energy. Sometimes we don't feel because we are so conditioned to give to others. In this exercise, we receive the positive into our body/energy system.
2. Do some form of exercise, or pat up and down on the body with your hands, as explained earlier. As you rest, receive the charge into your body.
3. Notice what you can, such as the touch of your clothes, hands, chair, wind, or breath. Once again, focus on what you can do, and let that be enough. Also, get support from a Me-B Guide to help you. Over time, with practice and support, we succeed.

OBJECTIVE 2: To assess our energy system so we can collect information about heath, energetic blocks, and Core Distortions in the body/energy system.

Begin by sequencing through the BCS 3 times, focusing only on the positive sensations as outlined in Objective 1 above. As you sequence through, notice where there are flows and no flows. If you are not sure, guess and use your imagination. Trust that you know more than you think you know.

Picking an area that might be misaligned, melt your awareness into the area you want to collect information from and ask a question you want to know the answer to. For instance, you might ask a question such as, "What negative belief about myself is held here?" *Make sure your Enlightened Observer is engaged and strong* as you connect deeply with your breath and awareness. You can also touch the area with your hand(s) and allow the energy from your hands to also meet the area.

Assessing Questions

Examples of what you can ask are:

- What Core Distortion is here?
- What wisdom can I receive?
- How am I sabotaging myself?
- What gift is here?
- What positive/negative belief is here?
- What Core Being aspect can I anchor into?
- What negative ego challenge needs support, and how can I best heal it?
- What am I pretending not to know?
- What nutritional/exercise/health changes support me?
- What are the lessons/gifts I can receive from this illness/emotion/difficulty?

The list is endless.

Either ask a question or set your intention to open to receive data. Information may come in the form of: direct knowing (7th chakra), visuals/images/symbols (6th chakra), auditory, smells, taste, sounds, words (5th chakra), intuition (3rd chakra), emotions/feelings (2nd chakra), and/or sensations (1st chakra).

OBJECTIVE 3: To ground more deeply into the physical dimension.

As you scan, in sequence, down though your body and the BCS, hold the intention of sinking deeper into your cells. Say the phrase, "release-down" *at every stage of the sequence*. For instance, say, "head: release down" . . . "tongue: release down" . . . "cheek: release down" . . . and so on. If you practice this enough, your field will automatically be programmed to ground anytime you say the words "release down."

After some time, with practice, you will be able to reduce the BCS exercise to just six stages:

1. "Head release down,
2. shoulders release down,
3. belly release down,
4. hips release down,

5. legs release down, and
6. feet release down"

until eventually, just saying the words "release down" grounds you.

OBJECTIVE 4: To balance and charge your field.

Complete the Body Connecting Sequence at least three times and follow the procedure outlined below.

Be in both the Auric Dimension and the Manifest Energy while you connect to the intention of balancing and charging.

As you move through the sequence the first time, focus on where there are stronger energy flows and where you can kinesthetically feel positive sensations. Remain 30 seconds or longer in the high vibrational areas where you see, sense, and/or feel good sensations or flows. As you do so, program the words "balance and charge" into your field. Remember to say the words during the process. Eventually, just saying the phrase "balance and charge" will create a huge improvement in your field.

Make sure you move more quickly through areas of no sensation or areas where you feel or imagine pain, blocks, discomfort, difficult emotions, or low vibrational frequencies. (Move quickly, but don't avoid the areas or judge them.)

During the second and third times through the sequence, remain even longer on the higher vibrational frequencies, melting into their sensation *and inviting them to spread to areas of no or low sensation. Be careful to invite and not to "move" the energy.* Release your judgment, or the energy won't be as free to expand. Re- peat the words "balance and charge" as you go.

Lastly, using awareness, breath, and intention together, invite your field to balance front/back, left/right, and top/bottom by melting collectively into the front of your body, then the back of your body, then the left, and then the right. If possible, even say the words "balance left/right, top/bottom, and front/back." Our field follows our words. As we practice this more, we can get to the point where all we say are these words, "balance and charge front/back, top/bottom, left/right," and our field is usually happy to reorganize to our wishes. **If you smile, giggle, or feel joy while saying the phrase, it even increases the positive energies.**

If done correctly and with practice, at the end of this exercise your field will be more balanced and charged. Over time, you can train yourself to actually feel energy in the body—so that tingles and flows can be felt strongly throughout at least 90 percent of the body. The skill of feeling sensations in the body links us closely to the subconscious. It is an important skill to develop.

NOTE ABOUT SENSATIONS

Remember, if you don't feel any sensations in your body, don't worry. In time, with focus and positive intention, this can change. Begin by at least feeling the place where your clothes touch your skin, or where you feel the touch of the chair against you. You can also run in place quickly (or do any physical movements) for 20 seconds, and then stop and try again. Running expands your field by charging it and thus makes it easier to feel.

Work with a Me-B Therapist to assist you and continue to focus on what you can do. That creates more of the same—whereas when we focus on what we can't do, we then get more of what we can't do, which is counterproductive.

OBJECTIVE 5: To program your energy field to respond to cues and install positive energy such as safety, self-esteem, strength, and comfort.

Our energy field responds to intention and is constantly being reorganized based on the signals we send it— even unintended signals from our subconscious. Our words and thoughts reflect our intentions. We can pro- gram words or thoughts into our field, and our energy system will follow the cue.

Just as our field responds to the cue "release-down," we can program other supportive cues such as safety, feelings of being enough, a sense of strength, feelings of compassion, and/or connection to Core Being. Any positive cue we choose can be programmed into our energy system. We already have so many negative cues programmed into our system; we might as well balance the scales by cueing or more deeply embedding positive expressions into our programming!

In times of stress, it may take longer for our energy system to restructure and accept a new cue. This is why there are three grades of cue programming. Grade 1 is the easiest stage to program because we program it for less stressful situations. Grade 2 is when we introduce a slight stress into our consciousness during the programming. Grade 3 is programming designed for high stress situations and takes quite a bit of skill to master.

To program a cue, you must first balance your field as explained in Objective 4 above then follow the procedure outlined next. You can program in various levels of each cue. The higher the level, the more solidly your energy system needs to be grounded into the cue.

To program safety, find an image that makes you feel safe, such as your bed or a hammock on a beach. If you are working with clients, they may have difficulty coming up with an image. Work with them to find one. As you move through the body connection sequence, at each body part say the words, "I am safe and secure" at the same time as you visualize the image of safety and feel positive sensations and energy in your body.

Grade 2 of this programming would be to expose yourself to a risky **visualization** that normally triggers fear (such as imagining you are doing the exercise at the same time as flying on an airplane or speaking in public) and then repeat the sequence until you are successful. Never move to Grade 3 until you have completed Grade 2 successfully.

251

Grade 2 and 3 Examples of Safe and Secure

I felt confident in my ability to feel safe and secure sensations throughout my body. My image was of sitting on the beach while I listened to the waves roaring. When doing the exercise, I was even able to conjure up the smell of salt in the air. Next, I imagined my father criticizing me, just imagined it. In the past I never said, "Dad, please don't say that, it hurts." I was always too scared to speak conflict directly to my father. Even on the little things.

I remember my dad took me to his favorite gym to exercise. I carried my water bottle, the one I used at my own gym. The lid was always secure, a yellow screw top with an aluminum cover. I loved it. As we walked into the exercise room, my dad kept commenting on what an awful water bottle I had—and couldn't I have found a "normal" one? What he really wanted was a normal child who fit into his tightly defined box. On and on he went about my water bottle. At the time, for me to even say, "Mine is OK," or "It doesn't feel good to have you criticize my water bottle," or "please stop" was much too much to even imagine.

So I used this example to cue my energy system to a Grade 2. While I sequenced through my body, I imagined my father complaining about my water bottle. I repeated the procedure, remembering to say the words, feel, and visualize (all three) until I could go through the sequence without my body or energy system negatively reacting to the image of the criticism.

Only then did I know I was ready to move to Grade 3. To achieve Grade 3, I repeated the words "I am safe and secure" internally to myself the next time my father or mother criticized me, while I spoke up in my own defense and said something like, "Please don't talk that way to me" or "Your judgments hurt." The first few times I did this, my field reacted in fear. But with practice, my field eventually responded strongly to the cue, and I was able to stay safe and secure. In the beginning, my parents took this change in my behavior harshly. How dare their daughter disagree with them? No one ever said no to my father. That was not ever allowed. But, eventually, because I could speak my truth without any angry charge, just clarity of intention, my parents and I became closer, for there was no fear or suppressed anger in the way.

As demonstrated in the above example, Grade 3 of the safety programming described above would be to place our self in a fearful situation while we run through the sequence. Practice this until your field and body sensations stay positive throughout the encounter. Fearful does not mean dangerous. This exercise is not meant to put us at unnecessary risk. Its goal is to normalize our abnormal responses to stress, so we can overcome fear that is based on past Core Distortions.

To program feelings of **"I am enough,"** the procedure is very similar to the programming of safety.

In fact, it is much more effective if we have already programmed in at least Grade 1 safety within our system, because feelings of being enough are often linked to needing external support or validation. If we can at least support our self in creating safety, then we are closer to the goal of programming self-validation— the focal point needed in order to program feelings of being enough.

As before, find a visualization that represents "I am enough." You might choose a symbol, picture, or example of a time when you actually felt "enough." Then as you visualize it, say the words, "I am enough" and move through the BCS, stopping and pausing at each part of the body and energy system as was detailed earlier. (Guide your client to find his or her own phrase that is correct for them.)

It is nice to finish this exercise with a Core Being connection exercise.

Depending upon an individual's personality type, just programming in the energy of being "enough" could be incomplete. This is true especially if the person is an Excel or Compassionate personality type.

Allowing Imperfection

Often we need to add an auxiliary program of: "even when I make a mistake or someone doesn't like me or approve of me, or they judge me, I am enough". As you know, mistakes in this human dimension happen. Allowing imperfection to be perfect is the key. Our imperfections and mistakes are simply signs leading us deeper into releasing the personality level. They are inevitable and do not decide our value.

If we operate from the premise that we are all whole and divine, and we are journeying to connect deeper to that wholeness, then a mistake is the light in the tunnel, shining the way. Our mind, ego, and cultural programming can argue with this statement, but who is in charge? Is it our wisdom and Core Being, or our past programming? We really can decide! We can use our energy system to create a boundary that says "no" to the past—or to a prison that locks us into our past.

NOTE: Other important components to program are **strength** versus collapse, and **sensations of comfort.** Follow the above procedures and remember to complete Grade 1 before moving to Grade 2. Then complete Grade 2 before moving to Grade 3.

OBJECTIVE 6: To program you or your client's field to be able to accept the reality that others will dislike us, judge us, and even hate us.

Separation from god occurs the first time we move from the frequency of unconditional love to the frequency where judgment, hate, and heartbreak can exist. It can feel overwhelming, as the energetic arrows can attack us when we might be the most open.

This one is a bit more difficult, because we will be visualizing someone who hates us or who is sending verbal/energetic arrows into us as we say, "___hates me." We will have to keep our Enlightened Observer energy at a very high frequency as we do the BCS. If we don't have a good connection to our Core Being, or if we are not at least at Stage 4 of Me-B Transformation™, it is best to wait on this exercise until the imagined energy of attack is sure to melt away into HVC.

OBJECTIVE 7: To program you or your client's field to quickly access and balance other dimensions and the consciousness held in those dimensions.

First, ground and balance your field as described above. Then connect to the dimension you want to program (such as Core Being, Manifest Energy, or Multi-dimensional Fabric of Interconnectedness). Say the name of the dimension as you connect with it.

As you connect to the energy dimension, say the name of the dimension and scan through the body. Eventually, just saying the name of the dimension will bring you into it, unless you are in defense or blocked by a Core Distortion. Then it might take longer, or you might need to look at the deeper issue that is in the way—a false belief, Core Distortion, trauma, etc.

OBJECTIVE 8: Anything we can think of—be creative.

The Universe really does want to support our intentions. Use this undeniable "cosmic" law to support yourself and your clients. Energy can be programmed for us to achieve our higher purposes. Use it to connect to meridians, organs, or whatever needs support.

How Often Do I Need To Program It? Whenever you feel *attached* to the energy of a negative program, it can be helpful to do a re-installment of the positive belief system. Thoughts move through us all day long. Some of them are positive, and some negative. It is our self-identification with the negative thoughts that causes problems. This self-identification or attachment is what needs to be transformed.

If you can detach from the energy of the thought and let it melt away, there is no need for deeper work. For instance, one teacher of mine said, "just don't feed the monster, and it will disappear." In these programming processes, we are learning how to not feed the monster. As we become self-empowered, we gain the ability to move beyond our past programming and invent our life based on our connection to our Core Being. *There are occasions when programming the positive doesn't shift the energy, and we need to go to the negative belief system and feel the intensity of it until it no longer harms us. This can only be done if you have an observer that is anchored into your Core Being.* This is the Enlightened Observer.

When part of you is aligned to your Core Being, you can then bring that energy into the body to melt the negative belief. This is basic trauma work, and it should only be done if the Enlightened Observer is strong enough and is operating at a high frequency that can be brought into the physical body to shift the negative. Ideally, you should be at least at Stage 4 of Me-B Transformation™ before you attempt this.

REVIEW QUESTIONS

1. Name three major components of Mindfulness.
2. Our subconscious is ____percent of awareness.
3. What areas of awareness would you most like to bring out of the subconscious and into the conscious mind? Why and how would your life change if you did this?
4. If #3 does not happen, or until it does happen, using the Me-B System explain how you can feel joyful and fulfilled now.
5. What information can be collected from the Me-B System?
6. Which chakras provide what psychic information?
7. Explain the PIN Wheel Technique. What is your way in?
8. What can you do to support yourself while learning to read the consciousness in energy? (Hint: When we focus on what we can do, this creates more of what we can do!)
9. What negative belief about yourself might inhibit your progress in developing your psychic awareness? Where do you imagine that this belief is held in your body? What positive

254

alternative belief could you bring in to help you?

10. Deepak Chopra writes that "the invisible world comes first." How do we make reality come closer? Explain.

11. How do you open up to your own Radical Intuition?

12. Practice the techniques below and write up what feels easy / difficult about them.
    - The Pendulum
    - Assessing Body Language
    - How to See Energy and Shifts in Consciousness Connection-Track-Intervention-Shift Sequence Assessing Subconscious Shifts
    - Seeing and Sensing Emotions/Core Distortions
    - Assessing Energy With your Hand
    - Seeing Energy when Someone is Absent
    - Moving and Tracking Energy at the Same Time
    - Look Mom, No Hands! Exercises
    - In the spirit of the Secret, please focus on what you CAN do—not on what you can't.

13. What subconscious Shadow material gets in the way of your seeing, sensing, and tracking energy and consciousness?

14. Every day, practice the BCS of programming positive sensations into your field.

15. List the ways in which you pick up information (for example: intuition, seeing, taste, feel, smell, hearing, direct knowing, or other).

CHAPTER 15

ANGER ENERGY TRANSFORMS SADNESS and ANXIETY

Personal transformation cannot happen unless we are skilled at working with our anger. Anger left unnoticed or denied can hurt us and those we most love. As we endeavor to find it, and listen to its wisdom, we let ourselves have better boundaries, more compassion and personal power.

Too often cultural taboos prevent us from looking at the juice behind anger. As long as we have a primal brain, we will have anger. After all, humans are animals! Denying our basic instincts creates **Spiritual Junk Food** and the opportunity to do more harm to our self and others. By acknowledging and looking for our more base emotions, especially anger, we have the opportunity to transform the challenging emotions and claim our Core Being.

There are two ways anger is used to reinforce old negative patterns—we either hold onto it or push it at another. If we are in our Compassionate or Heart-Centered distorted energies, we are likely to hold our anger inside us or take on someone else's anger as our own. If we are in our Excel or Leader distortions, we tend to blow up and push our anger at another. As we turn to anger as our teacher, we can listen and learn from our anger. Anger is our personal messenger holding up a "red flag" that says, "pay attention to me!"

We can practice regular "anger meditations" where we take the time to look at where anger is held in our body/energy system and discover the source of our anger. *Anger meditations are important even when we are not feeling angry.* This is because throughout the day we are subjected to energies so harsh that we can't help but be tainted by them. Regular clearing of anger (once a month) helps promote peace and harmony around us. I go in cycles based on my current **Rhythm of Flow**. I can go for two months and not need any anger meditations—and then I may find I need to do many anger meditations for two weeks straight. I have found that during huge growth opportunities (and usually also during very difficult times), I do more anger meditations. Riding my mountain bike up a hill is a great way for me to process my anger and to receive guidance and wisdom about it. Let's be committed to creating the space in our busy lives to discharge, transform and listen to the wisdom of our anger.

FOUR SOURCES OF ANGER

There are four major sources of anger. The first source is anger we take on from someone else and confuse with our own energy. Secondly, we may experience anger from our past Core Distortions and past trauma. Third is anger that we experience in the present, often activated when we have repeatedly failed to set healthy boundaries or when our boundaries are repeatedly invaded. Often this type of anger can trigger the releasing of anger from our past or even past lives. Finally, there is also "just" anger. This is when we react to a "terrible wrong," such as when a child is murdered or a major event such as 9/11.

If our energy field is too porous, we can let someone else's energy enter our field and think it is our own. **There are many reasons we subconsciously make our field too porous and take on someone else's anger.** Anytime we energetically merge with someone *because we are "caretaking" them instead* *of caring for them*, we take on their energy. Also, if we collapse into the negative aspects of the Heart-Centered or Compassionate Character Structures, our guilt and feelings of not being "enough" can magnetize our field so we take on someone else's anger.

ANGER WE TAKE ON AS OURS

Many of us feel guilty when we have to tell someone "no." I am no different. When I worked as a massage therapist, if someone showed up late or not at all, I let it pass—until one client kept missing appointments and I began losing money and feeling she was taking advantage of my kindness. I finally told her that the next time she missed an appointment and failed to give me 24 hours notice, I would have to charge her for the appointment. She agreed and didn't seem to mind. But it wasn't long until she missed another appointment and I called and told her she owed me the cost of a session.

She was extremely angry, pushed intense energy in my direction, and complained that it wasn't fair. Even though I knew she had agreed to the arrangement, I let her anger collapse me. I began to feel guilty and responsible, like I had done something terribly wrong. My mind knew what was true, but the consciousness in my body and energy system rebooted into an old program so that, even over the phone, I subconsciously let my energy field merge with her field and took responsibility for her anger. I held onto it for days before I noticed what I had done and *released it, and reclaimed myself.*

I learned so much from the experience. It became clear to me my complicity in the adventure. My lack of clarity around setting strong and healthy boundaries with people was programmed into me at a young age and I was still struggling with sending clear signals. Not only was my energy field **magnetized to not set boundaries; it was programmed to take on another's anger and to attract people to me who will take advantage of me**. This information has been of extreme advantage as I worked (and still work) to reprogram myself and live from Core Being. Now, whenever possible, I look for my CHOICE POINTS to facilitate change.

When we finally do set boundaries, as explained in the previous example, we can feel responsible for the other person's angry reaction. *Sometimes when we take on someone else's anger, we become angry and annoyed, but sometimes we feel sadness. Our Explorers Mind can help us discover which feeling we are experiencing.*

Leader and Excel types can run their energy very tightly. Their fields are less porous and don't often take on someone else's energy. Instead, they are more likely to push anger at others.

When we begin the process of being responsible for our anger and our unhealthy ways of storing or reacting in anger, we support ourselves. We do this by identifying the original source of the anger. By doing this, we learn and grow and understand any negative patterns that are programmed into us.

Sometimes a **Core Distortion** or trauma programmed into us by our past is the root of our anger and our present situation activates the past. Common **Core Distortions**/traumas of the past that bring anger into the present are situations where we have been invaded or "abused" by an authority figure in our life. "Abuse" is in quotes because, for a young child, it can feel like abuse when a big adult towers over them and yells—even if the yelling is to protect the child from danger.

Since there are various root causes of our anger, identifying the source helps us identify what lessons our anger is delivering to us. There is a saying, "keep death as an ally to help us make the right choices in the moment." I agree, and add, "Use anger as our ally." It says, "Notice me! There is something we missed and it urgently needs our attention."

In marriage or close relationships, anger (often spiked over petty small issues) is a red flag saying we haven't taken care of important unresolved business. *If we don't judge our obnoxious displays that explode outward, we can instead say, "Wow, what was that I just did? Something deep inside of me must be in awful pain—what have I not paid close enough attention to? What part of me is crying out for love?"* We can follow the 5 Steps, move through the 3 Rings, find real wisdom and reconnect to our Core Being. Doing the following Anger Meditation helps us keep up with the "cleaning" of the dense vibrations in this Dimension of Earth.

ANGER MEDITATION FOR TRANSFORMING ANGER BACK TO CORE BEING

1. Look at where anger is held in your body/energy system.
2. Uncover its source. Is it your anger, anger you took from someone else, anger from your past or "just" anger? (Not even "just" anger should be held onto, because holding on to any energy distorts it, lowers our consciousness and separates us from Core Being. This is when our Separated Self takes charge and prevents us from achieving our highest good. We can listen to just anger and take appropriate action to improve our lives.)
3. Receive the message of wisdom anger always brings—it often relates to a boundary issue or some unfairness of the past we can't accept and move through.
4. Then, using the HVC of our Enlightened Observer, feel the emotion of anger as a sensation in the body and let it transform and return us to our Core Being. To help in this process, as you bring in your Enlightened Ob- server's HVC, it helps if you exercise or move about. So dance around, ride your bike up a big hill, or, if you are very skilled, sit in meditation and allow the anger to transform to wisdom and personal power. Also practice the exercises at the end of this chapter that are designed to be helpful to you as you learn how to transform anger.

If it is too hard to feel the sensation of the anger, feel free to imagine the sensation of it, picture what you are angry at, and with positive intention feel and visualize the energy of your Enlightened Observer come into your field and transform the anger. Anger transformed becomes personal power, wisdom, positive intention and positive action so we support/protect our self in a healthy manner. This helps us make our future free and clear of our negative past programming.

NOTE: If we only touch the emotion, but don't transform it, we loop and charge the anger, miss the wisdom and can even hurt our self or others. **So don't loop or charge the anger.** More is discussed later on this because the difference between "charging or looping" and "discharging for transformation" is a crucial distinction rarely recognized. Our job is to access the anger (connect to it) and discharge it, not to charge the anger and loop in it. **If we don't feel more empowered and less angry, then we failed to transform it.**

Energetically, congested anger is typically held in the shoulders, head, thighs and lower chakras. It hides in fat tissues as well. (This is not to say that people with a lot of fat are angrier than others! In fact, Excel types tend to have less body mass but are great at compressing anger into their system.)

Migraines and headaches can often be the result of congested anger. By transforming anger in the upper and lower parts of the body we energetically connect and align our energy system. Anger has such power in it that if used as a raw material, it can solve many of our problems such as depression and anxiety.

Depression can be considered to be a "sucking in" of our energy field. Anger, by contrast, expands our field and makes it big again. Anger transformed returns us to Core Being and reconnects us to our personal power. *Also, it is vital to do more than simply feel the anger (or any emotion we are processing).* **When accessing anger, anxiety or sadness, we must be careful not to charge the emotion because it makes it more difficult to transform.** *If our Enlightened Observer isn't vibrating at a high enough frequency, then it is impossible to transform the challenging emotion. Instead, we end up charging it and making it bigger.*

Anxiety and fear are the hardest emotions to transform because they activate our sympathetic nervous system into fight and flight. Fear activates us into flight and anxiety actually triggers both fight and flight at the same time. For instance, imagine we are in a car and are pressing both the gas and the break; this is what anxiety does to our energy system. The energetic frequency of anger, when used skillfully, will balance this dichotomy of fast/slow and eliminate anxiety so we can take positive action toward our goals.

Some psychologist feel there is "no reason" for the panic attack or anxiety. A professor in graduate school whose wife had a panic attack in the local mall felt there was "no reason" for the mall to trigger her attack. He did know however, that her attack was somehow related to her being robbed the previous year but was confused as to why a mall would trigger such an event.

There are many "reasons" we have anxiety. One reason is that any sympathetic nervous system that is programmed to reactivity goes on hyper-alert and becomes reactionary to the most subtle thoughts and energies entering it. So the intense energy of the mall, as experienced by the professor's wife, can easily activate an over-stimulated nervous system.

Our ego also plays an important role in anxiety. It is common knowledge that depression and anxiety often go hand-in-hand. As mentioned earlier, depression is the shrinking of our energy field, often because our ego feels shrunken as well. If **our ego shrinks, so does our energy field, potentially paving the way for depression and anxiety to take hold.** Anxiety shows up as the "rescuer" of the attacked ego: "Come on," it says, "we have to protect our ego from being deflated!" It revs up its engines to take action, but because it is not sure exactly what to do to protect our attacked ego, it can't take action— thus the gas petal/break analogy. Taking action helps reduce the intensity of anxiety. For instance, when we feel we have not—or may not—accomplish some- thing, it creates anxiety.

Taking action toward our goals and making progress is very important. It helps to re-inflate our ego. However, once our nervous system goes on hyper drive, it can be difficult to turn off. Using the energetics of anger can help. Also, the **Neurological Upgrade Intervention** is very useful to deactivate an over-active system.

Some people find medication is helpful, yet some feel it doesn't help. I have no problem with properly prescribed and used medications. I do encourage people to find longer-term solutions so they can eventually become medication free. In my private practice, *clients who are successful at quieting their negative ego and can feel Core Being as a sensation in their body and connect to its consciousness in their mind* can get off medications (or never go on them) and heal their anxiety and depression.

When our nervous system is activated, it is very difficult to maintain a strong Enlightened Observer. However, as we bring in the energetics of anger, its strong frequency of fight helps mitigate the energy of flight. It is similar to rebooting our energy system so it rebalances. I even recommend getting mad at the anxiety (with an Enlightened Observer and strong Manifest Energy)—a strange enough reaction to startle our programmed responses.

Often people with depression and anxiety don't want to let it go. They consciously or subconsciously don't want to get better. If this is the case, they will win and the depression and anxiety will remain. This topic is discussed in more detail in the Chronic Illness Chapter.

SOME OF US WANT TO AVOID OUR ANGER ISSUES

Georgia was a yoga instructor and saw herself as moral and spiritual. She was proud about her commitment to helping and not hurting. Every time I suggested she look at anger she would disappear from therapy for months at a time. After the third time this happened, I pointed out to her that every time I brought up anger as an issue to address she would disappear. She explained that anger from others toward her causes her such deep pain that she didn't think it was right to ever feel angry.

I pointed out to her that when we don't address anger, it is most likely to spill out and hurt another. Georgia had just finished telling me how she "accidentally" ran over her boyfriend's foot and how during a different argument she had broken his finger "by accident" when she slammed the door. Finally, Georgia began to look at anger instead of suppressing or ignoring it.

Too often our judgments of anger keep us from examining how we can use its energy for good instead of harm.

People are either skilled at anger or sadness, one is always easier to feel than the other. It is important to learn how to feel and process both. Generally, Excel and Leader types are better at feeling anger and Compassionate and Heart-Centered types are better at feeling sadness. Those who are easily overwhelmed by sadness can have a central channel that is too far forward, the structured levels of the field are either under charged, or fragment too easily, or are too absorbent of negative energy. They hold trauma on levels 2 and 4 and they are not deeply connected to their Core Being. Instead of feeling anger and maintaining a charge in their field, they collapse their field into sadness because they don't have the detachment that the Manifest Energy and Enlightened Observer provide. Anger can help them maintain their charge and regain their connection to themselves.

Energy fields of people *not able to* feel sadness usually have a very structured field. The ego is afraid of the vulnerability sadness presents, and so they keep themselves protected from it. Learning how sadness can be energy that runs through us, and not something that defines who we are in the world, is the most important skill. I teach clients to *learn how to cry, sob, feel with a strong Enlightened Observer, and from Manifest Energy's Intention Line so what they are feeling becomes an energetic release and a deepening into self-love, compassion and Core Being.* **What if every time we cried, or needed to cry, it brought us deeper into self-love, kindness and Core Being?** Being skilled at transforming both anger and sadness leads us to a sense of freedom and helps us move to Stage 4 (and above) of Me-B Transformation™.

Mastering Anger is essential to overcoming depression. Mastering anger creates the charge necessary to overcome depression. Depression literally depresses the energy field. Using the charge anger provides can help clients re-inflate their field and reconnect with their power.

Depression happens when our "Power Sources" are no longer feeding us and our negative ego takes over. Situational depression is when circumstances in our life (such as a death, divorce, career lost) take away an important source of power to us. In the following exercise, we discover what our internal and external power sources are so we can eventually develop a long-term strategy to strengthen ourselves. That way, if we lose our job, our partner leaves us, or some other external tragedy happens, we have enough internal power to avoid becoming depressed—or at least can move through the depression more quickly. *When we lose our external power source, our ego becomes activated, and fear and anxiety grow. If we can work with our ego so it doesn't collapse into negative patterns and move back into Core Being, depression can be avoided.*

DISCOVER OUR INTERNAL POWER SOURCE

Joanne was proud of her progress in life. She was finally dancing, working hard in graduate school and feeling good about herself – until … Jan always had an "until" happening in her life. She would coast and expand, flow and glow until…. The "until" usually dealt with a male withdrawing love, or her family asking her to support herself, or some **external** source of power she depended upon would dry up and she would spiral downward into depression and anxiety. She would get sick, miss school, and stop dancing.

This trend continued until she started noticing that she was so dependent upon another's power source and when it dried up, there were not enough internal reserves to keep going. Over time, she slowly began to develop her own power source so that when her external support stopped giving, and her negative ego sprang forth, she could rely on the energy of her Core Being, the Multi-Dimensional Fabric, and other Universal Energies of Support.

In the beginning, Joanne didn't appreciate my suggestion that she find her own power source. With guidance, I suggested she sit up straight in her chair, align her spine, and connect to the energy current running through the center of her body. As she did this, she noticed the sensation of strength filling her body. I then suggested she receive energetic support from the universe and allow it to come in through every cell – front/back, top/bottom, left/right. For the first time she knew what it was to feel connected to her own power source, independent of another's whims/wishes. Although she found times when she was reluctant to realign back to her own power source, she was able to do it. She became able to stand strong and stay healthy.

Developing our own Internal Power Sources is about creating HVC in our Outer and Inner Energy Egg or, as described in the first chapter, making lots of white paint! Some Buddhists call this *Building our Container*. Refer to the exercise on *Building our Energetic and Biological Consciousness Container* for tips on this process and review the next exercise to assess what are our power sources.

WHAT IS YOUR POWER SOURCE?

Depending upon our or our client's personality type, we may find our self hooked into a power source other than that of our highest good. A Compassionate personality type may hook into someone else for power, a politician or performer may hook into the audience for their power, and an addict will hook into a drug. Even junk food can become an unhealthy power source for us. Knowing what power sources we are connecting to can help us understand what dependencies we may be cultivating, negative beliefs developing and traps we may be creating in our lives.

I've used food, my husband, and others' admiration as fuel to propel me forward. Now, I know the highest source of power is connection to Core Being and the external support of the Multi-Dimensional Fabric, god, nature and spirit. Universal energy is abundant and open to support us all if we are open to receive it. Career, family, friends and our partners support us, but if they fall short, leave or die, we need to open to other consistent internal and external support. It is essential to mastering **the 3 Skills of Adult Consciousness: giving love, receiving love and giving love to self even when we would rather receive.**

- Step 1: Notice what proportion of the day you are aligned to your own Core Being and/or Universal Energy as your power source.
- Step 2: Notice how often, in times of stress, you rely on unhealthy external power sources. List those power sources.
- Step 3: Throughout the day, when you want to use an external power source (food, alcohol, partner, friends, drugs, sex etc.) begin to fill yourself up with Core Being first. Fill yourself up as much as possible and then try to select the most healthy external power source possible. For instance, if you want cake, eat an apple instead. If you want pornography, make love to your husband, wife or partner. If alcohol is the choice, ask for the love and support of a friend.
- Step 4: Over time, gradually strengthen your own internal power sources and improve your choices of the external power sources you select. Review the exercise on Building Our Energy and Biological Consciousness Container.

Anger is the most important emotion for securing personal power and manifesting our dreams in this physical reality. Anger **transformed** is the energy of aliveness and personal power. It reconnects people and balances their field. It also charges the second chakra, the energy vortex for creativity, passion and manifestation. *In order to transform anger skillfully, we must be able to actually feel it as a sensation in the body.* Before transformation, anger can feel like heat. After the transformation it feels like tingles and flows. Positive pleasure and aliveness are created.

Negative pleasure comes when our Separated Self conspires against us. The Separated Self feels pleasure when it reacts out of anger. Pleasure from anger, how can that be? Few people recognize the endorphin-like energy anger sometimes provides. Yet, we all— yes, we all—have this experience from time to time – even if we just keep it inside us and loop negative thoughts about our judgment of another. It took me years to see I had anger — let alone pleasure from it. My ego wouldn't let me recognize my distortion. Through deep meditation and self-awareness I woke up enough to see that there are times my anger is fueled by the energy of negative pleasure. (Gossip is an example of one form of pleasure our Separated Self receives and feeds off as its power source.)

With hard work, today, I can benefit from the energy of pleasure yet rarely act out from my Separated Self. In the occasional moments that I catch my Separated Self being in control, I take responsibility for my negative actions and move more quickly back to Core Being. Anytime there is pleasure with anger, usually it is our Separated Self energetically feeding and artificially boosting our ego. Unfortunately, it feels good to be "better than" another, especially if they have hurt us in the past. It is almost as if we are taking back the energy they took from us, as if we were evening the score. Some of this is out of our control, or at least it feels like it. Our inner protector feels the surge of energy and reacts. Slowing the reaction down so we can consider our actions takes practice and aligned intention. Once again, our Manifest Energy and Enlightened Observer need to be very strong so they can overcome the lure of the endorphin-like energy of this anger-related negative pleasure.

Anger at self becomes hate at self. We all are "blessed" with a certain amount of self-hate. It is part of the human condition and is created by our negative ego, life experiences and our programmed personality. Finding where we hold it in our body and releasing it is a huge gift we can provide to ourselves. Self-Hate feeds the Separated Self, arrogance, addiction and abuse. We can use the Anger Meditation to eliminate the LVC of self- hate in our Me-B System.

Anger is not bad. It is about wisdom and boundaries. Every time anger appears, it has a message. It is a red flag saying, "pay attention to me." Usually the message deals with boundaries that are too weak. Often caretaking and codependency is involved. For instance, maybe:

- We didn't get enough in return for what we gave away;
- We kept giving because the other person didn't respond as we had hoped;
- We feel more comfortable giving instead of saying no; and/or
- We tend to care-take or are co-dependent.

Learning from the wisdom of the anger and taking corrective action is essential to transforming anger. Often this means holding stronger boundaries so the other person holds up their end of the agreement. Sometimes it means simply saying no when we usually would say yes. Other times it means speaking the truth about something we would usually keep quiet.

TEENS, BOUNDARIES AND PARENTAL ANGER

Although we are far from perfect, my husband and I work hard to support our children to set healthy boundaries both at home with us and with others. It is common for them to discuss boundaries that are too strong or need to be stronger or have been invaded. It is a common term known in our family and it is discussed often, especially now that they are teenagers and can push boundaries. This is not good or bad. Teens need to assert their independence and become individualized from parents. Negotiating teen boundaries without being angry is a huge parental challenge that I am learning to master

My 16-year old daughter, driving only a few days without me in the car, asked to drive herself to a play on a school night. I agreed, even though she thought she wouldn't be home until 10:30pm. When 11:00pm came and went, I was calm, saying to myself, "wait until 11:20 to react." When 11:30 came and went, I was having much more trouble remaining calm.

By 11:40, I was quite charged by anger, fear, and concern. I noticed I was probably over-reacting as I drove down the street to her high school where the play was being held. I prayed, "Please let the show still be playing." Let the parking lot be full and the lights be on. Although the school was only a few blocks away, time slowed as I checked the clock every few seconds. I wondered what to do if the school was empty. My husband was overseas in Indonesia, and I felt alone and unseasoned as a parent of a teen. Doubt and trust issues surfaced. It was only yesterday that she had begged to attend a rock concert on a school night. Could she have gone there instead? My mind was racing. Clearly, I was completely disconnected from Core Being and not able to think straight.

As I pulled up the hill, I anxiously looked over the steering wheel, hoping to see lights, cars—anything that showed signs of life. But the parking lot was dark and empty. My fears were confirmed. As I drove home, I said to myself, "Ok, don't overreact. Hopefully her car will be in the driveway. She has only lied twice to you and only over small things. She wouldn't push the boundaries on this…. The long and the short of it is that I *did* lose myself and overreact. I even called the school in the morning to see what time the play had ended, only to find out that she had done nothing wrong except trigger me. As we discussed what we now call "the event," my daughter promised to be more responsible and call when she was going to be late. I promised to loosen up the boundaries so she had more space to discover her own inner adult.

Boundaries, especially with teens, need to be negotiated so that everyone's needs are met and honored. Listening to anger's wisdom can help in this process. Learning to listen and not react is my personal goal!

When doing anger work, it is important we and (or our client) learn to access it, but not charge it. Learn how to take regular brakes to prevent disassociation, stay grounded and/or become grounded and connect to personal power. Sometimes we need to discharge anger before it is able to transform. Regular breaks are vital to integrate the work and prevent re-wounding and/or charging the unhealthy parts of our nervous system.

REVIEW

1. Personal transformation cannot happen unless you are skilled at working with anger.

2. People are either skilled at anger or sadness. Whichever one they can process less, they need to learn how to process the other.

3. Mastering anger is essential to overcoming depression and anxiety. Some people think depression is anger suppressed. Accessing the energy of anger creates the necessary charge and frequency needed to expand the field and come out of a depressed energy field. The fight energy of anger can help balance fear and anxiety if done skillfully. This means we must at least be in Manifest Energy and have a strong Enlightened Observer.

4. Catharsis is not healing. When we cry and process difficult emotions, if our Manifest Energy and our Enlightened Observer are strong, we feel the sadness, anger, depression, and anxiety in a manner that brings us deeper into self-love, kindness and Core Being.

5. Depression happens when our "Power Sources" are no longer feeding us and our negative ego takes over. Anger helps us locate an internal power source. As we develop enough strong internal power sources and heal our negative ego, we move out of depression more quickly, gaining wisdom and skills along the way.

6. The energy from anger, when transformed to HVC, is the most important emotion in securing personal power and manifesting dreams in the physical dimension. It makes our Manifest Energy strong, and connects us deeper to Core Being.

7. Anger is not bad. It is about wisdom and boundaries. As we better listen to the message anger brings, we also are more able to balance our lives.

USE PHYSICAL MOVEMENT, CARDIOVASCULAR OR STRENGTH EXERCISES TO SHIFT CHALLENGING EMO- TIONAL ENERGY

Free movement/dance expression, punching bag, yoga, weight lifting, and many other exercises can also be used to shift anger or any challenging emotion. Whatever physical activity we enjoy (hiking, biking, yoga) can be adapted to help us shift out of a negative emotion and back to Core Being. I teach Trinity, a weekly exercise class through the local recreation department where students get a great physical workout as they transform energetic and emotional challenges. Given how busy many of us are, using exercise as a way to shift our mind and energy systems lets us get more "bang for the buck!" Follow the exercises outlined below or create some of your own.

1. A common body-centered psychotherapeutic practice to "work" anger is to hit pillows with a bat. Whether we are hitting pillows or punching a bag, there are some crucial cautionary notes to follow.

2. Take breaks in-between sets to make sure we don't charge the anger. For instance, when hitting a pillow or punching bag I usually don't let myself or my clients hit more than 6-10 times without stopping and feeling the sensation of energy in their body. Hitting creates a charge, but pausing to take in the energy from that charge into the cells is vital. We can harvest it deep within us to balance our field.

3. It is important to notice if the energy and sensations in the body are evenly distributed. If the

energy is mostly in just the upper body or just the lower body, then transformation has not been complete.

Assess whether the emotion(s) have lessened or increased. If the energy of the challenging emotion has increased, and we have done at least four sets, it could mean that our Enlightened Observer is not strong enough, and we are not holding a strong Intention Line toward healing. If this happens, we can connect to the consciousness in our body with our Explorer's Mind to investigate if there is a negative belief, ego and/or negative intention preventing the transformation.

4. Sometimes we need to discharge anger before it will transform. It is like a volcano needing to blow its top off before the lava will flow. Assess if a discharge of anger is needed—and be careful to discharge, instead of looping and recycling the same anger over and over again. Recycling the same anger usually happens when we are in negative intention because we can't accept the past and move forward. Straightening our Enlightened Observer and Manifest Energy will help with this.

5. Since it is intention that moves energy (touch is not necessary), when hitting a pillow or an object, don't intend the pillow to be anyone in particular. For instance, if we want to process our anger about our father and, as we are hitting the pillow, (or whatever) we are thinking we are hitting him, *then we are energetically sending hitting energy at him. Instead, we can align our* Manifest Energy *Line to release our anger about him and any LVC we took on from him. Never intend to hit or hurt another.*

A summary of exercises we can do to transform into Core Being (Always get your doctor's approval before doing any exercise.)

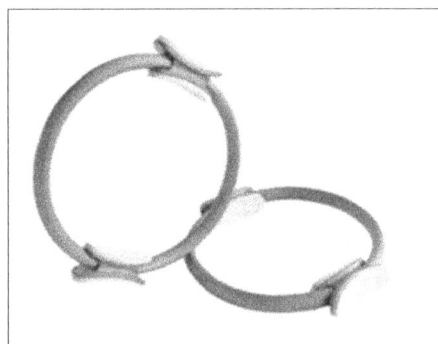

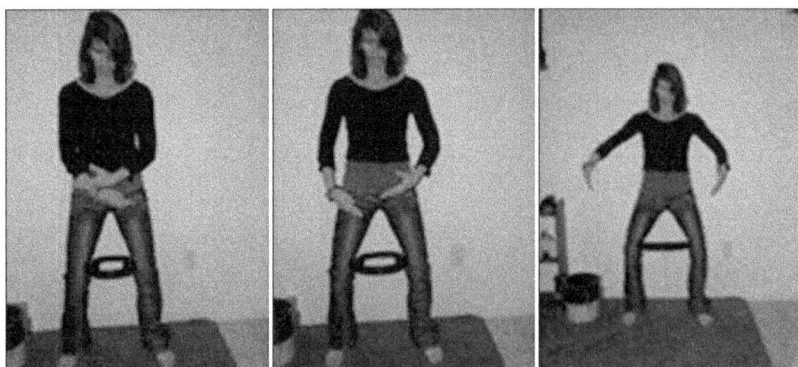

Magic Pilates Ring

266

When we want to move anger or move out of an energetic collapse that sadness can bring, we can use this **Magic Pilates Ring**. Breathe in, pressing it together as we bring our hands in; release the breath and bring the arms out. Repeat at least 3 times.

Staying in our Manifest Energy Intention Line, Enlightened Observer and positive intention, we can move through any anger/sadness cycle; we can discharge anger and release it; and we can move out of hopelessness and reconnect to Core Being. If this doesn't work, most likely there is too large a part of us fighting against getting better. Usually this is the Heart-Centered energy clinging to victim consciousness. Be patient! Manifest Energy, self-love and *giving up hope that another can save us* will eventually create the positive shift the other parts of us desperately want.

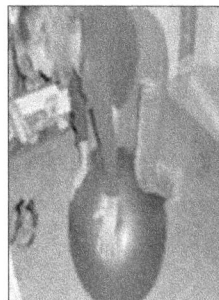

Balancing Techniques

Standing on one foot while standing on a Bosu or similar balancing device and sitting or balancing on a ball or Pilates roller can help us reconnect when we have dissociated or are overwhelmed by anger or sadness and want to reconnect to our Core Being. Centering in our Core Being means we are also energetically connected to our physical core. Where muscles are weak, so is our energy field. Energetics mirrors our physical health and strength.

We can also use balance as a diagnostic tool to see if our positive beliefs are strong energetically in the physical body and not just strong in the mind. For instance, a client explained how she was ready for a relationship. She was sure the anger she held about her past betrayal had been transformed and she was totally ready for love and marriage. So I asked her to balance on the ball. It was easy for her. I then asked her to balance while she stated out loud, "I am ready to meet my true love." She fell off the ball. We then tried, "I am afraid of love," she balanced perfectly.

The client then scanned her body to see where anger was still lodged from her past failed relationship. She felt it in two places-the back of her heart chakra and her pelvis. She also felt fear in the front of her third chakra, solar plexus area. Using the Magic Ring, she breathed inward, connected deeply to the anger with her Enlightened Observer, and on the out breath, she let her field expand so she could connect to feelings of strength and power. Repeating the sequence three more times she eventually used the energy of transformed anger to bring more of those feelings of strength and power into her third chakra. She balanced these sensations of HVC front/back, left/right, and top/bottom so they were evenly distributed throughout her body.

The client then tried again to balance on the ball and say, "I am ready to meet my true love." This time, she stayed strong. Then she tried, "I am ready to marry my true love." She stayed strong. Finally she said, "I love myself," again strong. Last month, I received a wedding announcement in the mail.

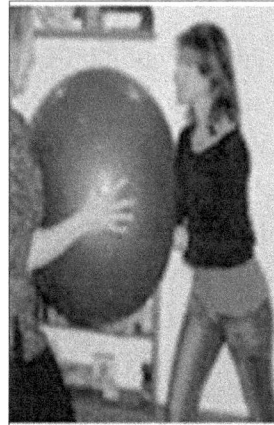

Releasing Anger We Want to Direct at Someone

Sometimes we or our clients harbor resentment toward an attacker, a parent, an ex-partner or co-worker that did them harm. It is not healing to hate or to direct negative energy toward them. However, we can release our resentment and regain our power! We can imagine we are pushing away the negative energy and reclaiming our strength and positive sense of self.

The physical act of pushing can be an effective energetic tool. Either pushing against me (the therapist or guide) or a wall, either way it is useful. The pushing against actually pushes the negative energy out of us and reconnects us to our strength. We make it clear that the intention is not to hurt the person we are angry at, but rather to release any residual effects of their "attack" on us and reconnect us to the power we let them take from us.

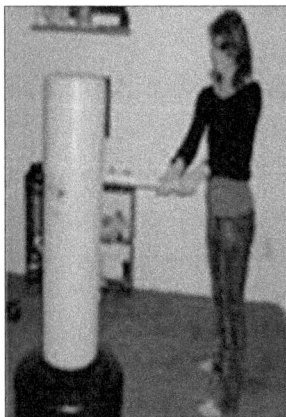

Using Words in Our Field To Help Release the Charge

Hitting something helps us release anger, **if we are not** imagining that we are hurting someone. Also, clear intention and a strong Enlightened Observer are needed. Saying key words to help deepen the release can be important as well. (Words are energy.) As a therapist, I often tune into the client's field in order to read what words could best help. Sometimes I will say the words out loud, guiding the client and sometimes the client needs to say the words out loud.

The 5th chakra and the 2nd chakra have a close relationship with one another. For instance, when one shuts down, it can shut the other down. Since the 5th chakra is about being strong in our own authority and the 2nd chakra gives us the personal power to be strong in our own authority, saying words out loud helps us open both our 2nd chakra and 5th chakras. To know what words to say out loud—as we use movement (or hitting) to discharge and transform anger and sadness—we can use our Explorer's Mind to investigate inside of us what words might be best. Sometimes saying, "I hate" or "I hurt" (without wanting to hate or hurt but wanting to release hate and hurt) can be very beneficial.

SHAKE RELEASE OF TRAUMA

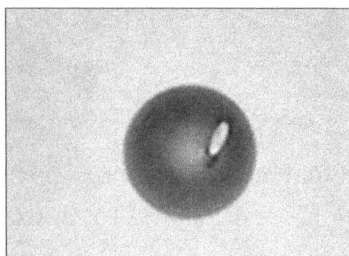

Place small ball (size of a tennis ball) on sacrum, mid-back between scapulas, gluteus (butt), hip, or any place where you think you need to release any stuck trauma (fight/flight/freeze energy) from your body. When the ball is on the sacrum, do pelvic tilts (anterior/posterior) very slowly, pausing every centimeter and melt into the ball. During the pause, using your Enlightened Observer, bring your mind into the sacrum and encourage the energy to run up and down your spine and legs. As the energy moves, your body may move, quake or shake during the release. This is good. Invite HVC into the areas that released and melt more, feeling and releasing any emotions as you do this. Sometimes when I do this I feel anger or sadness and tears often flow during the release. To keep my lower back out of pain, I do this at least once a month.

After the release is complete, always invite Core Being energy into the body to help balance the energy left/right, top/bottom, and front/back. The back of the heart chakra, hip rotator and the gluteus maximus (butt) are other good places to release trauma energy.

CARDIOVASCULAR EXERCISE

Aerobic (oxygen rich) cardiovascular exercise is great for shifting anger and anxiety. Often running up a hill, brisk walking where your heart rate excels to 75 percent of your maximum heart rate is a vital task in helping transform anger and anxiety back to Core Being. Check with your doctor or professional personal trainer to determine your maximum heart rate and how to stay aerobic. (Buying a heart rate monitor will help you too.) I notice when I have just anger my heart rate max is about 155 and when I am overly stressed and my cortisol hormone levels are high I might only be able to exercise at a heart rate of 135 and still be aerobic (oxygen rich).

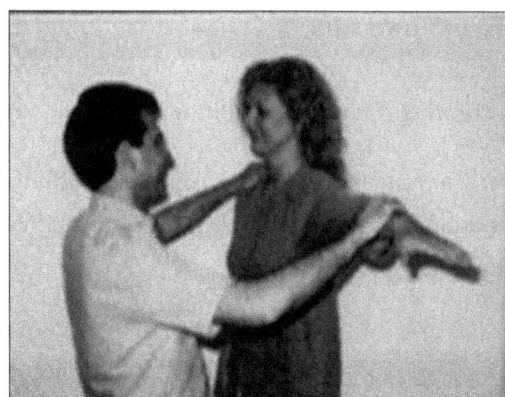

Lotus Flower Opens/Closes So We Program Positive Beliefs

While on a Pilates Roller, standing, or laying on the floor, we can shift negative beliefs into positive beliefs, at least temporarily. The beliefs may stay shifted, or they may return for more attention. Those who believe we can shift all negative beliefs forever are in Spiritual Junk Food. In times of stress, or as we take on new challenges, negative beliefs often reappear. This is because as humans, we have an ego. And as long as we have an ego, it will get activated with negativity. When this happens we will have challenging thoughts and negative beliefs. The good news is that we can notice when they return, release them, and return to Core Being. One teacher of mine once told me, "If you don't feed the monster, it goes away." Choosing not to feed the negative thoughts/beliefs that enter our mind helps us not feed the monster!

Muscle Testing Exercise

One way of eliminating negative beliefs is to muscle test for a specific belief that may be causing us pain. There are many great books on this subject. A very basic summary of the process follows. To muscle test, ask the person a question where the answer to the question is a clear "yes"— such as asking them their name. Then, press down on their arm to see how strong it stays. The level of strength you notice in their arm is the level of strength of a "yes" answer. Then ask them a clear "no" question—such as, "Is your name Mickey Mouse?" (or some other obviously incorrect name)—and press down on their hand to see how weak it gets. The level of weakness is an indicator of a "no" answer.

Make sure their eyes are looking downward as you muscle tests them. This will prevent the person from manipulating their energy and muddying the results. Also check to see if their Manifest Energy Line is adjusted for accuracy. Then ask them to say out loud the belief they think might test weak. For instance, the person being tested would say "I am enough" out loud as the tester pushed down on their arm to see if it tested strong. If the positive statement tests weak, we can reprogram it into our system so that it can eventually test strong.

One very effective method of reprogramming it so it tests strong (see picture) is to lay on the ground, let opposite hand and opposite leg come together (like a lotus flower closing) then come apart (like a lotus flower opening). Repeat three times – left hand/right foot; then repeat three times – right hand/right foot.

Do at least four sets before muscle testing the positive belief again. When I watch a client's field, I can usually tell if it has shifted or what needs to be done to help it shift. As we learn to tune into our selves and read our own field, we can also better read another's field. If the positive statement doesn't test strong after four or more sets, do the Containment Procedure and use your Explorer's Mind to assess what is creating the energetic block.

Some typical reasons why negative beliefs don't shift include: negative intention, ego merged with the negative belief, we want someone else to save us, and we are not connected to Core Being and/or our Enlightened Observer.

HOW EFFECTIVE ARE ENERGETIC TECHNIQUES THAT INVOLVE TAPPING & MUSCLE TESTING?

I feel that whatever works for us, is perfect. People have developed elaborate techniques to "tap" specific parts of our body, in an organized sequence, as a means to facilitate positive energetic shifts. Since energy is consciousness, and consciousness has ego, anger, projections, false sense of self and negative defenses, it is definitely possible to temporarily "tap" them away.

I teach clients tapping, bi-lateral movements, and other similar techniques when clients are in deep distress. I use it as an effective temporary method they can use to support themselves.

It is intention that moves energy and our mind is the most powerful energy tool. We don't have to "tap" or even "touch" to move energy. We *can simply place our mind in the body, scan our body with our Enlightened Observer and our Manifest Energy Line, feel positive sensations and create HVC for healing. It is that simple and easy for all of us.*

Tapping and some of the more popularized energetic techniques could become Spiritual Junk Food or a way to deny working directly with consciousness and taking responsibility for difficulties in the moment, as they arise. I find that the most simple, sweet, and effective technique to shift LVC of negative beliefs is to create HVC by using our Enlightened Observer to:

1. feel/sense/visualize the energy of positive sensations in the body that represent the positive belief; and
2. with positive intention and a strong Manifest Energy Line, anchor into Core Being. (What we focus on grows and expands.)

And, as often as possible, we can use the 3-Rings of Healing and the 5-Step Mindfulness Process to move from the outer circles back to Core Being. It is intention that moves energy. Tapping and touch is nice and can feel very supportive. Yet, as we develop a strong Manifest Energy Line and Core Being, we become free. Tapping (or any form of hands-on energy work) can be an important supplement to our deeper internal skills of self-mastery, but not a replacement for them.

ANGER/SADNESS CYCLES AND THE ROLE OF ADDICTION

When processing anger and sadness (grief), we can toggle back and forth between discharging anger and then discharging sadness. This is the Anger/Sadness Cycle and it is normal. Sometimes, however, we use it as a defense to avoid either anger or sadness because we feel more comfortable in one or the other emotion. When we cycle authentically between discharging anger, then sadness, then anger... if, at the end of the sequence, we feel better and more empowered, we know we are mastering both skills!

People with addictions often have deep anger/hopelessness issues to transform. I believe addiction is simply an attempt to connect to the energy of Core Being. Be it alcohol or harder drugs, the result of taking them is an expansive sensation of positive tingles and flows in the body. This experience resembles the Core Being frequency **but is not the Core Being energy**.

Addictions can be overcome when someone masters the Anger/Sadness Cycle and reconnects to the power of who they really are! Addiction is usually a symptom of disconnect from our Core Being. If it is also the result of an underlying physiological issue or mental illness such as schizophrenia, then medication may be needed in addition to deep energetic transformation.

As people learn to let go of being saved by another and commit to being here on earth, the new "addiction" can be their connection to Core Being! As we feel Core Being in the body, we can more easily overcome the difficulties the ego faces here on earth.

ANGER/SADNESS CYCLES TRANSFORMED

Joe, a former meth-amphetamine addict, often has thoughts of darkness and writes about them in a journal. In his life, he feels inadequate and disempowered to make changes. He explains that an enemy is out in the world working against him and that is why he can't change his life. He understands that anger can help him break this pattern but is confused about how. He has done enough personal work to have a strong Enlightened Observer that can support him during deep process work, so we proceed and investigate how can he connect to his Core Being and transform his victim consciousness.

As we begin, he first feels the anger only in his head. I instruct him to bend his knees, imagine his energy grounding deep into the earth and breathe. Eventually, after a series of movements, the anger moves into his heart. He thinks about how his dad was never emotionally supportive and wants to cry. Tears flow and then it turns into anger. As he melts into the sensation of the anger in his heart, the energy of the anger drops lower in his body. He now notices it in his pelvis and discovers feelings of deep hatred and shame toward himself. Sobs move through his body. I suggest he allow the energy to spread as a sensation to his inner thighs and lower legs to help it balance and transform.

As he and his Enlightened Observer allow the energy to spread to other areas of his body, the anger begins to transform to a sense of empowerment. He begins to let go of the shame and hatred—his posture changes. His shoulders move back and he holds his head high. Joy, happiness and pride flow. He turns to me and says, "For the first time, I really believe in myself; I believe I can change my life!"

These energies of victim consciousness visit again and again as we face difficulties, which are part of life. So Joe (and all of us) will revisit these emotional challenges and transform them again and again throughout our lives, at least 100 more times. Wishing we could do it once, and then be done, is Spiritual Junk Food. Knowing emotional challenges are part of life and knowing we are whole, even when they arrive, is self-mastery – especially as we get better at transforming them so we can anchor more deeply into our Core Being.

- **Step 1:** Using aligned intention (Manifest Energy) and your Enlightened Observer, connect to anger – or whichever emotion is hardest to process. Find where it is held in the body. Often anger is held in the back of the Heart Chakra and in the pelvis. Sadness is often held in the heart and throat.
- **Step 2:** As we melt into it with our Enlightened Observer and Manifest Energy, allow the energy in our 4th and 2nd levels of the Auric field (which hold emotions and trauma) to move

and expand. Allow ourselves to move between the anger and the sadness, following the Rhythm of Flow of energy as it expands and contracts-just as Joe did in the above example. Let one wave of emotion move through us and then open to the next as it unwinds anger to sadness, sadness to anger just as a twist in the string of a kite unravels so the wind can take it higher and higher. Organically it will flow as long as we keep supporting it by deepening into the next wave moving through us.

- **Step 3:** It is best if we are standing and doing one of the above exercises when we process at this level. Standing up and moving helps us bring more energy through our field so it stays larger than the painful emotions. If we lie down, we need to be careful that our field doesn't collapse into the pain, causing us to lose the HVC of our Enlightened Observer.

  If the Rhythm of Flow stops prematurely, we can follow the containment procedure (see Chapter 18) to stabilize our field before we move to Step 4 and bring as much of Core Being in as possible. Using our Explorer's Mind, we can investigate why we couldn't completely transform it. Remember, it is not good or bad that it didn't transform, it is just information we can use to better support ourselves. Time, patience and self-love help us develop and refine these skills.

- **Step 4:** Finish by bringing in the energy of Core Being to all aspects of our Me-B system. Using exercise, intention or whatever helps, bring it deep into our cells: front/back, top/bottom, and left/right.

USE ANGER TO SHIFT ANXIETY

Any of the previous exercises can be used to bring the energy of anger into anxiety and reconnect us back to Core Being. Then, follow the steps outlined below:

1. First, charge your field and expand it using any of the techniques already taught. Fill the central channel with strength.
2. Connect to your Manifest Energy and Enlightened Observer and make them strong.
3. Locate where the anxiety is strongest in the body-usually the heart or stomach. If the only place you sense it is in the head, then find a different place that is lower in the body to focus on. This is because focusing on the head could bring too big a charge into it and could result in a headache. Also, it could cause us to dissociate, and lose our grounding.
4. Next, find where in your mind/body you can tap into the energy of anger (such as the pelvis). It helps to think of something that makes you mad, such as 9/11; global warming or something personal in your life. Let the energy of anger expand throughout the lower body and let it blend and mix with your anxiety.
5. As you do this, engage your intention for the anger to transform to strength and melt away the anxiety. Breath, expand and let it melt. Breath, expand and let it melt.
6. As you melt away the anxiety with the now converted energy of strength, invite the HVC of Core Being to grow.

NERVOUS SYSTEM UPGRADE

This Intervention can be done on others or on ourselves. It can be done through both touch and non-touch techniques. Non-touch techniques work because it is intention, breath and awareness that moves energy. Our hands only support the movement of the energy guided by our intention. We can move energy in someone else without touching them simply by placing our awareness into their field and using breath, intention and awareness.

The Nervous System Upgrade is done when our own Nervous System (or our client's) becomes overactive and needs to be calmed and balanced. Do not underestimate the power of this positive resourcing Intervention. Personally, I found it very important after I had a near collision with my car. It was a typical Colorado winter; the roads were covered with ice and snow. Everyone was skidding and sliding like a slow-motion car ballet. It would have been beautiful if it weren't so terrifying, watching cars slide and smash into each other. When I arrived to teach my Me-B Transformation™ class, I was shaking. Franny, my student teacher, suggested that during the opening meditation I do a Nervous System Upgrade on myself so I was able to rebalance. Apparently, she had used it right after she had had an accident and it worked beautifully. Within five minutes of following this procedure, I was whole again and ready to lead class. Many of my clients have proclaimed its merits as well. Its effectiveness depends upon a person's ability to receive it and how strong their intention is to heal. It is helpful to have someone else work it on us so we don't always have to do it on ourselves.

Balance and charge our energy field. If working on a client, help them balance their field before following the steps below. For non-touch, where it says use our hands, we simple melt our breath and awareness into the body to move the energy of the new, more healed Nervous System.

1. Energetically connect to the healed version of our Nervous System. We do this by using intention. (When I ask for the healed Nervous System to arrive, I use my open hand, held upward to connect to the healed Nervous System. I can actually see it show up and feel it come into my hand.) Feeling our Manifest Energy aligned assists us in this process. Then, by feeling, seeing, and sensing the more healed nervous system, we energetically bring it into our or our client's field using our sixth chakra and Manifest Energy.

2. See it, visualize it, feel it, intuit it, know it and sense it sinking through first the 7 levels of the field from the 7th-1st; and then into the skin, organs, bone and muscle structure. Finally, drop it into the spinal column. (See illustration below.)

3. Then, starting at the tailbone, energetically glue it into the cells and the spinal column, while placing one hand at the base of the spine and one hand on the second chakra.

4. Notice where it feels it has melted into the spinal column. Integrate it into the energy field even more by placing one hand on the front of the body and one along the spine. Allow the energy from the hand by the spine to charge the spine, and the energy from the hand on the front to integrate it into the field and physical body. Just as porcelain fills a mold, allow the new nervous system to fill the mold left by the old. Because the new nervous system holds a higher frequency, it will dissolve, or melt, the energy of the old system.

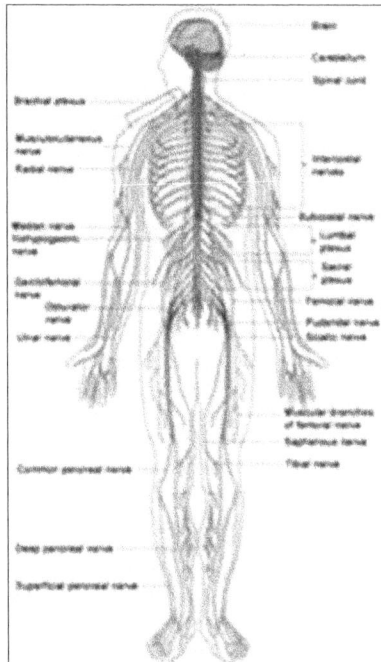

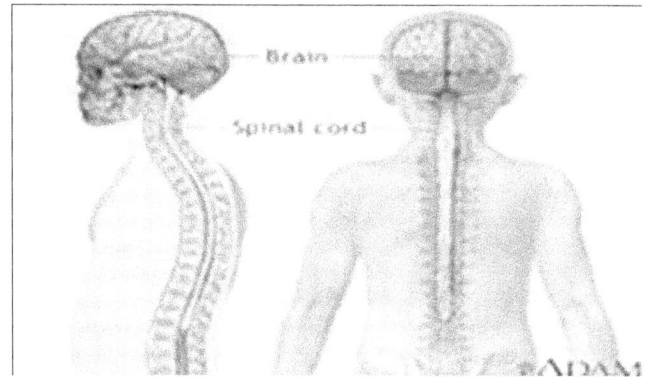

Work up slowly from the sacrum toward the base of the neck. Move upward inch by inch. Then integrate and work it deep into the base of the skull and neck. Then work through the arms and legs (see picture.) Lastly, imagine Core Being filling and wrapping around the new nervous system. Have it fill the spine, arms legs-every cell. Then expand Core Being front/back, top/bottom, and left/right.

Note: This is a very powerful healing so do not practice this on someone else unless you have been trained by an approved Mind Energy Body TransformationTM Instructor.

KEY STEPS TO TRANSFORM ANGER (or any difficult emotion)

Review of the 3-Rings of Healing and the 5-Step Mindfulness Process

- Feel where it is held in the body.
- Assess whether it is past or present anger and whether it is yours or someone else's that you took on.
- Listen to the wisdom it holds.
- Learn from the wisdom, especially if it deals with a boundary issue.
- Use your Enlightened Observer and strong Manifest Energy Line to feel the anger as a sensation in the body.
- Meditate, exercise or move to help discharge extra anger and transform it into aliveness and personal power.
- Take regular pauses to integrate the work and ensure you don't over-activate the nervous system.
- Be very careful not to collapse into sadness or charge the anger.
- Keep your Enlightened Observer and strong Manifest Energy.
- If sadness comes up when processing anger, don't identify with it or collapse. This will enable you to process it. But always check to see if the sadness is being used to avoid doing deep anger work.
- It is also very important to check to see if the anger is evenly distributed within the body energetically and in terms of sensations. If it is not, you need to discover why not.
- Is there a negative Image or Belief?
- Is there positive intention in the mind and body? If it is not equally transformed in both the upper half and lower half of the body, there is more work to do.
- If you don't feel more energized, balanced, alive and empowered in your Core Being, then you have not successfully transformed anger.
- Be patient.
- Keep your Enlightened Observer near and don't collapse or over-identify—stay out of the personality level.
- Practice, practice, practice — It gets easier!

CHAPTER REVIEW QUESTIONS

1. Why are anger meditations necessary?
2. Is it true we may need to process anger even when we don't feel angry? Explain.
3. What are the 4 sources of anger? Which ones create the biggest challenge for you? Explain.
4. Notice your Rhythm and Flow of Reality around anger, and then create time in your life to do Anger Meditations often enough to support yourself.
5. Practice the Anger Meditation and discover what is easy and what areas might need more support.
6. Describe how anger helps us transform and heal anxiety and depression and why.
7. What happens if you charge anger, or any emotion?

8. What can we do energetically to help us transform emotions and not charge them or collapse into them? Specifically, which dimension helps us and which Me-B Skills help us?

9. Why is it important to learn to process both anger and sadness? Which is easiest for you?

10. List some wisdom and/or messages anger has delivered to you. Be specific. How do you plan to integrate the wisdom into your life? Which changes are most frightening and might trigger you into the Void or to cause you to lose your current sense of self and need to develop a new sense of self (Stage 3-4 of Me-B Transformation^TM)?

11. What are the key factors that tell us transformation of LVC (such as anxiety, depression or anger) has happened?

12. If transformation doesn't happen, what does this signal?

13. After transformation of the emotions, why is it important to feel sensations in the body evenly throughout? If you only feel them in the upper body, what does that indicate?

14. Explain why pauses and breaks are important when we hit a pillow or punching bag to release anger.

15. Why is it important to (1) eliminate any negative intention that might make us hold onto the anger and (2) to be in our Manifest Energy when we hit a pillow or punching bag to release anger?

16. What physical movement(s) best helps you release and transform anger?

17. True or False: If you don't feel more energized, balanced, alive and empowered in your Core Being, then you have not successfully transformed anger.

18. Separated Self energy feels good. Explain why.

19. Why are anger meditations important, even when we are not angry?

20. If anger is often about boundaries, what boundaries might you need to change?

21. What are the reasons our energy field might get too porous and take on another's anger, depression or illness?

22. What is the difference between caring for someone and caretaking someone?

23. What are the hardest emotions to transform energetically?

24. Explain why the energy of anger, when transformed, can balance and melt away anxiety?

25. Why does our negative ego feed anxiety? What negative beliefs about our self might also be involved in feeding the charge of anxiety?

26. Addiction is a negative way of connecting to what?

27. Why is it important to be trained by a Me-B Instructor before you do the Neurological Replacement Healing on someone else?

28. Which physical movement exercises BEST help you move and transform anger or any difficult emotion?

29. Why is it important to take breaks when processing anger?

30. When processing anger by hitting a pillow (or anything), why don't we think of the pillow as the person we are angry with?

31. See the picture below of Intention and Balance. What helps bring balance into your life, and what helps you connect into Manifest Energy?

CHAPTER 16
5 SEEDS OF DISTORTION AROUND LOVE
With Every Step, We Either Create Love or Destroy It

The path to love and intimacy is sometimes mired in our unhealthy relational energy patterns. Notice them, so subtle yet so strong. They can crush our hope of receiving and giving healthy love.

Before conception, consciousness exists in/as a sea of bliss, love and joy. After conception, we enter this denser dimension of earth. Still somewhat protected, we enter the liquid warmth of the womb. This love and bliss fades further as we move through the birth canal out into the air. As a result, we all start life with the need to be loved. Unfortunately, because this need for love is not always met by our self and/or others, a separation from our Core Being evolves at deeper and deeper levels. This separation, caused by our attachment to joy, love and bliss, is where we forget our Core Being. As we develop a false understanding of who we are in the world, our distortions around love increase and **we carry these distortions into our intimate adult relationships.**

Psychoanalytic views would more or less hold that children are initially unaware of their separation from their primary "love," Mom. Over time, they begin to realize they are separate when their narcissism is shattered by the tardiness or perceived hostile behavior of their mother. Me-B Transformation™ believes this is when our ego-based personality grows to dominate our Core Being.

"Attachment" is an emotional bond to another person. An attachment disorder is an overly needy bond, an unhealthy bond, or an inability to bond. Psychologist John Bowlby was the first attachment theorist, describing attachment as a "lasting psychological connectedness between human beings" (Bowlby, 1969, p. 194). Bowlby believed that the earliest bonds formed by children with their caregivers have a tremendous impact that continues throughout life. The central theme of attachment theory is that mothers who are available and responsive to their infant's needs establish a sense of security.

The infant knows that the caregiver is dependable, which creates a secure base from which the child can then explore the world. Unfortunately, rarely were our environments and parents perfect. And even if they were, I still believe we would have attachment challenges *no matter how perfect our childhoods.* This is because the vibration here on earth is very dense, and this dense energy feeds our ego-based personality and our false sense of self and a disconnect from Core Being. **Our disconnect from Core Being is the source of attachment challenges.**

What every child wants to know is, "Do you see me? Does what I say matter to you? Does it mean anything that I am here?" We can carry these needs from childhood to adulthood.

We call these distortions around love the **5 Seeds of Distortion.** As we learn to recognize these seeds in our relationships and consequently develop the **Skills of Adult Consciousness,** *we reprogram and restructure our love relationships in a way that supports a more mature and empowering exchange of love.*

The Me-B 5 Seeds of Distortion outline (1) how we energetically reproduce our attachment challenges within our adult intimate love relationships, and (2) how we can heal from these disorders so we maintain long-term loving bonds with those around us. Review the information below, and take the following self-assessment test on bonding issues.

The "Betrayal Bond" Test

The following are a series of statements that describe traumatic bonding in which a person bonds on the basis of betrayal. The result is what we call a "betrayal bond". Please answer the questions by checking in the appropriate response and/or do it online at.

To complete the test, answer each question by placing a check in the appropriate yes/no column.

Yes No 1.   Do you obsess about people who have hurt you even through they are long gone?

Yes No 2.   Do you continue to seek contact with people whom you know will cause you further pain?

Yes No 3.   Do you go "overboard" to help people who have been destructive to you?

Yes No 4.   Do you continue to be a "team" member when obviously things are becoming destructive?

Yes No 5.   Do you continue attempts to get people to like you who are clearly using you?

Yes No 6.   Do you trust people again and again who are proven to be unreliable?

Yes No 7.   Are you unable to retreat from unhealthy relationships?

Yes No 8.   Do you try to be understood by those who clearly do not care?

Yes No 9.   Do you choose to stay in conflict with others when it would cost you nothing to walk away?

Yes No 10.   Do you persist in trying to convince people that there is a problem and they are not willing to listen?

Yes No 11.   Are you loyal to people who have betrayed you?

Yes No 12.   Do you attract untrustworthy people?

Yes No 13.   Have you kept damaging secrets about exploitation or abuse?

Yes No 14.   Do you continue contact with an abuser who acknowledges no responsibility?

Yes   No   15.   Do you find yourself covering up, defending, or explaining a relationship?

Yes   No   16.   When there is a constant pattern of non-performance in a relationship, do you continue to expect them to follow through anyway?

Yes   No   17.   Do you have repetitive, destructive fights that are no win for anybody?

Yes   No   18.   Do you find that others are horrified by something that has happened to you and you are not?

Yes   No   19.   Do you obsess about showing someone that they are wrong about you, your relationship, or their treatment of you?

Yes   No   20.   Do you feel stuck because you know what the other is doing is destructive but you believe you cannot do anything about it?

Yes   No   21.   Do you feel loyal to someone even though you harbor secrets that are damaging to others?

Yes   No   22.   Do you move closer to someone you know is destructive to you even though you do not trust, like or care for the person?

Yes   No   23.   Does someone's talents, charisma, or contributions cause you to overlook destructive, exploitive, or degrading acts?

Yes   No   24.   Do you find you cannot detach from someone even though you do not trust, like or care for the person?

Yes   No   25.   Do you find yourself missing a relationship even to the point of nostalgia and longing, that was so awful it almost destroyed you?

Yes   No   26.   Are extraordinary demands placed on you to measure up as a way to cover up exploitation?

Yes   No   27.   Do you keep secret someone's destructive behavior because of all of the good they have done or the importance of their position or ca-

Yes   No   28.   Does your relationship have contacts or promises that have been broken which you are asked to overlook?

Yes   No   29.   Are you attracted to "dangerous" people?

Yes   No   30.   Do you stay in a relationship longer than you should?

Go to www.sexhelp.com; click on do I have a sex addiction (go) then click on the Betrayal Bond. Six "yes" answers or fewer is considered normal.

How did you score? Note the areas you can improve as well as the areas where you already have healthy bonds.

Now that you are aware of how your relationships were influenced by your attachment patterns from your early significant relationships, I will unveil the **5 Seeds of Distortion Around Love**. As you learn about each "seed" and begin to identify yourself in the various "types" outlined below, you will open yourself to new knowledge and awareness. As you bring this new awareness to your family, friends and intimate relationships, *you begin an empowering process of shifting and enhancing these important relationships so you cultivate the mature love you long to give and receive.*

SEED 1

We attract what is familiar, even if it is unhealthy

How we run our energy and consciousness can attract friends, partners, and associates who will mistreat us just as we were mistreated in the past. It is like the south of a magnet, attracting its magnetic north. As we track our subtle relationship saboteur, we can reprogram it.

My Father Wanted Me to Be Like Him, So I Lost Me

My father showed his love by being controlling and asking his kids to fit into a specific box he felt was the "right box." Any time I acted or thought differently than the way he wanted me to, he would smash me down, obliterating any part of me that individuated from his views. As an adult, I noticed this trend continue when I connected to others. Any time I delivered a unique and advanced perspective, I often attracted criticism from my supervisors or peers. I became aware that the outer edges of the 2nd and 4th levels of my Auric Field shrunk every time I expressed my views and, in turn, this would make the other person's field expand and puff up.

Over time, I learned to better neutralize this effect by filling those levels of the field with Core Being energy. I also learned to keep my Manifest Energy Line aligned so I felt safe, even when another person disagreed with my perspective. It took many years until I had almost completely reprogrammed my energetic fear response. The more harmony I resonate in my field, the more harmony and positive reaction I attract back toward me. Even though my father never approved of my type of success, I eventually made peace with it, even at the most subtle energetic levels.

What Energy Within Us Attracts Others To Mistreat Us The Same Way We Were Mistreated In The Past?

Our brain and nervous system unconsciously orients towards bringing the traumas and difficulties of the past into our lives. This **orienting reflex** creates a "procedural learning" and subconsciously instructs us to be either too vigilant in our actions **(hyper-aroused)** or not vigilant enough **(hypo-aroused)**.

Review the following and assess if you are blind to seeing a good partner/friend/co-worker when they show up? Or do you instead attract a partner/friend/co-worker that are not in your best interest? Understanding the power of the law of attraction can help you glimpse your role in the equation. *(This law states that what you focus on grows. If you focus on fear, you attract a situation that will make you fearful. If you subconsciously relinquish your role as self-protector, someone will betray you so you learn to reclaim that vital self-care role for yourself!* **Learn to attract your high vibrational good and stop attracting your past traumas to replay in the present.***)*

What energy within us attracts others to mistreat us the same way we were mistreated in the past?

Take time to examine the people in your life who cause you pain. What could you energetically do differently on your part to promote more balance in the relationship and what are you doing to attract a negative form of love. For instance, do you sell yourself short, do you try to please too much, do you orient toward danger and chose the "wrong" person because they are more "exciting"? What Character Type are they, and what happens in your energy field that triggers a difficult energetic reaction in their field? What could you energetically do differently on your part to promote more balance? (Review the scenarios below to help you reveal any subconscious saboteur.)

REPROGRAM BOND DISTORTIONS

Spiritual-Types experienced their mother as being withdrawn and angry during the crucial months pre- and post birth. Thus, they often find people *who show their love by being hostile, who energetically disappear, or who intellectualize their love*. If they repeat this negative defense back, it perpetuates unhealthy pattern.

Leader-Types often choose to be with people *who show their love to them by being submissive.* However it is a mask of submissiveness. The Leader becomes the boss and the other is the follower. Equality in the relationship often takes work. And often, if the submissive partner changes the balance in the relationship by claiming his or her power, the Leader-type often ignites in anger. Instead of feeling supported by their friends, partners or work associates, the Leader-type will often feel betrayed.

Compassionate-Types often partner with a Leader-type because they are the underdog and want someone to mother them. In other words, Compassionate types find people *who show their love to them by taking care of them.* This allows the Compassionate Type to act needy and clingy in the relationship. They hope to choose someone that won't abandon them the way their mother/father abandoned them. The gift would be for them to learn how not to abandon themselves and heal their clingy insecurities and fill themselves up. The gift they could give their self is to know they are enough.

Excel-Types would find someone that would most likely be as "perfect" as possible. Excels have trouble making commitments because they don't want to make the "imperfect" choice. Their partner would *show their*

Excel-Types would find someone that would most likely be as "perfect" as possible. Excels have trouble making commitments because they don't want to make the "imperfect" choice. Their partner would *show their love for them by looking and being as perfect and appropriate as possible. There may use seduction and be competitive in the relationship as well.*

Heart-Centered Types would find someone *who shows their love for them by teasing them.* As a result, the heart-centered person would then feel shamed and they would hold in those feelings deep in their body until they eventually exploded. Finally the anger of the past would be released but only temporarily. Eventually it would build up again, release, build, release…. A positive alternative would be for the Heart-centered person to learn how to transform their anger into personal power so they can speak their feelings in the moment, set healthy boundaries and learn to love themselves.

SEED 2

We accept unhealthy behaviors as loving

What do we consider a loving response from someone? An extreme example would be a beating, or verbal or sexual abuse. Clearly, what we accept as loving behavior is not always worthy of being called love. Yet some of us will accept anything as long as it is "done out of love." We can instead learn to say "no" to unhealthy expressions of love—especially when the cost is too high to reap any benefit.

I Need You To Love Me, And I Don't Care What it Looks Like

Every night Ron would sit next to his father waiting for love—and every night his father, having consumed 4 double martinis, would tell Ron how disappointed he was in him. Why didn't he do this or that? He spent hours with his son, and gave him much attention but it was all negative criticism of what he was doing wrong. Ron never thought to say "No" to his father or to walk away. He was much too happy to at least get this type of love than no love at all. Today, Ron is 52 years old, chronically ill, unemployable, and a recovering drug addict. His father is the sole source of Ron's income, and Ron is still sitting at his father's feet being told he is no good.

Some of us will accept anything as long as it is "done out of love." We can instead learn to say "no" to unhealthy expressions of love—especially when the cost is too high to reap any benefit.

Do you have people in your life that are controlling and manipulative as a way of showing their love? Does anyone want to "fix" you as an expression of their love? Do they judge you and tell you what you do/think/feel is wrong as an expression of their love for you?

What We Accept As Love

Make note of how those you love best show their love for you. Notice what feels like love—and what does not feel like love, but you accept it anyway. When you accept it, what distortions do you feel in your energy field? What negative belief, trauma and/or Core Distortion are linked to the distortions in your field?

Especially notice what happens in the Manifest Energy Line and 2nd and 4th Levels of the field. Using positive intention, investigate how you can set healthy boundaries around what does not feel like love. Transform any distortions in your energy field and body with HVC.

Spiritual types might choose someone like their mother — someone who is *distant and hostile*. Or they may just move from one relationship to the next, *rejecting the other first* so they don't feel the pain of being rejected. Remember, withdrawal is their safest place. Lastly, they tend to *intellectualize love*. It is all in their head. There is nothing in their body because the body is vacant.

Companionate types believe if they ask, it's not love—and if they don't ask they won't get it. *Thus they never feel satisfied with getting love from others. They chose to be passive and depressed instead of energized and active. Energetically, they also try to hook you in. Sometimes they use hopeless and pleading eyes, or they speak softly…anything to get you, the substitute mother, to comfort them. They try to get you to energetically feed them the way they <u>were not fed</u> by their mother.*

Sometimes a Compassionate-type had a mother who was too good at comforting them. She never taught them how to comfort themselves. The mother made them dependent upon her, turning them into a "Peter Pan" type. They never want to grow up because they don't have to…mom will always be there for them.

Leader types might chose to get love from others in a manner *where they could always be in control.* They would create a situation where they could convince those around them that they were right. They would be manipulative in their love relationships.

Excel types might feel that either choice they make about getting love from others might be wrong. They don't want to make the wrong choice, so they may make no choice at all. If they do finally commit to being with someone, it would be the "perfect" person.

Heart-Centered types may *choose someone to love them who will invade their very porous boundaries. They in turn might* provoke them in the subconscious hope they can express the anger that they hide deep inside. They react with the message, "I will hurt myself before you hurt me."

SEED 3

What happens inside us when we are not loved?

When we really love or care for someone and they reject us, no matter how often this happens in our lives, it always hurts. I tell my children, one of the most important skills they need to learn in life is to learn to break up with someone and be broken up with. When you experience the aftermath, **only then do you really know if you have connected deep enough to your own internal self-love.**

Never, Never Again Do I Want to Feel Unloved

When she wasn't loved, Emily would think that something was wrong with her, and look at what she needed to change to be loved. Her construct was based solely on changing so she didn't get abandoned—because being abandoned would fill her with terror. Self-harm was another defense that she used when she didn't feel loved.

"Extra weight around my waist and thighs grow when I don't feel loved and accepted for who I am," said Emily. "I hurt myself by eating, drinking, and fill myself up with self-hate," she added.

As you risk loving and caring for another (be it a friend or intimate partner) and are rejected, you gain the gift of truly reflecting your positive **Core Being** back to the most important person in your life—You! **When you can be rejected and still feel whole, it opens you to a whole new sense of freedom and choice.**

What We Do When Our Love Is Not Returned

Take time to find your unhealthy way of reacting when you are not loved. Draw how your field changes when you don't feel loved. What energetic patterns are created, and what can you do to balance your field? Especially notice what happens in the 2nd and 4th levels of your Auric Field and your Manifest Energy Line.

REPROGRAM BOND DISTORTIONS

<u>Spiritual types</u> would obviously withdraw. They reject people before they are rejected. Energetically they try to hold it together. Fear and anxiety take over, but they escape so they can't feel it.

<u>Compassionate types</u> believe that they are not good enough when they aren't loved and they feel aban*doned* – yet it is they who abandon their own selves. Energetically they hold on.

<u>Leader types</u> energetically *hold up under the strain and feel once again betrayed, convinced that that they can't trust anyone*. They would attack or try to control those around them to prevent being left or being alone.

<u>Excel types</u> would try to be more perfect, disconnect further from their essence, and energetically hold back any feelings.

<u>Heart-Centered-types</u> would hold in the anger boiling within them. They would also feel shame and humiliation.

SEED 4

Unhealthy programming of how we "act out" self-love

Self-love, self-love, I know it is somewhere. Somewhere—I must have hidden it somewhere? Oh, yes, here it is! I find a very cute guy and have sex with him; I buy a new dress; I eat chocolate, "I cut myself."

Unhealthy demonstrations of self-love abound, such as: eating comfort foods, consuming alcohol, taking drugs, doing too much or too little exercise, cutting, excess shopping, etc. In addition, there may be deep self-hatred expressed in the form of thoughts, judgments and negative beliefs.

Where Has All the Self-Love Gone?

Self-love, self-love, I know it is somewhere. Somewhere—I must have hidden it somewhere? Oh, yes. Here it is. I find a very cute guy and have sex with him; I buy a new dress; I eat chocolate, "I cut myself"…. Unhealthy demonstrations of self-love can be numerous, such as eating comfort foods, consuming alcohol, taking drugs, doing too much or too little exercise, cutting, excess shopping, etc. In addition, there may be deep self-hatred expressed in the form of thoughts, judgments and negative beliefs.

Create a Plan to Cultivate Self-Love

Put together a plan to cultivate Self-Love. What are healthy energetic exercises you can do to support self-love? Where do you feel the depletion in your field? Often it is the back of the heart chakra and the front of the 3rd chakra. The Centered Oneness Healing is very effective for cultivating self-love. Also, you can practice filling up the third chakra with Core Being. Allow yourself to receive it in. Review the Positive Resource Interventions as possible support as well.

Spiritual types would be in *spiritual by-pass, withdrawal and intellectualization*. They would feel only the good and escape the more challenging aspects of being human. Learning how to exist, feel safe and love themselves—even the human parts—is their life task.

Compassionate types cannot *love themselves unless someone else confirms it.* They may eat or have an addiction to show how they love themselves, instead of fulfilling their life task of filling themselves up with essence.

Leader types may *be narcissistic in their love for self and hold an elevated view of who they really are in the world*. The life task of this type is learning how to NOT betray themselves even when others may betray them. They can learn how to create their own safety within, so they don't feel they need to battle, control or manipulate everyone else.

Excel types would also *have trouble with self-love*. They are extremely *judgmental of themselves and need to be perfect*. Their life task is to find their Core Being and not simply identify with the fake exterior.

Heart-Centered types unfortunately might hurt themselves, because they don't know how to truly love themselves. In order to truly love themselves, they need to be able to individuate and feel their own authority and Core Being.

SEED 5

We can make unhealthy "choices" around showing love for others

See All the Ways I Love You...

Seed One is what do we do to *attract* unhealthy love. Seed 5 is what do **we do to others that is unhealthy love**. For instance, are you invasive, manipulative, controlling, work too hard to please, co-dependent, shrinking, letting others dominate, or withholding from speaking the truth?

These are just a few examples of how we can make unhealthy choices around showing our love for others. What are your ways of participating in this dance? We all are human and are each capable of growing in this area.

See All the Ways I Love You...

Husbands and wives give so much to their families, sometimes too much. Jim was no different. He took care of every detail for his family. The bills were paid on time, groceries from the list purchased, taxes done, gas in the cars—everything. Although he could have asked for help, he never did. He was needed. He knew that and appreciated how important he was to his family. But, at the end of the day, he was short-tempered and difficult to be near.

Jim's wife, Rebecca, also cared for her family, but she played a different, more controlling role. She was careful to protect her children. They were never allowed to walk the two blocks home from middle school or to play outside without her carefully watching over them. She constantly reminded them of all the dangers they should avoid.

Being invasive, being controlling, working too hard to please, being co-dependent, shrinking, letting others dominate, not speaking the truth — these are just a few examples of how we can make unhealthy choices around showing our love for others.

Developing Good Programming

Throughout the week, explore any unhealthy ways you show love to others. Are they fear-based? What is at the root of the behavior? Is it insecurity or a need to be in charge? Review the chapter on boundaries and relationship coherency to help you investigate this seed of distortion and develop a new approach for showing love.

Spiritual types would *not be able to truly show love* until they become present with themselves. *They can talk and intellectualize about it*, but they can't go deeper.

Companionate types would show love *by trying to please you or getting you to please them.* They almost plead for you to confirm their validity and worth. The statement would be, "If I do things for you, you will in turn love me and not leave." They will be clingy and will want to be taken care of.

Leader types *will choose to show love to others as if they are in a battleground.* They have been betrayed throughout their lives and feel they can't trust anyone. They feel embattled and choose to show love for others with similar methods—such as control, attack, and manipulation.

Excel types would *try to be as perfect and appropriate* as possible; the mask would be the loving. They sometimes use seduction and are not connected to their own heart and sexuality.

Heart-Centered types would show love *in a co-dependent manner.* They may caretakers those around them but later resent it. The outcome of their unhealthy demonstration of love is their own victimization.

All of these five become the seeds of our Core Distortions. Find yourself in the Core Distortions and write out a plan that would help you shift your patterns of relating to others. In addition, look at how you would support different clients who hold these 5 seeds. How would you understand the underlying causes and energetic solutions?

How do they become our solutions? Overcome the Three factors play a large role in our false sense of self?

A part of our psyche gets confused about who we are. Three factors play a large role in our false sense of self: (1) our issues around love during the bonding stage with parents, (2) our relationships at school, and (3) to what extent we carry these same confusions about love and self into our adult life. These factors help create false belief systems and images that in turn create a false view of the truth of who we are.

As we increase our consciousness, we increase our awareness of our false images and beliefs and actions around these five seeds. Many of us begin to understand how to change, learn and grow. We discover that some of our old patterns create pain and don't get us what we think we want. During this discovery process, we can release our old programming and create healthier ways of being in the world.

5 Seeds of Distortion Overcome

Ways in Which We Can Re-Program For Healthy Love

Character Structures / Seeds to Distortions Of Love	SPIRITUAL (Schizoid)	Leader (Psychopath)	Compassionate (Oral)	Excel (Rigid)	Heart Centered (Masochistic)
Seed 1: Parents and/or Friends that show love for me by...	Staying Present With Us instead of Withdrawal, Hostility	Letting Others Give Us Unconditional Love without needing to control or dominate	Mothering Our Self instead of Demanding it from another	Letting Our Core Being be seen by another	Finding, then letting in unconditional love
Seed 2: Positive "choices" around receiving love from others	I chose someone who can be present to love	I don't need to be right and I don't need you to be submissive	I don't need you to love me but I accept the love you have.	I can commit. first to my own Core Being and then to you.	I can receive love in a healthy manner and not be invaded by you.
Seed 3: What happens inside us when we are not loved	I don't Withdrawal. I can exist, feel me, even when in deep pain.	If you betray me, I can trust again and feel self love and thus safety.	I won't abandon myself anymore! I am good enough even if you leave me.	I can connect to my essence and feel safe to love you even if you don't love me. I don't need seduction.	I won't hurt myself even if you hurt me.
Seed 4: How we "act out" self love.	I embody my love and can feel the sensation of it in my cells.	I find trust and safety within.	I self love and can confirm myself even when someone rejects me.	Because I am connected to core being I don't have to be perfect but can still enjoy achievement.	I am free! I no longer feel in a box of hurt and humiliation.
Seed 5: Good choices around "showing" love to others	I exist and am present in relationships, even if I am rejected.	I look for an equal. No need to control or manipulate or find someone submissive	I confidently take care of myself in life and in relationships.	My heart and sexuality are connected because I am present with my core being.	I don't need to provoke you and no longer look to be hurt.

5 SEEDS OF DISTORTION AROUND LOVE WORKSHEET
List your unhealthy programming for each seed
Print out and complete this worksheet

SEED 1

We attract what is familiar, even if it is unhealthy.

What to you attract in your relationships that are *familiar yet unhealthy?*

1. Write down how those you love best show their love for you.
2. Now list only the unhealthy ways they show their love for you.
3. What energy within you attracts others to mistreat you the same way you were mistreated in the past?
4. Write out how you can change your actions and energy field so you no longer attract these unhealthy expressions of love. For instance, do you resonate enough self-esteem in your field? Do you not show up to protect yourself when you should or do you see danger every-where and thus attract it to you? Be specific.

SEED 2

We accept unhealthy behaviors as loving.

1. Look at your relationships today,—What behaviors are unhealthy that you accept as loving? Write it down.
2. Look at what behaviors in past relationships were unhealthy that as a child you accepted as love. Write it down and compare your answers with your response to question #1.
3. What can you do to change this so you no longer accept unhealthy behaviors as loving? Write down a plan.

SEED 3

What happens inside us when we are not loved?

1. Take time to find your unhealthy ways of reacting when you are not loved. List them here.
2. How might your bodily sensations and energy field change when you don't feel loved? Write it down.
3. What can you do to balance your energy field and support yourself in transforming this pattern and reclaiming your wholeness? Write out a plan to fill yourself up when someone rejects you.

I believe this is the most important life skill. It creates a deep form of freedom to be who we truly are in the world, even if others don't like it!

SEED 4

Unhealthy programming of how we "act out" self-love.

1. List the unhealthy ways you show love for yourself (and/or act out self-hatred).
2. What is the negative belief that fuels these negative behaviors, thoughts and feelings?
3. Put together a plan to cultivate self-love and heal any negative beliefs and resulting actions.

What are healthy energetic exercises you can do to support self-love? Where do you feel the depletion in your body and energy field from lack of self-love? List powerful ways to support yourself in filling yourself with healthy actions of self-love so that you can move forward from this place of empowerment.

SEED 5
We can make unhealthy "choices" around showing love for others.

1. Throughout the week, explore any unhealthy ways you notice yourself showing love to others.
2. Who is the person you are most likely going to show unhealthy love towards?
3. Do you know why? Is it fear-based? What is at the root of the behavior? Is it insecurity or a need to be in charge? Write out an answer to these questions.
4. Now, develop a new approach for showing love to others.

REVIEW QUESTIONS

Explore the aspects of your programmed personality that were revealed during the 5 Seeds of Distortion exercises and describe any lessons learned. Be careful to explore and not judge yourself!

What was the result of the betrayal bonding test? What issues do you need to explore further that were highlighted as a result of the test? For instance, did you answer yes to staying in relationships too long? If so, what are the Core Distortions that cement you into an unhealthy pattern?

CHAPTER 17

THREE SKILLS DEFINING ADULT CONSCIOUSNESS

Turmoil is not harm. It is just a chance to distance ourselves from our ego and our false dream.
We just need to learn how.

Regarding turmoil, acceptance is rarely the card of first choice. We most often shoot for a door to open that will lead to a short-cut around our inner turmoil. This is because our turmoil is what reaches out to us most strongly. Our turmoil reaches out to us in an effort to support our transformation, yet we misjudge its intentions. Turmoil is not harm. It gives us an opportunity to distance ourselves from our ego and our false dream. Our Core Distortion's sole purpose is to help us "misbelieve" this so-called reality that we think is true. It is a gift toward remembering because as we feel the pain – and then "misbelieve" what we feel — we find truth. There is truth in seeing, truth in believing, and truth in living. The balance that comes from mastering the three skills of the triangle below is necessary to achieve adult consciousness. Therefore, as a mature and self-aware adult, we all strive to attain balance between these points of the triangle.

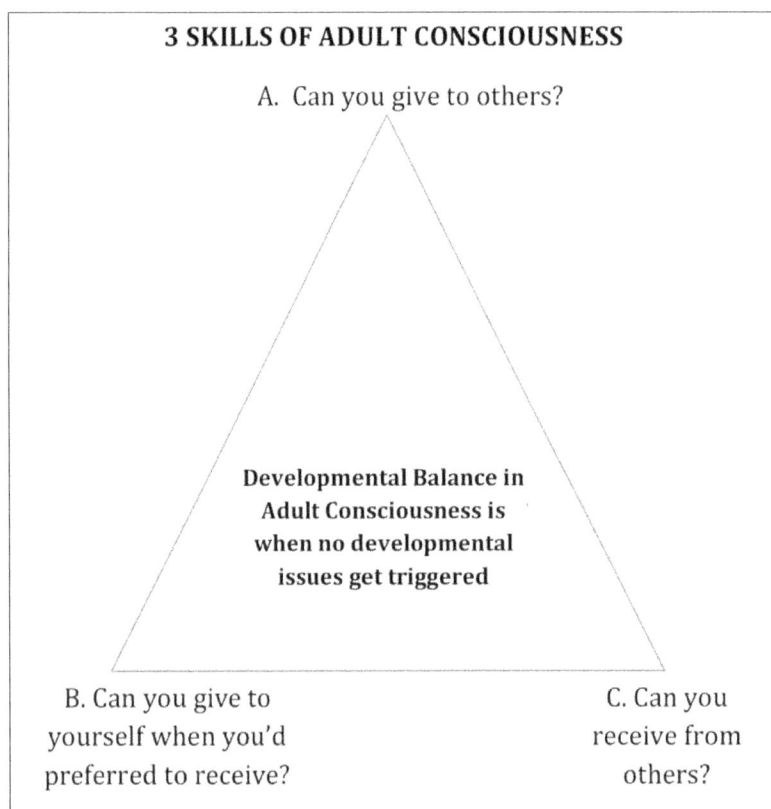

3 SKILLS OF ADULT CONSCIOUSNESS

A. Can you give to others?

Developmental Balance in
Adult Consciousness is
when no developmental
issues get triggered

B. Can you give to
yourself when you'd
preferred to receive?

C. Can you
receive from
others?

THREE ADULT CONSCIOUSNESS SKILLS

We, as well as our clients, will most likely have difficulty with one or more of the **Three Adult Consciousness Skills**. As we identify which skills to develop and/or refine, we support our adult sense of wholeness. Follow the 5 Steps and the 3 Rings of Healing to Shape-Shift our Realities so we return to Core Being and also return to Adult Consciousness.

1. **Give to self, especially when we would rather someone else give it to us**. If we have control

issues, and/or self-worth issues, this point of the Adult Consciousness triangle can be very difficult. The "Peter Pan" energies of being forever young also can cause us to have difficulty with this skill. Sometimes we feel we can't take care of ourselves and we need someone else to step in and help us achieve our dreams. Fortunately, our dreams can too easily become another's dreams if we are not the one creating them.

Yes, we can receive help, but can we be there completely and joyfully for ourselves when external support dries up? Even if we have a chronic illness?

The chapter on positive resourcing can help with this challenge. Adult Consciousness enables us to build our Energy and Biological Consciousness Container so that when energy is not being given to us by another, we are strong enough to give it to our- selves. It also outlines Positive Resourcing techniques to build and strengthen our connection to Core Being. Those who are lower in the Me-B Stages can have difficulty with this skill.

2. **Give to others, especially when you want to receive.** Sometimes we are not the takers in a relationship; instead, we can be the giver. Either giving too much or taking too much – in extreme ways — is a diagnostic indicator that we are **not** in Adult Consciousness. Balance between the three points of the triangle is possible when we make the commitment to explore our internal world.

3. **Receive from others, especially when we are more comfortable giving.** This means we must also **learn to ask for what we need**. This also necessitates our being in touch with our true needs. This is different from being "needy" and clingy. Asking for what we need can be risky, because someone may say "no." In that case, we could regress to child consciousness and get angry, run away, or collapse. As we are able to remain (or return to) Adult Consciousness, we can ask for what we need because we know that if they say "no," we can still give to self.

A **True Need**, for example, is when someone is yelling at us and we say, "Please, that hurts. Don't yell at me that way." There is no guarantee they will stop, but we can at least state our true need. Another example would be when we are in the middle of an emotional crisis, and we want support from a friend, and we say, "I would love a hug."

Knowing just what we need and then asking for it can be a difficult skill to master, especially during stressful times. It can feel overwhelming, and you may feel very vulnerable. Yet, from the "good enough" adult inside us, it can be exactly what is needed. Being able to receive energy, love, and support from another person can be a difficult skill, but it is essential to maintaining Adult Consciousness.

CHARACTER STRUCTURES AND ADULT CONSCIOUSNESS

Spiritual:

Must learn to be present enough for all three points of the triangle and feel and then transform the fear and pain their escape defense avoids. Getting out of the head and into the real work of the body is an important gift they can give themselves. This can take time and patience on the part of both the Me-B guide and the client.

Leader:

They must learn to give to self and receive from others without trying to control. It is important to help them learn that trust is an element within versus, something they control externally to create. They are givers and directors and sometimes manipulators. Can they give to self, when they would prefer to receive from another?

Also, can they claim their adult so deeply that they can give to self even when they think others are attacking?

Feeling safe even when fear arises is their life task. They need to learn to not meet the real or projected attack from a place of control, manipulation, and mistrust. Lastly, can their adult help them trust and stop projecting, which only creates feelings of attack and betrayal?

(LEADER AND EXCEL TYPES ARE MORE LIKELY TO MASTER THESE SKILLS.)

Compassionate:

They need interventions that support them in coming out of the contraction of Child Consciousness and into their adult. Positive Golden Shadow Resourcing Techniques are a good place to start but don't stay there.

They have to eventually feel the pain of you saying no. Only then can they transition to their adult by finding their own power through the anger they will feel when we say no.

Compassionate types will create situations for themselves where they think they need something from an- other, and then feel what they get from them is not enough. They will go into collapse or anger when they don't get it.

Interventions where you don't give them what they think they need but help them provide it for themselves can be very painful (it can ignite anger toward you), yet such interventions are necessary to help Compassionate types claim deeper levels of their fullness. Anger work can help them transform neediness and collapse into empowerment, where they will feel full, whole, and complete. Normally, compassionate types don't have enough charge in their field for self care. The anger can provide the charge necessary for deep transformation.

Heart-Centered:

Interventions can be tailored to (1) help them out of their energetic box, (2) help them see how they merge or hook into others, and (3) help them receive and take in support. If the support is not present externally, invite them to heal their inner "victim" and find their internal leader.

Sometimes they need to claim their internal "NO" before they claim their internal "YES." Learning how to process anger can be key to claiming their internal leader.

Excel:

To give to others even when it may not be perfect and to receive from others even when it may not be perfect will bring an Excel into their adult and out of their mask. The first intervention to make with this client is to help them find their true self. Many of the "resourcing' exercises we will practice today will help.

REVIEW QUESTIONS

1. In what area of your life (school, work, relationships, self-care, spirituality, recreation, hobbies) is it hardest to be in Adult Consciousness? Why?
2. In what area of your life (school, work, relationships, self-care, spirituality, recreation, hobbies) is it easiest to be in Adult Consciousness? Why?
3. Which point of the triangle is most difficult for you to master? Why, and what can you do to support.

CHAPTER 18

POSITIVE RESOURCING INTERVENTION TECHNIQUES
CAN BE USED FOR ANY OF THE Me-B STAGES

The word "HEALING" comes from the root Haelan, meaning to become whole. We are all whole, we just aren't always connected to our wholeness. Positive resourcing techniques help us reconnect and transform the LVC of our ego-based programmed personality so we can return to our true home within ourselves.

Mental or physical challenges cannot be present if: (1) intention is aligned, (2) the energetics of our Core Being is complete in all three systems, and (3) no contrary alignments are held in the shadow or subconscious. To understand the subconscious, it is vital that we and our clients learn to access the wisdom held within our physical body.

Our cells, tissues, bones, organs, fat, and muscles hold vital information. When we connect to our body, it sometimes brings up deep emotional pain. When this happens, it can feel overwhelming if we are not prepared. Practicing these Positive Resourcing Techniques helps us anchor more deeply into Core Being, and it helps us create a lot of "white paint" and move through the 3-Rings of Healing so we don't become re-traumatized when difficulty arises.

The common psychological term "Resourcing of Clients" originates in trauma/dark shadow work. Therapists noticed that if a client was not sufficiently "resourced" with a strong enough ego and sense of self, they reacted negatively to trauma/dark shadow interventions.

In Me-B Transformation™, it is counter-indicated for ourselves or a client to do deep trauma work, if we don't have a strong connection to Core Being. In fact, the deeper the work, the deeper the connection needs to be. When I see a new client, I spend most of the first few sessions helping them experience the energy of their Core Being before we address the LVC held in their presenting complaint.

In other words, if a person's connection to their true self is not stronger and higher in vibration than the trauma or dark shadow material—then they are susceptible to "re-wounding." "Re-wounding" is not bad or good. It can take time to *learn how to pace ourselves when transforming dark material. As we learn to better regulate our Me-B system, and not merge with the LVC, we take charge of our healing process.*

This means that clients (and we ourselves) need to become empowered and educated on our own system so we prevent re-wounding. I teach my clients about their Enlightened Observer, how to connect to it and how to self-assess and self-regulate so they are in charge of their healing process. In essence, I endeavor to empower them to the point that they eventually don't need me.

The following positive resourcing techniques help us become strong when messy edges in life show up. As we embrace our mistakes and transform challenges, growth is promoted. Also, as we accept that we (and others) will let ourselves down from time to time, we can accept imperfection and love others (and ourselves) in spite of these imperfections.

Perfection is not always possible; yet everything can be a gift of awakening. We can teach ourselves, and our clients, to positively resource so we are better equipped to deal with life's challenges. Bad news does not have to be such bad news, if we are resourced! This is because resourcing changes our perception so **we can find the gifts in the challenges.** Practice a different intervention every week and before you know it, you will have mastered them all.

BUILDING OUR ENERGY AND BIOLOGICAL CONSCIOUSNESS CONTAINER

Building our Energy and Biological Consciousness Container is the process of strengthening all 3 Me-B systems: our energy field, physical body and mind so we can run more energy through our field, and over a longer period of time. A stronger Container also means there is more "white paint" and HVC so any LVC (or black paint) dissolves easily. A stronger Container allows us to move to higher stages of Me-B Transformation™ and be in joy, even when hardship visits.

As we strengthen our Container, we also strengthen our ability to see, track and sense energy. We increase our intuitive ability, cleanse our field, and bring in HVC into our brain, nervous system, cells, and DNA. For in- stance, when I first began teaching energetic work, at the end of the day, I would be exhausted after holding my Container for the entire group and myself. Now I can easily teach an entire weekend and a much larger group and feel energized at the end of the day. This is because, over time, my Container grew. What once felt overwhelming, now feels easy.

It takes time and work to strengthen our Container. It doesn't happen overnight, but most things of value require focus to build and create. Our Container is no different. For example, I greatly enjoyed working with individual clients but felt ready to expand to teach groups, to writing a book, and hopefully to teaching internationally. Each of these steps is requiring me to continually strengthen my Container. And, step-by-step, I am achieving my goals.

Write down something you are passionate about achieving that feels difficult for you right now. Over the next several months, work to build your Container so you are strong enough to master your next steps, dreams and passions.

For instance, in the beginning of the Me-B training, new students who are not in the habit of transforming difficult energy and emotions find the days long and hard. After the first few months, if they have worked to strengthen their Containers, the transformation process becomes more effortless and their experiences deepen and become richer. Their ability to see and track energy grows as well. Doing deep process work helps.

Review the following categories and develop a plan to strengthening your Container.

Your Biology Can Cap Your Level of Consciousness:

Latest studies of our brain and biology suggest that our brain's neuro-network and our nervous system, DNA, cells and muscle memory can control our thoughts and reactions. Some researchers suggest the only way to heal yourself and raise your consciousness is to alter your body and brain's programming. In Me-B Transformation™ you learn to bring the energy of your Core Being into your biology to strengthen your container.

It is vital you learn to rewire any unsupportive habituations in your brain's plasticity and nervous system so it has appropriate arousal (hypo/hyper) and orienting responses. You also want to look at fostering High Vagal Tone (Social Engagement) and low Dorsal Complex (collapse energy). (See Chapter 20 on Trauma for more information about these topics.)

Mind/Thoughts:

Too much thinking can drain your field, especially if it is negative and ego-based thinking. We can review our random thoughts during Me-B Sessions and in daily life to become aware of the ones that tend to drain our energy field. Are there certain negative themes that run our thoughts?

When we work with our own energy field, one strategy for preventing our mind from wandering is to give it a job—the job of feeling the sensation of energy in our body. I ask my mind to feel and assess, feel and assess, as it scans through my body. As long as our mind has a positive job, it is easier to keep it from drifting into trouble by creating negative thought loops.

Assess what thoughts drain and/or support a strong Container and then develop an Action Plan to help yourself.

Energy:

Discover what can be strengthened and supported. Chi Kung, meditation and other energetic exercises practiced every day help make the energetic and Biology Consciousness Container stronger. Those with the strongest Containers can run very high vibrations and large amounts of energy through their bodies without negative effects. Also, individuals with strong Containers can feel LVC within them and around them without being too stressed. The Container can help convert those low vibrations to HVC.

Know what your energetic baseline is and work to improve it. Which chakras are weakest and need the most support? What does our Manifest Energy Line need for improvement? Every day notice your baseline and throughout the day take brief breaks to work your system so it improves. You may wish to do the Body Connecting Sequence (BCS) to scan and assess your system. Notice where there are flows, tingles or blocks. If done every day, it becomes an easy and positive habit for self care.

When I first started energy work, I had a large energy block in my spleen. It took two years for it to completely shift. Then, I noticed my second chakra held deep fear and my root chakra was weak. Now they are much better but require regular focus and support. Even though I am a decade older, my energy system is the strongest it has ever been. It is one area in life that can actually improve with age!

Throughout the day, assess your energetic baseline and work to support its improvement. Develop an Action Plan to help you achieve specific objectives and goals.

Body:

Exercise, nutrition, self-care, massage, alternative and traditional medical practices—all of these support strengthening our Container. The physical body is the densest vibration of the energy field. Illness first presents energetically at higher vibrations and then presents in the body. Using the body as a barometer can be useful—yet be careful to not over-identify with any pain or chronic illness that may present. We are not our body; we are our Core Being, if we choose to be. So use the body as a tool to strengthen our Container, and not as a reason to self-judge. Have long-term and short-term goals. *Because it is the densest vibration of our energy field, it can also be the most difficult to influence.*

My body was always a challenge for me, but it still made small incremental improvements. Then, when I was in graduate school, I went into early menopause and my health regressed dramatically. It took too many years to recover, and now that I am nearing 50, I find that my body takes much more focus and effort. Nevertheless, I am committed to making the necessary lifestyle changes to succeed.

> Have we had a physical lately? How are our dental practices? Do we floss daily? Do we know our hormone and cholesterol levels? How balanced is your sympathetic and parasympathetic nervous system? What trauma needs to be discharged and transformed? For instance do you have high vagus tone and low dorsal tone? (Review the section on Chronic Illness where this is discussed.) Is it time for a mammogram, breast exam or colonoscopy? Knowledge is power and both western and eastern medicine can help us assess and heal our body.

Write out a short-term plan and long-term goals to support your body. For instance, include the following categories to assess what you already are doing well and what needs improvement/change: exercise, lovemaking, nutrition, sleep habits, self-love, massage, alternative and traditional medical practices, community, friends, recreation, hobbies, spiritual practices...and more. Remember to focus on what you are already doing well and then build upon that.

Emotions and Depth of Processing:

The more deeply we are able to process challenging emotions or trauma without energetically merging with them, the stronger our Container and our ability to reconnect to Core Being will be.

Remember, simply feeling the emotions is not enough. We need to be able to transform them into HVC of Core Being. Seeing emotions, negative thoughts, and ego as energy that moves through us, and is NOT US, creates a strong Container. If we process too deeply without a strong enough Enlightened Observer, we can shatter our Container. This is not good or bad. In fact, sometimes shattering the Container can make it stronger if we have enough "white paint" and HVC to rebuild it more strongly. In the beginning, it can be hard to avoid shattering because we are learning how deep we can go. Deep process work is really an art form that takes time to learn.

It is important to know how to process emotions so we actively build rather than deplete our Container. Depression and anxiety can deplete our Containers. Spending more time in authentic self-acceptance, compassion, joy, gratitude and bliss are methods of strengthening our Containers. The Me-B interventions, meditations and exercises are also designed to strengthen our Containers.

Sometimes people process deeply and afterward get sick with what is known as "the fluky flu." The fluky flue resembles the real flu and cleanses our system deeply after we have transformed Core Distortions. It is actually good because it brings energetic material to the surface so it can be healed.

Also, it is important to carefully consider the timing of when we decide to process deep emotional material. If we or our client's life is too busy or stressful, going more slowly is better. Being able to process any emotion deeply without negative energetic or physical effects is diagnostic of a strong Container.

Help clients look at how they can strengthen their Container. This is especially true of "highly sensitive people." Part of their sensitivity is because their Container is weak. *We can learn how to have the benefits of being sensitive but with fewer challenges if our Container is strong. This means we are **not** living from the ego-based program personality and can skillfully move through the 3 Rings of Healing, Shape-Shift our Emotions, and anchor into Core Being.*

THE CONTAINMENT PROCESS

What happens if we lose our Enlightened Observer and can't get it back? Or if our Enlighten Observer's energy loses HVC and we merge with our pain? What do we do and how can we still reconnect to Core Being?

If our Container is not strong enough to process deep emotional material, we can use this Containment process and remove overwhelming emotional material from our Me-B System. This helps us re-balance and connect to Core Being. Until we are at Stage 4 or above of Me-B Transformation™, we can often lose our Enlightened Observer and collapse into physical or emotional pain. When this happens, we are no longer transforming — instead we are fostering the growth of LVC or metaphorical "black paint."

When we notice this happening, we can alter the Rhythm of the Flow of energy and stop ourselves or our clients from processing traumatic emotional material. We can then invite the LVC to leave our Me-B system and connect to our positive golden shadow/Core Being. If we connect to the Manifest Energy Intention Line, it helps us regroup so we can do the following containment process successfully. If we have already practiced connecting to Manifest Energy, it will be even easier. Some reasons why we may need containment include:

- the ego has merged with the pain and is over activated, and over-identified, nervous system over-activated (hypo or hyper-arousal),
- client doesn't want to go deeper,
- we are no longer anchored into Core Being,
- ran out of time to process the rest of the material, and
- the Me-B guide or therapist is not yet experienced enough to help the client and/or the Me-B guide's comfort
- level has been exceeded.

STEP 1: Alter the Rhythm of Flow of energy and connect to our Manifest Energy, moving away from the Auric Field.

STEP 2: Sense in the mind so we can name the pain, and locate where it is held in the body and energy system.

STEP 3: Imagine a Container we can energetically put the emotional material into. Also imagine a divine source to give the material to. Some people imagine a purple bag to place it in, or a trashcan, or a metal box.

STEP 4: Then imagine the energy of the excess material leaving our Me-B System and going into the Container. Feel it leave the body. Feel/imagine/send/see/sense/intend the energy of the negative images and thoughts go into the Container.

STEP 5: Give the Container to our divine source and ask them to transform it. Tell them that when we are ready to examine it more deeply, we can retrieve it from them.

STEP 6: Feel/sense/intend/experience high vibrations, colors, Core Being energy, and divine unconditional love filling up our energy system, mind, and body and replacing the "darker or lower vibrational energy."

STEP 7: If needed we can also (1) do any of the activities on the positive resource list, (2) get a massage, healing or outside support of a healer, therapist, friends, community or other, or (3) do physical movements, exercise, dance, sports, martial arts, yoga, chi kung or other.

GOLDEN SHADOW/CORE BEING RESOURCING INTERVENTION

The following Golden Shadow resourcing intervention provides methods to help us (or clients) claim their Core Being and golden shadow. They can also be used to alter the Rhythm of Flow of energy and transfer it to a higher vibration away from dark emotional material. Our Golden Shadow is our Core Being. It is the part of our Core Being we haven't yet discovered. I believe an infinite amount of our Core Being is available for us to discover. Every year I open to receive a little bit more and I am amazed at what I find, what we all can find if we just open to receive it. After all, we are already, in our essence, fully enlightened—we just aren't always connected to our enlightened state.

Adapting or gently implementing any one of the energetic meditations, interventions and exercise techniques already introduced can also be helpful. Be in the moment, trust guidance, and you will know which technique(s) you need in the moment to support yourself or your clients.

Core Being/Golden Shadow Dialogue Intervention Techniques

To begin, make a list that describes your Core Being and golden shadow. This is usually a difficult task for most people, especially if they are only at Stage 1, 2, or 3 of Me-B Transformation™. If we can't do it ourselves, we can ask people we love to help us, and/or we can look at the core qualities of people we admire; what we admire most in others is usually in us, just hidden. (The opposite is true too: What we judge in others tends to also be part of our dark shadow.)

Often we need to help clients come up with words that describe their Core Being. It is a dimension of truth, yet too often clients have yet to experience this dimension. Negative ego, self-judgments and cultural issues keep us separated. Through this dialogue intervention, the Me-B therapist helps the client move out of the personality level and opens them up to the energetics of their Core Being dimension. It is the dimension of the deepest reality.

Using a stream of consciousness technique, have the client speak whatever comes into his/her mind, or draw a picture of his/her golden shadow/Core Being. Once a list of about ten descriptive words has been generated, with the client either lying on a table or sitting in a chair, the Me-B guide follows these steps. (You can also do this on yourself. Never use the technique on someone else unless you have mastered it yourself.)

1. The Me-B guide connects to the Core Being dimension and brings the energy into the room, filling it.

2. Being aware of the energetics of her voice, The Me-B Guide calls off one word at a time from the list. Speak into the Core Being vortex and speak it three times.

3. The timing of the words should be called so they support the Rhythm of Flow of energy. We need to make sure we don't go too slowly or too quickly, or the client won't have time to take the frequency of the words into their body/energy system. If need be, have them speak the word out loud as well.

4. Guide the energy of the word in like a funnel into the Core Being vortex.

5. The Me-B guide works with the client to help them take the vibration of the words into their Core Being Dimension all the way down to the physical level of cells, bones, organs and marrow. The client is encouraged to feel the vibration, visualize it, and use all senses to experience the truth of who they are. It is important to assess if the energy has been absorbed or not. Keep practicing reading your own energy field and that will help you read another's field. Once the Core Being vortex is full, let the HVC spread throughout the body (front/back, top/bottom, left/right). It is important to track exactly where it fills and where a client's defenses prevent it from filling each and every cell. For instance, did it fill 50 percent or 70 percent? You don't necessarily have to tell the client to the extent it fills but at least ask them what they think is true. If they don't know or if they say it filled everywhere but it only filled a little bit then you know they have some deeper work to do down the line on facing their unhealthy defenses and ego.

Energetics of Table Work/Chair Work

If the client is on a table, the Me-B Guide places one hand on the second chakra and the other on the third chakra. The guide lets his/her Core Being dimension resonate to the level of the client's Core Being and to the words. This creates an energetic vortex so that the energy of the words can penetrate more deeply into the cells. If the client is in a chair, the Me-B Guide does the same process except his/her hands are not touching the client.

If we or our client cannot absorb the higher frequencies of this Intervention, usually it means the negative ego is in control. It may also mean that a part of the client is in negative intention. Patience, practice and patience!

— I have never had a client that didn't eventually succeed.

STRENGTHENING OUR ENLIGHTENED OBSERVER AND HELPING OTHERS STRENGTHEN THEIRS

It is **contra-indicated** for ourselves or a client to enter a stressful or challenging therapeutic space if we are over-identifying with the negative energy running through us. Therefore, we and our clients must have an Enlightened Observer that knows that the negative thoughts/emotions arising in the moment are not an expression of our true self. The Enlightened Observer must resonate with the deeper truth—

our existence is divine and whole. For some people, it may take a year or more until they have a strong Enlightened Observer that is able to hold a high enough frequency to transform the LVC of trauma and emotional pain into HVC.

When our Enlightened Observer's frequency is not high enough, our identity becomes too enmeshed with the pain and we can reinforce the negative instead of transform to embrace the positive. Ideally, our Enlightened Observer needs to clearly identify with the Core Being so the emotional and/or physical pain become vibrations and energy that moves through us.

If the Enlightened Observer is observing from the personality level, or from too low of a vibration, **it loses its empowerment** and we are re-wounded. We, or our clients, can loop and recycle the pain instead of transforming the pain. It's important, therefore, to follow the protocol outlined in the following steps:

Before a client connects to her sadness or pain, discuss the role of the Enlightened Observer. Teach your client how to access and maintain their own Enlightened Observer during deep emotional processing.

To teach them, I usually begin by explaining the three rings of healing. I draw them on the board in my office and provide them with a laminated handout. Outer ring is defense and mask, middle ring is wounding/pain trauma/false sense of self and the inner ring is our Core Being, our wholeness and divinity.

The client labels the rings and notices their common defenses, public personality and true self. We might stay at this level of just noticing patterns for many sessions while I help them develop a deep cognitive and energetic awareness of their Core Being. If during the noticing process they collapse into a regressed state or painful emotions, I do the containment procedure and re-direct them so they align with their Core Being. I tell them not to connect to any negative energy unless (1) their Enlightened Observer is anchored into their Core Being, (2) they know they are not the negative emotions/images/beliefs running through them, and (3) the Enlightened Observer is connected to a higher vibration. If they connect to a low vibration with more low vibration, they get more pain—but if they connect to a low vibration with a higher vibration (their Enlightened Observer) then they get transformation!

To help them connect to their Core Being and develop their Enlightened Observer I use positive resourcing techniques so they can feel their Core Being as a sensation in their body, an idea in their mind, and energetically. In the Trauma Chapter, we will discuss the technique of moving from pain – to Core Being—to pain—to Core Being. This technique is used to strengthen the Enlightened Observer so that it can be strong even when there is pain. (Stage 3 of Me-B Transformation™.) Once a client is strong in their Enlightened Observer, they can maintain Stage four of Me-B Transformation, holding two places at once.

A Me-B Guide must energetically track when the Enlightened Observer becomes lost and help the client regain his/her empowerment and true self. We make sure we have taught them the Containment Process and, if necessary, we use positive resourcing techniques to help them build their Container (in all three systems). We must also track the Enlightened Observer to make sure it is vibrating at a high enough level so that the energy shifts and doesn't loop or get stuck. The Enlightened Observer needs to be consistently in the mind/body and Core Being Dimension.

Hold the Enlightened Observer energetically for the client when the client can't hold it for him- or herself, and continue to reconfirm his or her Core Being so that the energy shifts to a higher vibration and the Enlightened Observer can become stronger.

ENLIGHTENED OBSERVER CAN SAVE THE DAY!

During a breath work session, I re-experienced the energy of my birth parents wanting my prenatal self-dead. I was conceived in the early 1960's. My birth parents were not married and they were terrified to find out that my birth mother was pregnant.

As I regressed back to that time, the raw realness of the experience consumed me. I could actually feel the constricting energy of the umbilical cord around my neck, pulling in both directions, choking me. I started sobbing as their hate toward "what I had done to them" filled me. They desperately wanted my unborn self to die.

This programmed prenatal experience was also representative of my life with my adopted parents. I grew up knowing they didn't appreciate my unique take on the world. They adopted a daughter who was very different from their "organized perfect" approach to how girls "should" behave. They were embarrassed that their 10 year-old started a school-wide campaign to end abusive leg-hold trapping. It just wasn't a normal thing for a young girl to do.

Looking back, I can see how the negative prenatal programming was just the start of feeling unloved, judged and worthless. After all, it was programmed into me from even before birth.

As I relived the pain of the past, because my Enlightened Observer was strong, instead of collapsing into the pain of self-hate, I was able to let go of the past and deepen into the truth of my divine self. I sent my young soul love and kindness and apologized to her that such a harsh experience had happened to her. I could feel my body's cells take in the "white paint" of the HVC of love and compassion. Like a sponge, I absorbed it. Although from time to time the pain of the past drifts into my field, it is much easier to transform.

This experience strengthened my Container and as a result, I am much more anchored into my Core Being and I am actually thankful. I am thankful this happened because it made me claim myself at a level I didn't think was possible. If my delicate young soul survived this experience, I am sure my adult soul can face the challenges that the future is sure to deliver. All this, thanks to my Enlightened Observer!

Too often new clients come to see me when they are feeling the cathartic experience of past trauma. They are excited about the "deep" experiences. Yet they complain about not having any tangible "real-life" results. Their old patterns remain stuck. **Just remembering or re-experiencing a past trauma in the present does not ensure healing or a raised consciousness.** What does ensure it is an Enlightened Observer that recaptures the deeper truth and re-patterns the past to the present in all three systems! Remember, time and space only exist in the mind. Bringing awareness and light to the present can change the past!

WATCH THE MOVIE

One way to practice using our Enlightened Observer is through the help of Hollywood. Yes, I practice watching movies that trigger me. I find that action suspense (Mission Impossible-style) is the most challenging for me. I resonate my Core Being, engage my Enlightened Observer and, without dissociating, I stay deeply connected to the action without letting myself get triggered. Sad Lifetime Channel movies also draw me in. So the next rainy day, rent a video and practice strengthening your Enlightened Observer.

CREATE AN ENERGETIC SAFETY NET

For some personality types moving out of the mental into the emotional levels so we can transform information—not only in the mind, but in the body and energy system can be a challenge. For some of us, feeling emotions in the present brings up the subconscious trauma from the past.

To support a client in feeling safety and trust on the emotional levels, help them create an energetic safety net following the steps outlined below to help their vibration rise to the level where transformation is possible.

Prepare Field to Accept Safety Net Frequency: Start by connecting to your hearts. Find that playful dolphin energy, the color is pink. Connect breath with awareness then feel, sense, intend that the pink energy of joy and happiness be brought into your body. Using awareness/intention/breath, run the energy of joy as you scan through the body. Begin at your head and follow it all the way down to your toes. Breathe.

As you scan downward through the body, simply notice where the joy wants to expand into areas of low or no sensation.

After a few scans up and down the body, use awareness/intention/breath, to allow the energy of joy and happiness to balance front/back, top/bottom, left/right—from toes to nose.

- **Step 1:** Resonate at Safety and Trust (by holding levels 1 and 5 of the Auric Field).
- **Step 2:** Feel, Sense, Imagine the energetic net (grid) it creates. Feel and sense it equally top/bottom; left/right; and front/back.
- **Step 3:** Using visualization, feeling and intention, bring the frequency of the safety net into the 7th level of the field, and let the trust and safety vibration fill the frequency of divine mind. Feel it as a safety net, moving downward in frequency, anchoring deeply.

Next move your attention to level 6 of the Auric Field, divine ecstasy. At your own pace, slowly let the frequency of trust and safety filter through all aspects of the fifth level of the field, divine will.

Then connect to the 4th level-love and relationship to others. Feel this safety net anchor very strongly into the4th level of the field. Feel the vibration of trust and safety in relationships. Let the frequency melt deep into the center of your bones. Trauma is often held in this level of the field. Notice how trust and safety can resonate deeply. Feel how solid the safety net can become. Let it be tangible and strong. Sense it in all of your cells.

Now allow safety and trust into the 3rd level of the field, yellow lines of light-mental clarity.

Next, let it deepen so it expands to the 2nd level of field- safety and trust related to self. Trauma is often held at this level of the field in the form of energetic clouds, negative beliefs about ourselves. Let the safety net vibrate strongly into this level of the field.

Lastly, let the safety net resonate at the 1st level of the field, blue lines of light. It is our physical body and represents being safe enough to fulfill our life task.

So this is your internal safety net. How many of us cling to external safety nets? What job, cake, wine, marriage is relied upon too much? Notice the fear that can come up when we let go of the unhealthy external safety net.

Trauma can hook into an over-reliance on unhealthy external support. Healing happens with healthy internal contact. This meditation can help us develop healthy internal support. It can also help us be strong enough to feel, sense and locate LVC (negative beliefs, false sense of self, trauma and difficult emotions) so it can be transformed into HVC and Core Being.

Without connection to the difficult emotions/traumas/negative beliefs, we can't transform the consciousness—the metaphorical lead—into gold. Contact does not mean identification with the challenging feeling, and it does not mean that the feeling has power over us. Let this energetic Safety Net help you heal when you are feeling difficult emotions, so that Core Being can be more present and transformation possible.

BEING HUMAN

We can put so much pressure on ourselves to be perfect that we forget that we are just human. Few of us easily connect to our humanness as being a benefit in life. We may spontaneously launch out of our body, energetically soaring skyward in the hope of finding peace and comfort. The spirit child inside us can remember what it was like, before the humanness. The innocent way we saw the world. Our confusion around the suffering, the petty meanness we encountered as we grew up can make us wish for something different-something that feels kind and fair.

It may seem like the only way we can make sense of the crazy-making in this world is to separate our spirit from the human part of us. Sometimes we forget the joys of being human. The love we feel in our hearts, an ice cream sundae, a mountain covered in snow or a sunset—all of these we experience because we are human. We smell, taste, and can feel so deeply the sun on our skin, the rain on our cheek and the joy of holding a newborn baby—all this because we are human.

So when our dear child-like spirit feels disheartened by the suffering human side of us, we can call in our angels, call in our god to hold our hand, to kiss our cheek and comfort us in the pain that sometimes comes from being human.

THE SUCCESS OF AN INCH WORM

Embarrassed by my humanness, I resign myself to acknowledge that just as an inchworm makes progress, bit by bit, I too continue to humbly make progress—inch by inch. Working away at my ego, inch by inch; meditating more deeply into my Core Being, inch by inch; and whittling away my unhealthy defenses, inch by inch.

Practice calling in support for your child-like spirit that can get overwhelmed by the human condition. Take a bath, get a massage, ask for a hug, walk in nature and reconnect your human part with your spirit by reinforcing the joys of being human while letting the pain fall away. It is our job to bring into balance our spirit in human form so the best of both can thrive. Some days this may feel easier than other days, but as long as we stay focused on the outcome of unity, we can succeed.

WHICH SYSTEM HOLDS THE TRUTH?

During the healing process, there will be times when the truth is held in one or two of the Me-B systems but not all three. For instance, sometimes we will speak what we think is the truth but our energy system says something completely different. Or, we can feel something somatically in our body, such as a pit in our stomach, but have no idea what it may mean.

By simply using the strength of one system, we can help shift the others. Or by tuning into one system that is out of alignment, we can assess our shadow and learn more about our personal process, Core Distortion, defenses and/or Core Being.

I AM OK AND I AM OK

Ned said everything was "okey dokey." Ned always said that, but sometimes his energy system said he was angry, or uncomfortable, scared or sad. His mind told him one thing, but his body reacted otherwise. Which system held the truth? Was he really ok or not?

When one system is out of alignment, there is a message being delivered by the other system. We can find the message and then bring all three minds, energy and body systems back to balance.

When Ned tuned inside to listen to the message, it told him an old trauma had surfaced in his field. As Ned remembered the incident that happened when he was young, he once again said it really didn't bother him. It wasn't a big deal. I explained that just because his mind was fine, it didn't mean his body was ok with what happened. I reminded him that our subconscious is held in the body and sometimes we have to listen to it and not just listen to our conscious mind. Skeptical but willing, Ned agreed to bring the HVC of his Enlightened Observer into his body/energy system and sense what was there.

Pictures of his past flashed across his mind screen. He then felt where the energy of the trauma was held in his body. We brought in the positive frequency that he was OK, deep into his cells to melt away the traumatic past.

Now when Ned senses his body is reacting negatively but his mind is reacting positively, he can use that positive energy from his mind, meet the LVC in his body and bring balance to all three systems- mind, energy and body.

Find a partner. Spend 10 minutes talking. One person acts as the Me-B Guide and one person acts as the client. The Me-B Guide tracks when the client's field said something different from his/her words. **Then:** Practice using the strongest system (often the mind) to help the other systems align.

And/Or: Practice sensing into your own three Me-B systems. Look for a personal shadow challenge and then determine which Me-B system holds the highest vibrational consciousness.

- If the strongest system is the mind then (1) connect to your 7th chakra (divine mind), (2) feel the positive energy/thoughts as a sensation in the body, (3) expand that energy throughout the body (4) focus only on the positive thoughts and sensations, (5) allow the body to shift.

- If the positive system is the energy system—connect to the chakras/energetic dimensions that hold the highest truth and then bring them into the body as positive sensations. Lastly, let the mind label them and "claim them" for the deeper truth they represent.

- If the body is the strongest system, focus on only the good sensations and let them spread to areas of low or no sensations until they replace any bad sensations. Then let the mind recognize the positive emotions and/or belief system that the sensations hold.

GRATITUDE BANK

We all can use a gratitude bank to call upon when our reserves run dry. Following the energetic universal law that "what we focus on, grows." As we focus on what we are grateful toward, we receive more things to feel grateful about. Gratitude is an action word. We need to show our gratitude and receive it daily so it grows.

As we can consciously notice, at least once a day, what we are grateful for, then that aspect of our life will improve. I have been practicing this for a few years now and I find the results life-changing.

We can train our *Mind Energy-Body System* to resonate at higher and higher states of grace- simply by focusing on gratitude. As we do this, there can be longer periods of time (within us, and around us) where life feels rich and complete. This is when everything seems to shine brighter as if God has touched it. Feelings of belonging fill our cells and we can see the perfection in every moment. Oprah speaks often about her "ah-hah" moments. This is what it feels like when we make enough deposits into our Gratitude Bank: a seemingly endless stream of "ah-hah" moments.

Gratitude delivers grace. Grace delivers inner peace and magical surprises that show up to support us. Some- times the support shows up just in the knick of time! This is a perfect ritual to begin to implement when the energetic consciousness of "thankfulness" is abundant and strong such as on Thanksgiving Day!

- **Step 1:**
  List what you are currently feeling grateful for such as: a place to live, food, pet, or family. Be specific and realize that we can even feel grateful for a difficult challenge as it can teach us very needed lessons.
  If you are having trouble finding something to feel grateful toward, consider that simply living in the United States is a blessing. I often travel to less affluent nations such as Africa and Asia. When I am in these countries, I am painfully aware of the harshness many citizens must endure. I see or hear of starving children and girls being given to older men to abuse and quickly, my problems shrink in comparison.
  So, a valid place to begin this meditation can be to focus on feeling grateful for living in a country of opportunity. Whatever you chose to list as the topic areas you feel thankful for, be as specific as possible.
- **Step 2:**
  Feel the energy of gratitude as a sensation and emotion in the body. Focus, one at a time, on where in the body you can feel it and surrender to receive it even stronger. Then move to the next item.
- **Step 3:**
  Now list the events, items, and topics you wish to feel gratitude toward. One at a time, feel the energy of gratitude toward these topic areas as if they have already manifested. Remember to feel them as a sensation and emotion in the body. Focus on where in the body you can feel it and surrender to receive it even stronger.
- **Step 4:**
  If you feel the energy or sensation of a negative belief or emotion that might prevent your

intentions from manifesting, be aware of that issue. Write the issue, emotion or negative belief down so later you can receive support to transform that lower vibrational consciousness (LVC) into higher vibrational consciousness (HVC) so that challenge transforms into a deeper connection to your wholeness, worthiness and Core Being. Then go back to noticing where in your body you can receive the positive sensations/emotions of it having already manifested. Remember, what you focus on grows! So please focus on where you can receive the sensations of energy that holds high vibrational consciousness and let them grow through surrender, acceptance and seeing the perfection in the moment. You intentions of what you want to manifest will come in the "right" and perfect time as you allow yourself to be grateful for what you can do, while trusting the rest is coming-perfectly timed!

- **Step 5:**
  Send yourself unconditional love and gratitude for who you are now and who you are becoming. And if you feel motivated, call a friend/family member or tell a pet, how much they mean to you. Lastly, align so every day you deposit some energy into your gratitude bank!

WEEDS GROW WHEN WE DON'T PLANT FLOWERS

Anytime we release LVC from our Me-B system it is important to plant the flowers of HVC and Core Being in its place. Just as a newly tilled field will eventually fill with weeds if no flowers are planted, our energy system will return to our old baseline if we don't plant anew with HVC. Spend time filling your cells with Core Being so the weeds of LVC don't take sprout. Also, do the BCS on feeling positive sensations to "plant" the seeds of Core Being.

NATURE AS RESOURCE

Living in Boulder, Colorado affords me the unique opportunity of having exquisite nature as a positive resource at my fingertips. I look out my window and a baby deer walks by with her mother. A beautiful hike in the snow-covered mountains is but a moment away. In the spring, I can take an hour off of work, bike from my house and see a fox or coyote cross my path.

I believe Nature wants to be our positive resource—so take time to hug a tree, sit on a park bench and let nature come into your Me-B system and fill you up with its positive energy. It can be one of the most bountiful positive resources for restoring our spirit and feeding our soul. And in exchange, we can offer nature support. We can recycle, use organic products and help our environment help us.

TOO MANY THOUGHTS AND THE WONDERING MIND

The strongest Container will have fewer random thoughts and longer periods of time in no thought, "no mind," or clear, focused thoughts. A powerful meditation technique to facilitate this is to focus on the center of the 6th chakra at the point where the front and back hook into the central channel. As we focus on this spot, just for a moment or two, we will find our zero point of no mind. Practicing this technique helps us limit circular thinking, negative thoughts and anxiety. It is helpful to have this ability programmed into our Me-B system during times of stress.

Circular and Looping Negative Thoughts

Habituation to negative thinking loops is common in our society. We spend so much time in our heads that it can be difficult to stop our thinking. As an example, a prospective buyer of my horse couldn't ride him, even though she said she was an expert. She accused him of having a weak front end. But in reality, he was young and his hind end was weak and needed much more growth and development. After she left, I let her words keep ringing in my head. I knew they weren't accurate, but I watched my sixth chakra reach out and grab onto her energy and bring it back into my field. This would prompt the loop of thinking to start up again. My En- lightened Observer thought this action was brilliantly superb. It said, "Wow, isn't that cool? Look what my 6th chakra just did." It had the voice of a proud parent noticing a new skill that its "chakra child" could perform. Never mind that it was not a useful trick!

Our Chakras don't always collect energy that is in our highest good. This is an example of how our negative patterns recycle until we reprogram them. To stop negative thoughts from looping, follow these four steps.

- **Step 1:** Notice how the sixth chakra can hook into negative thoughts so they keep replaying like a broken record. The sixth chakra can also recreate a scene from the past or make up a scene and project it into our consciousness. It is varied and creative in its skills. Using the Explorer's Mind, sense into what is happening energetically that is causing the looping to continue. If we weren't somehow feeding the energy, it would stop.
- **Step 2:** Place your hand over your forehead to prevent the sixth chakra from poking out and grabbing negative thoughts (or from projecting them into our mind). Connect to Manifest Energy and align to the intention of keeping the sixth chakra within so it doesn't grab externally.
- **Step 3:** Notice what part of you is bringing yourself down to a lower level of happiness. Usually it is a part of the ego that is accustomed to thinking negatively about yourself. Imagine sending that hurt part of you love and kindness. As you do this, let the kind loving energy fill and realign the Central Channel from the top of the head, filling it/aligning it through the center of the sixth chakra, down through the center of the 5th, 4th, 3rd, 2nd and 1st chakras and then finally into the ground.
  This helps balance the energy downward so there is less feeding of the looping. It also helps send love and acceptance to the part of us that hurts and needs support.
- **Step 4:** Repeat this every time you sense your sixth chakra bringing in the negative thought patterns. Remember love and acceptance is needed. Use Manifest Energy to diminish any self-sabotage energy that might try to return. Follow the containment procedure if this process doesn't work completely.

LISTEN TO THE VOICE THAT KNOWS

We all have an internal *voice that knows*. Then why do we fail to listen to it? It is our programmed personality that keeps us from listening. It gets fixated to react in a certain regiment so that when other, higher frequency data comes through, it can too easily be ignored. We pretend we don't trust *the voice that knows*. We act like it doesn't exist or we create excuses as to why it isn't the best time to listen. Spend one day listening to *the voice that knows* and ignoring the programmed personality. Write down what it says and gradually over time, practice listening more to the voice that knows. If, you don't have *an internal voice that knows*, then it is important to develop one. Review the exercises on connecting to our spirit guides. Also, practice resonating at the 7th level of the Auric field, divine wisdom and use the 5th chakra (that supports channeling our Core Being and our guides). Journal, paint, or draw the information you get when you resonate at the 7th level of the field and use the 5th chakra. This will strengthen your internal "muscle" to hear the *voice that knows*.

There is often a physical somatic response that tells us if it is an ego-based voice or the *voice that knows*. For me, the somatic indicator is the side of my head in which I hear the voice. If I sense it comes from the left side of my brain, it usually is my ego talking. If I sense it comes from the right side of my brain, it is *the voice that knows*. Practice and connect to the *voice that knows*.

> I am 48 years old now and I still don't always listen to my inner voice of wisdom when it cautions to me that I am going to say or do something that does not support my highest good. The voice comes from the 7th level of our Auric field, divine wisdom, and is a conduit to our Core Being.
>
> My excuse is that I have too many irons in the fire. Too much stress and too much work preventing me from being so aligned. Yet, didn't I create that reality too? I acknowledge that there are no excuses for not living my best life (a term borrowed from Oprah). I love and support those aspects of me that want to hurry and rush and thus create a sloppy and incoherent field.
>
> As I do this, I move away from the excuses and into positive action and self-compassion. Inch by inch, I get closer to listening to the *voice that knows*.

No Excuses

Some of us always have an excuse as to why we can't succeed. It becomes an addiction. We can become over-identified with our inner-victim and feed off of it out of habit and fear. When this happens, we can try the following "No Excuses" technique. Just for today, let's pretend there are no excuses and examine what might be going on underneath. Just for today, let's pretend there is no escape from facing ourselves and that **we DO have the power within us to succeed if we don't allow any excuses to get in our way.**

Another version of this intervention is to ask ourselves to **give up hope that anything outside of us will save us from our situation.** We can ask ourselves to surrender and accept that no one will save us. We can use our Explorer's Mind and say, "the only solution is the one within me." So, the only place I can turn is within.

Then, feel this intention within our Manifest Energy and within all three Me-B Systems and practice finding solutions and positive outcomes instead of excuses and wishes to be saved by another.

CHOICE POINTS FOR PEACE!

Critical point analysis is derived from the fact that in any highly complex system, "there is a specific, critical point at which the smallest input will result in the greatest change," says Hawkins. In Me-B

Transformation, we use our **Explorer's Mind** to uncover our **CHOICE POINTS** by unraveling the complexity of thoughts, energies and somatics in our Me-B System. Then, when we use our **Enlightened Observer** at the **CHOICE POINT**, we raise our vibration, end our distortion and exert change.

Once we find our **CHOICE POINTS**, a relatively small amount of energy is needed to stop the negative pattern. *This is true as long as the energy is exerted at the exact point at which we collude with the negative pattern.* We can all find these critical **CHOICE POINTS** so that we can create positive life patterns.

Only clear intention and continuous focus are mandated to eliminate the negative pattern. Hawkins uses the example of a ship in the ocean that is only a few degrees off course. If not corrected, the ship will quickly find itself miles off course. As we correct our "few degrees" of being off course in our lives, this correction has profound effects as well. Throughout each day, there are at least a few CHOICE POINT opportunities. If we took advantage of even one CHOICE POINT a week, our lives would significantly change. Begin to meet CHOICE POINTS from Core Being and not from the ego-based programmed personality. This can dramatically change your life. Once it feels easy to address your minor CHOICE POINTS, begin to look at more difficult CHOICE POINTS that take deeper personal work to change but produce more beneficial results.

For instance, to help pay for my son's college, we are selling our beloved horses. The process of finding the perfect home for our companions is an awkward and emotional journey. Weeks went by and there were no calls for anyone wanting our Billy until one weekend it seemed like everyone wanted our Billy. Tears flowed as the reality set in that this was really going to happen. Billy was going to leave us.

Every time I became worried that we wouldn't find a good home for Billy, I chose to calm my field, find my **CHOICE POINTS, and realign back to trust and Core Being.** I worked each **CHOICE POINT** to realign my field when "something bad" happened. **This created the energetic opening for something good to come.**

Over the next few weeks, as the events unfolded, I kept realigning, working **my CHOICE POINTS,** realigning, and working my **CHOICE POINTS.** My daughter and I kept following the **CHOICE POINTS** until they led us to the perfect situation for both horses.

This process is called "CHOICE POINTS for Peace" because every time harmony leaves us, we can connect to it and gradually steer our lives toward balance and harmony. I find this works very well in troubled relation- ships too. Many of us have conflicts with friends and family. We may want our boss or parents to treat us differently. We don't want their judgments, and we don't want them to manipulate and control. As we resent their ways, we create more energy for them to resent our ways. This process steers our boat many degrees off course and we can wonder why we are so miserable. As we hate and judge them, it supports them in hating and judging us—country-to-country, family-to-family, person-to-person.

One client explained she resented how her mother became bossy and unsupportive. Last week, when they had a family get-together to help Cindy and Eric remodel their new home, Cindy's mother apparently tried to take control over who did what. Her mother wouldn't cooperate with Cindy at all. Cindy explained that she resented the person her mother had become. I then asked her if that might be why her mother is so defensive and controlling around her?

Cindy considered looking for **CHOICE POINTS** so that instead of resenting her mother, she might chose to accept her mother for who she is and not who she wants her mother to be. Although she wasn't quite ready to do that, Cindy began the process of beginning to create happier CHOICE POINTS for Peace in the other areas of her life. It took a year, but after finding the CHOICE POINTS in her marriage and work environment, she eventually began to find them with her mother. Although occasionally there is tension, Cindy found enough **CHOICE POINTS** and developed a new paradigm of mutual respect and support with her mother.

WHAT IS THE DIFFERENCE BETWEEN OUR IDEALIZED SELF-IMAGE AND CORE BEING?

Each one of us has an idealized self- image. So what is the difference between Core Being and our Idealized Self-Image? Our idealized self-image is ego-based and is grounded in duality. This means that if an aspect of our "humanness" or dark shadow is revealed, it won't be loved and accepted by our idealized self. The idealized self will abandon and disregard our core distortions. It will avoid the pain the ego can cause creating a split in our third chakra.

Core Being, on the other hand, fosters unity and flow between all the chakras. It is based on non-duality and comforts the pain created by our ego. It won't judge us for being wrong and imperfect. It can provide the good enough mother energy to our wounded child parts. It can accept both our humanness and our divine. (Stage 4 and above of Me-B Transformation.)

The idealize self-image only feels safe when it is connected to our divine parts. (Stage 1-3 of Me-B Transformation.) This can cause huge distortions, confusion and conflict in our life because earth is a dense dimension and difficulty does happen. We can't ignore or isolate ourselves away from it. If we haven't learned to transform the dark into the light, the allure of escaping into our idealized self becomes powerful. We may follow it just as a fish swallows the bait. Until the house of cards falls and that strategy back fires.

To heal our need for our idealized self, we can learn to turn the pain into energy that runs through. As we do this, the pain becomes the raw material to connect us to our light. This is when our idealized self-image is no longer needed. (Review the 5-Step Mindfulness process helps us achieve this goal.)

So when we let the HVC of Core Being energy into the pain of our ego or wounded child, we will feel the pain but we won't be the pain. When we do this, we let our authentic Core Being incarnate deeper within us. We anchor deeper into the dimension of truth.

So what is the confusion? Why do we negate our pain in exchange for our idealized self?

This is a great question we all could benefit from answering. Of course, our ego, separated self and trauma programming play a role. Yet there might be a spiritual answer to this question as well. For instance, I think an aspect of our child consciousness remembers the lifetimes we lived on a different dimension or on a planet that wasn't dualistic. I believe our idealized image is part of that remembering.

Unfortunately on this dualistic earthly dimension we are messy, others are messy and imperfect and our light is not always honored and respected. When this happens, we want to escape from the rawness of the moment. I know my child often splashes about on earth as if it still lived on a planet of light. And, when my light isn't honored and respected I can become very hurt and confused. My child asks, "Where am I?" "Why don't you see this awesome beauty and light?" But others can't see it. They are too far lost in their own ego, negative program personality or idealized image.

Take some time now to give your inner child support so he/she knows the light. Invite Core Being into your wounded parts. Heal your idealized self-image and accept your authentic light.

- **Step 1:** Engage your Enlightened Observer and strengthen your Manifest Energy Line. Ground and balance your field front/back; left/right; top/bottom.
- **Step 2:** Scan your body and discover where your idealized self-image is held.
- **Step 3:** Imagine it dissolving. Feel the pain that keeps it in place as energy that runs through you and invite Core Being to fill in the space left behind.

I DON'T BELONG HERE

Where is my tribe? I don't fit into my family, my community—I just don't belong here! How many of us have felt this before? It is our ego working with our Separated Self. The two collude with our trauma, programmed personality and attachment issues and make us feel less than and out of place.

When this happens, we either judge others for not being like us, or we feel our victim consciousness taking hold and wonder what is wrong with us. Why don't they love and accept us for who we are? Why don't we fit in? The truth is that there are many CHOICE POINTS that we miss or fail to see that could allow us to be individuated, yet still part of the group. **Once we are comfortable with ourselves, we don't always have to be similar to feel we fit in and belong. Instead the consciousness of belonging stays with us, no matter what.**

I was the queen of not fitting in and was perfectly programmed that way since birth. I was adopted into a family where I woke up feeling as if I was reliving the movie *Invasion of the Body Snatchers.* "Who are these people I am living with?" I asked. To me, their whole worldview felt out of place. I remember reading the book *Alice In Wonderland*, knowing intuitively that there was a connection between her world and mine.

I didn't know anything about creating my reality or finding CHOICE POINTS. Back then, I collapsed and said nothing or I fought back lamely. These feelings of "not belonging" followed me to college. I joined a sorority because my parents told me I would be a failure if I didn't. During meetings, I would stand up at the announcement time and invite my sorority sisters to join me for an Amnesty International event or a protest or an animal rights campaign. Every week I stood up and happily invited them, and all the while they thought I was "off my rocker." Did I notice where I was and what they thought? No.

It is hilarious to look back now and say, "What was I thinking?" Naïveté fills me, even today. A part of me unconsciously asks to be met for who I am and does not honor what the other person is actually capable of doing.

So how do we deal with Low Vibrational Consciousness (LVC) when they push it our way? Or what do we do when their paradigm is not our paradigm? How can we find our place and still belong? This can be an overwhelming question to ask but an easier one to answer.

Hopefully, at this stage of the book we can begin to see a pattern of programming by our past that can replicate these patterns in the present. It is too easy for our trauma to be replayed again and again. It takes work to locate our CHOICE POINTS and create peace and harmony. But when we do the work and react in a new manner, the benefits spread into all areas of our life.

Now, when I enter a new situation or a new group, I take note of the past. I acknowledge what I am programmed to create and try to more accurately assess those around me. I do it not from judging them but from owning my own distortions and tendencies. I open to see where they are and what they are capable of doing.

Do I still make mistakes? Do I still enter groups where I don't feel as if I belong? Yes, but I am much more aware and much more successful. I remind myself that yes, I am ok—and my inner child doesn't have to keep reaching out to belong. I can feel the energy and sensation of belonging within me. I have nothing to prove. This helps create a coherent relationship energy field for mutual acceptance and support. I also find it is important to surround myself with people who are part of my own tribe, and who are similar to me.

This creates at least one safe haven of support. **We all need at least one safe haven of support** so that we don't try finding support in places (or in people) that are not capable of supporting us.

Now, from my Enlightened Observer, I watch my inner child reach out to **everyone** for support in the hopes of finally finding it. I watch her do this, but I don't follow her lead anymore. Instead, I send love and support to that part of me and remind her that she already belongs somewhere. This need has already been met within me.

If you don't feel that you have a "tribe" of supporters and/or family, begin the process of finding one.

When we are in a group that is different from us, we can still belong to ourselves and then we are more able to feel part of something external to us.

In some native cultures, a tribe member must pass a ritual before he or she belongs. Once they pass, they gain a sense of acceptance and feel a healthy attachment to the group. In our culture, this doesn't always happen and we can grow up never feeling like we belong. **It is vital to find somewhere we can belong so we can use the energy of belonging as a resource in life.** Although I didn't get the "sense of belonging" from my family of origin, I did get a sense of love and acceptance from the tribe I created once I grew up.

We can practice feeling the energy of belonging in all our Me-B systems. This helps support balanced relationship harmony and prevents the negative past from being replayed. Those who work with attachment disorders recognize the need to have at least one or two people/groups where we can feel safely connected. This sense of connection gives us an external safety net to support the safety net that we are developing within.

1. If we haven't had an experience of belonging, and of being loved and accepted for who we are, we can create our own tribe. Having a tribe can help provide a sense of "belonging" energy so we don't try to get it from sources that aren't capable of giving it to us.

2. Let the energy and HVC of belonging fill our body, cells and energy system.

3. We can belong to ourselves and resonate that energy of belonging to help us become part of other groups.

4. In the moment that we reach out to others and want to belong, we can instead bring the energy of "belonging" into our Me-B System. We can practice meeting the needs of our inner child so that this part of us doesn't reach out to others in a manner that will rewound us or make us feel unloved and rejected. If we can get more skillful at this, over time we can create a new and more aligned sense of belonging with those around us.

5. Accept that others, who are not part of our main tribe, won't necessarily appreciate all parts of us. We can notice who they are, and what they are capable of accepting. We can do this without judging them or our- selves.

6. The negative past repeats in the present. So if we have a history of feeling that we do not belong, then it will take deeper work to find our CHOICE POINTS so we can change our energy into wholeness and Core Being.

7. Trying to please others or be subservient to others will only create tension and in authenticity in our field. It is not a healthy way of belonging. This is an unhealthy defense of the Heart-Centered and Compassionate personality types. Knowing our unhealthy defenses and moving to wholeness and Core Being is an important component of belonging to ourselves so we can become connected to others. Kindness, patience, self-love, acceptance and wisdom help us succeed.

WHAT ARE WE PRETENDING NOT TO KNOW

A client came into his session and exclaimed that he found the most magnificent bumper sticker. It said, "What are you pretending not to know?" We spent the rest of the session exploring this very important idea.

Make a list of what you are pretending not to know. For me, the list often has to do with my weight, my level of self-care, and my relationship issues. I give myself a give-year plan of slowly making progress (in an inch-worm like way) on issues that otherwise I might normally pretend not to know. They feel easier to ad- dress when I give myself a few years for any significant progress to be made. Take a moment to write down what you may be pretending not to know! Then give yourself some time to resolve the puzzles they present.

PRAISE THE EFFORT

Sometimes we fail. Even when we have tried our hardest, sometimes we still fail. I promised myself that I would not gain back any of the weight I had lost. I would give up coffee too, and my book would be done within 14 days.

Well, it has been two months and five pounds . . . so I praise the effort, and not the outcome. This gives me the energetic boost to look at what dark shadow material sabotaged my progress. I engage my Explorer's Mind, connect to Core Being and praise my intention and effort. Tomorrow is another opportunity to succeed. Remember, 98 percent of success is showing up for our selves, again and again.

MY ACHING, BREAKING HEART!

OUCH! One of the hardest energies to battle is that of feeling left behind, rejected or abandoned by someone we love. The energy of being left and/or replaced can make us regress into deep child consciousness. When this happens, our negative ego often tells us we are not good. We can feel broken and incapable of being loved.

The HVC of our Enlightened Observer deflates as the energetic cords in our heart are ripped out. This tears the Heart Chakra and the 2nd and 4th levels of our Auric Field. So the emotional pain can also feel like physical pain.

The emotion of grief combined with loneliness and child consciousness can make us spiral downward. Anytime there is a death or a break up, it is very important to take positive steps and find internal and external resources to help us. For one, we need to repair our Heart Chakra and Auric energy field and prevent our ego from taking over our thoughts and emotions.

Steps for Transformation

- **Step 1:** On a very practical level, it is important to reach out to those who do love and support us. We can open ourselves to feel supported and comforted by our community and friends. This helps repair the rips in our Heart Chakra and Auric Field. Eventually, once we have taken in all of their love and support, we can move forward to the next phase.
- **Step 2:** Place one hand on the heart and one hand over the solar plexus, where your ego energy is held. Call upon your guides and Core Being to come into your body and energy system and repair the Auric Field. Imagine green energy filling the heart. Then imagine rose energy filling the heart. During this phase, if you feel the emotional grief/pain with the HVC of your Enlightened Observer, your "breaking heart" breaks open energetically and is restructured in a manner that *increases your ability to give and receive love*. Your Heart Chakra can actually grow stronger and bigger at this time.
- **Step 3:** Imagine yellow energy filling the solar plexus and then peach-colored energy filling the solar plexus.
- **Step 4:** After this is done, repeat the Core Being exercise and fill up the inside of your outer energy egg with the HVC of Core Being.
- **Step 5:** Throughout the next weeks, notice and name when your negative ego takes charge. Realign your Manifest Energy to release the negative ego and reconnect to Core Being. Release the energetic trash of the grief and emotional pain by bringing in the HVC of your Enlightened Observer. (In the beginning, you might need to repeat this process 100 times a day.)
  Eventually, once you feel stronger, write down the lessons learned from the past relationship and how you can support yourself in your next relationship. Commit to self-love.

POWER ANIMAL TO THE RESCUE

A shamanic-oriented exercise is to allow the energy of a power animal to support us in times of stress and strain. I have two main power animals that I call on for assistance from time to time. One power animal came to me during a meditation. The other one kept showing up in my life during times of stress and eventually I adopted him as support.

If we don't already have a power animal, take time to find one. The animal may be one that shows up on the day of reading this Intervention. Or it may be one we feel an affinity toward. There is no one correct way of finding our power animal. In meditation one may show up or we may wake up and find one on the front yard as I did. My husband and I were looking to buy a house and were having trouble finding a house that we both liked. Then, one day we were driving around the neighborhood and saw a huge tree in the front yard of a house with a for sale sign. Sleeping under the tree was a family of deer. A more obvious sign couldn't have been delivered. We are happily living there today.

Once we have selected our power animal, explore the qualities of the animal that we find most attractive and write them down. For instance, a deer has a very gentle loving energy. Notice where in the body and energy system we need the positive energy from the animal and, use intention to bring in its HVC. Feel it, imagine it, and sense it deep in our cells. Notice where it has been absorbed into the cells and melt into again- this time with the intention that it spread to other areas of the body. Then balance the energy front/back, top/bottom, and left/right.

If we have trouble sensing the qualities of the animal we have chosen, the book *Animal Speak* by Ted Andrews is a helpful aid to support our own intuition about the animal and discover some of the animal's most remarkable qualities that can support us.

HOLD THE LIGHT IN THE DARK

Helping ourselves or a client learn to hold the light in the dark supports balance and unity. Unity supports our connection to Core Being and reinstates any disruption in the Rhythm of Flow of the energy. **Stage 4 of Me-B transformation involves holding two places at once, or light and dark.** Whenever we or our client feels as if the "darkness" we are experiencing defines us, bringing in the light into the darkness is a useful process to initiate. Like many things in life, it often takes practice before we see success.

What is the light that we are supposed to bring into the darkness? The light is the HVC of Core Being, the blessing of god, the hand of Jesus touching our pain, self-love, kindness and compassion. Each of us has to define for ourselves what feels like light. One client said it was the sun. Another said it was when she felt Mother Mary hold her.

- **Step 1:** Identify where in the body/energy system the darkness is held.
- **Step 2:** Using (a) intention, (b) visualization, (c) feeling/emotion and (d) sensation, bring in the energy and consciousness of light. If we can't do all of a, b, c, d, then do as well as we or the client can do. It does take a high level of skill and much practice. Do containment if the light doesn't take hold and seek the support of a Me-B guide and/or licensed therapist.

Bring The Light Into Our Darkness

Jerry felt lost. Depression was a frequent visitor. Never before had he thought about bringing a higher vibration into his darkness. With practice, he was able to locate where he felt the darkness in his body. The solar plexus was the place he felt it most. He visualized a bright light, the sun, coming into his body beaming warmth and light. He noticed the old feeling of self-hate melt away and hope take its place. As this happened, the sensation of warmth, tingles and flows spread throughout his mid-section. He had successfully brought the light into his deep darkness.

MY FIELD KNOWS THE ANSWER—CAN I LISTEN?

Oftentimes we wonder, what is in my highest good? Should I buy a house, take this job, move? Do I love him? Does he love me? What is in my highest good? When we are not sure what action we should take or what we should choose, we can tune within for the answer. One way of tuning within is to assess how our energy field reacts when we state our highest good. If our field expands, the answer is yes. If our field contracts, the answer is no. Excel and Spiritual types might have trouble reading their fields if they are not grounded into the body or if they keep the structured levels of the field too tight. So before beginning this Intervention, we should charge and balance our field and connect to Core Being using any of the techniques already taught.

Then assess our baseline of flows and tingles on a scale of 0-10. Ten represents 100 percent flowing and tingling energy, and 0 representing no flows or tingles of energy. If we can't feel energy as a sensation in the body, then use visualizations or intuition to self-assess.

Once our field is charged and balanced and we have assessed our baseline, we make a declarative statement out loud: "It is in my highest good to_." For example, we might say, "It is in my highest good to divorce John," or "It is in my highest good to move to Tucson," or whatever the issue. After we make the statement we again assess the level of flows and tingles of energy to see if there was an expansion from our baseline or a contraction.

Then we state the opposite declarative to see how our field reacts. "It is in my highest good to stay married" or "It is in my highest good to stay in Chicago." Once again, assess our flows and tingles again. Notice if the energy expands more on one declarative than the other. An expansion is a yes answer and a contraction of energy is a no. If there is no change, then a Core Distortion is in the way of reaching clarity. Many times it is ego or child consciousness that feels threatened. Do a Core Distortion Intervention and then try this again. We can assess our own field in this manner or we can help a client assess their field.

I GLADLY CLAIM MY TALENT

A shadow aspect of avoiding Adult Consciousness is the inclination of some people to avoid claiming and then using their personal gifts and talents. All the chakras have aspects of our gifts but it is through our first chakra's energy that we use those gifts to fulfill our life task. When we don't use our gifts to fulfill our life task, depression and anxiety can overtake us.

- **Step 1:** Using any of the techniques already taught, balance and charge the energy field. Then connect to the 7th level of the Auric Field, divine wisdom. To do this, place your hand on the 7th Chakra, at the top of the head. Using intention, allow the frequency of that Chakra to come into the hand and spread throughout the body. Also visualize a golden grid of light filling the body. Then, receive information about your gifts and innate talents. Write down the information that comes. If nothing comes, review the chapter on sensing energy and review how you can connect to your spirit guides. You can also see a Me-B Guide to receive additional support and education on how you can better collecting data from our Me-B System.

- **Step 2:** Staying on the 7th level of the field scan downward connecting to the 6th chakra and ask the same question, what are my gifts and innate talents. See what comes through. Continue this process stopping at each chakra, (5, 4, 3, 2, and 1) collecting information and writing it down.

- **Step 3:** Repeat Step 2, but this time, instead of collecting the information and writing it down, collect the energy of the gift/talent into a golden energy ball. Allow the ball to move from the 7th chakra, down to the 6th, gathering and cultivating the gifts from each chakra as it moves downward, 5th, 4th, 3rd and 2nd chakra. Let the golden ball of energy grow. If the color/shape of the energy ball changes, let it evolve and grow with our gifts. Feel the sensation of the energy as well. Use all our senses. Then, when you get to the first chakra, let the energy of the ball charge the first chakra and open it—so that it is spinning clockwise. Bring the energy from the center of the earth into the first chakra as well so that you can actualize our gifts here in the physical dimension. Let the energy fill your inner thighs and expand to your legs, lower legs and lower body. Balance the energy front/back; left/right; top/bottom.

Over the next month spend a few minutes every day feeling the energy of your gifts/talents as a sensation in the physical body and own these qualities in all Me-B Systems. As we claim our golden gifts, we develop the strength to incorporate them into our life. This reminds us that we are gifted and capable of Adult Consciousness.

HIGHER BRAIN OVERRIDE

Unlike our four-legged friends, human animals have both a higher brain and a primal brain. Because of this, our higher brain may prevent us from finding LVC hiding within our primal response systems. Because our fears and emotions are not always rational to the higher brain, we (or clients) may freeze our process work by stating: "It doesn't make sense for me to be angry. I know I am safe, I don't understand why I reacted that way. I have no right to feel this way. He doesn't deserve for me to be so mad at him. I should not have reacted that way to the situation. In my mind I know I am ok."

We can help ourselves (or our clients) to purposefully override the knee-jerk reaction of the higher brain and its propensity to judge, discount or minimize the reactions of the primal brain. Begin to explore what the primal brain is trying to say. Learn from it. Usually the primal brain is saying, "I am in fear and don't feel safe." Sometimes this is because:

a. the ego feels threatened;
b. boundaries are being invaded;
c. we need to speak our truth;

d.   we are not listening to some wisdom held in the body; and/or

e.   the primal brain needs to discharge some lower vibrational energy from the past.

The Separated Self can take control if we don't listen to the physiology of the primal brain. When the Separated Self takes control, not only do we lose contact with our higher brain, we also can become separated from our Core Being. Candice Pert's research proved that emotions are held somatically in our body and its chemistry. Our higher mind often wants to be in charge and will tell us that there is no LVC present when in reality our child consciousness has been activated in our body. It could even be preverbal child consciousness that has no cognitive orientation. It is important to not let our higher cognitive reasoning disconnect us from clearing any trauma held in the body. Often we must learn how to connect to our somatic memory in the body in order to heal. Practice connecting to the energy in the body, and find old trauma or LVC and heal it. Be careful not to let your higher brain lead you a stray.

Practice listening to the more primitive part of our physiology and energetics then use the wisdom from Core Being to understand and transform any LVC of our Separated Self. Notice where the LVC is held in the body/energy system and bring in the energy of Core Being to transform it using positive intention, love and kindness.

GROUNDING BRINGS SPIRIT INTO THE BODY

What is Grounding and why is it Important? When we lose our grounding we lose our center and shrink. When we lose our center we disconnect from our Core Being and can become overwhelmed with the challenges of the day. Lack of grounding means we are in defense. We misplace our perspective and we lose the energy to interact from a place of balance. Our defenses lock us into our programmed personality limiting our divine expression.

At the mind level, lack of grounding can present as confusion, disassociation and/or lack of individuation. We may take on another's opinion or perspective as our own because we have lost independent thought and action. We become more judgmental of others and ourselves. We literally lose the ability to hold our own. Lack of grounding can also open us up to attack and can create situations that may be unsafe and definitely less secure. After all, we can't operate fully if we've lost us.

Lack of Grounding

Energetically in the Auric Field, lack of grounding can look like the following: Chakras: undercharged and in distortion.

Outer Energy Egg: becomes light bulb shaped with more energy on top versus bottom. Or the egg shape can become fragmented so that there is no energy egg or boundaries between us and the outside world no longer exist. This makes us vulnerable.

Energetically, there is a dimension that is always whole-Core Being. When we lose our grounding this dimension of deeper truth becomes more difficult to access.

Why Do We Lose Our Grounding?

It is a defense against something. Usually, it is an unhealthy defense that has been programmed over the years-maybe even before birth. We lose our grounding because we feel overwhelmed and unsafe. Sometimes if we don't eat correctly, are fasting or are sick we can lose our grounding as well.

****

SAMPLE GROUNDING EXERCISES

Oak Tree: Make a circle with our arms in front of us like our arms are hugging an Oak Tree. We can also go outside and actually hug a tree to do this.

Feel the trunk of the tree on the front of our body. Feel its strength flow through our body. Feel how solid the tree is between our arms. So solid in fact that we can imagine our arms are being supported by it.

Feel it run through our legs. Imagine our legs are part of the tree trunk. Imagine the energy from our legs deepening into the earth below, deep down to the core of the earth.

Imagine receiving the heat up through the bottoms of our feet. Let it flow through our body.

Lastly, feel the front and back of our body's trunk become at one with the tree. Allow our self to feel its strength and wholeness.

Horse: Stand with knees bent like you are going to sit on a high stool. Our coccyx is parallel to the ground. Imagine energy running from the top of our head, down the center of the body.

Then imagine three metaphorical legs of energy connecting us to the center of the earth. One connecting the perineum to the earth and two others running through the center of our leg bones and connecting to the earth.

> Follow the following body scan sequence outlined below and at each point say the words—"release down" and feel/imagine the energy flowing downward. Pause for 10 seconds or longer in any area of the body where you can imagine feeling sensations of comfort and say the words "release down." Feel all parts of your body—dismiss nothing.
>
> - Eyes, nose, ears, teeth tongue, lips, and jaw.
> - Neck—front and back Shoulders—front and back Chest, upper back
> - Arms, elbows, hands, fingers
> - Mid-back and Core Center
> - Lower back and Lower Abdomen
> - Pelvis—Sacrum
> - Legs, thighs, back of thighs, front/back of lower legs, Ankles, Feet, Toes
>
> Scan through the body 5 times—each time stopping at sensations of comfort and saying the words "release down."

Melt into the sensations of comfort and notice if they grow, intensify or expand.

Simply by focusing on the positive comforting sensations, you are charging them energetically. Helping them multiply.

Safety and Security: Repeat the exercise above with a slight variation. Instead of saying "release down," say "I am safe," and visualize a place that feels safe for you as you scan through the body feeling the positive sensations. Examples of safe places that people seem to like are: their bed, a partner's arms, the beach, or a quiet area in the house.

Develop Your Own: Grounding is about self-empowerment. Knowing what works for you is paramount so feel free to be creative. Adapt these exercises or develop your own. Meditation, Chi Kung, Hands-On Energy Work, exercise, acupuncture and personal process work are useful tools in helping us regain our grounding. Find out what works for you by experimenting.

Food and Supplements: Some foods and supplements have the effect of grounding and others detract from it. Know how your body reacts and adjust accordingly. Typical grounding foods are nuts, whole grains, and proteins.

CORE BEING CONNECTION: POP GOES THE WEASEL!

Another Core Being connection meditation is outlined next. This can be used in addition to the one outlined in the beginning of the book.

- **Step 1:** The vortex for the Core Being Dimension is an inch 1/2 above the navel. We are going to pump Core Being energy into an energy ball in the vortex then let it pop out (Pop goes the Weasel) and fill our inner and outer energy egg. Just as a black hole collapses inward, if we cultivate a "white hole" of Core Being, we can cultivate the energy within and then let it expand outward. Another example of this is the joke trick, "snakes in a can," which spills out when the lid is open. We can compact Core Being Energy and let it expand outward. Use breath, awareness and intention to let it spill and overflow throughout our cellular structures and outer energy egg.
- **Step 2:** Charge and balance our field using any of the exercises already taught. Then, using our favorite exercise, charge and run energy into our body for 30 seconds. (Run, bounce on ball, jump rope....) Then pause, and imagine the charge from the exercise filling an energy ball in the center of our Core Being vortex. (Imagine an energy ball about the size of a tennis ball of Core Being energy.) Repeat this 6-8 times, allowing as much energy into the Core Being energy ball as we can cultivate.
- **Step 3:** Once we feel there is a large charge filling the ball, place our awareness into the center, breathe and invite it to expand filling all the cells in our body and our outer energy egg. Repeat 3 or more times until we can feel the sensation of it intensify and spread throughout our Me-B system.

CHAPTER 19

ME-B GUIDE INTERVENTIONS HELP CLIENTS RESOURCE POSITIVELY

We Can Only Be What We Give Ourselves the Power to Be!

We all need help from time to time. It is the sign of an advanced soul when we are willing to ask for help. The below Me-B Guide Interventions can help clients receive HVC so they are more able to transform and move back to Core Being. If we have mastered these techniques on ourselves, we are more able to help others. Get trained as a Me-B Guide before practicing these Interventions on others.

SAFETY AND TRUST

Before any work with a client can be done, trust and safety must be present. Depending upon the client's character structure, we may begin the first sessions working on safety and trust. Remember, it is the relationship that creates the healing. Practice teaching the client the Safety Net Intervention discussed in the previous chapter. In addition, we can do touch and no touch interventions to teach ourselves and our clients how to connect to the energy of Safety and Trust as sensations/visualizations in the body.

- **Step 1:** Resonate at the first and fifth Levels of the Auric Field. If doing a Touch Intervention have one arm under the client's shoulders and one on the third Chakra.
- **Step 2:** Ask the client to pick a visualization of a time when they felt (or imagine they felt) the energy of safety and trust in their body. Use that visualization as they say "I am safe and trust." Ask them to imagine, feel and receive that energy into their body.

Ask them to feel the energy as a sensation in the body. As they focus on what they can feel, allow the energy to spread to areas of low or no sensation until they feel it balanced front/back, top/bottom, and left/right. As the client is doing this, the Me-B Guide guides the HVC of safety and trust to fill the client's body.

I AM SAFE ENOUGH TO TRUST

Janet, an extravert, and a very strong businesswoman told me she was looking forward to receiving a healing. We connected, I learned some of her history, and we moved to the table. Her field made it clear that I shouldn't place my hands on her. I waited and tracked her field. It eventually softened and I placed my hands on her legs. No energy flowed. Instead, fear filled the field again. I asked her if she was aware of any emotions.

She mentioned fear. Given her history I was not surprised. I asked her if she ever felt safety as a sensation in her body. It is quite common for a client to say no to that question. We used imagery and energy work to help her be able the access the energy of safety and trust in the body. It took three sessions before her field was able to resonate with enough safety for us to do deeper work.

CONNECT TO CLIENT'S GUIDES FOR SUPPORT

Be able to receive information from our guides and/or our client's guides for support before, during or after a session. Practicing this skill strengthens this skill. Often during a session with a client there are places in the Rhythm of Flow where it pauses. At this time we can check in with our guides and/or our client's guides so we can assess which direction to go with a client so they feel supported.

SEEKING SPIRITUAL GUIDANCE AS SUPPORT

The client was experiencing a deep contraction and was complaining about feeling stuck. The Heart-centered push/pull energy filled the room. I could feel her resistance to receiving help. Yet, at the same time, she was pleading for help. She slumped in the chair waiting for me to save her while resenting the need for help. I checked in with our guides for advice on what path would create an opening in the box where she had trapped herself. I then noticed an image in my head of her as a child. As I spoke the image, her eyes lit up. Contact was made. The rest of the session flowed and evolved effortlessly.

HOW TO WORK MULTI-DIMENSIONALLY

In many of the leading types of energy work, healers are taught to draw in energy through their head or through their feet/root chakra. Me-B Transformation enthusiasts work Multi-Dimensionally. This entails inviting energy to connect through all vortexes and dimensions. We can resonate our field at:

- Auric Levels,
- Intention Line,
- Core Being, and
- The Multi-Dimensional Fabric Dimension.

Then we can allow the energy to flow through: feet/all chakras/head and bring in energy from all dimensions in the room using mind/awareness and intention. This is working multi-dimensionally. It is still sometimes difficult for me to be in all these frequencies at the same time but each year it gets easier and becomes a positive and natural habit. Begin by practicing being in Core Being and the Intention Line at the same time.

- **Step 1:** Allow Core Being to resonate throughout the Intention Line.
- **Step 2:** Once that feels comfortable, practice Core Being and Auric Levels at the same time.
- **Step 3:** Then try Core Being, Intention Line and Auric Dimension all together.
- **Step 4:** Add in the Multi-Dimensional Fabric Dimension once we have mastered the other three dimensions. Practice, Practice, Practice!

FILL THE VOID WITH UNCONDITIONAL LOVE

As explained in the Stages of Me-B Transformation, when we or a client experiences the energetics of the "Void," it can feel overpowering. But, we can assist ourselves in filling the space with unconditional love and acceptance so we recover from its traumatic effects. Energetically, the void is held in the solar plexus area. So that is where we begin to fill it.

- **Step 1:**

    Invite a client (or ourselves) to imagine the love of the mother earth or spiritual guide, Jesus, or god-like energy as the source of the unconditional love. If doing hands-on work with the client on a table, the Me-B Guide places one hand on her solar plexus and one hand between her shoulder blades on the back of the heart chakra.

    If the Guide is using no-touch techniques, then the Me-B guide simply moves the energy with her awareness, mind, breath and intention. The Me-B guide helps the client energetically by vibrating their Core Being. Holding levels 2, 4, 6, the Guide calls in unconditional love.

- **Step 2:**

    Then, tracking the client's field closely, the Me-B Guide supports the client to receive the positive energy through her third chakra, and abdomen area. Often, it is difficult for the client (or ourselves) to receive and accept the love. Much patience and support is needed to make it easier for the client.

- **Step 3:**

    Once the area in the third chakra and abdomen fills, allow the energy to expand and fill the heart, pelvis and every cell in the body. If the client can't receive the energy in the third chakra, suggest she notice where in her body she can receive it. If she can't receive it anywhere, have her imagine receiving it. Sometimes we must "fake it to make it."

FILL THE VOID

Collin felt alone and empty. The void within him seemed endless. As he lay down on the table he felt that Mother Earth could be his source of unconditional love. Vibrating my Core Being and Auric Levels 2, 4, and 6, I put one hand on his solar plexus and one near the back of his Heart Chakra. I let my third chakra receive the unconditional love and deepened and slowed my breathing. Automatically he did the same. Slowly at first, he took in more of the HVC and let himself expand and fill.

THE WHOLE FEMININE/MASCULINE and the GOOD ENOUGH MOTHER/FATHER

This is similar to the previous Intervention of taking in unconditional love with the exception being receiving "good enough" mother or father energy and/or balanced feminine or masculine energy. It is a slightly different vibration than the energy of unconditional love but just as important.

The Me-B guide invokes the good enough mother/father energy (or the whole feminine/masculine) and the client opens to receive the balanced energy. The client chooses which mother/father (masculine/feminine) energy to receive.

Possible Sources of "Good Enough" Father/Mother Energy: The higher self energy of their mother or father, Mother Mary, Jesus, Buddha, Quan Yin, Guadalupe, or any other archetypal figure.

Possible Sources of Balanced Masculine/Feminine Energy: Archetypes such as Joan of Arc/Hercules, movie characters, or specific people in their lives they admire who represent that balanced Male/Female energies. In Chinese medicine, the left side of the body represents female energy of receiving and the right side of the body represents male energy of giving. Stereotypical male energy is someone who goes out into the world and "hunts" to bring home food for the family. It is a more external energy that is used to give and provide for others. Masculine energy fixes a problem where as feminine energy listens and is receptive and is inwardly focused and emotionally based.

Both masculine and feminine energy is equally important to all of us in this complicated and demanding life. These days, it is common for both mothers and fathers to both play the role of provider and nurturer.

Sometimes I use my horse, Zeus, to help clients feel the balanced masculine energy and his girlfriend, Windy, as a feminine energy resource. Whatever the source, it must hold the highest vibration possible.

Defenses against HVC

At first, HVC can be difficult for clients to assimilate, and they may fall asleep when the higher vibrations come into the body. Or, clients may subconsciously defend against receiving the HVC. If a Core Distortion gets in the way, it might take a client many sessions to shift decades (lifetimes) of not having the higher vibrational energy available to them.

(Remember the 3-Skills of Adult Consciousness: give, receive and give to self when we would rather receive.) If a client is more comfortable giving than receiving, it can be harder for them to open and receive. Also, if a client has trust and negative attachment issues, they may have difficulty opening their energy field. Excel and Spiritual energy types have difficulty opening and being connected to their bodies and emotions.

It is not "good" or "bad" when our defenses prevent us from receiving HVC. It is diagnostic of a challenge to overcome. Awareness is the first step. Going slow, shifting Core Distortions and being kind and patient with our self creates success. We and our clients can learn to receive our light. Nelson Mandela spoke about this during his 1994 inauguration speech. He noticed how it is our light that we are most afraid of receiving. He spoke, "Our deepest fear is not that we are inadequate. Our deepest fear is that we are powerful beyond measure."

Receiving Transformational Energies

- **Step 1:** Once a source of the HVC is identified, ask the client (or ourselves) to picture the source, feel the source as energy in the body and align their Manifest Energy Intention Line to open and receive.
- **Step 2:** If the client is on the table and we are doing Touch Interventions, place one hand on their Solar Plexus and one hand on the back of the client's Heart Chakra. The Me-B guide resonates at the frequency of the HVC (good enough mom/dad or divine masculine/feminine energy) and allows that energy to expand into the client's field. The Me-B guide also calls in this energy multi-dimensionally.

INTEGRATION OF PAST Me-B GUIDE TRANSFORMATION SUCCESS

Our growth proceeds in expansions and contractions of the Rhythm of Flow. A wonderful positive resourcing strategy is to help ourselves (or a client) notice the changes they have made and really integrate them into all three Me-B systems.

If working with a client, have them take notice of their transformational successes as tangibly as possible. We can even do a ceremony marking the passage and changes. I have a fireplace in my office for this reason. We can note any or all of the following victories:

- energetic improvements,
- ability to track, transform and self-regulate our energy/emotional systems,
- self-care/health successes,
- relationship improvements,
- career developments,
- abundance,
- self-love,
- healing of child consciousness,
- trauma resolution,
- cognitive changes in beliefs/images,
- more—be creative.

We can then encourage them to feel these successes as sensations of HVC in their body, mind and energy system.

SIMPLY SUPPORT THE FLOW

It is often helpful to spend sessions simply supporting the positive energy of the Rhythm of Flow by using supportive dialogue and energetic techniques. When we or our clients feel "burnt out" on life or deeper work, it can be revitalizing to receive a *Rhythm of Supportive Flows Session*.

Practice phrases such as:

- Why don't we just focus on the positive today?
- Let's create a supportive environment for you.
- How would it feel to find a comfortable place to lie down on these pillows and you just practice receiving?
- You know what impresses me about you?
- I have always admired....
- Where do you feel the most positive sensations in your body?
- What color vibrations do you imagine might feel the best?
- What positive pictures, images feel most nurturing (a beach, nature...)
- What positive issue do you want to focus on next?
- What do you find most successful about yourself?
- Let's feel the support of your spirit guides?
- Other—be creative.

Trust that you will know the next dialogue or energetic intervention for the next supportive flow.

JUMP AHEAD/JUMP BACK

If we jump too far ahead of where the client is able to go, or if we proceed too slowly, or if we inadvertently (or purposely) trigger a client into transference, it can interrupt the Rhythm of Flow of Energy. This is not necessarily "bad" or "good" as long as Me-B Guides use this technique with talent and purpose.

Jumping to the next place a client needs to discover, if not too far ahead, just one step ahead, can help support the Rhythm of Flow of Energy and thus support transformation. Jumping backward can help slow the Rhythm down enough to review the work that has just been done. It will help the mind understand and integrate the work the body/energy system just mastered.

ASSESS THE ENERGY OF A CLIENT'S STORY TO BRING IN HVC

Sometimes, it is important to limit cognitive exchanges. Tracking the energy while a client talks can provide insight into how to deepen the contact between us and the client and help raise her/his vibrations. As a client talks, if they talk about something that brings high vibrations into the room, ask them to bring those high vibrations also into their body.

USING THE CLIENT'S STORY TO CREATE HVC

I have been seeing Sara for over 2 years. She is a healer and a massage therapist and very talented. Today, she was in deep emotional collapse. At one point in the session she began telling me about a wonderful business trip. She described an artist colony she visited and the people she met. As she talked, I sensed the vibration of the positive experience come into the room. I invited her to feel the high vibration on the edges of her skin. I could feel it all around her but it was like her skin refused to receive a positive shift. However, all she needed was a little support. With a little guidance, the vibration filled her skin, her body and her cells. Her collapse transformed into an expansion.

SHOULD I LEAVE OR SHOULD I STAY?

Clients often come into therapy with a presenting complaint about their relationships. "Should I leave or should I stay in my marriage?" they ask.

For at least five years, I have stayed in my marriage asking this same question. I wondered if I was masochistic for staying, or if I was being altruistic. I just wanted someone to tell me what was true. My mind said one thing and my body/energy system said something completely different. Somatic therapists told me the body always held the truth and cognitive therapist told me to listen to my mind. I didn't want to leave the marriage only to repeat the same mistakes again.

The confusion I suffered came from me trying to make a decision from my wounded parts one moment, and from my Core Being the next moment. My "flip-flopping" was due to my inability to stay connected to Core Being. I too often let my insecurities and disempowered self be in charge of making a decision.

Over the next five years I did deep Core Distortion Trauma work to deepen into Core Being. Because of the hard work I did, eventually I reached a point where there was no longer indecision or a negative charge around the choice. It was clear what I needed to do. To help clients see what part of them is making the decision, help them practice the following exercise. This exercise can be used for any decision that is difficult to make.

- **Step 1:** Place two chairs in the room, in a gestalt-like practice. One chair represents Core Being energy and the other chair represents her wounded parts. Ask the client to resonate with Core Being and energetically fill the chair with her/his Core Being. Connect to whatever decision needs to be made and notice the Core Being perspective.
- **Step 2:** In the other chair, call in the energy of the client's wounded parts. Keeping the Enlightened Observer strong, notice the root cause of the wounded parts' pain. What is the negative belief, Core Distortion and/or child consciousness keeping the client in confusion and indecision? Is trauma involved?
- **Step 3:** Establish a longer-term transformation goal to heal the issues fueling the LVC in the wounded parts and help the client deepen into Core Being.

TRANSFORMING CHILD CONSCIOUSNESS INTO HVC

Once a client is at least Stage 4 of Me-B Transformation, we can notice when they have regressed and then work with the energy to help them transform the past and create a positive future. Methods to invoke regression follow.

Repetitive/Deep Breathing

Using deep repetitive breathing techniques can invite the subconscious to emerge. Often times, this process reveals child consciousness, trauma, birth challenges, and/or past life issues. There are many breath work workshops that train people in this area. Some use a plastic coke bottle with the bottom cut out. They breathe through the open spout for 15 minutes deeply to create the regression. Other techniques simple support sustained continuous deep breathing. It is important to never do this alone, under the influence and/or without a trained supporter.

Notice Triggers

Triggers often have their origin in child consciousness and/ or trauma. A dialogue intervention such as, "I noticed you were triggered." Or, "Your field seemed to be triggered," can help the client notice what is happening.

How Old Do You Feel?

When you notice a client is developmentally regressed, you might ask them how old they feel. This often deepens self-awareness and usually deepens them into the regressed experience. If they have an Enlightened Ob- server, transformation is possible.

Dialogue with the Emotion

Any of these dialogue interventions can lead to a regression.

- "I notice you are feeling an emotion."

- "That emotion feels strong."
- "Let's stay with that feeling and follow it more deeply."
- "Can we pause here and stay with that emotion?"
- "Keep exploring those feelings."
- "Let yourself deepen into that emotion."
- "Feel how young you were when that emotion was strongest."
- "What message does that emotion bring?"

Any of these dialogues usually brings clients deeper into the emotion or experience and into regression. If not, we can back up and reestablish contact with the client and check our field to make sure we are balanced. It is helpful to self-assess what is going on with us at this time and to assess the defenses/ego strength of the client.

Another method of dialoging with an emotion is to **read information about the emotion in the field and to make a comment based on the information we receive**. This will gently open the door to their inner child's needs, feelings or fears. Something like:

- "I wonder if you felt you had to do it all on your own."
- "Were you able to really let in all that love?"
- "Did you stop believing in yourself?
- "Speaking your truth must have been hard."

Transformation

Finding and feeling the energy of the wounded child is only the beginning. It can be easy to help someone identify their pain and past issues. (Stage 1-3 of ME-B Transformation.) The real work is to raise the vibration and consciousness of the past by being effective, clean and gentle in the present. Transforming child consciousness can be divided into two main areas:

- needs that were not met, and
- harm to undo.

> **Sometimes transformation can be accomplished simply by:**
> **(1) isolating a need, and (2) meeting that need.**

For instance, having a client speak up for themselves when they couldn't speak up as a child is a wonderful gift. Giving them the right to say "no" to Mom/Dad and claim their personal space and power back can be very transformative. And, as always, the Me-B guide can check to see if the issue has shifted in all three systems (mind, energy and body).

It could take many sessions to clear these unmet needs, and most likely the work will concern an issue they may have to revisit again, yet at a deeper level. (The issue may arise 100 times, and 100 times we may need to transform it.) The higher the client reaches in the 10 Me-B Stages, the deeper the work we can do be- cause the client can hold themselves and they know they are not the negativity that moves through them.

332

- **Step one** is to notice when the client (or we) are triggered.
- **Step two** is to feel where in the body the trigger is being held.
- **Step three** is to isolate what emotion, image or belief is being held there. Then, engaging the HVC of the En- lightened Observer, feel the feelings (levels 2 and 4 of the Auric field) and allow HVC to transform the pain back into Adult Consciousness. If the Enlightened Observer merges with the pain and loses its HVC, then we just create more pain. This is why the person must be at least Stage 4 of Me-B Transformation. They can use any of the techniques taught previously to help transform LVC. Carefully track the field to see if they are charging the negative feelings or transforming them. Do the containment procedure if they get stuck.

NOTE: As we do the transformation process, remember we need to eventually teach the client to hold a supportive space for themselves. They must be weaned from us and empowered within themselves. Help them transition at least to Me-B Stages 4-5.

TRANSFORMING CHILD CONSCIOUSNESS

Missy had an alcoholic mother and her father abandoned her when she was only one year old. She had no positive mirroring during her childhood and was sexually abused by her mothers' best friend when the friend was babysitting.

During one of our sessions, I noticed Missy's field was deeply regressed and it felt like she never had the support she needed. I commented, "So, you felt alone and unsupported." She began to weep. I offered her the chance to receive that support now. I put pillows in my lap and a blanket over her. (I find pillows make it more safe because the boundary between she and I are clearer. Close but not suggestively close.)

The weeping continued for a few minutes and then I suggested she might be able to take in the love and support. Her breathing changed, she stopped crying and her chakras began to spin clockwise again as she took in the love and support. This process continued on and off over six months before she could hold this loving Container for herself.

Bring In Adult Consciousness To Comfort the Inner-Child

Eventually, and as soon as possible, the client will have to master the technique of meeting their own needs by bringing in their own adult to comfort their own inner-child with love or compassion. If we can't yet do this for ourselves, set a goal to accomplish this skill. Let us not ask a client to do what we can't do ourselves.

This is a more advanced process and it may take a few sessions (or years) of us "playing" the good enough Mom/Dad, before clients can fulfill that role themselves. There are many methods and styles.

BECOMING OUR ADULT TO OUR WOUNDED CHILD

Dorothy was first abandoned by her mom in the hospital after she was born. Two weeks later, her mother eventually reclaimed Dorothy and yet held deep resentment toward her daughter. So deep was the resentment that as Dorothy grew up, her mother emotionally and physically abused her.

I began seeing Dorothy at the age of 50. She had been in therapy for over 20 years and was diagnosed with Dissociative Identity Disorder (DID). She has a strong spiritual and meditation practice that serves to support her, yet she was still shy about being touched, supported and loved. Table work was too intimate for her and it felt overwhelming.

Again and again she would regress to a very young age or disassociate, freeze and lose contact with herself. Eventually she was able to hold and send love to her young self.

She described this experience as "holding myself as I would hold a baby kitten." It marked a substantial shift in her personal process and empowerment. Her ability to hold her own inner child transformed her life in a way 20 previous years of therapy had not.

If our child consciousness holds a sexual/physical abuse or neglect issue, the theme may take months (or years) to completely re-pattern and then it may be revisited every year or so but at deeper levels. This is not bad news. Let it just be part of the human reality we must all face again, and again. Besides, the more we visit the same issues, the more refined and effortlessly our skills become. It is like learning to move from skiing on greens, to blues to black diamonds. As our skills increase, we can master harder challenges.

EYE OF THE HURRICANE

Locate a place in the body holding child consciousness and chaos. Using the imagery of the "Eye of the Hurricane," we and our client can connect to the "hurricane" of child consciousness energy and bring in Adult Consciousness of trust and safety. It is a very effective method to shift the chaos and lack of control.

MOVIE PICTURES

If our client is good at visualizing and has a creative mind, we can replay the movie of the past drama and change the ending to one that is more satisfying. Always check the field, however, to see if the ending visualized was integrated deeply into all three Me-B systems. If not, we can help see the Core Distortion in the way and gradually transform it.

The one rule I recommend is to hold clear intention to change the past mistakes by being conscious in the present. If time and space don't really exist, it is possible to eliminate the mistakes of the past energetically in the mind and body and reawaken to Core Being.

This work asks the client to move away from the personality level to the multidimensional reality available right here and now!
Change the reality created in the past by reprogramming the present.

334

TUNING INTO THE BODY

This process can be done one of two ways. First, start by asking clients what they notice in their body. Usually this question is asked because the Me-B guide notices a strong energetic holding somewhere in the body and wants to support the client in collecting information about the holding. Second, clients may present a complaint or emotional challenge and we may ask them where they think it is held in the body. We may then ask them to pick up information about the issue and let the session evolve.

Sometimes when we ask clients where they feel an emotion in the body, they say their head. Unless it is a physical pain or rage, chances are it is not in their head; they just don't have the skills yet to locate it in the body. So honor where they are, proceed slowly, and be supportive. Don't tell them they are wrong. You can suggest that it may also be in another location as well and encourage them to make an intuitive guess.

COLLECTING INFORMATION FOR SOMEONE

In Me-B Transformation we will most likely be asked to "read" the client. During the Me-B training, students have opportunities to practice this skill in a manner that supports the empowerment of the client and allows us to only be a vessel the information comes through and not the authority. I recommend the following three qualifications be met before we do a "reading" on a client: (1) Our guides and our client's guides feel it is in the client's highest good; (2) We have supported the client in gaining the information on his/her own first; and (3) Doing a reading is an exception to the transformation work and not the rule. It is only to support and in no way disempowers the client.

I had been seeing Tom for over three years and never did a "reading" on him even though he often requested one. During a table work session, I began to channel a reading for him about his relationship to anger and his inability to find a lifetime partner. As a result of the reading, Tom finally overcame his resistance to exploring and transforming his inner rage and is now in a long-term relationship.

SHARING OUR EXPERIENCE OF A CLIENT TO INVOKE THEIR EXPERIENCE

If we have a close relationship and trust has been developed — and the client has a strong enough connection to Core Being — then we can **share with them what it is like to experience them**. It can be an option that we employ, or not — depending upon what is in the client's highest good.

We can also notice how their energy is affecting us. For instance, if we notice our solar plexus contracting and we know it is not about us, we can say, "I just noticed my 3rd chakra contract; what are you experiencing?" Oftentimes this Intervention will take them deeper into their body and their experience.

Sometimes we will see/sense a major change in their field and we can make a comment on it. For instance, one client usually came into my office with yellow energy surrounding him. On one particular day, his field was very blue/green. As he explored what this meant to him, he discovered a beautiful part of his golden shadow and deepened his connection to Core Being.

Isabella was in the process of coming out of her Public Personality. She was in the beginning stages of finding herself yet still confused about the real her. When we began the session, I noticed her energy field was very small as if she was slightly insecure. "Are you feeling uncomfortable?" I asked.

Apparently, she had just left a meeting with her friend and the friend told her that she was a very distant and cold person. I asked her if she would like me to tell her how I experience her. She shyly smiled, "yes." I explained to her that I felt more and more how genuine and authentic she was and I could feel her warmth and inner light come through. Immediately her field returned to its normal balance. She then explored her own truth. Was she cold or warm? She began to feel the energy of her Core Being in her body and noticed when she felt trapped at the programmed personality level.

Another client I worked with was having trouble dealing with a group he had joined. He was afraid they didn't like him as much as some of the other people in the group and he wanted to know what I thought.

I told him that when he was around me, I sometimes felt a regressed, needy, insecure, child-like demanding energy from him. He said he had noticed this energy coming out of him too and expected that people in the group were probably feeling the same thing. He said, "I don't want to pull and feel demanding or needy; it is just hard sometimes not to feel that way." In time, he learned to fill himself up. As he shifted internally, so did his relationship to the group. He became one of them instead of an outsider.

In sessions, we even purposefully explored what it was like for him when I wouldn't or couldn't give him what he wanted or when I couldn't "fix," or "save" him like he sometimes felt I should. Before sharing this information he was stuck at Me-B Stage 3 for over two years. Afterwards, he quickly mastered Me- B Stage 4.

Sometimes we must risk "not pleasing" a client in order to help them move forward.

DISSOLVING THOUGHTS

Anyone who has circular or obsessive thinking knows how difficult it can be to stop the thoughts. Thoughts, like trauma or anything else, in their essence are simply energy. **Ask the client to circumvent the thinking of thoughts and invite them to feel the thoughts as sensations in the body.** This process helps the thoughts dissolve. (Review the Intervention *Too Many Thoughts and the Wandering Mind.*) As the client increases their skill level, thinking first slows, becomes intermittent, and then normalizes.

This technique is most effective during table work. The Me-B guide charges the field. One hand is on the top of the back of the head and one hand is on the neck or heart area. Direct the energy in the head to move downward. Open the flow of energy downward through the central channel — releasing any blocks along the way. If an area doesn't release, ask the client to connect to the area and feel any sensations they can, even the touch of your hand. Next, invite them to melt into the area like butter melts on a grill. If a thought happens, ask them to think the thought again and then to imagine feeling the energy of the thought first on the head or face, then neck, then heart... guiding them gently down the entire body.

Usually circular thinking is energetically "fed" by a deeper issue. Often it is about their ego feeling attacked. Ask the client to bring their 6th chakra downward and into the body where the emotion/Core Distortion is held most strongly. Engaging the Enlightened Observer, invite them to feel the difficult emotions as energy, and then imagining these difficult emotions melt away and transform into HVC.

INTERACTIONS ON PAST HISTORY OR CLIENT'S STORY

The process of doing a dialogue intervention during a personal history in-take will differ depending upon our style and the client's character structure. Dialogues such as "how was that for you" or "it must have been hard" can help deepen the relationship and begin working on transforming the past. Since Me-B Transformation focuses on what is happening in the moment, a client's history becomes supplementary information and not primary support. During intake, it is important to begin assessing the Client energetically. When we accurately track a client's field, then make a dialogue intervention on what we sense, we foster trust. Clients notice we are really seeing them at the deeper level.

Kathryn began talking about the death of her husband and how she had disconnected from her friends but badly wanted to reconnect to her old community. When she mentioned her intention to reconnect, her field became fragmented. When her story had finished, I shared with her what I saw in her field. She then confessed that she was afraid to reconnect with them and that she wasn't really excited about following through. Months later she is still using that incident as the moment she relaxed and began to trust our relationship—because I could see below the story to the real issue, even when she wasn't aware of it herself!

INTENSIFY TO MELT

Ironically, sometimes when we intensity a feeling/sensation in the body, this charges it just enough so that we can (1) deepen into it, (2) discover more about it and (3) energetically melt into it and let it shift.

Without conscious connection, energy cannot transform. We don't always have to know the deeper meaning for it to melt, but we must be in contact with it emotionally, and preferably in terms of physical sensations or tensions in the body. By sensing into the body, we create deep contact for energetic transformation.

Notice the client's body position and where the negative energy is being held. Ask the client to do the same. Then invite the client to tense the muscles and intensify the body position to activate what is hidden there. Remind them to engage their Enlightened Observer so they keep enough HVC for transformation.

Accentuate the Body's Hidden Form

Bart is a strong man with an Excel defense. Actually feeling emotions is challenging for him. He contains them in a low-grade depression. His girlfriend holds the Leader personality-type (same as his mother) and he often feels overwhelmed by her criticism. Energetically he takes on worthlessness every time his mother or his girlfriend yells, judges, or criticizes him. He soaks the worthlessness into his cells like a sponge.

I invited Bart to collapse into his overwhelm. This tall, six foot man let his body contort and roll into a ball. I encouraged him to move into it even more deeply and he fell to the floor—emotions started moving through him. He was careful to let them flow and not merge with the negativity. His Enlightened Observer was strong.

The tightness of the Excel defense melted away. Finely, he could feel his pain. Feeling his pain meant he could claim what he had subconsciously done to himself and thus change. When the Rhythm of Flow of the energy shifted, I suggested he slowly unwind his body and see if his authentic strength wanted to return.

Slowly he moved, each movement representing a reclaiming of his strength—first sitting, then standing tall and strong. I suggested he imagine his girlfriend and mother in front of him. He hesitated at first, questioning if he could still stand strong with their images looking at him.

He breathed, deepened his breath, made his pose taller and fuller and claimed his power and truth.

A similar method for shifting the energy is to accentuate a body movement or gesture and to alter a pose. For instance, if we see a client making a repetitive gesture such as shaking the hand, we can invite them to repeat it and accentuate the movement. It will provide a trigger to deepen the emotion and understand the shadow message. Also, we can ask the client to shift their position, for instance by pushing out their chest and bringing their shoulders back. We can also ask them what that feels like energetically in their body and to identify the positive (or negative) image or belief. This can deepen the therapeutic response.

If it is a positive belief, invite them to authentically claim it. If it is a negative belief, keep working with it, charging it and following the rhythm until we can bring it around to the positive. Remember to end the session with positive vibration.

INTERACTING WITH A CLIENT WHEN NON-VERBAL EMOTIONAL ISSUES PRESENT

If a client becomes developmentally regressed to a non-verbal state, cognitive and dialogue interventions be- come less effective. The first step is to be able to track when a client has regressed to this state. All of the 5 character structures can exhibit this trait, but the Spiritual-type's Core Distortions hold this the strongest.

Taping sessions or having a client **take notes** after the session is necessary to later integrate what happened into the adult mind. Once we have found a client has regressed, first asses their ego strength and if they are too dissociated and need to be brought back from the regression. When a client has regressed to a non-verbal state or has regressed too far, ask them to look around and find five examples of a particular color in the room. If they cannot, we know they probably have regressed too far.

Read their field and know their history. A field too regressed will be very diffuse and their central channel won't be defined. If they are too disassociated, use physical exercise, balance techniques, the containment procedure and positive resourcing techniques to bring them back.

If they are strong enough to do work at this level, working non-verbally with them either (1) on the table, (2) through physical movement, and/or (3) in non-verbal role-playing is most effective. The intention of the Interventions can be to **teach them how they can return themselves to strength and Core Being.** Also, **they can learn how to use the Manifest Energy Intention Line to transform the pre-verbal wound and discover its hidden wisdom**.

FEEL EMOTIONS AS ENERGY AND SENSATIONS IN THE BODY

Getting a client out of their head and into their emotions is necessary for transformation. Unfortunately, when this happens, they often let the feelings of hopelessness, self-hate, and loneliness take control and define them.

Clients can learn to feel emotions as energy and sensations in the body. It gives the mind a job so it can detach enough to bring in the Enlightened Observer. We all can learn to detach from *being* the emotions so we work instead toward *transforming* our emotions in the mind and body.

When a client is in the process of feeling an emotion, ask them to first identify the emotion. If they are not sure, ask them the basics: sad, angry, scared and/or happy. If they are ripe for this intervention, they will most likely be clear what the emotion is. Then ask them to feel the emotion as energy in their body — as an actual SENSATION running through them. Usually when this happens a client will quickly transform the energy of the emotion into a higher vibration. This intervention can be used with a client of the Excel or Spiritual Types as long as we know it might take a few sessions for them to be successful. Because their field tends to be tight, it can be difficult for them to connect to sensations in the body.

Dave often feels overwhelmed by his emotions. He can't easily distinguish the personality level from his Core Being. He also tends to "talk away" his emotions when they arise. As he attempted to "talk away" the emotion that just arose, I quickly suggested he pause and imagine he could feel that emotion as energy running through his body.

I invited him to breathe into his body and feel the sensation of the emotion. Reluctantly, he indulged my suggestion. He breathed deeply in. On the out breath, he began to feel the emotion in his body as energy and sensations. I guided him to continue to breath through the lower body, melt into the body and observe the emotion running through him as energy. As he connected deeply within, his body relaxed and responded. After a few minutes I noticed his field had shifted and light, brilliant energy floated through him. I asked him what he observed now. He said, "I am full and light. Maybe emotions don't have to decide how I feel about myself!"

DEEPENING THE WORK

When a client is ready, we can work at deeper and deeper levels of transformation. To deepen thoughts:

- link them to false images/beliefs
- link them to body sensations/negative energy patterns

To deepen false images and beliefs:

- Find the consciousness/thoughts that keep them from shifting
- Find the negative intention(s) that keep them in place
- Use the positive alternative
- Discover a paradigm shift

To deepen emotions/feelings:

- Find where they are held in the body
- Find the youngest time the client remembers having them
- Find the negative pattern in their life that supports them
- Find the paradigm shift that is needed to transform them

To deepen out of public personality:

- notice the qualities of the mask for the client
- notice how the public personality serves the client
- notice what is needed to let it go
- invite the higher vibration in of what is needed
- in the client's own space and time, allow it to release

WORDS IN THE FIELD

This is one of my favorite dialogue interventions because of its effectiveness and because it bridges the gap between the mind and energy/body. One method involves **sensing the effects of the client's words on the energy field and then using that information to consciously invite key words to deepen into the field.**

SPEAKING OUR HIDDEN TRUTH

Jean felt guilty because her marriage was failing. On the table, I asked her to use key words to describe how she felt. I asked her to own her hidden feelings and then together, as she spoke the words, we would work to energetically release the pain. I placed my hands on her body, focusing on key areas in resistance.

We worked together to help her acknowledge (but not over-identify) with the feelings behind the words. She began to make peace with the part of her she had so desperately wanted to ignore. "My marriage is falling apart," she said. Her cells resonated with the words and the truth behind them.

As we worked, she discovered what was real about those words and what was based on past Core Distortions. She moved toward healing, consciousness raising and choice about her life and no longer felt stuck in reaction and cover up.

Another method is when the Me-B guide reads the energy field to locate key words. The guide then asks the client to repeat the words with the intention of using the words to shift the client's field. This process is equally effective on or off the table. Usually when this is done off the table, it is done during physical movement or while processing anger.

POWER IN TRUTH

Angelica doesn't have anger. She feels her boyfriend doesn't respect her and give her the acknowledgement she deserves but she isn't angry or upset about it. She is spiritual and she meditates and does yoga. She also holds the Excel character structure strongly. She looks perfect and acts perfect. I suggest that maybe there is something more going on that she might not be aware of and ask her if she wants to explore the issue more deeply.

I give her something to hit. I suggest she try saying: "I hate you!" or saying, "I hate how you treat me," while hitting a bag in my office.

As she stands up in front of the bag, tears start streaming down her cheeks. She says, "I don't understand why I am crying right now." This is a typical response because the power of speaking the truth reveals the shadow.

Depending upon the client, this may be enough for one session, especially for an Excel client that is used to containing their emotions. Leaving clients more open but not collapsed into the energy is paramount.

NOTICE THE COMPUTER PROGRAM

Ask your client to feel into their body, energy system and/or thoughts and look at what feels like it has been programmed within them and what is authentic Core Being energy. Help them shift the program by helping them shift the programming in their body, energy system and mind. Some common programs are listed below.

- Pleasing others to get love.
- Fear of being assertive.
- If you tell the truth it will harm someone.
- It is not ok to let someone be mad at you.
- If someone doesn't like you, then you have done something wrong.
- If you are successful, you will be attacked.
- Don't let anyone think you made a mistake.
- If you have money, you are a success.
- To survive, you must be perfect and not rock the boat.
- If I am myself, I will not fit in.
- I will be alienated if I don't pretend to be something else.

TAKE OUT THE TRASH

Just as our house collects dust, our energy system collects energetic trash. Sometimes it is our own trash and sometimes it is trash we have picked up from someone else. We can also "volunteer" to help heal the pain of the Earth and take out its trash. Once I was processing deep grief and I knew it wasn't my own. It moved from the Earth upward, was transformed in my belly area and then it moved back into the Earth. My supervisor and I watched amazed as I played conduit for transformation to help heal our Earth. Since then, I have seen others do the same.

We can assist ourselves and clients to identify when – for whatever reason — a session on "Taking out the Energetic Trash" is needed. Working cognitively on taking out the trash is usually counter-productive. All that is generally needed at the mind level is to label it trash.

This can be done either on or off the table:

1. The Me-B guide and/or the client can identify where (energetically) the trash is being held, then
2. have the client feel the sensations of it, and
3. use any or all senses (visualization, taste, smell, intuition) to assist the trash in leaving the body.

Often the energy runs downward and out the bottoms of the feet/root chakra. Sometimes it will come out the back and the front of our body at the same time like steam comes off hot cement. Track, support its flow and release it. If it does not release, it may not be ready to release or there may be a negative intention preventing the flow outward. Be gentle and patient. I find most clients easily release the build up once they can name it as trash.

SHIFTING CORE DISTORTIONS BY BRINGING IN THE HIGHER VIBRATION, CLIENT INTERACTION

Begin by assessing where in the body or energy system the distortion is held. Assess what you think is held there. Pick up as much information as possible—such as images, beliefs, colors, flows, energetics, emotions, and consciousness.

Then guide the client to pick up an emotion, image or belief. If they pick up nothing, practice sharing information you received. Explore what the positive alternative could be and help the client bring in a higher vibration/consciousness. It is most effective if they can do this in all three systems at the same time: cognitively in the mind, sensations in the body as well as energetically using as many of the six senses as possible (visual, hearing, taste, smell, sensations, intuition).

HVC SHIFTS CORE DISTORTIONS

Joan noticed deep tension in her right shoulder. I led her to place her mind into the area of tension and pick up any information she could about it. Because we have worked together, she was familiar with this process and immediately felt her father. She explained that he would only loan her money if she signed his contract that depicted all of the mistakes she ever made with money.

With guidance, she realized the deep shame she felt by needing the money and by having all her mistakes thrown at her by her dad's written contact. The emotion was shame and the belief was that she would never be able to be financially successful. I helped her bring in the higher vibration of confidence in her ability to be a financial success. The pain in her shoulder became lightness and flows. She affirmed herself cognitively, energetically and with sensations in the body.

I IMAGINE

The "I imagine…" dialogue allows us to suggest what we think is going on in a very gentle way and possibly not activate the client's ego.

BREATHING ENERGY OUT—OVER/UNDERCHARGE

Energy can either be over- or undercharged. Often the back chakras and other areas of the body become congested from overuse. Too many of us push our way through life.

Invite a client to breathe out the back, or any place where the energy is overcharged. We and our clients can use our breath and/or the Me-B guide can use their hands to lessen the charge. The energy will rise off, like steam off hot cement.

If an area is undercharged a client might be in emotional collapse or a weakened state. Using intention, awareness and/or table work will help us connect to the specific area and increase the charge. Targeted physical exercises and/or movements also help with shifting both under- and overcharged areas of the energy field/body. Many times suppressed anger is the cause.

UNHOOKING THE ENERGY

A client or guide can get too focused on trying to make an area shift. Checking in on a regular basis and unhooking your 6th Chakra (or any chakra such as our back Chakras) from the stuck energy is helpful. If we have an "agenda" that the energy transform, we accidentally distort the energy. Unhooking from it will allow deeper true connection and stronger higher vibrational energy to flow.

ABSENT PERSON

I often have a client who needs support with a husband or boyfriend. Common questions are: should I stay married, is he cheating on me, does he love me, should I continue the relationship, and am I making the same mistake with this one…?

Being able to tune into the field of someone who is not currently in the room can be very useful. Even energetically calling the person into the room can help the client gain enough information to know how to shift their internal triggers in the matter. Usually when we mention the person's name, the room will fill with their energy and it can become easier to assess them. The two techniques I use to assess someone who is absent are:

- Using a chair or table and calling in the person's energy.
- Using intention to tune into them and see them on my mind screen.

Once the energy is present, there are many way we can work with it. We can use gestalt-like, body-centered, and role-playing techniques. Be creative and follow the flow of energy to see what evolves.

FINDING THE WORK

Once we have a good working relationship with a client, sessions begin to sequence toward isolating the work. Develop the ability to track the energy quickly to pinpoint what work is waiting to be revealed. We can serve as a detective to help isolate the work, NOT as a director of an agenda for the work. As the client sits down, and we begin the formalities of "meet and greet," we can energetically assess what is here now. Tips on this process include:

- Assess the client's field
- Check guidance
- Establish deep contact with client. (The deeper the contact, the more information we receive.)
- Be curious and open
- Notice any tension or difficult emotions
- Look for an opening to deepen the dialogue
- Inquire about any unique or repetitive body movements or choices of speech

Sara came in to the office and her energy field filled with bright throat chakra blue. Then the fifth level of the field began to quiver. This information, combined with guidance, led me to wonder if communication issues dealing with trust might be important to investigate.

She began talking about what was happening in her life. After listening to her, I decided to ask if she trusted her ability to speak her truth. She immediately began crying and the work was before us.

SUMMARY DIALOGUE

Summary dialogue is when we summarize what we think the client says and then get confirmation or clarification. This method helps mirror the client back to himself and helps establish trust and contact. As we do this, watch how the field reacts to our summary to find clues about hidden emotions and shadow material.

USE TRANSFERENCE

Use negative/positive transference and counter transference as a dialogue intervention. This can be one of the more difficult dialogue techniques, yet the healing results are great.

For instance, we can respond to the client's energetic defenses when we notice they are either putting us on a pedestal or projecting negatively upon us. We might say, "Did it feel like mom when I said/did that?" or "Who do I remind you of?"

When the client is experiencing positive transference, we can use the "good enough mom" energy to help them heal this issue before it changes and we become no longer perfect. This too can be used for their benefit.

NONSENSE TALK TO ELICIT EMOTION

If a client is afraid or embarrassed to tell us something, they can tell us energetically while they "make-up" a pretend foreign language. Saying nonsense words to elicit an emotional response from the shadow can be a gentle and private method for our client to share deep information. First ask them to connect to their 2nd and 4th levels of the field so they are more connected to their emotions. Then they begin talking and expressing sounds/ words/ pretend words. Whatever sounds emerge, let them be expressions of the deeper hidden emotions and feelings. Me-B Guides can practice this technique themselves, if they ever feel stuck and too intellectual about what might be happening below the surface. It is surprising what comes out and how effective this technique is at revealing the truth.

ENERGY TRACKING DIALOGUE

Dialoging around what you see/sense energetically with a client is a very effective. The client can share their experience and/or the Me-B Guide can share their experience.

ENERGY REVEALS ALL

I was having an equine psychotherapy session with a client and I noticed her energy felt like it was in a box. I mirrored that back to her and she began to cry. At first she didn't know why. Then she remembered her father's criticism every time she tried to expand and flow with her light.

The box comment reminded her of how painful it is for her to keep her light dimmed. The horses then helped her open and expand her light.

USING WHAT WENT WRONG

During an intervention, the Me-B guide may sometimes send a client's field into defense or somehow trigger it. Being aware of when that happens and simply saying any of the following comments can help:

- "I noticed that triggered your field."
- "Did what I said bother you?"
- "Last session, I wondered if it was too much for you when I _____."
- "Should I move my hands?"
- "Are you comfortable?"
- "I could have been more supportive."
- "That probably was not the best direction to take."
- "You are important to me."
- "What do you need right now?"

SYMPATHY DIALOGUE

Limiting the amount of advice we give a client can be hard but it is as important as being able to sympathize with a client. Dialogue we can use to be supportive follows. As always, after we make a dialogue intervention, track the field to see what effect it had on the client to say:

- "I hear what you are saying."
- "I understand. It must have been difficult."
- "I totally support you."
- "Ouch, that must have hurt."
- "I don't believe he said that."
- "It sounds difficult."
- "That was not OK!"

TELL ME MORE—AND ONLY DECLARATIVES

Too often therapists get stuck asking only questions. Practice a session stating only declaratives or just support the rhythm of the session by saying, for instance, "tell me more." Check to make sure your field is out of defense, you are in your Core Being and are deepening contact with the client.

"IF YOU WERE . . . THEN WHAT?"

We all find times where we see only part of our story. The phrase, "if you were __, then what?" can invite the client to look deeper.

> Jim always got nervous at his ballroom dancing class and he got nervous around girls. I asked him why? He said he didn't know why. So I said, "If you get nervous, then what?" He said, "I am afraid of making a mistake." I said, "If you make a mistake, then what?" "I am not perfect," he said. "So, if you are not perfect, then what," I added. "Then I am bad!" he declared.
>
> After his declaration, we then could look at where he felt the negative energy in his body/field and the origins in his mind and work to transform it.

SUBCONSCIOUS DIALOGUE

Look for the subconscious dialogue in the body, energy system or words that are unspoken. Then use the information you pick up from their energy field as a dialogue intervention with the client. See if you can help the client experience his/her own subconscious. For instance, Jack was on the table and he was energetically merging with his parents even though he hadn't lived at home for over a decade. I asked him to release his parents and feel completely separated from them at the cellular level.

As he imagined their energy leaving, sadness filled his field. It was as if a part of his child consciousness was waiting for the "good enough adult" to come to his aide. So I said, "I am so sorry the adults in your life never supported you. I am so sorry no one is going to come to your rescue." Tears flowed as I spoke the truth held within him. He released this hidden need, and worked to love and support himself.

ENERGETIC THERAPEUTIC RESPONSES TO 5 PERSONALITY TYPES

1. **SPIRITUAL** (schizoid): In response to the escape and withdrawal defense, resonate to their higher vibration so our field touches their field. Then, using intention, slowly bring our vibration back down to earth and them with us. Next, work with their nervous system so they balance and feel safe. The Neurological Upgrade and the Safety Net Interventions are helpful. In addition, support them with many of the other positive resourcing techniques taught, such as the BCS to help them reprogram safety, trust and learn to be present in their body. It is vital they learn how to feel sensations, flows of energy in their body and not just connect to the intellect. Feeling sensations of HVC must become a tangible, kinesthetic experience for the negative programming and terror to be overcome.

2. **COMPASSIONATE** (oral): Don't let them hook into us energetically. Turning to the side or placing our hands over our third chakra can help. Begin by filling ourselves up with essence. Then, fill them up from our overflow. This process can happen for many sessions until eventually, we will have to wean them from us so they can learn how to fill themselves. When we make this transition and stop filling them up, they usually become very angry and lash out. The anger can then be used as the charge that helps them fill themselves up. In fact, this stage of them being angry is pivotal to them learning how to fill themselves. This helps their psyche

differentiate and thus can help them discover who they are separate from another. Loneliness can become over- whelming at this stage so helping them connect to their Core Being is important.

3. **LEADER** (psychopath): Trust and safety is key. Vibrate our field at Auric levels 1 and 5 and bring this energy into the room to help them relax and feel more comfortable. Go slow and let the relationship develop. Their aggressive behavior brings aggression back to them at every turn. They want to prove we are wrong so they can feel correct. It is vital that we don't return aggression with aggression. We can fill the lower part of our energy field with green energy when they attack us. Remember, the attack is a mask and underneath it is their terror. So, we must ground deep into the earth. In arguments, vibrations tend to escalate. Let them feel heard and see them for their true self, and not their anger. If this is a difficult Character Structure for us, then support ourselves with deep work so we keep healing our own defenses and trauma that is often triggered. Ultimately, we need to feel safe and trust ourselves at a very deep level so we don't collapse, or attack back. Write down our defense that might be triggered when manipulated, controlled or attacked. Then do a Core Distortion intervention to support our healing.

4. **HEART-CENTERED** (masochist): A compassionate type person will take in all our suggestions; they will just always need more. However, Heart-Centered Types will reject everything we suggest. It is like they are trapped in a box. They can't get out without our help, yet they can't open to receive help. In other words, they can't heal without us but all of our suggestions will be wrong. There is push-pull energy about them and they can make us feel like we are controlling them. They need a lot of space and they need to claim and express who they are so they feel free and independent. Even though they will try to get us to invade them, we must keep good boundaries. Don't merge and don't let them merge with us or hook into our third chakra. Bring the frequency of our field to their field's frequency and then slowly move our field back until it touches only the edge of theirs. The goal is to help them feel their essence and to be complete yet separate from us. They must be- come their own authority and not need us. They can learn to feel themselves without us and they can learn to release their anger and transform it into power.

5. **EXCEL** (rigid): They need to learn how to feel their own Core Being. Because their field has so much structure, they are disconnected from their Core Being and their emotions. They can move out of the perfect movie of their life and into the truth in this world. Ultimately, help them reach the deeper truth of their Core Being. Resonate our Core Being and mirror their Core Being back to them so they can see it and experience it. Be the positive example they can follow, if they choose.

Me-B TRANSFORMATION TOUCH ENERGY CLEARING AND CHARGING SEQUENCE

Follow this basic energy sequence to clear and balance a client's energy field. This can be done while they stand or lie on a massage table. Place our hands following the format outlined and allow energy to run multi-dimensionally through us and out our hands into the client. Begin by doing the Core Being Meditation on your- self to prepare your field. Resonate at your Core Being (to the extent possible) front, back; top, bottom; left, right of your whole physical body. Resonate Core Being everywhere: in your organs, tissues, cells, bones, bone marrow and outer energy egg.

Begin by connecting to the client with your hands (resonating at Core Being) and your divine Core Being mind deeply within the client's body. Align for your Core Being to resonate and awaken/meet their Core Being frequency and allow the energy to expand. Our Core Being, meets their Core Being. It is divine presence of source that creates the energetic charge! Presence and deep connection is what expands the field - coupled with deep alignment to surrender to the highest good to move through you.

a. Dominant hand on bottom of the foot nearest you; non-dominant hand on knee. Energetically connect deeply with Core Being to Core Being. Feel the love and let the energy flow.

b. Dominant hand on bottom of the foot farthest from you; non-dominant hand on knee. Energetically connect deeply with Core Being to Core Being. Feel the love and let the energy flow.

c. Dominant hand on knee and non-dominant hand on hip. Energetically connect deeply with Core Being to Core Being. Feel the love and let the energy flow.

d. Dominant hand on knee farthest from you; non-dominant hand on hip. Energetically connect deeply with Core Being to Core Being. Feel the love and let the energy flow.

e. Dominant hand on 2nd chakra; non-dominant hand on 3rd chakra. Energetically connect deeply with love and let the energy flow. Energetically connect deeply with Core Being to Core Being. Feel the love and let the energy flow.

f. Dominant hand on 3rd chakra; non-dominant hand on 4th chakra. Energetically connect deeply with Core Being to Core Being. Feel the love and let the energy flow.

g. Dominant hand on 4th chakra; non-dominant hand on 5th chakra. Energetically connect deeply with Core Being to Core Being. Feel the love and let the energy flow.

h. One hand on each shoulder as we stand at the head of the client. Energetically connect deeply with Core Being to Core Being. Feel the love and let the energy flow.

i. Continue with the next phase of the Intervention (Core Distortion, multi-dimensional, centered oneness or whatever other intervention is needed....)

CENTERED ONENESS

This is an excellent positive resource intervention. It connects a person to the Centered Oneness of all dimensions. The higher self sometimes even reincarnates at deeper levels through this technique. It can be done both through touch and non-touch techniques. If non-touch, the client guides the energy into his or herself with the thumb and index fingers resting on opposite sides of his/her own bellybutton.

- **Step one:** using intention, access the cord to the Centered Oneness of all at the bellybutton. Your thumb and index fingers rest on opposite sides of the bellybutton.

- **Step two:** using intention, presence, deep contact with the Centered Oneness — invite the client to receive the Centered Oneness of all through the belly button in terms of sensations in the body. Allow the energy to first fill the whole belly. It will then expand to fill both up and down the body.

Once the flow subsides, slowly disconnect and let the client continue doing this without our help. (This is a good preparation for the Multi-Dimensional Fabric Alignment Healing or before the Star Child Healing.)

MULTI-DIMENSIONAL FABRIC ALIGNMENT HEALING

The depth of this healing is dependent upon (1) to what extent the Me-B Guide can connect to these dimensions, and (2) to what extent the client can open to receive that connection. Me-B Guides begin by first connecting to themselves and then outwardly expanding their field multi-dimensionally. He/ She returns to the place of expanded oneness with the world and then expands further to encompass worlds/planets and universes. Feel, see, imagine and experience it!

Now imagine rainbow ribbons (pastels, primary colors, opal essence, gold, silver) flowing through that oneness. The ribbon-like energy shines. It is strong and about six inches wide. Let the colors come in and flow from head to foot down the client's body: (1) head, torso to perineum, then (2) arm/leg on the left side of the body, and (3) arm/leg on the right side of the body — letting the ribbons flow on their own.

Watch to see which color comes next. If no color comes, imagine rose red flowing. Then, wait to see if another color flows. If it doesn't, then move through the pastel colors one at a time, pausing between in case the next color wants an opportunity to come without us directing it.

Feel the universes and worlds flowing and connected. Imagine the consciousness they bring. Let our consciousness resonate at that level. Breathe, bask, breathe. Let your own imagination and creativity ignite the process.

Then put your mind/awareness into the client's field. One hand is placed by her hip, closest to us. The other hand is resting on her arm closest to us. Allow this vibration to resonate from the anchor in our field to our client's. It can also anchor and resonate from the field in the room directly into the client.

Using your mind, hands, and whole field, deepen your connection to the client. Observe where the energy is transmitted from you to the client.

Move hands and mind/awareness to areas where the transmission is least. Then gently transmit more deeply. Continue moving hands/awareness to areas of least transmission until the energy is balanced equally throughout the client's field. Usually it takes two or three movements before the field becomes saturated and won't receive a deeper shift (about 15-20 minutes).

STAR CHILD HEALING

After the Multi-Dimensional Fabric Alignment preparation, the field tends to be very open to receive this healing.

We expand our field to connect to the stars. The energy that comes in looks like computer chips made of stardust. It contains the knowledge the client needs to fulfill their life task. If a client has never had or has had only a few incarnations on other planets and stars, only a few chips may enter. If they have had many, we may sense the whole belly cavity fill with the knowledge of the stars!

COMPLETING THE MULTIDIMENTIONAL HEALING

We sense the client's field has shifted as much as it will, place one hand on the hip and one hand on the client's arm nearest us. Using breath and awareness, raise our vibration to the Universal Fabric and allow the celestial blanket to descend and gently anchor in as it naturally covers the client's body. Take time to anchor it in! Carefully place your hands on hips, waist, chest, shoulder and anywhere else it needs help anchoring in. Let it vibrate and raise the vibration of the client. I recommend the client remain on the table 3-5 minutes once the process has finished so it can fully integrate.

HELP CLIENTS ASSESS, SHIFT AND TRACK THEMSELVES

Ultimately, the cornerstone of Me-B Transformation is self-empowerment. As clients learn to track themselves and shift to a more aligned place in all three systems, they become more empowered. This segment is organized according to client skill levels: beginning, intermediate and advanced tracking techniques.

Beginning Skills include regulation of the chakras, running colors through the field, grounding the energy into the earth, and basic Chi Kung Techniques. (Stages 1 and 2 of Me-B Transformation)

Intermediate Skills include being able to self-assess energetically and resonate the energy in all dimensions (Auric, Manifest Energy Intention Line, Multi-Dimensional Fabric, and Core Being). Individuals at this level can align the Central Channel so it is not too far forward (emotions) or to far backward (will); balance their outer energy egg; feel emotions as energy; and increase or decrease the structure in their field. They also can anchor into Core Being (Stage 3 and 4 of Me-B Transformation).

Advanced Skills include being able to transform LVC into HVC of Core Being, Manifest Energy Intention Line, Multi-Dimensional Fabric Alignment. Clients can find where the emotion/energy is distorted in the body and feel the sensation of the energy in the body. They can work emotional issues in two or more systems at the same time. For instance, they can notice and shift thoughts in the mind related to sensations and energy in the body.

Advanced clients understand their energetic defenses and can shift them. They also can track their intentionality, Image/Belief, Ego, Public Personality and Core Distortion, Separated Self, Core Being, Rhythm of the Flow of Energy, Transference/Counter Transference, and Boundaries. They are Stage 4 and above of Me-B Trans- formation and can move through the 3 Rings of Healing and follow the 5 Steps:

1. Self-Awareness (through deep connection within).
2. Detachment
3. Naming then owning the Core Distortion/Defense/Trigger.
4. Insight—linking the trigger to the past so the mind can understand why we have been triggered.
5. Transformation—shifting the energy and return to Core Being by bringing the energy of our Enlightened Observer (HVC) into the dense LVC of the Programmed Personality.

COMMON EMOTIONAL ISSUES TO TRANSFORM

COLLAPSE/VICTIM CONSCIOUSNESS: This presents during the first 3 Stages of Me-B Transformation. Jerry came in again. Collapsed and slumped in the chair, again. He hated his job, had no girl friend and was feeling over-whelmed. This can be a common scenario.

Solution: Shifting body position. Simply by inviting clients to change their body position, it can

351

change their field. Next explore and identify what is the specific emotion creating the collapse and where is it held in his body. Then Bring in the HVC alternative. Also explore breaks in his Manifest Energy Intention Line. He may have hidden negative intentions to have someone else save him- such as the right job or the right partner.

OVER-IDENTIFICATION OF EMOTION: What tends to come next is the client will over-identify with the emotion. They will believe they are the emotion instead of the emotion being just energy running through them.

Solution: Have them use the Enlightened Observer so they can let go and detach from the emotion. They can also connect to the Manifest Energy Intention Line to make this easier. They can also release the energy of the emotion and let it run through them into the earth or let it dissipate like steam, into the air. Next, the Centered Oneness Intervention and other positive resourcing techniques can be used to help them fill themselves up and reconnect to Core Being.

I AM EMPTY/I AM ALONE: Often over-identification and collapse is related to the energy of "I feel empty" and "I am alone." Hopelessness can become pervasive when this happens. Those of us who are on a spiritual journey can face this during *the death of the ego transformation process* we face during Stages 5, 6 and 7 of Me-B Transformation. The energy of feeling empty and alone may present at different times yet they are interconnected. The empty feeling connotes "lack" and feelings of not being enough. It is the energy of a lost soul. It is very painful and it may be challenging for the Me-B guide to help a client transform.

Solution: Healing emptiness and the "alone" energy entails finding one's self at a deep level. It is the journey to define who we are in the world based on the internal resource of our Core Being. Many of us know who we are by the roles we play in our family, community, and church— externally. Our career often defines who we are as well. I have had many clients come in after a job loss and feel alone, empty and deeply question who they are now.

This place of emptiness and aloneness is an exciting time for spiritual awakening. If we or our client is able to see it as an opportunity and not a curse, much of the work is done. Positive resourcing techniques, re-orienting to internal self-knowledge is the key. Ideally, we can claim the spiritual "emptiness" Buddhists discuss that feels vast and whole — a complete feeling that promotes happiness and feelings of contentment. This is the HVC we can use to replace the LVC.

THE VOID/ DEATH AND REBIRTH: I strongly recommend reading the book by A.H. Almaas entitled *THE VOID*. It outlines the perils and gifts of this energetic dimension. The void can be defined as the empty space between the death of our old ego and the re-birth of our new sense of self. It can feel overwhelming and terrifying. This is because we don't know who we are anymore. Who we were no longer fits us and we feel lost, alone and confused. Sometimes we are triggered into this place because we lost a job, a partner, or because we have done deep personal growth work. Pema Chodron wrote the book *Falling Apart* to help people make sense of this rite of passage. The new sense of self that is eventually reborn once we come through the void is more aligned and anchored into our Core Being. But when we are in the thick of it, it can metaphorically feel like we are climbing Mt. Everest without oxygen. Just as a snake must shed its skin so it can grow, we must shed our old ego identification so we can know our Core Being. Entering into the void is painful, but necessary for us to claim our true self here on earth.

> **Solution**: It is important to *help ourselves or our clients learn to feel safe and trust that something great is happening*, even though it is difficult and painful. Since we will go through this process more than once in our life, we can remember our past successes so we can have faith that we will come out the other side of this as well. If it is our client's first time in the void, we might want to schedule sessions with them more often and do much positive resourcing work. Helping them unravel the old self-identification is important. They can actually feel the energy and sensation of their old self no longer belonging to them. Once this happens, it is much easier for them to let go. Eventually, help them feel the energy and sensation of who they are choosing to become. (See next Intervention.)

I CHOSE WHO I AM: Whenever we let go of our old ego identification, we need to chose who we want to become. If not, we can lose ourselves. Depression and anxiety can take over.

So, it is important we learn how to cultivate the energy of our Core Being, bring its HVC deep into our Me-B System and evolve into a new, more enlightened state. As I write this book and it gets closer to being published, I keep allowing my old ego-identification to leave and open to discover who I might become. For me, I hope to become a clear vessel HVC can move through so my ego and its programmed personality dissolve and disappear for longer periods throughout the day. This is a tall order but inch-by-inch I hope to make my way closer to this ideal.

> **Solution:** This Intervention can be done in a chair or on the table. Ask clients to (1) connect into their Core Being and (2) to the extent possible, resonate its HVC throughout the body and (3) feel it as a positive sensation in the cells. (Review the Core Being expansion meditation to help guide them.) Then, once they can experience it in at least 25 percent of their body, ask them to receive information about who they are becoming and who they want to become. Create a list of at least four aspects of their new sense of self that closely reflects their Core Being. Then ask them to practice feeling the energy and consciousness of it in their Me-B system.

> Over time, our new sense of self becomes closer to the HVC of Core Being. We may never reach the pure enlightenment of Core Being, but with clear intention, we move closer. And what a ride it becomes! So much joy and adventure can be found. As we move higher in the Me-B Stages, the pain can be transformed more quickly and with more skill so the lows in life don't keep us down as long. We remember to move through the 3 Rings of Healing, Shape Shift our emotions, and return back to Core Being.

IF NO ONE EVER AFFIRMED ME, HOW DO I AFFIRM MYSELF? Clients often say, "how do I affirm myself if no one has ever affirmed me?" It is a great question to ask, yet difficult to answer. As clients strengthen their Enlightened Observer and learn to resonate to their Core Being, everything becomes possible.

> **Solution:** Clients can use a spiritual source to help. For instance, the positive resourcing techniques in this chapter and the previous chapter are designed to help clients connect to a

source outside of them and receive HVC. With a strong enough positive intention, they will definitely succeed. Sometimes negative intention gets in the way of success. Looking at the emotional issues around the negative intention speeds the process along. Also, mastering the 3 Skills of Adult Consciousness and learning to send love to our child consciousness brings us much closer to success.

I AM MY EMOTIONAL PAIN: This one was discussed earlier under the Collapse section. It is mentioned again as a reminder of the importance of learning that we are not our emotional pain.

> **Solution:** Detachment from the pain and positive resource.

IDEALIZED SELF IMAGE DESTROYED OR DEFENDED: All of us have an idealized self-image that can be released. The release of this idealized image enables us to destroy a level of our programmed personality that does not serve us.

> **Solution:** The Idealized Self is propped up by our Ego. We can learn to watch our ego and deepen into Core Being. (See the *Where is Waldo* exercise on the ego.) If we know we are enough, even when we totally screw up, there is no need for the idealized self. As the Me-B Guide, we may need to go slow. Let the client set the pace unless it looks like we are avoiding the "elephant in the room." Journaling about the idealized self can help bring it to the forefront of our consciousness. Acceptance of our imperfections and humanness relax our defenses so the idealized self can dissolve.

NEGATIVE EGO—Where is Waldo: There is a children's book called "Where is Waldo?" Children look at a complex picture that has many images and they have to find a picture of Waldo. Clients need to be able to recognize when their negative ego is in control and then learn how to move out of its programmed personality and back to Core Being.

> **Solution:** Yes, clients will often come into a session wearing their negative ego on their sleeve. Helping them see it as a sleeve and notice that it is not all of who they are helps them detach enough to find their positive ego and Core Being. Energetically the ego is held in the 3rd Chakra. The Centered Oneness Intervention is great and releasing the negative ego and reconnecting us to Core Being.

SURRENDER: "Just let go and surrender!" This can be a difficult challenge and helping a client with this is an advanced skill.

> **Solution:** If someone is not surrendering, then chances are their ego has been activated and they are in defense. Help them create trust and safety so they can let go. The Excel and Spiritual character structures can have the most difficulty with this. It is a definite skill and if our client is not deeply connected to their body and cannot feel sensations of energy then it is harder. Teach them how to feel sensations and then to melt into the sensations. Begin with them even feeling the touch of the table or their cloths on their skin. *Make sure they focus on what they can feel and not what they can't feel.* Where awareness goes, energy flows. If they focus on what they can do and what they can feel, then invite them to let that expand.

I AM NOT ENOUGH: This is a core belief most of us hold and almost every client will encounter at some point in their Me-B Transformation work. Know how to recognize when it comes up and how that particular client can be supported with positive resource techniques so they can anchor into their Core Being.

> **Solution:** Anchor into Core Being. From Core Being, we all are enough so that even in difficult times we don't lose connection with who we really are.

INTEGRATION: It is important to really allow time for our client to take in and integrate one level of growth before their energetic Container can be strong enough to launch into the next level of work.

> **Solution:** Integration must be done in all three Me-B systems. It is best if clients feel the "new growth" as somatic sensations in the body and then link it to a positive image in their mind. The Me-B Technique of "Which System Holds the Truth" can help with this.

SELF -SABOTAGE: Everyone has a shadow, so they also have a saboteur. If a person does deep enough work, they will ultimately confront their saboteur.

> **Solution:** The saboteur Is an archetype, and working with ancestral and archetypical energies can help clients shift the impact of the saboteur. Techniques are outlined in the next few chapters on this topic. We can also help clients feel the energy of their particular flavor of saboteur so they can know it very well and thus confront it at the deepest level. Working with the saboteur is working with our deep shadow. We can help clients explore their shadow and yet not be defined by it.

HITTING A WALL/BEING STUCK: In the Rhythm of the Flow of Energy, there is expansions and contraction in the rhythm. After a contraction, yet before the next expansion, it can feel like we are stuck or hitting a wall.

> **Solution:** Exploring negative intention, separated-self, and shadow work is crucial. Also, help our clients investigate why a part of them might think it is better to stay stuck. Have them explore the following questions:
>
> - How are they better served by staying where they are?
> - What does the metaphorical wall look like and what does it represent?
> - What positive aspects of their soul or Core Being need to return in them in order to feel safe and trust they can move forward?
> - What are the shadow aspects of the "stuckness?"

AUTHORITY ISSUES: We all have them. Depending upon our client's personality type, they may want to control others and become the authority over them, or they may enjoy being controlled by others so they never have to stand up and take charge. Ultimately, authority issues are about developing our own internal authority so we don't rely on someone else to define who we are.

> **Solution:** Help our clients find themselves at the deepest level so they know who they are even when someone else is defining them in a negative manner.

To do this, explore family dynamics. How did mom and dad act as positive or negative authority figures and what negative or positive images and beliefs grew out of this programming? Also, they can investigate their relationship to the "heavenly" father and mother. Sometimes authority issues develop into being angry with god. This issue often comes up again and again, yet at deeper levels. Help clients learn how to anchor into Core Being, even when they are attacked.

NEGATIVE INTENTION: Any time Me-B Guides feel they are doing more work than the client, the client may be in negative intention. In terms of the Rhythm of the Flow of energy, this tends to happen right before an expansion begins or during an unhealthy contraction.

Solution: Teach the client about negative intention and help them investigate how it subconsciously supports them. Oftentimes negative transference happens at this point. Explore this possibility with the client.

ROOT OF ADDICTIONS: The roots of most addictions are the feelings of wanting to be saved and feeling not enough.

Solution: If you are not a trained addiction counselor, make sure clients are getting additional professional support. The client may also need to join a support group such as AA or NA to compliment the work we are doing with them. At some point, an Me-B guide can help the client find and then transform the place of "no hope." They need to give up hope of ever being saved or rescued by another. They need to find enough internal strength. Eventually, we need to help clients know that even we can't save them. Doing developmental work (especially around young wounding and birthing issues) is extremely productive. I have seen miracles, yet it usually is a long-term therapeutic intervention. Trauma work and positive resourcing are important. As clients are able to feel the sensation of Core Being in their body and anchor into it, they gain the ability to support themselves and heal the addiction.

TO FEEL SATISFIED THROUGH AN INTERNAL SOURCE LETS US FIND TRUE HAPPINESS: Helping a client find this experience in their Me-B systems can be considered the ultimate goal. Core Being can provide this for all of us so that even when darkness visits, we feel whole, joy and bliss.

Solution: Clients can become strong enough to do deep trauma and shadow work. Then, over time, the client will discover his or her internal sources of bliss and joy that are so strong, that even in times of grief and stress, they can feel happy and whole.

PUER, PUELLA ETERNUS: Forever young energy (Peter Pan) can be stubborn to transform. Clients that hold this archetypal energy pattern don't want to grow up and be responsible. They hold negative images about what it means to be an adult. For instance, clients claim that to be an adult means they must give up their happiness, sense of fun and freedom. Ultimately these clients fear they can't provide for themselves and are not powerful. Many Peter Pan types have addiction issues as well.

Solution: Help them explore and change their false images and beliefs about what it means to grow up. Also help them master any feelings of inadequacy and negative beliefs about "not being big enough for the job." Often they feel they can't be successful or they want someone else to take care of them instead of them having the power and strength to create abundance.

Help them connect to the child consciousness waiting for the support of the "good enough adult." As they feel the emotion and pain, also help them feel the comfort of their own "good enough adult" energy entering their cells, comforting their wounded parts. As they master this skill, transformation happens. *Throughout the following years, every time their young wounded parts call out for support, they will need to meet them with the energy and comfort of their "good enough adult."*

It might take 100 more doses throughout their life of this type of self-love. They can program their Intention Line to provide this level of self-care and support every time it is needed. In fact, we all probably need to program into our Intention Line this level of support to our wounded or fragmented parts. This is self-mastery.

HIGH VIBRATIONS: A speech given by Nelson Mandela expresses this issue well. As he explains, it is our light we are most afraid of, not our darkness. Many clients will fight taking in their light.

Solution: Positive Resourcing and saboteur work helps shift this dilemma.

EXISTENTIAL FEAR: Everyone has it if they do deep enough work. If we can meet our existential fear, we do much to heal our shadow and to shift the subconscious and separated self. So much of our saboteur, separated self and shadow is to protect ourselves from feeling this fear. So facing this demon and knowing we can survive and even thrive afterward is an important milestone.

Solution: Table interventions work for this level of the work unless our client tends to collapse or disassociate on the table. Go very slow and combine it with positive resourcing. Make sure we don't over stimulate the nervous system.

CRYING WHEN IT IS ABOUT RECEIVING LOVE: Often when a client finally lets his or her self take in and feel love, instead of feeling happy and good, they cry. This is because they also feel the sadness around the times they didn't get love.

Solution: Explain this to them and over a period of time, the volcano of the past will dissipate and joy will take its place.

REVIEW QUESTIONS

A. Answer the following discussion questions using the Explorer's Mind. Use these questions as an opportunity to investigate your edges, challenges and gifts in the ME-B Approach.
   1. Is contact what creates healing?
   2. What is contact with yourself?
   3. What is contact with another?
   4. What is your definition of personal process and how would you describe this definition from a mind-energy-body perspective?
   5. What is your definition of the purpose of therapy?
   6. How do you personally work your process when you get triggered?
   7. How do you describe your core being in the mind-energy-body systems?

8. When you get triggered out of your center, what is it that gets triggered and how do you come back?
9. What does it mean to be whole, and how do you know when you are whole?
10. How do you resource in life and how do you resource yourself during an Me-B therapy session?
11. Who does the healing?

B. Review the following checklist to self-assess and discover if you are holding back or working hard during an Me-B Session. We all do some of these. Which ones come to the front for you?

— Your breath is forced, shallow or uneven
— You have an agenda
— Thinking too much
— Not in contact with self or client
— You think you know what should happen
— In the past or future
— You are doing more work than your client
— Judgments of client or self
— Energy, Ego, Physiology in Defense
— Needing the client to heal
— Over-identified with session material
— Over-identified with client's need to heal or healing process
— Ego Activated
— Wanting to do a "Good Job"
— Knowing what is "best" for the client
— Not following the Rhythm of Flow of Energy
— Counter transference
— Shadow
— Wanting to please the client
— Not supporting the next flow and Rhythm of the session
— Fear
— Wanting the client to like you
— Your client feels misunderstood or unsupported and they are NOT in transference with you

C. Check your progress in relation to the following energy competencies:

• *Energetic Diagnosis and Assessment.* (What are the core emotional issues and what is happening with the chakras and dimensions? For instance, is Core Being awareness strong, are structured or emotional levels undercharged, overcharged, etc.?)

▪ Me-B Guide Energetic Self-Care, Preparation and Readiness Tools. (What's happening in your field?)
▪ *Client Energetic Awareness and Adjustment Exercises.* (Using High Sense Perception (HSP) to determine if the exercises are working—are they doing it? Where are the clients still blocked? Sensing emotional issues related to block.)

- *Basic Skills of Tracking Self using* High Sense Perception *(HSP).* (During a session, do you know what is happening with your own energy system/related emotional issues)

- *Energetic Relational Dynamics using* High Sense Perception (*HSP).* (How is your energy field positively or negatively influencing your clients? What do you notice?)

- *Basic Skills of Tracking Client's Energy Field using HSP.* (What are the core emotional issues and what is happening with the chakras and dimensions? For instance, is core star awareness strong, are structured or emotional levels undercharged, overcharged, etc.?)

- *Energetic Awareness of Core Distortions/Images and Beliefs Being Reprogrammed or Recycled using HSP.* (What does the field say is happening and what are the deeper emotional issues that are hidden in the subconscious as read in the field?)

- *Did Client's Field Assimilate Intervention.* (How do you tell if it's working in the field or is it only in the mind using HSP)

- *Determine if Client's Story is Consistent with Client's Field—Using HSP.* (Is the client's field saying one thing and their words another?)

- *Energetic Healing Response to Client and Self—Using HSP.* (Do you know what is happening in your field and the client's?)

If a client falls asleep on the table when they are receiving a Me-B positive resourcing session, this is an indicator that they are receiving HVC and it is too strong for them to stay awake during the process. Is this good or bad? Explain.

CHAPTER 20

RE-PATTERN TRAUMA IN THE PAST AND CREATE JOY NOW

Our body houses the truth of who you are, who you are not and who you can someday become. Through the body, trauma heals with the HVC of your Enlightened Observer.

What is Trauma? It might be easier to say what *isn't* trauma. **In Me-B Transformation we define trauma as anything that disconnects us from feeling Core Being as a *thought, belief, sensation and emotion* in our mind and body.**

For instance, just before conception, there is a deep sense of knowing who you are at the level of source. Then, at the point of conception, as you move into the physical body there is a disconnect from Core Being. Then over your lifetime, a biological programming further distances you from Source. Your brain, emotions, limbic system, cells hold the illusion of ego, personality, judgment and pain. As a result, it becomes difficult or impossible to remember who you really are and reconnect to Core Being. As your ego energetically merges with your biological consciousness container, it creates your false sense of self and your negative beliefs.

For a little girl, trauma can be her father yelling at her for eating too much candy or her best friend teasing her and choosing to be friends with someone else. As these smaller actions repeat in similar scenarios over a lifetime, the accumulated affect imprints your brain, our nervous system, ego and sense of self. As a result you subconsciously orient to the world and yourself in a manner so you actually recreate the pains of your past in present-day experiences.

You don't necessarily repeat them exactly but the experiences of your negative past mirror the emotional wounding of the present. For instance, if you have been repeatedly rejected and teased by your friends in the past, these same experiences can continue throughout your lifetime until your sense of self changes and you orient and react differently to the world around you.

In this regard, trauma is also when the pain of your past negatively affects the present. (The middle ring in the 3-Rings of Healing holds trauma.) Trauma fosters negative transference and counter-transference and it creates a subconscious orientation to the world so you repeat your past. Your ego uses it to judge and your separated self feeds off of it so it remains in distortion.

Someone once explained it as there being a big "T" trauma and little "t" trauma. An example of big "T" trauma is rape or a severe car accident. A little "t" trauma is something less severe that still negatively affects your sense of self and creates or supports your negative belief systems and disconnects you from who you really are.

For instance, little "t" trauma is the accumulated affects of a negative repeated action, habituation of animosity and judgment toward ourselves or of others toward us. An example of this is the boy at school who repeatedly doesn't fit into any peer group; over time, as this continues throughout his childhood, it creates a traumatic orientation to social settings.

Although mental health professionals use a diagnosis of Post Traumatic Stress Disorder (PTSD) to label someone clinically traumatized, I believe all of us can benefit from understanding more about the physiological and psychological implications of trauma programming and how to re-pattern its unhelpful influence upon us. The brain has neuroplasticity and thus has great ability to change and heal. But we first must be aware of our negative programming. Hopefully this chapter offers an important step to identify and reorganize trauma within our Me-B System.

AWARENESS OF SECONDARY TRAUMA

There is also **Secondary Trauma.** This happens when we hear about and are deeply affected by another's trauma. For instance, during the 9/11 attack many of us watched over and over again the falling of the twin towers and some of us received secondary trauma from that episode. As a Me-B Guide, it is vital that we learn to protect our self from Secondary Trauma. Learn how to release any holding in our cells, body and energy system so we do not take on our client's pain.

Sometimes we take on secondary trauma when we empathize with another. This is when our energy field becomes more porous and merges with the LVC of a client. The unstructured levels of the Auric Field become overwhelmed and the structured levels can lose coherency. The heart chakra expands in front, and sometimes it breaks, or we push energy out of the heart chakra and send it to the client. Pushing energy out of a chakra often damages it so that LVC is more able to enter.

The most common cause of secondary trauma is when the Me-B Guide's trauma resonates to the same vibrational frequency as the client's trauma. In this case, the Me-B Guide's trauma is being activated and brought to the surface simply by being in the presence of comparable trauma. (Just as one tuning fork can set off other tuning forks in the same room, being around similar trauma can activate our trauma.)

The good news is it is being brought to the surface of consciousness, so the Me-B Guide can heal it. The challenging news is that the Me-B Guide must contain the trauma until he or she is ready to process and transform it. Therefore, an essential component of preventing secondary trauma is to practice the containment procedure. If we have already practiced it, we can use it when needed. It is also important to receive external support (such as therapy, supervision, energy healings, massage, etc.) so any trauma activated during Me-B sessions gets transformed. The more advanced we are in the Me-B Stages, the more skilled we are at preventing secondary trauma from happening.

PREVENT SECONDARY TRAUMA

Notice what happens to you when you empathize with another person. Does your field change? If so, how does it change? Especially look at what happens to the Heart Chakra. Design an Action Plan to adjust your field **before, during, and after** trauma sessions with clients so you don't take on their trauma.

In the Action Plan, address the following aspects. What happens to your field when you are working trauma issues with clients? How do you do self-care to prevent secondary trauma? What containment procedure do you chose to use if your trauma becomes activated during a session? What is your method to release holding before, during, and after an Me-B session? Also note which character structures within you have the most difficulty releasing trauma and what support they need.

TRAUMA REPEATS ITSELF AND CREATES SIMILAR TRAUMA

We become programmed mentally, physically and energetically to behave in the manner that re-ignites and actually invites past traumatic events to be replayed in the present.

"Long after the original traumatic event is over, many individuals find themselves compelled to anticipate, orient to, and react to stimuli that directly or indirectly resemble the original traumatic experience or its context. These individuals unconsciously and reflexively narrow the field of consciousness to reminders of the trauma, thereby failing to perceive cues indicative of safety and inadvertently maintaining an internal sense of threat. Alternatively, they may experience hypoarousal-related interference with the innate ability to orient to cues signaling either pleasure or danger; they may report feeling "shut down," unable to perceive their own emotions or body sensations, and fail to notice threatening stimuli (which can result in increased vulnerability to re-victimization)." (Pat Ogden, *Trauma and the Body*, p.65.)

This research accentuates the importance of using the body in the process of healing trauma. As we increase our ability to tune into bodily sensations (in addition to the energetics), we more easily notice our old program. When this happens, we can establish a new and improved program based on deep orientation to healthy belief systems that transcend the old consciousness of "victim or perpetrator" or "stuck and confused."

In Me-B Transformation, we use (1) aligned intention, (2) advanced mindfulness of our Enlightened Observer to transform trauma's LVC, and (3) reconnect to Core Being. We also use the interventions out lined in previous chapters including movement, exercises, the Body Connecting Sequence (BCS), Manifest Energy and a balanced energy field to reorganize unhealthy neurological programming, **release** trauma from our mind, our cells and energy system and then **re-pattern our responses and replace** (R & R2) trauma with HVC of Core Being.

STRESS ACTIVATES DORMANT TRAUMA

Stressful situations tend to activate trauma that was once dormant. This can be looked at as an opportunity to cleanse our nervous system and energy system at deeper levels. The Catch 22 is that trauma should never be processed unless there is enough time and space to support deep emotional processing. This presents a difficult therapeutic mandate. The best time to process deep trauma is when a client has a lot of time and space to self-care; yet, stressful circumstances bring up trauma.

In this case, containment and positive resourcing procedures taught in previous chapters are recommended. Holding the intention of melting the trauma by bringing in higher vibrations is vital. A client at Stage 4 or above of Me-B Transformation is much more equipped to deal with the challenges of trauma.

Eye Movement Desensitization Reprocessing (EMDR) techniques can also help to minimize the need to go too deeply into feeling emotional material. EMDR is a psychotherapeutic technique developed to send signals to the nervous system so that trauma is more easily healed. These days, a machine the size of an iPod is used. Wire leads are attached to the iPod- sized box. At the ends of the wire leads are dime-sized vibrators. One is held in each hand. A client typically holds the leads in their hands (or earphones are used that beep).

Energetically, the EMDR machine charges the field so there is more energy moving and thus more possibility of bringing in higher vibrations. (EMDR-trained therapists can use this technique and can attend my trainings on combining energetic work with EMDR reprocessing. The training is offered through the Mind Energy Body School of Transformation.)

At times of stress, it is even more important to not identify with the material as being the truth of who we are. Trauma is just energy and bio-chemical reactions. Our Enlightened Observer helps prevent us from merging with the LVC of trauma.

SIFTING INFORMATION

Traumatized people typically have trouble sifting through significant information from inconsequential information so they can determine if there is a threat. Their selection process may be biased by hypo-arousal/hyper-arousal states and a corresponding dulling/activating of the senses that interferes with the ability to select (Pat Ogden, *Trauma and the Body*).

In other words, we have trouble determining what really is a threat, and what isn't. As a result, we either over- or under-react. This can negatively impact social situations, relationships and careers. *We become our own saboteurs based on how we were sabotaged.*

EXTERNAL REALITY VERSUS INTERNAL SUPPORT

To mitigate your own internal saboteur, you can look at how you internally and externally orientate yourself in the world.

> *Our orienting reflex helps us remain appropriately (or inappropriately) open and able to decide how to react to information around us. So trauma survivors (everyone) have strategies for connecting to the external world that are based on unhealthy and subconscious relationship to our external and internal worlds (Pat Ogden, Trauma and the Body, p. 79).*

As mentioned earlier, some of us have a hypo-arousal (under-reactivity) to situations that merit arousal. Or, we become too alert to stimuli that should be ignored. Learning how to orient to situations is an essential component to energetically and somatically re-patterning the negative aspects of trauma. We can learn positive habituation and/or sensitization so we respond to stimuli based on appropriate arousal status.

June's Trauma Alignment

June reacted every time she was in a mall—it carried a smell that reminded her of her attacker. A cold sweat and racing heart signaled the trauma response. As the therapist asked her to re-orient herself from the past to finding four colors of red in the room, she was able to unhook from the past and become more aligned to what was happening in the moment. Her breath and heart rate normalized.

TRAUMA-ORIENTING RESPONSES

According to Pat Ogden, we can notice a trauma response in an activity as simple as noticing a door slam. If we are prone to too much arousal, we might immediately feel danger and be over reactive. Or if we are programmed to collapse, or are desensitized to danger, we might ignore the slammed door when in reality it could be something we should investigate (Pat Ogden, *Trauma and the Body*). Listed below are the eight indicators Ogden outlines that could signify a trauma response:

1. Activity arrest to gather information. Usually a person stops what they are doing to determine if there is something wrong (Pat Ogden, *Trauma and the Body*, p.79). If nothing is wrong, but our body stays on high alert, this might create anxiety and poor vagal tone. As we learn more advanced mindfulness techniques and how to better regulate our Me-B system, we can prevent this from happening.

2. Sensory Alertness. Senses of smell, taste, hearing, kinesthetic, direct knowing, and intuition kick in to determine if there is a real threat (Pat Ogden, *Trauma and the Body*, p. 79). If in hypo-arousal, a client will have dull senses; if in hyper-arousal, senses may be out of proportion to the situation. Either way, it is information to help us assess if we have to reprogram our sensory information so it is aligned accurately.

   Negative and positive transference and projection happen in the haze of trauma. We don't see others or the world around us accurately.

   Energetically, if there is a real threat, our energy system will already be in defense. This is because we pick up information in our energy system quicker than the cognitive mind can notice. Frequently I will notice my system in defense before I cognitively understand why. We can train ourselves and our clients to track at the subtle level of energy in order to determine if there is a threat or to notice if trauma has been activated. Self-awareness and transformation create self-mastery. We learn how to sense, look at the deeper truth and then realign our perceptions and raise our consciousness in all Me-B systems. This is deep empowerment for change.

3. Muscular adjustments. If there is a real or perceived threat, the muscles will fill with blood and react toward movement. If not, they will relax (Ogden, *Trauma and the Body*, p. 79). In the previous chapter, we explored using physical movement and exercises to shift energy. These techniques can be used to discharge any overcharged area of the body created by trauma and to complete any healthy physical defensive movement that might not have been completed during the time the trauma occurred. For instance, if a rape victim went into a freeze and never fought off her attacker, we might help her complete the action by encouraging her body to move in a healthy defensive manner. *The movements/exercises can charge any undercharged area of our body created by trauma and can dissipate any overcharged area of the body. Emotionally an overcharged area can be stuck anger (fight/flight) energy and an undercharged area can be freeze or immobilization energy. As we get the energy to move into balance we also rebalance our physiology.*

4. Scanning is the practice we use to help us determine how to react. The body symptoms are eye movement and then head movement (Ogden, Pat; *Trauma and the Body*, p. 79). If during a Me-B session, we notice a client's eyes scan the room, and then his or her head move—we might ask the client to look and see if there is a threat in the room. This scanning response

means trauma could have been activated and the client might not feel safe. As the Me-B Guide, we may have inadvertently helped trigger trauma and the client may be in transference. If we notice someone initiating the scanning response, we might want to check in to see what is happening with them. Energetically we may sense their energy become disorganized and/or defensive.

5. Location in space. Where is the threat? As our client looks around, paces, or moves, invite him/her to find the threat (Ogden, *Trauma and the Body*, p. 79). If it is not external, where might he or she be holding this old pattern in their body/energy system?

6. Identification and appraisal. Appraisal asks us to separate past from present in order to think, feel and attribute appropriate meaning to a present experience (Ogden, *Trauma and the Body*, p. 79).

   If trauma is activated, we or a client may not be able to accurately identify and appraise if there is a true threat because the trauma shuts down the higher brain functions and a conditioned response is initiated based on Procedural Memory/Learning behavior. This is when our Enlightened Observer can come to our aide. We can begin the process of working through the 3 Rings of Healing. The **outer ring** is when we notice if we are in defense and self assess if trauma has reared its head. Then we move into the second ring of healing and begin to transform the emotions so we can return back to Core Being (center ring). Awareness is the first step. (Review 5-step Mindfulness Process.)

   Procedural learning/memory involves learned patterns of behavior, movement, gestures, autonomic arousal patterns, and emotional and cognitive tendencies. Procedural Memory is often unconscious and reactive in nature. It is why the story repeats and choice is eliminated.

   Procedural Memory prevents us from being in charge of our actions. It can put us on autopilot. Because most often we don't know we have lost choice, we later judge and ridicule ourselves for our negative reactivity. Trauma from the past prevents us from functioning at a higher level of choice instead of taking action out of a programmed defense. So we can get stuck in the outer ring of healing and never make it back to center.

7. Action. If the appraisal is inaccurate, then the action will be too. So if action is based on an inaccurate appraisal then we or our client will replay the past in the present. This is one main reason trauma repeats itself (Ogden, *Trauma and the Body*).

8. As we are successful in transforming our trauma, reorganization happens. The system returns to home-ostasis, re-orienting to other objects, people, and relationships appropriately (Ogden, *Trauma and the Body*). We no longer base our responses on defense and/or a programmed personality. Our Enlightened Observer is strong and we can feel the sensation of Core Being in our body. This means that our body and energy system is re-patterned to adopt appropriate organizing responses. There may be muscular relaxation or slight tremors/quakes, depending on how much arousal, sensory alertness, and muscular mobilization have occurred (Ogden, *Trauma and the Body*).

   All of us, and our clients, can learn to make choices about how to orient in a healthy manner. We can learn to notice when trauma has been activated. Using our Explorer's Mind, we can create the awareness needed to shift our Me-B Systems back to balance so that we are less likely to replay the past (Ogden, *Trauma and the Body*, p. 79).

STAGES OF DEFENSIVE RESPONSE

1. *Marked change in arousal.* When a stimulus is evaluated as threatening, an instant and automatic change in the level of arousal occurs, usually emerging as an increase in arousal (Ogden, Pat; *Trauma and the Body*, p.98).

   For instance, an abused teenager may say, "oh no, there is my dad!"

2. *Heightened orienting response.* Sensory vigilance amplifies and all attention is drawn to the potential threat (Ogden, Pat; *Trauma and the Body*, p. 99).

   "And he is drunk," says the teen.

3. *Attachment and social engagement systems.* Once the orienting system has collected data and evaluated the danger, protective actions are employed. We may cry out for help or activate our social engagement system by attempting to negotiate with the perpetrator (Ogden, Pat; *Trauma and the Body*, p. 100).

   "Dad, please, I am not bad. Please stop yelling at me!" the teen pleaded.

4. *Mobilizing defensive strategies.* If the social engagement system doesn't work, according to Porges's polyvagal hierarchy theory, when social engagement fails, the next way we protect ourselves is to fight or flee (Ogden, Pat; Trauma and the Body, p. 100).

   Unfortunately the teen had no place to run. His father cornered him in his "office" and kept telling him how he would never measure up to his expectations. Crying, the teen was trapped. There was no escape.

5. *Immobilizing defensive strategies.* When fight or flight might cause more harm or are ineffectual, there are two main immobilizing freeze strategies presented by Ogden in her book. Type one is when the sympathetic nervous system is engaged with tense heart rate, arousal but no action is taken. Another type is feigned death with limp passivity, behavioral shut down. Memory access and storage can be impaired and amnesia may be expected (Pat Ogden, *Trauma and the Body*, p. 95).

   However, there can also be submission as an immobilizing defense-especially in the case of chronic abuse. It is not uncommon for traumatized people to respond to threat cues with mechanistic compliance or resigned submission. So, with Porges's polyvagal hierarchy, dorsal vagal complex comes into action when all other defenses fail to ensure safety. Individuals who suffered chronic abuse as children, even only verbal abuse, often must sometimes rely on immobilizing defenses. When physical escape proves impossible, these immobilizing defenses are the physiological and psychological measures that are thought to protect the person against further suffering (Pat Ogden, *Trauma and the Body*, p. 95-100):

   So in the case of our teenager, he would act compliant and agree with his father night, after night. "Yes dad, I am bad," the teen would say. Adding, "I really should think like you and be like you." But underneath it all, the teen just wanted his dad to love him for who he really was — even if he wasn't at all similar to his dad.

6. *Recuperation.* This is when the threat is over and the perpetrator is not around and physiological and psychological recovery takes place. Physiological recovery is when the de-escalation of arousal back to a more optimal baseline state occurs. When submission or dorsal vagal responses (parasympathetic) have been the dominant defense, recovery occurs as arousal elevates from hypo-arousal to a more optimal level. To do this, movement or exercise is helpful.

If sympathetically mediated defenses have been employed, then discharge happens in the form of shaking or trembling to release the pent up fight/flight energy (Ogden, *Trauma and the Body*, p. 100-101).

> Since there was no escape from his fathers repeated verbal attacks, the teen eventually resorted to drugs and alcohol as an escape and a way to numb from the abuse.

7. *Integration.* "People subjected to chronic or severe trauma are often not only unable to complete the recuperation stage, but fail to integrate what has happened to them over time. Instead, they wall off the parts of themselves that are hurt or scared, and continue their everyday activities as if nothing happened" (Ogden, *Trauma and the Body*, p. 102).

"The stage of integration occurs over a longer period of time than recuperation and varies depending on the severity of the threat, the kind of defense used, the success of the defense, the degree of completion at the recuperation phase, as well as the individual's history, abilities, and support system. Integration is a long-term process of reorganization that includes both the physical and the psychological assimilation of the traumatic experience" (Ogden, *Trauma and the Body*, p. 102).

> The teen never made it to the integration stage because he never made it through the recuperation stage. Today, his parents support him financially. He is chronically ill, a recovered alcoholic and clinically depressed. They claim that he was born damaged and they feel sorry for themselves that in their old age they must financially support their broken son.

To help yourself and/or your clients heal, you may need them to return to their Me-B system and complete these last two stages of trauma recovery.

TRAUMA TO DO LIST!

Accurately evaluate the apparent threat.

1. Integrate a wide array of stimuli as perceived by our Enlightened Observer, energetic awareness, and senses.
2. Notice our Orienting Responses and explore what is old trauma being activated.
3. Overcome Procedural Memory so we appropriately assess and reorganize/re-pattern trauma in our body/energy system. This may mean we need to move our body in ways that release the old learned behaviors.
4. Following the 5-Step Mindfulness Process to move through the 3 Rings of Healing and shape-shift old patterns so wholeness can be realized. Be careful we don't over-identify with the trauma.
5. Promote healthy vagal tone and mitigate unhealthy dorsal complex. (This is explained in more detail in the chronic illness chapter.) Overcome maladaptive defensive responses and to the extent possible complete any recuperation and integration phases.
6. Understand that when trauma is activated, we don't always have balanced function of our higher brain. We either become over-reactive to a situation or we minimize how we feel. Don't let the higher brain rationalize by saying, "I don't feel that way." Or "I don't have a good enough reason to be traumatized." Listen to what is held in the body and meet it's needs to discharge any fight/flight energy or reawaken from any demobilization. Be compassionate to ourselves and align our Manifest Energy so we don't over-identify.

IMPORTANT TO REMEMBER

When a traumatic event is so severe that the individual has no recourse but to freeze or submit, the defensive system becomes disorganized and overwhelmed. The common perpetuation factor in trauma-related disorders appears to be the persistence, even decades later, of altered defensive responses and maladaptive orienting responses (Ogden, Pat; *Trauma and the Body*, p. 79). Thus it is important for us (and our clients) to use our Explorer's Mind and recognize our orienting responses and the maladaptive defensive responses.

Next you will learn how to **release** LVC of trauma, **re-pattern** the body/energy system and **replace** it with HVC (R & R2). **Re-patterning is the process that occurs when the body's physiology and energy systems have released trauma and the body is reorganized to have healthier orienting responses.**

To assist in this process, the size of our (or our client's) energy field must foster maintenance of the Enlightened Observer. If the field shrinks too much during process work, we lose the HVC of our Enlightened Observer. We risk charging and expanding the trauma instead of eliminating it. Asking a client to stand up, or do some of the movement exercises outlined in previous chapters, will help restore the Rhythm of Flow and expand the size of their energy field so the HVC of the Enlightened Observer can return.

Without patience, we risk accentuating the dark instead of redeeming the light. When someone feels trauma, their field reacts quickly and shrinks. Guiding ourselves or our clients to expand their field so they don't over-identify with the trauma is necessary. They also must learn to feel the energetic sensation of HVC in the body as the replacement for the trauma. If we don't plant flowers in the freshly tilled field, weeds will grow.

If a field shrinks too much, clients will collapse and it may even cause harm. A Me-B Guide may need to spend many sessions:

- developing a safe and confident relationship with a client,
- resourcing the client,
- helping them feel the energy of Core Being as a sensation in the body, and
- teaching them about the Enlightened Observer, containment and their orienting responses.

After years of cognitive process work, some clients complain they still feel uncomfortable emotions. Many clients believe that once their trauma is healed, they will never have to feel difficulty and challenge. Unfortunately, we are never done. The deeper we go, the deeper we can go. Given the fact that our subconscious is always larger than our conscious mind, there is always more light we can let in by transforming the darkness.

Me-B Transformation is magical, but it is not magic. Many of us are looking for magic. On some level, we are looking for a way of escaping ourselves and a way of escaping difficulty and pain. When some of us do deep work, we can eliminate our pain and we think it will be gone forever. Later, when our pain or difficulty has returned, we feel defeated and lose patience. This is because we can cling to the belief that mastery means no pain, no stress, and no ego. In truth, mastery means our ability to not **over-identify** with the pain and discomfort. Mastery is the ability to unhook the painful effects of the ego and to reconnect to our divinity. It **does not** necessitate the absence of pain! As the Buddha says, "life is suffering." As Masters, we learn not to BE the energy of suffering that runs through us.

The source of all pain is perception.

Healthy Train Track

Anchoring into the Core Being and using the Enlightened Observer

The Ventral Vagal

We are the conductor!

Unhealthy Train Track

Over-identification with pain

Disassociating – Hypoarousal
Freezing or Immobilizing
Is Undercharged energy

The switch is consciousness.

We must learn how to flip the switch from identifying with the pain, the consciousness of separation, to identifying with the Core Being, the consciousness of wholeness. Flip the switch using Enlightened Observer and

"Peace is a thought away."
– Jill Bolte Taylor

HOW DOES TRAUMA PRESENT IN THE THREE Me-B SYSTEMS?

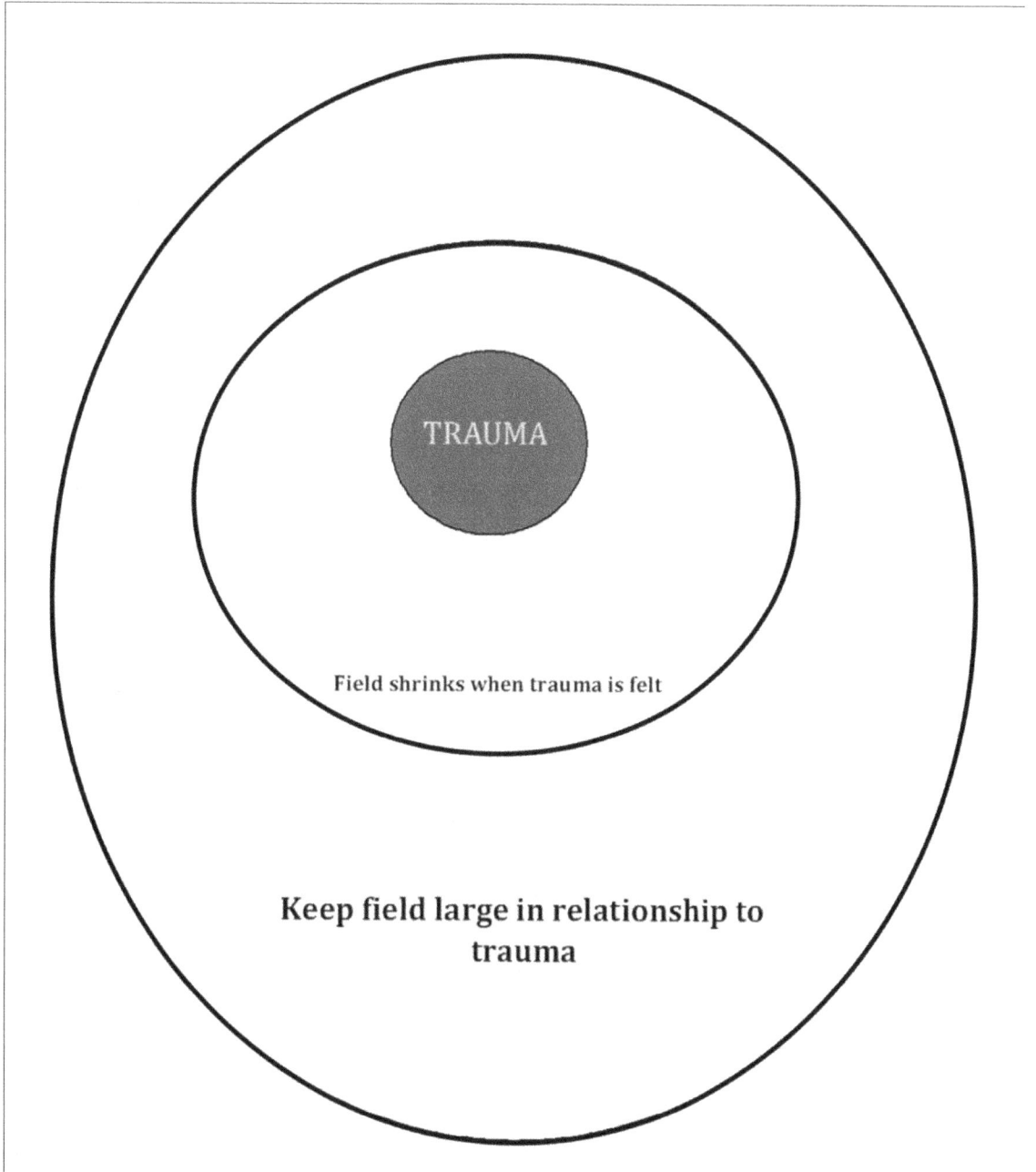

TRAUMA

Field shrinks when trauma is felt

Keep field large in relationship to trauma

TRAUMA IN THE MIND

Trauma presents in our mind in the form of negative belief systems and a false sense of self. Sometimes trauma affects sleep patterns, anxiety, circular thinking, obsessive thoughts, and difficult dreams. Because of the neuroplasticity of the brain, these negative patterns become deeply ingrained in our biology. This makes it very difficult to change. *It takes strong, relentless aligned intention and a deep anchor into Core Being* for us to follow our Choice Points and create long-term meaningful change.

False traumatic memories can develop from trauma. Therapeutically, when memories of the past (or past lives) arise during a Me-B Session, it is important to not question their validity but to work to create a healthier life in the present. After all, how real are any of our perceptions? At the source, it is just energy and consciousness.

If it is a false memory, it is at least a symbol of the truth. So work with it as a valid signal from the subconscious that is asking for help, love and transformation. The same is true about past lives. If we don't believe in past lives, don't judge them when they come up for ourselves or others—just work with it as "what is presenting in the moment."

Often victims of child abuse want to "know the truth." We can get trapped in "needing to know the truth" and don't move toward healing. Be understanding of this and gently assist in the Release, Re-pattern and Replace (R & R2) Process so we can move forward through needing to know to understanding our own divine truth. Isn't that what matters anyways?

The most important task of the mind is to let go of the memories or impressions of the past so there isn't an over-identification with the trauma. If a client over-identifies with trauma, they can't heal. The higher vibrations won't integrate into the mind and the R & R2 process is stilted.

For trauma to be healed, there must be movement toward the dimension of the Core Being and a release of the programmed-personality level. Support the process of movement in all 3-Me-B Systems.

TRAUMA IN THE BODY

The physiology of the body traps trauma. Working only cognitively in the mind rarely releases trauma in the body or energy system. Because the body is so reactive to trauma, during the R & R2 process, we must be careful not to re-traumatize. If we re-traumatize instead of transform the energy of trauma— the body's physiology **becomes more conditioned to trauma and not less.** We may end up with poor vagal tone and an un- healthy dorsal complex.

For instance, it is as if a traumatized body loops and loops, around and around, on an unhealthy train track. Our job is to create a bridge to a healthier train track. When this happens our Orienting Reponses become appropriate. A Me-B Guide must be careful not to create a deeper "groove" in the unhealthy track. As a metaphorical bridge is established, a deeper "groove" on the healthier track is created and it becomes ingrained and habituated.

We want the new healthier track to become so ingrained that eventually it can't jump back to the unhealthy track. This is the ideal! Some research suggests trauma and consciousness are held in the body's protein structures, nervous system, hormones, and higher and primal brain functions. Our work as a Me-B guide must be to positively influence these body physiology centers. Refer to trauma books that explain this in more detail such as Pat Ogden's book *Trauma and the Body* or Robert Scare's Book *The Body Bears the Burden*.

In these books, various aspects of trauma in our body are discussed. For instance, they present the Polyvagal Theory of Emotion and Vagal Tone. I am still trying to understand the complexity of this theory. A short review reveals that high dorsal vagal complex tone is not ideal because it promotes immobilization and freeze. In relation to our normal day-to-day life, this in not healthy, because it is associated with fear, helplessness, dissociation and lack of body awareness.

The Ventral Vagal Complex fosters social engagement and maternal infant bonding and complex social behaviors. High vagal tone promotes health and communication and social engagement (Robert C. Scare, MD; *The Body Bears the Burden*).

> "The basic blueprint of our map of the world and the way we move through it consists of connections between the arousal system of the brain (the reptilian brain) and the interpretive system of the mammalian brain (the limbic system). These connections organize how all animals, including humans, organize their responses to sensory stimuli—and these responses, first and foremost, concern movement." (Ogden, Pat; *Trauma and the Body*, p. xvii.) When trauma studies rediscovered the automatic activation of fixed action patterns in the mind and body it became clear, cognitive psychotherapy is ineffectual.

Based on past traumatic responses, these body systems become reprogrammed to respond in a certain way when they perceive a threat. Our higher brain functions are over-ridden, and we react as our body was programmed to react, both emotionally and in terms of physical movements. Typical unhealthy reactions include: anger, yelling, collapse, eating or control of eating (i.e., anorexia), and addictions—alcohol, sex, pornography, etc.

In humans, we often respond with lashing out or collapse in the face of a perceived threat. As we learn to feel what is being triggered within us, we then activate our higher brain to understand and discern if the threat is real or programmed. As this happens, our choices expand to include other options for responding.

HOW IS TRAUMA CONTROLLING OUR REPONSES?

Over the next month, explore the answers to these questions. Actually, we all probably would benefit from exploring these questions throughout our lives.

1. What is your typical programmed response? Do you lash out or collapse? Do you tend to be more in hyper- or hypoarousal?
2. How effective is your response, and what negative effects does your response have on those around you?
3. How does their negative response activate your negative beliefs and your false sense of self?
4. What is the trauma, Core Distortion, and/or negative beliefs feeding our Procedural Memory?
5. What could be a healthier way of responding that we could enlist?

The BCS helps us overcome Procedural Memory and reorient to our environment.

PROCEDURAL MEMORY OVERCOME

Jan's father was abusive to her. When he drank, he was aggressive, verbally abusive, controlling and sexually inappropriate. When he would do this, Jan couldn't escape. Her father was relentless and she was cornered. This programmed her to collapse. So when she was confronted with this energy in her daily life or work, she couldn't stick up for herself. Her brain and thought patterns froze and she couldn't think of another way to respond. She only collapsed and once again became the victim with the other person playing the role of perpetrator.

She had more appropriate Orienting Responses with people with whom she felt safe—like her husband. She married him because he was "different" from her father. However, overtime she found herself lashing out, being controlling and angry. She acted toward him in the same manner as her father had acted toward her. In this role, she was the perpetrator and her husband the victim.

As Jan healed her Post Traumatic Stress Disorder (PTSD), her higher brain functions returned and she was able to illicit more balanced and healing Orienting Responses instead of the programmed responses of the past. As a result, her outside life changed dramatically. She became empowered in her work and could stand up for herself. She also learned not to play the role of perpetrator with her husband. The family dynamics changed and their children began to thrive.

A Me-B Guide's work at the body-centered level is to help the client shift their physiology so they can have **new** behavioral responses to **old** programmed stimuli. As higher brain functions return, we have more opportunity to choose differently in the face of pre-programmed traumatic Orienting Responses.

In The Auric Field:

Energetically, trauma is held in the form of Core Distortions in the Auric Dimension. On the second and fourth levels of the field, trauma presents as darker or congested energy. It holds negative beliefs and a negative sense of identity. Negative emotions decrease the charge on all levels of the field—except anger, which creates a strong energetic charge. This may feel like heat or heaviness in the physical body.

The third chakra can tear or collapse and the second and first chakras will distort or run less energy. The fifth chakra tends to shut down. There is a relationship between the fifth and second chakras—if both are open and flowing, it is a good sign the trauma has been re-patterned and Orienting Responses will normalize.

The sixth chakra can hold dense energy of not really liking what it "sees." Depending upon the client's character structure, the seventh chakra may shut down and cut off from its spiritual support and the root chakra may close up and pull away from the earth.

If our trauma gets activated too strongly, the Auric Field will shatter. This means it becomes diffuse, undercharged and fragmented. If this happens, as it is bound to at times, we can rebuild it more strongly. For in- stance, sometimes a building needs to be demolished and rebuilt again from the ground up. So, if our field does shatter, we can use this as an opportunity to make it stronger. (See exercise on building our consciousness container.)

As we and our clients learn to self-regulate during trauma processing, we become more skilled at transforming trauma to the HVC of Core Being. All of us can learn to self-assess and (1) determine if there is enough HVC to transform the trauma and (2) know if our Enlightened Observer is strong enough. It is not the Me-B guide's job alone. Clients must take charge of their healing and Me-B guides are just assistants. Teach them how to recognize healthy body movements that promote high ventral tone and to decrease dorsal vagal tone. (Also explained in the chronic healing chapter.)

Manifest Energy Intention Line:

In the Intention Line, trauma presents as breaks or twists in the line. We can connect to where it is misaligned, feel the negative belief and/or Core Distortion and then allow it to realign.

Accessing Core Being To Heal Trauma:

- This is the dimension of our unique divine spirit. Bring this vibration into the trauma to create healing and a "healthy train track" within the body and mind.

Multi-Dimensional Fabric/Centered Oneness:

- As we heal our trauma at deeper and deeper levels, our ability to receive the support of the multi-dimensional fabric, Centered Oneness and star child dimensions grows.

Positive Resourcing Interventions

- Use any of the positive resourcing interventions that might be helpful.

TRAUMA CHOICE POINTS

1. Using the Explorer's Mind, over the next few weeks, examine times when you respond to a situation by being too careful or not careful enough. Also notice how by over- or under-reacting to a situation, you actually invite a negative experience.

2. Using this information, consider that you can eventually use your choice points to practice the R & R2 sequence-reprogramming physiologically, release trauma from your cells and Auric field, and replace with HVC of Core Being. (This process is detailed below.)

This is a life-long journey. We can think of the inchworm and make small incremental changes over time so we reprogram ourselves to react accurately to situations. Over time, we will reduce our tendency to over- or under- react (hypo- or hyper-arousal states).

CHOICE POINTS are easy to find, especially if we look at close relationships that often activate trauma (spouses/parents). For in- stance, Cathy loved her boy friend. They had been together for many years and yet, she didn't trust him. If he didn't return a call quickly, she was sure he was with another woman. She was conditioned toward hyper-arousal. Yelling at him as her cells filled with anger, she would collapse into feelings of worthlessness. Her mind raced, "He doesn't love me. No one will love me." Only later did she discover he didn't call her because he hadn't gotten the message. He had left his phone in the car.

Embarrassed by her over-reaction, she thought that more than ever, she was not worthy of love. This cycle continued. She would over-react and then judge herself as being unlovable. Again, and again, and again she repeated this cycle. Eventually, she drove both of them crazy. Not until she discovered that her hyper-arousal reaction was a trauma response did this sequence change.

Every time we over- or under-react to a situation, know it is the trauma in charge and our higher brain is not functioning properly. Then, using a CHOICE POINT, we can find a different way of responding. Patience and much practice are usually both needed for success.

RELEASE, RE-PATTERN, & REPLACE (R & R2) PROCESS

Body Cues

Using both body cues and energetic cues can help us track ourselves and our clients better. For instance, if we see a client's hand move in a repetitive pattern, we can ask them what they are experiencing.

If the hand moves up and down, they can accentuate the movement to explore what it is saying and what emotions it represents. Also, we can track the following body cues:

- breath
- head position
- scanning, looking down or away
- shoulders collapsed
- facial expressions
- feet—soles rolled inward or outward or tucked under
- tight or flaccid muscles
- posture
- body movements—especially eyes, shoulders, hands and feet
- body types as represented by the character structures
- notice our body—it often mirrors what is happening in the client
- promote forward movement of the body and healthy defensive movements
- other

R & R2 Intervention

I. Greeting.

II. Assess client's resourcing level and where they are in the 10 Me-B Stages of Transformation. Only do positive resourcing if they are not at least Stage 4 of Me-B transformation.

III. Over time, teach clients how to feel safety and trust as a positive sensation in the body.

IV. Gradually, teach clients about the 5-Step Mindfulness process and the 3 Rings of Healing. Help them learn how to self regulate their energy field back to Core Being and how to engage their Enlightened Observer and strengthen their Manifest Energy Line.

V. As the session progresses, once clients are ready to do trauma work, begin to guide them into their body/energy system to assess where the trauma is held. (Unless they are at least Stage 4 of Me-B Transformation don't guide them into the darkness. Instead bring the light into the pain.)

VI. Then we can use any of the methods outlined in previous chapters such as:

- Core Distortion Intervention—on or off the table;
- Physical movement/exercises to promote healthy body movements and healthy defenses;

- Trauma Core Distortion Work (below); and
- Other relevant Interventions taught.

Use our energy tracking techniques to determine which Me-B interventions to implement. Be creative, and explore. Make sure we **follow the next steps**:

1. Track HVC of clients' Enlightened Observer and help clients make adjustments if needed.
2. We must base Me-B interventions on what the client tells us and what their body/energy system tells us.
3. We can make sure we help clients **release** the LVC of trauma.
4. We then help them rewire their Me-B system to a healthier "train track" so they **re-pattern** and reorganize to healthy Orienting Responses in all three Me-B systems.
5. Lastly, we can help clients **replace** the LVC with a higher vibrational frequency and consciousness. Ideally, they will be able to anchor into Core Being.

NOTE: It is important we let clients know that trauma is never fully healed in the therapist's office. It takes implementing our new Me-B behavior patterns outside the office and in their everyday living environments. As they take the deeper understanding of their trauma and their issues into their love relationships, deeper healing takes place. This is why looking for our Choice Points and implementing them creates deeper peace.

Melting into Trauma R & R2 Sequence

If a Core Distortion does not shift by bringing in a HVC, AND if a client is at least Stage 4 of Me-B Transformation, we can help clients melt into the trauma with their Enlightened Observer and feel the depth of the pain in their body and transform it to HVC.

1. Identify the trauma in all three Me-B systems. Using the Explorer's Mind, discover any wisdom about the trauma. For instance, what image/belief, child consciousness, emotion, feelings about self and/or Core Distortions does it hold? If we can't identify it in the mind system, we can at least feel the energy of the trauma as an energy and sensation in the body.
2. Charge the negative energy (through hands-on healing, movement, intention, exercises...any way that works). We connect deeply to the trauma in our body with our Enlightened Observer and charge it with the clear intention that it **expand out** of our energy field and **melt** away.

If our Enlightened Observer is strong, the trauma will eventually dissolve so we can then reorganize our negative orienting responses and reorganize and self-regulate our Me-B System back to Core Being. Remember, catharsis is NOT healing. We need to be very aware of this so we don't strengthen the trauma.

As we energetically charge the trauma, the emotion of it can become overwhelming. Our body may shake, and we can feel deep emotional pain from every cell. If we feel the emotion (sob) from the upper chest, see if we can sob from the solar plexus or lower in the body. Ideally, if we can feel the emotion of the trauma in our pelvis, AND if we are not attached to its negative energy, it will open up our entire Me-B system from the top of our head to the bottom of our feet.

However, it can be very difficult to feel trauma low in our body. This is because energy is denser in the 1st and 2nd chakras than in the higher chakras. Dense energy holds LVC and can feel more painful.

Another reason why it can be difficult to feel trauma lower in the body is that many of us don't incarnate into our bodies completely. We like to stay in just the upper chakras where the energy can feel more comfortable and safe.

To prevent us from feeling lower in the body, we unconsciously constrict the 5th chakra to prevent too much energy from flowing down to the trauma. If we don't constrict the 5th, we may unconsciously try to constrict the 4th chakra, the diaphragm or the third chakra. As we are able to open up completely and release the trauma from all our cells (even the ones lower in our body), we can also open up to completely receive our light.

Continue to melt into the trauma with the intention that it diminish. (Our Intention Line needs to be aligned and strong.)

- Assess if we are, or the client is, at an appropriate stage of Me-B transformation with positive ego strength.

- Track if the energy is melting.

- Determine if the Enlightened Observer is strong enough.

- Review the effects of the process on the nervous system (social engagement).

- Promote healthy body defensive movements

- Assess if a HVC is replacing LVC. See if there is any charge of anger that can create a sense of strength and forward movement. Assess if the victim consciousness has shifted to strength and more leader energies. If not, we must do containment and look at any negative intention or ego energy preventing the transformation.

Me-B TRAUMA WORK

I had seen a particular client for over six months, and I knew she had a strong sense of self and much positive resourcing. She was at Stage 6 of Me-B Transformation. I noticed energetic congestion and significant trauma in her heart. I invited her to connect to the trauma, meet the sensation in her heart and collect information and wisdom. Almost immediately the tears began to flow. I reminded her to maintain her Enlightened Observer and that the energy within her was not her. Feeling the pain, she deepened but wasn't identified with the pain, so we could continue. As she brought in the HVC of her Enlightened Observer into the center of the pain, the darkness melted and Core Being began to spread throughout her body. Wholeness and wisdom returned.

Shifting Developmental Trauma R & R2 Sequence

There are many interventions that shift developmental trauma. We need to assess if a client has regressed to a younger age and then help them return back to adult consciousness. Cues a client is developmentally regressed are:

- voice change, body language, broken Intention line, dissociation,
- body posture,
- lost connection to core,
- structured levels of the field less defined,
- no filters on chakras or less strong filters on the chakras,
- energy system regressed and in defense,
- boundaries changed from normal presentation,
- typical facial expressions altered,
- 2nd and 4th levels of the field activated,
- emotional levels feel young, or
- old unhealthy body movement patterns are manifest.

Step 1: Find where the child consciousness is being held in the body.

Step 2: Ask what it needs? Usually he or she needs love support and acceptance from the adult, and the Core Being. Sometimes it needs to be accepted for all aspects of who he or she is. Also, it may ask for something it can't receive. For instance, one client wanted to be supported by his mother and father in a healthy and accepting manner. Unfortunately, that wasn't going to happen in the near future or perhaps at all. In this case, we had to commiserate with the child consciousness and gently let it grieve the fact that its needs would never be met.

Step 3: Bring in the HVC of our adult consciousness and Core Being to sooth and meet the needs of the child. Inviting the child to connect to his or her just anger is also helpful. The anger creates more charge in the field so more energy is available to wash away the trauma. In addition, anger when connected with the HVC of our Enlightened Observer becomes personal power and strength. *Promote healthy bodily defensive movements.* Let the child consciousness know how strong it must be to have survived. Have the child's self-identity be one of a survivor instead of one of a victim. In all Me-B Systems can the client feel the strength.

If the Enlightened Observer of the client is not strong enough to give the child consciousness support, then we as the Me-B guide need to provide support.

Step 4: Make sure integration of the HVC is felt as a sensation of energy in the body and an understanding in the mind. If the client wasn't ready to soothe their own child consciousness, later we can discuss with them if that might be a helpful longer-term goal.

Prenatal, Birth, Past Life, and Evolutionary R & R2 Sequence

This is done through table work. Begin by following and supporting a wave of energy that moves throughout the body from the 1st chakra ascending upward and the upper chakras descending downward.

As the charge waves through the body, the client begins to regress. Often this regression creates an urge for them to push. Help them push into the table, ask them to press their knees apart as you hold them together or ask them to press their knees together as you hold them apart. (Repeat this sequence six or more times to build the energy and allow it to move lower in the body.)

This brings the energy deep into the body and builds the charge. We can also have them push against us with their arms or head to deepen the regression. (We don't create the regression — we follow it.)

We don't make the wave happen. If a client is ready for this to happen, the wave starts on its own. We just support creating a strong charge of energy to run through them. We also assess them to see if their Enlightened Observer is strong enough so they don't re-traumatize.

If the client is ready, it often goes past the birth and neonatal phase and into past life and/or ancestral energies. Some ancestral sequences even go further, back through the evolutionary process. I never make a client go anywhere, I just follow the flow and support the energy to unwind and evolve. It is important we are trained in this before we practice it on someone.

Note: If a client wants to know about a past life, I help them "journey" within their body to locate the past life. If they can't do this on their own, I will do it for them. Shamanic work usually creates a journey by going into the earth or through a hole in the tree. I find the body serves as the instrument for the journey. Sometimes a past life just surfaces and you don't have to build the energy to bring it to consciousness. This tends to happen most with people who have done a lot of past life work or deep emotional transformational work.

PAST LIFE TRAUMA TRANSFORMED

Lilly is a massage therapist and healer. The energy of her as a dark sorcerer from a past life clouded her field and tainted her self-esteem. As we worked, her awareness deepened into her neck and heart. The energy increased and waved through her whole body. As this happened, HVC came in. The energy shifted and she became a white sorcerer. As a dark sorcerer, she had killed babies and stolen their essence. In her life as a white sorcerer she used the essence of the dead to create healing in the world. She undid the wrong of her past by helping in the present.

Whatever happens, and wherever the energy takes you, there are three rules to remember:

1. Don't let the client over-identify with the negative. Track their Enlightened Observer. Also, don't let the trauma of the client hurt us. Stay grounded and in Core Being.
2. Follow the flow using aligned intention, advanced mindfulness to accurately track the energy and consciousness and eventually invite the presence of Core Being into the client's Me-B System. Don't interpret the experience for the client. Let them have their own experience. Only in rare cases do I tell them what I pick up. I do sometimes use certain words in the field to help them go deeper.
3. Always end by bringing in a higher vibration.

5 TASKS OF TRAUMA RECOVERY

1. **Accept the Reality of the Trauma.** Name what has happened and notice where in the body we might be holding it. If we can't notice where in the body it is held, then imagine where it might

be held.

2. **Feel the Feelings of Trauma as Sensations in the Body** — Let the Energy of Trauma Move Through, Us But Don't Identify With It. See, visualize and sense the trauma as energy that we must move through versus being stuck in it. Once we move through those feelings and images of trauma, we then move toward the next step of recovery. Remember to separate what we are experiencing from the deeper truth of who we are. In other words, don't be the trauma we are experiencing. Remember we are much more than the energy, feelings or sensations moving through us.

3. **Consider What Could Replace the Trauma.** If a part of our psyche, body physiology, thought process is attached to or saturated with the energy of trauma—imagine what could possibly take the place of the negative energy. What could replace the past with a positive and healthy future? Imagine how it might feel in our body, mind and soul. Imagine how our body might move and our thoughts and energy reorganize in the absence of trauma. Let the body move and our Procedural Memory reorganize.

4. **Reinvest in Life**. Readjust to the environment without the trauma. Find our self again and be the new us in the world. Emerge from the Cocoon! Complete of the metaphorical death-rebirth process and discover who you are now.

5. **Anchor Into Core Being.** The old patterns and ways of thinking and acting may return; if this happens, just don't attach to them. Instead, anchor into Core Being. Imagine, feel and sense Core Being and our Intention Line. From the place of Core Being and our Intention Line, we can feel trauma, imperfections and defenses—we just don't attach to them.

Traumatic experiences change us. As we emerge from them, we are forever different. From difficulty the riches can be found. Find the internal riches of the deeper truth of who we are. Emerge!

REVIEW QUESTIONS

1. Define trauma.
2. Explain the difference between charging trauma and accessing trauma. Name some other do's and don'ts of working with trauma.
3. Explain Secondary Trauma and how to prevent it.
4. Why does trauma create similar trauma? What is the solution?
5. Explain the process of Sifting Information.
6. Explain the 6 stages of a health/unhealthy orienting response.
7. Name some techniques that help a client re-orient to reality versus being influenced by past programming.
8. When working with a client, what might be some key concepts to remember?
9. What do victims of child abuse want to definitively know that could hinder further progress?
10. If a past life/abuse issue is presented by the client and you don't believe in past lives or know what to believe, how should you deal with it?
11. What is necessary for trauma to be healed?
12. Can trauma be healed without accessing the body or energy system? Explain.
13. If you find people reacting negatively toward you, what could that be an example of?
14. What does it mean to re-pattern trauma in the body and energy system? Be specific. Why is re-

patterning so important? And what is it that is being re-patterned?

15. Explain Procedural Memory.
16. Explain the R & R2 sequence.
17. Case 1: Mary began to yell. It was like she had no other option. Case 2: John couldn't respond, inside he was shaking. What are these examples of?
18. Explain the energy/body/mind configuration of trauma.
19. What Stage of ME-B transformation must a client reach before they do deep traumatic processing?
20. As a Me-B Guide, why might it be important to alternate a trauma session with a positive resourcing session? Explain.
21. Oftentimes, once a client makes so much progress that they begin to think Me-B Transformation is magic. Explain why Me-B Transformation is magical but not "magic." What will always return?
22. What is mastery of trauma?
23. How do we ensure we are not abused by emotions but instead use emotions for our highest good?
24. How do you connect to your trauma and transform it to HVC of Core Being? What is easy and what makes it hard? How can you better support yourself when you transform trauma?
25. Discussion questions for trauma healings:
    - Was it easier to help the client bring in the vibration or to do it yourself? Why?
    - How might your personality type be an asset/detriment in this experience?
    - How might your client's personality type be an asset/detriment in this experience?
    - Did you share too much information? Why or Why not?
    - What was easy/ difficult? Why?
    - What would you do differently next time? Why?
    - What would you do again?
    - Did your trauma get triggered?
    - What does it mean if the trauma did not shift?
    - Did any transference/projections come up?
26. What are the 5 Tasks of Trauma Recovery?
27. When working with prenatal or pre-birth trauma, what is important to remember?

CHAPTER 21

ARCHETYPES, DREAMS and ANCESTRAL CONFLUENCE

Archetypes are energetic imprints that exist in our collective consciousness. They are symbols and concepts of consciousness and can be used to understand Core Distortions and the deeper aspects of the divine.

The term "Archetype" was popularized in the work of Carl Jung. He saw archetypes as the first original model from which all other similar persons, objects, or concepts are merely copied, patterned, or emulated.

Archetypes are innate prototypes for ideas, which may subsequently become involved in the interpretation of observed phenomena. By accessing the energy of higher vibrational archetypal structures that we would like to embody, we can shift ourselves or a client deeper into aspects of their divine spirit. Conversely, we can also help ourselves or our clients tap into negative archetypical patterns held in the Me-B system. Negative archetypical patterns such as the martyr and the victim exist in many of us.

As we tap into the negative, bring the shadow (LVC) into the light (HVC), we can then transform and support a more truthful frequency of the whole. Dreams and myths are constellations of archetypal images. Dreams are the vehicle that archetypes use to speak to us. By working with dreams, we can also work to access the collective wisdom that can aid us in our transformation.

There are many examples of common archetypes. Hopefully in this book, we are finding our own type of leader/healer/therapist/guide archetype to embody. In a horse herd, if a horse wants to take leadership, he will attack the leader in an effort to take control. Some people use this type of leadership in their personal interactions, as do many corporations and business models. It is one archetype of leadership. There are many different styles of leadership—working with archetypes can help us find our own style.

EMBODY THE ARCHETYPES OF CORE BEING

Choose an archetypical energy that you long to embody at a deeper level. It should be an aspect of your Core Being. Invoke the energy of the positive archetype to fill your body's cells. Feel it in your DNA, bones, muscles and throughout your Auric Field. Now imagine it filling your multi-dimensional fabric. Imagine it anchoring into the physical. Smell, know, feel, and visualize its embodiment within you.

RELATIONSHIP BETWEEN ARCHETYPES AND ANCESTRAL PATTERNS

Jung believed that archetypes could be linked to heredity and regarded them as instinctual. We are born with these patterns. They are held in our bodies and in the blueprint of our DNA as it is passed down through centuries. Jung even explored how archetypes are elemental forces that play a vital role in the creation of the world and of the human mind. Ancients called them "elemental spirits." One writer explains it this way:

> We all share a single universal unconscious. Mind is *rooted* in the unconscious just as a tree is rooted in the ground. Imagine the Universal Unconscious as a cosmic computer. Our minds are subdirectories of the *root directory*. If we look at our personal "work areas," we find much material that is unique to our historical universal patterns. If we humans have the courage to seek the source to which our account belongs, we begin to discover ever more impersonal and universal patterns. The directories of the cosmic computer to which we can gain access are filled with the myths of the human species.

(Source: www.iloveulove.com/psychology/jung/jungarchetypes.htm)

When doing Ancestral interventions, we will be looking for the energetic wiring, which looks like a black wire. We will unwind the energetic root from entangling and diminishing the flow of energy through the chakra system and the Auric Field. When we disconnect the unhealthy wires (root free), we reconnect ourselves to the source of the healthier ancestral pattern or the main archetypical "directory" or elemental force.

During Ancestral interventions, often times archetypical patterns emerge. The two often become the same thing. For instance, we may have lived lifetimes as an abused woman. This is the challenging archetype of the wounded woman. We can bring in the positive energy of the heroine archetype to transform the LVC of the wounded woman archetype.

The heroine or hero archetype is represented in the legends of Hercules and Joan of Arc —figures who are confronted in numerous battles alone, on behalf of others much weaker than themselves.

ANCESTRAL REWIRING

1. Imagine where your negative ancestral wiring is held in your body/energy system.
2. Name the Ancestral negative pattern. What Archetype relates to it?
3. Imagine, feel, and then dissolve the negative wiring.
4. Feel the energy of the positive alternative taking hold.

If this is too difficult, ask a trained Me-B Guide to assist.

It is important to track the energy accurately and not impose an intervention upon a client or ourselves. Rarely do clients present with an archetype or ancestral intervention until they have done a significant amount of developmental work and are at least at Stage 4 of Me-B Transformation.

SOLO ARCHETYPE INTERVENTION—TOUCH OR NON-TOUCH

- **Step 1**: Two options. Use this as a positive resourcing intervention and identify the positive archetype that your client identifies as a positive force. Or, you can notice your client discussing a negative archetype (such as victim) and suggest that you connect the cords of the opposite positive archetype (leader).

- **Step 2:** Come into your Intention Line and Core Being, resonating to its vibration. Let that vibration fill your field. Using intention, connect to the energy of the positive archetype you wish to bring into the client's field. If the energy does not come, try a similar archetype that might better connect to your client.

TABLE WORK: If doing table work, reach with your dominant hand upward toward the outer edges of your client's field. Connect to, feel, and sense the cord of the positive archetype and connect it into the client's Core Being vortex just above the navel and below the third chakra. Ask the client to use all of their senses. Visualize a symbol, picture or a time in the past when the client felt connected to the energy of the positive archetype. Ask your client to let the energy of the positive archetype into their body. Ask them to notice where it feels strongest and then focus on those areas and invite the energy to fill every cell, bone and organ.

(Note: If the energy does not download, then investigate if there is an unhealthy ancestral wire in the second, third and/or forth chakras. Usually, this means you need to explore an unhealthy ancestral cord that is blocking the positive archetype. This is no longer a Solo Archetype Intervention, and it becomes an Ancestral Confluence Archetype intervention. This is diagramed next.)

NON-TOUCH: Ask your client to resonate to their Core Being/intention line while you do the same. Use intention to sense the positive archetype and ask your client to do the same. Ask the client to use all of their senses. Visualize a symbol, picture or a time in the past when the client felt connected to the energy of the positive archetype. Ask your client to let the energy of the positive archetype into their body. Ask them to notice where it feels strongest and then focus on those areas and invite the energy to fill every cell, bone and organ.

- **Step 3:** If the energy covers at least 70 percent of the body, consider that a success and suggest they practice inviting the download of the positive archetype until you see them again. Eventually, you can explore what Core Distortion, negative belief or negative ancestral energy prevented the expansion throughout the body if they are not able to feel the sensation of the consciousness of the positive archetype throughout at least 90 percent of their body.

ARCHETYPE AND ANCESTRAL CONFLUENCE INTERVENTION

When a client follows the same negative pattern in life and you notice it is linked to the same negative pattern that their mother, father or ancestors followed, it is time for an Archetype and Ancestral Confluence Intervention. Confluence, by definition is a flowing or coming together of people and/or things. So by doing this intervention, you are able to transform any negative confluence in a person's life. Before practicing this on someone else, attend a Me-B training to learn how to do this intervention. It is complex and very technical. Get support and learn it well.

- **STEP 1:** Identify the negative ancestral pattern. Ask your client where they feel it in their body. Track the energy of it and investigate how the negative wire of this ancestral pattern presents in the client's energy system. Which chakras does it wind through?
- **STEP 2:** Identify the positive Archetype that can replace the negative Ancestral pattern.
- **Step 3:** If on the table, feel the negative wire of the unhealthy Ancestral Pattern between your fingers. If this is a non-touch intervention, you and your client will have to find the negative wiring by using intention.
  Resonate at the Core Being level. Follow the wire and let it dissolve or pull the wire out of the field. This also pulls out the unhealthy pattern.
- **STEP 4:** Once the negative ancestral pattern has dissolved, ask your client to identify a positive archetypical pattern to replace the negative ancestral pattern.

TABLE WORK INTERVENTION: If doing table work, reach with your dominant hand upward toward the outer edges of your client's field. Connect to, feel, sense the energy of the positive archetype to replace the energy of the negative ancestral pattern. Connect it into the client's Core Being vortex just above the navel and below the third chakra. Ask the client to use all of their senses. Visualize a symbol, picture or a time in the past when the client felt connected to the energy of the positive archetype. Ask your client to let the energy of the positive archetype into their body. Ask them to notice where it feels strongest and then focus on those areas and invite the energy to fill every cell, bone and organ.

NON-TOUCH INTERVENTION: If doing non-touch work, ask your client to resonate to the Intention Line/Core Being while you do the same. Use intention to sense the positive archetype and ask your client to do the same. Ask the client to use all of their senses. Visualize a symbol, picture or a time in the past when the client felt connected to the energy of the positive archetype. Ask your client to let the energy of the positive archetype into their body. Ask them to notice where it feels strongest and then focus on those areas and invite the energy to fill every cell, bone and organ.

WAKING UP FROM THE DREAM

Some of us believe that we are here on earth so we can learn how to "wake up" from the dream of life. This means that the reality we live is only something our mind has created. This world is only as real as our dreams at night—the only difference being that it is much more difficult to wake up from the dream of the everyday world.

Byron Katie's book, *1000 Names of Joy*, explains the view of reality she has held since 1984, when she "woke up" and began to view the world from the perspective of her enlightened mind. Katie states that everything is perfect and represents god's will 100 percent. If something happens, it is perfect, in her view—even rape, murder, death and tragedy.

For some, this is a rather radical view. For me, it requires a constant letting go of what I think "should" or "could" happen versus what DID happen or IS happening in the moment. Seeing life as a dream can help us stop judging what is happening.

Given how deeply I am committed to personal change and to facilitating change in others, it is a huge personal challenge to view the world as not needing change. It is probably one of the hardest things we can do to view every moment in the bliss of the unknown, knowing that what happens is always perfect. This is an ideal I am enjoying more and more every day. Working with our own or a client's dreams can help bring perspective to this ideal. *We know our dreams are not reality. Should we also view everyday life as a dream that is not a clear representation of reality?*

If we can do it, how might it even serve the greater good? How might it create more joy, peace and fulfillment in the world... or should I say, in the "dream" of the world?

BASIC TECHNIQUES FOR WORKING WITH DREAMS

- If it were my dream, I imagine it would mean….
- View each character in the dream as if the character represented an aspect of you.
- Retell it in the present first person narrative and feel the feelings/emotions/energy along the way. Process the deeper meaning.
- Explore symbolism in the dreams.
- Draw the dream.
- Find the biggest energetic charge in the dream and notice where we feel that same charge in our body and energy system. Work with that charge in a Core Distortion healing to shift the LVC into HVC.
- If the dream is too traumatic, you can have a power animal or a spirit guide come into the dream with you.
- Work with pillows in a Gestalt-like fashion. Let each pillow represent a part of the dream. You can add pillows or take them away. Usually work from the areas of lowest charge to the areas of greatest charge, or isolate one aspect of the dream to start.

Three Types Of Dreams:

1. Archetypical dreams—or, as Jung would say, dreams that represent collective consciousness.
2. Dreams that represent personal and developmental Core Distortions. Usually a person will begin seeing dreams in terms of developmental distortions and then progress to collective consciousness.
3. Precognitive dreams or dreams providing psychic information.

To make a dream less traumatic, we can ask ourselves or the client to view the dream as an issue of collective consciousness, so they are more detached. Many war dreams are about collective consciousness. After all, we are all one, so anyone tapping into the collective is also tapping into himself or herself.

Dreams can be subconscious or unconscious, and they can hold emotional material.

Even if we can only remember one aspect of a dream, we can still work with it. A teacher of mine told a story about one of their clients who could only remember a color in their dream. By working with that color, the client's true being was revealed. He discovered that he was not a computer programmer at heart—instead, he was gay, and his passion was to be a florist. It took over a year of therapy before this client's dreams opened up.

REVIEW QUESTIONS

1. What archetypes do you identify with? For a listing of archetypes, go to the following link:

   http://meta-religion.com/Psychiatry/Analytical_psychology/a_gallery_of_archetypes.htm

2. What negative ancestral patterns follow you throughout the day? What positive archetypical energies can help you realign?

3. Why might it be helpful or not helpful to view life as a dream? What are your challenges in viewing this life as a dream? What negative intention might get in the way of letting you receive the benefits of viewing life as a dream?

4. Watch your dreams for a week and write them down. Explore what wisdom they might hold.

CHAPTER 22

CHRONIC ILLNESS, DEATH and DYING

If the mind or body continues to fail and does not heal, it does not mean that we cannot still resonate as brightly. More than ever, chronic Illness necessitates that we learn to feel gratitude, whole and complete especially when darkness lingers. Utilizing the Buddhist wisdom of not clinging to health and not revolting against illness allows us to create the energetic balance of acceptance. Acceptance of what is happening in the moment helps us re-balance and align our manifest energy toward our highest good.

CHRONIC ILLNESS

We all can cultivate the energy of god. In Me-B Transformation, we call this energy Core Being and learn to bring it into our mind and body to heal ourselves. If there is any debate that Core Being is real...or if we still wonder if there is an actual energetic vortex of god within us, then a chronic illness can feel even more over- whelming.

I define chronic illness as any reoccurring symptom or pathology that is persistent, long-term and/or terminal. Both physical and emotional challenges can be considered chronic.

Examples of common physical chronic illness include but are not limited to: back pain, cancer, migraines, Multiple Sclerosis (MS), Parkinson's; heart disease; stroke; irritable bowel; and autoimmune diseases such as chronic fatigue and fibromyalgia.

Examples of mental illness that can be chronic and/or degenerative include: schizophrenia; bi-polar disorder; depression; anxiety; dissociative identity disorder and personality disorders such as border-line and anti-social.

Chronic illness presents the opportunity for deep personal, energetic and emotional transformation. Supporting ourselves or our client in becoming more than our illness is an important therapeutic intervention. Because our state of mind strongly influences our health, working with thoughts, energy, beliefs and the subconscious needs to be an integral part of healing. The text below summarizes common emotional and energetic obstacles and opportunities that chronic illness provides: disempowerment, lack of control, wisdom, self-care, wishing to be saved, empowerment and energetic challenges such as a broken Intention line or a disconnected Core Being.

Disempowerment, No Control

A typical person that finds his or herself plagued by a chronic illness often feels disempowered and victimized by their body and/or their illness. We are faced with the issue of no-control. If we are spiritual, we may even feel we have done something wrong to cause the illness and it is our fault. Typically, one of the first interventions must be to help us (or our client) establish influence and action over the illness. (This is the opposite of needing control over the illness.)

We may not be able to control everything that happens to us, but we do have influence, power, and the ability to turn a challenge into a gift. This may be all we can do. Illness, like any personal challenge, is a spiritual opportunity to create necessary life changes that would not otherwise be possible. As we open to this possibility, deeper healing, growth and transformation can occur. Michael J. Fox wrote a wonderful book on this topic en- titled *Always Looking Up*. Energetically, the Manifest Energy Intention Line and our Enlightened Observer can be useful to help us detach enough to find the internal strength to look up!

Gaining Wisdom

Gaining wisdom from illness includes accessing any feelings that arise such as anger, grief or loss. Nothing brings up personal issues more than a chronic illness, chronic pain or facing our mortality. An Me-B Guide, Nancy Battilega, wrote about her emotional journey to heal breast cancer in *A Story of Grace*. It is an uplifting story of self-exploration and is a testimonial to the power of surrendering to the healing powers of the god within us all.

TAKE TIME AND SPACE TO HEAL

Augusta was diagnosed with an abnormal mammogram. During an Me-B session, she connected to her breast cells. Breathing deeply, she connected even deeper. She felt them full—full with the pain of her family, friends, and country. She saw how her deep love and compassion for others led her to unconsciously take their pain and discomfort into her heart and breast tissue.

She began to let go of their energy and to create space for her own energy and essence to heal her cells. She made a personal note to have healthier boundaries and not take on other people's energy. Six weeks later when she had follow-up tests, she was given a clean bill of health. No cancer tumors were found! It only takes a moment to change our life! We can create the time and space for our healing moments.

When dealing with any severe illness, working one's personal process can feel more complicated emotionally. However, the basics are still simple. For example, illness exists in the absence of light. The internal light reflects the essence of the truth of the soul. It reflects one's Core Being.

This truth is simple, yet not easy to incorporate into our minute-by-minute experiences. As our skills advance, however, it becomes easier to allow our Core Being to fill up our cells, enzymes—the molecules of our being— and illness and distortion dissolve. Find where the LVC is held in our body/energy system then follow the 5 Steps so we can move through the 3 Rings of healing and back to Core Being.

Brain/Neurological Reactivity's Role in Perpetuating Illness

Research seems to indicate that dysregulation of our autonomic nervous system as a result of stress and/or trauma could contribute to illness and tax our immune system. In the book, *The Body Bears the Burden*; Robert Scare, MD outlines the neurological influences of stress and trauma on the body. Understanding some of the key factors to health and healing as outlined in his book (or similar books) may be important to helping ourselves or our clients heal.

Although much of the scientific data associating traumatic stress with adverse health effects is circumstantial and subject to debate and interpretation, many studies show physiological alterations in

PTSD [Post Traumatic Stress Disorder] that correlate with predictable diseases seen in its victims. There also appears to be a small cluster of poorly understood syndromes that have a compelling link to the physiology and incidence of trauma, including irritable bowel syndrome, gastroesophegeal reflux disease, interstitial cystitis, chronic pain syndromes, fibromyalgia/CFS, and RSD. All of these diseases are compatible with a dysregulated autonomic nervous system,, especially with parasympathetic dominance. Other so-called diseases of stress, including hypertension, peptic ulcer disease, ulcerative colitis, and atherosclerotic coronary artery disease probably also can be added to the list of diseases of trauma, although they primarily reflect the high cortisol-based diseases of stress (Robert C. Scare, MD; *The Body Bears the Burden*; P.127).

The body-mind connection to health still needs further documentation but until that time, anyone with a chronic illness might benefit from understanding more about (1) their Heart Rate Variability, (2) The Polyvagal Theory of Emotion, (3) the effects of kindling, (4) dissociative capsules, and (5) how to discharge any left-over freeze response. I offer only a brief introduction to these topics. *To adequately understand these very complicated and complex concepts, you will need further study and research. I offer only a taste and a very general overview.*

1. <u>Heart Rate Variability:</u> Heart rate normally increases with inspiration and decreases with expiration. In his book, Scare calls it the Respiratory Sinus Arrythmia (RSA). The greater the difference between these rates, the healthier and more stable the autonomic nervous system, a measure of homeostasis or optimal autonomic balance (Robert C. Scare, MD; *The Body Bears the Burden*).

2. <u>The Polyvagal Theory of Emotion and Vagal Tone:</u> I am still trying to understand the complexity of this theory. A short review deals with two parasympathetic nerve centers in the brainstem medulla: dorsal and ventral vagal nuclei. Dorsal vagal complex governs digestive, taste and hypoxic responses. In part, it provides primary neural control of abdominal organs. It also promotes change from mobilization to immobilization- the freeze response. High dorsal vagal complex tone may promote immobilization and freeze. In our normal day-to-day life, this in not healthy because it could deal with fear, helpless, dissociation, and lack of body awareness (Robert C. Scare, MD; *The Body Bears the Burden*).
   The Ventral Vagal Complex fosters social engagement and maternal infant bonding and complex social behaviors. High vagal tone promotes health and communication and social engagement (Robert C. Scare, MD; *The Body Bears the Burden*)
   In chronic illness, there is sometimes low vagal tone and high dorsal vagal tone. This might not create optimum health. Chronic illness in itself is trauma. Working to mitigate any additional trauma or stress to our emotional system might be important.

3. <u>Kindling and Autonomic Dysregulation:</u> Kindling is the development of self-perpetuating neural circuits through repetitive stimulation, said Scare. In other words, continued and repetitive stress and/or trauma causes an imbalance in our neural circuits. Kindled posttraumatic procedural memories provide repetitive, unconscious cue-related input to the sympathetic limb of the autonomic nervous system, leading to increased dysfunctional cycling and dysregulation, according to Scare. (Robert C. Scare, MD; *The Body Bears the Burden*)
   "Since the autonomic nervous system in PTSD may well be associated with the self-perpetuating central nervous system phenomenon of kindling, it is likely that the resulting continuous

perturbation of autonomic, vascular, endocrinological, and immune systems is required to contribute to the development of diseases of trauma. As diseases of kindling, they may be perpetuated by internal brain processes. They may be expected to progress in severity in the apparent absence of an ongoing identifiable pathogenic event...In this model, therefore, the pathophysiological effects of trauma might well provide the major impetus to development and perpetuation of many chronic diseases of un- known cause." (Robert C. Scare, MD; *The Body Bears the Burden*; P. 127).

4. <u>Dissociative Capsules created by procedural memories</u>: According to Scare, the number of one's Dissociative capsules is determined by the sum total of one's cumulative life traumas. He said that capsules consist of procedural memories from the past trauma, but are perceived as being present, and are therefore dissociative. This "living in the past" could stress our body-mind system.

   He lists some examples of capsule procedural memories: pain, numbness, dizziness; tremor, tics, paralysis; nausea, cramps, palpitations, anxiety, terror, shame, rage; flashbacks, nightmares or intrusive thoughts (Robert C. Scare, MD; *The Body Bears the Burden*).

5. <u>Discharge of the Freeze:</u> Lack of discharge of our bodies freeze response could create vulnerability to our body and health. As we learn to discharge any leftover freeze energy, we could support a more balanced system. In addition, we could reduce unhealthy hypo or hyper-arousal states that can cause stress on our body. As Core Being or HVC comes into our body, we often shake and quake away the freeze energy. As we can move our body in a healthy defensive manner in all Me-B Systems, we invite health and happiness.

Solutions

According to Scare, parasympathetic symptoms in PTSD include cramps, diarrhea, indigestion, fatigue, weakness, collapse, numbing, bradycardia, constriction, and cognitive dulling. He adds that sympathetic symptoms in PTSD might be arousal, anxiety, panic, phobias, muscular bracing, tremor, pain, and tachycardia (Robert C. Scare, MD; *The Body Bears the Burden*).

Although this is a brief and incomplete summary of our brain and nervous system's workings, it offers some understanding of the relationship between trauma/stress and chronic illness.

As we are able to relax our ego with Core Being energy and transform LVC into HVC we can often lower the dorsal vagal tone and create high vagal tone and a healthy RSA. In addition, as our skills advance at discharging LVC of the freeze response and replace the freeze energy with Core Being energy, we can sometimes reduce kindling as well. I also find the neurological replacement intervention taught earlier to be extremely helpful.

Pain Abatement

Scare writes, "In fact, I believe that the most common complaint in current medical practice, that of persistent and unexplained chronic pain, has its roots in the persistent changes in brain circuitry associated with unresolved trauma, and the continued tendency for dissociation to occur in the face of stress or threat...The pattern of defensive and protective movement at the time of a traumatic event is stored in procedural memory for the purpose of adaptation to future related threat and incorporated in regional neuromuscular detail into the kindled cycle of trauma." (Robert C. Scare, MD; *The Body Bears the Burden*; P. 23).

Self-Care

Self-care is needed to eliminate our past traumas and stresses and to heal from chronic illness. Many of us don't always take optimum care of ourselves. Too busy and too rushed, we live a fast-paced and overwhelmed life. If we have a chronic illness (or to prevent one), self-care has to take a high priority. I give my- self a 5-year self-care plan. I ask myself what incremental changes can I realistically make in 5 years and in all three Me-B Systems? For instance, energetically what is my baseline now, and where do I want it to be 5 years from now? At the mind level, how can I have more kind thoughts, work more effectively with my ego and stay present? In my body, how can I improve my exercise routine, nutritional habits and other support?

All the information in this book can be considered a self-care plan. Find what is most helpful and implement these steps, inch by inch.

SELF-CARE PLAN

1. What exercise, nutrition, vitamin, herbal, mineral or supplement self-care changes are needed? It's important to start slowly with any changes and build upon our successes.
2. Take a moment to look at our Rhythm and Flow of Reality. Do we have too much time and space? Do we run too fast, too slow? Do we need more space or less space in our lives? How tight or loose are our boundaries with others and ourselves? Are we able to maintain a level of abundance and balance? Write down what changes are needed. Remember to be kind and not judgmental.
3. Feel our cells and feel the ample space around our cells. Breathe. Within that space, notice distance and time, plenty of time. Breathe again. Now look at our life and the space and time we allow between activities in our life. Where might there be too much or too little and what solutions can you imagine?
4. What is your energetic baseline? What improvements can you realistically make in one year? What are the negative beliefs and LVC that can be transformed to improve your energetic baseline? Where is it held in the body/energy system? What do you imagine is their positive alternative? Often we work the same core issues at deeper and deeper levels. What are your core issues and what is your next level of healing around them?
5. Write out a self-care action plan that will bring you joy and kindness, and that builds slowly upon the skills that you have already, right now.

If we remain sick, does it mean we have failed?

No. Our body is only a temporary consciousness container for this light and we have no control over how long it will last—especially as we grow old. *So, if the body continues to fail and does not heal, we can still resonate as brightly (or more brightly than before).* Therefore, illness should not be taken to the extreme to mean that we cause our own illness or illness is our fault! Judgment never heals. It is all just a journey. Chronic Illness is only a bend in the rode and should not be judged as a mistake or an evil. In fact doing so misses the point of the gift. Illness is just a subconscious arrow pointing us in a direction to explore, not judge.

Use the Explorer's Mind to navigate all the bends in the road. They are perfect and necessary—otherwise they wouldn't be happening. Surrendering to acceptance, wisdom and compassion is the real lesson. Even if a bend in the road leads to physical death, it should not be looked upon as a failure. Death will happen to all of us. Who are we to say that remaining alive reflects more success than being successful at how we die?

I do believe in the benevolent universe theory that we are truly being held in love and compassion and wisdom, even in times of turmoil and trial—or rather, especially in times of turmoil and trial. All we can do is walk our path, learn, grow and enjoy the ride. After all, I believe we are never done. Even after we die, the journey continues—just in a different form and dimension.

To Be Saved

One key emotional issue many clients with a chronic illness share is a deep-seated (often subconscious) need to be taken care of, loved and supported. Part of us is waiting for someone to heal us, and/or fix and save us from the difficulties of the world. Some of us are looking for an escape—a way out of internal pain through an external savior. We can use chronic illness (subconsciously) as a means to achieve this unstated goal.

The following describes false images and beliefs that interfere with healing a chronic illness. All three represent poor vagal tone which significantly taxes our immune system.

1. To live—I had to please others (collapse).
2. To live—I need you to accept me.
3. To live—You must take care of me.

The positive image and belief a Me-B Guide can help their client master is: To live—I will support myself, be strong, not collapse and accept all parts of me. This represents optimum vagal tone and supports homeostasis and physical health.

As a Me-B guide, we can help clients to continually let go of the hope of being saved. In fact, it is vital we help clients let go of the hope of being saved by some human external source and help them reconnect to their internal source of power. This does not mean that they shouldn't continue to pursue alternative or conventional methods of medicine and healing. It means they don't seek help from a place of lack within themselves. In- stead, they seek help from a place of power and abundance. Being able to self-validate and reflect our own true spirit back to us is a key element to happiness and promotes health. Illness points out to us where in our body we hold Core Distortions. As we use our Explorer's Mind, engage our Enlightened Observer to move through the 3-Rings of Healing, we gain truth and promote health.

From this perspective, doctors and other external support are our employees. They don't hold the answer or the power to heal. We listen to them yet we stay connected to our own intuitive knowing and assess their advice and support. We take in the multitudes of advice coming our way, and design our own healing plan.

A FEAR-BASED SEARCH NEVER WINS

July, a mother with breast cancer, traveled all over the world seeing healers and doctors. She meditated and visualized light and wholeness. She ate organic foods and followed all the "rules." When I saw her I could tell the cancer was stronger, not weaker— despite her latest visit to a healer who had "performed miracles."

It was clear that July was going through the proper actions to heal herself but she felt victimized by her cancer. When confronted with this fact, she collapsed into tears, saying she did feel like a victim. She said that she had tried so hard to do everything perfectly—but her test results indicated the cancer was advancing. "It has even spread to my lungs!" she exclaimed.

After July did deeper work to claim her own authority and power over her healing, the growth of her cancer dramatically reduced and her lungs cleared. She realized that every act she had taken before had been about giving her power to someone else to heal her, instead of claiming her own authority and using others as supplemental support. After deeper Me-B work, July even got to the point of knowing that if the cancer ended up spreading, she would not collapse into victim mode. She would no longer let cancer, or her body, be a drain on her light!

Energetic Challenges

Illness moves from higher frequencies in the Auric Field downward to the denser frequencies of the first level of the Auric Field. So any energetic healing must focus on bringing the higher frequency of Core Being down into the 1st level of the Auric Field. One common energetic configuration of chronic illness is a broken Intention Line and distortions on the 1st, 2nd and 4th levels of the field.

1. Begin examining the Manifest Energy Intention Line and discover what negative beliefs/intentions created the breaks and misalignment. Simply working at this level can be enough to create healing.
2. Next explore what Core Distortions are held in the 2nd and 4th levels of the field.
3. Finally, as the Intention Line, 2nd and 4th levels repair and reprogram, integrate the HVC into the 1st level of the field. (Review previous chapters for interventions on how to bring in HVC into any LVC held in the Intention Line or the Auric Field. Remember that it is intention that moves energy and creates healing.)

Depending upon the illness, there are different protocols to energetically support healing. If it is cancer, we must be careful not to push energy into it. For most kinds of cancer, there is already an over-charge of energy. Using intention, inviting the energy out of a cancer tumor can help shrink and eliminate the tumor.

However, if we or our client has an autoimmune disease, the energetics of what is needed to heal becomes more complicated. If we bring in too much energy, it can deflate the energy field just as putting too much air in a tire can cause it to burst and deflate.

Energy has intelligence. We can learn how to follow the energy and support it to bring in HVC and transform the LVC of illness. As we use positive intention and develop our energy tracking and awareness skills we can feel confident in our abilities to assist others and our self. Always wait to work with someone who has a chronic illness until we are comfortable that we can support their highest good.

CORE BEING DISSOLVES ILLNESS

Deborah was crying when she came into my office. Her latest mammogram revealed a tumor, and she was scheduled for a biopsy the next day. Although Deborah was still learning how to connect to Core Being, within 30 minutes of table work, her cells had filled with Core Being's HVC. The next day when she went for the biopsy, they couldn't find anything to biopsy. The tumor was gone.

I worked with a Filipino healer that helped me greatly with the energetic aspects of healing. Leony Apilo calls herself a spiritual healer. Her type of healing can't be taught. She was born with the gift. She is very talented in pulling out energetic illness and bringing in HVC into the body. If we are ready for healing, she is great at energetically facilitating health.

Find Empowerment Within

Every chronically ill client can learn how to feel, sense, know, visualize and acknowledge their Core Being in a meaningful and tangible manner. Our Core Being is the savior we have been waiting for. It is our internal power source and helps us manifest and receive our external support. Many of the positive resourcing exercises taught in this book help in the process of finding our true spirit.

In addition, I often refer to the Adult Consciousness triangle of:

- learning to receive from others when we'd rather give, giving when we'd rather receive and,
- giving to self when we'd rather receive from others.
- Balancing all aspects of this triangle, coupled with feeling our Core Being as a sensation in the body, mind and energy system creates a tangible experience toward achieving self-empowerment.

CHRONIC ILLNESS EMPOWERMENT CHECKLIST

1. **TAKE CHARGE OF OUR HEALING.** No one is the expert on us. We must learn to tune within and discover what works. Doctors, family, alternative medicine, and others are only support. They are not the authority over us and they are not in charge of us. We must listen, learn, research and discover what works for us. We then use others to supplement our own inner knowing. This is the first and most important step. Strongly program into the Intention Line that (1) we are in charge of our healing process and that (2) we are succeeding. Depending upon the illness, "success" may look differently. Don't be rigid in its definition. There can be multiple types of success every day. Breathe in the gratitude of every win, every day. This creates the energetic opening for grace. This must be done without "attaching" to success in order to feel good about ourselves. Remember, energetically, if we "need" to heal to feel whole, it creates a distortion. We can instead enjoy and accept healing.

2. **DESIGN AN INTEGRATED SELF-CARE ACTION PLAN.** Make our action plan as comprehensive as possible. Write out a plan and make changes to it as needed. Be as specific as possible and have it solution focused so it helps us connect to our own personal power. We will have to work hard so we don't feel victimized by our illness or by our bodies/mind.

   - Who do we need on our team to help us? Also include what alternative/traditional medical care is needed? For instance, do we need an herbalist, massage therapist, acupuncturist, or Me-B Guide for energetic and emotional support?
   - What eating habits need to improve?
   - Do we need someone to help us navigate the insurance paperwork?
   - Do we need support to address any financial challenges?
   - What other support do we need?
   - If we have children, older parents, animals or others that are accustomed to being cared for by us- what changes are needed?
   - How can we reach out to our community and receive its support?
   - What emotional support do we need?
   - What energetic support do we need?
   - How can we find the gifts in this illness and not feel victimized?
   - Energetically feel the Action Plan aligned in the Intention Line.

3. **INTERACTING WITH TRADITIONAL and ALTERNATIVE MEDICINE.** When meeting with the doctor and/or alternative practitioner, there will be times we might need to take someone with us to take notes and collect information and receive clarification. Chronic illness can be overwhelming and it can be difficult to do everything ourselves.
   Also, feel free to **get a second opinion and learn as much as we can about our illness**. We must become our own advocate on healing and remember the doctor is our employee not our authority. Be careful not to give away our power to anyone "in-charge." Emotionally, chronic illness offers the possibility of claiming our personal power and Core Being at deeper and deeper levels.

Interacting with insurance companies can be frustrating, confusing and tiring. See what support we need internally for this challenge and what external support we can receive.

4. **TRANSFORM FEAR-BASED AND EMOTIONAL REACTIVITY.** Do not minimize the challenges of chronic illness but rise to meet them. Chronic illness is trauma- very strong trauma. So there is bound to be some fear-based reactivity, anger and other emotional and energetic challenges. This is especially true if there is a lot of pain or if the illness could become (or is) terminal. This is normal and it will happen! We can use our Explorer's Mind, notice when it happens, move through the 3-rings of healing, follow the 5 steps, and reconnect to Core Being. If the body continues to fail and does not heal, it does not mean that we cannot still resonate as brightly. More than ever, chronic illness necessitates we learn to feel gratitude, whole and complete even when darkness lingers.

5. **USE CHOICE POINTS: FIND THE GIFTS AND FOCUS ON THE POSITIVE**. We can look for OUR CHOICE POINTS to find the gifts in the illness and focus on the positive so we reprogram our past negative behaviors and negative beliefs

6. **WORK ENERGETICALLY.** Core Being is the HVC that helps heal chronic illness. To the extent possible, during the day feel the sensation of the HVC of Core Being in every cell.

Notes for Families and Caretakers

If we have a loved one with a chronic illness, it can be upsetting to the entire family system. There can be resentment, anger, grief, guilt and overwhelm. Once again, this is normal. We can **design a family Self-Care Action Plan** so we are more equipped to deal with the challenges. Have regular family meetings to address emotional and/or practical fires that flare up. To the extent possible, put out the small fires before they become too consuming. Finding someone qualified as a medical advocate is also very helpful.

Chronic illness often means there are some very difficult decisions to be made on choosing which medical treatment might be best and/or what alternative treatment might be supportive. Most of us are not educated enough to negotiate the complexity of the medical system. A trained medical advocate who can advise both the patient and the family of treatment options and to help them determine if there is a need for additional medical opinions and/or advice can be of great support.

Ultimately the family needs to be careful not to place their needs and worries upon their loved one. This can be very hard. In fact, one of the most common complaints I get from people with a chronic condition is that they are tired of everyone telling them what to do. They constantly get bombarded with "new ideas" of how to beat the illness. Quickly it can become too much and overwhelming.

PERSONALITY TYPES AND CHRONIC ILLNESSES

Heart-Centered: Their boundaries tend to be more permeable and their body types often hold more toxins. These two characteristics make their health challenges significant and they need to overcome any dorsal vagal complex. As a Me-B guide, you can teach them to firm up the structured levels of their field and to heal their victim energy and become physically active. Making these small but significant changes are important to long-term mental and emotional health.

Compassionate: This character structure is ruled by the false belief that they are not enough and their field can be undercharged. They wait to be saved and fed by another. This is the most difficult personality type to heal from a chronic illness. A Me-B Guide must focus on helping the client find strength, fullness and empowerment. This means that they need to overcome any dorsal vagal complex. Many times, the Compassionates Intention Line will be organized toward dependence on another. Teaching them how to reorganize their Intention Line toward independence and power is a good place to start.

Leader: This character type is most likely to succeed in healing a chronic illness. The Leader tends to tackle life as a battle. This can be helpful when healing a chronic illness. Call in the positive archetype of this character structure and keep reminding them they can succeed.

Excel: If the Excel person can overcome the emotional strain of being "imperfect" and feel (but not collapse into) they can then transform the deeper emotions and will have a high success rate in healing both mental and emotional illnesses.

Spiritual: Encourage the Spiritual to use their gift of connecting to higher vibrations to help them heal. What might be difficult for them is to bring those HVC into the physical body.

Spiritual types tend to be very disconnected from the physical body. As they learn to bring in the HVC of Core Being into the body they can heal. It will also help them overcome any negative beliefs and false sense of self that developed because of their young trauma. They will have to learn to transform the trauma of their past without disassociating. If a Me-B Guide helps them strengthen their energy and biological consciousness container (brain neuroplasticity, nervous system, limbic system, cellular memory...) they will eventually be able to transform any emotion or LVC life challenge and return back to the HVC of Core Being.

Do's and Don'ts of Energetically Working with Cancer/Heart Disease in the Field

- Cancer cannot live in high vibrational frequencies. Cancer is the absence of Core Being. Energetically, cancer can first be found in the upper levels of the field and eventually presents in the physical level. **Bringing in the HVC of clients Core Being helps heal cancer.**
- There was a study where healers sent loving energy into cancer and It grew. **Making sure we don't charge the cancer by sending energy into it is primary.**
- Emotionally, cancer often deals with having good boundaries. This means teaching a client to have good boundaries around what they allow to enter their energy field. This technique alone can help reduce and/or eliminate cancer. When I first learned energy work, I heard of a case where a boy healed cancer by visualizing a packman eating and destroying it. This is a good example of energetically saying "no" to what is allowed to live inside us.

Steps for Working With Cancer

Connect energetically with the consciousness of the cancer. Connect as deeply to the center as possible but be careful not to draw the cancer into your body.

Note: If the cancer has already metastasized and spread throughout the client's body and bones, start at the head of the person and work down—one quadrant at a time. Spread our intention to cover each quadrant of the body and connect into and feel the cancer.

Make sure you DO NOT bring the cancer into your body. **You work in the client's body**—*do not energetically bring the client into your body*. Also, be careful you don't resonate to the frequency of the cancer when you feel deep compassion for the client with cancer. I have made this mistake and accidentally brought cancer into my field. Make sure your energy field stays at a higher frequency than the cancer.

Gradually, using intention and awareness, expand your field to resonate to your Core Being dimension and fill your body with your Core Being creating HVC throughout yourself. Then allow **the client's Core Being** energy to fill reclaim the space/cells that the cancer took over. Allow his or her core to fill every cell and space in all parts of the body.

Lastly, because cancer (and most chronic illness) is caused by a malfunction in our immune system, work to support and stabilize the second chakra. Place one hand under the second chakra and one hand over it. Using intention, resonate orange throughout your field; let it spread through your hands and into the client. Allow the energy to flow between your hands until the chakra feels charged and balanced.

NOTE: If the client is having radiation or chemotherapy, first connect to the energy of the chemo or radiation and direct it into the center of the cancer. Each type of chemo will feel different and you may even be able to energetically tell when your client has changed the type of chemo and/or sense into the energetic effectiveness of the chemo or radiation.

Some chemotherapies may feel like burning brandy, while others can feel and taste metallic. After you direct the chemo into the cancer, energetically remove it from healthy cells. You can either: (a) energetically pull it out of the field or (b) energetically call in the vibration of Core Being and allow the chemo to dissipate out of the field.

Sensing Cancer In the Field

When I sense cancer in the Auric Field, it feels to me like pins and needles prickling my hand. As the cancer begins to die, and Core Being regains its space, I find the feeling changes to a more smooth flow and positive tingles. When I see cancer in the field it looks dark and solid.

PRACTICE WORKING WITH CANCER

1. Using a long distance technique, call in a volunteer client with breast cancer and place her energy onto a table or into a pillow.
2. Then, sense into the cancer. Be careful you don't let it come into your field. Call in the HVC of the volunteer client's Core Being, and allow it to melt away the cancer.

Heart Disease

The leading cause of death among women is heart disease. When working with heart disease in the energy field it is important not to pump too much energy into the chest. Instead, balance areas that feel overcharged by allowing the energy to move to areas that are undercharged. Then, check to see if there are any unhealthy Ancestral wiring or Archetypical energies preventing the heart from healing. Explore what Core Distortion might be feeding the heart disease? Over time, Core Distortions and Negative Beliefs can be healed and transformed.

SUPPORTING A CLIENT THROUGH THE DEATH PROCESS AND THE FAMILY THROUGH THE GRIEVING PROCESS

If a chronic illness is terminal, a client will need much support. The *Tibetan Book of the Dead* and Elisabeth Kubler Ross's books can be important resources in this manner. (Her books include: *On Children and Death; Life Lessons; On Life After Death; Rise Above It; Death is of Vital Importance; To Live Until We Say Goodbye;* On Grief and Grieving.)

Kubler speaks of the stages of death, dying and grief as movement through emotions such as denial, anger, bargaining, grief, and acceptance. In Me-B transformation, the grief and death process can be looked at as a continuum of movement through four major stages. Just as concentric circles deepen within each other, over time we move through the four stages at deeper and deeper levels.

FOUR TASKS OF GRIEF/DEATH AND DYING

Acknowledge the loss and the emotional pain. Emotions such as anger, sadness, and/or hopelessness. With our Enlightened Observer, feel and release the discomfort in the mind, energy and body systems. Open to the possibility that something positive could fill the gap left empty when the pain is gone.

Actually fill the gap in all 3 Me-B Systems with something positive. An internal positive could be Core Being and any self-awareness gifts/lessons we received during this difficult challenge. An external positive could be feeling more connected to community or rearranging priorities so that we find a new job or…. If we are in the grief process, we must eventually reinvest in life after the loss. This is what it means to "fill the gap."

If we or our client is on the verge of dying, filling in the gap could mean that we have found enough trust and safety to surrender to god in the form of our physical death. So, under the right circumstances, death from a chronic illness can become a positive form of transformation.

MEN AND WOMEN CAN RESPOND TO GRIEF DIFFERENTLY

Stereotypical Masculine responses to grief: Feelings held in or toned down; thinking precedes or dominates feelings; focus on problem solving rather than on the expression of feelings; outward feelings often involve anger or guilt; internal adjustments to loss are expressed through activity; intense feelings may only be ex- pressed privately; reluctance to discuss feelings with others; and intense grief is usually expressed immediately after the loss during funerals.

Feminine stereotypical reactions include: Feelings of anguish and tears of lament; socializing to be nurtured; not afraid to discuss grief or feelings; difficulty with expressing anger; able to seek support; and often act as care givers to others.

Get support so we can find our positive way of dealing with grief.

SUPPORTING THE FIELD OF A DYING PERSON

This process is about the client reclaiming their divinity. Life, like death, can be an effortless flow. Flow becomes the divine. What makes death hard is the ego at the personality level because a part of it doesn't want to let go. Instead, it wants to hold on to some concept of self. Through the death process we can help them let go and surrender to "no self".

Just as when we work with our clients we aspire to work from a place of Core Being or "no self", when we die we also endeavor to release old concepts of self and move toward being the open vessel that god can move through. In Me-B Transformation this is stage 7 and in some cases stage 8.

Our deepest passion and longing is to let go (and of course, part of us doesn't want to). When we fully let go we become the vessel for source to move through.

Being alone or with others

During the dying process, some people want to be alone. Think of the story of the older dog leaving home to be alone to die. However no death or person is the same, and some people want a witness to their experience and/or they may want a guide to help them travel through the dimensions and release their soul.

Me-B TRANSITION TO DEATH GUIDE

If you are helping guide someone to transition through death, learn how to regulate your field so it can harmonize with the outer edges of their field before you enter their field. Make sure you don't merge with them during the process.

- **Step 1:** Center yourself into Core Being
- **Step 2:** Let your field harmonize with their field. Usually this means that your field will become very etheric and unstructured. However, during this process don't merge with them. Keep your identity separate, present and strong.
- **Step 3:** If there are others in the room, they may be tearful, angry, emotional and feeling lost. This energy can be hard for a dying person to handle because they are so vulnerable, open and no longer have any structure or anchoring into their self. So it is vital the Me-B Guide be strongly connected to their Core Being, hold presence, safety and comfort in their field. When a person is in the dying process, according to Barbara Brennan, their field begins to dissolve at the 1st chakra, then the 2nd, the 3rd, and so on—with the last chakra being the 7th. In Buddhist tradition, leaving through the 7th chakra is considered optimal and an indicator of a higher state of awareness. I personally have noticed that dying clients leave through the heart chakra, fifth chakra and sixth chakra.
- **Step 4:** Death is a process of reclaiming divinity/back to source. What makes death difficult is when a part of us struggles to hang on to personality/concept of self at the ego level. So if you hold the frequency of being nothing/no concept of self/let go of concept of self/let go of the

brain and thinking it will help them do the same. Don't plan what you are going to do, show up with no mind.

- **Step 5:** Lastly, intend to surrender and help them to surrender and accept. This means they might have to forgive themselves for past deeds and actions. It also may mean they must make peace with past relationship challenges and life tasks that went unfinished.
- **Step 6:** Basics to Follow for Transition-to-Death Me-B Style. When doing hands on work, always work from the bottom up toward the head because the lower levels of the field are the first to dissipate.

Allow the client to set the stage for what they need next. Track the field closely and keep bringing in the seventh level of the field throughout the whole body.

After you feel the whole body filled though the seventh level, invite the client's consciousness to travel upward through the chakras, especially the crown. *However, remember to follow what the field tells you it needs. Never force it. Let the field and client tell you what they need, and then support that process.*

As a person dies, their field begins to disintegrate until only the upper levels of the field remain. During this stage, a dying person becomes very sensitive to their external environment. The veils between this dimension and the higher dimensional fields soften. Clients will often see and speak with family members who have passed on and may communicate with their spirit guides.

As a Me-B Guide it is important to honor the sensitivity of the client during their transition to the nonphysical form. Friends and family may be in a highly agitated state and unwilling to accept what is happening. Heighten emotions can make it harder on the person dying. Holding a strong Intention Line can help shift the mood in the room and create more trust and clarity. Just as a client walks in with their own healing, so does a client walk in with their own death process. Every death I have assisted in has been different. Being able to track and be supportive of the client's own way of leaving the physical body is crucial. There is no "right way!" There is only THEIR way.

My mother in law was waiting until her angels came to get her before she felt comfortable letting go. I connected first to her guides and loved ones. Using intention, I expanded my energy field to resonate to their vibration. I slowly allowed that energy to enter the outer edges of her field and then to enter into her physical body. Gray energy had filled her head (she was 89 and was rarely mentally clear). As the higher vibrations entered, the gray cleared and bright light sparkled. She died peacefully shortly after.

Andy only needed me to help him shift his emotional challenges by bringing in the vibrational frequency of the seventh level of the field. He surrendered to death two hours later. Once he left his body, he then needed support so he could release more emotional issues and embrace more light. This was done over a two-week period after his death.

Joan, a Buddhist mediator with a strong spiritual practice, did something I had never seen before. She allowed some of her consciousness to remain in her body after her death until after the final funeral ceremonies. She then flew by my house and knocked off a picture from my mantel as a wave good bye!

Janet took many trips out of her body before her final way out. She even visited me during a morning meditation while I was teaching a workshop. She didn't physically die until the next day. It is very common for someone to leave the body periodically, almost as a dress rehearsal, before their final departure.

Al was a quiet person and kept to himself, even during the death process. I had studied the "proper" way to help someone die and had many images of what I thought we "should" do so he would transition in a peaceful manner. Al taught me that the "should" is very individual. He didn't spend time learning about himself, reviewing his lessons or lamenting with his wife and children. His sense of humor stayed strong. He did it his way-quiet and alone. After his death, his soul quickly accepted the light. No drama, no emotions to explore. It was simply his way.

MENTAL ILLNESSES IN THE FIELD

Mental Illness is a debilitating form of chronic illness. It presents a Catch 22: if we don't have connection to Core Being we can't heal, but we can't connect to Core Being if our mental illness is too severe. If there are childhood traumas, addiction, or health issues in addition to mental illness, then the challenges abound. A strong Intention Line, grace and resiliency help. Below are brief descriptions of how mental illness presents in the energy field. Unless we have training and experience working with severe mental illness, we should not take on this type of client. Also, clients with schizophrenia, severe depression, mania, bi-polar disorder, and other chronic forms of mental illness often need medication in addition to Me-B support.

Young Wounding in the Field. When I looked at Beth's energy field—it was clear she had a lot of young prenatal and pre-birth trauma. As I watched her field, I noticed it over-reacting to stimuli and it filled with fear. Her energy was in her head and she was ungrounded. The 3rd level of the field was highly developed and the emotional levels held fear and trauma. She connected to me with her intellect and wisdom, which was brilliant and bright. Energetically levels 2 and 4 were in hyper-arousal and her upper chakras were stronger than the lower chakras.

Mania in the Field. All levels of the field are overcharged—and the chakras are in hyper-spin, bringing in too much energy. The energy is extremely ungrounded and the Intention Line is broken off at the 3rd and 5th chakras.

Depression in the Field. All levels of the field are undercharged. The size of the field is compressed. Mucus and Clouds are extensive on the 4th and 2nd levels of the field. Usually suppressed anger keeps depression in the field. Use a combination of the Me-B anger techniques, positive resourcing and trauma work to help clients shift out of depression. Regular exercise and a healthy diet are also helpful.

Schizophrenia in the Field. Typically, there are energetic tears in all or most levels of the field. The extent to which the levels are torn depends upon the person. Energetically, schizophrenia can look like Swiss cheese—or the outer energy egg can be so fragmented and diffuse that there is no clear egg. A Me-B Guide needs to be careful when working with a schizophrenic so as not to charge their field in a manner that could tear it more. Only if we have had additional training and experience with people diagnosed with schizophrenia should we be their primary support. Then we can work to help them develop their Enlightened Observer and teach them to track and heal their own field.

Boundary Issues in the Field. Energetically, boundary issues can look differently depending upon a person's character structure. Shanti, a spiritual/compassionate type, had a weak energy field. The structured levels were so weak and undercharged that the emotional levels of the field barely had any energy. Her immune system, liver, and kidneys were taxed. She was a psychotherapist and after every session, she would feel so drained that she had to make sure she saw only one person a day.

> Clients with Heart Centered energy configurations might have a large 4th level and a very strong and big heart chakra. Their first level of the field is often armored in a defensive pattern. They subconsciously invite invasion so they can feel their "victim" issues and heal them. As they learn to set stronger boundaries, and protect themselves before they are invaded, they will connect to authentic power and use it to manifest joy in their lives.

REVIEW QUESTIONS

1. What gifts/lessons can come from chronic illness and how best can we help a client master them? Why does chronic illness so often trigger our victim issues and feelings of being out of control?
2. The energy vortex for the HVC of god/source is located where in the body?
3. If we remain sick, or die, have we failed? Is sickness our fault? Why is this not Spiritual Junk Food or when is it Spiritual Junk Food?
4. The Intention Line needs to be realigned so it supports health. Explain why this is so important.
5. When sensing into cancer or any chronic illness, how do we make sure we don't get sick from its LVC?
6. When working with cancer, what do we want to be careful to avoid?
7. What are the most important strategies to remember when we are helping someone during the dying process?

8. What emotional issues must we address if we have a chronic illness? What are some solutions to them? Explain in detail.

9. Which character structure has the most difficult time healing chronic illness and which character structure has the easiest time? Explain.

10. Describe mania and depression from an energetic perspective.

11. Given your talents at tracking and assessing energy, which senses would you use to assess mental illness in the field?

12. What mental and physical illnesses make you feel uncomfortable and why? Would you accept a client with these illnesses? Explain.

13. Describe unhealthy energetic boundary configurations in the field.

14. How can we support people with schizophrenia?

15. What are your self-care challenges? Write up a self-care action plan.

16. Review the steps to help guide someone to transition through death and outline what might be easy for you and what might be challenging.

CHAPTER 23

DOs AND DON'Ts OF WORKING WITH SEXUAL ENERGY

Sexual energy is about power. Sex can be used as an addiction or a way to avoid intimacy. Connecting heart (4th Chakra) and sexuality (2nd Chakra) allows us to experience all colors of the energetic rainbow of love, intimacy and balance.

Just as anger is not bad, neither is sexual energy bad. In fact, sexual energy, when used appropriately, increases flow. Sexual energy initiates in the second chakra. According to Barbara Brennan, the front of the second chakra regulates the quality of sexual energy, and the back of this chakra regulates the quantity of sexual energy (Barbara Brennan, *Hands Of Light*). In addition, the second chakra (whose color is orange) is the area of personal power and creative energy. The 2nd Chakra is also the energetic doorway to the 2nd level of the field, our relationship to our self. Blocked or distorted sexual energy prevents life flow and reduces a person's ability to orgasm, have regular menstruation, get pregnant and feel empowered. It can also prevent deep intimate connection.

When working with energy, it is important to allow sexual energy to flow and mix with the energy coming through the other chakras. This creates a rainbow of colors and supports HVC. Using only sexual energy or ignoring sexual energy can cause or deepen our **Core Distortions**.

Using only sexual energy or ignoring sexual energy can cause a distortion.

Sometimes when we do energy work on ourselves or a client, sexual energies are awakened. Being aligned and clear can help a client overcome shame of their sexuality. If sexual energies arise in a client during a Me-B Transformation session, we can hold good boundaries and a safe space for the client to process these issues. We can also encourage them to blend their sexual energy with other energy in their bodies. As they do this, the mass of energy expands and can then be directed toward healing energetic blockages.

When a client comes in with marital problems or relationship issues, it is important to ask them about their sexual health in the marriage/relationship. How often do they make love? Are they satisfied? What are their feelings about masturbation? The health of a couple's sexual life is often linked to safety and intimacy issues. If they are having trouble in the bedroom, it can be an indicator of trouble in other aspects of the relationship.

Some people are afraid of sexual energy and/or prefer to be celibate, like a monk or priest. Celibacy does not mean that someone doesn't still work with his or her sexual energy—just as spirituality doesn't mean we don't work with anger. For people who choose to be celibate, we can recommend various sexual energetic practices so they maintain healthy sexual energy and ensure that their sexual energy isn't (1) inappropriately expressed toward someone else, or (2) held inside them in a way that is harmful, energetically or physically.

Don't let your own issues around sexuality interfere with your client's issues. If they have different morals, don't judge. They will know if we are uncomfortable. If they are considering or engaging in illegal behaviors, consult a supervisor for guidance on how to handle these issues professionally. (And know and follow the laws around abuse of children and confidentiality.)

LOOK AT OUR OWN ISSUES AROUND SEXUAL ENERGY

Answer the following questions to begin to assess the health of our own sexual energies.

- Do you have pre-ejaculation issues? If so, they tend to be about personal power. How can you connect to your own sense of Core Being and personal power?
- Do you have a healthy and active sexual life?
- Can you orgasm?
- Do you know how to self-pleasure?
- How do you feel about masturbation?
- How do you feel about sexual energy?
- Do you have a sexual addiction?
- Do you feel you rely too heavily on pornography?
- It is common for a woman to never have looked at her genitals or know how to self-pleasure. Have you addressed these issues?
- How can you improve your sexual intimacy experiences, and how can you better use sexual energy for your own healing?
- How comfortable are you talking about sexual issues with clients/friends/your children?
- If sexual energy comes up when working with a client, do you know how to adjust your field so you don't
- Push it at them and you connect heart with sexuality?
- Do you have risky sexual behaviors or unprotected sex? If so, what shadow material is linked to this issue?
- How safe do you feel when someone sends sexual energy in your direction?
- What role does your Separated Self play in your sexual challenges?

What sexual issues do you have that you have not yet addressed? What can you do to support yourself given what you have read so far in this book (and not judge yourself)? Everyone has some aspect of sexuality that can be improved. How can you tune into the wisdom within your body/energy system to better support yourself in the area of sexual intimacy and sexual energies? Write out a plan to assist yourself.

Meditation

Connecting Sexual Energy in your 2nd Chakra With Heart Energy in 4th Chakra

- **Step 1:** Get into your body. Dance, jump up and down, love yourself. Use the methods that awaken sensations in the lower body and grounded energy.
- **Step 2:** Put on some "feel good" music. Hips-waist width apart with knees slightly bent, imagine there is a pen attached to your tailbone and draw big circles with it. Really let the hips move and flow as you do this. Surrender to feel sensations of energy in the body so deeply that you can actually describe those sensations and feel the emotions/consciousness

associated with those emotions.

- **Step 3:** Keep drawing the circles but let the circles gradually get smaller until they are the size of a quarter or dime. Once again, really let the hips move and flow as you do this. Surrender to feel sensations of energy in the body so deeply that you can actually describe those sensations and feel the emotions/consciousness associated with those emotions.
- **Step 4:** Repeat in the opposite direction.
- **Step 5:** Now surrender to allow the energy from the center of the earth to flow up your legs, through the muscle, bone and bone marrow. Let it flow from the earth to the bottom of your foot, upward through your lower leg. Let if fill the thigh, pelvis. As you connect breath with awareness in all those parts of the body, surrender to feel sensations of energy in the body so deeply that you can actually describe those sensations and feel the emotions/consciousness associated with those emotions.
- **Step 6:** Now swing your arms and waist back and forth like a twister or windmill. Let your 3rd chakra charge and fill. As you connect breath with awareness in all those parts of the body, surrender to feel sensations of energy in the body so deeply that you can actually describe those sensations and feel the emotions/consciousness associated with those emotions. If the emotions become too intense, make sure your Enlightened Observer and Intention Line are strong.
- **Step 7:** With your hands pointed toward the ground, bend and straighten your knees and let the energy from the earth rise up again through your lower body, pelvis, sacrum, and upward to fill chakras 1-3. As you connect breath with awareness in all those parts of the body, surrender to feel sensations of energy in the body so deeply that you can actually describe those sensations and feel the emotions/consciousness associated with those emotions. If the emotions become too intense, make sure your Enlightened Observer and Intention Line are strong.
- **Step 8:** Allow the energy to fill the liver, kidneys, stomach, pancreases, spleen and intestines. As you connect breath with awareness in all those parts of the body, surrender to feel sensations of energy in the body so deeply that you can actually describe those sensations and feel the emotions/consciousness associated with those emotions. If the emotions become too intense, make sure your Enlightened Observer and Intention Line are strong.
- **Step 9:** Twirl again but with your arms extended shoulder height. We are now surrendering to charge the 4th chakra, check and upper back. Now really let the energy from your 1st- 4th chakras connect and expand. As you connect breath with awareness in all those parts of the body, surrender to feel sensations of energy in the body so deeply that you can actually describe those sensations and feel the emotions/consciousness associated with those emotions. If the emotions become too intense, make sure your Enlightened Observer and Intention Line are strong.

There are some very good Tantra workshops, books and videos on using sexual energy for self-healing and for healing intimacy issues that couples experience. Some of these resources may be too sexually explicit for your comfort level, so be selective when researching them to be sure you have the right fit for you. (For instance, some Tantric workshops involve participants practicing sexual acts in the same room and not privately at home.)

Sexual energy is very important, and it is important to learn as much about it as possible so we don't hurt anyone or ourselves. Mantack Chi and his wife have written books that use Chi Kung (Qigong) techniques to shift sexual energy. These books have been useful to many of my clients. Two other books for helping women are: *Becoming Orgasmic* (Julia Heiman) and *For Yourself* (Lonnie Barbach). (Available through my web site.)

Some common sexual issues clients present are:

- Pre-ejaculation in men.
- Usually deals with empowerment issues but there could also be a physical cause.
- Not able to orgasm.
- Often deals with shame, rigidity, Spiritual Junk Food, and safety and trust issues.
- Choosing to have sex with someone and then regretting it later. Women in particular "give themselves away" too quickly and then regret their decision. They feel shame and embarrassment.
- Sexual addictions or distortions. Usually deals with fear of intimacy and attachment issues.
- Couples stop having sex or have difficulty with sexual connection.
- Menstruation problems or infertility.
- Infidelity.
- Lack of sexual satisfaction.
- Sexual abuse.
- Needing sexual release yet not having a partner to release with.
- Engaging in risky sexual behavior.
- Sexual identity problems.

There are many different strategies we can use to address these concerns within ourselves and our clients. Begin by looking at any Separated Self energies behind your sexual challenges. What negative beliefs fuel the Separated Self in this subject area? For instance: sex is dirty; sex is bad; sex is about power and control; if they want to have sex with me that means I am worthy; I will use sex to manipulate; sex means they won't leave me; sex will hurt me; or sex is invasion.

Exercise to Awaken Deeper Understanding of Your Sexual Challenges

This exercise will help you awaken to any hidden sexual challenges that might get in the way of becoming a skillful Me-B Guide. In addition, as you practice this exercise, you will discover how to better work with a client that might push sexual energy your way.

Find a partner that you trust and practice the following exercise.

- **Step 1:** Stand facing each other about 3 feet apart.
- **Step 2:** One of you will be an A and the Other a B.
- **Step 3:** The A person will run sexual energy out their second charka at person B. Person A lets no connection to happen between their 2nd chakra and 4th, Heart Chakra.
- **Step 4:** Person B senses how familiar this feels to them and how common it happened or happened. Person B assesses what Core Distortion was/is created when this happens to them.
- **Step 5:** Person A senses how it feels for them to run just sexual energy at someone. How often do they do this in their life and what is their emotional reaction to doing this? What Core Distortion exists or was brought to the surface for them?
- **Step 6:** Now person A resonates a healthy sexual energy response and lets the sexual energy in his or her 2nd Chakra blended with the heart energy in their 4th. In essence, Person A allows the sexual energy to expand and include energy from all the chakras so no longer just sexual energy flows.
- **Step 7:** Both Persons A and B assess how their mind, energy and body system responds to this latest energy shift. Both A and B engages their Explorer's Mind and explores what healing can take place for them and how to foster more balanced sexual energy in their lives
- **Step 8:** Change Places and repeat so person A plays the role of B and person B plays the role of A.

Note: Make sure your Enlightened Observer is strong so you don't rewound and yet you do feel the challenging feelings that need to be transformed.

In our society, sexual displays abound. When I was young, rarely did I ever see kissing on T.V. Now, we can see woman kissing women and men kissing men on prime time. One episode of the popular T.V. show *Gray's Anatomy* even discussed how one doctor could teach his female co-doctor how to perform oral sex on another female co-doctor! Sex definitely seems everywhere. Be this good or bad, I don't know. I do know that it is important to establish a healing relationship within ourselves around our own sexuality—and that healthy sexual energy is paramount.

Go to www.sexhelp.com and take the following self-assessment tests to explore more deeply various aspects of your sexual health:

The Sexual Addiction Screening Test (SAST). Everyone should take this, even if you don't think you have an issue in this area. The SAST is designed to assist in the assessment of sexually compulsive behavior which may indicate the presence of sex addiction.

The Sexual Addiction Risk Assessment Test (SARA). Everyone should take this, even if you don't think you have an issue in this area. The Sexual Addiction Risk Assessment has been developed to help you better understand your behaviors. The assessment consists of 88 questions, which will take approximately 25 minutes to finish. You can then print out your results immediately. You will be provided with a detailed, personalized 23-page report to help you determine the best course of action for **you**.

The Internet Sex Screening Test (ISST). A test designed to access your Internet sexual behavior.

The "Betrayal Bond" Test. A test using a series of statements which describe traumatic bonding in which a person bonds on the basis of betrayal. The result is what we call a "betrayal bond".

In addition, a good meditation in relation to sexual health is to practice feeling Core Being energy in your genitals and second and first chakras. It is a great way to balance, ground, and create the energy needed to fulfill our life task.

NOTE: It goes without saying that we should never push sexual energy upon a client, and we should never touch a client in a sexual manner. In fact, I believe we should never date or become friends with a client or a former client. (The standard of practice nationally mandates a 2-year waiting period.)

HEALING FROM SEXUAL ABUSE

Healing from Sexual Abuse can mean different things to different people and the negative effects can vary. For me, it has been a long and hard road. In my own life I have noticed that because of the sexual abuse I suffered:

- I have had extreme challenges with my self-esteem,
- I found it very difficult to stand up to authority figures (especially if they have a lot of male energy),
- I could not touch myself or feel much in my body,
- I lost my ability to ask for what I need sexually from my partner, and
- I could not attract to me a sexual partner that would connect with me in a healing/loving manner.

Recovering from sexual abuse in all Me-B Systems can take time, aligned intention and advanced mindfulness techniques so you can collect the wisdom needed to heal. Every trauma has a gift and I know that I probably wouldn't have been so motivated to write this book if I hadn't been abused. I hope you or your client finds the following tips helpful. Also review the Trauma chapter, the information on Adult Consciousness, and the chapter on the 5 Seeds of Distortion around love.

Healing From Sexual Abuse – Three Tips

- **Tip 1:** Review your issues around intimacy, boundaries, attachment and bonding. Also review the 5 Seeds of Distortion. Design a plan to learn to give healthy love to yourself and others. Also learn to receive love in a healthy manner.
- **Tip 2:** Energetically people who have been sexually abused need to learn how to balance their

first and second chakras so they are open and flowing clockwise. These chakras also need to be hooked into the central channel and bringing energy in (review chapter on energy.) Lastly, allowing yourself to feel the flow of energy through the inside of the legs is paramount. When we are abuse, this energy stops flowing in a healthy manner. The energy also can hold deep core distortions. Get support to heal the core distortions so the energy flows through- out the inner legs (medial) as evenly as it flows through the outer (lateral) part of the legs-from the hip down. (For instance, look at the inside/outside of the pants leg seam. This is where we can invite the energy to flow and the emotions to heal.

- **Tip 3:** Commit to creating healthy sexual practices. Heal any unhealthy sexual issues.

REVIEW QUESTIONS

1. What sexual issues do you have that you have not yet addressed?
2. Based on what you have learned so far, what would you do to heal your sexual issues? Outline short-term goals and long-term goals then outline a plan for achieving these goals.
3. Connect to your Manifest Energy Line and program in aligned intention to address your sexual issues. We can make this commitment from a place of loving spiritual kindness toward ourselves and NOT from the negative judgmental ego.
4. What can you do to support yourself in claiming your personal power given what you have read so far in this book? How can you tune into the wisdom within your body/energy system to better support yourself in the area of personal power, sexual intimacy and sexual energies? Write out a plan to assist yourself.
5. Why is it important to connect our sexual energies with our heart energies? What is difficult for you in this area?
6. When supporting a client with their sexual issues, what might feel uncomfortable for you?
7. If a client tells you they are attracted to you, how might you handle this situation ethically?
8. Why is sexual touch and sexual interaction with a client never appropriate? What, if anything, might be challenging for you in this area?
9. Describe your results to the sexhelp.com assessments and describe any support you may need to give yourself in order for you to balance your sexual energies.

CHAPTER 24

CONCLUSION

Emotions and LVC are god's gift to help us connect deeper to source. If we avoid them they tend to come back at us stronger. Why is this so? How do we make sense of it? As we open to transforming emotions, they lead us deeper into our light.

Emotion is a bountiful natural resource within all of us. When we connect to it with aligned intention and right mindfulness it illuminates our way back home to wholeness. Every time an emotion explodes into our consciousness, what it is really doing is shining a light, pointing the way home, should any of us choose to follow.

As we stop using emotion as a weapon with which to wage war, or to hurl prejudice and judgments upon one another, we can discover the bigger plan for its use. *For instance, when we connect to* **the feeling and sensation** *of emotions with our Enlightened Observer, emotions become an energetic portal to connect us back to source.*

Spirit wants us to return to Source and provides us with the mechanisms to do so, through our emotions and the sensations of energy in our bodies. Each time we connect to an emotion—*any emotion—* e.g. grief, sadness, helplessness, anger, fury, bliss . . . this connection (if we use the Enlightened Observer) creates an opportunity for us to use that emotion as a *resource to feel god within us*.

As long as we feel/experience the sensation of emotion with the knowing that it is showing us the path, we can follow it to our wholeness. This is why the Enlightened Observer is so important. It creates the alchemy of HVC that is vital for transformation. **Without our Enlightened Observer, we are just observing our pain—and thus we can and likely will end up expanding that pain. With the Enlightened Observer, emotions become a portal to experience Source.** Me-B enthusiasts know this and use their emotions to heal, manifest dreams, and develop intimacy and closeness with others.

Joy, bliss, grace . . . all are emotions to remind us of what is already in alignment. Anger, jealousy, and hate, by contrast, are examples of emotions that are anchored deeply into false beliefs. They are dark shadow material that can be used as a marker to say, "Here it is—see the candle of light on the pathway back to Source." Ironically, it's only what we consider to be positive emotions that typically remind us of god; when in reality it is the "dark" emotions that — when connected with our Enlightened Observer – can also return us to Source and to our wholeness.

In the mental health community, many counselors and psychologists understand the importance of feeling emotions. However, it is easy to miss the technical aspects of transformation. Psychological groups can emphasize feeling—but too often, no transformation happens. Instead, there is just a connection to the emotional trash. This can look like a catharsis that is sometimes misinterpreted as a healing process.

Instead, we need to learn HOW to connect to difficult emotions (and thought-patterns and sensations) in a way that facilitates deeper connection to our light. As we take charge of our healing by taking charge of our most valuable natural resource – emotions — we can use them as the vehicle to connect us back to wholeness. **It takes much more than just *feeling* emotions for transformation to happen.** The "feeling" has to be done in a particular manner for it to result in "gold" and transformation.

We all can learn how to feel emotions in a way that actually reconnects us with our Core Being. As we do this, a **spiritual revolution can happen.** And I believe it needs to happen if our world is to create lasting peace, harmony, and kindness.

In this sometimes treacherous Earthly dimension, it can be hard to understand how things work and how our ego and mind can create havoc for us. Hopefully, the skills we gain from the exercises outlined in this book will help us negotiate the sometimes chaotic environments within and around us.

TEN TRUISMS THEY DON'T TELL US – BUT WE NEED TO KNOW!

1. *Life is unfair.* We can prepare ourselves so that when trials and tribulations happen, we are strong enough to use them for our benefit and not our demise. From Core Being, meaning can be found. From meaning, joy can be found. And from this place, we can comfort our most wounded heart. Seeking to avoid pain just creates more pain. We may numb ourselves, drink, and self-abuse to avoid the emotion—but what we are really avoiding is the gold that lies within the emotion, if we are skillful enough to find it.

2. *No one is "perfect." We won't be perfect and others will not be perfect in their treatment of us.* Through our Choice Points, we discover the hidden perfection, lessons, and gifts in each "imperfect" moment. Then the Explorer's Mind can ask, "Why is this happening? What can I learn? And what past programming is being repeated so it can heal?" As we answer these questions, we learn to connect more deeply to Core Being and to embrace our HVC.

3. *No one can save us.* Fame, winning the lottery, even finding that "special" love— nothing can save us. This is because wherever we go, there we are. We can never run so far that we leave ourselves behind. However, we can learn how to become more empowered as a result of our challenges. Core Distortions and LVC are part of being human. As we commit to transforming the parts of ourselves that interfere and cause us pain, we reconnect to Core Being and save ourselves. It is much richer to know how to come to our own aide than to wait helplessly for another.

4. Miracles are self-made. As we raise our consciousness, we become more empowered and thus more able to notice how to let them happen. Yet grace plays a role too. Many times throughout the day, there are "miracle" opportunities. Some we see in time to take advantage of; many we don't. Yet, sometimes, grace steps in, and we feel the loving arms of the divine intervene. We can't count on grace, but we can appreciate it when it hap- pens. Gratitude for what we have supports grace's presence. As we move higher in the Me-B Stages of Trans- formation, we become more aware, so miracle opportunities become more apparent. Our Enlightened Observer can remind us that the universe wants to support our intended creations. It can help us transform the LVC and Core Distortions that make it hard to see opportunities.

5. *Our mind lies to us and can't always be trusted to know the truth.* It may tell us we are

happy when really we are sad. We might feel sadness when there is joy and opportunity available. Our mind colludes with our ego and programmed personality to distort our perceptions. Remember to question your mind. Use the skills in this book and notice which system (mind, energy, or body) has the truth. The truth can return us to our divine spirit, our wholeness, our core.

6. *Faulty perception is the cause of most pain and it usually means the ego is in charge.* Our body houses the truth of who we are, who we are not, and who we can someday become. When uncovering this fountain of wisdom, the mind's cooperation is necessary—yet the mind rarely cooperates easily. It is like a tiger, protecting its false understanding of itself, because to do otherwise would mean the ego would die. As you free yourself from faulty perception, you also free yourself from the ego. When the ego takes over, feel where it is held in the body and bring in the HVC of your Enlightened Observer to transform it back to Core Being.

7. Trying to please others so they will like us is a trap. This is because people are sometimes mean, even if we haven't done anything wrong. Sometimes we won't be loved or even liked. People project their fears upon us, and we can invite projections from others based on our fears and past programming. It is inevitable. We can fill our cells and our outer energy egg with Core Being energy when this happens. It is the best protection—it provides a way to calm our ego and keep from judging others. When something happens to upset us, why do we always instinctively wonder, "What did I do wrong?" Maybe there are times the fault doesn't lie within us.

8. *Another painful challenge will always come. Accept this fact and prepare for it.* Just as dust collects on our mantle, over time it also collects in our Me-B System. On a regular basis, we must go within, find where in our Me-B System our "dust" has collected, and clean the LVC and Core Distortions. Every house needs cleaning on a regular basis. Our Me-B System is no different. How often we need to "clean" it depends upon our Character Structure, our level of stress, our support systems, the strength of our consciousness container, and our ability to feel Core Being. Cleaning out our "trash" on a regular basis helps us anchor into Core Being and readies us to find the next gift and transform the next challenge. If we don't find the "dust" and transform it to HVC, we can feed our internal saboteur.

9. *We can't be happy until we learn to find internal peace — even in our darkest moments.* Since we can't control our external circumstances, happiness needs to be an internal experience. Happiness can become something that we can find anytime and anywhere, so we feel connected to wholeness, bliss, and fun—even during our most challenging times. **The ability to create our own happiness gives us true freedom.** From the dimension of Core Being, brought into all 3 Me-B Systems, it is possible to maintain internal happiness. Until we experience it, it can be hard to believe how good it feels! This is the Holly Grail, and it is available to every- one!

10. *Everyone has a wounded child and everyone must learn to love and protect him or her with our adult energies and Core Being.* Find your child consciousness. Where are you holding it in your body? Wherever the child consciousness resides, when it calls out, send it love and support from your Adult Consciousness. This process can be tricky

417

because usually it calls to us during times of stress and difficulty. It takes strong intention to develop this skill. Let your Core Being and Enlightened Observer help you meet the needs of your inner child.

I hope this book creates an energetic "wake" that makes it easier for you to ride the wave of self-empowerment. Remember that it takes (1) aligned Intention, and (2) advanced Mindfulness to discover the wisdom needed to be present enough to then (3) return to Core Being. I thank all of the teachers before me upon whose wakes I have ridden. This book wouldn't have been possible without all the love and support of my teachers, students, clients, family, and spiritual guides. At its best, this book is a product of me being the vessel that the material moved through. Therefore, any thanks or appreciation can be sent back to Source and sent back to you, the reader-participant.

In my lifetime I have been very blessed. I have trekked in Nepal, visited China when people still wore Mao jackets, performed Tai Chi on a remote beach in Thailand, and lived in magical Cambodia . . . but the most profound and challenging journey I have taken is the one to the center of my Core Being. This is where I began to discover who I am and what I can be. And, everyday, I get to take this journey again and again. Although I have a long way to go—and, at times it is very difficult—for the majority of my days, I reside in joy. I feel loved and grateful. I send blessings and kindness as we journey together back to wholeness.

APPENDIX A - ME-B APPROACH SKILL COMPETENCIES TO MASTER

Rate your ability to work these skills within yourself and in relationship with a client.

P=POOR
F=FAIR
G=GOOD
E=EXCELLENT

TOUCH and NO-TOUCH ENERGY SHIFTING SKILLS

SKILL	P	F	G	E
Manifest Intention Line				
Auric Level Dimension				
_____Balance Chakras				
_____Levels of the Field				
_____Opening Central Channel				
_____Micro-Cosmic Orbit, Healing Sounds, Smile Down, Tree				
Core Being Dimension				
Centered Oneness Healing				
Multi-Dimensional Fabric Healing of Interconnectedness				
Star Child Healing				
Positive Resourcing Interventions				
Working Multi-Dimensionally				
Core Distortion Healings With/Without Dialogue, Touch and Non-Touch				
Body Scanning and Re-Programming				
Connection-Track-Intervention-Shift Sequence				
Making Your Consciousness Container Stronger and Helping a Client Do the Same				
Containment				
Grounding Techniques				
No-Touch Energetically Shift Client				
Teach the Enlightened Observer				
Teach a Client the 3 Rings of Healing; Shape-Shifting Practice				
Teach A Client to Self Assess				
Move Energy with Mind				
Move Energy with Hands				
Move and Track Energy at Same Time				

Assess Which System Holds the Truth				
Work with Energy of Person Not Physically in Room Such as a Boyfriend, Partner, Parent, Etc.				
Programming Words into The Field				
Intervention and Dialogue Techniques for Character Structures				
Intervention and Dialogue Techniques for Developmental				
Trauma and other Trauma				
Intervention and Dialogue Techniques for 5 Seeds of Distortion				
Intervention and Dialogue Techniques for Adult Consciousness				
Intervention Dialogue Techniques for Positive Resourcing—Helping				
Them Connect to Their Core Being, Strength, and Safety				
Movement and Exercise Techniques for Anger/Emotional				
Transformation				
Intervention Techniques for False Images and Beliefs				
Other Misc. Intervention and Dialogue Techniques				
Helping A Client (and Self) Build Their Consciousness Container				
Working with Sexual Energy				
Tracking and Working with Client's Subconscious Shifts				
Assessing a Better Power Source				
Neurological Rebuilding Technique				
Ancestral Lineage Transformation				
Archetypical Transformation				
Energetic Dream Protocol				
Cancer Protocol				
Chronic and/or Terminal Illness Transition Protocol				

TRACKING SELF AND OTHER, HSP SKILLS

SKILL	P	F	G	E
Balance Own Field Before Session				
Assess Client's Over/Under Charge/Flow				
Assess Client's Core Distortions (Auric, Manifest Intention Energy, Physical Dimensions)				
Know How You Collect HSP Information				
Can Assess When You're in Defense and Support Self				
Can Assess When Client Is in Defense and Support Self and Them				
Can Assess How Connected Client Is to Core Being and Support Them In Finding It				
Sensing Energy; PIN Wheel Technique				

	P	F	G	E
Pendulum, Visual, and/or Hand Scans				
Can Assess Own Energy Field				
Can Assess Others' Energy Fields				
Body Connecting Sequence				
Opening to Radical intuition				
Healing Response to Character Structures				
Tracking ME-B Systems in Client				
Tracking ME-B Systems in Self				
Assessing If Intervention Worked and If Enlightened Observer is Present				
See Energy of Person Not Physically in Room Such as a Boyfriend, Partner, Parent, Etc.				
ID Core Being of Client				
Muscle Testing				
Character Structure/Personality Types Assessment				
Assess Client's Developmental Levels				
Assess Client's Subconscious Shifts				
Reading Words from Client's Field				
Assess Client's Emotions				
Assess Client's Images/Beliefs				
Assess Client's Me-B Stages				
Assess Client's Level Of Resourcing				
Tracking Trauma/Shock Response Energetically in Client				
Assessing Subconscious Shifts				

Me-B SELF-MASTERY/TRANSFORMATIONAL SKILLS (ASSIST CLIENT/SELF)

SKILL	P	F	G	E
Explorer's Mind				
Intention				
Core Being				
Enlightened Observer				
Personality Level:				
_____Defenses				
_____Public Personality				
_____Core Distortion				
_____Separated Self				
_____Ego				
Beliefs				

Transference/Counter-Transference				
Boundaries				
Rhythm of Reality				
Let Go and Let Flow				
5 Seeds of Distortion - Can Shift Within Self				
Adult Consciousness – Can Shift Within Self				

APPENDIX B - ENNEAGRAM, MYERS BRIGGS, AND CHARACTER STRUCTURES COMPARED

PERSONALITY TYPES

PERFECTIONIST – 1; Excel; Judging

HELPER/GIVER – 2; Heart-Centered; Extrovert/Sensate

PERFORMER/ACHIEVER – 3; Excel/Leader; Extrovert/Feeling

TRAGIC/ROMANTIC - 4; Compassionate/Heart-Centered; Intuitive/Feeling; Perceiving

OBSERVER – 5; Spiritual/Rigid; Introvert/Thinking

QUESTIONER/DEVIL'S ADVOCATE – 6; Heart-Centered/Spiritual; Introvert

ADVENTURER/THE EPICURE - 7; Excel; Extrovert/Intuitive

ASSERTER/BOSS – 8; Leader; Extrovert/ Intuitive/ Thinking/ Perceiving

PEACEMAKER/MEDIATOR – 9; Compassionate/Heart-Centered/Rigid; Intuitive/Perceiving

ENNEAGRAM ENERGETIC CONSTRUCTS

1. PERFECTIONIST (Similar to Excel and Judging)
    The Perfectionist judges self and others. They feel there is only one correct way, and they know the correct way. They hold a feeling of superiority. They use words like "should" and "must" a lot. They have a fear of failure or mistakes.
    In the Perfectionist, the structured levels of the Auric field are developed, and the mental level is overcharged. The Hara tends to be strong toward achievement.
    The life task of the Perfectionist is to develop the ability to know that when they are wrong and/or messy (imperfect), they can still feel safe and loved. A deeper connection to Core Being or god self is needed.
    The Image or belief that keeps this client from attaining Me-B Stage 7 or above is: "If I am imperfect, I am nothing." Learning how to make themselves the ultimate authority in their lives is key. They need to be correct or righteous to legitimize their anger. Instead, they could learn how to feel the anger as energy that can be transformed into personal power and a deeper connection to their Core Being.

2. HELPER/GIVER (Heart-Centered; Extrovert/Sensate)
    The Helper/Giver demands affection and approval and seeks to be loved and appreciated by becoming indispensable. These individuals can present a different face to each friend depending upon who they are—they are chameleon-like.
    The structured levels of the field are underdeveloped in the Helper/Giver. These individuals need more boundary containment so they don't take on others' feelings as their own. The Auric field is sometimes undercharged and depleted in Helper/Givers, especially in the upper body.

If you are a Helper/Giver, to reach Stage 7 of Me-B Transformation, you must overcome any co-dependent attitudes and develop the ability to say no to others. In addition, when others say no to you, you must learn not to feel unloved. In other words, you must develop the ability to hold yourself even when you are being turned down.

3. PERFORMER/ACHIEVER (Excel/Leader; Extrovert/Feeling)

These individuals seek love and acceptance through performance. They are obsessed with image and external approval.

In Performer/Achievers, the backs of the chakras are overused by too much will. They can hold a full charge in their fields, especially in the upper body, but the pelvic and Solar Plexus areas remain cut off from Core Being.

Developing the ability to be authentic and to transcend the personality level is key for Performer/Givers. To do this, they must learn to feel emotions but not to be overwhelmed by them. They must also learn to balance will and emotion. In addition, learning to look at the "internal" versus "external" sense of self is vital to achieving Stage 7 of Me-B Transformation.

4. TRAGIC ROMANTIC (Compassionate/Heart-Centered; Intuitive/Feeling; Perceiving)

Tragic Romantics are attracted to the unavailable. The ideal is never here and now. These individuals are tragic, sad, artistic, and sensitive. They remain focused on the absent lover, or on the loss of a friend.

The Tragic Romantic needs more structure in field and less emotions. They should move the vertical power cord from too far in front toward the back. They also benefit from learning to allow their feelings while not collapsing into feeling or being overwhelmed by it. As this person learns to let emotions run through them—instead of letting emotions define them—they will reach Stage 7 of Me-B Transformation.

5. OBSERVER (Spiritual/Rigid; Introvert/Thinking)

Observers are emotionally distant and private. They protect their privacy and don't tend to get involved. They defend against the outside world by doing without, because they feel drained by commitment and by other people's needs. They compartmentalize obligations, detaching from feelings and people and things. They are Monk-like as a form of escape—not an obligation.

Grounding is very important for Observers. Learning how to come into the body and feel safe is key. For these individuals, the emotional levels of the field are greatly underdeveloped and are protected by boundary containment.

To achieve Stage 7, they will have to claim their essence in the physical body and learn how to fill themselves up when they are actively connected to others. Being present and not finding an escape are also important.

6. QUESTIONER/DEVIL'S ADVOCATE (Heart-Centered/Spiritual; Introvert)

These individuals are fearful, dutiful, and plagued by doubt. They often tend toward procrastination—thinking replaces doing—and they are afraid to take action because exposure leads to attack. They tend to identify with underdog causes; they are anti-authoritarian, self-sacrificing, and loyal to a cause.

For the Questioner, the upper levels of the field could be stronger, as well as the second and third charkas. The Hara is displaced away from the Earth and spirit. It is misaligned toward fear of attack.

Finding safety within and a deeper connection to spiritual guidance is the task of the Questioner. These individuals also must learn how to deal with their anger in a manner that empowers them toward action and connection.

7. ADVENTURER/THE EPICURE (Excel; Extrovert/Intuitive)

A *"Pueraeternus"* (eternal child) or Peter Pan-type energy describes this personality. Commitment is hard, and emotional chaos is promoted. Completion can be difficult.

Adventurers have overly structured fields but with many energetic leaks through the emotional and mental levels. The Hara has breaks that if filled could assist in helping the person complete their tasks. The back of the 5th chakra spins backwards.

Adventurers need a deeper connection to Core Being or god self. They need to learn how to meet their own insecurities with self-love instead of external accolades. These qualities are key to their Me-B Transformation.

8. ASSERTER/BOSS (Leader; Extrovert/Intuitive/Thinking/Perceiving)

Asserters have combative, take-charge attitudes, with a tendency toward needing to control to feel safe. Confrontation helps them feel themselves. They often have a split between the higher self and lower vibrations in the body.

The Auric field holds a strong charge in these individuals. However, the back or will energy tends to be overworked. Their 3rd chakras are one of their strongest, as are their mental centers. They have strong Intention Lines geared toward constructive activity.

For Asserters, it is important to learn to trust and surrender that the universe supports them. Bringing in the higher self, demonstrating compassion, and developing relational energies in their fields is important for Me-B Transformation through the stages. Learning not to merge, be aggressive, or disconnect in relationships is key for Asserters to they develop healthy and appropriate methods of being in deep relationship.

9. PEACEMAKER/MEDIATOR (Aspects of the Compassionate/Heart-Centered; Rigid; Intuitive/Perceiving) Peacemakers are obsessively ambivalent . . . they can see all sides to an issue. They don't typically take a stance and will easily shift their viewpoint toward another's perspective. This type has addictive tendencies.

Energetically, the Peacemaker doesn't have a deep anchor into Core Being or their true self, so there are wide fluctuations in the energy field. They experience distortions and tears in their third chakras and no connection between the second and third chakras. They need to be better grounded, with a balance between top and bottom energetically.

To move through the Me-B Transformational Stages, this personality type needs to learn how to meet their own needs and how to deepen their discernment between the personality levels and the level of Core Being.

DSM IV

- Obsessive/Compulsive; compulsive side dominates
- Histrionic or Dependent
- No correlation—Type A personality
- Depressed or Bipolar
- Schizoid or Avoidant

- Paranoid
- Narcissistic
- Sociopath/Anti-Social Personality
- Passive Aggressive or Obsessive/Compulsive; obsessive side dominates

APPENDIX C - MEYERS BRIGGS SUMMARY OF KEY POINTS

NOTE: The Meyers Briggs approach uses terminology that may be erroneously interpreted. When considering the terminology, keep these points in mind:

- "Extrovert" does not mean talkative or loud;
- "Introvert" does not mean shy or inhibited;
- "Feeling" does not mean emotional;
- "Judging" does not mean judgmental; and
- "Perceiving" does not mean perceptive.

EXTROVERSION

These individuals like to focus on the outer world of people and activity. They direct their energy and attention outward and receive energy from interacting with people and from taking action. They are attuned to the external; they prefer to communicate by talking; they work out ideas by talking them through; they learn best through doing or discussing; they have broad interests; they are sociable and expressive; and they readily take initiative in work and relationships.

Connecting to an extroverted person first cognitively and personally is very important. Meditative techniques may be less effective. Try using more active and external methods first. One strategy can be to give them something to "do" externally versus asking them to "be" internally. Table work that is more interactive may also be useful.

INTROVERSION

People who prefer Introversion like to focus on their own inner world of ideas and experiences. They direct their energy and attention inward and receive energy from reflecting on their thoughts, memories, and feelings. They are drawn to their inner world; they prefer to communicate in writing; they work out ideas by reflecting on them; they learn best by reflection and mental practice; they focus in depth on their interests; they are private and contained; and they take initiative when the situation or issue is very important to them.

For these individuals, meditation and accessing inner guidance (especially if they are also Intuitive Types) can be great strategies. Table work should have minimal interaction. In fact, you might be careful to censor how much information you share so you limit it to the most pertinent facts.

If you share too much, you might distract them from their own inner experience. Feel free to check in and ask them if you are sharing too much. I even recommend you ask them what they are experiencing first so that you stay connected to them as they progress through their inner world. Watch the rhythm of the energy to help you determine what is enough interaction and what is too much.

SENSING

People who prefer to sense like to take in information that is real and tangible. They are observant about the specifics of what is really happening. Oriented to present realities, they are factual and concrete. They focus on what is real and actual, building carefully and thoroughly toward conclusions. They understand ideas and theories through practical applications, and they trust experiences.

I have been working with a sensing type client for over two years. And still he says to me, "I don't understand it, but I can feel the benefits." We always spend at least 30 minutes cognitively expressing ideas and theories as practically as I can to help him trust the experience on the table. He came to me to help him deal with anxiety that had increased dramatically during his premarital preparations. His anxiety decreased in a real and tangible manner, so he continued to come for sessions and be open to additional benefits.

In Me-B Therapy, working with this personality type can be challenging. If need be, there are wonderful resource materials that can provide factual and concrete information if the clients are open enough to receive it.

INTUITION

People who prefer Intuition like to take in information by seeing the big picture and focusing on the relationships and connections between facts. They want to grasp patterns and are especially attuned to seeing new possibilities. Oriented to future possibilities, they are imaginative and verbally creative, focusing on the patterns and meanings in data and remembering specifics when they relate to a pattern. Intuitive types move quickly to conclusions, follow hunches, trust inspiration, and want to clarify ideas and theories before putting them into practice.

Giving an Intuitive some structure could be beneficial, to assist them in working through their process and seeing the big picture. Even giving them an inventory of personality traits such as Meyers-Briggs, Enneagram, or Character Structures could help them map out their internal landscape. Using this knowledge, an Me-B Therapist could encourage them to rely on their own hunches and trust their own inner knowing.

THINKING

People who prefer to use Thinking in decision making like to look at the logical consequences of a choice or action. They want to mentally remove themselves from the situation to examine the pros and cons objectively. They are energized by critiquing and analyzing to identify what's wrong with something so they can solve the problem. Their goal is to find a standard or principle that will apply in all similar situations. Thinking types are analytical; they use cause-and-effect reasoning; they solve problems with logic; they strive for an objective standard of truth; they are reasonable; and they can be "tough-minded" fair.

Because these clients are fair-minded and examine the pros and cons objectively, they quickly understand their process and make changes. They are often dream clients. They reach conclusions and seem motivated toward implementing change. The Me-B therapist can strive to support their need for clarity and understanding.

FEELING

People who prefer to use Feeling in decision making like to consider what is important to them and to others involved. They mentally place themselves into the situation to identify with everyone, so they can make decisions based on their values about honoring people. They are energized by appreciating and supporting others, and they look for qualities to praise. Their goal is to create harmony and treat each person as a unique individual. Empathetic, and guided by personal values, they assess the impact of their decisions on people, striving for harmony and positive interactions. They are compassionate, they may appear tenderhearted, and they are also fair.

> *Clients who use feeling as a major component of transforming have the benefit of being able to access sensitive information (even shadow material). Yet, they can sometimes get lost by merging with the material and thus risk over-identifying with it. They need to be supported in finding their own authentic perspective. If they collect too much information, they may need support in filtering through it. In addition, the Me-B therapist from time to time might check in with the client to ensure they don't take the therapist's point of view out of a misguided sense of compassion or need for harmony.*

JUDGING

People who prefer to use their judging process in the outer world like to live in a planned, orderly way, seeking to regulate and manage their lives. They want to make decisions, come to closure, and move on. Their lives tend to be structured and organized, and they like to have things "settled." Sticking to a plan and schedule is very important to them, and they are energized by getting things done. They tend to have organized lives and to be systematic and methodical. They make both short- and long-term plans; they like to have things decided; and they try to avoid last-minute stresses.

> *Finding a style of Me-B Therapy that meets the needs of this client type is necessary. I had one Judging client that liked to use a pendulum. I helped her work with false images and beliefs by using a very structured method of energy work. I read false images and beliefs in her field. She tested their validity with the pendulum. Then she tested to see if the energy work we did together shifted the energy of the beliefs and for how long.*

> *She developed a graph to look at which beliefs needed deeper work and which ones were no longer a hindrance. She used this method to move through her issues in an organized and systematic manner and to document progress. Although my way of working typically is very different, I was able to shift my style to meet the needs of my client. This was very crucial to the success of the Me-B Therapy— meeting the client where she needed to be met.*

> *Muscle testing techniques can also be helpful to this type of client.*

PERCEIVING

People who prefer to use their Perceiving process in the outer world like to live in a flexible, spontaneous way, seeking to experience and understand life, rather than control it. Detailed plans and final decisions feel confining to them; they prefer to stay open to new information and last-minute options. They are energized by their resourcefulness in adapting to the demands of the moment. Spontaneous, flexible, casual, and adaptable, they are comfortable with leaving things open-ended and changing course as situations change. They like to "keep things loose"—they are open to change, and even feel energized by last-minute pressures.

> *Clients that come to my office and thrive on this style of working generally match my typical manner of working. Yet, regardless of your typical style, it is paramount to track the energy in the moment, follow*

the rhythm of the client's energy, and help the client track it within themselves (to the extent they feel comfortable). Being flexible enough to sometimes do things the client's way demonstrates the talent of the therapist. If you find yourself needing more structure and formality and less spontaneity than your client feels serves them, you can learn to adapt and become more fluid in your style. Depending upon your personality type, you might find this to be a deep challenge or an exciting possibility. Either way, it must be done.

I once had a client ask me to leave the room while they processed a piece of themselves. I gladly gave them the space. It took three sessions before they felt comfortable enough to be in the same room for the full hour.

APPENDIX D - EMDR R & R2 TRAUMA TIPS

NOTE: You cannot use EMDR methods unless you have been specifically trained in EMDR.

STRATEGIES

Important EMDR components (with slight alternations) that might be useful for any trauma session include:

1. Determine the negative belief system the client's trauma holds. It must begin with an "I" statement. "I am. . . ."

    Examples of some of the most common "I" statements are: I am bad, not good enough, afraid, unsafe, broken, imperfect, angry, sad, alone, hurt, wrong. . . .

    Ask them when is the youngest time they remember feeling that way. Then ask them to come up with an image that represents the negative statement.

2. Determine the positive opposite. For instance, "I am enough," or "I am empowered." Never use negatives.

    The body doesn't recognize the "no" or the "not."

3. Ask them to say the negative statement silently, to visualize it, and to feel it, with the intention of melting the negative and opening space for the positive.

    Remember, if possible, they should go back to the youngest (or most charged) time that they felt that way. This focus on past feelings is used to help deepen the experience and to help visualize it.

    On a scale from 0-10, ask the client to assess how large the charge is. Usually, the client will say 8 or 10. If they are disassociated from the charge, they may say a 2. If they give any ranking below a 5, reassess if this is the best intervention at this time. Usually the ego and negative self-image (defenses) keep a client from really feeling the trauma. Never force them to feel it—instead, use the dissociation as a sign that the client needs more positive resourcing.

4. You can skip Step 3 if you think a client is not ready for trauma work and instead just do the positive resourcing technique.

    Ask the client to feel, visualize, and say the positive statement. (Example: "I am safe . . . .") They must feel the words as sensations in the body, and as visualization. It is best if they can visualize a particular time when they felt the positive statement. If they can't, then they can visualize a symbol or person that represents the positive statement.

    Ask the client to state the positive statement out loud, unless you are confident they are able to stay focused and not go to the negative. It is paramount that they stay in the positive and not go to the negative. Shorter sets make this easier. Continue the sets until the client feels they are a number 7 out of 7 or at least a 5 or 6 out of 7.

    Check to see if the field/body assimilates the intervention. You may see it as energy waves deepening into the muscles. You can also tell if the breath is deep and full through the whole chest and lower abdomen, and you see relaxation in the body. Assess whether the energy field reflects the number the client identifies. If they say the positive energy is a 10, but their energy field says it is only a 2, you might discuss this with the client.

Also, if the number does not move up to a 7, do containment and revisit this issue at the next session.

WHO SETS THE SETS

Before you begin, determine who is in charge of the timing of the frequency and duration of the sets.

APPENDIX E

SUGGESTED READING LIST FOR Me-B TRAINING

(Ask Us About how to Register for Our Certification Training!)

CORE BOOKS:

Explorer's Mind-A Map to Freedom, Carolyn Eberle

Hands of Light-A Guide to Healing Through the Human Energy Field, Brennan, Barbara

Light Emerging, Brennan, Barbara

Trauma and the Body, Pat. Ogden 2006 (The best trauma book I have ever read.)

OTHER VITAL BOOKS:

Biology of Belief, Bruce Lipton

Brainstorm; The Power and Purpose of the teenage Brain; Daniel J. Siegel, M.D.

Attached: The New Science of Adult Attachment and How It Can Help You Find and Keep Love; Amir LevineFacing

Love Addiction: Giving Yourself the Power to Change the Way You Love, Pia Mellody, Andrea Wells Miller and J. Keith Miller (Apr 29, 2003)

Hardwiring Happiness; Rick Hanson, PhD

Hold Me Tight: Seven Conversations for a Lifetime of Love, Sue Johnson

Healing Developmental Trauma; Laurence Heller, PhD; Aline LaPierre, PsyD

In An Unspoken Voice; How the Body Releases trauma and Restores Goodness, Peter A. Levine, PhD

Issues and Ethics in the Helping Professions; Corey; Callanan

Molecules of Emotion, Pert, Candice

Why our Brains are Wired to Connect, Mathew Lieberman

Wired for Love: How Understanding Your Partner's Brain and Attachment Style Can Help You Defuse Conflict and Build a Secure Relationship, Stan Tatkin PsyD

You're Not Crazy-You're Codependent, Jeanette Menter

If you are not currently an MA in mental health or licensed as a mental health professional, please read any recent Abnormal Psychology book.

Go to my web site: www.mindenergybodyinstitute.com and click on free downloads. At some point you can review papers and documents and read. It is being updated so wait until end of November. Thanks

The two writers best known for working on prenatal trauma are: David Chamberlin and William Emerson. If you google them you can find their papers online. The book by Chamberlin on Looking at The Mind of Your Newborn Baby is an easy read and explains how aware prenatal babies are.

If you have time, I suggest…..

The Intimate Couple and Body, Self and Soul, Marjorie Rand and Jack Lee Rosenberg 1991

The Subtle Body; an Encyclopedia of your Energetic Anatomy; Cyndi Dale

Codependent No More: How to Stop Controlling Others and Start Caring for Yourself, Melody Beattie

Chakras and their Archetypes – Uniting Energy Awareness and Spiritual Growth, Ambika Wauters

The Feeling of What Happens, Anthony DeMasio;

The Anatomy of Change, Richard Strozzi Heckler

Infinite Mind – The Science of Human Vibrations, Hunt, Valeries.

Sensing, Feeling, and Action; The Experimental Anatomy of Body-Mind Centering; Bonnie Cohen

Energy Medicine, Eden Donna.

The Listening Hand – Self -healing through the Rubenfeld Synergy Method of Talk and Touch, Rubenfeld, Ilana.

The Body Remembers, Babette Rothschild 2000 (very technical)

The Body Bears the Burden: Trauma, Dissociation and Disease, Scaer, Robert C.

Waking the Tiger, Peter Levine 1997 (easy read)

Training Your Brain To Adopt Healthful Habits: Mastering The Five Brain Challenges; By Jodie Trafton, Ph.D.; William P. Gordon, Ph.D. Supriya Misra, M.A.

Characterological Transformation: The Hard Work Miracle, Stephen M. Johnson

The Polyvagal Theory, Stephen Porges

Healing the Split, John Nelson, M.D.

DSM V

Gallbladder

Liver

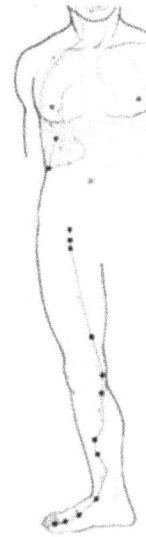

Kidney

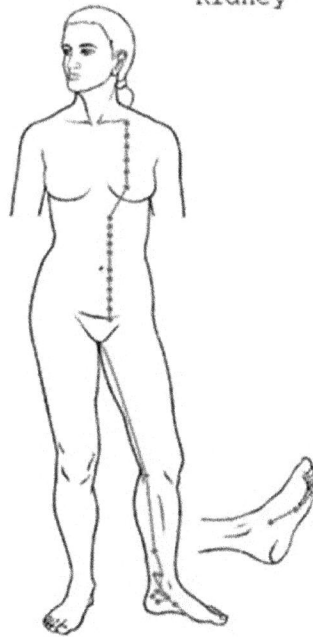

Urinary
bladder

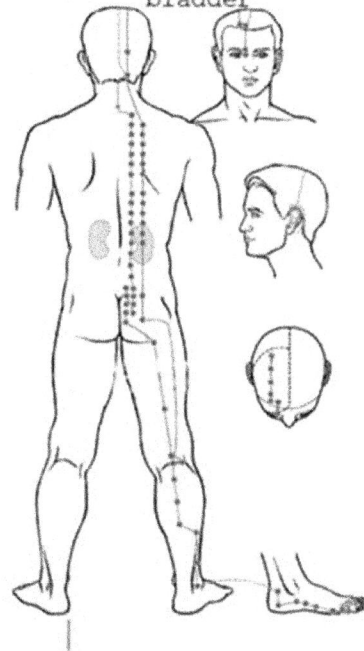

Small
Intestine

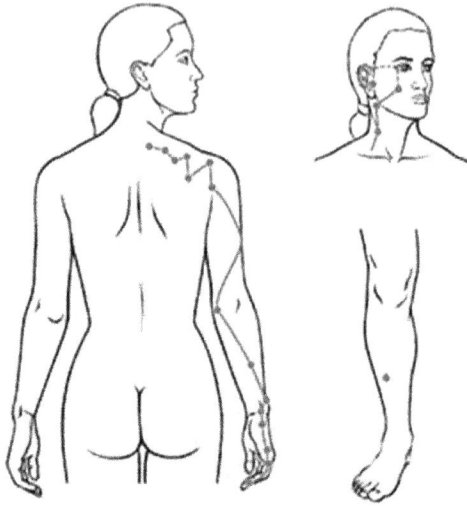

Heart

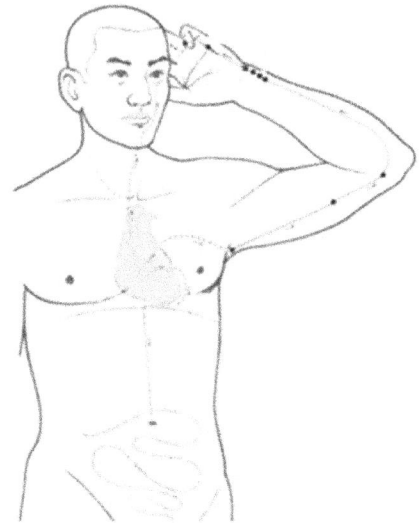

Pericardium

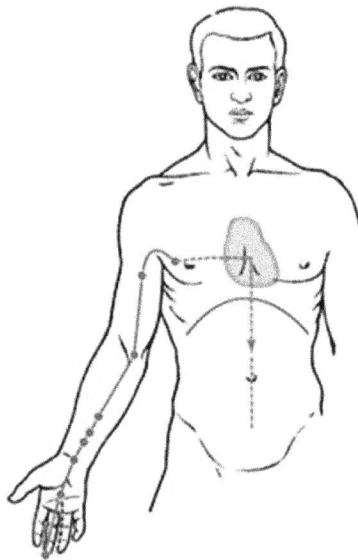

Triple Heater

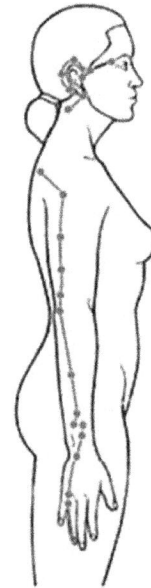

436

Stomach

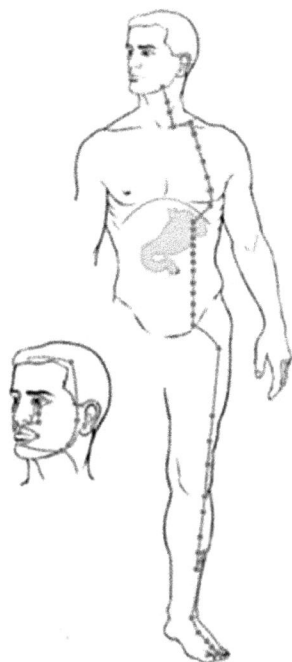

Spleen

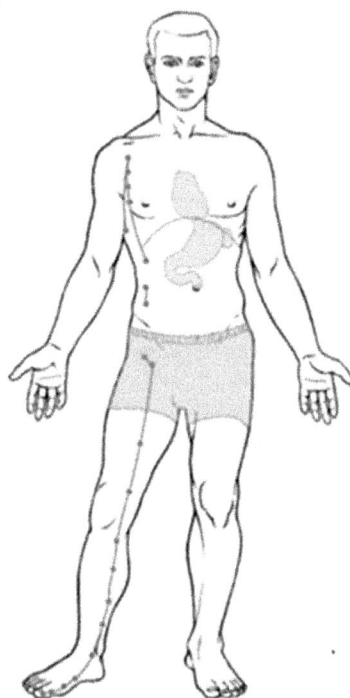

Lung

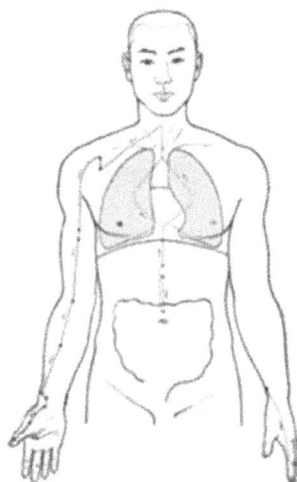

Large
Intestine

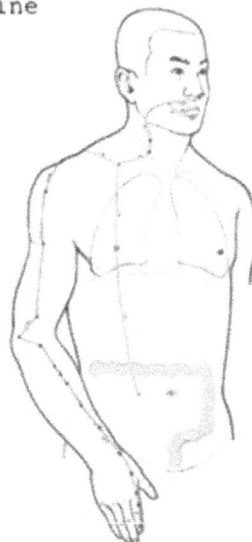

437

Governing
Vessel

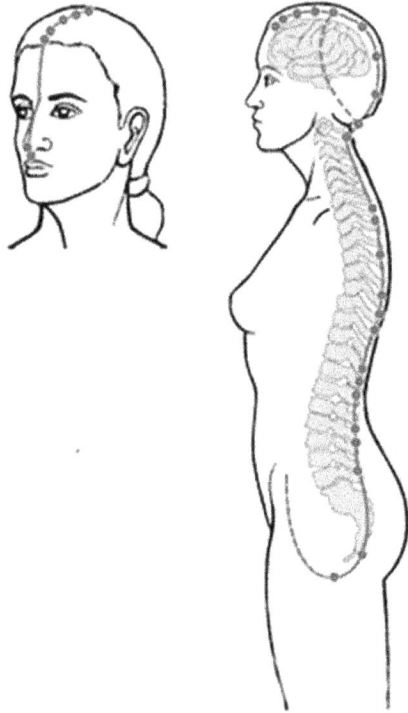

Conception Vessel

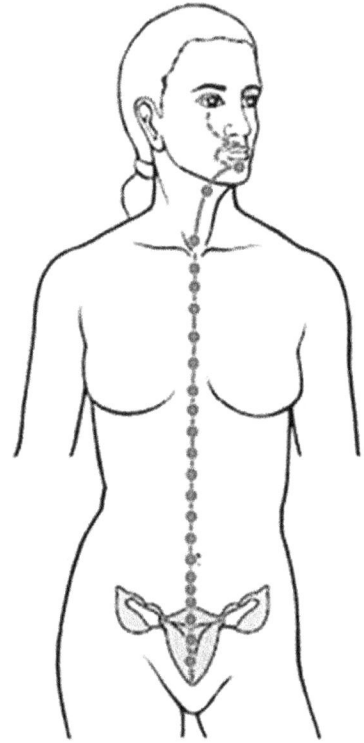

www.ingramcontent.com/pod-product-compliance
Lightning Source LLC
Chambersburg PA
CBHW081426270326
41932CB00019B/3109